Drawing Down the Moon

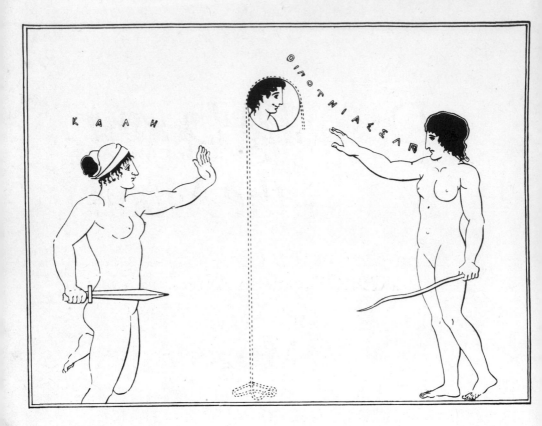

Drawing down the moon: one of the few known depictions of this ancient
ritual, from a Greek vase probably of the second century B. C. (*New York
Public Library.*)

Drawing Down the Moon

Witches, Druids, Goddess-Worshippers, and Other Pagans in America Today

Margot Adler

REVISED AND EXPANDED EDITION

Beacon Press • *Boston*

Beacon Press
25 Beacon Street
Boston, Massachusetts 02108

Beacon Press books are published under the auspices
of the Unitarian Universalist Association
of Congregations in North America.

92 91 90   8 7 6

Library of Congress Cataloging in Publication Data

Adler, Margot.
  Drawing down the moon.

  Bibliography: p.
  Includes index.
    1. Witchcraft—United States. 2. Cults—United
States. 3. Women and religion. I. Title.
BF1573.A34   1986   299'.93   86-70551
ISBN 0-8070-3253-0

Contents

IV. The Material Plane

Illustrations follow page 152

Preface to the Revised Edition

On All Hallows' Eve, 1979, Drawing Down the Moon *was published in New* York. On the same day, Starhawk's *The Spiral Dance* was published in California. These two books continue to be many people's introduction to Neo-Paganism, Wicca, and Goddess spirituality. In the seven years that have passed the world is much changed, but strangely, although many details in this book have become outdated and many groups and organizations no longer exist, the root ideas in *Drawing Down the Moon* seem more relevant now than they did in 1979.

It is easy for strangers to Witchcraft, feminist spirituality, and Paganism to get sidetracked by odd words and customs and to think that a book like this is really about "cults" and "odd sects." If this had ever been the book's main subject, it might well not be in print today, for cults and sects come and go.

The real message of *Drawing Down the Moon* is that the spiritual world is like the natural world—only diversity will save it. Just as the health of a forest or fragrant meadow can be measured by the number of different insects and plants and creatures that successfully make it their home, so only by an extraordinary abundance of disparate spiritual and philosophic paths will human beings navigate a pathway through the dark and swirling storms that mark our current era. "Not by one avenue alone," wrote Symmachus sixteen centuries ago, "can we arrive at so tremendous a secret."

The dominant spiritual trend of the 1980s is militant fundamentalism worldwide. Children in Iran are sent to die as martyrs in Iraq; Christians in America throw textbooks in the flames; Sikhs war in the Punjab; and in Israel Jewish fundamentalists continue to destroy the hopes of Israeli and Arab peace activists. When *Drawing Down the Moon* was published, the Iranian revolution was still new, Ronald Reagan had not entered the White House, and "détente" was still a word in common usage.

The fundamentalist impulse—coupled with the inevitable rise of apocalyptic millennialism as we approach the year 2000—is, along with nuclear war, the most dangerous peril facing the human race. Most fundamentalists, whatever the name of their religion or country, are at war with the diversity of life and ideas. Like corporations that reduce Latin American countries to poverty by turning all acreage to sugar, the belief that there is one word, one truth, one path to the light, makes it easy to destroy ideas, institutions, and human beings. As the historian James Breasted wrote almost seventy-five years ago, "Monotheism is but imperialism in religion."

Perhaps most dangerous, most fundamentalists do not believe this world, this earth, these bodies we inhabit are holy. Since they see this world as sinful and this time as evil, they seek only a world that comes after. Several hundred years ago, the Inquisitors felt they were acting with the greatest human kindness when they tortured, burned, and hanged those they called "Witches" in order that their souls might be saved. They are not so different from their descendents in the 1980s who wistfully yearn for salvation, even if it takes the form of nuclear war.

Drawing Down the Moon espouses radical polytheism. It is grounded in the view that reality is multiple and diverse. It stands against all of the totalistic religious and political views that dominate our society. It says, "Strive to be comfortable in chaos and complexity. Be as a Shaman who walks in many worlds. Try to feel strong and whole and at home in a world of diversity." The book's basic assumption is that your own spiritual path is not necessarily mine. In fact, Islamic and Christian fundamentalism are seen here as appropriate *individual* spiritual paths as long as each is seen as merely one flower in the garden. Polytheism always includes monotheism. The reverse is not true.

The book focuses on modern Neo-Paganism and Witchcraft because these religions turn out to be a surprising and amazing attempt by Westerners in the heart of our industrial society to create non-authoritarian and non-dogmatic religions. There are many anti-authoritarian religious groups from liberal Christians to Unitarians. What's unusual about modern Pagans is that they remain anti-authoritarian while retaining rituals and ecstatic techniques that, in our culture, are used only by dogmatic religions or are the province of small and forgotten tribal groups.

While Neo-Paganism and modern Wicca are very anarchistic religions and it is probably wrong to say all Pagans believe this or that, there are some basic beliefs that most people in this book share:

> The world is holy. Nature is holy. The body is holy. Sexuality is holy. The mind is holy. The imagination is holy. You are holy. A spiritual path that is not stagnant ultimately leads one to the understanding of one's own divine nature. Thou art Goddess. Thou art God. Divinity is imminent in all Nature. It is as much within you as without.
>
> In our culture which has for so long denied and denigrated the feminine as negative, evil or, at best, small and unimportant, women (and men too) will never understand their own creative strength and divine nature until they embrace the creative feminine, the source of inspiration, the Goddess within.
>
> While one can at times be cut off from experiencing the deep and ever-present connection between oneself and the universe, there is no such thing as sin (unless it is simply defined as that estrangement) and guilt is never very useful.
>
> The energy you put into the world comes back.

If you go far enough back, all our ancestors practiced religions that had neither creeds nor dogmas, neither prophets nor holy books. These religions were based on the celebrations of the seasonal cycles of nature. They were based on what people did, as opposed to what people believed. It is these polytheistic religions of imminence that are being revived and re-created by Neo-Pagans today. This book is the story of that Pagan resurgence.

This book is the only detailed history of the origins of Neo-Paganism in the United States. In preparing this new edition, there was a constant tension between keeping the book as a piece of history and the desire to bring people up to date. Many people wrote to me requesting that there be additions instead of changes. Moreover, there was no time for a truly massive reconstruction of a book that took more than four years to write. In the end, I took a middle course—leaving most of the book intact, adding several new sections, making small changes here and there, and creating an extensive Resource Guide to Pagan groups, festivals, and journals.

There are new sections on Norse Paganism and men's spirituality as well as a new section on Pagan festivals and their extraordinary impact in creating a national Pagan subculture. There is also new data compiled from a survey conducted in 1985. There are some new developments in the history of Gardnerian Wicca in light of writings by Stuart Farrar and Doreen Valiente. The Resource Guide reflects the extraordinary expansion of groups and newsletters. There are now more than one hundred Pagan periodicals worldwide, and more than fifty regional and national Pagan festivals in the United States, Australia, and Canada.

While there are more Pagan and Wiccan organizations in the United States and Europe today than ten years ago, some of the groups described in detail in this book no longer exist, or no longer participate in the broader Neo-Pagan community. It is important to remember that many of these organizations set the terms of the Neo-Pagan religious critique. They originated or developed key concepts that play an important role in creating a modern Pagan viewpoint—concepts like the difference between a tribal and a credal religion, between a religion of imminence and one of transcendence, between a polytheistic and a monotheistic outlook, between religions based on words and religions based on experience.

Finally, remember, no one *converts* to Paganism or Wicca. You will find no one handing you Pagan leaflets on the street or shouting at you from a corner. Many people came across this book, or *The Spiral Dance* (or any of a number of related books), in some isolated corner of America or the world. Often they found it in a small-town library, or in a used bookstore, or stashed away on a friend's bookshelf. Upon opening its pages, perhaps they said, "I never knew there was anyone else in the world who felt what I feel or believed what I have always believed. I never knew my religion had a name." To these people, this edition is dedicated.

Preface

"Paganism in America" . . . This simple phrase stirs deep responses in many people.

A book on Paganism in America today might be many things, since *pagan* has been defined as everything from decadence to sensuality, to a return to the primitive, to a stance against religion. It might be yet another book on narcissism in our time, or it might be a sensationalist study of religious cults. It could be a book on satanism. It could be a book on atheism. No matter how precisely the word is defined—and it *is* defined precisely in the pages that follow—the word *pagan*, like *anarchist* or *communist*, calls forth conflicting expectations in readers.

The thousands of people in the United States today who call themselves Pagans or Neo-Pagans use the word *pagan* in a very different way. These people—the subject of this book—consider themselves part of a religious movement that antedates Christianity and monotheism. By *pagan* they usually mean the pre-Christian nature religions of the West, and their own attempts to revive them or to re-create them in new forms. The modern Pagan resurgence includes the feminist goddess-worshippers, new religions based on the visions of science-fiction writers, attempts to revive ancient European religions—Norse, Greek, Roman, Celtic—and the surviving tribal religions.

The Pagan movement does *not* include the Eastern religious groups. It includes neither Satanists nor Christians. Almost every religious group that has received massive exposure in the press, from the Hare Krishna movements to the Unification Church to the People's Temple, lies outside the Pagan resurgence. The many hundreds of Pagan religious groups, by and large, stand in contrast and opposition to these authoritarian movements. The Pagan vision is one which says that neither doctrine nor dogma nor asceticism nor rule by masters is necessary for the visionary experience, and that ecstasy *and* freedom are both possible.

Part I of this book is somewhat theoretical. Chapter 1 describes the broad outlines of this movement and defines troublesome words like *pagan* and *witch*. Chapter 2 describes my own entry into this world fifteen years ago as an observer-participant, and discusses how entry into these groups differs from the conversion process so familiar in many religions. Chapter 3 is about the Pagan world view: how the polytheistic perspective of many Pagan groups demands—at least in theory—a stance against authoritarianism.

Part II describes the Witchcraft revival, its history, its links with Britain and certain British folklorists, its current expressions, practices, "beliefs," and sects. One chapter describes the role of magic and ritual in these groups; another discusses feminist Witchcraft covens, and the broader interest of feminists in goddess worship and ritual.

Part III looks at other Neo-Pagan groups; the revivals of ancient European religions, the creation of religions based on fantasy and private visions, and a potpourri of groups that originated as satire, from Hasidic Druids in the Midwest to the worshippers of Eris, goddess of chaos.

Part IV considers the relationship of all these things to the "real world." It begins a discussion of how scholars and writers have interpreted and misinterpreted these movements, and describes the attitudes of many Pagans to worldly concerns: technology, progress, politics, ecology, work.

This book could not have been written without the aid of hundreds of people. Many of their names appear within.

The original draft of *Drawing Down the Moon* was read and criticized by a diverse group of friends, scholars, and Neo-Pagans: Isaac Bonewits, Sharon Devlin, John Gliedman, Aidan Kelly, Morgan McFarland, Penny Novack, Theodore Roszak, and Jeffrey Burton Russell. Their comments led to many important changes.

Somewhere between one hundred and two hundred hours of taped interviews were transcribed by volunteers. Special thanks to Patricia Holub and Elena Le Pera. Also, Susan Advocate, Doug Berk, Arlene

Coffee, Alice Elste, Mary Joiner, Melvin Jones, Jackie Kelly, Jean Kononowitz, Herb Penmen, Maureen Scherer.

For three months I traveled thousands of miles to groves and covens in the United States and Britain. I attended ritual gatherings, conducted interviews, and met hundreds of people. Often I was housed and fed by people who had never before met me. Often I was driven hundreds of miles by people who had only heard, by word of mouth, that I was "trustworthy." Special thanks to: Alison Harlow, Athena and Dagda, Otter and Morning Glory Zell, Judy and Michael Myers, Doris and Vic Stuart, Morgan McFarland, and Mark Roberts.

The Neo-Pagan journal *Green Egg* published my long questionnaire and I received hundreds of pages in response. In preparing for the second edition, a new questionnaire was published in *Panegyria* and handed out at three Pagan festivals in 1985. One hundred ninety-five responses arrived by hand or in the mail.

A number of libraries and institutions were invaluable: the C. G. Jung Foundation in New York and its library; the Institute for the Study of American Religion, headed by Reverend J. Gordon Melton; the Lesbian Herstory Archives in New York City; and the New York Public Library. The book was written, in part, in the Frederick Lewis Allen Room of the New York Public Library, a special room for writers with a very special atmosphere. The writers there gave warmth, support, and a companionship that is truly rare.

Mary Card and the City and Country School provided a twelve-year-old child with the legends of the Greek gods and goddesses; without that experience, the journey would never have been taken. Gilbert Rose provided me with the rudiments of the Greek language seven years later, and thereby allowed my thoughts to continue in unusual directions.

The people of Coeden Brith gave poetic inspiration. The ideas of many were valuable: Lindsay Ardwin, Bruce Kenyon, Arnie Sacher, Kathleen Pullen, Zana Miller, Ernst Becker, Ernest Callenbach, John Schaar, Ursula Le Guin, Bill Monaghan, and Bill Lee.

Many people helped make the revised edition of *Drawing Down the Moon* a reality. In particular, four people went out of their way to share their libraries, files, and resources, as well as to give ideas and information: Selena Fox, Bob Murphy, Christa Heiden, and Larry Cornett. Many other people gave important insights and information, among them: Judy Harrow, Oz, Starhawk, Isaac Bonewits, Ginny Brubaker, Doreen Valiente, and the folks who ran the following 1985

Pagan festivals: Rites of Spring, Pagan Spirit Gathering, the National C.O.G. Festival, and the Festival of Women's Spirituality.

Lastly, Jane Rotrosen talked me into doing this book and believed in the project before I did. She gave me the push and supported me at every stage. Deepest thanks to my three editors: Edwin Kennebeck, Alida Becker, and the woman who made the revised edition possible, Joanne Wyckoff.

A Note on Names and Language

A number of those whose names appear within are using "Craft" or "Pagan" names instead of their given names. This may be for reasons of job security, because of the community in which they live, or because, for any one of a number of reasons, they do not wish to be "public" about their religion. Their wishes have been honored.

Throughout the book I do not use "man," "mankind," or "he" as generic terms. At the present time these terms mean "male" rather than being truly generic. Many of those I quote do use these terms and their quotes are left intact. There are also several quotations that contain words with intentionally unconventional spellings, such as "womin" and "thealogy."

. . . the Thessalian witches who draw down the moon from heaven . . .
—PLATO, *Gorgias*

If I beheld the sun when it shined, or the moon walking in brightness; and my heart hath been secretly enticed, or my mouth hath kissed my hand: this also were an iniquity to be punished by the judge: for I should have denied the God that is above.
—Job, XXXIII, 27–8

I. *Background*

I

Paganism and Prejudice

In the last twenty years, alongside the often noted resurgence of "occult" and "magical" groups, a diverse and decentralized religious movement has sprung up that remains comparatively unnoticed, and when recognized, is generally misunderstood. Throughout the United States there are many hundreds, perhaps thousands, of groups in this movement, each numbering anywhere from several to several hundred. Eclectic, individualist, and often fiercely autonomous, they do not share those characteristics that the media attribute to religious cults. They are often self-created and *homemade*; they seldom have "gurus" or "masters"; they have few temples and hold their meetings in woods, parks, apartments, and houses; in contrast to most organized cults, money seldom passes from hand to hand and the operations of high finance are nonexistent; and entry into these groups comes through a process that could rarely be called "conversion."

While these religious groups all differ in regard to tradition, scope, structure, organization, ritual, and the names for their deities, they do regard one another as part of the same religious and philosophical movement. They have a common name for themselves: Pagans or Neo-Pagans.* They share a set of values and they communicate with one

* "Pagan" and "Neo-Pagan" are capitalized since the words are used here to de-

3

another through a network of newsletters,[1] regional and national gatherings.

Most Neo-Pagans sense an aliveness and "presence" in nature. They are usually polytheists or animists or pantheists, or two or three of these things at once. They share the goal of living in harmony with nature and they tend to view humanity's "advancement" and separation from nature as the prime source of alienation. They see *ritual* as a tool to end that alienation. Most Neo-Pagans look to the old pre-Christian nature religions of Europe, the ecstatic religions, and the mystery traditions as a source of inspiration and nourishment. They gravitate to ancient symbols and ancient myths, to the old polytheistic religions of the Greeks, the Egyptians, the Celts, and the Sumerians. They are reclaiming these sources, transforming them into something new, and adding to them the visions of Robert Graves, even of J. R. R. Tolkien and other writers of science fiction and fantasy, as well as some of the teachings and practices of the remaining aboriginal peoples.

Most of these groups have grown up in cities, where the loss of enrichment from the natural world is most easily perceived and where, also, the largest number of intellectual tools to enlarge such a perception exist. Fueled by romantic vision, fantasy, and visionary activies, empowered by a sense of planetary crisis and the idea that such a nature vision may be drowned in an ecocidal nightmare, Neo-Pagans have often allied themselves with other philosophical and political movements.

Since 1972, I have moved freely among a large number of Neo-Pagans. I have visited groves and covens across the country and have attended many festivals and gatherings. I have also visited groups in Canada and the United Kingdom. This book charts the resurgence of these contemporary nature religions.

In the late 1960s it was fashionable to characterize the counterculture and the psychedelic movement as a visionary, "neo-sacral," "neo-transcendental"[2] movement which joined a mystical view of the

---

scribe members of a religion, in the same way as one would describe a "Christian" or a "Jew." "Witch" will be capitalized when it is used to refer to members of the modern Witchcraft religion, Wicca or the Craft.

† Reference Notes begin on page 415.

cosmos to a countercultural life style and worldly politics. In the last decade that movement has virtually disappeared and its place has been taken by large well-financed religious groups usually characterized by authoritarianism and asceticism. The Unification Church of Sun Myung Moon and the International Society of Krishna Consciousness of Swami Prabhupada are two examples among many.

In contrast, the Neo-Pagan groups described in these pages have something of that original "neo-sacral" impulse of the 1960s. They do not regard pleasure as sinful, nor do they conceive of this world as a burden. While many of their members lead quite ordinary, and often successful, lives in the "real world," they are able to detach themselves from many of the trends of the day, maintaining a sense of humor, a gentle anarchism, and a remarkable tolerance of diversity.

I have noticed that many intellectuals turn themselves off the instant they are confronted with the words *witchcraft, magic, occultism,* and *religion,* as if such ideas exert a dangerous power that might weaken their rational faculties. Yet many of these people maintain a generous openness about visionaries, poets, and artists, some of whom may be quite mad according to "rational" standards. They are fascinated by people of diverse professions and life styles who have historical ties with, let us say, the Transcendentalists or the Surrealists, as long as the word *occult* is not mentioned.

If Neo-Paganism were presented as an intellectual and artistic movement whose adherents have new perceptions of the nature of reality, the place of sexuality, and the meaning of community, academics would flock to study it. Political philosophers would write articles on the Neo-Pagans' sense of wonder and the minority vision they represent. Literary critics would compare the poetic images in the small magazines published and distributed by the groups with images in the writings of Blake and Whitman. Jungian psychologists would rush to study the Neo-Pagans' use of ancient archetypes and their love of the classics and ancient lore.

But words like *witch* and *pagan* do not rest easily in the mind or on the tongue. Pop journalists present a Neo-Paganism composed of strange characters and weird rites[3] or describe bored suburbanites dancing naked in a circle in their living rooms.[4] More serious journalists see in it a dangerous trend toward the irrational. Psychologists dismiss it as a haven for neurotics who seek power in magical cults.

The reality is very different. This *religious* movement of people who often call themselves Pagans, Neo-Pagans, and Witches is only partly an "occult" phenomenon. Often it is interwoven with the visionary and artistic tradition, the ecology movement, the feminist movement, and the libertarian tradition.

A few scholars and specialists have studied and come to understand Neo-Paganism, but the public continues to have an inaccurate picture of it. Misunderstandings begin at the most basic level, with the meanings of words used to describe beliefs and attitudes. Let us take the word *magic*. Most people define it as *superstition* or *belief in the supernatural*. In contrast, most magicians, Witches, and other magical practitioners do not believe that magic has anything to do with the supernatural.*

A personal example may help to illustrate the depth and complexity of these differences. During my travels I came across a coven of Witches living on a farm in the plains of Colorado.[5] This small group was led by a couple who called themselves Michael and Judy. On their farm livestock were raised and sold, goats were milked, pigs were slaughtered, vegetables were grown, canned, and put away, jewelry was crafted—in general, the seasons turned and work proceeded. The people living on this farm were Witches under the modern religious definition of that term. They were members of a polytheistic nature religion who worshipped a goddess and a god and regarded themselves as priests and priestesses of the Earth-Mother. Outside of this, they lived quite ordinary lives, like their neighbors, who also grew crops and raised animals. Unlike most of their neighbors, however, they had no television and spent their few hours of spare time each day studying music and reading books on mythology, Celtic history, or the history and philosophy of magical practice.

---

* An entire chapter could be written on the several definitions of the word "magic" that can be found in dictionaries. The *Oxford English Dictionary*, for example, calls it "The pretended art of influencing the course of events . . . by processes supposed to owe their efficacy to the power of compelling the intervention of spiritual beings, or of bringing into operation some occult controlling principle of nature," then adds what amounts to a brief historical essay implying that yesterday's magic is often today's science.

Their rituals marked the seasonal turnings of the year and provided a focus for various creative activities—from the writing of poetry and drama to a large number of activities that, in this society, are the domain of artists, not farmers.

They planted by the phases of the moon (as do thousands of farmers), they used herbal remedies to heal wounds in their animals, they used ritual to unite themselves with the natural world. They experienced the deaths and births of animals and plants. They used the events of the *real world* (the joys and tragedies on the farm) to provide their students with an initiation sublimer than the ornate passage rituals of secret magical orders.

Now, what did *magic* mean to this group of Witches? And how would their definition differ from the notion commonly held by the public and from the views of scholars? What, in fact, was a real instance of magic at the farm?

Although this group has now disbanded, I visited the farm in 1974 and 1976. On a hot and dry day, four of us—myself, two weekend volunteers who were studying with the coven, and one full-time member—were asked to go down to the river, which habitually dried up in the late summer until, by September, nothing remained but a cracked riverbed. Each year as the river dried up, the fish inhabitants died. Our project was to catch the dying fish in two buckets and fill an entire small truck with the creatures, which would then be used as composting materials for an organic garden.

A few of the fish were floating on the surface, but most were still quite lively and dashed away to survive a few more hours, perhaps days. It was slimy, messy, and unsuccessful work. At the end of three hours we were caked with mud up to our thighs. We returned with only two buckets of fish. It seemed an impossible task.

When we arrived back at the farm, Michael said that they would go back with us to the river, that the job *was* possible, and that, more to the point, the fish were needed. I was skeptical. In the truck on the way to the river he spoke a few words about magic (this may have been the only time I heard the word during my stay at the farm). "Magic," he said, "is simply the art of getting results." He noted that the fish were dying and that they might as well be put to good purpose fertilizing the earth. He impressed upon us the necessity for our actions.

Michael then began to describe how bears catch fish with their paws. He asked us to visualize ourselves as bears, to place ourselves in the position of a hungry bear in need of food. I began to imagine the essence of a bear's life. In such a mood, we waded to the middle of the river, where the water came up to our waists, and began slapping our hands together very quickly, catching the fish between our hands and throwing them over our heads and onto the beach. We continued this process of slapping and throwing until the beach was covered with fish. An hour later, we gathered them up in buckets and took them to the truck, which was soon filled almost to the top.

If I may presume to broaden Michael's definition of magic, it might read something like this: Magic is a convenient word for a whole collection of techniques, all of which involve the mind. In this case, we might conceive of these techniques as including the mobilization of confidence, will, and emotion brought about by the recognition of necessity; the use of imaginative faculties, particularly the ability to visualize, in order to begin to understand how other beings function in nature so we can use this knowledge to achieve necessary ends.

This magic did not involve the supernatural. It involved an understanding of psychological and environmental processes; it was a kind of shamanism, a knowledge of how emotion and concentration can be directed naturally to effect changes in consciousness that affect the behavior of (in this case) humans and fish. It is important to stress that this naturalistic definition of magic is not unique to the farm in Colorado, but is common in one form or another to the other groups mentioned in these pages.

Interestingly, traditional occult definitions of magic have rarely included the supernatural. For example, in Aleister Crowley's famous definition, magic is "the Science and Art of causing change to occur in conformity with Will,"[6] and more recently Isaac Bonewits has defined magic as "folk parapsychology, an art and science designed to enable people to make effective use of their psychic talents."[7] Most of these definitions link magic to an understanding of the workings of the mind. Actually, the idea of the supernatural, of something outside nature, is a thoroughly modern notion unknown to the ancients.

Magic is only one of many terms about which there is misunderstanding. Others are *Pagan* and *Witch. Pagan* comes from the Latin *paganus*, which means a country dweller, and is itself derived from *pāgus*, the Latin word for village or rural district.[8] Similarly, *heathen* originally meant a person who lived on the heaths. Negative associations with these words are the end result of centuries of political struggles during which the major prophetic religions, notably Christianity, won a victory over the older polytheistic religions. In the West, often the last people to be converted to Christianity lived on the outskirts of populated areas and kept to the old ways. These were the Pagans and heathens—the word Pagan was a term of insult, meaning "hick."

Pagan had become a derogatory term in Rome by the third century. Later, after the death of Julian, the last Pagan emperor, in 362 C.E.,* the word Pagan came to refer to intellectual Pagans like Julian. Gore Vidal, in his extraordinary novel *Julian*, wrote a fictional description of this event in which the Pagan orator Libanius, after attending the funeral of a Christian notable, writes in his journal: "There was a certain amount of good-humored comment about 'pagans' (a new word of contempt for us Hellenists) attending Christian services. . . ."[9] Julian, by the way, has long been one of Neo-Paganism's heroes, and an early Neo-Pagan journal was called *The Julian Review.*[10] Centuries later the word *Pagan* still suffers the consequences of political and religious struggles, and dictionaries still define it to mean a godless person or an unbeliever, instead of, simply, a member of a different kind of religion.

Pagan is also often associated with hedonism. This makes some sense, since many ancient Pagan religions incorporated sexuality into ecstatic religious practice. One scholar, writing on the use of mystical experience by young people in the 1960s, observed that a characteristic of many groups was "the idea of paganism—the body is a temple in which there is nothing unclean, a shrine to be adorned for the ritual of love."[11] New attitudes toward sexuality play a part in some, but not all, Neo-Pagan groups, and the old Pagan religions had

---

* C.E. (Common Era) is used throughout this book to replace A.D.; B.C.E. (Before Common Era) is used to replace B.C. This is fairly common usage among scholars. See *Webster's New International Dictionary*, 2nd ed. (F. C. Merriam Company, 1958), pp. 540 and 866; *Encyclopaedia Judaica*, Vol. I (New York: The Macmillan Company, 1972), p. 73.

their share of ascetics, but generally, Neo-Pagans seem to have healthy attitudes toward sex.

I use *Pagan* to mean a member of a polytheistic nature religion, such as the ancient Greek, Roman, or Egyptian religions, or, in anthropological terms, a member of one of the indigenous folk and tribal religions all over the world. People who have studied the classics or have been deeply involved with natural or aboriginal peoples are comparatively free of the negative and generally racist attitudes that surround the word *Pagan*.

Isaac Bonewits uses the term *Neo-Paganism* to refer to "polytheistic (or conditional monotheistic) nature religions that are based upon the older or Paleopagan religions; concentrating upon an attempt to retain the humanistic, ecological and creative aspects of these old belief systems while discarding their occasional brutal or repressive developments, which are inappropriate. . . ."[12] Another Neo-Pagan writer, Otter Zell of the Church of All Worlds, has written that Neo-Pagans see divinity manifest in all the processes of nature. According to his view, Neo-Paganism is a constantly evolving philosophy that views humanity as a "functional organ within the greater organism of all Life. . . ."[13]

Since many of the groups I interviewed for this book consider themselves to be Witchcraft covens of one description or another, it will be impossible to understand their nature if one is burdened by stereotyped notions about Witches. The mere words *witch* and *witchcraft* unlock a set of explosive associations that inspire unease if not fear.

Dictionaries define Witches as (primarily) women who are either seductive and charming (bewitching) or ugly and evil (wicked). In either case, the women are supposed to possess a variety of "supernatural" powers. The lexicographical definitions of *witch* are rather confusing and bear little relation to the definitions given by Witches themselves. Participants in the Witchcraft revival generally use *Witch* to mean simply an initiate of the religion Wicca, also known as the Craft.

Followers of Wicca seek their inspiration in pre-Christian sources, European folklore, and mythology. They consider themselves priests and priestesses of an ancient European shamanistic nature religion that worships a goddess who is related to the ancient Mother Goddess in her three aspects of Maiden, Mother, and Crone. Many Craft traditions also worship a god, related to the ancient horned lord of animals, the god of the hunt, the god of death and lord of the forests. Many Neo-Pagan Witches, and Neo-Pagans generally, see themselves as modern-day heirs to the ancient mystery traditions of Egypt, Crete, Eleusis, and so on, as well as to the more popular peasant traditions of celebratory festivals and seasonal rites.

The word *Witchcraft* comes from the Old English *wicce* and *wicca*, referring to female and male practitioners, respectively. Many Witches have said that these two words derive from the root "wit" or wisdom. Others (including myself, in the previous edition of this book) have said the word derives from the Indo-European roots "wic" and "weik," meaning to bend or to turn. According to this view, a Witch would be a woman (or man) skilled in the craft of shaping, bending, and changing reality. This definition would apply well to what happened with the fish in Colorado. Although this definition emphasizes the flexible and non-authoritarian nature of modern Wicca, most dictionaries say something quite different. *The American Heritage Dictionary of the English Language*, for example, says that the word "witch" is derived from the Indo-European root "weik," which has to do with religion and magic, and this differs from "weik," to bend. Most members of the Craft define *Witchcraft* as the "Craft of the Wise," and anyone who reads the literature of modern Wicca will come across this definition many times, of Wicca as Wisecraft or Wiccacraeft. Whether or not this idea is etymologically correct, it is understandable, since the old Witches were often the wise people of the village, skilled in healing and the practical arts.

In this book *Witch* refers to the followers of the Craft unless otherwise stated. Neo-Pagan Witchcraft is seen here as one of a number of modern polytheistic religions. I use the word "religion" broadly, to refer to any set of symbolic forms and acts that relate human beings to ultimate conditions of existence, cosmic questions, and universal concerns. Since we live in a world denuded of religious

---

* In all fairness, the scholarly debate around the word *witch* is complex. For example, *The American Heritage Dictionary of the English Language* says that the word is derived from the Indo-European root *"weik²,"* which has to do with religion and magic, and this differs from *"weik⁴,"* to bend. Isaac Bonewits has written that the word comes from a root *wic*, meaning to bend or twist. His arguments are as reasonable as any I have seen. And they are compelling because they emphasize the flexible and non-authoritarian nature of modern Wicca.

and mythic variety, most people in the West tend to associate the word *religion* with the type of religion they are used to. They assume that religion must contain "beliefs" and "dogmas" and must involve a remote and transcendent deity, usually male, though occasionally neuter, and often removed from human interaction. The idea of a "nature religion" seems almost a contradiction in terms.

Neo-Pagans look at *religion* differently; they often point out that the root of the word means "to relink" and "to connect," and therefore refers to any philosophy that makes deep connections between human beings and the universe.[14] The science fiction writer Joanna Russ once told a convention that science fiction was a "religious literature." Many Neo-Pagans would agree. Similarly, the literature of ecology—for example, the work of Loren Eiseley, René Dubos, Marston Bates, and Barry Commoner—is seen by many Neo-Pagans as religious. One of the foremost characteristics of Neo-Paganism is the return to the ancient idea that there is no distinction between spiritual and material, sacred and secular. We generally think of spiritual concerns as apart from mundane concerns. This idea is entirely opposed to the Pagan perception. A group of women in a feminist Witchcraft coven once told me that, to them, spiritual meant, "the power within oneself to create artistically and change one's life." These women saw no contradiction between their concern for political and social change and their concern for "things of the spirit," which they equated with the need for beauty or with that spark that creates a poem or a dance. This is similar to views I have noticed among many tribal peoples who are fighting to preserve their culture.

People who want a convenient box to place these groups in frequently ask me whether they are "occult." Usually this question is asked by people who do not wish to consider them at all, and if I say yes, they feel relieved that they don't have to. The real answer is yes or no, depending on the definition of occult. Yes, because many of these groups deal with hidden or obscure forms of knowledge that are not generally accepted, and no, because a number of groups regard themselves as celebratory rather than magical or occult.

Harriet Whitehead, in an article on scientology, science fiction, and the occult, makes the point that, contrary to the popular assumption, most occultists have an intellectual style, "a process of sorting, surveying, analysing and abstracting." One of the hallmarks of that style is lack of dogmatism. "The occult world," she writes, "offers to the individual a 'free marketplace' of ideas. . . ." What this resembles, "and not by coincidence, is the intellectual democracy of the scientific and academic communities." She writes that the difference between these two communities and the occult world is that occultists refuse "contentment with the finite" (the phrase comes from William James). Occultists continually affirm that "certain experiences do not cease to exist simply because there is no place for them in our customary order." Occultists display an extraordinary ability to shift from one dimension of reality to another with ease, feeling that the whole world "hangs together in one unified piece."[15] While some Neo-Pagans consider themselves occultists and others do not, Whitehead's characteristics seem to hold true for the groups I've observed.

2

A Religion without Converts

How do people become Neo-Pagans? This question assumes great importance when we consider that Neo-Pagan groups rarely proselytize and certain of them are quite selective. There are few converts. In most cases, word of mouth, a discussion between friends, a lecture, a book, or an article provides the entry point. But these events merely confirm some original, private experience, so that the most common feeling of those who have named themselves Pagans is something like "I finally found a group that has the same religious perceptions I always had." A common phrase you hear is "I've come home," or, as one woman told me excitedly after a lecture, "I always knew I had a religion, I just never knew it had a name."

Alison Harlow, a systems analyst at a large medical research center in California, described her first experience this way:

"It was Christmas Eve and I was singing in the choir of a lovely church at the edge of a lake, and the church was filled with beautiful decorations. It was full moon, and the moon was shining right through the glass windows of the church. I looked out and felt something very special happening, but it didn't seem to be happening inside the church.

"After the Midnight Mass was over and everyone adjourned to the parish house for coffee, I knew I needed to be alone for a minute, so I left my husband and climbed up the hill behind the church. I sat on this hill looking at the full moon, and I could hear the sound of coffee cups clinking and the murmur of conversation from the parish house.

"I was looking down on all this, when suddenly I felt a 'presence.' It seemed very ancient and wise and definitely female. I can't describe it any closer than that, but I felt that this presence, this being, was looking down on me, on this church and these people and saying, 'The poor little ones! They mean so well and they understand so little.'

"I felt that whoever 'she' was, she was incredibly old and patient; she was exasperated with the way things were going on the planet, but she hadn't given up hope that we would start making some sense of the world. So, after that, I knew I had to find out more about her."

Harlow is now a priestess in the Craft, working in a self-created tradition that deals mostly, but not exclusively, with women. As a result of her experience, she began a complex journey to find out about the history and experience of goddess worship. This search led her, through various readings, into contact with a number of Craft traditions, until she ended up writing a column on feminism and Witchcraft for the Neo-Pagan magazine *Nemeton* (now defunct). It is perhaps only fair, at this point, to describe my own entry into this same world.

When I was a small child, I had the good fortune to enter an unusual New York City grammar school (City and Country) that allowed its students to immerse themselves in historical periods to such an extent that we often seemed to live in them. At the age of twelve, a traditional time for rites of passage, that historical period was ancient Greece. I remember entering into the Greek myths as if I had returned to my true homeland.

My friends and I lived through the battles of the *Iliad;* we read the historical novels of Mary Renault and Caroline Dale Snedeker[1] and took the parts of ancient heroes and heroines in plays and fantasy. I wrote hymns to gods and goddesses and poured libations (of water) onto the grass of neighboring parks. In my deepest and most secret moments I daydreamed that I had become these beings, feeling what it would be like to be Artemis or Athena. I acted out the old myths and created new ones, in fantasy and private play. It was a great and deep secret that found its way into brief diary entries and unskilled drawings. But like many inner things, it was not unique to me.

I have since discovered that these experiences are common. The pantheons may differ according to circumstances, class, ethnic and cultural background, opportunity, and even chance. There are children in the United States whose pantheons come from "Star Trek,"[2] while their parents remember the days of Buck Rogers. The archetypal images seem to wander in and out of the fantasies of millions of children, disguised in contemporary forms. That I and most of my friends had the opportunity to take our archetypes from the rich pantheon of ancient Greece was a result of class and opportunity, nothing more.

What were these fantasies of gods and goddesses? What was their use, their purpose? I see them now as daydreams used in the struggle toward my own becoming. They were hardly idle, though, since they focused on stronger and healthier "role models" than the images of women projected in the late 1950s. The fantasies enabled me to contact stronger parts of myself, to embolden my vision of myself. Besides, these experiences were filled with power, intensity, and even ecstasy that, on reflection, seem religious or spiritual.

As I grew up, I forced myself to deny these experiences of childhood. At first I missed them; then I did not quite remember what I missed. They became a strange discarded part of youthful fantasy. No one told me directly, "People don't worship the Greek gods anymore, much less attempt to become them through ritual and fantasy," but the messages around me were clear enough. Such daydreams did not fit into the society I lived in, and even to talk about them was impossible. It became easier to discuss the most intimate personal, emotional, or sexual experiences than to talk of these earlier experiences. To reveal them was a kind of magical violation.

Religion had no official place in my childhood world. I was brought up in a family of agnostics and atheists. Still, feeling that there was some dimension lacking in their lives, I embarked on a quasi-religious search as a teenager. I felt ecstatic power in the Catholic mass (as long as it was in Latin); I went to Quaker meetings and visited synagogues and churches. Today it seems to me I thirsted for the power and richness of those original experiences, though I found only beliefs and dogmas that seemed irrelevant or even contradictory to them. I wanted permission for those experiences, but not if it would poison my integrity or my commitment to living and acting in the world.

I remember coming across the famous words of Marx on religion: "Religion is the sigh of the hard-pressed, the heart of a heartless world, the soul of soulless conditions, the opium of the people. . . ."[3] And having no place to put this experience of Goddess nor freedom enough to continue the ancient practice I had stumbled on, I gradually left it behind, and set my sights on the soulless conditions. It was 1964, I was in Berkeley, and there were many soulless conditions with which to concern myself.

In 1971, while working as a political reporter for Pacifica Radio in Washington, D.C., I became involved in various environmentalist and ecological concerns. During that year John McPhee wrote a series of articles for *The New Yorker* called "Encounters with the Archdruid," later published as a book. The articles narrated three wilderness journeys made by David Brower (president of Friends of the Earth and former head of the Sierra Club) in the company of three of his enemies on environmental issues. Two passages from this book come to mind as emotional springboards to the events that followed. The first was Brower's statement that the ecology movement was really a spiritual movement. "We are in a kind of religion," he said, "an ethic with regard to terrain, and this religion is closest to the Buddhist, I suppose." In the second quote, one of Brower's enemies, a developer, spoke against the practices of conservationists and called Brower "a druid." I began to search for a religious framework that might be appropriate to ecological principles. I started by searching for druids.

The two quotes struck me deeply and I began to search for a religious framework that might be appropriate to ecological principles. I started by searching for druids.

Around that time two noted historians, Arnold Toynbee and Lynn White, wrote essays in which they claimed that there *was*, in fact, a religious dimension to the environmental crisis.

Toynbee's article appeared in 1972, in the *International Journal of Environmental Studies*. Its main point was that worldwide ecological problems were due in part to a religious cause, "the rise of monotheism," and that the verse in Genesis (1:28), "Be fruitful and multiply and replenish the Earth and subdue it," had become biblical sanction for human beings to assert their rights over all nature. Toynbee felt that his education in pre-Christian Greek and Latin literature had had "a deeper and more enduring effect on my *Weltanschauung*" than his Christian upbringing:

> In popular pre-Christian Greek religion, divinity was inherent in all natural phenomena, including those that man had tamed and domesticated. Divinity was present in springs and rivers and the sea; in trees, both the wild oak and the cultivated olive-tree; in corn and vines; in mountains; in earthquakes and lightning and thunder. The godhead was diffused throughout the phenomena. It was plural, not singular; a pantheon, not a unique almighty super-human person. When the Graeco-Roman World was converted to Christianity, the divinity was drained out of nature and was concentrated in one unique transcendent God. "Pan is dead." "The oracles are dumb." Bronsgrove is no longer a wood that is sacrosanct because it is animated by the god Bron. . . .

The Judeo-Christian tradition gave license for exploitation. Toynbee advised "reverting from the *Weltanschauung* of monotheism to the *Weltanschauung* of pantheism, which is older and was once universal."

> The plight in which post-Industrial-Revolution man has now landed himself is one more demonstration that man is not the master of his environment—not even when supposedly armed with a warrant, issued by a supposedly unique and omnipotent God with a human-like personality, delegating to man plenipotentiary powers. Nature is now demonstrating to us that she does not recognize the validity of this alleged warrant, and she is warning us that, if man insists on trying to execute it, he will commit this outrage on nature at his peril.[5]

While Toynbee stopped short of advocating a return to polytheism, and implied that many of the pre-Christian deities were too crude for our age, his basic perception was strikingly similar to the impulse that led to the creation of many Neo-Pagan groups.

The article by Lynn White had appeared several years earlier in *Science* and had begun quite a controversy. While much of White's article, "The Historical Roots of Our Ecologic Crisis," dealt with changes in methods of farming and agriculture over the centuries, a few of its points were strikingly similar to Toynbee's. White observed that "the victory of Christianity over paganism was the greatest psychic revolution in the history of our culture."

> Christianity in absolute contrast to ancient paganism . . . not only established a dualism of man and nature but also insisted that it is God's will that man exploit nature for his proper ends. . . . In antiquity every tree, every spring, every stream, every hill had its own *genius loci*, its guardian spirit. . . . By destroying pagan animism, Christianity made it possible to exploit nature in a mood of indifference to the feeling of natural objects.[6]

In the following years I searched in books and articles for an ecological-religious framework compatible with my own politics and commitment to the world. I soon entered into a lengthy correspondence with a coven of Witches in Essex, England. Being no less a victim of stereotypes than most, I pictured the couple who led this group as in their thirties and middle class. But Doris and Vic Stuart turned out to be in their late forties and fifties. He was an old unionist and socialist and she was a factory worker.[7] At this period, I also contacted a Pagan group in Wales. Frankly, at the time I thought that corresponding with Witches was bizarre and even amusing. I certainly had no thought that there might be any link between these groups and my own experience of Goddess, which still came to me, unbidden, at odd moments.

One day the coven in Essex sent me a tape recording of some rituals. The first one on the tape was called "The Drawing Down of the Moon." I did not know it then, but in this ritual, one of the most serious and beautiful in the modern Craft, the priest *invokes* into the priestess (or, depending on your point of view, she *evokes* from within herself) the Goddess or Triple Goddess, symbolized by the phases of the moon. She is known by a thousand names, and among them were those I had used as a child. In some Craft rituals the priestess goes into a trance and speaks; in other traditions the ritual is a more formal dramatic dialogue, often of intense beauty, in which, again, the priestess speaks, taking the role of the Goddess. In both instances the priestess functions as the Goddess incarnate, within the circle.

I found a quiet place and played the tape. The music in the background was perhaps by Brahms. A man and woman spoke with English accents. When it came time for the invocation, the words came clearly:

> Listen to the words of the Great Mother, who was of old also called Artemis, Astarte, Melusine, Aphrodite, Diana, Brigit and many other names. . . .[8]

A feeling of power and emotion came over me. For, after all, how different was that ritual from the magical rituals of my childhood? The contents of the tape had simply given me *permission* to accept a part of my own psyche that I had denied for years—and then extend it.

Like most Neo-Pagans, I never converted in the accepted sense—I never adopted any new beliefs. I simply accepted, reaffirmed, and extended a very old experience. I allowed certain kinds of feelings and ways of being back into my life.

I tell these stories in a book that contains little personal history in order to respond to the statement I frequently hear: I don't *believe* in *that!* This is the standard response to many of the ideas and people with which this book is concerned. But *belief* has never seemed very relevant to the experiences and processes of the groups that call themselves, collectively, the Neo-Pagan movement.[9]

In my fifteen years of contact with these groups I was never asked to *believe* in anything. I was told a few dogmas by people who hadn't ridded themselves of the tendency to dogmatize, but I rejected those. In the next chapters you will encounter priests and priestesses who say that they are philosophical agnostics and that this has never inhibited their participation in or leadership of Neo-Pagan and Craft groups. Others will tell you that the gods and goddesses are "ethereal beings." Still others have called them symbols, powers, archetypes, or "something deep and strong within the self to be contacted," or even "something akin to the force of poetry and art." As one scholar has noted, it is a religion "of atmosphere instead of faith; a cosmos, in a word, constructed by the imagination. . . ."[10]

My own role has been that of observer-participant. I began by trying to find reasons for my involvement and then traveled across the country to visit hundreds of people in order to contrast my own experiences with theirs. By the end of my travels I found that many of my early assumptions were incorrect.

For example, I found that Neo-Pagan groups were very diverse in class and ethnic background. My first experiences brought me in touch with a much broader spectrum of people than I had known in the student movements of the 1960s. The first three covens I encountered in New York and England were composed largely of working-class and lower-middle-class people. Later, I met covens and groups composed predominantly of upper-middle-class intellectuals. Then I met groups whose members worked as insurance salesmen, bus drivers, police, and secretaries. All my class stereotypes began to fall by the wayside.

Another assumption, and one I was slow to drop, was that the Neo-Pagan resurgence was, fundamentally, a reaction against science, technology, progress. My own involvement had come through a kind of Luddite reaction, so I assumed it was typical. But in many interviews Neo-Pagans and Witches supported high technologies, scientific inquiry, and space exploration. It is true that most Neo-Pagans feel that we abuse technology; they often support "alternative" technologies—solar, wind, etc.—and hold a biological rather than a mechanistic world view.

In general, I have tried to be aware of my own biases and to make them clear so that, if you wish, you can steer between the shoals.

Lastly, a few words about the reasons for this Neo-Pagan resurgence. One standard psychological explanation is that people join these groups to gain power over others or to banish feelings of inadequacy and insecurity. Obviously (some of the studies referred to later show this) some people do join magical and religious groups in order to gain self-mastery, in the sense of practical knowledge of psychology and the workings of the psyche, so they can function better in the world. But this reason was not among the six primary reasons that Pagans and Witches gave me in answer to the questions "Why is this phenomenon occurring?" "Why are you involved?"

Many of their reasons are novel, and completely at odds with common assumptions.

Beauty, Vision, Imagination. A number of Neo-Pagans told me that their religious views were part of a general visionary quest that included involvement with poetry, art, drama, music, science fiction, and fantasy. At least four Witches in different parts of the country spoke of religion as a human need for beauty.

Intellectual Satisfaction. Many told me that reading and collecting odd books had been the prime influence in their religious decision. This came as a surprise to me. In particular, most of the Midwesterners said flatly that the wide dissemination of strange and fascinating books had been the *main* factor in creating a Neo-Pagan resurgence. And while class and profession vary widely among Neo-Pagans, almost *all* are avid readers. This does not seem to depend on their educational level; it holds true for high-school dropouts as well as Ph.D.'s.

Growth. A more predictable answer, this ambiguous word was given frequently. Most Pagans see their lives not as straight roads to specific goals, but as processes—evolution, change, or an increase in understanding. Neo-Pagans often see themselves as pursuing the quests of the mystery traditions: initiations into the workings of life, death, and rebirth.

Feminism. For many women, this was the main reason for involvement. Large numbers of women have been seeking a spiritual framework outside the patriarchal religions that have dominated the Western world for the last several thousand years. Many who wanted to find a spiritual side to their feminism entered the Craft because of its emphasis on goddess worship. Neo-Pagan Witchcraft groups range from those with a mixture of female and male deities to those that focus on the monotheistic worship of the Mother Goddess. The latter, the feminist Witches, are among the newest and most outspoken members of the Neo-Pagan revival.

Environmental Response. Many of those interviewed said that Neo-Paganism was a response to a planet in crisis. Almost all the Pagan traditions emphasize reverence for nature. Many Witches consider the Craft a repository of survival skills, both psychic and physical (like the things one might be taught in an Outward Bound camp). Other Pagans told me that a revival of animism was needed to counter the forces destroying the natural world.[11]

Freedom. Another unexpected answer. The Frosts, who run one of the largest Witchcraft correspondence courses in the country, described the Craft as "religion without the middleman." Many people said that they had become Pagans because they could be themselves and act as they chose, without what they felt were medieval notions of sin and guilt. Others wanted to participate in rituals rather than observe them. The leader of the Georgian tradition, a Craft tradition with a dozen covens in the United States, told me that freedom was his prime reason for making an independent religious decision.

This last reason seemed most remarkable. The freedom that is characteristic of the Neo-Pagan resurgence sets the movement far apart from most of the new religions of the 1960s and 1970s. How is this freedom possible? Why have these groups refused to succumb to rigid hierarchies and institutionalization? And how is it possible for them to exist in relative harmony, in spite of their different rituals and deities? These groups can exist this way because the Neo-Pagan religious framework is based on a *polytheistic* outlook—a view that allows differing perspectives and ideas to coexist.

3

The Pagan World View

We gaze up at the same stars, the sky covers us all, the same universe encompasses us. What does it matter what practical system we adopt in our search for the truth? Not by one avenue only can we arrive at so tremendous a secret.

—SYMMACHUS, 384 C.E.[1]

Monotheism is but imperialism in religion.

—JAMES HENRY BREASTED[2]

While most Neo-Pagans disagree on almost everything, one of their most important principles is polytheism, and this is generally understood to mean much more than "a theory that Divine reality is numerically multiple, that there are many gods."[3] Many Pagans will tell you that polytheism is an *attitude* and a *perspective* that affect more than what we consider to be religion. They might well say that the constant calls for unity, integration, and homogenization in the Western world derive from our long-standing ideology of monotheism, which remains the majority tradition in the West. They might add that monotheism is a political and psychological ideology as well as a religious one, and that the old economic lesson that one-crop economies generally fare poorly also applies to the spiritual realm.

If you were to ask modern Pagans for the most important ideas that underlie the Pagan resurgence, you might well be led to three words: animism, pantheism, and—most important—polytheism. Neo-Pagans give these words meanings different from the common definitions, and sometimes they overlap.

Animism is used to imply a reality in which all things are imbued with vitality. The ancient world view did not conceive of a separation between "animate" and "inanimate." All things—from rocks and trees to dreams—were considered to partake of the life force. At some level Neo-Paganism is an attempt to reanimate the world of nature; or, perhaps more accurately, Neo-Pagan religions allow their participants to reenter the primeval world view, to participate in nature in a way that is not possible for most Westerners after childhood. The Pagan revival seems to be a survival response to the common urban and suburban experience of our culture as "impersonal," "neutral," or "dead."

For many Pagans, *pantheism* implies much the same thing as animism. It is a view that divinity is inseparable from nature and that deity is immanent in nature. Neo-Pagan groups participate in divinity. The title of this book implies one such participation: when a Craft priestess becomes the Goddess within the circle. "Drawing down the moon" symbolizes the idea that we are the gods, or can, at least, become them from time to time in rite and fantasy. This idea was well expressed in the quotation at the beginning of the *Whole Earth Catalog*: "We *are* as gods and might as well get good at it.'" The Neo-Pagan Church of All Worlds has expressed this idea by the phrase: "Thou Art God/dess."

The idea of *polytheism* is grounded in the view that reality (divine or otherwise) is multiple and diverse. And if one is a pantheist-polytheist, as are many Neo-Pagans, one might say that all nature is divinity and manifests itself in myriad forms and delightful complexities. On a broader level, Isaac Bonewits wrote, "Polytheists . . . develop logical systems based on multiple levels of reality and the magical Law of Infinite Universes: 'every sentient being lives in a unique universe.' "[5] Polytheism has allowed a multitude of distinct groups to exist more or less in harmony, despite great divergence in beliefs and practices, and may also have prevented these groups from being preyed upon by gurus and profiteers.

In beginning to understand what polytheism means to modern

Pagans we must divest ourselves of a number of ideas about it—mainly, that it is an inferior way of perceiving that disappeared as religions "evolved" toward the idea of one god.

The origin of this erroneous idea can be traced to the eighteenth century. We can see it, for example, in the works of the philosopher David Hume, who wrote that just as "the mind rises gradually, from inferior to superior," polytheism prevails "among the greatest part of uninstructed mankind"; and the idea of a "supreme Creator" bestowing order by will is an idea "too big for their narrow conceptions. . . ."[6] Until recently many writers labeled tribal religions "superstition," while dignifying monotheistic beliefs (usually Christianity and sometimes Judaism) with the term "religion." These notions are usually not stated so boldly today, but they persist.

Many anthropologists have long disputed the notion that religions "evolve" in linear fashion. Paul Radin more than fifty years ago wrote that monotheism exists in some form among all primitive peoples. Ethnologists must admit, he said, that "the possibility of interpreting monotheism as a part of a general intellectual and ethical progress must be abandoned. . . ." He showed that monotheism often existed side by side with polytheism, animism, and pantheism. Radin regarded monotheism and polytheism merely as indicators of those differences in philosophical temperament that exist among all groups of people.

As for monotheism in our society, Radin observed, "The factors concerned in the complete credal triumph of monotheism in Judaism, Christianity and Mohammedanism have never been satisfactorily explained, but they are emphatically of an individual historical and psychological nature." He added that no progress in solving this riddle will be made "until scholars rid themselves, once and for all, of the curious notion that everything possesses an evolutionary history," and that the great mistake lies in applying Darwinian thinking to analyses of culture. Radin considered primitive societies to be as logical as modern ones, often having a truer, more concrete sense of reality. Most primitive societies exhibit all types of temperaments and abilities: "The idealist and the materialist, the dreamer and the realist, have always been with us."[7]

Harold Moss, a Neo-Pagan writer and priest of the Church of the Eternal Source, wrote several years ago that monotheism existed in many tribal societies; many later societies developed a polytheistic theology as they became more complex and sophisticated. "Today," he said, "in place of a single Christianity with multiple Gods, we see a shattered Christianity, each sect worshipping a slightly different God."[8]

Another problem confronts us when we attempt to look at old and new Pagan religions with fresh eyes: the notion of "idolatry" and the image of dull natives abasing themselves before a stone idol. I remember seeing this image often in books I read as a child—*The Story of Chanukah* is one that I recall vividly. It was easy to feel pity for the poor heathens, as well as a patronizing superiority. The entire issue of idolatry seems to be a residue of Judaism and fundamentalist Christianity. Both religions have long assumed that the worshipper who stands before a statue or a grove of trees can see no further than that statue or grove, that such a worshipper invests divinity in those things and nothing more, and, contrarily, that other people's worship of neutral, omnipotent, and unknowable deities is necessarily pure and sublime.

The best refutation of these notions is in Theodore Roszak's *Where the Wasteland Ends*. The statue and sacred grove were transparent windows to experience, Roszak says—means by which the witness was escorted through to sacred ground beyond and participated in the divine. The rejection of animism, first by the Jews and later, most dogmatically, by certain Christian groups, resulted in a war on art and all imaginative activities. Roszak finds no evidence that the animist world view is false. He notes that none of us has entered the animist world sufficiently to judge it existentially.

Prejudice and ethnocentrism aside, what we know for a fact is that, outside our narrow cultural experience, in religious rites both sophisticated and primitive, human beings have been able to achieve a sacramental vision of being, and that this may well be the wellspring of human spiritual consciousness. From that rich source there flow countless religious and philosophical traditions. The differences between these traditions—between Eskimo shamanism and medieval alchemy, between Celtic druidism and Buddhist Tantra—are many; but an essentially magical worldview is common to them all. . . . This diverse family of religions and philosophies [represents] the Old Gnosis—the old way of knowing, which delighted in finding the sacred in the profane. . . . I regard it as the essential and supreme impulse of the religious life. This is not, of course, religion as many people in our society know it. It is a visionary style of knowledge, not a theological one; its proper language is myth and ritual; its foundation is rapture, not faith and doctrine; and its experience of nature is one of living communion.[9]

Our idea of idolatry is therefore a kind of racist perception grounded in ignorance. For Roszak, if there *is* any idolatry, it exists in our society, where artificiality is extolled and religion viewed as something apart from nature, supernatural. Roszak has called the modern view "the religion of the single vision."

Much of the theoretical basis for a modern defense of polytheism comes from Jungian psychologists, who have long argued that the gods and goddesses of myth, legend, and fairy tale represent archetypes, real potencies and potentialities deep within the psyche, which, when allowed to flower, permit us to be more fully human. These archetypes must be approached and ultimately reckoned with if we are to experience the riches we have repressed. Most Jungians ..rgue that the task is to unite these potentialities into a symphonic whole. One unorthodox Jungian, James Hillman, has argued for a "polytheistic psychology" that gives reign to various parts of the self, not always leading to integration and wholeness.

In theological circles the champion of a new polytheism has been David Miller, professor of religion at Syracuse University. Miller relies heavily on Jungian ideas. For him, polytheism is the rediscovery of gods and goddesses as archetypal forces in our lives. Miller's arguments, set forth in *The New Polytheism*, are similar to the views of many Neo-Pagans. Yet at the time of publication Miller was apparently unaware of the widespread emergence of Neo-Pagan groups; he only reported that his students had become deeply drawn to the Greek myths, at the same time that theologians and psychologists were reappraising the idea of polytheism. Theologian William Hamilton, for one, had said at a conference that students are now seeking access to all the gods, "eastern and western, primitive and modern, heretical and orthodox, mad and sane." These gods are "not to be believed in or trusted, but to be used to give shape to an increasingly complex and variegated experience of life." Hamilton added, "The revolution does not look like monotheism, Christian or post-Christian. What it looks like is polytheism." This remark was the beginning of Miller's journey.

By the end of it Miller had come to believe that the much talked of "death of God" was really the death of the one-dimensional "monotheistic" thinking that had dominated Western culture from top to bottom, influencing not only its religion but its psychology and politics as well. Polytheism, by contrast, was a view that allowed multiple dimensions of reality.

> Polytheism is the name given to a specific religious situation . . . characterized by plurality. . . . Socially understood, polytheism is eternally in unresolvable conflict with social monotheism, which in its worst form is fascism and in its less destructive forms is imperialism, capitalism, feudalism and monarchy. . . . Polytheism is not only a social reality; it is also a philosophical condition. It is that reality experienced by men and women when Truth with a capital "T" cannot be articulated reflectively according to a single grammar, a single logic, or a single symbol system.[10]

Far from being merely a religious belief, polytheism, for Miller, is an attitude that allows one to affirm "the radical plurality of the self." In psychology, for example, it would allow one to discover the various sides of one's personality. Beyond that, it becomes a world view that allows for complexity, multiple meanings, and ambiguities. Like Roszak's "Old Gnosis," it is at home with metaphors and myths. Yet this new polytheism is "not simply a matter of pluralism in the social order, anarchy in politics, polyphonic meaning in language"; the gods, for Miller, are informing powers, psychic realities that give shape to social, intellectual, and personal existence.

Miller disagrees with a number of theologians who espouse monotheism—in particular, H. Richard Niebuhr, who says that the central problem of modern society is that it *is* polytheistic. Niebuhr, defining gods as value centers, sees modern polytheism as the worship of social gods such as money, power, and sex. Against this social polytheism Niebuhr opposes a radical monotheism that worships only the principle of being.

Miller's reply calls for a deeper polytheism. He sees the gods not as value centers but as potencies within the psyche that play out their mythic stories in our daily lives.

Miller believes that we can experience multiplicity without jeopardizing integration and wholeness. He observes that polytheism *includes* monotheism, but the reverse does not hold true. For most people, religious practice comes down to a series of consecutive monotheisms, all within a larger polytheistic framework.

Here Miller is close to the modern Neo-Pagans who devote themselves to one of a number of gods and goddesses or one of a number of traditions, without denying the validity of other gods or traditions.[11]

Miller relies heavily on James Hillman's essay "Psychology: Monotheistic or Polytheistic." Hillman said that psychology had long been colored by a theology of monotheism, especially in its view that unity, integration, wholeness, is *always* the proper goal of psychological development and that fragmentation is always a sign of pathology. Hillman argued that the images of Artemis, Persephone, and Athena collectively formed a richer picture of the feminine than the Virgin Mary. Carrying this idea to the extreme, Hillman suggested that the multitude of tongues in Babel, traditionally interpreted as a "decline," could also be seen as a true picture of psychic reality. He then argued that some individuals might benefit from a therapy that, at times, led to fragmentation.

In the end Hillman advocated a "polytheistic psychology" that would allow many possible voices:

> By providing a divine background of personages and powers for each complex, it would find a place for each spark. . . . It would accept the multiplicity of voices, the Babel of anima and animus, without insisting upon unifying them into one figure. . . ."[12]

Hillman's contention that Jung always stressed the self as primary and considered all exploration of archetypes as preliminary to something higher is open to dispute. His views have not been accepted by most Jungians. Still, his question, "If there is only one model of individuation, can there be true individuality?" is close to the Neo-Pagan religious and social critique.

Miller's and Hillman's ideas about polytheism at times seem too much like the liberal notion of pluralism, a kind of competition of factions. Most Neo-Pagans that I know see polytheism not as competitive factions but as facets of a jewel, harmonious but differing. Many Neo-Pagans *do*, however, see the gods in Jungian terms. The late Gwydion Pendderwen, one of the best-known bards in the Craft, told me, "The gods are really the components of our psyches. We are the gods, in the sense that we, as the sum total of human beings, are the sum of the gods. And Pagans do not wish to be pinned down to a specific act of consciousness. They keep an open ticket."

Miller writes that the task at hand is to incarnate the gods, to "become aware of their presence, acknowledge and celebrate their forms."[13] These gods, he observes, are worlds of meaning; they are the comings and goings, the births and deaths within our lives. They are generally unrecognized because our culture is not in harmony with them.

He notes that the old ways of knowing (such as mysticism, alchemy, and gnosticism) still exist, but most of us are divorced from them. The recent widespread interest in occultism is, in part, a wish to reclaim them. These systems are richer in imagery than the Judeo-Christian tradition as it has come down to most of us. Despite this, both Miller and Hillman worry about a Pagan revival. Hillman is apprehensive about a "true revival of paganism as *religion*," fearing that it would bring dogmas and soothsayers in its wake. He advocates a polytheistic psychology as a substitute.[14]

Miller advocates a return to Greco-Roman polytheism because we are "willy-nilly Occidental men and women" and other symbol systems are inappropriate.[15] Much of the remainder of Miller's book is an attempt to use Greek mythology to explain modern society. He sees the problems of technology as the playing out of the stories of Prometheus, Hephaestus, and Aesclepius; the military-industrial complex is Hera-Hephaestus-Heracles; the outbreak of the irrational is Pan; and so forth. This may be fine for students of ancient Greek polytheism, but most Neo-Pagans diverge from him at this point.

When Miller's *The New Polytheism* appeared, one Pagan journal called it a "stunning victory for our point of view." Harold Moss, on the other hand, wrote that Greco-Roman polytheism was not a suitable framework for today.[16] And one of the strongest criticisms of

Miller's book came from Robert Ellwood, professor of religion at the University of Southern California, in his *Religious and Spiritual Groups in Modern America.*

Ellwood accurately picked up the Neo-Pagan complaint about Miller when he wrote, "One may feel he [Miller] gives our revitalized heritages in Celtic (Yeats), Nordic (Wagner), African (LeRoi Jones), and Amerindian (many names) polytheistic religions short shrift." Ellwood's credentials are impressive by default: he is one of the very few scholars to have studied Neo-Paganism with any depth, insight, or integrity. His book contains an extraordinary chapter on Neo-Paganism titled "The Edenic Bower." Judging by that chapter alone, he should be considered the best outsider to have written about the Pagan resurgence to date.

Ellwood is no proponent of Paganism, but unlike Miller he has spent some time among Pagans and Neo-Pagans. He asks, "Is Polytheism in practice what Miller makes it out to be? What would a serious polytheistic stance in modern America be like?"

Ellwood first looks at the practice of Shinto in Japan and sees polytheism there as a binding, structured system, a reaction, in fact, to increased multiplicity, a means of structuring it into an empire, a cosmos. He argues that polytheism in the past appealed to organizers of the official cults of empires and that the fervent cults of the dispossessed were, largely, monotheistic—the mystery religions, Christianity, and the new religions of Japan.

As for Neo-Pagans in the United States, he acknowledges their "reverence for sun and tree," their sincerity, and the reality of their experience. "The personal vision of some of the Neo-Pagans is deep and rich; they are seers if not shamans," he says. But he sees these groups as unstable, and concludes that "polytheism puts a severe strain on group formation and continuity," and that it "can only be an intensely personal vision," the vehicle for the subjective. Each group is "tiny, struggling, and probably ephemeral"; he finds it difficult to believe that Neo-Paganism as a religious view can deal adequately with human alienation. He claims that polytheism has never been a cause, only a backdrop against which causes have moved.

Ellwood considers the great spiritual problem of the day to be "dealing with multiplicity," but implies that Miller's position, and polytheism in general, lead ultimately to a life of "anchorless feelings," constant changes in life styles that will eventually precipitate a backlash. One such form of backlash, he notes, can be seen in the Jesus Movement with its slogan "One Way," and of course there are many other new monotheistic movements. Certainly one would have to agree that Neo-Paganism is a minority vision, struggling amidst the majority trend toward authoritarian cults.

Ellwood sees polytheism in the United States as the "polytheism of the lonely poet" rather than that of the temple priest. It is epitomized by the lonely shaman, withdrawn from common feelings and goals. Such images are already staked out, Ellwood says; they can be seen in the personages of Ged in Ursula Le Guin's Earthsea trilogy, Gandalf in J. R. R. Tolkien's *Lord of the Rings* trilogy, and Don Juan in the series of books by Carlos Castaneda. These are all persons who form no lasting groups, have no lasting friends; they share an intuitive knowledge and wisdom, but ultimately remain alone and sad.[17]

For Ellwood, polytheism can never provide social cohesion, nor can it increase multiple options except in private ways. He implies that it is fundamentally antipolitical and antisocial.

Practicing Neo-Pagans might say to Ellwood that their religion is not at odds with the experience of wholeness, that the "instability" of Neo-Pagan groups is a virtue. Individuals may move freely between groups and form their own groups according to their needs, but all the while they remain within a community that defines itself as Pagan. The basic community remains, although the structures may change. Neo-Pagans might argue that the volatility of groups reflects the need of people who are growing and changing, that their religion is not an institution that needs to perpetuate itself or engage in empire building. The Pagans I have met do not equate community and social needs with "largeness" or with the cohesiveness of organized temples, churches, and governments. They say that communities formed for mutual aid and sustenance should break apart when those needs no longer exist, or are met in different ways. In fact, there *is* a broad stability. I have seen hundreds of groups begin and end, but the basic ties remain. The only real question is whether such a loose structure can survive for more than one generation. So far, Neo-Pagans have not been successful at forming lasting communities, but in the last few years there has been a trend toward institutionalization: the creation of legally recognized religious organizations, the proliferation of nature sanctuaries and even a few seminaries. It is unclear whether this trend will change the nature of Pagan groups and, in the end, prove Ellwood wrong.

Most Neo-Pagans would agree with Ellwood that "only monotheistic or monistic religions 'convert' nations. We are not likely to see a temple to Hera, Heracles or Hephaestus on the lawn of the Pentagon." Most would also regard this as a great strength of polytheism—that it does not lend itself to holy wars. Even David Hume's fierce condemnation of polytheism as idolatry and superstition was mitigated by his acknowledgment of polytheists' tolerance of almost any religious practice, in contrast to the intolerance shown by almost all monotheistic religions.

In practice, Neo-Pagans give a variety of reasons for their polytheism.[18] "A polytheistic world view," wrote one, "makes self-delusion harder. Pagans seem to relate to deities on a more symbolic and complex level. Personally I think all intellectualizing about deities is self-delusion." Others told me that polytheism was more likely to encourage reverence for nature. A woman wrote to me: "Polytheism and particularly animism demand the cherishing of a much wider range of things. If you are a monotheist and your particular god is not life-oriented, it is easy to destroy the biosphere you depend on for sustenance—witness where we are right now."

A third reason given to me is the one most emphasized by Miller: diversity and freedom. Alkmene, a Craft priestess in New York, wrote to me:

> A monotheistic religion seems analogous to the "one disease—one treatment" system still prevalent in modern medicine. When worshippers view deity in a single way this tends to feed back a homogenous image. The worshippers begin (1) to see homogeneity as good and (2) to become homogenous themselves. Eccentricity becomes "evil" and "wrong." Decentralization is seen as a wrong since what is wrong for "A" cannot possibly be right for "B." A polytheistic world view allows a wider range of choices. A person can identify with different deities at different times. Differences become acceptable, even "respectable."
>
> The old pagan religions did not have much trouble seeing that many different names were "at heart" the same. Of course, their cultures and politics clashed, but they had relatively few holy wars. All of our wars seem to be holy wars of one kind or another.

This idea of diversity and tolerance was also stressed by Isaac Bonewits, who told me, "The Pagans were tolerant for the simple reason that many believed their gods and goddesses to be connected with the people or the place. If you go to another place, there are different gods and goddesses, and if you're staying in someone else's house, you're polite to their gods; they're just as real as the ones you left back home." Bonewits called monotheism an aberration, but "particularly useful in history when small groups of people wanted to control large numbers of people." In *The Druid Chronicles* he observed that monotheism, "far from being the crown of human thought and religion as its supporters have claimed for several bloody millennia, is in fact a monstrous step backwards—a step that has been responsible for more human misery than any other idea in known history."[19]

Many other Neo-Pagans emphasized that polytheism allowed for both unity and diversity, and several asserted that they were monotheists at some moments and polytheists at others. Penny Novack, a Pagan poet, once wrote that glimpses of the One could make her happy, awed, and excited, "but I can't imagine a religion based on it."

Still another wrote to me:

> I do not believe in gods as real personalities on any plane, or in any dimension. Yet, I do believe in gods as symbols or personifications of universal principles. The Earth Mother is the primal seed—source of the universe. . . . I believe in gods perceived in nature; perceived as a storm, a forest spirit, the goddess of the lake, etc. Many places and times of the year have a spirit or power about them. Perhaps, these are my gods.

And those Neo-Pagans in the Craft, the followers of Wicca, might well be considered "duotheists," conceiving of deity as the Goddess of the Moon, Earth, and sea, and the God of the woods, the hunt, the animal realm. Feminist Witches are often monotheists, worshipping the Goddess as the One. Morgan McFarland, who heads the Dallas covenstead of Morrigana, told me, "I consider myself a polytheist, as in the statement Isis makes in *The Golden Ass* when she says, 'From me come all gods and goddesses who exist.' So that I see myself as monotheistic in believing in the Goddess, the Creatrix, the Female

Principle, but at the same time acknowledging that other gods and goddesses do exist through her as manifestations of her, facets of the whole." One male polytheist said that certain portions of the Craft were afflicted with "the curse of Goddess monotheism which is apparently driving so many Witches mad."[20] Of the many answers to the question "What does it mean to you to be a Pagan and a polytheist?" the answer that remains most in my mind is that of the California systems analyst who is also a priestess, Alison Harlow:

> I am confronted very often with trying to explain to people what I mean by Paganism. To some people, it seems like a contradiction to say that I have a certain subjective truth; I have experienced the Goddess, and this is my total reality. And yet I do not believe that I have the one, true, right and only way.
>
> Many people cannot understand how I find Her a part of my reality and accept the fact that your reality might be something else. But for me, this in no way is a contradiction, because I am aware that my reality and my conclusions are a result of my unique genetic structure, my life experience and my subjective feelings; and you are a different person, whose same experience of whatever may or may not be out there will be translated in your nervous system into something different. And I can learn from that.
>
> I can extend my own reality by sharing that and grow. This recognition that everyone has different experiences is a fundamental keystone to Paganism; it's the fundamental premise that whatever is going on out there is infinitely more complex than I can ever understand. And that makes me feel very good.

That last sentence struck me profoundly. What an uncommon reaction to people's differences and how unlike the familiar reactions of fear and hostility! What kind of a person is able to say this—to celebrate differences? This is the question I struggle with. Who are those who can embrace polytheism, accepting a bit of chaos in their spiritual perspective without denying rational modes of thinking? Who are those who are able to suspend belief and disbelief at will and are equally comfortable with scientific discourse and magic ritual? Who, in short, can afford a nonauthoritarian religion? Are we talking about a broad-based phenomenon in this country? Surely not. Are we talking about ways of being that are available only to those strong enough to break with certain aspects of the dominant culture?

My own experience with the Pagan resurgence has made me reluctant to categorize Neo-Pagans according to simple age and class divisions. I am not comfortable with the "radical" analysis that says that the recent rise of occult groups is a white middle-class phenomenon. It is too simple, although many of those I subsequently met did fall into this category.

My tentative conclusion is that Neo-Pagans are an elite of sorts—a strange one.[21] The people you will meet here may be some of those few who, by chance, circumstance, fortune, and occasionally struggle, have escaped certain forms of enculturation.

Some of the worst analyses of occult groups slip into one of two stereotyped positions: the first sees these groups as escapist diversions for the bored and privileged; the second insists that if, like them, we all change our consciousness and train ourselves to use magical and psychological tools, the world's problems will all be solved.

In my own view Neo-Pagan and other psychic groups do use certain techniques to achieve a fuller and richer life, but these techniques are available only to those who have already gotten off the treadmill and have a certain kind of inner strength or spark. These people are at home with themselves and with others.

The one exception may be those groups that have grown out of the feminist movement. Many feminist Witchcraft covens have, as we shall see, attracted women from all walks of life. But even there, most of these women have already been strengthened by the feminist movement, or by consciousness-raising groups, or by an important experience such as divorce, separation, or a homosexual encounter.

Most Pagans are avid readers, yet many of them have had little formal education. Few are addicted to television. They are, one priest observed to me, "hands-in-the-dirt archeologists," digging out odd facts, "scholars without degrees." They come from a variety of classes and hold down jobs ranging from fireman to Ph.D. chemist. But as readers, they are an elite, since readers constitute less than twenty percent of the population in the United States.

The paradox of polytheism seems to be this: the arguments for a world of multiplicity and diversity, a world that concentrates on processes rather than goals, are made by those few strong enough and fortunate enough in education, upbringing, or luck to be able to disown by word, life style, and philosophy the totalistic religious and political views that dominate our society. Perhaps in my own fascination with the Neo-Pagan resurgence I am hoping that these attitudes can become the heritage of us all. They may be the prerequisite to living a fully human life. The questions posed by the controversy between Miller and Ellwood are these: Has the polytheistic affirmation of diversity come at a time when most people increasingly fear complexity and accept authoritarian solutions? Is Neo-Paganism doomed to be a delicacy for the few? I am not sure.

II. *Witches*

4

The Wiccan Revival

What can we learn of this witch figure? . . . She takes energies out of consciousness and pulls them toward the unconscious to forge a link between the two mental systems. . . .

We know the roots of our consciousness reach deep into the nonhuman, archaic unconscious. . . . The witch archetype makes visible to us the very depths of what is humanly possible, the great silences at the edge of being. . . .

She stirs up storms that invade whole communities of people. She conducts vast collective energies to our very doorstep. . . . These undirected unhumanized spirit forces are symbolized for us as ghosts, dead ancestors, gods and goddesses come up from the world below. . . .

What do we gain from this vision? A sense of perspective . . . . The witch-seer makes us see into the proportions of life. . . .

The radical impact of the witch archetype is that she invades the civilized community. She enters it. She changes it. . . . She heralds the timeless process of originating out of the unconscious new forms of human consciousness and society.

—Dr. Ann Belford Ulanov[1]

The word witch *is defined so differently by different people that a common* definition seems impossible. "A witch," you may be told, "is someone with supernatural powers," but revivalist Witches do not believe in a supernatural. "A witch," you may be told, "is anyone who practices magic," but revivalist Witches will tell you that Witchcraft is a religion, and some will tell you that magic is secondary. "A witch," you may be told, "is a worker of evil," but revivalist Witches will tell you that they promote the good. The historian Elliot Rose observed that the word *witch* is "free to wander, and does wander, among a bewildering variety of mental associations,"[2] and the occultist Isaac Bonewits has asked:

> Is a "witch" anyone who does magic or who reads fortunes? Is a "witch" someone who worships the Christian Devil? Is a Witch (capital letters this time) a member of a specific Pagan faith called "Wicca"? Is a "witch" someone who practices Voodoo, or Macumba, or Candomblé? Are the anthropologists correct when they define a "witch" as anyone doing magic (usually evil) outside an approved social structure?[3]

Bonewits does away with some of this confusion, as we shall see, by dividing Witches into many types, including Classical, Gothic, Familial, Immigrant, Ethnic, Feminist, and Neo-Pagan. And in this book we are (mostly) talking about Neo-Pagan Witches—the revival, or re-creation, or new creation (depending on your viewpoint) of a Neo-Pagan nature religion that calls itself Witchcraft, or Wicca, or the Craft, or the Old Religion(s). This religion, with its sources of inspiration in pre-Christian Western Europe, has a specific history—clouded though it may be—and a specific way of being in the world.

We saw that the word *witch* comes from the Old English *wicce, wicca*, and these words derive from a root *wic*, or *weik*, which has to do with religion and magic. We saw that many practitioners of Wicca will tell you that Wicca means *wise*, and that, in any case, the Wicca are seekers of wisdom. Others will tell you that Wicca comes from a root meaning to bend or turn, and that the Witch is the bender and changer of reality.

But etymology does not help one to confront the confusing feeling that lies behind the word *witch*. The very power of the word lies in its imprecision. It is not merely a word, but an archetype, a cluster of powerful images. It resonates in the mind and, in the words of Dr. Ulanov, takes us down to deep places, to forests and fairy tales and myths and friendships with animals. The price we pay for clarity of definition must not be a reduction in the force of this cluster of images.

Among the Wicca, there is division over this word *witch*. Some regard it as a badge of pride, a word to be reclaimed, much as militant lesbians have reclaimed the word *dyke*. But others dislike the word. "It has a rather bad press," one Witch told me. Another said, "I did not plan to call myself Witch. It found me. It just happened to be a name—perhaps a bad name—that was attached to the things I was seeking." One Neo-Pagan journal stated that the term *Witchcraft* is inappropriate as "it refers to a decayed version of an older faith."[4]

Some Witches will tell you that they prefer the word *Craft* because it places emphasis on a way of practicing magic, an occult technology. And there are Witches—the "classical" ones of Bonewits' definition—who define Witchcraft not as a religion at all, but simply as a craft. Others will say they are of the "Old Religion," because they wish to link themselves with Europe's pre-Christian past, and some prefer to say they are "of the Wicca," in order to emphasize a family or tribe with special ties. Still others speak of their practices as "the revival of the ancient mystery traditions." But when they talk among themselves they use these terms interchangeably, and outsiders are left as confused as ever.

Sadly, it is only poets and artists who can make religious experiences come alive in telling about them. Most descriptions of mystical experiences are monotonous and banal—unlike the experiences themselves. And that is why, after all other chapters lay finished, this one remained unwritten. I had stacks of notes lying in piles on tables: descriptions of Witchcraft by Witches; definitions of Witchcraft by scholars; theories of the Murrayites and anti-Murrayites; theories of modern Neo-Pagan writers like Aidan Kelly and Isaac Bonewits; a hundred stories and anecdotes.

But Ed Fitch, a Craft priest in California, told me, "To be a Witch is to draw on our archetypical roots and to draw strength from them. It means to put yourself into close consonance with *some ways that are older than the human race itself.*" I felt a slight chill at the back of my neck on hearing those words. And then I remembered a quotation from Robert Graves' *The White Goddess* that the true "function of poetry is religious invocation of the Muse," that all true poetry creates an "experience of mixed exaltation and horror that her presence excites." Graves said that one must think both mythically and rationally, and never confuse the two and never be surprised "at the weirdly azoological beasts that walk into the circle."[5]

So perhaps the best way to begin to understand the power behind the simple word *witch* is to enter that circle in the same spirit in which C. G. Jung consulted the I Ching before writing his famous introduction to the Wilhelm-Baynes translation. Do it, perhaps, on a full moon, in a park or in the clearing of a wood. You don't need any of the tools you will read about in books on the Craft. You need no special clothes, or lack of them. Perhaps you might make up a chant, a string of names of gods and goddesses who were loved and familiar to you from childhood myths, a simple string of names for earth and moon and stars, easily repeatable like a mantra.

And perhaps, as you say those familiar names and feel the earth and air, the moon appears a bit closer, and perhaps the wind rustling the leaves suddenly seems in rhythm with your own breathing. Or perhaps the chant seems louder and all the other sounds far away. Or perhaps the woods seem strangely noisy. Or unspeakably still. And perhaps the clear line that separates you from bird and tree and small lizards seems to melt. Whatever else, your relationship to the world of living nature changes. The Witch is the changer of definitions and relationships.

Once on a strange and unfamiliar shore a group of young and ignorant revivalist Witches were about to cast their circle and perform a rite. They were, like most modern Wiccans, city people, misplaced on this New England beach. They had brought candles in jars and incense and charcoal and wine and salt and their ritual knives and all the implements that most books on the modern Craft tell you to use. The wind was blowing strongly and the candles wouldn't stay lit. The charcoal ignited and blew quickly away. The moon vanished behind a cloud and all the implements were misplaced in the darkness. Next, the young people lost their sense of direction and suddenly found themselves confronting the elemental powers of nature, the gods of cold and wind and water and wandering. The land—once the site of far different ancient religious practices—began to exert its own presence and make its own demands upon the psyche. Frightened, they quickly made their way home.

The point of all this is simple. All that follows—the distinctions, the definitions, the history and theory of the modern Craft—means nothing unless the powerful and emotional *content* that hides as a source behind the various contemporary forms is respected. This content lies in the mind. There is something connected with the word *witch* that is atemporal, primordial, prehistoric (in *feeling*, whether or not in *fact*), something perhaps "older than the human race itself." The story of the revival of Wicca is—whatever else it may be—the story of people who are searching among powerful archaic images of nature, of life and death, of creation and destruction. Modern Wiccans are using these images to change their relationship to the world. The search for these images, and the use of them, must be seen as valid, no matter how limited and impoverished the outer forms of the Wiccan revival sometimes appear, and no matter how misreported this revival is in the press.

The Myth of Wicca

Many have observed that myths should never be taken literally. This does not mean that they are "false," only that to understand them one must separate poetry from prose, metaphorical truth from literal reality.

The Wiccan revival starts with a myth, one that Bonewits used to call—much to the anger of many Witches—"the myth of the Unitarian, Universalist, White Witchcult of Western Theosophical Britainy."

It goes something like this: Witchcraft is a religion that dates back to paleolithic times, to the worship of the god of the hunt and the goddess of fertility. One can see remnants of it in cave paintings and in the figurines of goddesses that are many thousands of years old. This early religion was universal. The names changed from place to place but the basic deities were the same.

When Christianity came to Europe, its inroads were slow. Kings and nobles were converted first, but many folk continued to worship in both religions. Dwellers in rural areas, the "Pagans" and "Heathens," kept to the old ways. Churches were built on the sacred sites of the Old Religion. The names of the festivals were changed but the dates were kept. The old rites continued in folk festivals, and for many centuries Christian policy was one of slow cooptation.

During the times of persecution the Church took the god of the Old Religion and—as is the habit with conquerors—turned him into the Christian devil. The Old Religion was forced underground, its only records set forth, in distorted form, by its enemies. Small families kept the religion alive and, in 1951, after the Witchcraft Laws in England were repealed, it began to surface again.[6]

At this point the Wiccan Myth branches in many directions. Different Wiccan traditions (or sects) have a different story to tell. Many will mention the work of Margaret Murray, whose *Witch-Cult in Western Europe* (1921) popularized the idea that Witchcraft is the surviving pre-Christian religion of Europe. Many will mention Charles G. Leland, whose books, written at the turn of the century, described a surviving Pagan religion in Italy, including a Witch cult that worshipped Diana, and a host of ancient Etruscan survivals. Others will mention Gerald B. Gardner, a retired British civil servant who was supposed to have been initiated into one of the surviving ancient English covens in 1939. Convinced that the Witch cult was dying from lack of knowledge about it, Gardner published some of what he had learned in a novel, *High Magic's Aid*, and after the repeal of the Witchcraft Acts in 1951, published *Witchcraft Today* and *The Meaning of Witchcraft*. British Witches will often mention the work of the Witchcraft Research Association and its short-lived magazine *Pentagram*, which did much to aid the revival.

The elements of this Myth of Wicca can be found—in much lengthier form—in almost all the introductory books on the modern Craft that were circulating prior to 1980, including works by Gardner, Doreen Valiente, Justine Glass, Patricia Crowther, Stewart Farrar, and Raymond Buckland. Many elements are unquestionably true—such as the idea of pre-Christian survivals in Europe. Others are sharply contested by scholars—in particular, Margaret Murray's theory of a *universal, organized* Old Religion.

Until about a decade ago most of the Wicca took almost all elements of the myth literally. Few do so today, which in itself is a lesson in the flexibility of the revival. Many scholars refuted the literal accuracy of the myth and then wrongly dismissed the modern Craft itself as a fraud. This they still tend to do. One cannot really understand the revival of Witchcraft today without first becoming familiar with some of the sources that formed the Wiccan Myth and gave birth to the revival. These sources include the matriarchal theorists, such as J. J. Bachofen and Friedrich Engels; the British folklorists; Margaret Murray's theory of Witchcraft in the Middle Ages; and the books of the revival, in particular Gerald Gardner's writings in the 1940s and 1950s.

The Murrayite Controversy

While modern Wicca has very little to do with the witchcraft of the Middle Ages, the revival was strongly influenced by Margaret Murray's writings. Her work must be understood, because those who denigrate Wicca often do so by proclaiming that Murray's theory is mistaken, and that anything arising from a mistake must also be an error.

Although there have been many different approaches to the study of medieval European witchcraft, until about sixty years ago there were two main opposing theories, humorously called by the historian Elliot Rose the "Bluff" school and the "Anti-Sadducee" school.[7] The former, reflecting the rationalism of the late nineteenth and early twentieth centuries, concluded that witchcraft was a delusion invented by the Inquisition. Rationalist scholars said that "supernatural elements" in reports of the trials—accounts of flying through the air and transformations into animals—made them totally suspect. In addition, the Inquisition's use of torture to obtain these accounts rendered them useless as evidence. Opposing scholars, such as Montague Summers, believed in the reality of Satan and accepted all trial reports as accurate and literal.

In 1921 Margaret Murray published *The Witch-Cult in Western Europe*. Murray was foremost an Egyptologist and secondarily a folklorist and anthropologist. After reexamining the trial documents of the Inquisition, she argued that witchcraft could be traced to "pre-Christian times and appears to be the ancient religion of Western Europe" centered on a deity which was incarnate in a man, a woman, or an animal. One of its forms was the two-faced horned god known to the Romans as Janus or Dianus. Murray wrote that the feminine form of the name—Diana—was found throughout Western Europe as the leader of witches. Because of this, Murray called the religion the Dianic Cult, although she wrote that the god rarely appeared in female form and a male deity had apparently superseded a female one. This "organized religion" was, according to Murray, primarily a fertility cult, in the tradition described by Sir James Frazer in *The Golden Bough*. It was a cult of the god who dies and is reborn, and whose birth and death are reflected in the cycle of the seasons and the cycle of crops. According to Murray, this cult had originated with an aboriginal British race of small people who were the reality behind the fairy faith. The cult had participants in all classes from the peasantry to the nobility. The two main festivals of the cult, on May Eve and November Eve, were described as "pre-agricultural," having more to do with the fertility of animals than of crops.

Murray wrote that witches practiced a joyous religion. They met at the eight great festivals (sabbats) and at more general meetings (esbats) in covens of thirteen. They feasted and danced and had shamanistic visions. She argued, in fact, that the trial reports of accused witches describing themselves as flying through the air and changing their shape into animals were "ritual and not actual," a "clear account of the witch herself and her companions believing in the change of form caused by the magical object in exactly the same way that the shamans believe in their own transformation by similar means." Murray also argued that the coven, the sabbat, and all other aspects of the accusations made against witches had a reality behind them. The Inquisition had simply turned the god of the witches into their devil and substituted evil for good.[8]

Murray's later books, *The God of the Witches* (1933) and *The Divine King in England* (1954), were even more controversial, particularly the latter. In that book she argued that the idea of the sacred king was a reality in Britain and that many English kings had been ritually murdered; she contended that most of Britain's royalty had been members of the Dianic Cult. Most scholars dismissed this book as the work of a crackpot who had the audacity to publish at the age of ninety. (Murray was a remarkable woman who lived to be a hundred. She published her autobiography, *My First Hundred Years*, in 1963, the same year she died.[9])

Murray's theories held sway for quite some time. In the last twenty years, however, they have come under increasing attack. The arguments against her are many: that she took as true stories that may have been fabricated under torture; that, while she gave good evidence for Pagan survivals in Britain, she did not give evidence that an *organized* Pagan religion survived, or that this religion was universal, or that covens or sabbats existed before they appeared in Inquisitors' reports.

The primary value of Murray's work was her understanding of the persistence of Pagan folk customs in Britain and her realization that Witchcraft could not be examined in isolation from the comparative history of religions or from the study of anthropology and folklore. But most scholars today view her work as filled with errors.

Studies of European witchcraft, particularly of what has come to be called the witch craze of the sixteenth and seventeenth centuries, are so vast that to summarize scholarship after Murray would be impossible in a book of this nature. But a few examples will illustrate the kind of thinking that scholars have brought to the subject in the last ten years. Here is a brief summary of the opinions of three writers, only one of whom gives even indirect support to Murray's thesis. Although often highly critical of earlier scholarship, these views are modern variations on three traditional approaches: (1) that European witchcraft was a delusion fostered by the Inquisition; (2) that it was an invention of the Inquisition for political and social purposes; (3) that it was the survival of archaic Pagan traditions.*

Norman Cohn:
Witchcraft as Delusion

The most recent exponent of the "delusion" view is historian Norman Cohn, author of *Europe's Inner Demons* (1975). Cohn has turned the old dismissal of witchcraft as "the delusions of hysterics" into a more sophisticated argument worthy of our psychoanalytical age.

The stereotype of the witch, Cohn writes, comes from a specific fantasy that originates in antiquity. This fantasy—that there exists in the midst of the larger society a small clandestine society engaged in antihuman practices, including infanticide, incest, cannibalism, bestiality, and orgiastic sex—is an age-old tradition. It was first used by the Romans to characterize Christians, and later by the Christians to characterize Jews as well as heretical Christian sects such as the Cathars, the Waldensians, the Manichaeans, the Montanists, and groups such as the Knights Templar.

* At least one scholar has asked me why I chose these three writers. He argues that, taken together, they do not give a complete picture, and individually they may not be the best examples. But their views have captured the popular imagination. These authors have been reviewed in literary magazines and are widely read outside the field of their specialty. They have had an impact, and they are taken seriously.

Cohn doubts that a sect of witches ever existed; therefore his book is the history of a "fantasy." He argues that folklorists Jacob Grimm and Girolamo Tartarotti—long considered the originators of the view that witchcraft is a pre-Christian religion—merely drew attention to the persistence of pre-Christian folk beliefs that later contributed to the stereotype of the witch. Karl Jarcke in 1828 first stated that witchcraft was the former Pagan religion of Germany, surviving among the common people. Ten years later Franz Joseph Mone described German witchcraft as an underground esoteric cult. Neither of these theories, Cohn says, is convincing; neither Jarcke nor Mone could show that the worship of ancient gods was "practised by organized, clandestine groups in the Middle Ages." Cohn's next victim is the historian Jules Michelet, whose famous book on witchcraft, *La Sorcière*, appeared in 1862. He characterizes Michelet as an "aging romantic radical with neither time nor desire for detailed research." He argues against Michelet's view that witchcraft was a protest by medieval serfs against an oppressive social order and that those serfs came together in secret to perform ancient Pagan dances and satires of their oppressors. Such a view, writes Cohn, was prompted by "a passionate urge to rehabilitate two oppressed classes—woman, and the medieval peasantry," but there was no evidence behind it.

Next, Cohn takes on the idea of witchcraft as the survival of a fertility cult. He writes that Frazer's *The Golden Bough* "launched a cult of fertility cults," and in 1921, when Murray's theory of the Dianic cult appeared, "the influence of *The Golden Bough* was at its height." He is completely contemptuous of Murray. Because she was sixty years old when she put forth her theory, he is convinced that her mind was rigidly "set in an exaggerated and distorted version of the Frazerian mould." (In fact, throughout the book Cohn uses age as a reason to dismiss a scholar or an idea.) He argues—as do many other scholars—that Murray does not prove the existence of an organized cult. But his main criticism is that she eliminates the fantastic features of the witch trial reports and gives a false impression that realistic accounts of the sabbat exist. If there are parallels between the descriptions of the sabbats and fertility rites, they are, he observes, meaningless. For him the sabbats are a complete delusion, a fiction. He rebukes such historians as Elliot Rose and Jeffrey Burton Russell for still being under Murray's influence despite their criticism of her work; and he vents his dismay that Murray's work has "stimulated the extraordinary proliferation of 'witches' covens' in Western Europe and the United States during the past decade, culminating in the foundation of the Witches International Craft Association, with headquarters in New York."

Cohn's main point is that no story with "impossible elements" should be accepted as evidence. "Nobody has ever come across a real society of witches," he writes, adding:

> Taken as a whole, that tradition itself forms a curious chapter in the history of ideas. Over a period of a century and a half, the non-existent society of witches has been repeatedly re-interpreted in light of the intellectual preoccupations of the moment. The theories of Jarcke and Mone were clearly inspired by the current dread of secret societies; that of Michelet, by his enthusiasm for the emancipation of the working classes and women; those of Murray and Runeberg, by the Frazerian belief that religion originally consisted of fertility cults; those of Rose and Russell, maybe, by the spectacle of the psychedelic and orgiastic experiments of the 1960s.[10]

According to Cohn, scholars have simply been "grossly underestimating the capacities of human imagination." He writes that the many "fantastic" notions about witches had a long history in folk beliefs—that they practiced evil, that they changed shape and flew through the air—but were never significant until new Inquisitorial procedures began to investigate ritual magic. At that point, small-scale trials of individuals accused of consorting with demons took place. These were minor affairs, and most of the accused were priests. It was not until all parts of the "fantasy" were put together and believed by those in authority that the witch persecutions could really begin. For most peasants, witches were simply those—mostly women—who harmed by occult means. The other notion, that witches were members of a secret sect headed by Satan, came from educated Church leaders and Inquisitors when the Inquisitors themselves had become convinced of the *reality* of the sabbat and nocturnal flights. (Murray, as we have seen, never considered the nocturnal flights to be real, but believed them to be shamanistic visions similar to those reported by religious visionaries around the world.)

At the end of *Europe's Inner Demons* Cohn, unfortunately, leaps into his own fantasy. He adopts whole hog the most popular witchcraft religion of our day—psychiatry. The origins of witchcraft in the Middle Ages lie in our unconscious, he writes. It is a fantasy at work both in history and the writing of history. The witch hunts would never have taken place without "the fantasy of a child-eating, orgiastic, Devil-worshipping sect." The only continuity is in the fantasy. And where do those fantasies come from? Cohn's answer is that they represented "the innermost selves" of many Europeans, "their obsessive fears, and also their unacknowledged, terrifying desires." These fantasies of cannibalism and infanticide appear in all folklore, and their roots are in childhood, part of the "wishes and anxieties experienced in infancy or early childhood, but deeply repressed and, in their original form, wholly unconscious." The creation of a society of witches was, therefore, an unconscious revolt against Christianity as too strict and repressive.

One of the problems with Cohn's argument is his limited conception of what is possible in reality. For example, he considers all reports of orgies to be fantasy. He states, "Orgies where one mates with one's neighbour in the dark, without troubling to establish whether that neighbour is male or female, a stranger or, on the contrary, one's own father or mother, son or daughter, belong to the world of fantasy." Here he is surprisingly ignorant of the history of sex and ritual. Orgiastic practices were a part of religious rites in many cultures of the ancient world. And while most modern group sexual encounters lack a religious dimension, one has only to read reports about modern sex clubs to know that orgiastic experiences are not merely a product of fantasy.

H. R. Trevor-Roper: Witchcraft as a Political Creation

Many writers have viewed the witchcraft of the sixteenth and seventeenth centuries as a creation of the Inquisition brought about not by the unconscious but by policy—to achieve political goals. One of the clearest expositions of this view can be found in the work of historian H. R. Trevor-Roper. Unlike Cohn, Trevor-Roper sees the witch craze not as a delusion but as a clear product of social and political forces.

Pagan folk beliefs and magical beliefs, says Trevor-Roper, were universal, and during the "Dark Ages" the Church did much to dispel them. He cites a statement by Saint Boniface that belief in witches was "unchristian." He cites Charlemagne's decree that those who burned witches would be put to death. He cites the much-quoted Church document of the eighth century, the *Canon Episcopi*, which declared the powers of witches to be illusion. This document remained official Church policy until it was systematically reversed by the Inquisition. By the end of the fifteenth century a new doctrine had been established—*not* to believe in witches was heresy—and the *Canon Episcopi* became an "inconvenient text of canon law."

Trevor-Roper argues that European witchcraft was not "the old pre-Christian religion of rural Europe." Yes, he writes, Pagan customs did survive, including beliefs in the night-riding goddesses Diana and Herodias. Yes, what came to be called witchcraft did include elements of Pagan belief. But, he adds, one must not "confuse the scattered fragments of paganism with the grotesque system into which they are only long afterwards arranged." These survivals only became an organized system when the Church took the older beliefs and fragments and created an "organized, systematic 'demonology,'" complete with new elements, including the pact with the devil, the coven, and the sabbat.

At first, he writes, the new stereotype was woven into a system by the Catholic Church and was used in local struggles against groups it would not assimilate. Then it might have died, had it not been revived in the century of the Black Death and the Hundred Years' War, and had it not received new strength from the struggle between Reformation and Counter-Reformation, which "revived the dying witch-craze just as it had revived so many other obsolescent habits of thought: biblical fundamentalism, theological history, scholastic Aristoteleanism."

Trevor-Roper contends that in the sixteenth and seventeenth centuries this new demonology "acquired a momentum of its own" from the struggle between Catholicism and Protestantism. He asserts that every major outbreak of the witch persecutions in the 1560s and after took place in the frontier areas between the two religious groups. For example, persecution in England was fiercest in Essex and Lancashire, where Catholicism was strong. In Catholic France most of the witches were Protestant and often came from "Protestant islands" like Orleans and Normandy.

The new mythology of witchcraft became part of the social structure and the structure of thought. The best minds of the age believed it. It "was the social consequence of renewed ideological war and the accompanying climate of fear." And Trevor-Roper argues that this is the real reason that the confessions at the trials sounded the same and that identical answers were given, even in places where judicial torture did not take place. These confessions were not always obtained through torture, nor were the beliefs expressed in them merely delusion, "detached or detachable from the social and intellectual structure of the time." They were, rather, the creation of social and political struggles. And only when the social structure of the society changed could the myth be destroyed.[11]

Mircea Eliade:
Witchcraft as an Archaic Pagan Survival

The most interesting recent support for the Murrayite position—albeit very indirect support—has come from the historian Mircea Eliade. He observes in an essay, "Some Observations on European Witchcraft," that while Murray's work is filled with errors and unproven assumptions, more recent studies of Indian and Tibetan documents "will convince an unprejudiced reader that European witchcraft cannot be the creation of religious or political persecution or be a demonic sect devoted to Satan and the promotion of evil."

> As a matter of fact, all the features associated with European witches are—with the exception of Satan and the Sabbath—claimed also by Indo-Tibetan yogis and magicians. They too are supposed to fly through the air, render themselves invisible, kill at a distance, master demons and ghosts, and so on. Moreover, some of these eccentric Indian sectarians boast that they break all the religious taboos and social rules: that they practice human sacrifice, cannibalism, and all manner of orgies, includ-

ing incestuous intercourse, and that they eat excrement, nauseating animals, and devour human corpses. In other words, they proudly claim all the crimes and horrible ceremonies cited ad nauseam in the Western European witch trials.[12]

Eliade points to the cult of the *benandanti*, unearthed by Carlo Ginzburg. On the four great agricultural festivals of the year these Italian wizards fought a battle (in trance) against a group of evil wizards, the *stregoni*. They went to their assemblies *in spiritu*, while they slept, and their central rite was a ceremonial battle against the *stregoni* to assure the harvest. "It is probable," writes Eliade, "that this combat between *benandanti* and *stregoni* prolonged an archaic ritual scenario of competitions and contests between two opposing groups, designed to stimulate the creative forces of nature and regenerate human society as well." The persecution of the *benandanti* took place in Italy in the sixteenth and seventeenth centuries and in most of the trials the accused were charged with adhering to a cult of Diana. The Inquisitional model pressed upon the accused had an effect and "after fifty years of Inquisitorial trials, the *benandanti* acknowledged their identity with the witches (*strighe* and *stregoni*)." They began to speak of the sabbat and pacts with the devil. Eliade argues that though this example gives no evidence for Murray's horned god or for her organized system of covens, it is, nevertheless, "a well-documented case of the *processus* through which a popular and archaic secret cult of fertility is transformed into a merely magical, or even black-magical, practice under pressure of the Inquisition." Incidently, Norman Cohn dismisses the *benandanti* because their experiences were all under trance and therefore, to him, illusory.

Eliade also describes parallels in Romanian studies, significant because there was no systematic persecution of witches in Romania, no institution analagous to the Inquisition, and the "archaic popular culture" was therefore under "less rigid ecclesiastical control." Romanian witches were reported to change their shape, to ride on brooms, and to fight all night at specific festival times until they became reconciled. The Romanian Diana was connected with the fairies, and the Queen of the Fairies came to be associated in name with Diana, Irodiada, and Aradia—"names," Eliade writes, "famous among western European witches."

Eliade concludes that "What medieval authors designated as witchcraft, and what became the witch crazes of the fourteenth, sixteenth, and seventeenth centuries, had its roots in some archaic mythico-ritual scenarios comparable with those surviving among the Italian *benandanti* and in Romanian folk culture."[13]

Modern Wicca, while retaining the use of such terms as *esbat, sabbat* and *coven*, bears no resemblance to the European witchcraft that the scholars have discussed. There are no beliefs in Satan, no pacts, no sacrifices, no infanticide, no cannibalism, and often not even any sex. Still, the theories of Margaret Murray were strongly influential in stimulating the revival of Wicca, and it can be argued that her work alone generated a number of British covens.

Other Sources of the Revival

It is clear that many of the revivers of Witchcraft, such as Gerald Gardner, came into contact with various books promoting the idea of goddess worship including, at the very least, Lucius Apuleius' classical witchcraft romance, *The Golden Ass*[14] (in which Apuleius becomes a priest of Isis after the goddess appears in a beautiful vision), and Charles G. Leland's *Aradia, or the Gospel of the Witches*, published in 1899.[15]

If scholars have contested Murray's thesis, they have totally dismissed Leland by saying either that he was the victim of a bad joke or, since he had written satire in the past, he could not be taken seriously. Jeffrey Burton Russell, author of *Witchcraft in the Middle Ages*, has said that *Aradia* does not contain useful evidence.[16] Elliot Rose has called it a product of art rather than a folk product. The most informative treatment of C. G. Leland can be found in Leo Martello's *Witchcraft: The Old Religion*.[17]

Charles Godfrey Leland (1824–1903) was an American writer and folklorist who, according to the accounts of his niece and biographer, Elizabeth Robins Pennell, was a political rebel, an abolitionist, an artist, an occultist, and a folklorist. He lived with native American tribes; he studied with gypsies; he compiled gypsy lore, learned Romany, founded the *Gypsy Lore Journal*; he learned the Celtic tinkers' language, Shelta; he became president of the first European folklore congress in 1899; he went to Italy and wrote a series of remarkable books that traced the persistence of Pagan religious beliefs. One of these books, *Etruscan Roman Remains* (1892), is a gem. In it Leland traces the names of Etruscan deities as they degenerated through time into lesser sprites and spirit beings who persisted in chants, rhymes, and incantations.[18] He achieved a measure of fame for writing a series of satiric verses about German-American immigrants, the *Hans Breitman Ballads* (1872), but few scholars have taken him seriously as a folklorist.

The controversy that surrounds Leland concerns his meeting with a woman named Maddalena who claimed descent from an old Witch family. She brought Leland what she said was the local Witches' book, a mixture of myths and spells. Leland called it a translation of an early or late Latin work. The myths tell of Diana (or Tana), Queen of the Witches, and two different versions of her union with Lucifer, the sun. From this union was born a daughter, Aradia, who was to go to earth as the messiah of Witches and teach the arts of Witchcraft to oppressed humanity. Leland wrote that this was a sacred gospel of the Old Religion (*la Vecchia Religione*). He said this religion still prevailed in entire villages in the Romagna in Italy.

Elliot Rose dismisses the book and writes that "The whole work reads much more as if one of its authors was consciously seeking to establish that the witch-cult was a cult of this particular nature, and grafted material calculated to prove it onto an existing straightforward book of incantations."[19] Whatever the case, clearly there are elements from *Aradia* in some of the rites of modern Wicca. Several beautiful stanzas from *Aradia* appear little changed in the rite known as "The Charge of the Goddess." In *Aradia* this appears as follows:

> Now when Aradia had been taught, taught to work all witchcraft, how to destroy the evil race (of oppressors), she (imparted it to her pupils) and said unto them:
>> When I shall have departed from this world,
>> Whenever you have need of anything,
>> Once in the month, and when the moon is full,
>> Ye shall assemble in some desert place
>> Or in a forest all together join
>> To adore the potent spirit of your Queen
>> My mother, great *Diana*. She who fain

> Would learn all sorcery yet has not won
> Its deepest secrets, them my mother will
> Teach her, in truth all things as yet unknown.
> And ye shall all be freed from slavery,
> And so ye shall be free in everything;
> And as a sign that ye are truly free,
> Ye shall be naked in your rites, both men
> And women also: this shall last until
> The last of your oppressors shall be dead. . . .[20]

In the modern Wiccan rite "The Charge of the Goddess," as published, for instance, in *The Grimoire of Lady Sheba*, this is only slightly changed and depoliticized.

> Whenever ye have need of anything, once in the month and better it be when the Moon is Full, then shall ye assemble in some secret place and adore the Spirit of Me, who am Queen of all the Witcheries. There shall ye assemble, who are feign to learn all sorceries who have not as yet won my deepest secrets. To these will I teach that which is as yet unknown. And ye shall be free from all slavery and as a sign that ye be really free, ye shall be naked in your rites and ye shall sing, feast, make music and love, all in my presence. For mine is the ecstasy of the Spirit and mine is also joy on earth. For my Law is love unto all beings.[21]

Interestingly, many writers have taken *Aradia*'s political references as a sign of the degeneration of the text. The historian T. C. Lethbridge says that *Aradia* is "much distorted by political propaganda."[22] Craft priest and writer Raymond Buckland cóncurs.[23] Doreen Valiente notes that "Its sexual frankness—which Leland has toned down in his translation—its attacks on the Christian Church, its anarchistic attitude toward the social order, all contributed to make it a book that was pushed aside."[24] Leland was himself a political radical. The more modern Wiccan version fits, perchance, the desires and dreams of a very different man, a man who spent much of his life as a government official in the British Empire.

Still, it is in *Aradia*, and in Leland's other books, that the phrase *"la Vecchia Religione"*—the Old Religion—appears. And that is where the term, now applied so often in the Wicca religion, may have originated. And *Aradia*'s importance in helping to create the revival cannot be stressed enough. In contrast to Murray, Leland as far back as the 1890s said that women were given an equal, perhaps superior, place in the religion. He wrote that whenever "there is a period of radical intellectual rebellion, against long-established conservatism, hierarchy, and the like, there is always an effort to regard woman as the fully equal, which means superior sex." And he noted that in Witchcraft, "it is the female who is the primitive principle." Leland's book is most popular with the feminist groups in the Craft, partly because the myth of the creation of Aradia and Diana places the feminine principle first and partly because the feminist Witches—the most political Crafters—are very sympathetic to the idea of a link between Witches and oppressed peoples. In the appendix to *Aradia* Leland wrote:

> The perception of this [tyranny] drove vast numbers of the discontented into rebellion, and as they could not prevail by open warfare, they took their hatred out in a form of secret anarchy, which was, however, intimately blended with superstition and fragments of old tradition. Prominent in this, and naturally enough, was the worship of *Diana* the protectress. . . . The result of it all was a vast development of rebels, outcasts, and all the discontented, who adopted witchcraft or sorcery for a religion, and wizards as their priests.[25]

Along with Murray and Leland, Robert Graves has been very influential in the Witchcraft revival. *The White Goddess* and some of Graves's lesser-known works, particularly such novels as *Watch the North Wind Rise* and *King Jesus*, had an enormous impact on people who later joined the Craft. Several noted that after World War II a number of books put forth the idea of goddess worship as a way to turn humanity from its destructive course.[26]

Bonewits told me, "Graves is a sloppy scholar. *The White Goddess* has caused more bad anthropology to occur among Wiccan groups than almost any other work. It's a lovely metaphor and myth and an inspirational source of religious ideas to people, but he claimed it was a work of scholarship and that people were to take what he said as true. There are still a few groups of Neo-Pagans who use Graves and Murray as sacred scripture."

It is likely that certain members of the Craft have interpreted

Graves too literally. Graves himself said that he wrote the first draft of *The White Goddess* in a few weeks, in a storm of passion, and from the beginning it was very clear in his mind that the book was poetic metaphor.[27] His attitude toward Wicca has always been one of bemusement. In 1964, writing in *The Virginia Quarterly Review*, he attributed the spread of organized Witch covens to Margaret Murray's anthropological works. He argued that Witches existed in Britain from early times and that several covens had survived, but that Murray's "sympathetic reassessment of organized witchcraft made a revival possible." Graves looked at the Craft with some amusement, finding it numbered among its members idealists as well as "hysterical or perverted characters." "Yet the Craft seems healthy enough in 1964, and growing fast," he wrote. "It now only needs some gifted mystic to come forward, reunite, and decently reclothe it, and restore its original hunger for wisdom. Fun and games are insufficient."[28]

If much modern scholarship has dismissed Murray as a crank, Leland as a satirist, and Graves as a writer of poetic fancy, Gerald B. Gardner is usually put down as a "fraud" or a "dirty old man." And yet it is impossible to understand the revival of Witchcraft without coming to terms with Gardner and his influence—an influence that is much greater than one would think from reading about his life or reading his works.

The most sympathetic accounts of Gardner's life have been J. L. Bracelin's poorly written biography, *Gerald Gardner: Witch*, Doreen Valiente's beautifully written account in her *The ABC of Witchcraft Past and Present*, and the accounts of various Gardnerians, neo-Gardnerians, and ex-Gardnerians including Patricia Crowther, Stewart Farrar, and Raymond Buckland.[29] The most negative accounts can be found in the works of the occult writer Francis King and the historian Elliot Rose.

Here is the story as put forth by Bracelin, Valiente, Buckland, and others. Since certain parts of it are in controversy, this story can be thought of as part of the Wiccan Myth.

Gerald B. Gardner (1884–1964) was an amateur anthropologist and folklorist who lived much of his life in the Far East, working as a rubber planter and tea planter in Ceylon and Malaya and later as a British customs officer. He wrote a book on Malay weaponry in 1936

(*Keris and Other Malay Weapons*) and went into retirement that same year, settling in Hampshire, England, with his wife. He joined a naturist society, apparently having become a nudist early in life.

It was in 1939 that Gardner, according to the story, contacted the Witch cult in England. Valiente, who, according to her own account, was initiated into the Craft by Gardner in 1953, writes that Gardner joined an occult society, the Fellowship of Crotona, which had constructed a community theater called "The First Rosicrucian Theatre in England." Among the members of this occult fraternity was the daughter of Annie Besant, the Theosophist and founder of Co-Masonry, a masonic movement for women.[30]

Bracelin writes that Gardner noticed among the members of the Fellowship a group that stood apart from the others.

> They seemed rather browbeaten by the others, kept themselves to themselves. They were the most interesting element, however. Unlike many of the others, they had to earn their livings, were cheerful and optimistic and had a real interest in the occult. They had carefully read many books on the subject: Unlike the general mass, who were supposed to have read all but seemed to know nothing.[31]

According to Bracelin, Gardner was taken to the house of a wealthy neighborhood woman named "Old Dorothy" and in 1939 was initiated by her into Wicca. Until recently little was known about "Old Dorothy" and many scholars assumed she was a fiction. Valiente wrote that the lady was known to her, but to tell the public who she is would "be a breach of confidence."[32] More recently, in an appendix to *The Witches Way*, Doreen Valiente describes her long and ultimately successful search for the birth and death certificates of Dorothy Clutterbuck.[33] In Bracelin's account, Gardner was halfway through the initiation ceremony "when the word Wica was first mentioned: 'and then I knew that that which I had thought burnt out hundreds of years ago still survived.' "[34]

Gardner wanted to write about the Craft openly, but could not because of the Witchcraft Acts in Britain (the last of these acts was repealed in 1951, largely through the efforts of the spiritualist movement). In 1949 Gardner published *High Magic's Aid* under the penname "Scire." It was a historical novel about the Craft and contained two initiation rituals, but there was no reference to the Goddess.[35] After the last Witchcraft Act was repealed, Gardner came out with two books under his own name, *Witchcraft Today* (1954) and *The Meaning of Witchcraft* (1959). In 1951 Cecil Williamson set up a museum of Witchcraft at Castletown on the Isle of Man. Gardner joined Williamson as the resident Witch and began creating quite a bit of publicity. Valiente writes:

> G.B.G. decided that the time had now arrived for members of the Craft of the Wise to come out into the open and speak out to the world about their rituals and beliefs. . . . Whether or not he was right in this decision is still a matter of controversy among present-day witches, and seems likely to continue to be so.
>
> There is no doubt that G.B.G.'s action was a complete break with the witch tradition of silence and secrecy. I have reason to think that it was also contrary to the wishes of his associates. Today, many persons inside the witch cult regard G.B.G. as having done far more harm than good by his publicising of witchcraft. Furthermore, they do not agree that G.B.G.'s version of the Craft is an authoritative one. . . .[36]

Gardner's version of the Craft was very different from that described by Murray. To him, Witchcraft was a peaceful, happy nature religion. Witches met in covens, led by a priestess. They worshipped two principal deities, the god of forests and what lies beyond, and the great Triple Goddess of fertility and rebirth. They met in the nude in a nine-foot circle and raised power from their bodies through dancing and chanting and meditative techniques. They focused primarily on the Goddess; they celebrated the eight ancient Pagan festivals of Europe and sought to attune themselves to nature.[37]

Valiente wrote that some of Gardner's critics felt the publicity he generated was undignified, but, "looking back," she decided that Gardner was "sincere." Gardner's coven "was mostly composed of elderly people" and he was afraid the Craft "was in danger of dying out." She writes that many considered his insistence on nudity to be his own invention and that, while a very old and valid magical idea, it was unsuitable in the cold and damp of England. She also noted that many other Witches regarded much of Gardner's writings as "a reflection of his own ideas." She noted the use of Masonic phraseology in Gardnerian rituals and the use of quotations from Aleister Crowley.* She wrote:

> When I pointed out to him that I thought this inappropriate for the rites of witchcraft, as it was too modern, he gave me to understand that the rituals he had received were in fact fragmentary. There were many gaps in them; and to link them together into a coherent whole and make them workable, he had supplied words which seemed to him to convey the right atmosphere, to strike the right chords in one's mind. He felt, he said, that some of Crowley's work did this.
>
> From my own study of these rites and traditions, I believe that this old coven which Gerald Gardner joined has fragments of ancient rituals; but fragments only. These were in the hands of the few elderly members that were left. Gerald Gardner, believing passionately that the old Craft of the Wise must not be allowed to die, gathered up these fragments and, with the assistance of his own knowledge of magic, which was considerable, and the result of many years' study all over the world, pieced them together, and added material of his own, in order to make them workable. In doing so, he of necessity put the imprint of his personality and ideas upon them.[38]

The controversy surrounding Gardner is over whether he was initiated into an authentic surviving coven from ancient times, and how much of revivalist Wicca is his own invention or Crowley's or Doreen Valiente's or anyone else's. Most writers who are not members of the Craft or sympathetic to it dismiss the entire revival as "a fraud" created by Gardner.

Francis King, the English writer, has a brief chapter on the Witchcraft revival in *The Rites of Modern Occult Magic* (1970). He estimated that between one and two thousand people in Britain were, at the time he wrote, members of covens that "are practicing, or believe that they are practicing, traditional witchcraft, which they suppose to

---

*Valiente, in her book, *Witchcraft for Tomorrow*, notes with amusement that she is the author of two Craft poems that have appeared in many published (and unpublished, I might add) versions of Craft rituals. She writes that she and Gerald Gardner wrote "Darksome Night and Shining Moon" (a poem used in countless rites that already has numerous spin-off versions) in 1954 or 1955. Her poem "Invocation to the Horned God" has been misquoted in *Lady Sheba's Book of Shadows*, where it appears as part of an ancient rite. Valiente notes that the poem was published in *Pentagram* in 1965 under her name and copyright mark.

be the still-surviving fertility religion of prehistoric Europe." King said that he believed that pre-Gardnerian covens did exist (although they may date no further back than the publication of Murray's thesis), but he attributed the growth of the movement to Gardner's writings. King argued that Gardner *was* initiated into a coven; that he did not find "their simple ceremonies to his liking," and so decided "to found a more elaborate and romanticised witch-cult of his own." To do this, he "hired Crowley, at a generous fee, to write elaborate rituals for the new 'Gardnerian' witch-cult and, at about the same time, either forged, or procured to be forged, the so-called *Book of Shadows*, allegedly a sixteenth-century witches rule-book, but betraying its modern origins in every line of its unsatisfactory pastiche of Elizabethan English."[39]

In fact, there has never been a single piece of real proof that Aleister Crowley was hired to write the Gardnerian rituals. King asserts it, but no one, to my knowledge, has seen any documentation. There are elements of Crowley in the rituals, just as there are elements of Ovid, Leland, and Kipling. Still, this idea was floating around in the 1970s, and one priestess, Mary Nesnick (who worked in both the Gardnerian and the Alexandrian* traditions before creating her own combination tradition known as Algard Wicca), wrote to me:

> Fifty percent of modern Wicca is an invention bought and paid for by Gerald B. Gardner from Aleister Crowley. Ten percent was "borrowed" from books and manuscripts like Leland's text *Aradia*. The forty remaining percent was borrowed from Far Eastern religions and philosophies, if not in word, then in ideas and basic principles.

The most devastating critique of Gardner comes from Elliot Rose in his lively book *A Razor for a Goat*. Rose admits his biases. He is an Anglican who believes Witchcraft is foolish, and while it was "once rational to fear witchcraft," it has "never been rational to admire it."

Rose considers the Witchcraft revival to be a sort of literary production by a group of English men and women who were "sorry to see England going to the dogs" after World War II, and felt that a return to goddess worship would prevent this. The Witch cult, writes Rose, "would happily combine the more aesthetically tolerable *motifs* of several former creeds and the least controversial ethical statements of all ages. Gods with Persian names and Greek bodies would prove, on examination, to have thoroughly Bloomsbury minds."

Rose describes Murray's Witch cult as "male-oriented." The myth of the Goddess, he feels, "reeks of twentieth-century literary fashion," and was not easily available before 1930. He writes: "I doubt if at any date much before 1930 enough of the appropriate literature yet existed for many people to feel that to be truly pagan one must be 'matristic.'" He disregards Engels and Bachofen. He does note Apuleius' *Golden Ass* but calls its "syncretistic" goddess religion Paganism "of a very literary kind." He also mentions Leland's *Aradia*, which was published in London in 1899, but dismisses it as another literary production. He calls the book "post-Christian," "not very pagan," and "not very religious at all." It is his position that the Italian Church had so thoroughly taken over the old festivals that it had "quite as good a claim to represent the old paganism as a cult that talks about Diana. . . ." As for Gardner, Rose calls his version of Witchcraft "syncretic," full of Greek names and no Celtic ones, and even describes Graves's contention that goddess worship is a part of the British heritage as a Nazi view.

Since Rose is judging the revival of Wicca on the basis of its claim to "old traditions," he can become quite acerbic, as when he observes:

> Those who seek here for a mystical profundity hidden from common men will seek in vain, and wander in the same fog hand-in-hand with the eager latter-day necromancer on their left and on their right the Comparative Religionist spying out the elder gods. If they should pick up ten moonstruck companions, let them form their own coven to prove their own points; it will be as traditional, as well-instructed, and as authentic as any there has been these thousand years.[40]

While various writers were dismissing the revival, within the Craft the debate for many years focused on the question raised by Valiente: Was Gardner's version *authoritative?* Or was he merely an "upstart" and was there some other, older Craft that was authoritative? The second issue of *Pentagram*, the newsletter put out by the British Witchcraft Research Association, reprinted an address to the association in which Valiente paid tribute to Gardner and observed that many people assumed wrongly that he had invented the religion. *Pentagram*, she said, was beginning to contact surviving traditions that had had no contact with Gardner; the Craft had "survived in fragments all over the British Isles," and each group had its own ideas and traditions of ritual and practice. And sure enough, other traditions, declaring themselves to be older, generally calling themselves "traditionalist" or "hereditary," began to provide a counterpoint to the revivalist Craft described by Gardner. Various members of hereditary covens criticized the followers of Gardner and disagreed that Witchcraft was "a simple religion for simple folk."[41]

Almost all the writers in *Pentagram* took the view that the old traditions were fragmented, that these fragments once formed a coherent whole. They saw the Witchcraft Research Association as a kind of "United Nations of the Craft" that would open the way "for a truly great work to be performed; namely, the piecing together of all the true parts of the ancient tradition. . . ." In other words, *Pentagram* accepted the idea that Witchcraft was once the *universal religion*, which had been driven underground to survive in secret, with much being lost. Many articles encouraged the joining of traditions "before it is too late," as the heritage was in danger and time was running out.[42]

A Revisionist History of the Craft

How is one to reconcile all this controversy with the idea of Wicca as a serious movement? Did Gardner simply make it all up? Are there hereditary Witches? Are there covens that predate Murray and Gardner? Did Gardner have access to a family tradition?

As we have seen, until a few years ago most scholars dismissed all segments of the modern Craft as a hoax. Some Witches said they were of very old traditions that existed long before the time of Gardner. Others said that Gardner's version of the Craft was a "pure" tradition. And in America descendants of European immigrants insisted that they were Witches through family tradition, and that their Witchcraft didn't resemble Gardner's in the least. What's more, many of them said that Witchcraft was first and foremost a *craft* and only secondarily a *religion*. At the same time, covens sprang up in many places, and coven leaders declared themselves to be heirs of traditions that were thousands of years old. Many of these were soon discovered to be liars. One Wiccan priestess told me, "I've never seen a really old Book of Shadows. I'm not saying they don't exist . . . but like unicorns and hippogryphs, I've never seen one!"

What does this controversy have to do with the reality of the modern Craft? Fortunately, not much. In the last few years, while writers and scholars have been dismissing the Craft as "silly" or "fraudulent," Neo-Pagans and Wiccans have begun to reassess who they really are and what the Craft is really about. And during this time a number of Neo-Pagan American writers tried to piece together a revisionist history of the Craft.

In the beginning of this chapter it was noted that Isaac Bonewits had divided Witches into several categories. Now is the time to look at his arguments more closely, particularly as they are related to the origins of the Craft and the place of Witches outside the revival.

The history of Bonewits's interaction with the Craft is a stormy one. He is a magician and occultist, who was for many years a priest of the New Reformed Druids of North America. He currently heads a revivalist Druid group called *Ar nDraiocht Fein*. From the beginning, when he wrote *Real Magic* (1971), Bonewits has been a bit snide about Wicca. He dismissed the "Myth of Wicca" a little too bluntly, a little too easily, and a little too *early*, and thereby angered many in the Craft. At the time of *Real Magic* and his later article, "Witchcult: Fact or Fancy?" most Witches accepted literally the idea of a universal Old Religion such as that described by Murray. Since Bonewits's views were close to those of more inflexible scholars, he was branded by some as unfriendly to the Craft community. In the book, written when Bonewits was barely out of college, he argued (as he still does) that there never was a unified European-wide Old Religion. There were Pagan religions—many of which were very vital—and many European communities retained Pagan beliefs and even, perhaps, groups well into the Christian era; but Bonewits argued that the "Unitarian Old Religion of White Witches" existed in fancy, not in fact, "the product of local cultural egotism and bad ethnography."[43] His final sally in *Real Magic* caused even more friction:

> Some of the witch groups claim to be Christian, and except for the fact that they often do their rites in the nude, you could find more paganism and witchcraft at a Baptist prayer meeting. Other groups claim to be revivals or remnants of the nonexistent "Witch-Cult of Western Europe"

(made so popular by author Margaret Murray). They get their "authority" from their Secret Beliefs Handed Down for Generations of Witches in My Family, etc. This sort of witchcraft tends to be a mishmash of half-forgotten superstition, Christian concepts, and Hindu beliefs. Thus, their "fertility rites" are done for "spiritual fertility" rather than physical fertility, though they like to hint that their ceremonies are really very exciting (they're not—they are hideously boring to anyone who's been to a good love-in)."

Several years later Bonewits addressed a meeting of Witches in Minneapolis. His remarks were later published in *Gnostica* as "Witchcult: Fact or Fancy?" He later refined these arguments in a series of articles that appeared in *Green Egg* in 1976–1977 under the title "Witchcraft: Classical, Gothic and Neopagan."

Bonewits's division of Witches into categories is meant to clear up some of the confusion surrounding the word *Witch*. For example, the "classical witch" is defined as:

> a person (usually an older female) who is adept in the uses of herbs, roots, barks, etc., for the purposes of both healing and hurting (including midwifing, poisoning, producing aphrodisiacs, producing hallucinogens, etc.) and who is familiar with the basic principles of both passive and active magical talents, and can therefore use them for good or ill, as she chooses.

This "classical witch" would be found among most peoples. In Europe this woman (or man) would be an old peasant, perhaps, "a font of country wisdom and old superstitions as well as a shrewd judge of character." For this kind of witch, writes Bonewits, *religion* was fairly irrelevant to *practice*. Some considered themselves Christians; some were Pagans. In Ireland many said that their powers came from the fairies. Relatively few classical witches exist today in Europe. But Bonewits thinks that most people who call themselves "witches" today are "Neoclassical"—that is they use magic, divination, herbology, and extrasensory perception without much regard for religion. According to Bonewits, 70 percent of the Witches in America today are "Neoclassical."[45]

Bonewits's "gothic witches" are those who appear in trial reports between 1450 and 1750. They represented a reversed version of Roman Catholicism, including pacts with the devil, the devouring of babies, and other pieces of propaganda that the Church used during the Inquisition. Gothic witchcraft, according to Bonewits, is a Church fiction. He refutes the Murrayite thesis of a universal Old Religion with the contention that witchcraft in Europe was a creation of the Inquisition, complete with descriptions of the sabbat, covens, and orgies. He regards contemporary Satanism as neogothic witchcraft because it descends from the gothic witchcraft created by Christianity. Most modern Satanists pattern themselves on the ideas created by the Church and proceed from there. (I would amend this to say that a few modern Satanists seem to be misplaced Neo-Pagans who have not been able to get beyond Christian terminology and symbolism.)

Bonewits does accept the survival of Neo-Pagans into the Christian era, although he is convinced that by the eleventh century most of them had gone underground or had been destroyed. Essentially he takes the orthodox scholarly position that until the middle of the fourteenth century witchcraft simply meant sorcery—the attempt to control nature—and was never an organized survival of Paganism; that the word acquired a new meaning in the fourteenth century, when it was identified as a heresy and was elaborated upon and spread by the Inquisition for its own political ends. We have met his arguments before: official Church policy that witchcraft was illusion was reversed; a new form of witchcraft was created by the Church to root out heresy; many of the old charges against Jews and Gypsies were "dusted off" and combined with the new inventions of the witches' sabbat and the Black Mass to persecute and destroy between two hundred fifty thousand and several million people.

Bonewits believes that some European families may have kept Pagan traditions alive (he notes that rich families often don't get persecuted) but that there is no solid evidence of an underground organized religious movement during the European Middle Ages.[46]

Bonewits uses the term "Neopagan Witchcraft" to refer to Wicca. In 1976 he estimated that of the thousands of people in America who consider themselves Witches, a statistical breakdown might look something like this:

Neopagan	10 percent
Neogothic	2–3 percent
Neoclassical	70 percent
Classical	1–2 percent
Family Traditions	1–2 percent
Immigrant Traditions	1–2 percent
Others (Voodoo, Amerindian, etc.)	10 percent[47]

Today, he splits the first category into feminist Witches (5 percent) and Neo-Pagan Witches (5 percent). Like many others, Bonewits believes that folklore and literature gave birth to Neo-Pagan Witchcraft: the folklore of Frazer and the theories of mother-right, and Leland's studies of Pagan survivals among the Italian peasantry. He says that the fields of folklore, anthropology, and psychology really began to develop between 1900 and 1920, as did psychical research and ceremonial magic. He speculates:

> Somewhere between 1920 and 1925 in England a group of social scientists (probably folklorists) got together with some Golden Dawn Rosicrucians and a few Fam-Trads [see below] to produce the first modern covens in England; grabbing eclectically from any source they could find in order to try and reconstruct the shards of their Pagan past.[48]

Bonewits attributes most Neo-Pagan Witchcraft in the United States to Gerald Gardner's influence, and writes that Gardner took "material from any source that didn't run too fast to get away."

Family Traditions

Bonewits is most illuminating when he talks about the reality of Family Traditions (Fam-Trads). He accepts the idea that some "Classical witches" could have preserved folk traditions and agricultural festivals. While this was no organized universal cult, isolated and powerful families may have preserved many traditions, each family suffering contamination over the years. "There is plenty of evidence," he writes, "of ancient Pagan traditions surviving under thin Christian veneers in isolated parts of Christendom," but "there is almost nothing logical to suggest that the people leading these traditions were in touch with each other or shared more than the vaguest common beliefs."[49] These families often call themselves Witches now, but whether they did a short while ago, or whether they have anything in common with modern Wiccans, remains in question.

Bonewits stresses the contamination of the European family traditions, as well as of those families that immigrated to the United States (Immigrant Traditions). Classical witches were becoming fewer in number, and "Scientism was rapidly becoming the supreme religion in the West."

> Most members of Fam-Trads made efforts to conceal their "superstitious" beliefs and Pagan magical systems. Instead they became involved in Freemasonry and Rosicrucianism in the 18th century, Spiritualism and Theosophy in the 19th; for all of these movements were considered more respectable than witchcraft, and still allowed the Fam-Trads to practice occult arts. . . . So as the years went by, members of the Fam-Trads absorbed more and more from non-pagan magical sources and handed their new information down to each generation, often carelessly letting the descendants think that a Rosicrucian spell or alchemical meditation was a legitimate part of their Pagan heritage. So even today we have Fam-Trad witches who are far closer to being Theosophists or Spiritualists than to being Classical or Neoclassical witches.[50]

Almost everyone who has met members of family traditions notes that their Craft is far different from the Witchcraft of the revival. They far more easily fit Bonewits's description of "Classical witches." As one Midwestern priestess observed to me, "I know about family traditions—there are lots of people who have been taught how to do various things. But it's rarely called *Witchcraft*. Later on, of course, these people begin reading and they say to themselves, 'I was taught to do *that*, and here they say it's Witchcraft!' "

In Bonewits's analysis, the Family Tradition Witches are essentially "Classical witches" who changed with the times. As he told me, "In order to stay unpersecuted, they had to use a lot of protective coloration. When Rosicrucian terminology was in, they would train their kids with that terminology. When Theosophy was in, they were Theosophists. When Spiritualism was in, they were Spiritualists. And this means that from an anthropological point of view, the Fam-Trads are extremely contaminated. The later generations don't know what's from the family and what's been inserted.

"There may have been Family Traditions who read Frazer and Murray and said, 'Oh, that's what we've been doing,' and copied down all this stuff, thinking, 'This is our long-lost tradition brought back to us by this anthropologist or this folklorist.'

"And when a Family Tradition comes to the United States—an immigrant tradition—they'll start to mishmash their family belief system with the folk customs of the people they're living with. Today, many of these people are sitting on the borderline between being a neoclassical witch and a modern Wiccan Witch."

Do the Witches of these Family Traditions speak about themselves as Bonewits describes them? The answer is, pretty much, yes, as we will see from a few examples.

Lady Cybele is a Witch who lives in Madison, Wisconsin. Her roots are Scots and Welsh, and the main family magical traditions come from her father's side. Both her father's parents were from Craft traditions. After arriving in New York, most of the family settled in Wisconsin and Minnesota.

Cybele told me of family gatherings of over two hundred people at which a small group would get together on the side and talk about "the old ways" or "the way we used to do things." Her family was wary about letting the neighbors know that they had any unusual practices. And to them Witchcraft was a *practice*. She said, "The religious aspect was very simple—worship of Mother Nature. God was in Nature and Nature was female. The Goddess was the earth. The oak tree, not the sun, manifested the male principle. That was about all the theology.

"When I was growing up, the spiritual aspects were not stressed as they are now. The Craft has taken a lot of influences from high magic. I think that's a fine thing, but it's fairly new to the Craft."

Cybele's tradition did not contain written laws. "If the Fam-Trads have a law," she said, "that law would be: 'If it works, do it; if not, throw it out.' The Craft has always borrowed from every culture we've come in contact with." Since the family lived close to the land, she was taught primarily agricultural magic—weather working and crop magic.

"I was shown how to do certain things, practical things. How do you make your garden grow? You talk to your plants. You enter into a mental rapport with them. How do you call fish to you? How do you place yourself in the right spot? How do you encourage them?"

For most of her life, Cybele was unaware of the Wiccan revival. "It wasn't until college that I found out there were other people in the Craft, and I didn't know there were many of us until 1964, when my husband came running home from the library where he worked, bubbling with excitement, saying, 'There are more of us in the world.' He had Gerald Gardner's book and we read it through and he said, 'This is incredible! They're not like us completely, but, *yes*, we do this, and we do that, and whoever heard of *that?*' "

Cybele said that in her experience most Fam-Trads were loners who had difficulty working in covens. Occasionally Fam-Trads would work together, but seldom would it be a formal ritual gathering. More likely it would be a series of telephone calls: "Hey, did you hear about Sam Smith, who is going in for cancer tests Tuesday at eight o'clock? Think about it!" Cybele said that most of the Fam-Trad Witches she knew worked in street clothing and used common kitchen implements for tools. "I've added things from other traditions," she said, "because I think they're fun."

I also talked with Bonnie Sherlock, a Craft priestess in Lander, Wyoming, before her death in 1976. She described the teachings of her Irish immigrant grandmother in similar terms.

"Her beliefs were Pagan, although her room was full of Roman Catholic statues and pictures. She never used the terminology that's used in the Craft today. She called a pentagram a 'star.' If you had the ability, she referred to it as 'the power.' She did not use the term 'aura,' she would say 'light.' She never called it 'Witchcraft,' but simply 'having the power.' She called the summer solstice 'the Middle of the Summer,' and Beltane [May 1st] was 'May Basket Day.' Yule was 'Yule' and Samhain was 'Hallows-een.' She made incense from ground cinnamon in the pantry and pine needles.

"I learned from her that the Craft is a religion of hearth and fireside. The tools of the Craft are kitchen utensils in disguise. It's a religion of domesticity and the celebration of life."

Despite having these teachings, Bonnie Sherlock needed an impetus to begin working in the Craft. As with Cybele, that impetus came from outside and sounds strikingly similar.

"I got an advertisement in the mail and it had a list of books by Gerald Gardner. I decided to subscribe to the British magazine *Pentagram.* Then I saw a letter from Leo Martello in *Fate* magazine, setting up a method of getting Craft people together. Through Leo, I began corresponding with a man who became my High Priest."

But this was still not enough. "You just can't go around saying, 'I'm a Witch.' Perhaps it all boils down to the idea that you have to prove yourself to yourself before you can prove yourself to anyone else. I felt I had to have some kind of initiation. And so I went to a Native American Medicine Man. I went through a ritual, a three-day fast and a vision quest. In creating our Delphian tradition, I used a combination of traditions, including Celtic and Native American material as well as things I remembered from my grandmother."

Michael Myer, a Witch from Colorado, also told me of his experience with a family tradition. He had, despite being partly Jewish, grown up in an "Irish sort of ghetto," a small agrarian community in Kansas. A small group of people there who were interested in psychic phenomena operated a family grocery store, where he went to work doing odd jobs. Everyone in the community belonged to the local church, but this group would suggest books on mysticism to Michael, as well as Folkways recordings and selections from the Fate Book Club. One day they gave him Patricia and Arnold Crowther's *The Witches Speak.*[51] Patricia Crowther is an English priestess who worked with Gardner for a while.

"I was reading the book," Michael told me, "and suddenly I thought, 'Wait a minute . . . this is *home*. This is what I feel comfortable with.' I mentioned this to one of the people and he said, 'How interesting.' From that moment on I became more formally tied."

Michael said he had no idea how old this tradition was, only that the families of most people in the area had come over from Ireland during or right after the potato famine. They did call themselves Witches. They celebrated May Day and Halloween and the solstices and would often meet together on the night of the full moon or on the sixth night of the new moon. They had no written laws, their teachings were oral, but, he said, they did form covens of twelve members.

Here is yet another story from a Family Tradition Witch, this one a man from Minnesota:

"I was brought up with a sort of old-fashioned American Pagan-occult background. Mostly, I've revolted against this in much the same way most Neo-Pagans and other counterculture people have revolted against their Judeo-Christian backgrounds. Only a couple of members of my family were people I consider even remotely Aquarian, and they're dead now.

"I was raised as a Pagan. My whole family are 'old-fashioned witches.' This doesn't mean they're anything like the Neo-Pagans or the Pagans of ancient Europe. Mostly it means they're *not* Christians, Jews, Moslems, or modern intellectual atheists.

"Other than reference to 'Mother Nature' and the like, I was never exposed to the Pagan deities as described by Robert Graves and others, and the 'magic' my grandmother, mother, aunts, etcetera, practiced was derived from a wide variety of sources, mostly modern Masonic and Rosicrucian techniques, Spiritualism, 'Gypsy' card reading and divination, Theosophy, and so on. I have an idea the whole thing is rooted somewhere in the past in the Celtic Old Religion, but if so, the elements are so worn down as to be impossible to identify for sure.

"Most of the ways in which my upbringing differed from a standard American one are little nonverbal details. Like being put to nurse on a sheep-dog bitch when my mother ran short of milk, instead of being put on a bottle filled with cow's milk and refined sugar. Cutting my teeth on meat gristle instead of a plastic pacifier. *Lighting* instead of blowing out the candles on my birthday cakes. Bringing home a 'Christmas tree' in a tub, roots intact, and planting it again in the spring. Those are the only things that I remember, but my personality turned out radically different from those of the kids I went to school with. For instance, I *never* had any true understanding of the Christian concepts of 'sin' and 'guilt.' As long as I can remember I've simply realized that if you do something 'wrong,' you get 'punished,' maybe by other people, maybe by the workings of Nature, but never by yourself.

"My family used the word 'Witch' rather loosely for anyone who practiced 'magic'—it had nothing to do with going through any particular *religious* rituals, only operational rituals [spells]. The 'magic' I learned as a child was mainly what you might call 'extrasensory perception'—knowing if an outsider was friendly or hostile, lying or telling the truth, having flashes of knowledge about the future or past of a person or object, locating lost things. As I got older, my aunt and uncle started teaching me from all sorts of 'standard' magical sources: the holy books of a dozen or more religions, the occult and spiritualist books of the last century and this. They also taught me their 'personal' system, which was a hodgepodge from many different magical systems, as well as a lot more that wasn't magic at all but all the con-man tricks necessary to make my living as a magician if I wanted to. (They spent about thirty years traveling around the country calling themselves 'Gypsies' and supporting themselves mostly by doing various kinds of divination. They also gave people 'profound spiritual experiences' by turning them on with peyote without telling them what they were doing.) So I'm really not a 'Witch' in the sense the term is used among modern groups calling themselves by that name, even though I've used that term all my life. 'Magician' would be more descriptive, and it's what I now use to describe myself, leaving 'Witch' to apply to the people who practice Pagan religions loosely derived from Celtic and other Indo-European Old Religions."

As a final example, here is the story of Z Budapest, the feminist Witch of Los Angeles. This is what she told me of her childhood in Hungary:

"I was a Witch before I was a feminist. My family kept a book of who had lived and who had died, starting in 1270. There were quite a few herbalists in my family. At one point our family had a small pharmacy in a little town. My father was a doctor and many people in my family were healers.

"I observed my mother talking to the dead. I saw her go into trance and feel presences around her. She is an artist and her art often reflects Sumerian influences. She presents it as *peasant*, not *Pagan*, and so she gets away with it in Hungary. And in Hungarian, the word is the same.

"Many country folk buy my mother's ceramics. She uses ancient motifs, such as the tree of life, flower symbology, and the idea of the

Goddess holding a child within a circle of rebirth. She does spontaneous magic and chants, and rhymes. She tells fortunes and can still
the wind."

When Z was sixteen the Hungarian uprising occurred and she became a political exile.

"In one day I saw a total change occur. Suddenly the people of my
county came out and loved each other. Hungarians usually hate each
other. It was my first initiation into revolution. It made me decide to
change my life. I wanted to live. I wanted to thrive. I decided my
country was wiped out. I decided to check out the West."

But when Z came to New York she discovered a new form of oppression. The Ford and Rockefeller foundations were giving scholar-
ships to refugees. Men would get a reasonable income, but women
could get very little money. They had to become waitresses to even
get through high school. She ended up in a traditional role: wife and
mother. After twelve years, feeling limited and enslaved, she was
driven to make a suicide attempt. During this attempt she had a vision in which she died and death was not fearful. She told me:

"After this vision, I regained my true perspective of a Witch, how
a Witch looks at life—as a challenge. It is not going to last forever,
and it's all right on the other side, so what are you going to *do?*

"And once that happened inside me, I just packed up and stuck
out my thumb and hitchhiked from New York to Los Angeles. And I
picked up a paper and there was a women's liberation celebration on
March 8th. And I thought I would check out these people. And I
knew them. They looked like me. Some of them had my wounds;
some of them had different wounds.

"I began to talk about the Goddess. I knew a lot of Pagan customs
that my country had preserved, but which had lost religious meaning—although not for me. I also began to read about Dianic Witchcraft, the English literature. A year later I began, with several other
women, to have sabbats. In 1971, on the Winter Solstice, we named
our coven the Susan B. Anthony Coven."

The pattern is clear. The family tradition begins quite close to
Bonewits's definition of "Classical Witchcraft": a heritage of magical
teachings, mostly oral. The religion is simple. There are no elaborate
initiations. Ritual is at a minimum. It is a *craft*. Then there is contact
with revivalist Wicca, in many cases with the "English literature"—

Margaret Murray and Gerald Gardner, among others. From this comes a new outward direction toward activity, and in some cases the adoption of more formal structures, initiations, and rituals.

The literature of the revivalist Craft had influenced almost everyone I met. And whatever Gardner had done in England for good or ill, his books had served as a catalyst or springboard for many covens and traditions that did not necessarily "look" Gardnerian. These covens had little of the minor trappings of Gardner's Craft—the nudity, the scourge, the use of particular rituals. But the influence was there.

My interview with the poet and shaman Victor Anderson is a case in point. This was among the most mysterious of my encounters. His was the only story I heard that was clearly from the land of faery. It was pure poetry.

Anderson, the author of a beautiful book of Craft poems, *Thorns of the Blood Rose*,[52] told me of his meeting with a tiny old woman who said to him, at the age of nine, that he was a Witch. He was living in Oregon when he came upon her sitting nude in the center of a circle alongside a number of brass bowls filled with herbs. He said that he took off his clothes, knowing instinctively what to do, and was initiated "by full sexual rite." He then told me of the vision he had in that circle.

"She whispered the names of our tradition and everything vanished; it was all completely black. There seemed to be nothing solid except this woman and I held on to her. We seemed to be floating in space. Then I heard a voice, a very distant voice saying 'Tana, Tana.' It became louder and louder. It was a very female voice, but it was as powerful as thunder and as hard as a diamond and yet very soft. Then it came on very loud. It said, 'I am Tana.' Then, suddenly, I could see there was a great sky overhead like a tropical sky, full of stars, glittering brilliant stars, and I could see perfectly in this vision, despite my blindness.* The moon was there, but it was green. Then I could hear the sounds of the jungle all around me. I could smell the odors of the jungle.

"Then I saw something else coming toward me out of the jungle.

---

* Anderson became almost totally blind as a child.

A beautiful man. There was something effeminate about him, and yet very powerful. His phallus was quite erect. He had horns and a blue flame came out of his head. He came walking toward me, and so did she. I realized without being told that this was the mighty Horned God. But he was not her lord and master or anything like that, but her lover and consort. She contained within herself all the principles and potencies in nature.

"There were other strange communications, and then the darkness disappeared. We sat in the circle and she began to instruct me in the ritual use of each one of the herbs and teas in the circle. Then I was washed in butter and oil and salt. I put my clothes back on and made my way back to the house. The next morning when I woke up, I knew it had really happened, but it seemed kind of a dream."

After the description of this vision had settled, I asked Anderson, "When did you decide to form a coven?" And he replied, "It was when Gerald Gardner put out this book of his, *Witchcraft Today.* I thought to myself, 'Well, if that much is known ... it all fits together.' "

On the other side of the country I questioned another Neo-Pagan leader, Penny Novack, one of the early leaders of the Pagan Way, a Neo-Pagan group that in theology was closely allied with Wicca. She described her entry into a religion of goddess worship.

"I was working as a cleaning lady for a small college in Vermont. There was a terrible snowfall and I was out on the road, hitching. The moon was up, a beautiful full moon, and I was walking along the road.

"Now, me and God had this relationship. I always yelled at God and God always said, 'If you get off your ass and do something, it will straighten out.' And sometimes it would and sometimes it wouldn't.

"So I'm walking along this road, shaking my fist at the moon and saying, 'Why am I not growing any more? What am I supposed to do?' And I'm furious and I'm shaking my fist at the moon and getting more freaked by the whole situation when I get this message. I didn't hear a voice. I just got this message: 'Your problem is that your concept of the Eternal One is masculine, and until you can know the One as Feminine, there's no way you're going to grow.' So I said to myself, 'That's weird. I never would have thought of that, but I'll give it a try.' "

When Penny and her husband, Michael, moved to Philadelphia, Michael began to get interested in Witchcraft. Penny told him, "I'm *not* interested in magic. I want something that deals with *goddesses* and *spiritual* growth.

"And Michael is saying, 'I read these books by Gerald Gardner, and it sounds like a real nature religion,' and I'm saying, 'Don't talk to me about *Witchcraft.*'

"A week later, in December of 1965, the local Republican committeeman came to call and, in passing, mentioned some Witches he'd like us to meet. He brought over a Gardnerian pamphlet, and things took off from there."

Gardner in a New Light

In the late 1970s, Aidan Kelly, a founder of one of the most vital and beautiful Craft traditions in America—the New Reformed Orthodox Order of the Golden Dawn (NROOGD)—began to write about the origins of the Gardnerian tradition. His yet unpublished manuscript has gone through many permutations as Kelly himself has changed his views. These changes are partly the result of his scholarship and partly because of his return to the Catholic Church.

The early versions of the manuscript were titled "The Rebirth of Witchcraft: Tradition and Creativity in the Gardnerian Reform." Within this work, Kelly did something quite new. He labeled the entire Wiccan revival "Gardnerian Witchcraft." "I refer to this current religious movement as 'Gardnerian,' " he writes, "because almost all the current vitality in the movement was sparked by Gerald B. Gardner, a retired British civil servant who instituted a reform (and I use this word very precisely) in the 1940's."[53]

Most modern Witches use the term "Gardnerian" to refer either to those specific covens that derive through a chain of apostolic succession from Gardner's coven on the Isle of Man, or to those covens that use Gardnerian rituals, a large number of which have been published in books. NROOGD fits into neither category. But Aidan was saying something different—that the influence of Gardner on the modern Craft revival is much greater than most people realize, and that many groups have, often unknowingly, assimilated his main contributions.

The manuscript focused on the problems we have been considering—the Wiccan movement's claim to historical continuity—since most members of the Craft (at least until recently) have said that their practices descend in a direct line from the pre-Christian religions of Great Britain and Northern Europe. As Aidan observes, most Witches see their religion as a "native Pagan religion of Britain and northern Europe that, according to Margaret Murray's theory, underlay the politico-religious struggle that culminated in the witch trials of early modern time." But, as we have seen, most scholars dismiss Murray's theory and the entire movement as fraudulent. The truth, wrote Aidan, in the late 1970s, lies somewhere in between.

Since the late 1970s, Kelly's manuscript has gone through many revisions. The changes in his thinking can be seen from the change in title. The manuscript is now called "Inventing Witchcraft," and Kelly now believes—"with 99 percent assurance," he says—that Gardner had no access to an original coven or Pagan tradition.

Aidan pores over various versions of the Gardnerian *Book of Shadows*, the "sacred cookbook" or "liturgical manual" of the movement. He looks at various versions and drafts of this book: there are working drafts typed by Gardner, which Aidan Kelly received through Llewellyn Press; and there are some of Gardner's magical notebooks and papers that were turned over to Ripley's International Ltd. when Gardner's museum on the Isle of Man was sold to Ripley's by Monique Wilson. After the sale Ripley set up museums of witchcraft and magic in various parts of the United States and Canada.*

At the time *Drawing Down the Moon* was published, Aidan was arguing that there was no way of proving whether Gardner had access to any traditional elements or whether a New Forest coven actually existed. He wrote that if such a coven existed, its procedures were so rudimentary that new ones had to be invented. More important, whether or not Gardner had "traditional information" or simply took basic concepts out of books, he transformed the concepts "so thoroughly that he instituted a major religious reform—that is, as has happened so many times in history, he founded a new religion in the apparently sincere belief that he was merely reforming an old one" and although this religion may have

---

* Many of Gardner's working tools can be seen in the Ripley Museum of Witchcraft and Magic in San Francisco. Unfortunately, the exhibit is tacky; the museum plays up the sensational and, from a Wiccan point of view, it's pretty sacrilegious.

elements of the Old Religion, it is "no more the same religion than the first Buddhists were still just Hindus, or the first Christians were still just Jews."[54]

The concepts that were new—the focus of Gardner's reform—were: the preeminence of the Goddess; the idea of the woman as priestess; the idea that a woman can *become* the Goddess; and a new way of working magic that was particularly accessible to small groups. The last was a combination of the "low magic" common to folklore the world over (spells and recipes) and the "high magic" of the ceremonial *grimoire*. Added to this was the idea of the circle as a place to contain power. Sources used by Gardner included Ovid, Crowley, Kipling, Leland, and the Order of the Golden Dawn.

Could Gardner have been initiated into a group that persevered in worshipping a goddess? Aidan now believes no. But in his early writings he said only that it was unlikely. Some old families in Britain could have maintained belief in the goddesses of the Celts, mainly because the conversion to Christianity there was slow and the persecutions relatively mild. But Aidan wrote that while remnants of goddess worship may have persisted, their continued existence by Gardner's time would have been unlikely in view of increasing scientific skepticism.

But, Aidan wrote, it *really makes no difference* whether or not Gardner was initiated into an older coven. He invented a new religion, a "living system," and modern covens have adopted a lot of it because it fulfills a need. This new system has little to do with the rituals that are labeled "Gardnerian." It has little to do with the few covens that "are part of the 'orthodox apostolic succession' of Gardnerian initiation." The reform consists of these new concepts, the primary ones being the worship of the Goddess and a new way of working magic, a kind of middle-class magic (although Aidan did not use that term). The appeal of the Goddess makes the movement more significant than its size would indicate.*

Aidan observed that Gardner's reform took place during the same

---

* Doreen Valiente writes in *Witchcraft for Tomorrow* that the idea of British covens led by a priestess was in no way original with Gardner, but was the hallmark of nine hereditary covens led by George Pickingill, who lived in England from 1816 to 1909. This concept, she writes, was "allegedly derived from Scandinavian and French sources" and was unacceptable to some "hereditary leaders of the witch cult." In addition, she notes that Pickingill's antiestablishment attitudes and strong opinions against Christianity did not gain him support. Valiente also writes that Aleister Crowley may have been a member of one of these nine covens.

period in which Robert Graves published *The White Goddess* and Gertrude Rachel Levy wrote *The Gate of Horn.*[55] He wrote that

> the essence of Gardner's reform is that he made the Goddess the major deity of his new movement, and it is the Goddess who captures the imagination, or hearts, or souls, or whatever else they are caught by, of those who enter into this movement. It is as if western civilization were ready to deal again (or finally) with the concept of Deity as Female. Whatever the reasons may be why this readiness exists, it is this readiness which justifies and sustains the Gardnerian movement, not a pseudohistory traceable to the Stone Age.[56]

It was Aidan's view that Gardner had never been given credit for creative genius. He had a vision of a reformed Craft. He pulled together pieces from magic and folklore; he assimilated the "matriarchal thealogy" set forth in Graves and Leland and Apuleius. With these elements he created a system that grew.

Gardner, for whatever reasons, preferred to maintain the fiction that he was simply carrying on an older tradition. This fiction, wrote Aidan, has put modern Craft leaders "into the uncomfortable position of having to maintain that stance also, despite the fact that doing so goes, I suspect, against both their common sense and better judgment." He argued strongly that the Craft does not need to depend on such "traditions." It is valid on its own terms. Why? Because it is a religion based on experience. The Craft is a religion that allows certain experiences to happen. It doesn't need dogma. Its covens are linked by their focus on the pantheons of pre-Christian Europe, by their ethic of "An ye harm none, do what ye will," and, primarily, by their worship of the Goddess.

In the last few years, Aidan Kelly has changed and refined his arguments and has engaged in a long dispute with Doreen Valiente, who he now believes was responsible for the tradition's Pagan theology. They have never met, but their opposing views have been set forth in numerous Pagan journals, such as *Iron Mountain, A Journal of Magical Religion.*

In an article entitled "Inventing Witchcraft, the Gardnerian Paper Trail," Kelly writes that there is absolutely *no basis* for the claim that Gardnerian Witchcraft derives from the ancient Pagan religion of Europe, "specifically from an ancient pre-Christian religion that focused on a great Mother Goddess as its supreme deity." Using the same kinds of tools one would use in doing New Testament textual criticism, Aidan Kelly—in this article, as he does in the various versions of his manuscript—examines various documents of Gerald Gardner. His main argument depends on his discovery of one of Gardner's working notebooks, *Ye Bok of Ye Art Magical*, which is in the possession of Ripley's International Ltd. Many things were copied into it, including passages from the *Greater Key of Solomon* that appear in Gardnerian rituals and the initiation rituals that are found in Gardner's novel *High Magic's Aid*. Kelly contends that the book did not start out as a "Book of Shadows" but "had become one—in fact, the very first one—by the time it was filled up and retired." Kelly argues that by looking at the documents it is clear that up until 1954 all the rituals were adapted from the Cabalistic procedures in the *Greater Key of Solomon*. There was, in his view, no emphasis on the Goddess as a major deity and on the high priestess as the central authority in the coven until after 1957, "when Doreen Valiente became the first such 'Gardnerian' high priestess and began to adopt Robert Graves' 'White Goddess' myth as the official thealogy of her coven." According to Kelly, it was only after the publication of *Witchcraft Today*, in 1954, that the Goddess and the priestess became dominant. Writes Kelly: "Valiente's major work from 1954–7 was the creation of a Pagan theology on which rituals could be based; she also created rituals based on this theology by adapting the cumbersome procedures of the HOGD (Holy Order of the Golden Dawn) system to the needs of a small group. As such things go, I must consider this a major advance in magical technology."[57]

In the summer 1985 issue of *Iron Mountain*, Doreen Valiente replies. She says that she did contribute many things to the present-day Book of Shadows of "what has come to be called Gardnerian Witchcraft," but she says her contribution is by no means as extensive as Kelly believes. She says she was not the first Gardnerian priestess and that Gardner already had a working coven when she was initiated in 1953. Valiente says the existence of a pre-1939 coven in the New Forest area does not stand or fall on an analysis of the Gardnerian documents, that independent testimony about such a coven was given to the occult writer Francis King by the writer Louis Wilkinson. Valiente then describes her own search for "Old Dorothy," the high priestess who initiated Gerald Gardner in 1939. After a long search, Valiente found copies of her birth and death certificates and asserts that her background corresponds to the account given of her in Bracelin's biography of Gardner, and that she was living in the same area on the edge of the New Forest as were Gerald Gardner and his wife in

1939. Valiente also asserts that Kelly is simply wrong to say that there was no emphasis on the Goddess as a major deity and on the high priestess as the central authority in the coven until 1957. "The worship of the Goddess was always there," she writes, "and according to Gerald always had been there."[58]

In the last few years, Doreen Valiente has been revealing pieces of missing information. Some of it can be found in her book *Witchcraft for Tomorrow*, and the Farrars' *The Witches' Way* reveals more. But there are many questions that remain unanswered. I asked Valiente, "What do you think did exist in 1939?" In a series of letters over the summer and fall of 1985, Doreen Valiente wrote that she believes Gardner did not invent the basic skeleton of the rituals. "I base this belief," she wrote, "on what old Gerald told me, and on the rather disjointed state of the rituals which he had when I first knew him. They were heavily influenced by Crowley and the O.T.O., but underneath there was a lot which wasn't Crowley at all, and wasn't the Golden Dawn or ceremonial magic either—and I had been studying all three of these traditions for years." She writes that she believes the initiations were more or less as they are today, as were the concept of the Goddess and the God and the role of the Priest and the Priestess. "Yes, I am responsible for quite a lot of the *wording* of the present-day rituals; *but not the framework of those rituals or the ideas upon which they are based.* On that I give you my word."

Valiente also says she never believed "Gardnerian" or any other Witchcraft rites had "a direct line to the paleolithic." On the contrary, she says, "I think that our present-day rituals bear the same sort of relationship to the ancient days that, for instance, the Sacrifice of the Mass in a present-day cathedral bears to the little ritual meal that took place under dramatic circumstances in the upper room of a tavern in Palestine somewhere around 33 A.D." She writes that she is intrigued by Isaac Bonewits's suggestion that a group of folklorists in the 1920s got together with some Fam-Trads and some Golden Dawn Rosicrucians to produce the first modern covens in England.

Valiente also has some words that modern American Gardnerians would find surprising. Noting the tendency to use the titles of "Queen," "Lord," and "Lady" within some American covens, she writes: "All this bowing and scraping to 'Queens' and 'Ladies' makes me sick! The only Queen whose authority I acknowledge lives in Buckingham Palace!" She claims such ideas were introduced into America by Monique Wilson.

The priestess she is most impressed with these days is Starhawk. "Some years ago," she writes, "I did some scrying at a Sabbat, in the course of which I predicted that a new young priestess would arise who would do a great deal for the Craft in the future. When I read Starhawk's book I felt that my prediction was coming true." So I asked Valiente, "How do you assess 'validity'? What makes someone valid?" She wrote back, "Well, to paraphrase Gertrude Stein, 'a witch is a witch is a witch is a witch.' If someone is *genuinely* devoted to the ways of the Old Gods and the magic of nature, in my eyes they're valid, especially if they can use the witch powers. In other words, it isn't what people know, it's what they are."[59]

The Primary Craft Tradition: Creativity

Today most revivalist Witches in North America accept the universal Old Religion more as metaphor than as literal reality—a spiritual truth more than a geographic one. And while the first issue of *Pentagram* (in 1964) proclaimed that the old traditions were once a coherent whole that only needed to be pieced together again, many Witches never viewed Wicca monolithically and only a few dogmatists would view it so today. Bonewits's old definition of Neo-Pagan Witchcraft would now be disputed by most Wiccans. And he himself has modified his views. But he once wrote:

> "Neopagan Witchcraft" refers to people who also call themselves "followers of Wicca," "Wiccans," and "Crafters." These people are Neopagans who have a duotheistic theology (a Goddess and a Horned God), who believe firmly that once upon a time everybody in Europe worshipped the same way they do now, that the Witches were the priests and priestesses of the Universal Goddess Cult driven underground by the Christians, and that someday every ordained Witch will become the leader of a congregation of Neopagans just as their predecessors supposedly led congregations of Paleopagans.[60]

Bonewits, of course, was describing the Myth of Wicca early in its development in America, at a time when most Wiccans were newly initiated or were obsessed with re-creating "traditions." But by 1975 this had all changed. Many Witches no longer accepted the Murrayite thesis totally. While some still talked of "unbroken traditions," few of them thought Gardner—or anyone else—had a direct line to the paleolithic. And people in the Craft were beginning to regard the question of origin as unimportant. Most had become comfortable with the idea of creativity and originality as the springboard to the Craft. As more and more of the Wicca came to see that there was no such thing as a totally unbroken or uncontaminated tradition, they began to reassess the meaning of their movement.

Many of the Witches I talked to spoke forcefully about Pagan survivals. Many spoke of different traditions of ancient Pagan peoples. Many spoke of a rich Pagan past. Many spoke of ancient mythology and folk traditions. Many talked about the names of goddesses throughout the world. But they did not accept the Wiccan Myth as it was commonly described five years ago.

Many of them feel no link with the witchcraft of the Middle Ages, preferring to look farther back to the ancient Greeks, the Celts, and even the Egyptians. If they organize in "covens," it is certainly not primarily because "covens" appear in some descriptions of sixteenth- and seventeenth-century witches, but rather because groups of seven to twelve people have proved over time—in encounter groups, therapy groups, and consciousness-raising groups—to be the best size for like-minded people to work together effectively. Modern Wicca descends *in spirit* from precisely those fragments of pre-Christian beliefs and practices that nobody denies: myths, poetry, the classics, and folk customs.

The comments of modern Witches are instructive. Ed Fitch, creator of the Pagan Way rituals, Gardnerian priest, and one of those who was attacked in the past for adhering dogmatically to the Wiccan Myth, told me:

"I think all of us have matured somewhat. After a while you realize that if you've heard one story about an old grandmother, you've heard six or seven just like it. You realize that the hereafter must be overpopulated with grandmothers.

"Ten years ago, even less, people like Raymond Buckland and myself did agree that the Craft was very ancient. For a while I think I believed the Gardnerian Craft literally descended from rituals depicted in the paleolithic cave paintings in the Caverne des Trois Frères at Ariège, France.

"I think all of us went through this sort of thing. I know I did. But now, of course, the realization has come around to everyone that it doesn't matter whether your tradition is forty thousand years old or whether it was created last week. If there is a proper connection between you and the Goddess and the God in the subconscious, and other such forces, then that's what matters."

Ed Fitch's wife, Janine Renée, said she felt that Murray's chief contribution was to show the prevalence of Pagan survivals in Europe. She felt the Craft was connected to horticulture and that its origins were pre-Germanic and pre-Celtic.

Gardnerian priestess Theos told me:

"Certainly the Great Mother and her horned Consort were venerated in ancient times. But I do not personally subscribe to the idea that cavemen were Witches, as many seem so eager to attempt to prove. Nor do I feel that those many later societies who related to those forces were Witches; nor am I certain that those who were accused of being Witches in the seventeenth century were into the same thing we are into in modern Wicca."

Carl Weschcke, a Craft priest in the American Celtic Tradition and the publisher of Llewellyn Press, told me that the universal Old Religion may not have existed geographically, but it existed in the Jungian sense that people were tapping a common source. "We are reaching back; we're trying to rediscover our roots. Nobody I've met seems to have a truly living tradition. Everyone seems impoverished. But it's coming to life, coming to life."

Moria, a priestess from northern California, told me:

"I've seen people lie to get into the Craft, to be accepted as a 'real' bonafide Witch. They feel that in order to be accepted, they have to have this history behind them. But what good is a lineage? You either have the energy or you don't.

"I've seen a lot of people in the Craft get hung up on fragments of ritual and myth. Some people accept these fragments as a dogma. And dogma is the worst thing you can have in the Craft. The Craft has to be a living, breathing religion, something that is alive, and growing."

Many Witches expressed these same feelings, agreeing that the subject of prehistory was filled with unknowns and that it was the spiritual connection that was important. Dianic priestess Morgan

McFarland of Dallas said that goddess worship had "an ancient universality about it," but that it had appeared in different places at different times, changing from place to place. Still, she said, "at this point it really doesn't matter whether or not it existed. If not, invent it! The people I know in the Craft are so desperate to bring back some balance to the Mother before she is totally raped and pillaged that we are, through that desperation, creating it or re-creating it."

Priestess Alison Harlow took a similar position. "It doesn't matter if the Craft is ancient. What does matter is learning to accept the process of intuition that occurs, that rings a bell. When you are doing a ritual and you suddenly get the feeling that you are experiencing something generations of your forebears experienced, it's probably true.

"I don't think we will ever find a *true* history of the Craft, simply because too much time has gone by and all history is lies, often received second or third hand."

Leo Martello put it this way: "Let's assume that many people lied about their lineage. Let's further assume that there are no covens on the current scene that have any historical basis. The fact remains: they do exist *now*. And they can claim a *spiritual* lineage going back thousands of years. All of our pre-Judeo-Christian or Moslem ancestors were *Pagans!*"

A few Witches were downright cynical. Herman Slater, a Craft priest in New York City and the proprietor of the occult shop, The Magickal Childe, told me:

"I have been initiated into several traditions. All their origins are questionable. The coven I practice with *now* is democratic. We are oriented toward celebration. We are Gardnerian in outline of rituals with a lot of bullshit thrown out. We are Welsh in background and mythology. Personally, I think Murray and Lethbridge were pretty good propagandists for the movement, but that's as far as it goes."

Almost all Witches stressed the value of creating *new* rituals as opposed to being handed a lot of *old* ones on a plate. "I always stress very strongly the improvisational part of the Craft," Z Budapest said to me. "It's not rigid. Our Book of Shadows is a pattern for others to get inspired and create their own books." A Witch from Minneapolis began to describe to me "the beautiful creativity which is happening in us, which is more important than all the old texts." She said thoughtfully, "If we could really get hold of an old Book of Shadows, it probably wouldn't fit where we're at now. Today, when we have a festival, we first sit down and talk about what that festival means and how can we apply it in terms of how we live now. It makes you think. Those groups that go strictly by somebody's book are really very impoverished."

Glenna Turner, priestess of NROOGD, said, "Following traditions may be a mistake. It's more important for the Craft to answer needs we have today." And Tony Andruzzi, a Sicilian Witch from Chicago, mused, "Yes, my mother taught me a few things. But maybe she got them out of the blue! Who knows if she got these things from *her* grandmother. The important thing is that I'm *working* with a fragment. I'm not just accepting it, putting it in my pocket, burning a candle to it, or wearing it around my neck on a gold chain."

One of the most impressive statements came from the late Gwydion Pendderwen, songwriter, bard, and Craft priest. He said, "We make up all of our grandmothers. We make them up whether or not we actually had a grandmother who taught us anything or not. It doesn't matter whether the grandmother was a physical reality, or a figment of our imagination. One is subjective, one is objective, but we experience both."

Gwydion said that he did not feel the Craft was ever a single entity. "What has come down is so minimal, it could be thrown out without missing it. Many groups have received nothing through apostolic succession and do not miss it. Objectively, there's very little that has gone from ancient to modern in direct succession. But subjectively, an awful lot is ancient. It is drawn from ancient materials. It represents archetypal patterns."

As I talked to Gwydion and heard him sing some of his songs, I remembered the long piece by him that had appeared in Hans Holzer's *The Witchcraft Report*[61] several years ago. It was on the traditions of Coiden Brith, the two hundred acres of land held by the Neo-Pagan group Nemeton. I had read those pages and had known from my own experiences there that parts of the essay were pure fantasy. "What about that fantasy?" I asked. "What do you feel about that essay now? Does it bother you? Was it a lie?"

Gwydion replied, "Yes, I wrote a fantasy. It was a desire. It was something I wished would happen. Perhaps that's why there are so many of these fantasies running around in the Craft today, and people trying to convince other people that they're true. It is certainly so much more pleasant and 'magical' to say 'It happened this way,' instead of 'I researched this. I wrote these rituals. I came up with this idea myself.'

"So I sent it to Hans Holzer and I didn't think he would print it without checking the facts. And then I began to regret it. And when it came out, I regretted it again. And I began to get inquiries from sincere people and from friends.

"Then I had a long talk with Aidan Kelly. I told him I shouldn't have done it—that Holzer was a fool and a bad journalist for not even checking the facts. But then Aidan said a most extraordinary thing. He said it didn't really matter because the *vision* I had had was a valid Craft tradition."

It was only a few years ago that the sociologist Marcello Truzzi wrote:

> Basically, witchcraft constitutes a set of beliefs and techniques held in secret which the novice must obtain from someone familiar with them. The normal, traditional means for obtaining such information is through another witch who knows these secrets. Traditionally, this can be done through initiation into an existing witch coven or by being told the secrets of the Craft by an appropriate relative who is a witch. Any other means of obtaining the secrets of witchcraft, such as through the reading of books on the subject or obtaining a mail-order diploma, is not a traditional means and is not considered to be legitimate by traditional witches. Because most witches today have not been traditionally initiated into the Craft, they often create other links to the orthodox as a means of gaining legitimacy. Thus, many of today's witches claim hereditary descent from some ancient witch or claim to be the current reincarnations of past witches.
>
> In general, ascertaining the source of legitimacy in witchcraft groups is very difficult, especially since almost all claim ancient, traditional origins. However, intense investigation usually reveals that the group's secret sources are not as claimed.[62]

But just a few years later one priestess told me, "It's better to get training from experienced people, but lacking that, we just stole it out of every book we could!" And another Witch observed, "Recently, I've begun to see personalities which were once dominant in the Craft recognizing their own inadequacies, being able to admit them and become students again."

Traditionally, religions with indefensible histories and dogmas cling to them tenaciously. The Craft avoided this through the realization, often unconscious, that its real sources lie in the mind, in art, in creative work. Once people became comfortable in the Craft, the old lies began to dissolve. That they did so quickly is an insight into the flexibility of Wicca.

In a brief period many Craft leaders did complete turnarounds. Perhaps the most noteworthy of these leaders is Raymond Buckland, who, along with his wife, Rosemary, brought the Gardnerian tradition to the United States in the 1960s. In 1971 Buckland published *Witchcraft from the Inside*. Speaking as a Witch, he snubbed all "homemade" traditions:

> It says much for the success of Gerald Gardner in obtaining recognition for the Craft as a religion, for its imitators are those who, unable to gain access to a coven, have decided to start their own. These do-it-yourself "witches" would, on the face of it, seem harmless but on closer scrutiny are not so. They are causing considerable confusion to others who, seeking the true, get caught up in the false. The majority of these latter-day "witches" have usually read, or heard of, at least two books—Gardner's *Witchcraft Today* and Leland's *Aradia*. From these they pick out as much information as they feel is valid and make up whatever is missing. . . .
>
> Why do people start such "covens"? Why not wait and search? For some it is just that they have no patience. They feel so strongly for the Craft that they *must* participate in some way. By the time they eventually do come in contact with the true Craft it is too late.[63]

A mere two years later Buckland, in conflict with his own tradition, his marriage broken, created a new tradition—Seax Wicca or Saxon Wicca, a tradition that would be accessible to anyone who opened his new book, *The Tree* (1974). He now believed that there were many valid paths and that he had been guilty of a limited view "in earlier days." Writing in *Earth Religion News*, Buckland said, "While others fight over which is the oldest tradition, I claim mine as the youngest!"[64] And when *The Tree: The Complete Book of Saxon Witchcraft* appeared, it contained these words:

Those searching for the Craft *can* have ready access to at least one branch, or tradition, of it. . . . With this, and the explanatory material, it is now possible to do what I just said, above, cannot generally be done: to initiate yourself as a Witch, and to start your own Coven.[65]

Seax Wicca was a new tradition created—rumor has it—as a joke by Buckland in conjunction with a number of well-known and still practicing Gardnerian Witches. As Buckland later developed it, Seax Wicca became an accessible tradition available to anyone, and it was the first book of public Craft rituals to appear since Lady Sheba had published what were essentially (with a few modifications and a number of omissions) the Gardnerian rituals. Sheba had said the Goddess told her to do it. Her action was greeted with intense anger by many Witches, particularly Gardnerians. Reaction to Buckland's action ranged from pleasure (expressed by those who had fruitlessly searched for admittance into an existing tradition) to indifference (by most others).

Buckland wrote in *Earth Religion News* that the new tradition was created as an answer to internal conflicts in the Craft. Since most Wiccans were "tradition-oriented," he had given his tradition some historical background, a Saxon background. But: "By this I most emphatically do *not* mean that there is any claim to its liturgy being of direct descent from Saxon origins! As stated above, it is brand new."[66]

Buckland is just one example of the trend away from musty old Books of Shadow and dubious claims of ancient lineage. It could be said that he was following the most authentic and hallowed Gardnerian tradition—stealing from any source that didn't run away too fast.

5

The Craft Today

Validity

I know of one instance where, some years ago, a person obtained the Book of Shadows of an existing coven after he had been turned down for membership in that coven. Based upon that Book of Shadows, he then established himself as a Witch, performed initiations and the people he initiated went forth into the world and formed their own covens, . . . initiating others in turn. If the first person of this pyramid were not "initiated" does this make all of the initiations invalid? I don't think so. Despite the original fraud those people went through the ceremony with sincerity and apparently received the illumination that comes with true initiation.

—Joseph Wilson[1]

If anyone can become a member of the Wicca by reading books, if people can create their own "tradition," if one comes to the Craft out of a sense of homecoming, if the Craft works because of the archetypal content of the human mind, is there such a thing as a "valid" tradition or an "invalid" one? Is any tradition that *feels* right appropriate? How does one decide on validity in such a religion? Does one need an initiation to become a Witch? Here is a true story that may serve to illustrate this problem and provide a key to its solution.

Five years ago, only two years after the beginning of my own Craft journey, I went to England and looked up Alex and Maxine Sanders. Alex Sanders had founded the Alexandrian tradition of Wicca. He claimed that in 1933, at the age of seven, he found his grandmother standing nude in a circle in the kitchen. She then initiated him into the Craft. An account of this tale can be found in June Johns' *King of the Witches* and also in Stewart Farrar's *What Witches Do*.[2]

Alex and Maxine Sanders became celebrities in London. Their pictures have appeared in dozens of popular books on the occult. Many of the Alexandrian rituals have been published, and they so resemble the Gardnerian rituals that Alex's story of their origin is often questioned.

At the time I visited London, in the summer of 1973, Alex had left Maxine for a time and she was running the coven alone, as well as conducting a training group and several occult classes. I called her up with some trepidation. I was newly initiated into the Gardnerian tradition and tended to tread softly in strange pathways. I told Maxine I was "in the Craft" and she quickly invited me to attend a circle that night. I expected her to check me out and was surprised that she did not. She asked the name of my "tradition," but little else.

I put my athame and a necklace in my bag and proceeded to the Sanders home. One entered by way of a long foyer that was quite dark. A rather prim woman in a black dress asked me my purpose. I told her I had been invited by Maxine to attend the circle, that I was an initiate from another tradition, and that I was here to see Maxine. "Maxine is very busy now," the woman told me brusquely, "but just go on back and change in the loo." I was also informed that I, as a guest, would not have to pay the normal fee of fifty pence to attend the circle.

I was beset by a variety of strong emotions. Here I was, a stranger to this Wiccan circle of another tradition, invited by this priestess who, when I arrived, did not even have the time to greet me and take me in hand. And the money . . . that seemed a violation of every Craft principle I had been taught. I had brought food and wine to many circles, but had never seen a coin change hands. But, undaunted, I went into the bathroom and took off my clothes. The Alexandrians, like the Gardnerians, worked "skyclad."

As I undressed, a woman opened the bathroom door and entered. Let us call her Jane. She is the real heroine of our story. Jane easily weighed over two hundred pounds. She was young, perhaps eighteen. As she undressed, it became painfully obvious that she was nervous and scared and shy and upset about her figure. She was so heavy that her stomach hung down, making her vagina invisible. Since I myself was thirty pounds overweight, her appearance, I regret to confess, cheered me immeasurably. Here was a comrade-in-arms. I suddenly felt calm, cool, an experienced Craft priestess, a woman of the world.

Jane told me that tonight was her initiation into the Craft. She was excited and nervous. "Do you know what's to happen?" she asked me. She had been to three previous circles and a certain number of classes. I told her that I was an initiate of a tradition similar to this one and that she should not be worried; she would have a beautiful experience. Together we walked out of the bathroom—both of us completely nude except for a necklace. I had a sheathed athame in my hand. Together, we walked into this strange and darkened hall.

Everyone else had disappeared, except for the prim woman in black. "Where do we go?" I asked.

"Stay here a minute," said the woman.

Then, two young men appeared. They had taken off their shirts, but they were wearing pants. They blindfolded Jane and bound her hands behind her back. In this way, according to the Alexandrian tradition, she would be brought into the circle. I waited. "Who's the High Priestess?" one of the boys asked the woman in black. At this point I began to feel a sense of unease. Wasn't Maxine Sanders the priestess? And where *was* Maxine, anyway?

In response to the man's question the lady in black turned to him, pointed to me (standing nude in the darkness), and said, "She is."

"What?" I said, not believing her words.

"She is," the woman repeated.

I reacted with absolute amazement. "Wait a minute!" I said. "I've just stepped off the street from another country, from another tradition. I have never been in an Alexandrian circle in my entire life. I have no idea what you even *do!* I just don't think this is right at all, and anyway, I don't know how you conduct your rituals!" I was babbling by this time.

"Oh, it's all right," she replied. "It's all in the book, just follow the book!"

"No," I replied. "I won't do it. I just don't think it's right." And I began to repeat my arguments. "Here I am, a complete stranger, I just don't think this is right."

Meanwhile Jane was standing against the wall, bound and blindfolded, awaiting her sublime experience of initiation and hearing this unbelievable exchange. All of a sudden Maxine Sanders appeared, almost out of nowhere. She was dressed in a long white gown; her blond hair flowed down past her waist. She looked even more beautiful than any of the pictures I had seen of her. "What's the matter?" asked Maxine.

"She won't do it," said the woman in black, pointing at me.

I repeated my arguments to Maxine who told me, "None of the other women have shown up."

Soon several things became clear. The circle-to-be was Maxine's training coven and, within their tradition, first-degree initiations took place in this training group. The priestess of the training group had apparently left after a tantrum over some minor matter. Jane, myself, and six or seven men remained. Jane, by the way, was still standing bound and blindfolded while this explanation was going on. I still refused. Maxine accepted this and said they would make do without a priestess.

One strange event superseded another. For a few moments after we entered the room where the circle was to be held there didn't seem to be an available priest for this training group either, until Maxine threw a small fit. "What kind of Witches do we have here?" she shouted at the seven men in the room. "Why is it always the same person who volunteers?" Finally, someone put his hand up, and everything could begin.

Finally the circle was cast and the ritual was begun. Maxine Sanders listened from outside, on the other side of the room. Power was raised through dancing and chanting: "Eko, eko Azarak, Eko, eko Zamilak, Eko, eko Karnayna, Eko, eko Aradia."

The circle was fairly monotonous. The energy level seemed low, as one might imagine after the disputes. Lines were read and chants chanted without much feeling. If I hadn't still been in a state of shock, I would have been slightly bored.

Then Jane was led through the initiation ceremony. She was consecrated in the names of the God and the Goddess of the tradition:

Karnayna and Aradia. She was asked if she wanted to go through with it. She did. She was welcomed with the passwords, "Perfect love and perfect trust." She was ceremonially scourged. She was given an oath. She was anointed with water and wine. She was presented each of the circle tools and welcomed into the coven. The details of this ritual can be found in Stewart Farrar's book.

At the end of the ritual everyone dressed and convened at the local pub, which seemed a much livelier place than the circle. But there was Jane, dressed once more, and her eyes positively glowing in that peculiar and extraordinary way that betokens—as sure as anything—a powerful experience inside oneself, an experience that may have begun a process of great change in her life.

And so we come to the peculiar fact that even if Sanders's story is bogus, even if there was no priestess to cast the circle, even if all the "traditions" were violated, even if untalented students botched the event, still Jane may have gone through a true rebirth.

Many in the Craft have come to see initiation as an inner process. Leo Martello, writing in the *Wica Newsletter*, notes that whereas European traditions say, "A Witch is born, not made," Anglo-American covens say, "A Witch is made, not born." Martello has often observed that a valid initiation depends more on the one receiving it than on the initiator.[3] And New York City Craft priest Myrdden wrote:

> I don't think that our Goddess would deny worship . . . to someone . . . just because they were not initiated by an initiated witch. . . . Also who can tell whether the "witch" doing the initiating has really been initiated herself? . . . Many of our origins are obscure and documentary evidence . . . is not usually available. . . . [Sometimes it is] extremely difficult to locate someone who will initiate.
>
> Initiation is primarily a method to protect the institution of the Craft from people calling themselves "witches" who are insincere, "evil" or would give the Craft a bad name. But does it really stop anyone from calling himself a witch? No. . . . The mysteries and secrets of the Craft can be discovered independently of the Craft: we do not have the only way. The Gods can be discovered independently of the Craft. . . . The Gods, only, can make a witch; man can only confirm it.[4]

And Craft priest Phoenix made a similar observation:

I have come across those who have carefully and proudly constructed their own "Traditions," initiated themselves, and have gone on to keep their secrets and to function with inspiration, sincerity and effectiveness. On the other hand, I think we have all, from time to time, had contact with those who are apparently well able to substantiate a so-called "valid initiation" (in fact, more than likely a dozen initiations, the majority being "honorary" or otherwise non-working and non-learning) but to whom the Wicca means little or no more than a publicity gimmick, or a way of supporting themselves, a power/ego excursion. . . . Who of these, then, is *truly* of the Wicca?[5]

Who Defines the Wicca?

How do modern Witches define themselves?

Since the Craft is decentralized and each coven is autonomous, no single definition applies to all Wiccans. In the United States most attempts to create a common set of principles and definitions have met with failure. Most of those who join the Wicca do so, in part, because of its implicit autonomy—"It is religion without the 'middleman,' " to repeat the words of one Craft priest. Despite this, there have been several attempts by United States Witches to meet and define this slippery term *Witch*. One attempt to create an ecumenical definition of modern Wicca that would be acceptable to many traditions began in the fall of 1973 when Llewellyn Press, the occult publishers, sponsored a meeting of Witches in Minneapolis. Seventy-three Witches from different traditions attended. They formed the Council of American Witches and, during the winter of 1974, began collecting statements of principle from various groups. These were printed in the Council's newsletter, *Touchstone*.

Carl Weschcke, publisher of Llewellyn, wrote in *Touchstone* that many Witches felt that a common definition was necessary as a "self-policing" mechanism "to protect ourselves from misunderstanding brought about by those whose personal power trips have exposed all of us to ridicule and injury."[6] It was also felt that a common statement would help dispel the sensationalist image pushed in the media, which continued to link Wicca with Satanism.

It turned out that there were many differences among Wiccan groups, a few of them conflicting. Here are some of the answers to the question, "What is a Witch?"

A Witch *above all* worships the Triple Goddess and her Consort, The Horned God, in one form or another. A Witch works Magick within a definite code of ethics. A Witch acknowledges and uses the male-female polarity in his/her rites. A Witch takes *total* responsibility for her actions, herself, and her future.

—NROOGD (New Reformed Orthodox Order of the Golden Dawn)

Witchcraft is an initiatory mystery religion whose adherents seek, through self-discipline, to live a life dedicated to the pursuit and practice of knowledge, wisdom and compassion under the guidance of the Gods.

—Coven of Gwynvyd, St. Louis, Missouri

A Witch is a member of a religion which by its own internal definition is monotheistic. [This definition was obviously in conflict with the others.]

—School of Wicca

Wicca can be defined as a pagan mystery religion with a polarized deity and no personification of evil.[7]

—Lady Cybele

Some Witches refused even to take part in this process of defining the Craft, feeling that a common statement of principles implied an unacceptable degree of centralization. One Witch wrote to *Touchstone*:

> In the early days of the Church, we of the Wicca were persecuted for not joining with the common belief of the church fathers because we refused to join, be baptized or pay our tithes to their God. We were tortured, burned, hanged and placed in vats of ground glass. We preferred to live simply, worshipping our old Gods of Harvest, and doing as we had for years before, and as our fathers had done. . . .
>
> The Church sent in spies who reported on us into our worship circles, and those of us who were caught were humiliated and killed because we were as we were . . . and of course the Church wanted the money and wanted to oppress the people.
>
> Now it seems to us old Wicca that that is what you younger's are doing . . . oppressing us, trying to force us to join in an organization, and criticizing us for wanting our freedom and our belief in freedom. . . .

Let us not quarrel among ourselves. Leave us be and we shall do the same for you. Worship as you see best and allow us also the same right. This is the true Wicca way . . . and the free way.

—From an anonymous Witch
(because it is my right to be so)[8]

Other conflicts arose between people bound by strict oaths of secrecy and others who wished to share their information openly. Some felt that little should be "secret" except for the names used for deities and initiation rituals, so that their psychological impact would not be lost. Another problem was "validity." Many felt that initiation was an internal process and that one could receive a valid initiation in a dream or vision, or even at the hands of frauds. Others felt that only certain traditions were "valid."

The groups were closest on ethics. All agreed with the basic Wiccan Creed—"An ye harm none, do what ye will." Most affirmed Aleister Crowley's famous statement: "Do what thou wilt shall be the whole of the Law. Love is the law, love under will." Most agreed that it was unethical to "forcefully violate a person's autonomy." Most affirmed the divinity of all living beings. NROOGD's statement was the strongest.

An it harm no one, do you as you will.
You may not alter another's life/karma without his permission.
Solve the problem, no more, no less. All power comes from the Goddess.
You must help your brothers and sisters in the Craft as best you can.
If you stick your hand in a flame, you'll get burned.[9]

The Council of American Witches, meeting April 11–14, 1974, in Minneapolis, finally did hammer out a statement of principles:

PRINCIPLES OF WICCAN BELIEF
The Council of American Witches finds it necessary to define modern Witchcraft in terms of the American experience and needs.

We are not bound by traditions from other times and other cultures, and owe no allegiance to any person or power greater than the Divinity manifest through our own being.

As American Witches we welcome and respect all Life Affirming teachings and traditions, and seek to learn from all and to share our learning within our Council.

It is in this spirit of welcome and cooperation that we adopt these few principles of Wiccan belief. In seeking to be inclusive, we do not wish to open ourselves to the destruction of our group by those on self-serving power trips, or to philosophies and practices contradictory to those principles. In seeking to exclude those whose ways are contradictory to ours, we do not want to deny participation with us to any who are sincerely interested in our knowledge and beliefs, regardless of race, color, sex, age, national or cultural origins or sexual preference.

1. We practice Rites to attune ourselves with the natural rhythm of life forces marked by the Phases of the Moon and the Seasonal Quarters and Cross Quarters.

2. We recognize that our intelligence gives us a unique responsibility toward our environment. We seek to live in harmony with Nature, in ecological balance offering fulfillment to life and consciousness within an evolutionary concept.

3. We acknowledge a depth of power far greater than that apparent to the average person. Because it is far greater than ordinary, it is sometimes called "supernatural," but we see it as lying within that which is naturally potential to all.

4. We conceive of the Creative Power in the Universe as manifesting through polarity—as masculine and feminine—and that this same Creative Power lives in all people, and functions through the interaction of the masculine and feminine. We value neither above the other, knowing each to be supporting of the other. We value Sex as pleasure, as the symbol and embodiment of life, and as one of the sources of energies used in magical practice and religious worship.

5. We recognize both outer worlds and inner, or psychological, worlds—sometimes known as the Spiritual World, the Collective Unconscious, the Inner Planes, etc.—and we see in the interaction of these two dimensions the basis for paranormal phenomena and magical exercises. We neglect neither dimension for the other, seeing both as necessary for our fulfillment.

6. We do not recognize any authoritarian hierarchy, but do honor those who teach, respect those who share their greater knowledge and wisdom, and acknowledge those who have courageously given of themselves in leadership.

7. We see religion, magick, and wisdom-in-living as being united in the way one views the world and lives within it—a worldview and philosophy-of-life which we identify as Witchcraft, the Wiccan Way.

8. Calling oneself "Witch" does not make a witch—but neither does heredity itself, or the collecting of titles, degrees and initiations. A Witch seeks to control the forces within him/herself that make life possible in order to live wisely and well, without harm to others, and in harmony with Nature.

9. We acknowledge that it is the affirmation and fulfillment of life, in a continuation of evolution and development of consciousness, that gives meaning to the Universe we know, and to our personal role within it.

10. Our only animosity toward Christianity, or toward any other religion or philosophy-of-life, is to the extent that its institutions have claimed to be "the only way" and have sought to deny freedom to others and to suppress other ways of religious practice and belief.

11. As American Witches, we are not threatened by debates on the history of the Craft, the origins of various aspects of different traditions. We are concerned with our present, and our future.

12. We do not accept the concept of "absolute evil," nor do we worship any entity known as "Satan" or "The Devil" as defined by the Christian tradition. We do not seek power through the suffering of others, nor do we accept the concept that personal benefit can only be derived by denial to another.

13. We acknowledge that we seek within Nature for that which is contributory to our health and well-being.[10]

After the statement of principles was adopted, additional differences surfaced. The Council soon became moribund.

A more successful attempt to form an alliance of Wiccan groups took place in northern California on the Summer Solstice in 1975. Thirteen covens and several solitary Witches ratified the Covenant of the Goddess (COG) after a number of covens in California expressed the desire to build closer bonds, in part out of a concern over harassment and persecution.

When the meeting to form the Covenant was called in the spring of 1975, several months earlier, representatives of forty covens appeared. Many never joined. As Alison Harlow, an officer of COG, told me, "Many came out of a desire to make sure that nothing was going to be pulled on any of their covens behind their backs."

The Covenant, like the Council, came face to face with the decentralism of the Craft. As Alison said, "How could we build an organization that, in fact, did not dictate to anyone? How could we create a

charter and bylaws we could file with the state as a legal religious organization without giving away the reality of what we're doing?"

The Covenant wisely accepted the basic anarchism of Wicca as
not only inevitable, but desirable. They could not define the religion:

> We could not define what a Witch is in words. Because there are too
> many differences. Our reality is intuitive. We know when we encounter
> someone who we feel is worshipping in the same way, who follows the
> same religion we do, and that's our reality, and that has to be under-
> stood, somehow, in anything we do.

When the Covenant of the Goddess organized, Aidan Kelly suggested that it base its structure on the bylaws and charter of the
Congregational Churches, so that it would be a religious body governed by autonomous congregations—in other words, covens—and
not by ruling popes or bishops (or priests and priestesses, for that
matter). This suggestion was adopted and Aidan wrote many of the
bylaws. Originally, the "members" of the Covenant were covens and
each coven got two votes on the Covenant's council. When there
were enough covens (five) in a local area, a local council was formed
to handle its own affairs.

Some of the items in COG's philosophy are instructive in under-
standing the eclectic nature of modern Wicca. For example, take the
Preamble to the Covenant, as summarized by Alison Harlow in *The
Witches Trine:*

> We establish this Covenant to bring us closer together and to help us
> serve the Craft and the Pagan Community.
>
> We define ourselves: (1) We all worship the Goddess, and many others
> honor other deities. (2) We are bound by Craft law, not necessarily iden-
> tical in all traditions. (3) We recognize each other as being in the Craft.
>
> We are not the only Witches. Witches who do not choose to join us
> are nonetheless Witches.
>
> Each coven is autonomous. Any authority given to the covenant is by
> the choice of each coven, and can be withdrawn.[11]

In addition, the charter made clear that the Church or Covenant
could not dictate policy, belief, or practice; that it could not, by itself,

create a coven or initiate a Witch. Its board of directors had to consist—at all times—of members of more than one tradition.

Its code of ethics was also illuminating:

1. An ye harm none, do as ye will.
2. No one may offer initiations for money, nor charge initiates money
to learn the Craft.
3. Any Witch may charge reasonable fees to the public.
4. Witches shall respect the autonomy of other Witches.
5. All Witches shall respect the secrecy of the Craft.
6. In any public statement Witches should distinguish whether we are
speaking for ourselves, our coven, or our Church.
7. All these Ethics are interwoven and derive from Craft Law.*

The personal definitions of Witchcraft by Witches were much
richer than these more formal statements. In answering the questions, "What does it mean to be a Witch? What does it feel like?" almost everyone stressed that it was, more than anything, an attitude
toward life—a way of living.

Z Budapest told me, "I relate to the Goddess every day, in one way
or another. I have a little chitchat with Mommy. I love my freedom. I
love my independence. I like to be silent. I can go for days by myself.
I like to reach out to crowds. I see the presence of the Goddess
everywhere, how she's given me this or that—even hamburgers. I've
gotten a whole lot of nourishment from this religion; it has maintained me through difficult times.

"A Witch's approach to life is one that says, 'When evil comes
upon you, turn it around, make it work for you.' It means to bend; to
be wise.

"Also, the past is a mirror. And the Craft presents women with
their past. They look into this mirror and say, 'Look at what we did
back then! We are strong.' They look into this mirror and they like
what they see and, eventually, they say, 'Let's do something *more!*'

"And being a priestess of the Craft means responsibility for the

---

* Several lists of Craft Laws—such as those that come by way of Gardner and
Sanders—have been published. Several versions of these laws are in Aidan Kelly's
"The Rebirth of Witchcraft: Tradition and Creativity in the Gardnerian Reform," un-
fortunately unpublished. Published versions can be found in *The Grimoire of Lady
Sheba* and Stewart Farrar's *What Witches Do.*

collective experiences of the circles I am serving. It means being sensitive to those in the circle. I can touch on my divinity and, also, I can be a tool for others' growth."

Alison Harlow told me that Wicca implies a "sense of connectedness, of cherishing all the forms in which life manifests." Janine Renée said that being a Witch means "trying on the archetypes within you and *becoming them*, by taking on these archetypal powers, expanding the ego until it stands with the gods, and drawing strength from these roots, now, in a world where so much strength has been atrophied by depersonalization."

Others did not stress such cosmic goals—some even found them objectionable. "I'd be happy if most Witches stopped trying to become like the gods," said Leo Martello, "and simply developed as human beings." Many stressed that the Craft was a life style. Cybele told me, "It's a way of viewing yourself as a very natural being. You are at one with the stones and at one with the stars. It stresses practical knowledge, not blind belief. It's practical. It permeates absolutely everything I do. Craft people haven't lost touch with what's real. They haven't allowed themselves to be bombarded with stimuli, or, if they have at one point in their lives, they've found their way back." Bran Tree, a Witch, said, "A Witch is someone who sees more than the mundane things of life, who can become excited over the feel of a pebble or the croak of a frog," and Aidan Kelly told me, "What really defines a Witch is a type of *experience* people go through. These experiences depend on altered states of consciousness. The Craft is really the Yoga of the West." Morning Glory Zell said that a Witch is a type of European shaman, and being a Witch involves being a priestess or priest, a psychopomp, a healer, a guide. "It is the sum of those things. You sense a community. The community may be the whole world or a handful of people."

Most Witches stressed that the goal of the Craft was helping people to reclaim their lost spiritual heritage, their affinity with the earth, with "the gods," with the infinite. Most said it was not a religion for everyone. Many felt the religion would always be small. Many felt the "fad of the occult" was ending; their response to that was relief. Some emphasized the pragmatic side of the religion— practical magic to get various jobs done. Others emphasized the experience of ecstasy and joy. Still others expressed larger goals: responding to the needs of the planet in crisis, or actualizing the divinity within oneself.

How Many Are the Wicca?

How many people in the United States consider themselves of the religion Wicca? Again, the decentralism of the Craft makes all estimates suspect. The Witch Sybil Leek estimated that there were "several thousand covens in the United States" in 1971.[12] Sociologist Marcello Truzzi put the figure at three hundred.[13] Leo Martello told me in 1977 that there could be as many as thirty thousand. Isaac Bonewits who, if you remember, estimated that Wiccan Witches constitute about 10 percent of the Witches in the United States, thought there are between three thousand and six thousand Neo-Pagans here, about half of them Wiccan. Aidan Kelly of NROOGD observed to me that he was personally *familiar* with about one hundred covens in the United States. I have had contact with about the same number, but I estimate that for every coven I know of there may easily be five to ten others.

Susan Roberts wrote in *Witchcraft, U.S.A.*: "Witches don't know how many of them there are—much less where they are. There is no census, no master mailing list. Anyone who claims to have such a list is either lying or deluded."[14] At most, one can make an estimate from the number of people who subscribe to Neo-Pagan and Craft publications, and that's probably where the number three thousand comes from. No more than three thousand ever subscribed to *Gnostica*, although many thousands more issues were published and sent out free. No more than two thousand ever subscribed to *Green Egg*, and the number that subscribe to other coven newsletters and journals is far lower. But then, most of the people I have met who are in covens don't subscribe to *any* Neo-Pagan journals. And I am continually surprised to find new covens who have created themselves after reading a few introductory books or hearing a few lectures. Since the Craft is so decentralized, since each coven is autonomous, there is no way to compile accurate statistics. While such and such a tradition with a line of apostolic succession may have a record of thirty or forty covens, and another tradition a record of fifty, there is no way to estimate the frequency of the spontaneous creation of new covens and new traditions through the reading of books. It is impossible to know how many people have, let us say, heard a radio interview, gone to their local library and emerged two years later with a "tradition" or started a coven. There may be many groups that have no links with what we have been calling the Neo-Pagan movement. Many may not even have heard the term. Since some of the most vital Craft traditions—NROOGD, for one—started this way, it is a valid route. Probably no more than ten thousand people in the United States identify themselves with the broad Neo-Pagan phenomenon, with its journals and newsletters, its covens, groves, and groups. But many other groups and individuals may exist without such links.

Sabbats and Esbats—How Covens Work

A coven simply means a group of people who convene for religious or magical or psychic purposes. Not all Witches form covens. Certainly the "Classical Witches" of Bonewits's description were most often solitary, and many scholars would argue that the idea of covens was an invention of the Inquisition that was later adopted by the revival. Among the Gardnerian and Alexandrian Craft laws is one that states, "Ye May Not Be a Witch Alone." So, one would think that at least there are no solitary Gardnerian or Alexandrian Witches, but even that isn't true—many Gardnerians and Alexandrians have decided to function without covens. (In this religion there is an exception to *everything*.)

Whether the word and concept of *coven* was invented by Witches or by Inquisitors, it works. A traditional coven in Wicca is twelve or thirteen, but in practice it is any number from three to twenty, depending on the group's philosophy, the size of the working circle (if it's nine feet in diameter, twelve is a crowd!), and the available members. Again, the coven works, not because of its mysterious nature, but because small groups, working together, are effective.

Some covens work in couples, emphasizing male/female polarity. These will be even-numbered. Other covens do not emphasize polarity and may be more flexible in number and size.

Most Wiccan covens work within a circle, "a portable temple," as one Witch wrote to me. Certain groups in England have been known to set up a psychic "castle," and many Witches will tell you that their circle is really a sphere. The circle is the declaration of sacred ground. It is a place set apart, although its material location may be a living room or a backyard. But in the mind the circle, reinforced by the actions of casting it and purifying it, becomes sacred space, a place "between the worlds" where contact with archetypal reality, with the deep places of the mind—with "gods," if you will—becomes possible. It is a place where time disappears, where history is obliterated. It is the contact point between two realities. It is common for Witches to contrast their circle with the circle of the ceremonial magician. The Wiccan circle is not a "protection from demons" but a container of the energy raised.

Craft ritual usually starts with casting and creating this magical space and ritually purifying it with the ancient elements: fire, water, earth, and air. The circle is cast with a ritual sword, wand, or athame (a small, usually black-handled and double-bladed dagger that is used by almost all covens, whatever their tradition). Different covens have different symbologies, but often the sword represents fire, the wand (or incense burner) air, the cup water, and the pentacle—a round, inscribed disk of wax or metal—earth.[15] When the circle is cast, often the gods and goddesses are invoked.

Some covens use music, chanting, and dancing to raise psychic energy within the circle. Psychic healing is often attempted, with varying degrees of success. The most common form of "working" is known as "raising a cone of power." This is done by chanting or dancing (or both) or running around the circle. The "cone of power" is really the combined wills of the group, intensified through ritual and meditative techniques, focused on an end collectively agreed upon. Usually a priestess or priest directs the cone; when she or he senses that it has been raised, it is focused and directed with the mind and shot toward its destination.

Many covens also engage in more "spiritual" or "religious" workings. Many of the revivalist covens have rituals in which the Goddess, symbolized by the moon, is "drawn down" into a priestess of the coven who, at times, goes into trance and is "possessed by" or "incarnates" the Goddess force. Similarly, there are rituals where the God force is drawn down into the priest who takes the role of the God in the circle. In these rituals Witches *become* the gods within the circle, actualizing that potentiality. When done well, these can be among the most powerful experiences. I have seen people really change in such rituals. I have also seen these rituals become shams.

This is perhaps the place to talk about sexual rites, which are often described in popular books on Wicca. I have found very few covens that engage in explicitly sexual rituals. Many use sexual symbolism and poetry, but rarely is the sex act actualized. The reason for this is a strange one. Most coven leaders I have talked to feel that incorporating sex into rituals is playing with explosive chemicals, because the people in their covens are simply not ready for it. Of course, there are some groups that do use sex in ritual. And, in its highest form, the "Great Rite," often alluded to by the media, is a sublime religious experience. Properly understood, it is not—as the press would have us believe—the carryings on of bored suburban swingers. The idea behind the "Great Rite" is that a woman who, through ritual, has "incarnated" or *become* the Goddess, and a man who, through ritual, has "incarnated" or *become* the God—in other words, two people who have drawn down into themselves these archetypal forces, or, if you will, have allowed these forces within them to surface—can have a spiritual and physical union that is truly divine. It is the modern form of the sacred marriage, or "hierogamy," that appears in many ancient religions.

Most covens meet for spiritual, psychic, and social types of "work." I have known covens that wrote poetry, others that put on mystery plays or simply worked for the good of their members. I have known covens that created astral temples to Athena and Demeter, or spent most of their time in reforestation work, or put their energy into the feminist movement.

Most covens meet at "esbats." Most scholars believe Murray invented this term. These are working meetings that can occur at the full moon, or the new moon, or every weekend, or once a week, or whenever. Covens also usually meet on the "sabbats," the eight great festivals of European Paganism, the Quarter days and the Cross Quarter days. The lesser four are the solstices and the equinoxes. The greater sabbats are: *Samhain* (Halloween or November Eve); the Celtic New Year, the day when the walls between the worlds were said to be thinnest and when contact with one's ancestors took place; *Oimelc* (February 1), the winter purification festival, the time of the beginning of spring movement; *Beltane* (May 1), the great fertility festival, the marriage of God and Goddess; *Lughnasadh* (August 1), the festival of first fruits and, in some traditions, the time of the fight between the bull and stag god for the Lady, or the death of the Sacred King. These are the briefest of descriptions, and different Craft traditions, following different myth cycles from different parts of Europe, treat the festivals in diverse ways. But almost all traditions at least celebrate Samhain and Beltane.

These festivals renew a sense of living communion with natural cycles, with the changes of season and land. But many Wiccans, almost always an innovative group, are perfectly capable of changing the festivals and their meanings. As one priestess from a city in Ohio remarked to me, "We were sitting around trying to decide what we were going to do for the Summer Solstice [June 21]. What did the solstice mean to us here? And we realized it didn't mean a hell of a lot. So why were we celebrating? We decided that we would try and celebrate new festivals, tied in to things that really mean something to us."

In fact, a few Witches have totally rebelled against most of the festival rituals that have come down to them. One man wrote to me:

> Most Craft rituals that I've observed are completely absurd, because they're rooted in traditions alien to the people who are performing them. Very few people involved in re-created Celtic Paganism even bother to learn Old Irish or Welsh, let alone go beyond that and really try to understand what the various symbolisms were supposed to mean. . . . I've been trying to get together a group of people to invent a Pagan ritual based on modern English and symbolism that has real meaning to a modern American.
>
> Everyone says, "That's obvious," when I point out that the true modern equivalent to a sword to a modern American, even a "liberated" one, is a .38 police special—like they see on TV shows—or a military rifle, or possibly the Colt .45 of Western movies, but swords are still used in magical and Pagan rites and people think it's absurd to even suggest substituting guns.

Personally I have no desire to handle guns, and swords have a beauty and romanticism that I find acceptable, but the point is well taken; many feel that the festivals and rituals of Wicca must begin to fit changing times and changing needs.

The deities of most Wicca groups are two: the God, lord of animals, lord of death and beyond, and the Goddess, the Triple Goddess in her three aspects: Maiden, Mother, and Crone. Each aspect is symbolized by a phase of the moon—the waxing crescent, the full moon, and the waning crescent. In general, there is a great divergence among the Wicca as to what these "gods" are. Are they thought forms, built up over centuries? Are they archetypes? Are they literal entities? The answer depends on whom you talk to.

The names used for the gods also differ, depending on tradition and group. Most often the names are Celtic, Greek, or Latin. Most Witches do say that the polytheistic personification of the gods is what allows them to make contact with Divine Reality; that while Divine Reality may ultimately be unknowable, personification allows one to begin to approach it.

Most Witches believe in some form of reincarnation. Many believe in the "threefold law": that whatever you do returns to you threefold. Some Witches don't believe in the threefold law, but most believe that you get back what you give out. And I must stress that I have met priests and priestesses in the Craft who are agnostic on all "beliefs," who joined the Craft simply because they found its poetry beautiful or its "path" self-actualizing.

Some covens meet in robes, some in street clothes. Some work nude—the revivalist term is "skyclad"—generally because of the freedom they feel nudity engenders or because of its leveling quality. Gardner may be responsible for much of the nudity in the Craft. Many covens in the United States follow the sensible custom of nudity in the summer and clothes in the winter.

Most covens have an entry or initiation ceremony. Sometimes it's very simple; sometimes it's complex, involving a test, an oath, and a symbolic rite of death and rebirth. The concept of initiation is certainly a rich one. A woman who had just been initiated into a coven wrote:

> The push in the Magic Circle was like the slap given the newborn, welcoming it into a new life. The room was crowded with people I could not see, but whose presence made me feel I was on a witness stand.

My ankle was tied—neither bound nor free. What is this strange state of limbo that causes me to run in circles, stumbling as I do in everyday life . . . but not really circles? I felt I was racing through a long tunnel. In a sense I felt bound in a special way to living my life with a fresh consciousness, glowing and unconfined . . . a dedication of who I really am . . . a responsibility. My forehead on the altar awakened me: my mind must become the altar for the Mother, my body the living temple for the Gods.

The abrupt, almost harsh order to kneel reminds me of the kind of acceptance I must make when things in my life do not go pleasantly for me.

Blood rushing through every cell in my body felt warm and glowing. I am Blessed![16]

The Modern Craft Traditions (Sects)

Many books attempt to describe what Wiccans do—how they work in the circle, what traditions they follow, what rituals they perform, what tools they use, what beliefs they hold, what festivals they celebrate. Many revivalist traditions—particularly Gardnerians and Alexandrians—have been overly described. Each step in casting a circle and using a tool is fully given. And yet, having attended circles in many Craft sects, including Gardnerian, Alexandrian, NROOGD, Dianic, and various "traditionals," I am left feeling that these books tell little about how each coven radiates its own identity, which often has nothing to do with the supposed "tradition" it follows or with the particular rituals it performs.

Before we look at "traditions" it is important to be clear that these categories may have little to do with what is actually happening in a coven. Decentralism and individualism in the Craft seem to overshadow any "tradition" or "ritual." One cannot begin to understand any coven without first understanding this fundamental independence. And so while I can tell you that a certain tradition has a number of covens in the United States, and that it usually celebrates such and such a festival, the reality may be that the ten or twenty covens within this tradition are doing very different things.

In the past most writers broke down the Craft traditions into "Hereditary," "Traditional," "Gardnerian," "Alexandrian," "Dianic," and sometimes "Continental." All these terms now have vague boundaries and mean less as the years go by. Stewart Farrar had some fairly amusing things to say about "traditions" in his book *What Witches Do.* He wrote:

> The Hereditary witches are those, of course, who have kept the Craft alive in a direct family line. The theory is that those lines descend un-broken from the Old Religion itself; how true this is only the families know, if indeed they do know.

Turning to the "Traditional," Farrar observed wryly:

> Quite what it is that the Traditionals do (except that they apparently wear robes for their rites) I cannot say. They keep themselves to themselves, and I have never to my knowledge met one. . . .

Then he turns to the Gardnerians and Alexandrians, whose history is fairly easy to chart.

Most descriptions of traditions fall flat because they concentrate on the *forms*—the rituals, for example, which lose almost everything in description—and ignore the eternals, the nonverbal things, the experience of people. To quote Farrar again, the "detail of form" does not matter, "but the spirit and whether it works" matter greatly. In all the descriptions of traditions that follow it should be remembered that these differences are important for their richness and diversity, but most people join "the Craft" and *not* a particular tradition. Farrar, for example, joined the Craft because he found "its symbolism beautiful, its ritual satisfying, its tolerance (and indeed encouragement) of individual attitudes civilized, its deep roots nourishing, its small-group organization comradely and effective. . . ."[17] It just happened to be an Alexandrian coven he wandered into on a newspaper assignment.

Similarly, Valiente writes:

> I have danced at the Witches' Sabbat on many occasions, and found carefree enjoyment in it. I have stood under the stars at midnight and invoked the Old Gods; and I have found in such invocations of the most primeval powers, those of Life, Love and Death, an uplifting of consciousness that no orthodox religious service has ever given me.[18]

The fact that Valiente worked with Gardner at one time really seems irrelevant. Most people who join the Craft join the "tradition" that happens to be "around," that exists in their particular area. And no matter what "tradition" they enter, the stories of how and why they entered the Craft are similar. For example, New York City priest Lyr ab Govannon described his entry into the Craft.

"I entered a Protestant seminary at the age of nineteen, partly because I came from a cultural milieu in which this was a high calling and partly because I am an innately religious person. But within a very short time I began to have doubts about what I was being prepared to teach.

"Then one day, I came across *King Jesus* by Robert Graves. The book treats Jesus as a Sacred King in the old tradition. It was a startling idea to me. Midway through the book there is a chapter in which Jesus seeks out Mary the Hairdresser, a priestess of the older religion which worshipped the Goddess, whom Mary calls, 'My Lady of The First Eve,' meaning Lilith. Pow! There was a concept of the deity as feminine, not just a subsidiary Virgin Mary, but THE big one.

"A year later, Robert Graves came out with *The White Goddess*, and by then I knew what he was talking about and I agreed. From then, it was a long odyssey in search of . . . my people, I suppose . . . and believe me, I found some of them in pretty peculiar places. And we were always surprised to meet each other, because each of us thought we were somehow singular.

"I found the Goddess worshipped in a lot of places, under a lot of different names. And I sometimes found lip service being given Her when it was actually the same old patriarchal image that was being perpetuated. In Vedanta, for example, the great Sri or saint is Ramakrishna, a man who had been an intense devotee of the Divine Mother all of his life. He was drunk with Her! But his so-called followers do not pay homage to the Goddess. They worship a good old patriarchal image, Sri Ramakrishna.

"I began candle meditations and began to get flashes of pictures. I was led step by step. One time I saw a tall figure in the distance. It was a woman in a long cloak. The cloak hid everything but her face, and from that face there was a brightness so that I couldn't see her features. Often, I felt I had little choice in my direction. I fought against it, but was drawn back again.

"One day, a fellow sent me a book called *The Divine Mother*. It was like the top of my head came off. There were other worshippers. Not just one or two, but groups. I heard about a Witchcraft magazine called *The New Broom*, and then an organization called Nemeton. Suddenly everything seemed to blossom, and I moved into the mainstream of the Craft."

Carolyn Clark, a priestess from St. Louis, also described her process of entry:

"I got interested in Witchcraft when I was twelve. When I was a little kid, about nine or ten, I had the good fortune to live on the outskirts of a small town, surrounded by woods, and I used to go out in the woods and take a candle with me and find a tree stump and put the candle up, light it, bring flowers, and pour out a little honey, usually, because I didn't have any wine, to make an offering to Apollo and Diana.

"I read everything I could about Witchcraft and the paranormal. I took the School of Wicca's correspondence course, but since I was primarily interested in goddess worship, I ended up creating my own tradition.

"It was difficult. I had to find the sources. I raided the St. Louis public library to find books on Celtic mythology. I tried to track down the Tain and the Mabinogion. I picked up a little here and there. I had a few contacts and I began to put together a tradition and some rituals.

"I was turned on to the Goddess. It was the religion. I didn't care if I acquired any personal power. The Goddess just sort of flicked her finger and said, 'Hey!' "

These stories, more than any of the traditions, reveal the nature of the Craft. The people I meet rarely enter a tradition out of deliberate choice. They seek "the Craft." They get in contact, perhaps, with whatever group they run into. This group or coven gives them a plan of study, often lasting a year, sometimes more or less. Then, if they seem to mesh with the people of that group, they enter it. Usually that coven has a particular practice and tradition, but often that's the least important thing that's going on. Obviously, the tradition *can* matter. A person may respond to a particular myth cycle or a particular set of rituals, but often these are not the essentials. Often a person may enter Wicca *in spite of* a particular tradition, like this woman who spent a number of years with a Welsh-oriented group:

"I am a Witch. A Witch is a person who uses one set of tools—gods, rituals, and objects—to do the same things other Pagans do. For me, the Craft is my way of actualizing myself, my life; I am constantly exploring why this is so. The only real answer I can give is that there is an affinity between me and the Craft. But I do not know why that affinity and not some other. Perhaps it is because my anima has been rising and in rising has met the Goddess. But there are forms of goddess worship other than the Craft, and other crafts than goddess worship.

"The Craft is home to me. Not to say I do not have problems with it, and by 'it' I mean my own particular 'tradition.' I do not like hierarchical structure and some of its means of expressing itself via dualities which may or may not be part of nature. There are aspects of my tradition that institutionalize things I do not find institutionalized in myself. These are real problems.

"But I name myself Witch. I am named Witch, and Witch I am and I like it. But both me and my Craft are *always* changing. It is discovering what will endure.

"I do not believe Witches are different from other people, or that they have different powers. The Craft has helped me actualize these aspects of my being. I have allowed them in me."

Although the Craft is eclectic by nature, there are some useful distinctions that can be made about each sect or "tradition" within it.

TRADITIONALIST WICCA

Despite Farrar's humorous remark that the only thing he knows about "traditionalist" Witches is that they wear robes, there *are* many covens in the United States that follow the myths and folk traditions of a particular country and regard these traditions as more important to their craft than the forms of the revival. In the United States there are scores of covens calling themselves "Irish traditionalist," "Welsh traditionalist," "Scots traditionalist," "Greek traditionalist," and so on. In general, they are less prone to work nude, and less prone to use sexual symbolism. To give an example, one

"Welsh traditionalist" coven that I know of uses the Welsh Mabinogion myth cycle as the prime source for its rituals, poetry, and names
of deities. The "tradition" of these covens is often the heritage of literature and scholarship related to the pre-Christian beliefs of a particular people. Those who are drawn to a particular "traditionalist"
coven are often those whose ancestry is in that tradition and who are
searching for their own culture.

GARDNERIAN

As we have seen, many Wiccans use this word to describe those
covens in the United States that descend in a line of "apostolic succession" from Gardner's coven on the Isle of Man. Of the Witches
quoted in this book, several came to Wicca through this route, including Rosemary and Ray Buckland, who started a Gardnerian
coven in the United States in 1964; Theos and Phoenix of Long Island, who took over the Buckland coven in 1972; Donna C. Shultz
and Athena, the priestess and scientist.

But, as we have also seen, the term *Gardnerian* can be used to describe any coven that uses Gardnerian rituals, many of which are
publicly available. Occasionally these covens call themselves Neo-
Gardnerian or Gardnerian eclectic.[19] Some of the more well-known
external elements of Gardnerian Witchcraft include: the 162 (more
or less) Craft Laws, now accepted by many covens; ritual nudity; a
circle of nine feet; the symbolic use of the scourge to purify; a quasi-
ceremonial form of casting the circle with similarities to rituals in the
Key of Solomon; the use of the "Great Rite," either symbolically.or actually; the Charge of the Goddess, much of which derives from *Aradia*; three degrees of advancement; and the ritual known as the
Drawing Down of the Moon.

C. A. Burland, the English writer and ethnographer, wrote of this
tradition in *The Magical Arts*:

> [These covens] studied the subject, and mostly held their ritual dances
> around a magic circle in houses. They realized that the ancient rituals
> have to be revived, and used a magic circle with symbols of the kind
> shown in sixteenth-century paintings. The priestess was equipped with
> her two traditional knives, the black and white knife, and wore necklace
> and tiara. Many prayers were used, and they are again of older origin,
> some coming from *Aradia*. The purpose of the movement has been to

bring peace of heart to its members and to help them to gain a knowledge of the powers of Nature which witches have always known as a kind mother force.[20]

Most Gardnerian covens in the United States have a matrilineal system that passes leadership through successive priestesses. Each coven is autonomous. Some are primarily Goddess-oriented; others stress a balance between male and female principles. Many have become quite flexible. Priestess Donna C. Shultz, who leads a Gardnerian coven in Chicago, told me that her group often wore robes, had abandoned the use of the scourge, and played down much of the sexual symbolism. Instead, they stressed more general forms of occult practice.

Many Gardnerian covens spend more time with their "family of covens"[21] than in ecumenical activities with other Neo-Pagan/Craft groups. One common charge leveled against certain Gardnerians in the United States is that they are too concerned with structure and hierarchy, problems that may stem from their British origins. I have heard this charge less often in the last few years.

When I asked the priestess Theos for her opinions on structure and autonomy, she said, "Any successful group must have the advantage of some roots upon which to build, some knowledge of previous mistakes and successes, some information as to symbolism and myth. But then they must forge ahead to new frontiers, trying different concepts, approaching the gods in a manner which is suitable to their own needs, and gaining contemporary insights into the various philosophies and teachings which they have been given." She said that she had seen many groups that became so concerned with insignificant ritual details that they missed out on any opportunity to evolve.

Many Gardnerian rituals can be found in *The Witches' Way* by Janet and Stewart Farrar. This is the most complete published version of the rituals. Some of the rituals have also been published in *Lady Sheba's Book of Shadows*. Three of Gardner's books are also relevant: *High Magic's Aid*, *Witchcraft Today*, and *The Meaning of Witchcraft*.[22]

ALEXANDRIAN
The Alexandrian tradition comes out of the coven started by Alex Sanders in England, the same coven into which "Jane" was ini-

tiated.* It often seems as if half the photos of Witchcraft rituals in the media show Alex and Maxine. Alex claimed he was initiated by his grandmother in 1933, but many Alexandrian rituals are almost identical to Gardnerian ones, with a little more emphasis on ceremonial magic. Alex told his story at a time when almost all Witches were creating fabulous tales about their origins.

At any rate, Sanders did much to popularize the Craft. Perhaps one of his most astute acts was to initiate the English journalist Stewart Farrar, whose books continue to be some of the better introductory books on modern Wicca. Farrar later formed his own coven and went his own way.

Many Alexandrian covens have formed in the United States. Almost none have any present connection with Sanders. Some have wonderful names like Bandia Grasail, a coven that, until recently, functioned in Boston.

Mary Nesnick, an American who was initiated into both Gardnerian and Alexandrian traditions, combined them in 1972 (which wasn't very hard) and created a new tradition called Algard. In 1976 Nesnick claimed there were over fifty Algard covens in the United States. During the period when I was doing my research (1975–1977), however, I came across none of them. This either means that I did not look hard enough or that—as I suspect—there are not so many of them.

NROOGD

The covens of NROOGD—the New Reformed Orthodox Order of the Golden Dawn—are described in detail later.† Aidan Kelly, one of the founders of NROOGD, has been known to say that poetry led him to the Craft, and this is as good a clue as any to the tradition.

NROOGD, one of the most vital traditions in the United States, was created entirely out of research, poetry, inspiration, and the gathering of a small group of good friends. Those Witches quoted in this book who came from NROOGD include Glenna Turner and Aidan Kelly. NROOGD published a lovely Wiccan magazine called *The Witches Trine* from 1972 to 1976.

* See pp. 93ff.
† See pp. 159ff.

GEORGIAN

This is an eclectic revivalist tradition founded by the late George Patterson of Bakersfield, California. The members publish a small private newsletter,[23] and seem to have quite a large number of lively covens scattered throughout the country. It's a very open composite tradition that lays great emphasis on freedom. When I visited the Bakersfield coven I was told, "You don't *become* a Pagan. You *are* a Pagan. Most Craft teachings are really unbrainwashing—attempts to let you think for yourself so you can be free to live your own life in your own way without hangups."

DIANIC

The term *Dianic* describes a number of traditions. It stems, of course, from Margaret Murray's description of Witchcraft as "the Dianic cult." In the United States all the groups that call themselves "Dianic" are linked by one thing: their emphasis on the Goddess.

There are at least two primary streams of Dianic worship in the United States. The first comprises the entire movement known as the feminist Craft, which is treated in a later chapter.* Members of this portion of the Craft, with their many covens, look for their roots in the matriarchal tradition. They ally themselves with the women's movement and the women's spirituality movement. In the 1970s the most famous coven in this tradition was Z Budapest's Susan B. Anthony Coven of Los Angeles, which spawned many others, including the Amelia Earhart Coven in New York and the Elizabeth Gould Davis Coven in Florida. In the 1980s there are hundreds of Dianic covens, many of them with no connection to Z Budapest and her teachings. This Dianic stream conceives of Wicca as "womin's religion." Men are excluded.

Covens within this stream of Dianic worship use Leland's *Aradia* and Z Budapest's *The Feminist Book of Lights and Shadows* as sources for ritual. In addition to creating their own rituals, they call upon the literally hundreds of new writings on women's spirituality, the works by Starhawk, Hallie Iglehart, Diane Mariechild, Marija Gimbutas, Mary Daly, Chris Carol, and others too numerous to name. They also emphasize the works on matriarchy, such as books by J. J. Bachofen,

* See pp. 171ff.

Robert Briffault, E. G. Davis, Helen Diner, Merlin Stone, and Barbara Walker. In general, this stream of Dianic worship is high on creativity, high on psychic skills, high on politics, and low on structure and formal rituals.

The other Dianic stream in this country began in Dallas with the Dianic Covenstead of priestess Morgan McFarland. While McFarland is no longer leading a group, there are many active covens that derive from her original work. This tradition exalts the feminine but does not exclude men from the worship. When I visited Morgan McFarland in 1976, she was priestess of three covens, one of them exclusively female.

McFarland and her priest, Mark Roberts,* see the Dianic tradition as that which maintains its links with the ancient matriarchies in terms of myth and power. Dianic covens worship the Goddess more or less monotheistically. The Goddess is seen as having three aspects: Maiden-Creatrix, Great Mother, and Old Crone, who holds the door to death and rebirth. It is in her second aspect that the Goddess takes a male consort, who is as Osiris to Isis. To show this relationship, Dianics quote a phrase attributed to Bachofen: "Immortal is Isis, mortal her husband, like the earthly creation he represents." Thus there is a place for the God, but the female as Creatrix is primary. Dianics also see the Goddess symbolized in nature as the Triple Creatrix: as the moon, the Queen of Mysteries; as the sun, Sunna, the Queen of Stars, provider of warmth and care; and as Mother Earth, to whom all must return.

Mark Roberts told me that Dianics are also pantheists, since they recognize the sacredness of all that exists. But, he said, "The Goddess is the touchstone to this planet and this life cycle." And in this spirit Mark and Morgan seemed to be—of all those I interviewed— the most concerned with the ecological fate of the planet. In *The New Broom*, an occasional Dianic publication, Roberts wrote that there was less distinction between "mortal" and "deity" than there was between those who had lost touch with nature and those beings whose rhythms and pulse were attuned to the universe. He also wrote:

---

* As of 1978, Mark Roberts was no longer involved with the covenstead, and had formed his own Craft tradition, Hyperborea.

The lifestyle of a Dianic is a composite of three values and ideals. First, an awareness of self. Second, an increasing and evergrowing kinship with Nature. And third, an open sensitivity to the pulsebeat of the cosmos. As we near the common goals of awareness, kinship, and sensitivity, we attain the level of attunement that outsiders call "magic." We are well aware that in our workings we have achieved and produced nothing supernatural: we have simply reached our level of natural capacity.

In a society obsessed with artificiality, our lifestyle seems strange, "unnatural," even revolutionary. . . .

And we are revolutionary: in the sense that we whirl about the axis who is the Goddess and are completing the cycle that sees her worship returning in strength; and we are advocates of a drastic and radical change from the pell-mell, break-neck, destructive world in which we find ourselves; and in that, in a technological age where mechanical improvements take their increasing toll in human sensitivity, we train reawakening sense to a level of awareness that frees the human to once again be whole and independent and alert. In a patriarchal culture that becomes increasingly authoritarian, we find no choice but to stand as rebels against dehumanization. . . .[24]

In connection with these principles the Dianic Covenstead had one of the best series of exercises and techniques for regaining kinship and attunement with nature.

The origin of the Dianic Covenstead in Dallas goes back about twenty years. Morgan McFarland, the daughter of a minister, lived part of her youth in the Orient and then moved to the American South. She was trained in a Southern Witchcraft coven. It had no name for its tradition, simply calling it Witchcraft. She adopted the term *Dianic* later. The rituals of this coven placed great emphasis on the moon, were very "Gravesian." They focused on the myths, lore, and mystery behind the thirteen lunar months and their connection with the Beth-Luis-Nion tree alphabet of ancient Britain.*

---

*Much of Robert Graves' *The White Goddess* is a metaphoric investigation of this alphabet, said to be an ancient druidical alphabet. It has eighteen letters—thirteen consonants and five vowels—and each has a corresponding tree known well in European folklore. Beth is birch, Luis is rowan, Nion is ash, and so on. The consonants are often used for the thirteen lunar months. The covenstead of Morrigana uses this system. So do many recent lunar calendars, such as those by Nancy Passmore, published by Luna Press (Boston).

While both men and women could become initiates, those women who had experienced the rituals of all the lunar months could go through an additional five "passage" rituals, after which they could "hive" off and start their own covens. Within the tradition, it is the women who choose their priests, and they may revoke their choice at any time.

I asked Mark the obvious question: how it felt to be a priest in such a heavily matriarchal tradition. He said, "I'd rather be first mate on a ship that is solid than captain on a ship that has a rotten hull, a ship that is sinking. Patriarchy is such a ship."

I asked Morgan to talk about her feelings on the difference between her two covens that include men and the one that doesn't. She said, "We have found that women working together are capable of conjuring their past and reawakening their old ascendancy. They are capable of putting together many of the pieces. This does not seem to happen when men are present. Perhaps this is a societal thing. It seems that in mixed covens, no matter how 'feminist' the women are, a kind of competition begins to happen. Among the women, alone, none of this occurs, and a great reciprocity develops, unlike anything I have seen before."

Morgan McFarland has been a housewife, a lecturer on feminism and Witchcraft, and the owner of a small business in plants and baskets. She is currently working up the professional ladder at a large corporation. She has two children. I spent a week with Morgan and Mark during the period they were working together. I found them to be lively, spontaneous, and wonderful people.

Their circles were primarily celebratory. As Mark worte in *The New Broom*:

> We do perform healing and problem-solving, scrying and protective measures, but the majority of our ritual circles are for the praise and worship and contact of and with the Goddess. The protective spirit of our circles is more to shield us from the 20th century than to protect us from malicious harm. Our circles are a haven from the present that frees us to touch the past and to restore our old attunement to nature.[25]

Within the circle, all were equal, despite the "feminist" edge, and there was much room for innovation in regard to ritual, tools, clothing (or lack of it), size, and structure. In 1986, Morgan and Mark are no longer working together and neither have active groups. But there are scores of Dianic groves and covens that originated from the work they did in the 1970s and early 1980s. Over one hundred small groups corresponded with McFarland and Roberts, and followed their training exercises and preliminary rituals. Many of the Dianic covens in Texas and elsewhere owe their origins to this work.

SCHOOL OF WICCA

The School of Wicca is the largest correspondence Witchcraft school in the United States, and one of the few allied with the Wiccan community—although it is a strange ally.[26]

It is debatable whether the School of Wicca should be included in this book about Neo-Paganism and about Wicca as a branch of Neo-Paganism. The School of Wicca does not consider itself "Pagan," and Gavin and Yvonne Frost, who head it, define Witchcraft as a monotheistic religion.

Still, the School of Wicca may have created a hundred covens through its activities, and the Frosts have often been at the center of Neo-Pagan ecumenical ventures, as well as numerous disputes within the Craft—disputes over sexuality, homosexuality, monotheism versus polytheism, to mention only a few. Meanwhile, some forty thousand students have begun their twelve-lesson Witchcraft course, although only a couple of hundred have ever finished it.

Part of the controversy surrounding the Frosts comes from Gavin Frost's wry and rather bizarre sense of humor, and his tendency to say almost anything to get a rise out of someone. Because of this, the Frosts have been much misunderstood. For a time their opposition to homosexuality in the Craft raised a great debate. Since their particular tradition stressed heterosexual sex magic, this attitude was somewhat understandable, as long as they stopped short of claiming that their methods were "the Way"; unfortunately, Gavin did not always do this.

They made another mistake. They wrote a Witchcraft book and called it *The Witch's Bible*—or, at the least, their publisher did.[27] When it appeared, many people in the Craft were outraged and labeled it a "Witchcrap book." This book, with its emphasis on an asexual monotheistic deity, described a religion very different from that practiced by most Wiccans. There were also questionable statements about sex and race. There were descriptions of the use of artificial phalli—an old magical tradition, but one not familiar to most people in Wicca. The title of the book was the worst part. Many Witches fumed at the word *The*, since the book, in their view, had nothing to do with their religion.

In person, the Frosts are delightful. Gavin, a man in his fifties, is kind and humorous. Yvonne, who has long gray hair down to her waist, is forthright and even a bit prim. When I visited them in 1975 they lived in southern Missouri, near a town aptly called Salem. (They have since moved to New Bern, North Carolina.) They lived with their daughter in an old red schoolhouse on fourteen acres of land, and they ran a pig farm. The sense one got of their life was *solidity*. Despite my strong religious and political differences with them, I left thinking that they had truly translated the Craft into a living philosophy that placed a high value on techniques of survival and simple rural living. They had many rural-based covens connected with their school and church. This was a welcome change from the mostly urban covens I had encountered.

Gavin Frost told me that he was an iconoclast who believed in an abstract monotheistic deity. He divided "gods" into two types. On the one hand, "God" was abstract, unknowable, beyond the need for worship. But there were also "stone gods," the gods we "create" for a purpose. These gods are used as storehouses of energy. They are necessary for magic. Gavin said that people make "stone gods" or "idols" in order to have something to put energy into, so that later they can draw power out. Both kinds of deities "exist," but "stone gods" are of one's own creation. Gavin said he was not a "Pagan" because he did not worship "stone gods." "What do you mean?" I asked, as we sat around the cozy schoolhouse farm. At this point, the following conversation took place:

M.A.: You both say you are not Pagans, is that true?

Gavin: Absolutely!

Yvonne: I do not consider myself a Pagan. I do not worship any nature deity. I reach upward toward the unnameable which has no gender.

M.A.: How do you define "Pagan"?

Gavin: A Pagan is someone who worships a nature spirit.

Yvonne: Or a named, finite deity.

M.A.: Or many of them.

Yvonne: I say there is one deity, without gender.

Gavin: Okay, but if you want to make something happen, magically, you have no problem or objection to worshipping a statue of Isis, and then dumping power.

Yvonne: Oh! My mascot? *My* deity is my Volkswagen ignition key. That's what makes it happen for me. I do not reach up to it. But if I am going to work a procedure, that is the deity or mascot I use.

Gavin: And you don't have any objection to calling on Mars, let us say, if Mars seems to be appropriate for magical procedure.

Yvonne: But that is not a *reverence.*

I asked them if, had they known *The Witch's Bible* would create such a furor, they would have changed anything in the book.

"Maybe we'd change the title to *A* instead of *The*," Gavin said.

And Yvonne added, "If there are still masculine overtones in regard to deity in the book, we might change them to asexual ones."

Gavin Frost's interest in the Craft began when he was working for an aerospace company on the Salisbury plains. He told me that there, "surrounded by monuments," it was easy to become interested in the druids. When he came to the United States, he said, he was initiated by a group in St. Louis. Gavin said his tradition was "thirty seconds old" and that "we have a bunch of traditional stuff, but it keeps changing all the time and we encourage people to experiment and change." And while the Church of Wicca—an organization connected with the School of Wicca—includes many covens, several follow their own path, which has no connection with the Frosts' tradition; they chose to affiliate themselves with the Church in order to obtain the tax-exempt status of a religious organization.

The Frosts are militantly public, and they have stated that "the conscious decision to be a Witch should be at least semi-publicly acknowledged and admitted." They believe firmly that communication between groups should be fostered and that "secrecy brings with it persecution, for fear of the unknown results in destruction and death."

Here are some of the things that distinguish the teachings of the School of Wicca from other Wiccan traditions.

1. Monotheism: the view that Witchcraft is not a Pagan nature religion.

2. No particular emphasis on the feminine.

3. A very structured concept of "the astral," called *Side*, by the Frosts. The *Side* has ten levels.

4. Very structured beliefs in progressive reincarnation as the primary learning tool of human beings and all "souls." They also told me that they believe that overpopulation is causing "inferior souls" to reincarnate on the earth plane.

5. Kundalini sex practices, including "introitus," a practice in which sex without orgasm is used as a form of surrender to God.

6. The use of the Egyptian ankh as a symbol of regeneration. The use of artificial phalli.

7. An antimatriarchal bias. Gavin called the theory of matriarchy "a Marxist heresy."

The beliefs of the School of Wicca are often stated as follows:

> One individual cannot define a path in another's reality.
> God/ess is not definable. In Bardic language,
>
> There is nothing truly hidden but what is not conceivable;
> There is nothing not conceivable but what is immeasurable;
> There is nothing immeasurable but God.
>
> An it harm none, do what you will
> Power is gained through knowledge.
> Reincarnation is for learning
> The Law of Attraction (good begets good, evil begets evil)
> Harmony of man with the psychic and physical worlds.[28]

The Frosts continue to be the focus of much controversy within the Craft, although, compared to a few years ago, the criticism has indeed subsided. Some Wiccans still fault them for charging money for lessons in Witchcraft, feeling that this violates Craft Law. Feminist Witches charge them with sexism. But most have come to feel that the Frosts are simply practicing a different religion, and only wish they would stop calling it Wicca. The Frosts feel that everyone else is on an erroneous path. Despite this, the Frosts seem to get on well with most other Witches, most of the time.

Again, these traditions are not "hard and fast." As one priestess from the Midwest wrote humorously, "Mary Nesnick began as a Gardnerian, Jesus Christ began as a Jew, I began as an Alexandrian. None of us stayed that way.''[29] Most people in the Craft are coming to feel that traditions should be guides, no more, no less. "A tradition," one New York Craft priest wrote to me, "should be rich enough in associative values and nuances not to wear thin, but to lead to deeper pathways, deeper mysteries. Its images and symbols must not be trite. It should give you supportive values and relationships that aid growth with people or growth with other planes of reality. It should offer an introduction to the world of spirit, but be balanced in regard to the world of the senses and the flesh. In short, it should be stable enough to offer a pathway, a guideline, but it must not be so rigid that all spontaneity is lost."

In 1986, there is a lot of ferment and change within the traditions. Many English traditional covens are beginning to join together, pooling their resources. For example, the New Wiccan Church is an organization of English traditional covens from a variety of traditions—Alexandrian, Algard, Georgian, Kingstone, Majestic, Gardnerian, and Silver Crescent. One member of that organization told me in 1985, "In fifty years we may not have such fragmentation. All these different traditions may well come together, share their information and end up, simply, as English traditional Wicca."

If some of the older traditions are consolidating, new traditions are springing up almost every day. Those described here are simply some that are fairly well known, have a following of several covens, and have been around for at least a few years. In my travels across the country I found that easily half the people I interviewed in the Craft were forming their own traditions or changing the ones they were involved with. Here are some examples:

—Alison Harlow, trained in Victor Anderson's "fairy" tradition and in the Gardnerian tradition, began a coven with four women, all from different traditions. They combined their teachings and rituals and, presto, they had a new tradition: the Tanic.

—A Craft priest named Bran Tree wrote to me that he and his priestess had started a tradition called "Natural Witchcraft." He told me that he knew of lots of people who had never heard of the Craft or the Goddess, but were natural Witches because they saw wonder and mystery in everyday life. They formed their coven with this idea in mind.

—In northern California there is a coven called the "Compost Coven." The idea behind this name is that it takes a lot of manure for the flowers to grow.

—Ed Fitch and Janine Renée are a priest and priestess in the Gardnerian tradition. But for several years they have been spending most of their Craft energy researching the mythology of the dark, night-riding goddess of the wild hunt. They emphasize myths that talk of Holda, Habundia, Berata, of pre-Germanic mythology. Fitch is writing a new series of rituals out of this mythos. These rituals may, in the end, create a new tradition.

These Witches could be said to be following the advice that Witch Diana Demdike gave in the British magazine *Quest:* The best thing Witches could do, she said, would be to make a huge bonfire of all their carefully copied old books of rituals and then "drink the water of knowledge fresh from its source," which was "the light of the moon, the shape of the clouds and the growing of green things."[30]

Witches and Persecution Today

Despite the constitutional amendment that gives citizens of the United States the freedom to practice their religion—"Congress shall make no law respecting an establishment of religion, or prohibiting the free exercise thereof . . ."—Witchcraft is not accepted as a valid minority religion by most people in the United States, and many of those I interviewed told me of persecution they had encountered once they were identified as Witches. There were stories of firings from jobs, of children taken away from parents and placed in the custody of others, of arrests for practicing divination. There were stories of stones thrown through windows, and several tales of people who moved away from an area after fundamentalist groups decided to take literally the biblical injunction: "Thou shall not suffer a witch to live."

Among the Witches quoted in this book, Judy Myer lost custody of her children in a divorce proceeding after her husband said she was practicing Witchcraft. Z Budapest was "set up" by a police informer and arrested for doing a tarot reading for which she charged ten dollars; the informer told the court that the reading seemed quite accurate, but Z was convicted and fined three hundred dollars. Local teenagers tried to set fire to Bran and Moria's house; they threw tomatoes through the windows, as well as stones and other objects. This happened after Moria appeared on the "Tomorrow Show" to talk about the Craft. As a result, Bran and Moria picked up and left for northern California; they told me they regarded the incident as a "sign from the Mother" that it was time to get out of Los Angeles.

Among other incidents is the probable murder of a man by his "caring" relative who wanted to make sure his soul would be saved, and the case of Robert Williams, a psychologist who, after he mentioned the Craft in an interview in a local newspaper, was fired from his job at a Kansas reformatory and shortly after committed suicide.[31]

Most persecution is not this blatant. It takes the more subtle form of the images of Witches portrayed in television shows and in films like *Rosemary's Baby* and *The Exorcist*.

Leo Martello, long an activist for civil and gay rights, organized a "Witch-in" in New York's Central Park on October 31, 1970. He had to fight, with the help of New York's Civil Liberties Union, to obtain a permit from the Parks Department. Martello then formed the Witches Anti-Defamation League, devoted to securing religious rights for Witches.[32]

Several years later Isaac Bonewits and a number of other occultists formed the AADL—the Aquarian Anti-Defamation League—an organization dedicated to fighting legal battles on behalf of Pagans and occultists. Writing in *Gnostica*, Bonewits gave details of anti-occult laws and statutes on the books in many states. For example, in Delaware pretending to be able to do magic, divination, or "deal with spirits" makes one a vagrant. In Massachusetts to "pretend" fortune-telling for gain is larceny and fraud. In Michigan any form of divination is illegal, including dowsing. (It's all right, though, if you happen to be a member of a spiritualist church.) In Montana all forms of divination and all forms of magic are illegal. (Presumably, if you consult the I Ching in your own home you can get away with it, in the same way most people get away with smoking grass.) In

Ohio (and many other states) it's illegal to practice astrology, palmistry, and so forth without a license. In New York it's illegal to claim you have "occult powers." Reading cards for a fee is also against the law.

Bonewits observed in an article called "Witchburning ... Now and Then" that since most people don't consider Witches members of a "real" religion, they often don't get the protection the law gives to churches. In addition, since many states have laws against certain forms of sexual behavior ("victimless crimes"), many of the harmless acts—and rituals—of Pagans and Witches are illegal.[33]

The idea for AADL occurred after Bonewits and a number of other occultists were approached by some apparently sympathetic people who said they were trying to make a documentary on the occult. They turned out to be a fundamentalist group. The film, *The Occult: An Echo from Darkness*, was narrated by Hal Lindsey, the author of *Satan Is Alive and Well on Planet Earth*, *The Late Great Planet Earth*, and other such books. Bonewits observed:

> The film is a venomous, vituperative propaganda picture. Its sole purpose is to warp and confuse well-known data of world history and comparative religions, to convince ignorant viewers that all occultism, from newspaper horoscopes and tarot cards to Witch meetings and ritual magic, to ESP laboratories and mind training systems, is a unified Satanic plot to enslave the world and destroy Christianity. Every single person in the film, except the preachers, is equated with a young girl who "confesses" that she helped burn a baby to death in a Satanic ritual.[34]

Bonewits said that the film, a full-color production costing at least a hundred thousand dollars, used misquotes and trick editing. Many Neo-Pagans, psychics, Witches, and Neo-Christians appeared in it, including Bonewits.

The AADL was formed in response to this kind of problem, but the organization died from a lack of volunteers to do the work and a lack of funds.

Attitudes within Paganism and the Craft concerning persecution vary widely, and seem evenly divided between two schools: "If we're respectable and quiet, we won't get persecuted—only flashy trouble-makers do," and "It's time we stood up and fought for our religious rights." Priestess Theos, for example, told me that she felt that most of the establishment was totally unaware of the Craft. "I go my way, they go theirs," she said. A Pagan from the Midwest told me, "I've suffered a hell of a lot of persecution in my life, but since I belong to the 'shoot back' school of how to deal with persecution, I have no intention of talking about it in any detail. My advice to Aquarians who are persecuted is: Keep your eyes open, your mouth shut, and your shotgun behind the door, and hope you never need to use it. Don't tell your neighbors you're a Pagan unless they are Aquarians. Don't tell people at work. Use a nom-de-guerre, or several of them. If they don't know where you live, they can't burn your house down." But most Witches I talked to lived quietly, ignoring harass-ment if it occurred.

Essentials

A great many modern witches feel that they have brought back the ancient reli-gion of pre-Christian times. In so far as they have retained the love of nature and followed the festivals of the turning sky they have an argument in their favor. Those were the essentials of the ancient belief.

. . . In this environment of growing threats to human existence there is a surge toward the works of life. Hence the growth of witches of the old greenwood type, the dancers of the gods. Nakedness, sex, song and dance are their marks, and their hearts are mostly innocent and happy. The newly invented groups have a validity which springs from the emotional needs which created them. Often without any con-scious planning they throw up from within themselves echoes of ancient ceremonies. . . .

Witchcraft is in its essence the worship of the powers of this world, beautiful or terrible, but all in a circle under the turning sky above which is the One.

—C. A. BURLAND[35]

Most popular talk about Witchcraft is about *trappings*. This misleads and mystifies. Our society teaches us to regard objects as the essen-tials. Thus we are apt to focus on ritual daggers and spells and strange herbs and all the paraphernalia of modern Wicca, thinking that these *are* the Craft.

"Why did you put a *red* cloth on the altar?" a novice asks a priest of Wicca, framing the question softly, as if a big secret is about to be revealed.

"Because I just happened to *have* a red cloth," the priest replies.

We should not make the novice's error. Rather, we should heed the words a woman recently wrote to me:

> It sounds as if there are really very few beliefs that one needs to be a Witch. In fact—correct me if I'm wrong—the only thing one *really* needs, the only thing all varieties of Witches have in common, is a belief in the power of what I shall call the moon principle (for lack of a better term)—that from which springs the intuitive, the psychic, the mysterious, that which is somehow aligned with the female, the hidden, the unknown.
>
> This is a vague concept, true, but I think necessarily so, for two reasons: (1) Our culture, being so strongly based on the antithetical principle, has few means of dealing with this side of life other than to clothe it in ambiguous shadowy terms or condemn it as evil. (2) Being so vague, it is closer to being universal than the more rigidly defined religions or philosophies; more different types of people, as you found, can associate themselves with it.
>
> I have no trouble believing in such a principle, for there *are* things in life which cannot be explained by logic and rationality. There is the evidence of my senses, the feelings which cannot be denied. And I have no doubt at all (on a gut level) that I can grow to experience the principle at first hand.
>
> For the time being, then, I am quite willing to do spells, perform rituals, to chant over candles at midnight, because I've come to believe that this is a way to the power. The principle comes from within us, the source of it or the channel through which it manifests itself. (I'm not sure which, yet, though I suspect it's the latter.)
>
> But knowing that intellectually does not help us gain access to it; we don't order it to come forth with our rational minds, for it does not obey rationality. Therefore I chant, I gaze at a picture of a triune Goddess through incense-smoke as it wavers in candlelight, I turn off my rational mind for a while, and soon I feel it flowing through me like electricity, breathlessly, and I am the same and not the same as I was before. . . .

Goodness, it's easy to get poetic when talking about this! I guess poetry comes from Her/It/Me too. . . . But the trick is to keep from forgetting that candles, incense, images, etc., *are* props.[36]

The Witch, as we said, is the changer—the one who bends. Wicca, at its best, is the most flexible and adaptable of religions, since it is perfectly willing to throw out dogmas and rely on these types of experience alone.

By the time this book reaches print, some of the covens mentioned may have dissolved and entirely new ones may have sprouted. Don't look to find exactly what has been described in these pages. You may not find it, or, everything may all be a little different. That is the real beauty of Wicca when it is true to itself.

6

Interview with a Modern Witch

The following interview took place in the winter of 1976, in Oakland, California. The woman, Sharon Devlin, is an American of Irish descent. She is a member of the Craft; she is a mother; she is a weaver, a player on the Irish harp; she is an Irish civil rights activist; and she works in the field of health. She is *not* typical—if there is such a thing as a "typical Witch," which I doubt. Devlin's views would be considered very controversial by most modern Wiccans. In particular, her views on drugs, sex, and politics must be considered a minority position within the modern Craft. Still I chose this interview out of all of the others because of its peculiar richness and depth, because it is my favorite interview, and because it touches on many of the themes in this book.

Q. How did you come to be a Pagan and a Witch?

A. First of all, I am a hereditary Witch, but this does *not* mean that I have a direct lineage from mother to daughter, although [laughter] I did allege this as a neurotic teenager. What it does mean is that I am from a Witch family. My great-great-grandmother on my father's side was named Mary MacGoll. She was a fat, little, pudgy, brown-eyed woman of Scots descent (whom I am supposed to resemble). She was a local midwife and healer, basically a faith healer. I doubt she would have described herself as a Pagan. She was raised as a

Presbyterian and she remained a devout Christian, but her Christianity was of the peasant variety; it was centered on the Virgin Mary. She got her power from the Tuatha De Danaan. Most people called them the Gentry or the Sidhe or the Shining Ones. And there are many stories about the fairies that are associated with her.

She fell in love with an impoverished but apparently terrifically lovable Catholic named Jenkin Devlin, who is my great-great-grandfather. She eloped with him after she became pregnant and her family disinherited her because she had married a Catholic. She was an intense clairvoyant and she foretold to her family that because they had robbed her unborn child of its inheritance, they would be childless, and that someday they would come begging her descendants to take back what they had not freely given. And this prediction was fulfilled. I was told many other stories of things that she did. She apparently was taught artificial respiration by the fairies and she revived "dead" children. She did not live long. She died during the potato famine in County Tyrone.

I was brought up as a strict Irish Catholic, but this did not have the negative connotations people generally associate with it. My family was basically working-class Irish. They were not lace curtain in any way.

Q. How did you come to enter the Craft?

A. It was an independent decision on my part because at the time I didn't believe that anyone else had the same interests. When I was a young girl I was deeply religious and I was looking desperately for an ecstatic and deep religious experience. As a result I wished to become a nun and enter a contemplative order. My parents were radically against it. They felt it would be a copout. For a young girl faced with the terrors of sex, chastity is a very comfortable way out. The convent situation is one which lends itself to safety, and I found that attractive. Of course, as I matured, this alternative became less and less attractive.

The peak of my "convent period" was when I was about fifteen. I entered a convent for a brief time—about six weeks—and then was forcibly removed by my parents. My mother went to bed and simply refused to get up unless my father removed me. My father told the Mother Superior that he didn't want my tits to dry up on me as hers had. So I was spirited from my spiritual refuge and back into the world.

Well, back in the world, I soon became aware of the narrowness of the philosophical viewpoint of orthodox Catholicism. At the same time a strange awareness began to dawn on me of something of far greater potency. Now, I had been into a thing of praying to the point of ecstasy. This is one of the more positive aspects of Catholicism. I have met a few priests and nuns who have actually achieved enlightenment this way. Most of their personal views were pretty heretical, and this was one of the tools my parents used to get me away from the convent. They located a famous artist and nun, Sister Corita, and I spent a summer working for her at Immaculate Heart College in Los Angeles. She told me that the best thing I could do for my spirituality was to *work out my own.*

During that crucial sixteenth year I started to read philosophy. I read a lot of the classics, a lot of Attic and Roman philosophy. I stumbled onto the Hermetic tradition and I found some books on alchemy. I began to talk about alchemy with a wonderful high-school chemistry teacher, and one thing led to another, and before I knew it I'd gone to Larsen's Books on Hollywood Boulevard and had bought a copy of *The Greater Key of Solomon.* I began to work spells. It was at this point—after I had worked my first spell—that it flashed on me that I was fulfilling something to do with my ancestry.

After that I went down to UCLA and sat in on a bunch of classes on the language and mythology of the Welsh and Irish Celtic peoples. I read every book on Irish mythology that I could get hold of. Before the year was out I was calling myself a Witch because I knew that was what I was.

Later my grandmother gave me a beautiful cast-iron cauldron which had been brought over from Ireland as part of the personal possessions of our family. It had belonged to my great-great-grandmother, Mary MacGoll. In her time an iron pot was an investment of several months' cash money. Irish families cooked their entire meal of buttermilk and potatoes in the pot. This was probably the biggest possession my family had. So I have my great-great-grandmother's potato pot, which may or may not have been used as her cauldron. And although I told people some "ugga bugga" about being initiated by my grandmother and being given the cauldron, the fact is, I *was* given the cauldron and I was told the story.

Q. What is your present relationship to Catholicism?

A. It's an uneasy truce. I believe that Christ was a genuine avatar of the Great Mother—a Dionysus incarnation, pretty much. His worship has been desperately perverted. They have turned him into this dreadful sort of pathetic thing instead of the sacrificial god of Inspiration. I go and eat his Body and Blood every once in a while, and I consider that to be valid. But to "confess my sins" to people who refer to themselves as his "minions" but do nothing but assassinate his character and purpose, I would find that pretty sacrilegious. I know without doubt that if I lived in a Catholic community and if it were known that I was practicing magic, I would be asked not to communicate. I just go into various churches and take advantage of the social confusion that Berkeley offers.

Q. Do you consider yourself a Pagan?

A. What I actually am is an offshoot of Paganism and early Irish Christianity. I follow beliefs which formed the basis of the Culdee Church. The Culdee Church was the only true union of Paganism and the real teachings of Christ; it was brutally stamped out by the papacy. The Culdee Church continued to believe in the ancient Celtic gods. It continued to believe in the Danu and the Dagda and it considered all the ancient heroes and heroines of Ireland to be saints. They had women clergy. They did not believe that sexual intercourse was sinful and, as a matter of fact, on all the church doors was a big portrait of the Great Mother giving birth with her clitoris exposed and her labia pulled wide and her mouth open because she is in the birth ecstasy. Those are called Sheila-Na-Gigh.

Q. Do you consider yourself a polytheist?

A. I believe that all so-called gods are thought-form emanations of human beings toward the One Consciousness of which we are a part. I believe that there are many races of sapient beings in the universe, some of which are physically greater than we are or, perhaps, have nondelineated bodies, like the Shining Ones, or who live on a different dimensional plane. All these things are within the realm of possibility. It has been our nature to call these "gods." What is a god? A god is an eternal being, and in that sense we, too, are gods. So yes, I am a polytheist. But I also believe there is a unity to the whole trip and in that sense I'm a monotheist. There is one Spirit, but a multitude of delightful forms from which to choose, or to create new ones, as you will.

Q. What does it mean to you personally to be a Witch?

A. Well, unfortunately, it means that I have set myself off from humanity to a large extent. I do not see myself as a leader and I have no desire to be a leader. I would, however, like to help initiate a change of spirit in the world. I think that it is time for humanity to stand up and take a pro-life stand on everything. To say *no* to killing, *no* to the destruction and rape of our environment, *no* to the valuing of goods above human life, *no* to the senseless divorcement from our aged parents and our little children, *no* to the force that cuts us off from our ancient past, *no* to all these things that are meant to enslave us.

I'm not saying we should return to the ox cart. That is obviously ridiculous. To a large extent I believe, along with Bucky Fuller, that if we get the right head-set, this technology that we have can be used in a really beautiful way. But we've got to get off this rape-head. And I think Witchcraft offers an ethical alternative to this. Now, Papa Crowley was a fucked-up man in many ways. But, contrary to popular belief, he led a life of intense suffering, and his life of suffering was for one purpose, and that was to say, "Do what thou wilt shall be the whole of the Law. Love is the Law, love under will." They should inscribe that on the Rock of Gibraltar. It should be hung up in flags from the top of the Empire State Building and the Golden Gate Bridge. It should be carved on the book that the Statue of Liberty is holding. . . .

Q. If you were to paraphrase Crowley's statement in a way many people could understand, what would you say?

A. It means this: So you think you are helpless. You think all this is just happening to you. Well, that's bullshit! Because you are not just a son or a daughter of God. To be a son or daughter of God means you are equal to God and you have a responsibility to the One to get it together and make your Godhood count for something, because other than that, you are just another fuckin' insect. Now that's what it means. It also means that if we were all doing what we *really* wanted to do, we would do it in perfect harmony. Why do people kill and rape each other? This is an expression of the denial of love in that person's life. Now, I have been attacked, but frankly, I believe in my heart of hearts that the one who kills is enduring greater suffering than the one who is killed and that all "evil" is an expression of ignorance, an expression of the frustration of the Law of the One. And the Law of the One, whoever She is, in all Her many forms, is that we give to each other constantly. I am not talking about giving to the negation of self, I'm talking about giving to the glory of self. If you were what you could be the best and you did what you loved to do with all your might, you would create such light and such power that it would give pizazz to everybody in your immediate area, and even to those distant, perhaps.

Q. But how does this relate to the Craft's purpose—if it has a purpose?

A. I would say the ultimate purpose is to become that. If we become those kinds of people we will create an energy source for the regeneration of the whole world. We won't have to proselytize. We won't have to sell it on the street. That is what I consider my task to be, to bust my ass to achieve my Godhood. And if I fail to do that, I have become hopelessly debauched.

Q. Could you talk about ritual? One of the things about the Craft is that we do a lot of ritual. Why ritual? What is its purpose? Why do it?

A. The purpose of ritual is to change the mind of the human being. It's a sacred drama in which you are the audience as well as the participant, and the purpose of it is to activate parts of the mind that are not activated by everyday activity. We are talking about the parts of the mind that produce the psychokinetic, telekinetic power, whatever you want to call it—the connection between the eternal power and yourself. As for *why* ritual, I think that human beings have a need for art and art is ritual. I think that when we became sapient, we became capable of artistic expression. It is simply a human need.

One of the things I am deeply involved in is that I am trying to recreate the sacred music and dances of the Culdee tradition. I have reconstructed what I believe to be a good approximation of the circle dances, since few Irish circle dances have survived.

Q. It has seemed to me that much of the modern Craft and the

Neo-Pagan movement lacks real music and real dance, in comparison to indigenous Pagan religious movements.

A. That's absolutely true. Many things are lacking in modern Paganism. For example, in all indigenous Paganism possession of the participants by the gods and goddesses occurred frequently. This is not occurring frequently among Neo-Pagans and I consider it to be a sign of ill health in the Pagan movement. I attribute this to our loss of skill in the use of music, rhythm, dance, and psychogenetic drugs. In the Irish tradition music was essential to the success of the rites. I have finally initiated a traditional Irish piper so that we would be able to have the pipes, the harp, and the drums together in our rites. Another thing that was essential to the rites in ancient times was ritual drunkenness and sex. And I find this also lacking. We have to create those ecstatic states again. We have to offer people an energy source and a theological alternative, and we can only do this by offering real experience. We have to introduce real sacraments.

Look at what's going on in South America. Mark my words, the biggest thing that is happening politically in South America is voodoo. *That* may be the first Pagan United States. The juntas may find themselves thrown out on their asses, not by a military takeover, but by a spiritual regeneration.

But here the negative aspects of Christianity—the fascist political Christianity which has become the pervading form of Christianity in the world—this form of Christianity has produced fear of ecstatic states, fear of intelligent use of hallucinogens, fear of intelligent and sensitive use of sexuality to produce ecstasy. Now those are the three elements that have really been lacking, and worse still than any of that, Christianity has produced fear of personal responsibility for spiritual development. It has produced fear of independent thinking.

Q. What is your position on the use of drugs in the Craft? Most people I have interviewed take a very strong antidrug stance. Contrary to popular report, I came across very few groups that permitted any use of drugs in ritual.

A. I think that drugs, used with intelligence (like anything else), are important. Flying ointment was used in ancient times. Our ancestors definitely used drugs. Frankly, most Pagans and Witches are stumbling around in the dark. A Diabellero would laugh at us. A Southwestern Indian would think us ridiculous. I want people to start getting off. Drugs and sex are an essential part of magical rites. Some of the heaviest power is obtained that way. Do you know that there was a period in Irish history when people were so liberated that they were able to make love in any public place, without shame.

Q. I would find that very difficult.

A. Well, it's hard for me too, but I think this is the ideal we should attain to. I'm not saying we should fuck each other in public, but at least let's do it in private. Much of Neo-Paganism lacks the same content I've described before. The raising of power is an accidental occurrence among most of us at the present time. I find that difficult for my own self-esteem. It makes it difficult to work with people. I don't like going through empty ritual with anybody, especially my closest friends. Only once have I been to a Pagan gathering that happily enough "degenerated" into a Great Rite, and that was only because the Lady chose to give it to us at that time. I personally believe that anyone who calls themselves a Witch should have the capability to deal with different types of ecstatic states. But of course, these things have to be done with intelligence.

I want to tell you a story that fills me with humility, about a time I almost killed myself through stupidity. I was living on a commune that was situated in the middle of an apple orchard that was shaped like a long oval dish. And a peculiar thing that used to happen was that the dogs would start to bark at one end of the dish as if something was walking around the lip of this dish, and then they would stop. They would bark all the way around, and then stop. This happened a lot. My daughter was two months old at the time and when this "presence" would go around, I would get sensations of cold in my daughter's room. So on Halloween night I went out under the moon and I put on my ritual gear and I went out to look for this entity. The dogs began to bark. It was so beautiful out and I felt really strong. I suddenly felt this presence and I felt I was looking at an old Indian man, an old Pomo Indian. I couldn't see him, it was a feeling of his presence. I asked him what he was doing and he said he was a shaman and that he had died and needed help to get to the other world. He said he had been the last, and that there was no one left when he died to help him, no one who knew how to do it. So I stuck my knife in the ground and out of my knife came a path of light— again, I saw this in my mind. Well, he started to walk up this path like someone would walk up a staircase and when he was just about out of sight he looked down at me and said, "By the way, I give to you everything that comes into your hands if you close your eyes and walk back to the house."

So when he was up there, I pulled up the knife and put it back into my sheath, closed my eyes, and walked back through the orchard toward the house, and I realized at that point that I was in a field of belladonna. When I got to the house my hands were filled with the leaves of the "devil's weed" and I put the belladonna in a little velvet bag that I had and hung it up on the wall and kept it there for a long time.

One day I decided to make a flying ointment. I was doing it in front of a student who I wanted to impress. Well, I made it about a thousand-fold stronger than I should have because I was using denatured alcohol instead of spirits of wine to extract it, which is what they did in the old days. And instead of lard I was using hydrophilic ointment. As a result I increased the potency about two hundred to three hundred percent, and I got enough under my fingernails just by mixing it to kill me. And I would have died if it hadn't been for a friend of mine who was a doctor and a magician, whom I called immediately. I learned a very hard lesson. It was my first heavy experience with death, and a lot of bullshit pride went down the toilet with the rest of the flying ointment. So, that was my gift from the old Indian man.

Q. How much of the Craft is really ancient?

A. I don't think it matters. I think a lot of it is. I think the important part is, again, that we get on it and produce these ecstatic states in which real generation of energy occurs.

Q. It's always seemed to me that it is going to be difficult to write an accurate history of the Craft revival because so many people lied for so many years about their origins.

A. Well, that's true, but I'm owning up to my bullshit. I'm not an adolescent anymore. As a matter of fact, I was an adolescent with a streak of psychological difficulties that was a mile wide. But I'm perfectly willing to admit that I was not passed all of this "shit" down and that what I had was largely intense scholarship and, thank Goddess, a little bit of real inspiration.

Q. Do you think there was a universal Old Religion such as Murray describes?

A. Not necessarily. I think people have always been very diverse. You get three people together over on one side of a village and three people on the other, and before you know it, you have two magical systems because somebody on one side had a dream about goats and someone on the other side had a dream about frogs. So you end up with a goat god on one side and a frog god on the other. What difference does it make how universal it is? Universality of form, *no!* Universality of content, *yes!*

And Margaret Murray missed another point. In Ireland all of the great Witches like Biddy Early were potato diggers. They were not aristocrats. They were among the so-called ignorant. They were denied formal schooling, but they flocked to the hedgerow schoolmasters to get a classical education. They ended up as hard-drinking old peasants with dirt on the floor and no plates to eat their spuds out of, but they were honored by poor people, because they were poor people.

Let me tell you a story, an Irish national liberation story associated with Biddy Early, the greatest of all Irish Witches. Biddy Early lived from the late 1700s to just before the famine in the 1870s. She was from West Clare, and when she died she was a very old lady, well into her nineties. She was a normal woman in many respects. She had a husband and two children. Her first husband died quite young. She married again and survived her second husband by about twenty years. After Biddy Early had been widowed for the last time, she lived in a stone cabin a little way out from town. I visited her house and everything she owned has been carefully preserved by the people in the town of Feacle. The townspeople love her so much, even though she has been dead for a hundred and thirty years. I was shown her grave and I talked to a woman who swears that her son, who almost died of infantile paralysis, was saved from death by the fact that she took him while he was dying and laid him on Biddy Early's grave, and I saw him walking around, so . . .

Like most Irish Witches, she would not necessarily have called herself a Pagan, even though she always used to say that she got her powers from the fairies. She was not on friendly terms with the orthodox Catholic clergy, but the people loved her, and finally she so proved her worth that the parish priest was completely won over to her way of thinking.

She was a drunk during the latter part of her life. She had rheumatism very bad and, like most Witches, she could not heal herself, so she drank to blunt the pain. Well anyway, Biddy Early became old and weird, and her power increased. She saved cattle, healed people, helped women to get pregnant, saved babies, prognosticated, and in general, excited the admiration of everybody so that people came from all over to be with her.

There was a man in the area who was what they call a "cabin hunter," which means he got bounty from the landlords by hunting out and evicting people who were squatting on basically useless pieces of land without paying rent. In those days dispossession from your home was tantamount to death by starvation, and a cabin hunter was, without doubt, one of the most ruthless and revolting kinds of men to arise on Irish soil.

After this guy had dispossessed a few families, Biddy Early confronted him. She showed up at church one day to everybody's amazement. She walked up to the guy and grabbed him by the collar as he was going out of the church and forced him down on his knees and she said, "I'm putting you down on your knees because I want you to realize that's where you are going to be by the time I get through with you, if you do any more of this to people." Well, the guy was terrified, but he didn't pay any attention to her, which was a big mistake. He had amassed quite a decent amount of money and had a good-sized farm and a number of servants. Well, word came to Biddy that he was at it again. It was a pouring rainy night and she was at a Ceili—which is a big musical event very common among Irish people. She was sitting around and the rain was pouring down and she said, "Well, he's up and at it again." "Who?" they asked. And she said, "That cabin hunter." And she picked up a burning stick near the fire and she blew on it a little, and at that moment the granaries and home of this guy were seized with a terrific fire in the middle of the rain. Everything the guy owned was burned to the ground. Nobody was killed, but his wife and kids barely managed to escape with their clothes. He was reduced to the same level of pov-

erty as the people he had fucked over, and he came begging forgive-
ness to Biddy Early and she just told him to get out of the district or
she would kill him.

Q. I guess I have to ask you at this point—because many people
in the Craft would raise this question—what do you think about interfering magically in that way? Many in the Craft would say that
was unethical. What do you say about such an action, burning down
someone's house?

A. I would ask whether it was justified under the circumstances. I
would say that if a grave injustice of that sort was committed, it was
permissible. I myself have never willfully attacked anyone. But one
of the things about the old Witches, *they protected their community from
oppression to the greatest of their ability to do so.* And you would admit
that this person was an alien to that community. He had made himself an alien, a tyrant. He was no longer a member of that community.

Q. This brings up a related question. Many Neo-Pagans and Craft
folk feel the Craft is apolitical and should remain so. But I gather you
think of yourself as a political person. First of all, how would you
describe your politics?

A. I would describe myself as a spiritual socialist. I grew up in an
anarchist family and, frankly, I love the statement, "There's no government like no government," but what I believe, undoubtedly, is
that the answer is equal distribution of goods. In the one period of
successful Pagan society that my people enjoyed, we enjoyed perfect
socialism.

Q. What period do you mean?

A. I am talking about ancient Ireland, the period between the time
that Ireland was so-called "Christianized" and the time that the Vikings interrupted the socialist economy and forced Ireland to revert
back to the chieftain system in order to get enough military organization together to fight the Vikings. And then, once the chieftains
found themselves in power, they started boogying with the English
. . . so need I say more? There was a hundred-and-fifty-year "Golden
Age." But the problem was, we forgot that everybody else in northern Europe (despite the Aryan myth) had just barely swung down
from the trees . . .

Q. Let's get back to this idea of Paganism being apolitical . . .

A. It is not! Nothing could be more "political" than an idea of this kind. But this is the knotty problem: I could see how in the foreseeable future, if there were a straight Marxist takeover, I would be just as much a threat to them as I am now, despite the fact that I am a socialist. A *truly* socialist culture would be working for the same ends as I am working for as a Pagan—the elimination of all constraint. But few socialist regimes are working for these goals. So, I cannot love this "rape-head" that our exploitative society produces, but at the same time the belief in socialist ideology based on materialism is, unfortunately, hollow. It leads to many of the same abuses that the rape-head does because it tends to ignore the true spiritual needs of human beings which are, in many cases, as important as material ones—although, frankly, I'd be the last person to tell someone who's starving that it will be all right in the next world. I don't think there is a next world. *This* is the next world!

Q. You mean reincarnation?

A. Yes. Like I said, *this* is the next world. I think we keep coming back. We are our children, so we had better get with it and make it better.

Q. Do you think the Craft poses an alternative, a counterthrust? Are we a threat to the status quo?

A. We always have been. We are for the absolute liberation of the human spirit from all constraint. We are for the godlike beauty and development of all persons.

Q. Do you have a fantasy of what an ideal Pagan-Craft life would be like, *for you?* And what kind of society would it be?

A. I would like to be the local nurse-Witch-midwife of a good-sized Irish village, the person people consulted when they got in trouble. The society would be socialist, Gaelic, free, and Culdee.

Q. I keep coming back to this, but how do you reconcile your socialist politics with the common viewpoint on the left that the occult is a "copout"—you know, "Religion is the opiate of the people," et cetera.

A. The problem is this: Many people go into rabid politics to escape self-examination, just as many people go into heavy guru trips or straight religious trips to escape self-examination. A commitment *only* to politics is as much of a copout as anything else because it avoids the responsibility of developing the god-self along with developing the political self. I'm trying to do both. I think it's quite possible to do both.

As for religion being the opiate of the people, I'd say that opium is the religion of the people, at the present time. The real problem is that *institutional* religion is indeed an opiate and, in the form Marx saw it, religion was appallingly evil; it was satanically evil in that it crushed the free will of people and dulled their will to resist injustice. But you've got to remember that in his day and age the women and children were dragging coal carts through three-foot-high caverns in England, getting killed by the hundreds, never seeing the sun rise, working until they cast themselves down exhausted onto beds of rags, or drank themselves into insensibility, and then had to go out and "hook" to get enough money to feed their kids. Then these bastards would get up in the pulpit and refer to rich people as the "betters" of these people, these martyrs who patiently endured the most horrible insults to humanity. Sure, religion was the opiate of the people, but it was debased religion, *not* magic. Magic is not the opiate of the people.

Q. What do you think is the relationship between feminism and the Craft? What do you think of the feminist Craft, of people like Z Budapest?

A. I think that because the present rape-head is very antiwoman, the feminist Craft has a great amount of validity. And what Z and others are proposing—the idea of a purely woman's religion— has a definite place in Paganism. I think a lot of women need it in order to heal themselves of their terrible wounds. I think Z and the others are doing something important. But I do not find the feminist Craft *personally* important to me, largely because I did not go through a stage in which I was sexually subjugated. Most women have not been so fortunate. I think Z has been persecuted because she is a threat to everything straight people represent—and if you ain't a threat, you ain't worth much. But for me, the idea of a purely woman's religion is difficult. My own preference would be to draw power with males and females of equal number and equal levels of dominance.

I don't believe that there are any psychological differences between men and women. In fact, I think the big mystery of our society is that men and women are exactly alike and that this truth is being hidden under an incredible load of bullshit. I think that women are just as capable of being dominant and men are just as capable of being kind and loving. The proof of the latter is that men are dying off in droves at an early age because their emotions are being crushed. Now, I have driven bulldozers. I have shoveled shit. I have built barns. I have flattened men on their backs and fucked them until their eyeballs popped out. I have carried a knife from time to time. But also, I am incredibly tender and loving to my children. I am the biggest nurturer you ever saw in your whole life. I also cook well. What I want to see the end of is the frustration of the male father instinct, which is being diverted into violence, and the end of the frustration of the female lioness instinct, which is being diverted into bitchiness.

Of course men and women are physically different and that is really pleasurable, but I don't think their minds are that different. Men and women seem physically stronger than each other in different ways. Women have far more endurance than men. They have to, in order to endure the childbirth experience. Men are capable of brief, intense bursts of muscular output which were meant to be used in hunting down deer and whatnot.

As for religion, remember that in the ecstatic state it is very common for male gods to possess females and for female gods to possess males. As a matter of fact, the reversal of male and female roles in a body has long been considered a typical sign of the true ecstatic state.

Q. Do you believe there was a former matriarchal period?

A. Yes, at least in my culture—Ireland. Let's put it that way.

Q. Do you believe a future one would be desirable?

A. No, I do not. I do believe in a society in which all beings, male and female and neuter (if such should arise), would be valued. Some people do not ever want to define themselves sexually and I believe they should have that freedom.

Q. Do you have any thoughts on homosexuality and bisexuality in the Craft?

A. I consider bisexuality, by and large, a higher state than simply homosexuality or heterosexuality because it offers a greater number of alternatives. You should be able to love all people that you love freely. If you desire to give physical expression to that love, that should be permitted. If men choose to make love only to men, and if women choose to make love only to women, that's fine, but they should remember it is just as limiting as restricting yourself only to a member of the opposite sex.

Q. As a Witch looking at our present civilization, how would you describe it? Since Witches look to pre-Christian sources for inspiration, what of the past should we look to, and what should we reject?

A. First of all, I agree with the Tantric Buddhists that this is an age of darkness. This is an age of darkness greater than the darkness of the Middle Ages. We are seeing humanity's catastrophic hour in which we can either rise above it to greater glory than we possibly can imagine, or we can be obliterated as a species by the Great Mother.

After stating that idea of doom, I must say that I have hope. I'm just an optimist. If I weren't, I wouldn't be having any children. I do think we have progressed. I think scientific knowledge is wonderful and I think it has tremendous possibilities for increased spirituality. For one thing, it has opened to us the possibility of contact with other beings, ultimately. It has given us a far greater comprehension of the vastness of the cosmos than we ever had before. This is such an essential breakthrough.

There is no doubt in my mind that human beings as a species are growing up. The problem is we are in a sort of shaky adolescence. This is a critical point. The teenager can either commit suicide or it can accept life and go on to adulthood. The tendency to reject everything is the hallmark of evolutionary adolescence. And I think it is the duty of those of us who can see the writing on the wall to look with a mature eye on what our ancestors actually had before we progressed.

I do not believe that the past age was the Golden Age. Any time in which children are sacrificed or old people are sacrificed, or where slavery exists or where blatant sexism exists, is not a Golden Age. In ancient Ireland, for example, there are many myths that reveal a past history of both matriarchal and patriarchal abuse.

As far as those things from the primitive which should be preserved—the rites of passage, which are basically the links between ourselves and the natural cosmos which give our lives rhythm and meaning. *That* is the biggest message primitive life had to offer. It was the only thing that made it survive. Often they did not have a pot to piss in, or a window to throw it out of. If they didn't have good mysteries, they did not make it. There was tremendous discomfort and suffering that people had to face every day to survive. Primitive life is not idyllic. It is incredibly difficult, and the only thing that made it possible was that they had a spiritual technology which enabled them to survive the terrible physical hardships.

I went through a period in which I thought all technology was evil. But for those of us who have lived on farms, let me tell you, you go out and bust your ass in the hot sun for a while and you'll find out how much time you have for thinking about your life.

Q. But don't you think there is too heavy a reliance on technology in our society, and a resultant limitation of our sensory awareness, of our faculties?

A. Oh yes, but that's due to the stage of society we now live in. We live in a society where technology is used to *diminish* human faculties. That is why I say this is an age of darkness. People are turning away from their faculties generally, not because of technology, but because of the head-set of the present society, the present exploitation-oriented culture in which goods are the measure of personal achievement, *not the development of faculties.* In ancient Ireland, during the period I was talking about earlier, we had a tremendous burst of artistic and intellectual expression. And the reason we had it is that people's honor was defined not by how many cows they had, or goats, or boar tusks, or gold coins; their honor depended on how well they could sing, how well they could produce poetry, how well they could make things of incredible beauty. It was those things that brought status. The arts of poetry and music became important because they were detached from goods.

Q. What do you think is the relationship of Paganism and the Craft to the ecology movement?

A. Paganism is the spirituality of the ecological movement, and the people's spirituality has always been a threat to the state.

Q. Why do you think this resurgence of Paganism is happening?

A. I think there is a deliberate rebirthing of a large group of people. We have to begin to address ourselves to the amazing question of why we are all here and its obvious underlying purpose. And I think we have to prepare for a real regeneration of the world. We have to begin to offer people these energy sources and these alternative experiences.

Wicca priestess Elspeth consecrates the salt. *(Photo by Govan)*

1

3

4

2

Four Wicca priestesses: (1) Moria, (2) Theos *(Photo by Phoenix)*, (3) Z Budapest, and (4) Sharon Devlin.

Otter and Morning Glory Zell with one of their unicorns. *(Photo courtesy of The Living Unicorn)*

Above: A community feast at the 1982 Pagan Spirit Gathering in Wisconsin. *(Photo by Selena Fox)*

Below: Preparing for the Women's Ritual at the 1985 Pagan Spirit Gathering. *(Photo courtesy of the National Film Board of Canada)*

A Druid procession in California—the New Reformed Druids of North America.

The late Gwydion Pendderwen in ceremonial robes. *(Photo by Selena Fox)*

Above: Dancers performing in the Temple of the Sabaean Order in Chicago.

Below: A May Day celebration at the 1982 Rites of Spring Festival in Massachusetts. *(Photo by Selena Fox)*

The Church of the Eternal Source stages its annual Egyptian New Year's party in Los Angeles. *(Photo by Church of the Eternal Source)*

Selena Fox and friends gather herbs at Circle Sanctuary in Wisconsin. *(Photo courtesy of the National Film Board of Canada)*

The moon is drawn down on priestess Elspeth. *(Photo by Govan)*

7
Magic and Ritual

The craft of the Craft is the craft of producing altered states of consciousness, and, traditionally, always has been.

—AIDAN KELLY

Ritual is to the internal sciences what experiment is to the external sciences.
—TIMOTHY LEARY[1]

Magick is a science in which we never know what we're talking about, nor if what we are saying is true.

—The Abbey of Thelema (magical order)[2]

"The candles, the incense, and the images are props," the woman wrote to me. The spells, the chants, the dances are props. These things are not *magic.* The magic is the art (or science) of using the props. But to say this implies that magic and ritual have some purpose beyond the aimless activities of the ignorant, uneducated, and superstitious. Bonewits observes that "as intellectuals, we have been raised to have a kneejerk reaction to such terms as 'magic,' 'the occult,' 'ritualism,' 'the supernatural,' etc., so that we can only think about these subjects in the ways that we are supposed to."[3]

I have found it impossible even to discuss these subjects with certain upper-middle-class intellectuals; they elicit an almost religious response. Those who uphold the secular religion of rational human-

153

ism put up more blocks to such discussion than adherents of any other ideology.

I am hoping that most readers will adopt, at least temporarily, a more open position: a position that assumes that most of what has been written about magic is nonsense and that the truth about psychic realities lies under a thick web of ignorance, passivity, and conditioning. Perhaps the best approach is to allow yourself to play with the idea of magic in the way that Robert Shea and Robert Anton Wilson in their book *Illuminatus* allowed themselves to play with the idea of Eris, the Goddess of Chaos, letting her lead them in some unexpected directions. According to Wilson, that's precisely how magic works.

> The most advanced shamanic techniques—such as Tibetan Tantra or Crowley's system in the West—work by alternating faith and skepticism until you get beyond the ordinary limits of both. With such systems, one learns how arbitrary are the reality-maps that can be coded into laryngeal grunts by hominids or visualized by a mammalian nervous system. We can't even visualize the size of the local galaxy except in special High states.[4]

We have seen that most Witches and Neo-Pagans do not link "magic" with the "supernatural." The best comment on this subject comes from Leo Martello, author of *Witchcraft: The Old Religion*. He writes: "I make no claims as a witch to 'supernatural powers,' but I totally believe in the *super* powers that reside in the *natural*."[5]

Bonewits calls magic "a combination of an art and a science that is designed to enable people to make effective use of their psychic talents. These techniques have been developed for centuries all over the globe."[6] While "paranormal" events are extremely difficult to chart, or to repeat under laboratory conditions, much recent research has shown that the chances these events will occur increase dramatically during altered states of consciousness—in dreams, hypnosis, drugged states, sensory deprivation, deep meditation, and highly emotional experiences. Those who do magic are those who work with techniques that alter consciousness in order to facilitate psychic activity.

In *Real Magic*, one of the most intelligent explorations of this topic,

Bonewits writes that the only real difference between magic and science is that magic is an art and a science that "deals with a body of knowledge that, for one reason or another, has not yet been fully investigated or confirmed by the other arts and sciences." He adds:

> The physical Universe (assuming it's there) is a huge *Web* of interlocking energy, in which every atom and every energy wave is connected with every other one. The farthest star in the sky has *some* influence on us, even if only gravitational; the fact that this effect is too small to measure with present equipment is totally irrelevant.[7]

Bonewits also points out that all the traditional definitions of magic have been well in accord with natural philosophy. The popular belief that magic comes from a source alien and outside the natural contradicts the opinions of all the practitioners of the art throughout history. Bonewits gives copious examples, including: S. L. Magreggor Mathers, one of the founders of the Order of the Golden Dawn, who wrote that magic is "the science of the control of the secret forces of nature," and Aleister Crowley who called it "the Art and Science of causing changes to occur in conformity with Will." In fact, almost all definitions of magic seem to use the word in connection with "will," "concentration," and "attention." Among some more recent definitions, the English Witch Doreen Valiente says that magic resides in "the power of the mind itself," and that "the mind, then, is the greatest instrument of magic."[8] And the noted scholar of religions Jacob Needleman writes that "attention is the key to magic, both as deception and as real power." Needleman observes that most people's entire lives are characterized by misdirection and suggestibility, the very traits that are manipulated so successfully by the stage magician. This passivity of attention, says Needleman, may be the most important human failing. In contrast, almost all who study real magic work vigorously to strengthen their attention.[9]

Some occultists say that there is really no need to talk about any "sixth sense," that the truly awakened use of the five senses by themselves produces what we think of as "paranormal" activity. Colin Wilson implies this in his lengthy study *The Occult.* Wilson talks about "Faculty X," which is not a "sixth sense" nor an "occult" faculty, but an ordinary potentiality of consciousness. "It is the power to grasp reality, and it unites the two halves of man's mind, conscious and subconscious." "Faculty X" is latent within everyone; it is the key to all poetic and mystical experience. It is "that latent power that human beings possess *to reach beyond the present.*"[10] Doreen Valiente states a similar idea in *Natural Magic:* "By using our five senses rightly, the inner sixth sense is added to them."[11] A training manual put out by the Dianic Covenstead of Morrigana in Dallas says:

> Before you begin to doubt my use of the word magic, let me describe a study that was done on the Aborigines of Australia. . . . It was verified that they really knew where a herd of game was though it grazed beyond the horizon; knew when a storm was approaching; and knew where water was—though it lay some 10 feet below the surface. These are abilities that our society calls "magic." . . .
>
> These talents are achieved, not by any sixth sense, but by using the five senses to their full capacity. The native of Australia is no more supernatural than your dog. Keep your dog out in the woods long enough without access to water. . . . Your dog will scout around a bit, then dig a hole. As a reward for his efforts *and* his ability to *smell*, he'll receive a puddle of water. We accept this as a natural ability in a dog but think it's impossible for a human because, too often, we relate to cement and steel as our natural habitat. It becomes possible once we recognize our real environment and begin to regain our kinship with it. The Aborigines knew about the distant animals because they *heard* them. In the same, but more obvious way, Amer-Indians heard distant sound by placing an ear to the ground. The Aborigine knows when a storm is forming through a very important sense. The aware native *feels* the storm, feels the change of barometric pressure. That same highly developed sense of feeling can also . . . increase the odds for the storm to bring rain.[12]

This definition equates magic with those techniques that lead to an awakened, attentive, attuned sense of being.* Seen in this light, the

---

* Not all occultists agree that magic is merely another way of talking about changes in consciousness. In particular, Bonewits has said that these kinds of definition muddy the water; they "pretty-up" magic. In a letter (winter 1978) he writes:

As science gave people more control over areas that, previously, were only controlled haphazardly by magicians and priests, priests began to redefine magic in *religious* rather than *engineering* terms. They began to define it as a change in consciousness. A change in consciousness is certainly *required*, but when magic is various fads for meditative disciplines, the weekend courses in "Mind Control," "Mind Dynamics," and other brand-name growth programs such as Arica and est, are, quite simply, brief magical-training courses that attempt (with more or less success and with a greater or lesser use of unnecessary and even harmful dogmas) to reawaken imaginative faculties, to increase concentration, attention, and self-confidence, and to facilitate a student's ability to enter altered states of consciousness at will. The wide interest in these programs can be explained as part of the contemporary search for self-mastery and initiation into a process of growth and change. The regenerative aspects of such programs should be applauded while the dogmas that grow out of them should be opposed.

Just as Neo-Pagans and Witches define magic in a pragmatic way, the trappings surrounding Witchcraft and other magical systems can also be understood without mystification. Chants, spells, dancing around a fire, burning candles, the smoke and smell of incense, are all means to awaken the "deep mind"—to arouse high emotions, enforce concentration, and facilitate entry into an altered state. Again, Bonewits has said some of the most sensible words on this subject, observing that "mandalas," "sigils," "pentacles," and "yantras" are all pictures to stimulate the sense of sight; "mudras" or "gestures" stimulate the kinesthetic sense; "mantras" or "incantations" stimulate the sense of hearing. The use of props, costumes, and scenery can also be seen as a method of stimulating the senses. In addition, drugs, alcohol, breathing exercises, and sexual techniques can serve to alter one's state of consciousness. According to Bonewits, these techniques function in the same way for a Witch or a ceremonial magician as for a Native American shaman or a Catholic priest. To say that these methods never cause psychic and psychological changes in the people involved is as absurd as other common attitudes—that certain religions have a monopoly on these experi-

---

really magic it involves changing the world as well as the interior person doing the magic.

Most of the people who emphasize that magic is a system of enlightenment, or a system for spiritual development or changing consciousness, or that it is a way of seeing things, are people who for one political reason or another do not *dare* to suggest that magic can be a way of actually changing the physical world due to the control of psychic energies. It's much safer politically and socially to pretty-up magic as a spiritual development system.

ences and that certain religions worship "God" while others worship "demons." These techniques have existed for thousands of years and were developed by human beings for the purpose of widening their perceptions of reality and changing their relationship to the world. They can be used creatively or destructively, for the enhancement of self or the destruction of self.[13]

Often our conceptions of psychic reality and the magical techniques we might use are simply a function of the particular culture we live in. Robert Wilson humorously observes:

> Modern psychology has rediscovered and empirically demonstrated the universal truth of the Buddhist axiom that phenomena *adjust themselves* to the perceiver. . . .
>
> Take Uri Geller as a case in point. . . . Geller saw, probably, the Looney Tunes in which wizards bent metals and he saw, probably, class-B Hollywood Sci-Fi in which interstellar beings had names like "Spectre." Mr. Geller can now bend metal by thinking of bending it and gets messages from interstellar beings named "Spectre." . . .
>
> The fairy-folk are like that. They come on as Holy Virgins to the Catholics, dead relatives to the spiritualist, UFO's to the Sci-Fi fans, Men in Black to the paranoids, demons to the masochistic, divine lovers to the sensual, pure concepts to the logicians, clowns from the heavenly circus to the humorist, psychotic episodes to the psychiatrist, Higher Intelligences to the philosopher, number and paradox to the mathematician and epistemologist.
>
> They can even become totally invisible to the skeptic. For nearly 200 years all transmissions were cut off to the university-educated portion of European-American civilization. (It is doubtful that the Hottentots, the ants, the fish or the trees have ever been cut off for even 200 seconds.)[14]

Many people mistakenly identify magic with its opposite—religious dogma, or what some have called "failed magic." The concept of "failed magic" is often expressed by both scholars and Neo-Pagans. Jane Ellen Harrison, in her monumental *Epilegomena to the Study of Greek Religion*, writes that the dancer who plays a god in a sacred rite "cannot be said to worship his god, he lives him, experiences him." Only later, when the god is *separated* from the worshipper and magic is seen to fail, is religion born, and later, doctrine and dogma.[15] Robert Wilson expresses it this way:

Most of humanity, including the theologians of all faiths from Catholicism to Mechanistic Scientism, represent a point where magic stopped, i.e., where the results of previous research inspired no further investigation but instead solidified into dogma.[16]

Or, to echo Sharon Devlin, religion was the opiate of the people, not magic.

Another way of looking at magic and at psychic reality would be to use the image of the ceremonial magician's circle with its "demon" as a metaphor. The circle is the microcosm of the universe, a place apart from the world and protected. It is a positive environment in which the serpents of one's own psyche can reveal themselves creatively. Within the circle the psychic barriers we erect to survive in the world can be eased down and those parts of ourselves that we seldom confront in daily life can be brought to the surface— here we face Graves's azoological creatures who "come to be questioned, not to alarm." Traditional warnings against the use of magic and occultism suddenly seem similar to warnings against the use of psychedelic drugs. Certain strengths are necessary before using both—a knowledge of oneself, a correct environment—so that these new perceptions can come to us in a manner that encourages our growth rather than our harm.

While it is generally and rightly stressed that rituals in the Craft and other Neo-Pagan religions are quite different from those of ceremonial magic, some of the same ideas apply. A Witch's circle generally serves as a reservoir to hold group energy, which is then directed. No "demons" or "angels" or other thought forms from a Judeo-Christian context are used. But psychic barriers do fall, energy is "felt" and exchanged, and azoological creatures do occasionally appear.

A beautiful description of psychic reality appeared in NROOGD's journal, *The Witches Trine*. The art of divination, one writer observed, is "a process by which the conscious and unconscious minds of a particular person . . . cooperate to draw relevant information out of chaos, in answer to a question posed." The author describes this experience as "allowing one's mind to float upon the stream of the Tao, and observe the patterns of the current and the shapes they form." He then describes psychic reality:

I am an unabashed Jungian in regarding the mind and the personality as if it were an island in a psychic sea: what we perceive of ourselves, the conscious mind and the will, is like that part of an island above water; the edges and margins, outlines and heights, are pretty clear, but vary somewhat with the tides and waves on the surrounding ocean. . . .

Lying below this area, there is a vast and swarming depth of mystery which Jung calls the "collective unconscious," and it is from this deep and awe-full sea that the powerful, compelling archetypes rise up in their magical majesty, like a great whale or sea monster broaching the surface of consciousness, sending ripples and waves of change and renewal across the becalmed surface.

It is precisely these dwellers in the psychic deeps, with their protean shape-shiftings and vast power and numinosity, which are the gods and the powers consulted in divination. Their essence is perhaps objective—we cannot see to say—but their appearance is certainly subjective, moulding and shaping the stuff of an individual's mind into shapes which have meaning for her, and which she must, in turn, try to signal to other islands.[17]

If one conceives of reality in this fashion, "magic" becomes the development of techniques that allow communication with hidden portions of the self, and with hidden portions of all other islands in this "psychic sea."

Bonewits, Aidan Kelly, and Wilson each approach magic from very different perspectives. Bonewits is a magician and Druid priest, Aidan's approach has been in terms of poetry and the Craft, and Wilson seems to combine his own iconoclasm with the theories of Timothy Leary and Aleister Crowley. Despite this, they all seem to agree that Neo-Pagan magical systems are "maps" for learning about what appears to be an objective reality but often defies analysis. This reality lies within the unconscious mind, although, Aidan observes, "Actually, it's not unconscious at all; it is you and I who are unconscious of it, but it is definitely real."[18]

Once we accept the notion of reality as this kind of psychic sea, from which a minority have been able to extract certain kinds of information, at least one purpose of ritual becomes clear: it is a sequence of events that allows this type of communication to take place. I asked Aidan, when I visited him in Oakland, "Why do you think people do rituals? What is the purpose of ritual?"

"No one really knows. It's a wide open question. Most theorizing that goes on about ritual goes on in a Christian context and Christians tend to be very heady people. The theories focus on what people 'believe.' But you do not understand the religion of a culture unless you know what people *do*, and what people do is their ritual. Why do you do a ritual? You do a ritual because you need to, basically, and because it just cuts through and operates on everything besides the 'head' level. And in this culture, this heady, agnostic, Christian, scientific, materialist culture, ritual is ignored. And since ritual is a need, and since the mainstream of Western civilization is not meeting this need, a great deal of what's happening these days is, simply, people's attempts to find ways to meet this need for themselves."

Bonewits has defined ritual as "any ordered sequence of events or actions, including directed thoughts, especially one that is repeated in the 'same' manner each time, and that is designed to produce a predictable altered state of consciousness within which certain magical or religious results may be obtained."[19] The purpose of a ritual is to put you into this altered state "within which you have access to and control over your psychic talents." He has also written that magical rituals are psychodramas, "designed to facilitate the generation of psychic energy and the focused disposition of that energy, in order to accomplish a given result."[20]

> Almost every magical-religious ritual known performs the following acts: emotion is aroused, increased, built to a peak. A *target* is imaged and a goal made clear. The emotional energy is focused, aimed and fired at this goal. Then there is a follow-through; this encourages any lingering energy to flow away and provides a safe letdown.[21]

A much more complete and complex explanation of how rituals work can be found in *Real Magic* and in "Second Epistle of Isaac," published in *The Druid Chronicles* (*Evolved*).

It is important to note that when Neo-Pagans use the word *ritual*, they mean something far different from what most people mean. For the majority, rituals are dry, formalized, repetitive experiences. Similarly, myths have come to mean merely the quaint explanations of the "primitive mind."

From my own experiences of Neo-Pagan rituals, I have come to feel that they have another purpose—to end, for a time, our sense of human alienation from nature and from each other. Accepting the idea of the "psychic sea," and of human beings as isolated islands within that sea, we can say that, although we are always connected, our most common experience is one of estrangement. Ritual seems to be one method of reintegrating individuals and groups into the cosmos, and to tie in the activities of daily life with their ever present, often forgotten, significance. It allows us to feel biological connectedness with ancestors who regulated their lives and activities according to seasonal observances. Just as ecological theory explains how we are interrelated with all other forms of life, rituals allow us to re-create that unity in an explosive, nonabstract, gut-level way. Rituals have the power to reset the terms of our universe until we find ourselves suddenly and truly "at home."

How do these principles work in practice? Many Neo-Pagan or Craft groups could serve as illustrations, but perhaps the best example is the New Reformed Orthodox Order of the Golden Dawn (NROOGD), a tradition that has always emphasized ritual, poetic intuition, and vision.

NROOGD had its beginning in 1967. In 1972 an article in the order's journal, *The Witches Trine*, declared:

> The NROOGD (and we got that name from the Goddess) is an assemblage of natural anarchists, bootstrap witches and alienated intelligentsia. . . . By us, a major vice of Christians is that they take themselves Very Seriously; we don't. Our motto: It is all real; it is all metaphor; there is always more; all power from the Triple Goddess.[22]

NROOGD took its rather mystifying name from the original nineteenth-century Order of the Golden Dawn, but added *New Reformed Orthodox* "because we aren't the old one . . . we're trying to operate on different principles from theirs . . . we're trying to cast back to principles that are much older than theirs."[23]

NROOGD is an entirely self-created Craft tradition. It has no lineage and most of its decisions are made by consensus. Fourteen NROOGD covens have functioned in the San Francisco Bay Area at various times over the past ten years. There have also been public sabbat festivals with as many as two hundred people attending.*

The inception of NROOGD is revealing. It began not with one person's vision, but with a *ritual experience* that happened to a group of people almost by accident. Aidan Kelly, a founder of the group, described the event in an issue of *The Witches Trine.*[24] He calls his account "true to the spirit, fictive like all human craft, and, like anything that has ever been written, incomplete." A woman called Morgana was taking an arts class in ritual at San Francisco State College. After the professor told the class that "the only way you can learn anything important about rituals is by doing them," she decided, having read Robert Graves's *The White Goddess* many times already, to attempt a Witches' sabbat. She invited a few close friends, including Aidan Kelly and Glenna Turner. Aidan composed a ritual outline after combing through his notes on the writings of Robert Graves, Margaret Murray, T. C. Lethbridge, and Gerald Gardner. He wrote:

> Reading through them, I began to feel intrigued and challenged. All I had was fragments, hints, innuendos, a riddle, a puzzle. But I also had some ideas about what general principles might weld these fragments into a whole. . . .

The outline was turned in, the professor said, "Do it," and a large group of friends gathered to work on the ritual.

* In 1976 eight covens existed in NROOGD and large public sabbats were held often. Each coven was autonomous. All members spoke as equals, and issues were talked through until a decision was reached that all could accept. Decisions that involved the Order as a whole were made by the Red Cord Council, which was composed of the members of NROOGD covens who had belonged for more than one year and had attained the second degree (Red Cord). The covens, however, remained autonomous, and Red Cord Council decisions were treated as advisory for any one coven. The council merely suggested guidelines—that each coven observe the basic Craft Laws and keep its requirements for initiation at least as strict as the ones generally in force in the Order. In 1976 the Red Cord Council was dissolved. NROOGD declared itself to be no longer an organization, but a "tradition."

"How can such a system work? I asked one priestess, who laughed and told me, 'It took a lot of self-control.' " Aidan Kelly added, "Being a group of friends, we would discuss things the way friends would, until we reached an agreement. Later, we realized that this is what tradition says about how a council has to work, and the information that's available from anthropology says this is how tribal councils work."

As we sat about the room, looking at copies, Glenna asked, "I assume there must be some point to all this, but what is it?"

"If I understand Gardner right," I said, "the point is to raise the energy he talks about, and everything that goes on in the ritual is directed toward that raising. . . ." "Is there *really* such energy?" "Well, I dunno," I said.

The group polished the ritual, practiced it a number of times, and performed it for the class on January 11, 1968.

We all enjoyed ourselves immensely. However, we realized afterwards that the ritual had not worked for us: we had noticed no unusual changes in our perceptions or emotions either during it or after it. . . . We made no plans to do the ritual again. . . .

However, Aidan noted, "a subtle change came over us." And the meetings of friends that had once been for games and gossip turned into an informal occult study group. And the ritual "refused to fade into the past; we found ourselves talking about it again and again." In the summer of 1968 the group decided to do the ritual again, this time as part of a wedding, a genuine participatory celebration rather than a performance, and this time something *did* happen. "As we lay around on the grass afterward, . . . some singing, some listening, and talking about the ritual, a comment kept cropping up, in one form or another, until it finally dawned on us what we were all saying: *this time I felt something.*" As a result, the group decided to do the ritual again, with a few changes, but this time on a true sabbat, Lammas, on August 1, 1968, in a grove of redwood trees. Again the group—this time numbering over forty—experienced a change.

As Glenna began the opening conjuration of the ritual, a silence fell over the circle. Through the castings and chargings of the circle, through the invocations of the Goddess, it grew, and as Albion and Loik and Joaquin Murietta hammered out a dancing rhythm on their drums, as we whirled in a double sunwise ring, that silence swelled into waves of unseen lightness, flooding our circle, washing about our shoulders, breaking over our heads.

Afterwards we wandered about the gardens, laughing and clowning, drunk on the very air itself, babbling to each other: it worked!

"We were hooked," Aidan told me. "And the thing has been going strong ever since." In the written account he added:

> I had already hoped, of course, but that day I became sure that the Craft could be religion for us skeptical middle-class intellectuals: because it did not require us to violate our intellectual integrity, because it operated nonintellectually, striking deep chords in our emotional roots, because it could alter our state of consciousness. Thus, that day began our actual evolution toward becoming a coven.

By the end of 1969 the members of NROOGD knew that what they were doing was, in fact, their religion. They initiated each other, began to have meetings (esbats) during the full moon, and declared themselves a potential coven. Then, during the Fall Equinox, during that time when, traditionally, the Eleusinian Mysteries were held, Aidan broke the usual order of the ritual and led the group in a torchlight procession through a state park, crying the ancient words, "Kore! Evohe! Iakkhos!"

> . . . down the hillside, across wooden bridges, down to a spring, where, as I recall, I first spoke the myth of Kore's gift, then back to the circle, where with nine priestesses, we invoked the full Ninefold Muse, whom I, as Orpheus, audaciously led in a chain dance about the fire; then all joined the chain, and we danced until all but Isis and I had dropped from exhaustion, until again that silent energy rose and lapped its waves around us filling the entire campground with a warm mistiness that was everywhere except where I was looking.

By the end of 1971, "we knew," Aidan wrote, "we had somehow been transformed, that we had indeed become Witches."

All Craft groups talk about this "raising of energy" or "raising the cone of power." But how is this done? And what does it mean in terms of *ritual?* Since the methods used by a particular group are usually considered part of the "secrets" of a tradition, this information is often unavailable. But the best published explanation I have seen comes, again, from NROOGD:

> The coven, holding hands, and alternating male and female as closely as possible, dances sunwise, at first slowly, then gradually faster, perhaps

singing, perhaps chanting a spell made up for the specific purpose the energy is to be used for, perhaps with music, perhaps silently. When the Goddess is the one who has been invoked, the Priestess stands in the center of the circle, in the persona of the Goddess, holding the appropriate tool. When she feels the energy reach its peak she calls out or signals a command to drop, which all in the circle do, letting go of the energy which the Priestess then directs onward to its intended goal. . . .[25]

Aidan notes that this explanation leaves all real questions unanswered. *How* are these things done? What does the energy *feel* like? How can the priestess tell when the energy has *peaked?* How do those in the circle *let the energy go?* The answers to these questions, he writes, can be learned only by experience, and it is precisely such experience that constitutes the "higher secrets" of the Craft.

Many Craft rituals—NROOGD's included—are primarily religious and mythical. The rituals touch on the mythic themes of birth, death, and regeneration and assert the unity of mortals and deities. It is these aspects that seem to link the Craft (as well as a number of other Neo-Pagan religions) to the mystery traditions. What is striking about both Neo-Paganism and the mystery traditions (from our limited information about them) is that both assume that human beings can become as gods. In some traditions (as with the Church of All Worlds concept of "Thou Art God")* the idea expressed is that we *are* the gods, only some of us (perhaps all of us) have not realized it. In other traditions the idea expressed is that we are gods in *potential.* Many Western magical traditions have thus sought a path to the divine by strengthening the self rather than by obliterating the ego. And many Neo-Pagan groups have kept to this tradition, which is one reason why most of them have been blessed by a relative absence of authoritarianism, as well as a lack of "gurus," "masters," and so forth. The entire shamanistic tradition seems to assume that humans can, as I. M. Lewis has written, "participate in the authority of the gods."[26]

Aidan writes that all rituals in the Craft, at some level, celebrate the myth and history of the Goddess. That is similar, of course, to Graves's description of the true function of poetry as religious invo-

* See pp. 265ff.

cation of the Goddess, or Muse. Aidan describes the beginning of NROOGD rituals, all of which start with the Meeting Dance.

> The dance begins with all facing outward, alternating male and female, and holding hands. We begin dancing withershins, the direction of death and destruction, singing, "Thout, tout a tout, tout, throughout and about," which are the words the Witches of Somerset used to begin their meetings. The men dance with the left heel kept off the ground, in the hobbling gait of the bullfooted god, the lamed sacred king. The Priestess who leads the dance lets go with her left hand, and leads the dance in a slow inward spiral: Ariadne leading Theseus into the labyrinth to face the sacred bull; Arianrhod leading Gwydion into Spiral Castle, where his soul will await rebirth. When the spiral is wound tight, the Priestess turns to her right and kisses the man next to her, as the Snow-White Lady of the Briar Rose kisses the prince who sleeps in the Glass Castle, to awaken him to a new life. The Priestess leads the new spiral outward, sunwise, the direction of birth and creation, and she (and each other lady) kisses each man she comes to. The spiral thus unwinds into an inward-facing circle, dancing sunwise. In this dance, withershins is transformed into sunwise, destruction into creation, death into rebirth, and those who dance it pass symbolically through Spiral Castle: here all the traditions and myths of the Craft are pulled together into a single, moving symbol. In a very real sense, all the other rituals of the Craft are merely "explanations" of this dance.²⁷

To go through this experience with understanding is to repeat symbolically the initiatory experience each time the circle is formed and the dance completed.

Another point where initiatory symbolism occurs in many covens is during the invocation of the "Lords [although they may as easily be Ladies] of the Watchtowers." Aidan observes that these "Lords of the Towers"—the Craft may have stolen the term from Masonry— are archetypes, both human and immortal, who serve to remind coveners that they have "risen through the spiral of life and death and rebirth," and who thus represent "the goal toward which the spiral of reincarnation strives: to become both fully human and fully divine." An invitation for these "beings" to join the coveners and aid them in their work comes near the beginning of most modern-day Craft rituals, particularly those in the Gardnerian, Neo-Gardnerian, and Alexandrian traditions. These archetypes are also called "the Mighty Ones."

Most covens operating in these ways also have a ceremony of "cakes and wine," during which the ritual dagger or athame is lowered into the cup and the cakes and the wine are consecrated. Aidan writes out of his experience with NROOGD:

> This is the sacred marriage, the "great rite" of fertility, in a single image. . . . But notice, then, that the sacred marriage is not just between male and female, but also between "spirit" and matter, between the heavens and earth, between the worlds of gods and men, between death and birth. What is being said by the symbols is therefore something like "Sex is a true vehicle for the spiritual evolution of humankind for death and rebirth are the two halves of the cycle that drives us up the spiral to the Goddess's realm."[28]

It was Aidan Kelly who first made me aware that the phrase "Drawing Down the Moon" originates in antiquity. "The Drawing Down of the Moon" and the "Drawing Down of the Horned God" are, perhaps, the two most extraordinary parts of Craft ritual, as performed in the covens of the revival. For here, in true shamanistic tradition, the Priestess (or Priest) can become the Goddess (or God) and function as such within the circle. Aidan notes that:

> The Priestess may begin by standing in the arms-crossed position called "Skull and crossbones" which symbolizes death, then later move to the arms-spread position called the "Pentacle," which symbolizes birth. She may also dance sunwise around the circle, from the quarter corresponding to death, to that corresponding with birth, and, back again. . . . What is thus symbolized, as in the Meeting Dance, is the Goddess's gift of immortality through reincarnation.
>
> What the Priestess does internally during this process is—either purposely or "instinctively"—to alter her state of consciousness, to take on the persona of the Goddess, whom she will represent (or even, in some senses, be) for the working part of the ritual.[29]

I have seen priestesses who simply recited lines and priestesses who went through genuinely transforming experiences. I have seen a young woman, with little education or verbal expertise, come forth with inspired words of poetry during a state of deep trance. I have heard messages of wisdom and intuition from the mouths of those who, in their ordinary lives, often seem superficial and without insight.

In a diary that Aidan wrote several years ago there is an unusual entry concerning the training of a new coven—unusual, certainly, from the point of view of the common assumptions of what covens are and how they work. It reads:

> Read them some poetry, explained how tetrameter couplets or quatrains work; assigned them each 8 lines of rhymed tetrameter on horses for next study group.[30]

Elsewhere, within his *Essays toward a Metathealogy of the Goddess*, he writes that poetry, "being emotionally charged language that operates on many levels of meaning at once, can arouse the interest of the Lady and open up a channel of communication with Her, whereas ordinary prosaic speech has no such effect."[31]

This is another key to the distinction we have been making between *belief* and *ritual experience*. The prosaic and poetic ways of looking at the world are different. But within the polytheistic framework of multiple realities, both can be maintained in a single individual. Once one comprehends this, much else becomes clear. One understands why the theories of Robert Graves have remained so popular throughout Neo-Paganism, despite the many criticisms of the scholarship in *The White Goddess*. One understands that it is precisely this visionary aspect of the Craft, with its emphasis on poetry and ritual, that is responsible for the creation of a group like NROOGD. Glenna Turner, a former atheist, described to me how she once told a newcomer to her coven (to his apparent shock) that she remained quite skeptical about all gods, goddesses, and psychic reality. This, however, had nothing to do with the fundamental reasons for her being in the Craft.

"I'm in the Craft because it feels right. I'm a visionary. The Craft is a place for visionaries. I love myth, dream, visionary art. The Craft is a place where all of these things fit together—beauty, pageantry, music, dance, song, dream. It's necessary to me, somehow. It's almost like food and drink."

Aidan and Glenna are not alone in stressing the relationship of poetry and art to the Craft. Almost half of all Neo-Pagans and Craft
members interviewed for this book told me, unasked, that they
wrote poetry and created rituals. Many of them have had their work
published, at least in the pages of Neo-Pagan journals. It is no accident that those who are most respected within the Neo-Pagan movement are the poets, bards, and writers of rituals. These include, first
and foremost, Gwydion Pendderwen, whose extraordinary *Songs of
the Old Religion* are used throughout the Neo-Pagan movement; Selena Fox and Jim Alan of Madison, Wisconsin, whose tapes of Pagan
ritual songs are circulating throughout the United States; Victor Anderson, the blind poet and shaman; and Ed Fitch, the creator of an
enormous number of Pagan and Craft rituals used in both this country and England. But these are not all. The poems of Penny Novack
(writing often under the name of Molly Bloom), Caradoc, Aidan
Kelly, Morning Glory Zell, Isaac Bonewits, and countless others stud
the pages of Neo-Pagan magazines. Some of these people were always poets, but others told me that Neo-Paganism had opened a
wellspring within them and led them to write poetry for the first time
since childhood.

We have been focusing on NROOGD as a way to talk about Neo-
Pagan (in this case Craft) poetry, magic, and ritual. But the emphasis
on ritual in Neo-Paganism has other implications. A religion with
such an emphasis is bound to have a different kind of theology and
organization.

Aidan Kelly has been in the curious role of theologian (or, more
correctly, thealogian) in a most nontheological religion. His writings
on the Craft seem to show more clearly than others the strongly
antiauthoritarian nature of the Craft, since "No one has to believe
anything" and "There is no authority in the Craft outside each
coven." And if this were not so, we "would never have touched it
with a ten-foot broom. We value freedom above all."[32] Aidan has
said that the Craft, unlike Christianity and other world religions, is
totally defined in terms of the ritual—of what people *do*—and not
what people *believe.* The religion therefore demands a creative response from people.

"It's a religion of ritual rather than theology. The ritual is first; the
myth is second. And taking an attitude that the myths of the Craft

are 'true history' in the way a fundamentalist looks at the legends of Genesis really seems crazy. It's an alien head-space. This is one of the ways in which the Craft *is* a type of mystery religion, because the classical mysteries functioned similarly. The promise of the mystery religions in the classical world was that of immortality and regeneration, something like that. And in one of the associated legends, after death the soul confronts the Guardian of the Portals and is asked the question, 'Who are you?' The reply given was never, 'I believe in such and such,' but a statement like: 'I have eaten from the drum. I have drunk from the cymbal. I have tasted the things within the holy basket. I have passed within the bridal chamber.' These are statements of having passed through certain experiences. And this seems to be very much the Gestalt and tradition of the Craft as well. . . . What makes a person a Witch is having passed through certain experiences, experiences that happen down on a subconscious level and bring about a type of transmutation."

A Witch, writes Aidan, is one who is "pliable, adaptable, changeable, in short, able to learn." He notes that those who change their opinions often appear "wicked" to others:

> But anyone who believes in an orthodox truth—is like a great tree, which will be toppled and destroyed by the hurricane of change that blows through this century, where the Witch is like the reed, which bends with the wind and survives.[33]

This emphasis on ritual rather than creed makes the Craft a "shrew," not a "dinosaur." It is small, but can adapt and survive. It is not encumbered by those structures that have characterized the major religions of the last five thousand years. Aidan contends that the major religions evolved to rationalize an agriculturally based civilization, a civilization that has been breaking down for the past two hundred years. The Craft never developed in cities where complicated religious structures evolved; it operated out in the country among people who were close to the land and "who were still, in effect, living in villages like the first villages that evolved ten thousand years ago." And, ironically, considering the many pronouncements against Witchcraft as a threat to reason, the Craft is one of the few religious viewpoints totally compatible with modern science, allowing total skepticism about even its own methods, myths, and rituals. This ability to coexist with modern science, writes Aidan, is a great strength, since "for many reasons one can strongly suspect that any belief system incapable of such coexistence has no future."[34]

Noting the tendency for some persons within the Craft to regard it as merely another ancient and revealed religion, Aidan told me that, were that so, the Craft would have no chance of surviving. But, as he wrote in "Aporrheton No. 1," the Craft is "not an ancient system of knowledge or metaphysics or doctrine, but an ancient way of perceiving reality that is again becoming available."

> A major reason why the Craft is reviving now is that it depends on an "open" metaphysics, the only kind that can work in this century. The explanation I have evolved of such an "open" system is this: Reality is infinite. Therefore everything you experience is, in some sense, real. But since your experiences can only be a small part of this infinity, they are merely a map of it, merely a metaphor; there is always an infinity of possible experiences still unexplored. What you know, therefore, may be true as far as it goes, but it cannot be Whole Truth, for there is always infinitely further to go. In brief: "It is all real; it is all metaphor; there is always more." Everything in the Craft, no matter how useful, no matter how pleasing, even the Great Metaphor of the Goddess, is still only a metaphor.
>
> Knowing that all truths are merely metaphors is perhaps the greatest advantage you can have at this point in history. Thinking that you know the "Whole Truth" keeps you from learning anything more; hence you stagnate; hence you die. But knowing that every truth is merely a metaphor, merely a tool, leaves you free to learn and to grow, by setting aside old metaphors as you learn or evolve better ones.[35]

If you asked Aidan, "Is the Goddess 'real'?", he would reply that She *is* real "because human energy goes into making Her real; She exists as a 'thought form on the astral plane,' yet She can manifest physically whenever She wants to. She does not exist independently of mankind, but She is most thoroughly independent of any one person or group." And yet, he continues, "She is a metaphor because, great though she may be, She is finite, like any other human concept, whereas reality is infinite."

Why do we need such a concept? "Because the human mind

seems unable to grasp an undifferentiated infinity," he continues. "By creating our own divinities we create mental steps for ourselves, up which we can mount toward realizing ourselves as divine."[36] But he cautions that any such name for this reality "is an attempt to map (part of) psychic reality that seems all too willing to accommodate itself to any map you use, and you will get nowhere in trying to understand that reality if you don't keep its plasticity firmly in mind. The reason that dogmatism about magical systems is so poisonous is that everyone seems to live in a unique psychic universe. The magical system that works for one person may be totally contradictory to the system that works for another."

The lack of dogma in the Craft, the fact that one can *worship* the Goddess without *believing* in Her, that one can accept the Goddess as "Muse" and the Craft as a form of ancient knowledge to be tested by experience—these are precisely the things that have caused the Craft to survive, to revive, and to be re-created in this century. "This is a paradox," writes Aidan, but "the Lady delights in Paradoxes."[37]

In 1986 there were a number of active NROOGD covens from California to Connecticut. NROOGD still puts on large public gatherings in California. As for Aidan Kelly, he returned to the Roman Catholic Church. In the late 1970s he began to explore the male aspects of divinity; he began to go to Mass in 1977 and found himself able to reconcile fully with the church early in 1978. He wrote to me:

> I feel at peace with myself about it. No doubt rumors will become thick about how "Aidan's become a Christian! He joined the Inquisition!" Very few people have noticed that I'm primarily a poet and that I am in no way a true believer in anything, neither in the Craft nor in Christianity.

In a recent version of his manuscript, *Inventing Witchcraft*, Aidan Kelly writes that he began to have mixed feelings about Paganism and the Goddess in 1977. When he began teaching at a Catholic university in San Francisco in 1979, one night he entered the library stacks to find his field of vision entirely filled with books about Mary. He writes, "At this moment a voice spoke in my mind, saying, 'Aidan, didn't you ever know it was always me you sought?' " He wrote a poem which reads in part:

> Oh, yes, it is always me you seek,
> Me whom once you sang more clear

Than you have in recent years.
And perhaps you'll sing more sweet
Now that you know somewhat
Of who and where I'm not.
And when you are lost and heartsick,
When all logic fails, you'll sit at my feet
And weave me daisy crowns and clover wreaths
Until your heart will let you be, at peace.[38]

Aidan has now turned the tables upside down. He now believes that all visions of a universal Goddess come from the influence of Christianity—not the reverse. The Goddess movement is not Pagan, he says, but a radically dissenting type of Christian sect. It is not Mary who is a pale reflection of the Great Goddess, he argues, it is the idea of a Great Goddess that is dependent on ideas about the Virgin Mary. The Goddess, he says, is merely a "de-Christianized and backdated" version of Mary. Even the vision of Isis in *The Golden Ass* by Apuleius is, he believes, a creation influenced by Christianity. Aidan says further that the gentle, loving Goddess talked about by Wiccans and feminist religious groups "plays essentially the same role of personal deity and redeemer for them that Jesus plays in Christian belief." He also says that if you look at the ancient goddesses—Artemis, Orthia, Kali, Cybele, the Morrigan—they were often fierce and uncompassionate. He calls the goddess described in current feminist and Neo-Pagan literature "saccharine," a figure which "has not been restored from history, but has been created by investing the Blessed Virgin with some of the divine attributes of her son. In this sense the concept of the Goddess is Christian, and has never been anything else."[39]

While the modern revival of Goddess spirituality is hard to trace (in writing) much further back than the ideas of J. J. Bachofen and Friedrich Engels and while there are a few goddess-worshipping groups that do treat the Goddess as redeemer, and even a couple of very "Catholic" groups in England that see the Goddess as a monotheistic deity than can grant salvation, most Pagan goddess-oriented groups are growing more and more polytheistic. In fact, the main trend is to see goddesses as personal sources of inspiration and power and to look to *all* the goddesses. While Aidan dreams of the Mother at whose feet he may sit, his heart finally at peace, most women are dreaming a very different dream. They see many goddesses: the warrior, the amazon, the law giver, the giver of wisdom, the creator of worlds, the one who lets loose the elemental forces of nature, the giver of life, and even the destroyer. All of these they draw down into themselves and *become*.

8

Women, Feminism, and the Craft

I. D.

I am a secret agent
Of the moon
            Ex-centric
            Extra-ordinary
            Extra-sensory
            Extra-terrestrial
Celestial subversive
Con-spiritorial
Spirita Sancta
            Holy
                Holy
                    Holy
And then some
And I have friends.

—BARBARA STARRETT[1]

For rebellion is as the sin of witchcraft. . . .
—I Samuel, 15:23

There are few moments in life, for most of us, when one feels as if one has stepped into a Minoan fresco or into the life of a wall painting from an Etruscan tomb. But on a full-moon summery night, in the un-likely borough of Staten Island, I entered such a moment.

Nineteen women, including a visiting Italian feminist and a well-

176

known writer, sat nude in a circle in a darkened room. Molded candles of yellow hung by thongs from a loft bed. The small, bright flames cast a pattern of light and shadow. The room seemed powered by the muted oranges and reds of the bed coverings, and by the sweet scent of damiana mixed with marijuana, and by the pungent incenses that permeated the air, incenses with names like Vesta and Priestess.

A bathtub was filled with cool water, scented with musk and flower petals. A flutist played soft music while the women, one by one, entered the water, bathed, and were towel-dried by the others. There was laughter and a sense of ease.

After a short ritual a goblet was filled to the brim with wine and passed sunwise around the circle. The most powerful moment was yet to come: the pouring of libations to the goddesses and heroines of old. Each woman took a sip, then dipped her fingers into the wine and sprinkled a few drops into the air and onto the floor. As she did so, she invoked a particular goddess, gave thanks, or expressed a personal or collective desire. The well-known writer asked for the inspiration of Sappho to aid her in the work on her new book. The Roman Goddess Flora was thanked for the coming of spring and summer. Laverna—Roman goddess of thieves—was invoked to help a woman gain acquittal in a court case. Laverna was invoked again by a woman who had been caught using "slugs" instead of tokens in the New York subways.[2] Demeter, Isis, Hecate, Diana—the names continued. The goblet passed to each woman three times and the requests became more and more collective. Concerns were expressed for the coven as a whole, for women in struggle everywhere, for women in prison and in mental wards, for the feminist movement. And great hopes for the future were expressed by all. The ritual ended with the music of drums and flutes.

Fruit was brought out and shared—a large bowl carved from a watermelon, filled with blueberries and pieces of honeydew and cantaloupe. There were plates filled with olives and dates. There was a foamy strawberry drink and a huge block of ice cream covered with berries, and one large spoon. It was easy to feel transported to another age, some great festival, perhaps, an ancient college of priestesses on a remote island somewhere in the Aegean. . . .

This meeting was not unique. Such rituals have been taking place in many parts of the country. Feminist covens are springing up all over the United States, some of them showing more creativity, more energy, and more spontaneity than many of the more "traditional" groups that have been in existence for years. I have had personal contact with nine of these covens, located in Texas, California, New York, Oregon, Florida, and Massachusetts. There are others in Missouri, Illinois, Pennsylvania, and, almost certainly, many other states.

The presence of the feminist movement as a force that connects with Neo-Paganism and modern Witchcraft has had many ramifications. Links have been forged between these groups and new strains have been created. Many men (and some women) in the more mainstream Craft groups are upset by the growth of feminist covens, since many feminist Witches have purposely rejected some principles, norms, and structures of the modern Craft. Moreover, a number of feminists have stated that women are Witches by right of the fact that they are women, that nothing else is needed, and feminist Witch Z Budapest has at times declared the Craft to be "Wimmins Religion," a religion not open to men. In addition, feminist Witches have stated that Witchcraft is not incompatible with politics, and further that the Craft is a religion historically conceived in rebellion and can therefore be true to its nature only when it continues its ancient fight against oppression.

In most of what we still may call the "counterculture," the split between the political and the spiritual seems to be widening. In contrast, portions of the feminist movement seem to be combining political and spiritual concerns as if they were two streams of a single river. In the past four years there have been a number of feminist conferences on questions of spirituality; several have attracted more than a thousand participants. On the same agenda with discussions of Witchcraft, matriarchies, and amazons and workshops on the psychic arts, such as tarot, astrology, massage, psychic healing, and meditation, are discussions and workshops on the relationship between political, economic, and spiritual concerns.[3] It has become clear at these conferences that many women regard political struggles and spiritual development as interdependent, and feel that both are needed to create a society and culture that would be meaningful to them.

Linking feminist politics with spirituality and, in particular, with Witchcraft is not a new idea; the connection, which may be very ancient, was noticed in 1968 by the founders of WITCH, a group of women who engaged in political and surrealist protest actions. In its first manifesto WITCH stated that the link between women, Witchcraft, and politics is very old:

> WITCH is an all-woman Everything. It's theater, revolution, magic, terror, joy, garlic flowers, spells. It's an awareness that witches and gypsies were the original guerrillas and resistance fighters against oppression—particularly the oppression of women—down through the ages. Witches have always been women who dared to be: groovy, courageous, aggressive, intelligent, nonconformist, explorative, curious, independent, sexually liberated, revolutionary. (This possibly explains why nine million of them have been burned.) Witches were the first Friendly Heads and Dealers, the first birth-control practitioners and abortionists, the first alchemists (turn dross into gold and you devalue the whole idea of money!) They bowed to no man, being the living remnants of the oldest culture of all—one in which men and women were equal sharers in a truly cooperative society, before the death-dealing sexual, economic, and spiritual repression of the Imperialist Phallic Society took over and began to destroy nature and human society.[4]

The organization came into existence on All Hallows Eve 1968. The original name of the group was Women's International Terrorist Conspiracy from Hell, a name that certainly ruffled the feathers of conservative members of the Craft. But actually, only the letters were fixed; the name kept changing to suit particular needs. At a demonstration against the policies of Bell Telephone the group emerged as Women Incensed at Telephone Company Harassment. This kind of change happened a number of times.

At the time WITCH was founded it was considered a fringe phenomenon by the women's movement. Today its sentiments would be accepted by a much larger number of feminists, albeit still a minority.

Up to now we have seen the Neo-Pagan revival as a movement of men and women attempting to live a way of life and uphold values that have been a minority vision in Western culture. In general, Neo-Pagans embrace the values of spontaneity, nonauthoritarian-ism, anarchism, pluralism, polytheism, animism, sensuality, passion, a belief in the goodness of pleasure, in religious ecstasy, and in the goodness of *this* world, as well as the possibility of many others. They have abandoned the "single vision" for a view that upholds the richness of myth and symbol, and that brings nourishment to repressed spiritual needs as well as repressed sensual needs. "Neo-Pagans," one priestess told me, "may differ in regard to tradition, concept of deity, and ritual forms. But all view the earth as the Great Mother who has been raped, pillaged, and plundered, who must once again be exalted and celebrated if we are to survive."

Most women and men who have entered Neo-Paganism have done so because the basic tenets or the actual practices of one or another Neo-Pagan group came close to feelings and beliefs they already held. It "felt like home." It provided a spiritual and religious framework for celebration, for psychic and magical exploration, and for ecological concern and love of nature.

But in the last few years many women have taken a different path to Neo-Paganism. These feminists have a history of political action. They view all human concerns as both spiritual and political, and they regard the separation between the two as a false idea born of "patriarchy," an idea unknown before classical times and one that has produced much bitter fruit—the splitting of human beings into "minds" and "bodies." In this country, as we shall see, the writings of Native Americans often make this same point: that there is a relationship between the political and the spiritual. What is the nature of this understanding? How have feminists come to it? And how has this led to an identification with Witches and Witchcraft?

The two women who edited the *New Woman's Survival Sourcebook*[5] describe what they found on a cross-country journey:

> . . . we found wherever there are feminist communities, women are exploring psychic and non-material phenomena; reinterpreting astrology; creating and celebrating feminist rituals around birth, death, menstruation; reading the Tarot; studying pre-patriarchal forms of religion; reviving and exploring esoteric goddess-centered philosophies such as Wicce. . . . When we encountered this trend on our first stops, our initial reaction was indifference bordering on uneasiness and apprehension, a

frequent reaction among feminists who are intellectually oriented or who are political activists.

Susan Rennie and Kirsten Grimstad said that they began to feel that their early impressions stemmed from a conditioning that had led them to suspect and ridicule anything that could not be "scientifically validated" and that they had always associated things spiritual with reactionary politics. They soon changed their view. As they traveled, they came to feel that women were becoming sensitized to "the psychic potential inherent in human nature," that women are "the repository of powers and capabilities that have been suppressed, that have been casualties of Western *man's* drive to technological control over nature." They put forth the idea that women have an even deeper source of alienation than that which comes from the imposition of sex roles; that, in fact, patriarchy has created the erroneous idea of a split between mind and body and that women's exploration of spirituality is "in effect striving for a total integration and wholeness," an act that takes the feminist struggle into an entirely new dimension. "It amounts," they said, "to a redefinition of reality," a reality that challenges mechanistic views of science and religion as well as masculine politics.

> As we listened to women (these were the long night sessions) telling about their discoveries, explorations, experiences of the spiritual, nonmaterial in their lives, our conviction grew that this trend is not reactionary, not authoritarian, not mystical, not solipsistic. The effect we observed was that this reaching out for a broader conception of our natural powers, a larger vision of wholeness, is energizing, restorative, regenerative.[6]

Morgan McFarland, feminist and Witch, told me that for years she had kept her feminist politics and her Witchcraft separate. She said that when she first "blew her cover" and told her feminist friends that she was a Witch, she did so because she wanted to share with women a perspective that was broader than political action.

"I felt they were standing on a spiritual abyss and looking for something. And also, that I was looking for strong, self-defined, balanced women who were capable of perpetuating something that is beautiful and vital to the planet. Within my own tradition it is the women who preserve the lore and the knowledge and pass it on from one to another. I have begun to see a resurgence of women returning to the Goddess, seeing themselves as Her daughters, finding Paganism on their own within a very feminist context. Feminism implies equality, self-identification, and individual strength for women. Paganism has been, for all practical purposes, antiestablishment spirituality. Feminists and Pagans are both coming from the same source without realizing it, and heading toward the same goal without realizing it, and the two are now beginning to interlace."

The journey of feminist women toward a spirituality that does not compromise political concerns took less than five years. It probably began with the consciousness-raising group, which gave women a chance to talk about their seemingly private, personal experiences and find them validated by thousands of other women. The great lesson of CR was that personal feelings were to be trusted and acted upon, and that the personal was political. The step from the CR group to the coven was not long. Both are small groups that meet regularly and are involved in deeply personal questions. Only the focus differs.

Consciousness-raising provided an opportunity for women (some of them for the first time) to talk about their lives, make decisions, and act upon them, without the presence of men. Women used such groups to explore their relations with women, men, work, motherhood and children, their own sexuality, lesbianism, their past youth, and the coming of old age. Many women began to explore their dreams and fantasies; sometimes they tentatively began individual and collective psychic experiments.

Most of the original CR groups no longer exist. Most of the women have moved on into political action or, in many cases, into the exploration of women's history, which has led a number of them into research on matriarchy. This research has turned up legends of the amazons and the myth cycles involving ancient goddesses and heroines; it has led woman to the Great Mother Goddess in all her aspects. It has also led many women into magic and psychic work. Jean Mountaingrove, a coordinator of *WomanSpirit*, talked with me about this process.

"Feminism tells us to trust ourselves. So feminists began experiencing something. We began to believe that, yes indeed, we *were* discriminated against on the job; we began to see that motherhood was not all it was advertised to be. We began to trust our own feelings, we began to believe in our own orgasms. These were the first things. Now we are beginning to have spiritual experiences and, for the first time in thousands of years, we trust it. We say, 'Oh, this is an experience of mine, and feminism tells me there must be something to this, because it's all right to trust myself!' So women began to trust what they were experiencing. For example, a woman has a dream about stones and she goes to the library to see what there is about stones. Then she finds Stonehenge. Then she gets interested in the Druids and discovers that people do ceremonies and that this is often called Witchcraft. Then this woman becomes interested in Witches, and goes to them to find out what's going on. I think that's how connections are made."

Enter one of the many feminist bookstores in this country and look at the titles of poetry and literary magazines with names like *Hecate, 13th Moon, Dykes and Gorgons, Hera, Wicce,* and *Sinister Wisdom,* and you will have an idea of the connection between Witchcraft and goddess worship and the women's movement. Almost all these magazines identify women with the Goddess and with Witches. The Witch, after all, is an extraordinary symbol—independent, antiestablishment, strong, and proud. She is political, yet spiritual and magical. The Witch is woman as martyr; she is persecuted by the ignorant; she is the woman who lives outside society and outside society's definition of woman.

In a society that has traditionally oppressed women there are few positive images of female power. Some of the most potent of these are the Witches, the ancient healers, and the powerful women of preclassical Aegean civilizations and Celtic myth. Many women entering on an exploration of spirituality have begun to create *experiences,* through ritual and dreams, whereby they can *become* these women and act with that kind of power and strength, waiting to see what changes occur in their day-to-day lives. After all, if for thousands of years the image of woman has been tainted, we must either go back to when untainted images exist or create new images from within ourselves. Women are doing both. Whether the images exist in a kind of atavistic memory thousands of years old (as many women believe) or are simply powerful models that can be internalized, women are beginning to create ritual situations in which these images become real. Priestess McFarland writes:

> We are each Virgin Huntresses, we are each Great Mothers, we are Death Dealers who hold out the promise of rebirth and regeneration. We are no longer afraid to see ourselves as her daughters, nor are we afraid to refuse to be victims of this subtle Burning Time. The Wicce is Revolutionary.

The images are especially powerful for women who have made the biggest break with the society at large: the lesbian separatists, many of whom seek to remove themselves entirely from the mainstream of a society that they view as contaminated by masculine ideology. Thus, while most of the members of the Neo-Pagan movement are heterosexual or bisexual, and the feminist movement includes women with every conceivable attitude toward sexuality, the feminist Craft and the movement toward feminist spirituality seems to have a larger percentage of lesbians than either. But lesbianism today seems to be only partly a sexual orientation. It is also, perhaps primarily, a cultural and political phenomenon. For example, I have met a number of women who call themselves "lesbians," but from a purely sexual definition would be considered asexual or celibate. A large number of lesbian separatists have essentially made a political choice, often leaving husbands and families as part of a reaction against patriarchal attitudes.

Special issues of such feminist magazines as *Quest, Country Woman,* and *Plexus* have been devoted to "spirituality" and its relations to feminist politics. For example, an editorial in *Country Woman's* special issue noted that women's experiences, both political and spiritual, have never been part of noticed events. Women political leaders have been figureheads for the most part; women religious leaders have usually been considered "minor" or "eccentric," as opposed to the male "gurus" or "messiahs." The editorial also noted that just as the private emotional experiences of women turned out to have been shared by countless numbers, "the hidden, private, unconfirmed experiences of our spiritual search" should be revealed, "in the belief that they too are shared by many women, and are significant." The editorial then observed that while many women believe that politics and spirituality are incompatible, the division between the two is artificial, a product of the patriarchal misconceptions built into the language:

> Two streams are developing in women's consciousness—a political and a spiritual stream. Since women are noticing different parts of their experiences and categorizing them in terms used by the patriarchal culture, they feel suspicious of each other.
>
> To "political" women, "spiritual" means institutions and philosophies which have immobilized practical changes and have channeled women's energies into serving others to their own detriment. To "spiritual" women, "political" means institutions and philosophies which deny the unity of people and have channeled women's creativity into destroying and fighting each other. But each stream is trying to examine deeply the human experience—on the material and on the non-material levels. Women are revolutionizing their consciousness in both directions and challenging the patriarchal ideas and institutions of religion and government by holding to their own women's experience of life.[7]

An article in *Quest* took a similar position:

> The so-called division between cultural feminism and political feminism is a debilitating result of our oppression. It comes from the patriarchal view that the spiritual and the intellectual operate in separate realms. To deny the spiritual while doing political work, or to cultivate the spiritual at the expense of another's political and economic well-being is continuing the patriarchal game.[8]

The enormous response to the "spirituality" issue of *Country Woman* gave birth to the quarterly *WomanSpirit*. It comes out of Oregon, coordinated by Ruth and Jean Mountaingrove and a changing collective of women who often move around the country, issue to issue, to give a new group of women a chance to get involved with the magazine. *WomanSpirit* comes together in an unusually cooperative and collective manner. Nothing is "pushed," and both Jean and

Ruth have said that they feel the magazine is subtly guided. Each issue carries poetry, art, and articles filled with personal experiences—a kind of consciousness-raising effort of the spirit.

Jean and Ruth have described their editorial policy as open, growing, and evolving. "We feel we are in a time of ferment. Something is happening with women's spirituality. We don't know what it is, but it's happening to us and it's happening to other people. *WomanSpirit* is trying to help facilitate this ferment. Ruth and I feel that women's culture is what we want. We want so much to live what we can glimpse. Now that we understand what our oppression has been, and have fantasized what it would be like not to be oppressed, we want to *live* like that. That is what we're looking for; we want the world to be a wonderful place for us to live in; and we don't want it in three thousand years; we want it this afternoon; tomorrow at the latest."

Most feminist Witches feel the spiritual and political can be combined. They are moving toward a position that would, in the words of Z Budapest, "fight for our sweet womon souls" as well as our bodies.[9]

Others, such as writer Sally Gearhart, have maintained the division between spiritual and political, arguing strongly against the effectiveness of most present-day political action. Gearhart has written, in the pages of *WomanSpirit*, that the three known strategies of political action—political revolution, seizing power within the system, and setting up alternative structures—have failed, and that only a fourth strategy, "re-sourcement," finding a "deeper," "prior" source as powerful as the system itself, can threaten it and lead to change. She has noted that thousands of women have separated themselves from society and the world of men to lead isolated lives with other women, and she has called upon women who choose to remain in the mainstream of society, or women who have no choice, to set up a buffer state to protect the separatist women until they can gain the strength to create a new women's culture.[10]

But other women, such as Z Budapest, believe in the firm, continuing connection between spirituality and day-to-day political action. As an exile from Hungary, feminist, Witch, and leader of the Susan B. Anthony Coven in Los Angeles, Z has made her life a vivid example of this connection. We have seen how she left Hungary in 1956, but soon found her oppression as a woman in the United States equal to her oppression in Hungary. Z brought the status of Witchcraft as a religion to public attention with her trial in 1975 on the charge of violating a Los Angeles statute against fortune-telling. This law is one of the countless vague antioccult laws that exist in almost all cities and states. Ostensibly they exist to prevent "fraud," but they ban divination of all kinds, not merely divination for money. The Los Angeles law forbids the practice of "magic," clairvoyance, palmistry, and so forth. Since Z does tarot readings professionally, she was "set up" by a woman police agent who telephoned for a reading. Z was brought to trial, convicted, and fined. Many witnesses, ranging from anthropologists to Witches, came to her defense.

Z told me she regarded the trial as important to establish the right of women to define their own spirituality and to practice their own talents independent of religious and behavioral codes set up by men. Since fortune-tellers are numerous in Los Angeles, Z felt she was singled out because of her feminist politics and the visibility of her small shop, The Feminist Wicca, which is a center for women and Witchcraft. Some Neo-Pagans objected to the manner in which the case was fought; they felt it could have been won if it had been argued differently, and that losing established a dangerous precedent. There were also objections to the slogan of the trial: "Hands off Wimmin's Religion." Z replied that most fortune-tellers pay their fines quietly and go on practicing, and that her court battle had been useful in awakening the community to the links between politics, women, and religion; "winning" was irrelevant.

Z Budapest is a dynamic woman full of energy and humor. Despite the fact that her feminist and separatist politics have alienated her from much of the Neo-Pagan community, she has inspired love and respect in Californian Neo-Pagans who have come to know her, no matter what "official" attitudes toward politics and feminism they hold. For a while, articles and letters in the Neo-Pagan press denounced her. But many members came to her defense, including one of the most esteemed bards of the Craft: Gwydion Pendderwen. Gwydion, to the surprise of many, went further than mere support. He repeated several times his view that the feminist Craft has some of the truest representatives of the Goddess; as might be imagined, this view has not won him praise from all quarters. "I have seen women in a lot of different head-spaces," he told me in 1976, "but never, until this past year, had I seen the Goddess incarnate. I've seen the most supreme expression of Woman in these lesbian feminist Witches. Often the women are in their late thirties or forties. They have gone through an incredible load of bullshit in their lives; they have found their true selves and have risen above it. They look head and shoulders above the rest of us. The combination of feminism and Witchcraft has produced some Amazons, some true giants."

Z Budapest, with a few other women, started the Susan B. Anthony Coven on December 21, 1971. When I visited Z in 1976, the coven had twenty to forty active members and a larger group of three hundred women who joined in some activities. Related covens had been started in at least five other states. The Manifesto of the coven says in part:

> We believe that in order to fight and win a revolution that will stretch for generations into the future, we must find reliable ways to replenish our energies. We believe that without a secure grounding in womon's spiritual strength there will be no victory for us. . . . We are equally committed to political, communal and personal solutions.[11]

Z told me that "religion" was "the supreme politics." "Religion is where you can reach people in their mysteries, in the parts of their being that have been neglected, but that have been so important and painful; and you can soothe and heal, because self-images can be repaired through knowledge, but only experience can truly teach. The experience is to allow us these conditions again. Let us be priestesses again. Let us feel what that feels like, how that serves the community."

Z's vision for the future is a socialist matriarchy. Like many feminist Witches, she has a vision of a past matriarchal age, during which "the Earth was treated as Mother and wimmin were treated as Her priestesses." The manifesto accepts many of the theses proposed by Elizabeth Gould Davis in *The First Sex:* that women were once supreme and lost that supremacy when men, exiled from the matriarchies, formed into bands and overthrew the matriarchies, inventing rape and other forms of violence.

The Craft, Z wrote, is not a religion alone.

> It is also a life style. In the time of the Matriarchies, the craft of wimmin was common knowledge. It was rich in information on how to live on this planet, on how to love and fight and stay healthy, and especially, on how to learn to learn. The remnant of that knowledge constitutes the body of what we call "witchcraft" today. The massive remainder of that knowledge is buried within ourselves, in our deep minds, in our genes. In order to reclaim it, we have to open ourselves to psychic experiences in the safety of feminist witch covens.[12]

Z's interest in the idea of matriarchy is not unique among women involved with goddess worship and Witchcraft.

Matriarchy

It is not surprising that spiritual feminists, in their explorations of the hidden and distorted history of women, have been attracted by the idea of a universal age of goddess worship or a universal stage of matriarchy. These women have been reexamining those philosophers, historians, anthropologists, and psychologists who have argued that women in the ancient world held a position of relative power. Sometimes that power is political, as in the Marxist theories of a prehistorical classless society (as stated, for example, by Friedrich Engels and, more recently, Evelyn Reed); sometimes it is mythic or religious or psychological, as in the theories of J. J. Bachofen, Helen Diner, C. G. Jung, Erich Neumann, Robert Graves, and Esther Harding.[13]

The idea of matriarchy has ramifications that go beyond the question of whether or not the matriarchy ever existed in reality. When a feminist reads Strabo's description of an island of women at the mouth of the Loire, or when she reads an account of an ancient college of priestesses or Sappho's academy on Lesbos, or the legends of the Amazons, a rich and possibly transforming event takes place.

It is easy to get sidetracked by details, and that is the game many scholars play. We will play it also for a while. Prehistory is a wide open field. There is little agreement on what the word *matriarchy* means, and even less on whether ancient matriarchies existed, or if they did, on how "universal" they were. It is fashionable for scholars to dismiss the idea. This seems due partly to the lack of conclusive evidence in any direction and partly to (predominantly male) scholars' fear of the idea of women in power. The question may never be answered satisfactorily. Sarah Pomeroy, in her careful study, *Goddesses, Whores, Wives, and Slaves*, observes that most questions about prehistory remain unanswered. She allows herself to wonder why archeologists have unearthed four times the number of female figurines as male statues, why Minoan wall frescoes portray many more women than men, why the lyric women poets of Sappho's time appear to have so much freedom and independence, and what meaning lies behind the strong, dominant women depicted in those Greek tragedies and myths that speak of the preclassical age. It is as foolish, she notes, to postulate male supremacy in preclassical times as it is to postulate female supremacy.[14] According to Bonewits, we may have to wait until the field of archeology and prehistory is no longer dominated by men. Most women, however, are not waiting.

Many scholars have seemed to delight in showing certain weaknesses in the arguments of some of the more popular feminist writers on the subject of matriarchy, such as Elizabeth Gould Davis in her book *The First Sex*.[15] It's fairly easy to argue that one cannot always take myths literally, as Davis often does, nor can one assume that societies that venerated goddesses necessarily gave power to women. Such "reasonable" arguments have been used, however, to avoid dealing with the central thesis of the matriarchy argument: that there have been ages and places where women held a much greater share of power than they do now and that, perhaps, women used power in a very different way from our common understanding of it.

We face here the same problem we faced earlier in relating the modern Craft to the history of witchcraft scholarship. In that case, scholars such as Elliot Rose and Norman Cohn argued (quite possibly correctly) that witchcraft in European history was almost totally invented by the Inquisition. These scholars then used that argument to discount the Neo-Pagan and Craft revival and its *real* links to Paganism in the ancient world, to indigenous Paganism today, to oral traditions, folk customs, myths, and fairy tales. The situation in regard to matriarchy seems similar. Many ideas of the theorists of the matriarchy may prove incorrect, but that does not diminish the force of the central idea.

It is therefore important to stress that, contrary to many assumptions, feminists are viewing the idea of matriarchy as a complex one, and that their creative use of the idea of matriarchy as *vision* and *ideal* would in no way be compromised if suddenly there were "definite proof" that few matriarchies ever existed. In the same way, Amazons may prove to be fictions or creations of the deep mind, or, like Troy, they may suddenly be brought to the surface as "reality" one day. In either case, the feminist movement is giving birth to *new* Amazons, a process that is bound to continue no matter what we unearth from the past. An illustration may be helpful.

In Gillo Pontecorvo's extraordinary film *The Battle of Algiers*, Algerian women confront the French by giving out an eerie yell, a high ululation that makes the flesh crawl. These women have a great sense of power and strength, perhaps the power of the maenads. After the film appeared I occasionally heard the same cry in the demonstrations of the late 1960s, but never in the way I have heard it more recently, in meetings of women. Amazons are coming into existence today. I have heard them and joined with them. We have howled with the bears, the wolves, and the coyotes. I have felt their strength. I have felt at moments that they could unite with the animal kingdom, or ally themselves with all that is female in the universe and wage a war for Mother Nature. These women are creating their own mythologies and their own realities. And they often will repeat the words of Monique Wittig in *Les Guérillères*:

> There was a time when you were not a slave, remember that. You walked alone, full of laughter, you bathed bare-bellied. You say you have lost all recollection of it, remember. You know how to avoid meeting a bear on the track. You know the winter fear when you hear the wolves gathering. But you can remain seated for hours in the tree-tops to await morning. You say there are no words to describe this time, you say it does not exist. But remember. Make an effort to remember. Or, failing that, invent.[16]

These spiritual feminists do not feel their future is contingent on a hypothesized past. They do not feel they need the words of scholars to affirm or deny their reality. "After all," I was told by Z Budapest, "if Goddess religion is sixty thousand years old or seven thousand, it does not matter. Certainly not for the future! Recognizing the divine Goddess within is where real religion is at."

In other words, the *idea* of matriarchy is powerful for women in itself. Two feminist anthropologists have noted that whatever matriarchy *is*, "the whole question challenges women to imagine themselves with power. It is an idea about what society would be like where women are truly free."[17]

There is no consensus on what the word *matriarchy* means, for either feminists or scholars. Literally, of course, it means government by mothers, or more broadly, government and power in the hands of women. But that is not the way the word is most often used. Engels and others in the Marxist tradition use the word to describe an egalitarian preclass society where women and men share equally in production and power. A few Marxists do not call this egalitarian society a matriarchy, but most in the tradition do.

Other writers have used the word *matriarchy* to mean an age of universal goddess worship, irrespective of questions of political power and control. A number of feminists note that few definitions of the word, despite its literal meaning, include any concept of power, and they suggest that centuries of oppression have made it impossible for women to conceive of themselves with such power. They observe that there has been very little feminist utopian literature. (The exceptions are the science fiction of Joanna Russ,[18] Monique Wittig's *Les Guérillères*, and some of the fiction published in the feminist small presses.)

Elizabeth Gould Davis and Helen Diner do see matriarchy as a society in which women have power; and they conceive of *female* power as qualitatively different from *male* power. This has led many feminists to define *matriarchal* as a different kind of power, as a realm where female things are valued and where power is exerted in nonpossessive, noncontrolling, and organic ways that are harmonious with nature.

Echoing that kind of idea, Alison Harlow, the feminist Witch from California, told me that for her the word *patriarchal* had come to mean *manipulative* and *domineering*. She used *matriarchal* to describe a world view that values feelings of connectedness and intuition, that seeks nonauthoritarian and nondestructive power relationships and attitudes toward the earth. This is far different from the idea of matriarchy as simply rule by women.

In addition to feminists, a number of Neo-Pagans have been exploring the question of matriarchy, and ending up with similar views about power. Morning Glory and Tim Zell, of the Church of All Worlds, told me they disliked that term "or any 'archy' " and preferred to use the word *matristic*. The Zells call themselves *matristic anarchists* and, noting the views of G. Rattray Taylor in *Sex in History*,[19] say that they consider matristic societies (generally matrifocal and matrilineal) to be characterized by spontaneity, sensuality, antiauthoritarianism; embracing, in other words, many of the values Neo-Pagans share today.

There are a number of ways to approach the question of ancient matriarchies. Many have their roots in the historical theories of J. J. Bachofen and Friedrich Engels. Both men wrote in the nineteenth century, and although they had very different perspectives, both set forth the idea of a universal matriarchy in terms of historical laws and universal stages of evolution. The idea of a universal stage of matriarchy was, in fact, widely accepted until the twentieth century; it is now, like Murray's theory of the witch cult, out of favor.

Engels and the Marxists who followed him based their views on the theory of historical materialism. According to Marxist theory, a primitive egalitarianism prevailed before class society; women and men shared equally in production and power. Feminist writers such as Evelyn Reed continue to base their views on an evolutionary perspective and to define matriarchy as this kind of egalitarian society. Reed, it should be emphasized, has many original ideas in her book *Woman's Evolution*, including a novel speculation on the origin of the incest taboo as women's control of cannibalism.

J. J. Bachofen also sought universal laws of history, although he based these on religious organization, myth, and symbol rather than on materialism. In his *Myth, Religion, and Mother Right* (1861), he wrote that matriarchal societies were characterized by universal freedom, equality, hospitality, freedom from strife, and a general aversion to all restrictions. His works were attractive to poets, artists, and psychologists. Some of the feminists who come out of the Bachofen tradition, such as Davis and Diner, have dropped all reference to evolutionary theory, but accept the primacy of myth and symbolic forms. Davis has a cyclic and cataclysmic theory of history, influenced greatly by Immanuel Velikovsky. Patriarchy is seen as a degeneration, morally and even technologically.

Interestingly, it is non-Marxists such as Davis and Diner who are able to envision a dominance matriarchy with women in power, although that power is exercised in a very different fashion. Some feminist anthropologists have also noted contradictions in Davis's work; for example, she says that the rule of the matriarchies was totally benevolent, but that one reason for their downfall was the revolt of men who had been cast out. One feminist, knowledgeable in both Marxist theory and current feminist thought, told me that she was sympathetic to the argument that wars exist because of masculine aggression, but she noted, "I'm suspicious of it. I've read enough Marxist theory to feel that such a view may be a reactionary way of looking at things."

Since theories of stages of evolution in history are hard to "prove," most leading anthropologists and archeologists outside the Marxist tradition refuse to concern themselves with them. Many feminists, likewise, tend to drop the arguments for a universal stage of matriarchy and instead simply state that goddess worship was widespread in many ancient societies, and that archeological evidence continues to mount, with the unearthing of ancient societies such as Çatal Huyuk and Mersin, both of which may have been ruled by women. Matriarchy may not have been *universal*, and present matrilineal societies may be oppressive to women, but there *is* plenty of evidence of societies where women held greater power than they do now. For example, Jean Markale's studies of Celtic societies show that the power of women was reflected not only in myth and legend but in legal codes pertaining to marriage, divorce, property ownership, and the right to rule.[20]

Many women are also looking at the idea of matriarchy from points of view other than those of political theory, history, archeology, and ethnography. They are reexamining those writers, poets, and psychologists who have talked for years about *feminine symbols*, *feminine realms*, the *anima*, and so forth. The theories of C. G. Jung, Esther Harding, and Erich Neumann are being reexamined, as well as those of poets who have claimed to get all their inspiration from the Great Goddess—Robert Graves and Robert Bly, for example. Neumann, in *The Great Mother*, asserts that matriarchy was not a historical state but a psychological reality with a great power that is alive and generally repressed in human beings today. Writers like Neumann and Graves, in the words of Adrienne Rich, have seemingly rejected "masculinism itself" and have "begun to identify the denial of 'the feminine' in civilization with the roots of inhumanity and self-destructiveness and to call for a renewal of 'the feminine principle.' "

The recurrence of strong, powerful women in myth, legends, and dreams continues, and Rich observes:

> Whether such an age, even if less than golden, ever existed anywhere, or whether we all carry in our earliest imprintings the memory of, or the longing for, an individual past relationship to a female body, larger and stronger than our own, and to female warmth, nurture, and tenderness, there is a new concern for the *possibilities* inherent in beneficient female power, as a mode which is absent from the society at large, and which, even in the private sphere, women have exercised under terrible constraints in patriarchy.[21]

Philip Zabriskie, a Jungian, has also noted the power and *presence* of the ancient archetypes of goddesses and ancient women, and has stated that they can be evoked in one's present psychic life.[22] It is obvious that even the Greco-Roman classical goddesses who were known in a patriarchal context are much richer images of the feminine than we have today, although it is equally true that such images can be used to repress as well as to liberate women.

As we have seen, women are looking at the matriarchy from a complex point of view. They differ as to the existence of past matriarchies, and even as to what a matriarchy means in terms of power. Some, such as Davis, see childbearing as the source of women's ancient power, the innate difference that creates a kind of moral superiority stemming from closeness to nature and life. Other feminists, starting with Simone de Beauvoir and continuing through Shulamith Firestone, see in childbearing the root of women's oppression.

Feminists also differ on the question of matriarchy as a "Golden

Age," a view expressed forcefully in Davis's *The First Sex*. Some see matriarchy as, above all, an *idea* about women in freedom. They often picture the ancient matriarchies as societies governed by the kind of loose, supportive, anarchic, and truly unique principles that many of today's feminist groups are organized around, principles developed from the tradition of consciousness-raising. But others see the matriarchy rather as a place that *was* better for women, but had problems and difficulties of its own. Alison Harlow, for example, told me that she once had a vision, a small glimpse of the matriarchy.

"I was standing with my mother, father, and sister as a long procession passed by. A priestess was being carried along. She pointed at me with a long wand. I was chosen. Suddenly I was taken away from everything I knew. Now, maybe I loved it, but the lack of freedom scares me. A theocracy is only good if the priestess is always right. Now perhaps they were more intuitive than us, but . . ."

The matriarchy, according to Alison, was a period of thousands of years when women functioned strongly in the world.

"I do not consider there was ever a matriarchy that was a utopia. I do not consider it the ultimate answer to all our problems. I do think there were values from the ancient matriarchal cultures that we would do well to readopt into our present lives. I've spent a long time trying to come to grips with what it would mean to live in a goddess-centered theocracy, where people belonged to the Goddess, where cities belonged to the Goddess, where you are born to serve Her will. Concepts of human freedom as we understand them are not very compatible with any sort of theocracy and I am very committed to individual freedom."

If feminists have diverse views on the matriarchies of the past, they also are of several minds on the goals for the future. A woman in the coven of Ursa Maior told me, "Right now I am pushing for women's power in any way I can, but I don't know whether my ultimate aim is a society where all human beings are equal, regardless of the bodies they were born into, or whether I would rather see a society where women had institutional authority."

In any event, most women who have explored the question do see a return to some form of matriarchal values, however that may be expressed, as a prerequisite to the survival of the planet. We might note that Robert Graves wrote in 1948:

I foresee no change for the better until everything gets far worse. Only after a period of complete religious and political disorganization can the suppressed desire of the Western races, which is for some practical form of Goddess worship ... find satisfaction at last.... But the longer the hour is postponed, and therefore the more exhausted by man's irreligious improvidence the natural resources of the soil and sea become, the less merciful will her five-fold mask be....[22]

The idea of a matriarchy in the past, the possibility of matriarchy in the future, the matriarchal images in myths and in the psyche, perhaps in memories both collective and individual—these have led spiritual feminists to search for matriarchal lore. The road is not merely through study and research. It involves the creation of rituals, psychic experiments, elements of play, daydreams, and dreams. These experiences, women feel, will create the matriarchy, or re-create it.

Ritual

In Chapter 7 we looked at the idea that ritual may be seen as a way human beings have found to end, at least for some few moments, their experience of alienation from nature and from one another.

To reiterate, theorists of politics, religion, and nature have often viewed the universe in a strangely similar way. Many have noted the interconnectedness of everything in the universe and also the fact that most people do not perceive these connections. Spiritual philosophers have often called this lack of perception "estrangement" or "lack of attunement"; materialists have often called it "alienation" or, in some cases, "false consciousness." Perhaps theory, analysis, and the changing of society can end our experience of alienation on the conscious level. Ritual and magical practice aim to end it on the unconscious level of the deep mind.

By ritual, of course, we do not mean the continuation of those dry, formalized, repetitive experiences that most of us have suffered through; these may once have produced powerful experiences, but in most cases they have been taken over by some form of "the state" for purposes not conducive to human liberation. We are talking about the rituals that people create to get in touch with those powerful parts of themselves that cannot be experienced on a verbal level. These are parts of our being that have often been scorned and suppressed. Rituals are also created to acknowledge on this deeper level the movements of the seasons and the natural world, and to celebrate life and its processes.

Many strong priestesses in the Craft have talked about the primacy and importance of ritual.

Sharon Devlin: "Ritual is a sacred drama in which you are both audience and participant. The purpose of it is to activate those parts of the mind that are not activated by everyday activity, the psychokinetic and telekinetic abilities, the connection between the eternal power and ourselves. . . . We need to re-create ecstatic states where generation of energy occurs."

Z Budapest: "The purpose of ritual is to wake up the old mind in us, to put it to work. The old ones inside us, the collective consciousness, the many lives, the divine eternal parts, the senses and parts of the brain that have been ignored. Those parts do not speak English. They do not care about television. But they do understand candlelight and colors. They do understand nature."

Alison Harlow: "It is a consciousness-altering technique, the best there is. Through ritual one can alter one's state of consciousness so that one can become perceptive to nonmaterial life forms, whatever you choose to call them, and through this perception one can practice subjective sciences."

In what additional ways do feminists think about ritual? Jean Mountaingrove began by telling me that, since dreams seem to speak from our unconscious mind to our conscious mind, perhaps ritual is the way our conscious mind speaks to our unconscious mind. She and Ruth would occasionally share water from a stream, she said, to symbolize the sharing of the waters of life. She added, "If I want my unconscious mind to understand that I love Ruth and that she is my partner, then we engage in a ritual together and the connection is very deep. All the words we say to each other may not do that. Ritual makes the connection on another level."

Jean observed that ritual has a particular and radical relevance for feminists. "Since our culture—the one we share with men—is so contaminated, often when a group of women get together we only have words to use, and these words are all conditioned. Often we can argue and use words to divide. But our actions have not been so limited by men's definitions. So we need to find actions that have clearness about them, that do not have hierarchical connotations . . . because some of our symbolic behavior has also been contaminated. If I pat someone on the head, it may mean that I am bigger and better than she is; it may be condescending . . . but if we can find ways, like washing each other's hands, actions that we do mutually and that have not been contaminated, we can use such actions as a kind of vocabulary that cuts underneath all the divisiveness and unites us."

Women are creating this new language. They are developing psychic skills in workshops with names such as "Womancraft" and "Womanshare"; they are reinterpreting events related to women in a new light and using these insights to create new ritual forms. For example, a number of women are using "Moon Huts" for retreats during menstruation. In doing this, they are re-creating an experience common to women in ancient times and in many tribal societies today. These women are convinced that, contrary to popular scholarly assumption, such retreats were not forced on women because of "uncleanliness" but were introduced by women themselves to celebrate their mysteries and to have a time of collective interchange. It has also been theorized that before artificial light and modern forms of contraception all the women of a tribe often menstruated at the same time.

Some women have begun to work with their dreams. In one instance, twelve women spent a weekend in the wilderness together. They slept in a circle with their heads together, facing inward, their bodies like spokes of a wheel. They wove "dream nets" from wool and fibers and sewed "dream pillows" filled with mugwort and psyllium seeds. A woman who experienced this weekend told about her dream:

> I am with a mass of chanting women under the deck of an old ship which we are rowing across the sea. All the women are looking for their city. We have come to this land and see a man standing on the shore. He

asks, "Why have you come here?" We say, "We came here to find our city." He says, "Go back. Your city is not here." We pay no attention to him but start through this forest right at the edge of the water and walk down an inward-turning spiral road which leads us down to a city in its center. At the bottom is an old woman. We say, "We have come to find our city." She says, "This is an old city. This is not your city. Your city is not here. You have to look further." The women then disperse to look for our city.

WomanSpirit commented:

Margaret's dream tells me that we will not find our culture in the men's world, but neither will we find it in our ancient woman culture. It is still to be found.[24]

One example of a simple and powerful ritual is described in an early issue of *WomanSpirit:* an attempt to come to terms with the concept of Eve. Feminists and Neo-Pagans naturally feel that the story of Adam and Eve, as commonly interpreted, has probably done more to debase and subjugate women than any other such tale in Western history. In addition, the story has been used to inculcate demeaning attitudes toward mind, body, sensuality, and the pursuit of knowledge. *WomanSpirit* suggests that only by turning over biblical tradition and regarding Eve positively, as the bringer of knowledge and consciousness, can we end permanently the split between mind and body and the hatred of both that was foisted upon us by Christianity and much of the classical and Judaic traditions from which Christianity sprang. In an article titled "Eve and Us" a woman leading a class in theology speaks of coming to acknowledge Eve. She presents a counterthesis: Eve was "the original creator of civilization." The Fall was really "the dawn of the awakening of the human consciousness." The class notes that it is Adam who is passive. Eve is persuaded logically and rationally to become "as the gods." "Eve and the serpent were right," said the leader of the discussion. She opened up "a whole new world of consciousness. Every advance in literature, science, the arts can be traced mythically back to this event and in this light it is indeed Eve who is the original creator of civilization . . . and we women have the right and the responsibility to claim her as our own."

At this point in the class a spontaneous ritual occurred. Unlike many rituals in the Craft, which are learned carefully, this came from an immediate need to affirm women's being. A woman produced an apple and "the apple was ceremoniously passed around the circle and each woman took a bite, symbolizing her acceptance of and willingness to claim Eve as her own and recognize our mutual oneness with her."[25]

Women have also begun to create lunar rituals. The association of women with the moon is, of course, an ancient association.

> Last night [one woman writes] we hung out of the east windows and howled at the moon, incredible orb gliding up over the eastern hills . . . and made up a song to her. During the night I fell into a dream that enabled me to undersee the belly of death, as the giver of life. . . .[26]

Another wrote of a celebration of the New Moon in June 1974:

> Women seemed to be coming up the hill for hours. I hear voices and flutes in the distance. . . . We sit in a large circle in front of the cabin. We join hands and follow each other down to the meadow, down into the darkness. We tell stories of darkness. Ruth tells the myth of Persephone being abducted by the lord of the dark underworld. . . . We begin a free word and sound association from the word "darkness." This is very moving. Words and sounds come fast and flowing and die down again. There are images of fear as well as power and strength expressed, a lot of images of calm, warmth and rest. A large candle is lit. . . . [Billie] has made ten small bags with drawstrings, each from a different material. Each has a black bead attached to the drawstrings, signifying the dark moon. She gives them to us to keep. We are very pleased as the bags are passed around the circle. . . . We find seeds inside the bags. Seeds, the small beginning, the New Moon. . . . We stand for a farewell of Robin Morgan's 'Monster,' ending with us all shouting, 'I am a monster!'[27]

Confronting the "Goddess"

It is not surprising that women involved with these rituals and perceptions should begin to confront the idea of a feminine deity. They have found the Goddess, or have been led to the Goddess, and the idea of "Goddess" is fraught with problems and potentialities for feminists.

No matter how diverse Neo-Pagans' ideas about deities, almost all of them have some kind of "Thou Art God/dess" concept, even though a few whom I have met would say that such a concept as articulated by the Church of All Worlds contains a bit of hubris. Nevertheless, most would agree that the goal of Neo-Paganism is, in part, to become what we potentially are, to become "as the gods," or, if we *are* God/dess, to recognize it, to make our God/dess-hood count for something. This is a far different notion from the common conception of deity in Western thought as something "exclusive," "above," "apart," and "outside." Tim Zell has said that in Neo-Paganism deity is *immanent*, not *transcendent*. Others have said that it is *both* immanent and transcendent.

But whatever "deity" is for Neo-Pagans, there is no getting around the fact that the popular conception of deity is *male*. And this is so, despite the countless esoteric Christian and Jewish teachings that say otherwise. The elderly Neo-Pagan author W. Holman Keith, whose little-noticed book *Divinity as the Eternal Feminine* came out in 1960, noted:

> In spite of all that Christians say to the contrary, they conceive of deity as male. They will protest that they do not believe in anthropomorphism, that God is spirit, etc. But these protestations do not completely dispose of the above contention.[28]

More recently Mary Daly has written extensively on the idea that all the major religions today function to legitimate patriarchy and that since "God is male, then the male is God," and that "God the father" legitimates all earthly Godfathers, including Vito Corleone, Pope Paul, and Richard Nixon.[29] Since this image called "God" is the image beyond ourselves, greater than ourselves, it becomes the image of power and authority, even for most of those who profess atheism. It functions as a powerful oppressive image, whether or not we believe in "him"; it can also affect one's self-image. And this remains true whether "man" created "God" in "his" own image or the other way around. As many occultists would say: There is a continuing relationship between the human mind and its creations, and those creations affect all other human minds.

Western women have been excluded from the deity quest for thousands of years, since the end of Goddess worship in the West. The small exception is the veneration paid by Catholics to the Virgin Mary, a pale remnant of the Great Goddess. So, if one purpose of deity is to give us an image we can *become,* it is obvious that women have been left out of the quest, or at least have been forced to strive for an oppressive and unobtainable masculine image. Mary Daly has proposed to answer this problem with the idea of "God as a verb," but many women find this too abstract and prefer to look to the ancient goddesses.

A female deity conceived of as all-powerful and all-encompassing can create contradictions and other problems in an anarchistic feminist community that emphasizes the value of self. But the attractiveness of the Goddess to women was inevitable. She touched a deep chord and has been celebrated in the music of Kay Gardner and in a number of feminist songs, ranging from Cassie Culver's humorous "Good Old Dora" to Alex Dobkin's extraordinary hymn to the Goddess and the Goddess within all women, "Her Precious Love."[30]

Many women have had powerful experiences with deity as feminine. "It never occurred to me to create my own religion," wrote one woman, "or more importantly, that god was female. Discovering that femaleness gave me a tremendous sense of relief. I felt her blessing touch me for the first time. I felt a great weight drop from me. I could actually feel my last prejudices against my own female mind and body falling away."[31]

Jean Mountaingrove, who spent twenty years as a practicing Quaker, told me of her first experience of deity as feminine.

"There was this Quaker meeting at Pendle Hill, a Quaker retreat center outside of Philadelphia. We used to have meetings every morning and lots of weighty Quakers came to these meetings. And I sat in the back row, morning after morning, listening to all these messages coming through about 'the fatherhood of God' and 'the brotherhood of Man' and 'he' and 'him.' And one morning, after about thirty minutes, that feeling inside of me that I have always learned to trust as guidance just swelled and swelled until I was shaking, a feeling that I should say something. And I felt if I didn't say it, I would be betraying something I had learned to trust. All I said was, 'Mother. Sister. Daughter.' And it fell like a rock through this still pool of fatherhood and brotherhood. But then, everyone in the stillness could reflect on what that might mean. I had declared myself. I had declared myself as being—what shall I say?—on the fringe. My feminism was considered 'in poor taste.' But several women came up to me afterwards and hugged me, and that meant a lot."

Jean told me that years later, at a commune in Oregon, she began getting impressions from a special grove of trees. "I had a scientific background which makes fun of this sort of thing," she said. "I thought it was pretty kooky. But Ruth had a background in Jungian psychology and had read *The White Goddess*, so she watched all of this happening with a lot of understanding which I myself did not have. I was drawn to the tallest tree in the grove and I would come to it and just cry; and it was tears of joy and relief; and I would feel that I was whole and perfect; my own judgment of myself was that I was very inadequate, but the spirit of the tree, which I called Mother, seemed to think I was all right."

Some of the women I met had an easy and long-term relationship with the Goddess. One woman told me that she would go hunting with her father and brother as a child, and would call upon Diana as mistress of the hunt. This recalled my own invocations to Artemis and Athena when I was twelve.

Other women had a problem with the idea of "Goddess." "It's amazing," one wrote, "how much the basis of my life now has to do with the things I was raised not to believe in and to some extent still don't . . . that goddess business makes me very antsy too. I would like to know more about how spirituality ties in (or doesn't tie in) with what I call 'real life'—going to work, having relationships, getting sick, doing or not doing politics."[32]

In another example the editors of *WomanSpirit* described the results of a discussion among a group of women:

> Many of us had a real difficulty with the concept of a goddess. Who was this goddess and why was she created? We felt she represented different forms of energy and light to different people. Even though we had trouble with the words, we felt that the force of the goddess was inevitable, she was flowing through us all by whatever name, she was the feel-

ing of the presence of life. Goddess was a new name for our spiritual journey, the experience of life.[33]

The obvious criticism is that the idea of a single Goddess, conceived of as transcendent and apart, creates as many problems as the male "God." Trading "Daddy" for "Mommy" is not a liberation. A woman takes up this question.

> I have been thinking for days and weeks about Goddess. The word, the concept, the idea, the projection, the experience. For many months I have been experimenting with the word, using it freely, reverently, longingly. That is my strongest experience in regard to it, one of longing—oh that there were a Goddess to pray to, to trust in, to believe in. But I do not believe in a Goddess.
>
> Not a Goddess who exists as a being or person. Yes, the goddess who is each of us, the one within. . . . She is the inner strength, the light, the conscious woman who knows her own perfection, her own perfect harmony with the cosmos. . . .
>
> This common existence of all things is holiness to me. . . . I understand that the word "Goddess" is used to express this unity reality in a symbolic way. So too is "God" used. There is no one called "Goddess" to seek outside of ourselves or to enter into us. There is only in each our own center of unity energy which is connected to all. . . .
>
> But I do not believe that changing the sex of that concept does away with its problems. Not at all. To say Goddess instead of God still continues the separation of power, the division between person and the power "out there!" . . .[34]

I doubt this dilemma exists as forcibly for women in the Craft, perhaps because some of them have never considered these ideas. But, more importantly, as priestesses, they are taught that within the circle they *are* the Goddess incarnate. And they have been taught to draw that power into themselves through the ritual of Drawing Down the Moon. Women who have come to the Goddess outside the channels of Neo-Paganism and the Craft are beginning to find rituals and concepts that allow for the same idea. They are finding the Goddess within themselves and within all women. And, as might be expected, those feminists who have found joy in ritual, and who have discovered that the concept of "Goddess" feels right inside, are often drawn into the Craft.

"Feminist Covens" and "Traditional Covens"

Today the Craft has been adopted as "the religion" of a large portion of the feminist spiritual community. In a few cases feminists have joined with other women (and very occasionally with some men) in the more "traditional" Craft. In other cases feminists have formed their own covens. The word *traditional* is used here as a convenient way to distinguish between feminist Witches and those who have come to the Craft and Neo-Paganism by routes previously described. But someday we may find that feminists were being much more "traditional" than the "traditionalists." To understand the differences between "feminist" and "traditional" Witches, it is instructive to look again at the leaflets put out in 1968 by the feminist group WITCH.

Almost all the qualities that distinguish feminist Witches from members of the "traditional" Craft appear in the leaflets. One assumption of WITCH was that any group of women can form their own coven and declare themselves Witches by simply making the decision to do so and enforcing it magically.

> If you are a woman and dare to look within yourself, you are a Witch. You make your own rules. You are free and beautiful. You can be invisible or evident in how you choose to make your witch-self known. You can form your own Coven of sister Witches (thirteen is a cozy number for a group) and do your own actions. . . .
>
> Your power comes from your own self as a woman, and it is activated by working in concert with your sisters. . . .
>
> You are a Witch by saying aloud, "I am a Witch" three times, and *thinking about that.* You are a Witch by being female, untamed, angry, joyous, and immortal.

It is obvious that these ideas easily come into conflict with notions of formal training, priesthoods, and hierarchical structures. The second assumption of WITCH was that Witchcraft is inseparable from politics.

> Witchcraft was the pagan religion of all of Europe for centuries prior to the rise of Christianity, and the religion of the peasantry for hundreds of years after Catholicism prevailed among the ruling classes of Western

society. The witchcraft purges were the political suppression of an alternative culture, and of a social and economic structure. . . .

Even as the religion of witchcraft became suppressed, women fought hard to retain their former freedom. . . .

Thus, the witch was chosen as a revolutionary image for women because they did fight hard and in their fight they refused to accept the level of struggle which society deemed acceptable for their sex.

The third assumption that WITCH made in its leaflets was that it was necessary to create new rituals, "festivals of life, instead of death." These three assumptions have continued as the wellsprings of feminist Witchcraft, but they—particularly the first two—have often been at odds with the assumptions of the mainstream Craft.[35]

We end up with a kind of paradox. Thousands of women have suddenly found the Craft. They have come to it, as most people do, not by conversion but by a kind of homecoming. As the woman told me at the lecture, "I always knew I had a religion, I just never knew it had a name." But often these same women find a Craft somewhat different from the one we've been talking about. They have defined it differently to meet their own needs. And, having found the Craft through inspiration, poetry, reading, dreams, feminist politics, and discussion, they are often ready to throw all the "traditions" and structures and initiations to the winds. The "traditional" Craft has frequently reacted with shock and horror, but then been forced to change from within. The impact of feminism on the Craft in the United States has been enormous in the last few years. The impact of the mainstream Craft on feminism is harder to see. But each has been affected by the other.

Neo-Paganism in general and the Craft in particular have been good for women. Women have strong positions in almost all the Neo-Pagan religions discussed in this book, not only Witchcraft. This chapter concentrates on Witchcraft because most feminists do not seem to be interested in other Neo-Pagan religions. Witchcraft is one of the few "new age" religions where women can participate on an equal footing with men. Outside of Neo-Paganism in general, and Witchcraft in particular, the "Aquarian Age" new religions have not been particularly comfortable with the idea of women as strong, independent, powerful, self-identified persons. One has only to peruse the pages of "new age" journals such as *East West Journal* or the Buddhist *Maitreya* to conclude that most of the new spiritual organizations are still in the dark ages when it comes to women. Neo-Paganism, from its inception, has been less authoritarian, less dogmatic, less institutionalized, less filled with father figures, and less tied to institutions and ideas dominated by males. The religious concepts and historical premises behind Neo-Paganism and Witchcraft give women a role equal or superior to that of men. It is important to state these things before qualifying them. For while all these things are true, they are not always or completely true. It is important to find out how the role of women is defined in the Craft; how the "traditional" Craft is perceived by feminists; and how these feminists are perceived by the "traditional" Craft.

The question of attitudes toward women in the Craft, and in much of Neo-Paganism, is complex. For example, Robert Graves, whose book *The White Goddess* has had an enormous influence on women, the Witchcraft revival, and the creation of groups such as Feraferia, has often been viewed as a sexist. But *The White Goddess* is one of the few books by a male author that is easily found in most feminist bookstores. Published in 1948, it contains extraordinary passages about the Great Goddess, and Graves has often said that the return of Goddess worship is the only salvation for Western civilization. He writes:

> The age of religious revelation seems to be over, and social security is so intricately bound up with marriage and the family . . . that the White Goddess in her orgiastic character seems to have no chance of staging a come-back, until women themselves grow weary of decadent patriarchalism, and turn Bassarids again.[36]

Despite this, Betty and Theodore Roszak in their book *Masculine, Feminine* place Graves among notably sexist authors such as Nietzsche and Freud. They accuse Graves of placing women on a pedestal, one of the oldest tricks in the fight against women's rights. They contend that Graves, while appearing to support freedom for women, actually views them as outside the real world and maintains a position not far removed from orthodoxy. In "Real Women," the selection chosen by the Roszaks, Graves writes, "A real woman's main concern is her beauty, which she cultivates for her own pleasure—not to ensnare men." The real woman, he says, "is no feminist; feminism, like all 'isms,' implies an intellectual approach to a subject, and reality can only be understood by transcending the intellect." He says further, "Man's biological function is to do; woman's is to be," and that "womanhood remains incomplete without a child."[37] Most feminists would find these statements highly objectionable.

To take a less-known example: Pagan theologian W. Holman Keith wrote in 1960 that the fundamental religious error of our time has been "to substitute force as the divine and ruling principle in place of beauty and love, to make destruction, in which the prowess of the male excels, more important in life than the creativity of the female."[38] Keith seeks a Neo-Pagan revival in which nature will be seen as divinely feminine, in which the divine Mother is worshipped again as the Goddess of love and beauty. Keith has also written, in articles for the Neo-Pagan press, that feminist liberation has to do with carnal sex and that "only the fair sex can ennoble eroticism." He has said that "Beauty and graciousness are the ideal attributes of the woman; manly strength of the man,"[39] and that therefore men must acknowledge the leadership of women in the movement of the human spirit.

While Keith, like Graves, is an ardent supporter of the matriarchy, while he supports the right of women to be lesbians, most feminists would argue that his vision has no place for the old woman, the hag, the crone, the woman who is "ugly" according to classical standards, the intellectual woman, the woman who desires to be celibate or who is simply uninterested in sex. Feminist Witches would argue that Keith's position denies certain aspects of the Triple Goddess—most particularly the Goddess of the waning moon, the dark moon, the Crone—that such a position condemns women to be maidens, mothers, and creatures of sensual play. They would say that archetypes are fine until they become stereotypes, whereupon they become repressive and destructive. One Neo-Pagan priestess put it this way:

> Those who insist upon seeing the Goddess as a stereotype as opposed
> to an archetype have lots of "Tradition" on their side. For instance, I'll

bet you can't think of a single mythic Goddess whose attributes include being a musician, poet, painter, sculptor, or any other example of what we would call a fine artist. The exception being Isis/Hathor who is sometimes shown with a sistrum. The Goddess appears as a Muse but never as an artist. So much for Pagan "Tradition" . . . I will not be bound to the albatross of patristic Paganism, no matter how bloody traditional it is. Traditions are merely roots and roots are only one part of the whole tree.[40]

It's no wonder that the pages of Neo-Pagan journals reflect a diverse spectrum of positions on women. Despite what some psychologists say, no one really has the slightest idea what a woman (or, for that matter, what a man) is. We do know that whatever a woman is, it is hidden under thousands of years of oppression. We will need at least a century of living in a society devoid of prescribed role divisions to begin to answer that question. Since everyone is operating in the dark, the two prevalent views among feminists, and the views of others, are all simply opinions, or perhaps intuitions.

The opinion of many women today is that there are no important differences between men and women, with the exception of anatomy; all the rest is simply conditioning. In most societies that we *know* about, child raising and domestic chores are done by women, but there are a few societies in which this is not true; anthropology has shown us societies where women exhibit those characteristics we tend to think of as "male": concern and involvement in warfare, politics, and so forth. And there are societies where men exhibit characteristics we tend to label "female." The advantage of this view is that it produces a great amount of freedom from role stereotyping. It leaves us free to become what we want to become. Devlin, for example, once told me that she had been raped by a woman, one of the most horrible experiences of her life. To repeat her words, "I think, that the great mystery of our society is that men and women are exactly alike and this truth is hidden from us under an incredible load of bullshit."

Another view, accepted by many feminists, is that there is, in fact, a specifically female nature. Freud, we know, said that biology is destiny. And while most feminists would oppose his interpretations, not all of them oppose his idea. Feminist writer Sally Gearhart has repeatedly said that women *are* receptive; they are nurturers; they are the source of life, the symbol of creativity; they are more intuitive and more magical then men. "We are *not only* those things," she writes, "but neither is it accurate to say 'we are also aggressors, penetrators, attackers, etc.' "[41] The advantage of this view is that it gives a convincing explanation for the present rape of the earth, the abuses of technology, and the desperate need to return to a world centered on woman and the idea of a Goddess. A world ruled by women would be a better world, the argument goes; end male dominance, and human beings will live again in harmony with nature.

Women have been discussing these issues seriously. When men like Graves or Keith begin to define the "real woman," real women get angry. Then when male writers of less stature begin to echo these arguments in articles defining what a woman "is," and what her "proper" role in religion and magic should be, the anger increases. Until quite recently Neo-Pagan journals were filled with self-congratulatory articles by men on how women in the Craft have no need of "women's lib." Here is an example from *Waxing Moon*, in which the author first talks about the important position women have in the Craft. He then observes:

> This is not to say that female witches are domineering, mannish creatures . . . nothing could be further from the truth.
> Likewise they are not Women's-Lib types. Most Witches view the Lib as a "masculinizing" outfit reminiscent of the "Anti-Sex League" in Orwell's *1984*. There are advantages which society must grant to women, as their right, but not at the cost of throwing away a woman's deepest strengths and most splendid powers.[42]

As Alison Harlow once remarked to me, "Until several years ago most Craft people had bought the media image of the feminists. For these people, the popular stereotype of the radical feminist and lesbian is more frightening than the traditional stereotype of the Witch is to people outside the Craft."

Thus, for a period of time, a number of letters and articles appeared in the Neo-Pagan press denouncing feminist Witches as "sexists" and "bigots," and expressing a general fear of any alliance between feminism and the Craft. A subtle reaction against a total emphasis on the Goddess began. Several articles called for more emphasis on male gods and on the male principle, a return to balance between male and female. Some of these were written by women. Also, a number of women and men expressed concern over the oppression of men, "tangled in the shadow of Yahweh's crippling image."[43]

In return, some feminists called the Neo-Pagan movement "contaminated." One woman wrote to *Earth Religion News* that the newspaper was simply "an extension of the patriarchy"[44] and made a mockery of the Goddess. Z was more reflective. "*Green Egg* was just polluted with men's fears," she said, "but then it cleaned itself up." Among all these articles and letters, one truly serious criticism of feminist Witchcraft has emerged, albeit often under a pile of chauvinistic garbage: the fear that exclusive goddess worship can lead to a transcendent monotheism, whereas the diverse, polytheistic outlook of Neo-Paganism is the main reason for its freedom, flexibility, and lack of dogma. "Mother Hertha," writes Morning Glory Zell, "spare us from Jahveh in drag!"[45]

In all fairness, several Neo-Pagan men have taken strong public stands supporting the liberation of women—notably Leo Martello, Gwydion Pendderwen, and Isaac Bonewits. Bonewits, in his short but brilliant editorship of *Gnostica*, refused any manuscripts of a racist or sexist nature. In one editorial he noted the tendency of Neo-Pagan articles to imply that any woman not interested in homemaking, religious activities, and raising children "is somehow a psychic cripple; that she is an incomplete and inferior image of the Goddess." This notion, Bonewits said, was not so far from the Nazi conception of women: *Kirche, Küche und Kinder* (church, kitchen, and children). He wrote that Neo-Pagan men have a tendency to praise women "for the very qualities that many women consider sexist traps designed to prevent them from their full development as human beings," an attitude reflecting the dominant Christian schizophrenia that treats women as either Virgin Mothers or whores. "The priestess of Artemis," he wrote,

> or Morragu, or Kali is not going to be a simpering idiot or a Kirche-Küche-Kinder sort of woman. She is more likely to be a strong, domineering, combative intellectual. If you find that frightening, go ahead,

admit it. But don't accuse her of being "unfeminine" or of trying to castrate every man she meets. . . . Similarly, a priest of Apollo, or Oberon, or Balder is quite likely to be gentle, intuitive, receptive, and very creative. This you may find frightening too. But again, it is more honest to admit your fear than to call him "unnatural," "a queer," "unmasculine," etc.

"Why," he asked an unnamed author whose manuscript he rejected, "do you forget the Norse and Mongol women, who picked up their swords and fought beside their men? Why do you forget the many societies of Pagans in which the men did the cooking, weaving, and art while the women plowed the fields and handled the trading?" Bonewits concluded that these articles continue to appear because millions of men are struggling with the question of liberation, and because it is easier to *sound* liberated than to go through the difficult psychological changes necessary to *become* liberated from sexual stereotypes.[46]

Leo Martello, author, graphologist, and Witch, has defended the feminist movement from the beginning, as he has defended all civil-rights movements. Martello once wrote that in medieval times "the only liberated woman was the witch."

> All others were programmed into roles of wife, mother, mistress or nun. The witch was totally independent. She slept with whom she damn pleased. She was a threat to the establishment and to the church. . . . Of all the religions, especially Western, witchcraft is the only one that didn't discriminate against women.

Martello went further; he struck to the root of the problem in a number of articles by noting that women *within* the Craft are still oppressed and unfree. He pointed out that many women came to the Craft because it offered them a sense of self-esteem, and their self-esteem had been "badly bruised by the male chauvinism-sexism predominating in our society." These women then overcompensated for their sense of personal inadequacy or inferiority by becoming big fish in a small pond (the coven). They might be forced to play house-wife-mother-mistress in their daily lives, but they held great influence over a coven of five to thirteen people. Instead of becoming feminists, they perceived feminism as a threat to their status in the coven.[47]

This is a common problem. Many priestesses I have met lead lives that are not fulfilled in regard to work and other endeavors outside the Craft. Often they remain meek and silent, allowing husbands, who are often less intelligent, to hold forth. But magically, when the candles are lit and the circle is cast, these women become, for a short while, priestesses worthy of the legends of old. Two Witches, Margo and Lee, write about this problem in *The New Broom*.

> When a Witch steps into the consecrated Circle, she steps beyond time. Within that circle, the High Priestess assumes Woman's rightful role as a leader with power equal to and sometimes greater than man's. The women of Wicca, like the women of the matriarchies of old, are proud, free, confident, and fulfilled . . . within the Circle.

The two women note that it is chiefly men who speak for the Craft; men write most of the books about the Craft, found the Witchcraft museums, and give their names to the traditions, such as Gardnerian and Alexandrian. "The truth is that today no Wicca woman speaks with authority to the public outside her Circle."[48] This is not completely true. The most notable exception is, of course, Sybil Leek. But all you have to do is leaf through the pages of this book to see how true it is most of the time.

One might almost say that the Craft at times acts as a "safety valve" for the establishment, providing an outlet for oppressed women but stopping short of true liberation. If so, the Craft in these cases becomes a conservative force, making real change even more difficult.

I. M. Lewis, in his study of ecstatic religions, makes a related point: that the cult of Dionysus and other cults that produced ecstatic states were often forces for real change, centers of defiance and rebellion. He observes, however, that women's possession cults in Africa often existed in those societies where women lacked more direct means for getting their aims. These women would use the cults as a method of protest against men, but were always contained by mechanisms clearly designed to stop true insubordination.[49]

The Craft is a religion using ecstatic states that has been a force for change. It has put women in touch with powerful energies within themselves and it has given them a self-image that equates women with the divine. But in our society it operates within the same kinds of constraints that Lewis is talking about. And so it is no wonder that many fear the coming together of feminism and the Craft. Together, they might be a truly revolutionary force.

At any rate, a few women within the Craft who also consider themselves feminists have explored these questions. They have written articles in *Nemeton* and *The New Broom*, the two Neo-Pagan magazines that included a regular, specifically feminist column.

Margo and Lee, in their *New Broom* article, note that many in the Craft have been disturbed by the appearance of feminist Witches outside the "traditional" Craft, as well as the emergence of all-women covens.

> A Feminist calls herself Witch and claims, "Witchcraft is totally ours." The Craft rustles uncomfortably. She has never been initiated into a Coven. She knows little of Coven Law and myth, but proudly states, "I worship the Mother, I am a follower of the Old Religion, I work for the restoration of matriarchy under the Goddess." Wicca squirms. *Witch* is our name, our identity, our life. How, we demand, can these political women drain our identity of its deepest emotional and religious significance? Do they have any right to our name?

Yes, say the writers.

> Feminist "witches" are seeking their own heritage as women. They are reaching back, beyond five thousand years of patriarchy. Independent of *any* help from the Craft, they have found the Goddess. They have found Her in the past; they have witnessed Her rape in the man-ravaged earth; they have found Her within themselves.
>
> What the feminist Witches hold is a new, yet ancient, essence of pure worship. They hold the future.
>
> And they come, as the North Wind: with the chill of change, and the freshness of rebirth.[50]

Another article suggests that women in the Craft, instead of criticizing feminism, should come to terms with the idea that they continue to be oppressed in this society.

Despite the criticisms, we feel that Wicca women must admit to one thing: as women, we are surrounded in day-to-day contact with the Outside World, so to speak, by open and accepted chauvinism in our male-run, male-dominated, man-made society. The temporal power and spiritual sway of its majority are male-oriented. No matter how early or late in this, our present life, we came into Witchcraft, no matter what position we hold within it, no matter how self-assured, self-identified, self-confident we are as Witches, we are none of us isolated from the contemporary state of everything. The twentieth century woman is the end product of two thousand years of suppression and oppression. The Craft, too, has suffered drastically in this same time. The deliberate erasure of truth and history, both about women and about Wicca, seems to go hand in hand. It helps little, in our opinion, that Witchcraft is being more open and openly tolerated if women are no closer to their proper, egalitarian position as people than they are at this moment.

The writers note that many in the women's movement are "feeling a flash of recognition, a call from a distant past," and are reexamining their religious as well as their political beliefs. "Somehow to us, the touching of Feminists and Witches happens at numerous important points . . . these two groups are entwined closely and irrevocably."[51]

Alison Harlow expressed much the same point of view when she wrote in *Nemeton* that the Craft and the feminist movement were "two tributaries flowing to form a single river"[52]—the Old Religion providing the psychic interaction and the women's movement the political context, both seeking to transform the society and provide a more open life for all.

It must be emphasized, however, that positive reactions to feminism are not prevalent in the Craft; that Alison Harlow is presently working with a coven composed mostly of women, although she is far from being a separatist; and that *The New Broom* spoke for the Dianic tradition of the Craft, a tradition that conceives of the Goddess almost monotheistically. Other articles have expressed opposition to any feminist direction in the Craft as a whole, and have stated that such a direction lacks balance.

But those women who do accept feminism as an integral part of the Craft are beginning to compare that other Craft, which the feminist Witches are creating by themselves, with the Craft into which they were born, brought, or trained. Some are experimenting with all-women covens, and in the last few years all-women covens have been accepted as a valid form by some of the larger Craft organizations, such as the Covenant of the Goddess in California. (There have also been some experiments with all-male covens.)

Only a few short years ago the idea of an all-woman coven was considered impossible by the mainstream Craft. The traditional Craft is solidly based on the idea of male-female polarity, which is basic to most Craft magical working and ritual symbology. The Craft Laws within the revivalist traditions state that Witchcraft must be taught from male to female and female to male, and books and articles on Pagan and Craft magic often say that the use of male-female polarity is absolutely necessary to produce psychic energy, that it's "more natural," "better," "stronger," and the like. The new feminist covens don't work with such polarities.

For example, a coven of eight Dianic women, many of whom had worked previously in mixed groups, told *The New Broom* in an interview that they had decided to work with women because they felt "free enough as women together to totally know our strengths and weaknesses and to trust each other and ourselves because of this knowledge." In response to the argument that they were going against "the natural current," they said, "If the natural current isn't within each person, just where is it?"[53] History and legend, the article noted, give many examples of all-women mystery religions and colleges of priestesses.

Some feminists have also challenged the idea that energy works male-to-female. Deborah Bender, writing in *The Witches Trine* about her coven, Ursa Maior, said that the "male principle" had not been found to have any usefulness in their work.

The original study group, "Woman, Goddesses, and Homemade Religion," out of which Ursa Maior developed, was offered through a feminist free university. The people who came to our first meeting were women who would have greeted the statement, "You can't do it without a man," with extreme scepticism. Most members of the study group had previously participated in various woman-directed and -operated enterprises (bookstore, health clinic, theater group, newspaper, living-group) and expected working in the exclusive company of women to be a source of strength and creativity, not weakness. This has proven to be the case. . . .

Our rituals are the expressions of the energies of seven very different personalities, energies which are different every time we begin a ritual and continue to change during it as we respond to the ritual and to each other. If a polarity exists, it is not twofold, but sevenfold.

We take as a working hypothesis that there is such a thing as specifically female energy. However, we do not have some model in our heads of what that energy is like, which we then attempt to achieve. Rather, we try to set up circumstances such that each of us feels encouraged and accepted however she chooses to express herself. Whatever good energy is released in such a situation is female energy as far as we are concerned. The ideas any of us might already hold about female energy are likely to be distorted by the repressions and lies we have been subjected to in our upbringings in a patriarchal society. Only by growth and experimentation can we find out our true powers. To impose male and female polarities upon ourselves would not only be irrelevant to our work, it would interfere with our ability to notice the kinds of exchange of energy that are taking place between us.[54]

Another difference between strictly feminist and mainstream covens is evident in their use of symbols. The Craft in general has a fairly fixed set of symbols, stemming from Western magical traditions. The God is represented by the Sun; the Goddess is the Moon in her three aspects and phases. The Horned God is most often pictured as lord of animals, lord of the hunt, lord of death. The Goddess is the lady of the wild plants and growing things, as well as the giver of rebirth. Symbols and elements that most of Western occultism has long associated with the "male," such as air and fire, sword and wand, are similarly associated in the Craft. Likewise, the "female" is most often associated with water, earth, cup, and pentacle.

These polar opposites have much less application for feminist covens. Typically "female" symbols are often still used: the moon, the cup, the cowrie, the turtle, the egg, etc. But feminists celebrate sun goddesses such as Sunna and Lucina. They look at all goddess myths worldwide, and often take the attitude that it is merely certain cultures that have determined what is "masculine" and what is "feminine." The moon, after all, is a masculine word in the German, Celtic, and Japanese languages, and there are a number of myths with moon gods and sun goddesses. In other words, feminists reject most of the polarizing concepts common to Western occult circles: male-female, active-passive, light-dark, and so forth.

In an article called "I Dream in Female: The Metaphors of Evolution," Barbara Starrett, a feminist poet, writes that "male" structures are dependent on such pairs of opposites. She notes that women have long been associated with the "unknown, the irrational, the 'bad' half of the good/evil binary." Men, in contrast, are always linked with "the logical, clear, luminous, systematic half of that same binary." Starrett says that women should embrace *both* sets of symbols. They must see the traditional feminine symbols equated with the dark, the unconscious, the receptive, and so on as positive, but, she adds, "We need not relinquish their opposites. We will, in embracing the female symbols, incorporate within them the meanings of the male symbols, nullifying the binaries."

> When women replace the symbol of the father with that of the Mother, we, too, are committing a political act. The image of the Mother does not lose its old connotations of earth, intuition, nature, the body, the emotions, the unconscious, etc. But it also lays claim to many of the connotations previously attributed to the father symbol: beauty, light, goodness, authority, activity, etc. . . . What is significant here is that the duality, no matter which opposite is preferred, gives us only two choices. We may choose the reasoning, observing, dominating ego; or we may choose the annihilation of the personality. But if we learn to think beyond that binary, beyond the given choices, we can honor, equally, the conscious and the unconscious mind.[55]

Women in feminist covens seem to agree with Starrett, and so their rituals differ greatly from those in the "traditional" Craft.

Deborah Bender described the kind of ritual that might take place at a meeting of Ursa Maior. First the women might do a breathing exercise to achieve an interconnectedness within the group, "to make the 'circle' a present reality instead of an abstraction." Bender then described one case where the group worked to help one of its members, a woman who was upset and had been threatened with losing her job. The purpose was to replenish the energies of the woman and give her new strength. After all the women breathed and chanted together, a woman began to chant the woman's name, let us say "C": they chanted, "C strong woman, C strong woman." Other women joined in, adding new verses created spontaneously: "Like a redwood, strong; like a she-bear, strong; mountain-strong, strong woman." Bender said, "We spent a good half hour singing and praising C, calling out images of strength and sending her energy through our clasped hands." The woman in question said she felt much more self-confident, and she kept her job.[56]

It's important to stress that feminist covens, like most of the Witch covens we have been talking about, are diverse, autonomous, and difficult to generalize about. Since most successful covens are places where personal growth is a major concern and no dogma prevails, they are constantly changing. This situation of great flux has been noted by a number of academics who have judged, rightly, that the Neo-Pagan scene is even more fluid than the general situation pertaining to "cults." Since they believe in the great value of stability, they judge such fluidity to be a weakness. Only if a religion becomes institutionalized, is it judged "successful." But Neo-Pagans and Witches often regard fluidity as a strength, since the more institutionalized groups are less able to put primary emphasis on the personal growth of their members.

Occasionally, a feminist Witch coven will come together because of the energy and leadership of one particularly dynamic woman. Such was the case with the Susan B. Anthony Coven and Z Budapest. But most feminist covens do not have, and in some cases do not want, a strong, leading priestess. These covens have certain advantages and certain weaknesses. Most feminists have had strong experiences in collective decision-making without leaders or stringent rules beginning in their consciousness-raising seminars and continuing in their feminist organizations and other groups. It is therefore not surprising that most women who come to the Craft from the feminist movement favor a nonhierarchical, informal structure. In general, they are suspicious of rules and formalized rituals—at least at first. Bender stated it this way:

> We take a questioning, even sceptical attitude toward all traditions, formulas, the ways of talking about the Goddess, covens, magic, and Witches. We have two final criteria for using anything: Does it feel right? Does it make sense to me? If one member feels uncomfortable with

something we are doing or saying, we drop it and look for another way that feels right to all of us.

Feminist Witches seem to prefer the loose types of decision-making that have evolved in other radical feminist groups. This includes rotation of responsibility and leadership. In Ursa Maior, for example, leadership was based on initiative and knowledge rather than degree or length of experience. And any commitments, any bonds or oaths, were purely voluntary.

Bender gave me a series of characteristics that seem to distinguish many feminist covens:

1. They have no men.

2. They do not work from a handed-down Book of Shadows. Bender said she personally believed that such books were a nineteenth-century innovation, adding, "The medieval and premedieval traditions must surely have been oral. Ursa Maior adapts freely from published books of shadow and from the poetry and ritual of tribal peoples." The main source for rituals, however, is the women themselves. If a good ritual is created by the coven, or a song or dance or new mode of organization, it might well be published in a feminist magazine or newspaper.

3. While feminist covens generally adhere to the basic Craft Laws pertaining to ethics, money, and self-defense, they often disregard those pertaining to coven structure and regulations. Bender said, "Since we regard our circle as an institution with roots in time preceding the persecutions and the adoption of the secret-cell coven structure, we do not regard ourselves as bound by those laws regarding initiation and coven governance."

4. Feminist covens often attempt to recover matriarchal ideas and institutions through means of research, art, play, psychic exploration, and daydreams. These covens, in contrast to heterogeneous ones, are attuned to women's experiences, bodies, and needs.

5. Feminist covens, unlike most mixed covens I know of, actually serve a viable community: the feminist community. Bender told me that Ursa Maior devoted about 10 percent of its time to work within the community, and that this was one of the reasons for the coven's existence.[57]

In 1976 Ursa Maior was a small, intensive, active group of women who worked well together. Their experimentation and spontaneity apparently led to great creativity and growth. This has not been the case with all such groups. In some covens, where the group has not solidified or where the group is too large, the distrust of structure and formal ritual can lead to none at all, and an unwillingness to take responsibility for making things happen. As one woman wrote to me, "These covens and groves seem to melt like spring snow." In contrast, the mixed covens that exist through the survival-revival situation have a large body of formal ritual and practice, rules, chants, psychic exercises, and oral teachings, but often lack the energy and spontaneity of some of the feminist groups.

In the winter of 1977 the members of Ursa Maior dissolved their coven by mutual consent. Two of the members wanted to explore more deeply the "traditional" Craft. The others wanted to continue to involve themselves in feminist spirituality and holistic healing. In 1978 one former member wrote to me:

> At present, I am putting my energy into learning more of the hierarchically structured, semi-secret side of the Craft (Dianic when possible, but this is difficult when there are not trained Dianic priestesses in the neighborhood). I am working to some extent with men. I do not see this as canceling out what I was doing before. I am trying always to find solutions to certain weaknesses in the feminist Craft. Also, I have always wanted to learn the Craft in its fullness and not just a few parts of it. Perhaps after some years I will be able to find a synthesis.

Meanwhile Deborah Bender and another feminist Witch have begun the *Women's Coven Newsletter*,[58] "to provide some kind of accessible institution outside of the small groups that appear and disappear," as well as "to help build a large body of formal ritual and practice, rules, chants, psychic exercises and oral teachings, that seem to be one of the strengths of the mixed covens."

The Streams Converge

On a Friday night in Boston, April 23, 1976, some one thousand women sat down on the benches and pews of the old Arlington Street Church. The benches filled up and the women spilled over onto the floor and into the aisles, and became silent as the flute music of Kay Gardner created a sense of peace. The lights were dimmed and Morgan McFarland, Dianic High Priestess, came to the front, wearing a long white robe, accompanied by four members of her women's coven, the same coven that we have seen mentioned in *The New Broom*. The occasion was a ritual: "Declaring and Affirming Our Birth," to mark the beginning of a three-day women's spirituality conference, with the unusual name "Through the Looking Glass: A Gynergenetic Experience." The conference was attended by over thirteen hundred women, and besides an address by feminist theologian Mary Daly, the conference was most noteworthy for the large number of Witch priestesses who attended from as far away as Texas and California.

This relationship between feminist spirituality and the Craft is complex. Perhaps, if we had to choose one instant to catch all the qualities, problems, strains, and enormous potentialities in that uneasy relationship, this ritual would be such a prism. There are Morgan and the women in the coven standing in the church, looking a bit apart, somewhat too elegantly dressed, too stereotypically "feminine." I remembered how much more at ease they were working a ritual in a Dallas living room, where none of us wore anything except a string of beads. But here they are, standing in front of the altar of a church, holding candles, while a thousand women watch and wait. Most of these women are taking it in for the first time, realizing that they are all here to begin the creation of a new culture. Morgan steps out in front and speaks.

"In the infinite moment before all Time began, the Goddess arose from Chaos and gave birth to Herself ... before anything else had been born ... not even Herself. And when She had separated the Skies from the Waters and had danced upon them, the Goddess in Her ecstasy created everything that is. Her movements made the wind, and the Element Air was born and did breathe."

A candle is lit in the East. Morgan speaks.

"And the Goddess named Herself: Arianrhod—Cardea—Astarte. And sparks were struck from Her dancing feet so that She shone forth as the Sun, and the stars were caught in Her hair, and comets raced about Her, and Element Fire was born."

A candle is lit in the South.

"And the Goddess named Herself: Sunna—Vesta—Pele. About her feet swirled the waters in tidal wave and river and streaming tide, and Element Water did flow."

A candle is lit in the West.

"And She named Herself: Binah—Mari Morgaine—Lakshmi. And She sought to rest Her feet from their dance, and She brought forth the Earth so that the shores were Her footstool, the fertile lands Her womb, the mountains Her full breasts, and Her streaming hair the growing things."

A candle is lit in the North.

"And the Goddess named Herself: Cerridwen—Demeter—the Corn Mother. She saw that which was and is and will be, born of Her sacred dance and cosmic delight and infinite joy. She laughed: and the Goddess created Woman in her own image . . . to be the Priestess of the Great Mother. The Goddess spoke to Her daughters, saying, 'I am the Moon to light your path and to speak to your rhythms. I am the Sun who gives you warmth in which to stretch and grow. I am the Wind to blow at your call and the sparkling Air that offers joy. I give to all my priestesses three aspects that are Mine: I am Artemis, the Maiden of the Animals, the Virgin of the Hunt. I am Isis, the Great Mother. I am Ngame, the Ancient One who winds the shroud. And I shall be called a million names. Call unto me, daughters, and know that I am Nemesis.' "

Later, the cauldron is filled with fire and the chanting begins, at first very softly: "The Goddess is alive, magic is afoot, the Goddess is alive, magic is afoot." Then it becomes louder and louder until it turns into shouts and cries and primeval sounds. Morgan speaks for the last time.

"We are Virgins, Mothers, Old Ones—All. We offer our created energy: to the Spirit of Women Past, to the Spirit of Women yet to come, to womanspirit present and growing. Behold, we move forward together."

At the end of the ritual the women in the church begin to dance and chant, their voices rise and rise and rise until they shake the roof.

Later, a few women said they didn't want priestesses standing apart on pedestals and altars; they did not want to see energy sent "upward"; they wanted it aimed "at the oppressor." Despite this, acknowledging this, the uneasy, explosive, potentially powerful alliance between feminism and the Craft was apparent for all to feel, during this conference where many women said they felt, for the first time, that a new "women's culture" was a reality.

Morgan and her priestesses stand at the crossroads. This Dianic coven was perhaps the most feminist of the "traditional" groups. But that night in Boston many women found it too formalized and structured. These women were determined to set their own terms and start from scratch.

Alison Harlow also stands at the crossroads. She told me that her greatest mission is to be a bridge between feminism and the Craft. Still, she has doubts. She wondered out loud what, if anything, feminists want or need from the "traditional" Craft. She talked candidly about the intolerance she has felt from some separatists toward her bisexuality and the personal enjoyment she gets from associating with Neo-Pagan men. We both wondered if separatism was the ultimate answer for these women, or whether it was but a necessary time of healing and renewal. We both felt that one thing the Craft did have to offer feminists, outside of its knowledge of ritual and lore, was the polytheistic perspective and its view toward diversity and flexibility. And I expressed to her my own feeling that some of the feminist groups had a startling lack of curiosity about other forms of working outside their own.

What can the two Crafts give each other? Perhaps the most important thing that the feminist Craft can give the "mainstream" Craft is the understanding that Witchcraft is a religion and a practice rooted firmly in rebellion. Feminists see the Craft as a people's survival tool; as a source of affirmative power and strength; as a way of living and working creatively with vital energies; as an empirical *folk wisdom*, but one that is *never far removed* from daily life and from human needs, human problems and "mundane" concerns. "Paganism," Z once told me, while remembering her youth in Hungary, "fits the common people like bread." Many feminist Witches see the Craft as a kind of village woman's wisdom, the knowledge of village midwives and healers. This notion of folk wisdom is often denied by more "traditional" groups, who still tend at times to be impressed by ideas of royalty and by titles such as "Lady so-and-so," and by "bloodlines" and lineages. These groups also fall victim to the illusion that they can exist and practice comfortably within our society by simply pulling the blinds and dancing in secret in darkened rooms. "Mainstream" Craft members often split their lives in two; they have two sets of friends, two sets of interests. This kind of split life leads easily to the notion that something called "politics" is separate from something called "spiritual life."

The feminist Craft is brashly political and spiritual at once. Many feminist Witches would argue that the split life ultimately leads to self-imprisonment, to being cut off at the roots, to alienation. These women might argue that to live such a life is to perpetuate an ultimately sterile fantasy, as opposed to making a real attempt to create an integrated life.

The feminist Craft can build a good case for this argument because it has so much vitality and spontaneity. In addition, its suspicion of hierarchy and structure is good medicine for the rest of the Craft. But its "politics" have upset many in the "mainstream," who have accused the feminists of "using the Goddess for their own ends." The feminists say the reverse: "The Goddess is using the feminist movement to bring Craft principles to a wider variety of women than could have been possible otherwise."

The "mainstream" Craft can offer the feminist Craft the open-mindedness characteristic of polytheists. Feminist groups often have a tendency toward dogmatism, substituting "Big Mama" for "Big Daddy." The problem of Goddess monotheism will have to be resolved if the feminist Craft is not to become just another One True Right and Only Way. The feminist Craft groups often dismiss the "mainstream" groups as "hopelessly contaminated by patriarchy," but the groups, having been around longer, have a rich knowledge about how rituals work and how the coven structure can function. Their healthy distrust of hierarchy often leads feminist groups to abandon all structure, and this has resulted in the dissolution of many groups. Likewise, the fear of ritual as too "formalized" has at times led to stagnation. Ironically, many women within the "mainstream" have visited feminist covens and groves, have gained new knowledge based on new experiences, and then have made significant changes in their original groups or formed new groups altogether. This has not often happened the other way around. Lastly, the Neo-Pagan movement as a whole is rich in humor and ease. These are qualities the feminist Craft often lacks.

One difference between the two Crafts can be seen in the lives of two women who shall remain nameless. The first is the priestess of a Gardnerian coven in the West. During working hours she is a top scientist with a major corporation. No one at her job has any idea of her religious affiliation. Despite her prestige and success, and her integration into "normal" society, she remains afraid that her job would be imperiled if her religious activities become known. The second woman is better known. She was once a political fugitive wanted by the FBI. She made a growing commitment to feminism, and during the period when she turned herself in and was brought to trial she was initiated into a Dianic tradition from the Southwest.

It can be said that, generally, most members of the "mainstream" Craft function outwardly as "ordinary" members of society, while at least some members of the feminist Craft live on the edge of society; that the feminist Craft serves, at least in part, as a source of renewal for women who are among the dispossessed and the oppressed—a function of the Craft that may be most "traditional."

> And thou shalt be the first of witches known;
> And thou shalt be the first of all i' the world;
> And thou shalt teach the art of poisoning,
> Of poisoning those who are the great lords of all;
> Yea, thou shalt make them die in their palaces;
> And thou shalt bind the oppressor's soul [with power] . . .
> And ye shall all be freed from slavery,
> And so ye shall be free in everything;
> And as the sign that ye are truly free,
> Ye shall be naked in your rites, both men
> And women also: this shall last until
> The last of your oppressors shall be dead. . . .[59]
> —*Aradia: The Gospel of the Witches* (1899)

Recent Notes

The women's spirituality movement is now so large and undefinable that it is like an ocean whose waves push against all shores. There are some who have estimated that Starhawk's book *The Spiral Dance* has *alone* created a thousand women's covens and spiritual groups. It is absolutely impossible to estimate how many women began to meet with each other after reading a book or attending a workshop by Diane Mariechild, Carol Christ, Chris Carol, Z Budapest, Merlin Stone, Hallie Iglehart, Starhawk, Mary Daly, Margo Adair, and literally hundreds of other women. Workshops, classes, and lectures on women's spirituality and the power of the ancient goddesses are everywhere, at adult education centers, at feminist bookstores, and new age institutes. Jewish and Christian women are examining the feminine. Unitarian women are creating women's rituals.

Much of this previous chapter is now history. The tensions between the feminist and traditional Craft are much less evident. Women's circles and men's circles happen routinely at Pagan festivals and even in the traditional Craft. English traditional covens are creating rites of passage for boys and girls. In the feminist Craft separatism has diminished—at least in the United States. More lesbian women are seen at mixed Pagan festivals and more women from the mixed traditions have gone to women-only gatherings.

There are still many men within the English traditions who are deeply angered and threatened by feminism, and there are even a few men from these traditions who believe that women goddess-worshippers should not be called Witches. Ironically, separatism is still very strong in England, and this is certainly true at places like Greenham Common. In the United States, although most women's groups prefer to work rituals separately, there is increased contact between feminist women and men in the larger Pagan community. Starhawk, by focusing on feminist Witchcraft but including men, has had a great impact.

The idea of the Goddess has entered mainstream literature and ideas. It is absolutely common for women to mention the Goddess in public and have the person next to them actually know what they are talking about. Feminist spirituality has led to the publishing of non-sexist reinterpretations of tarot, astrology, Qabala, and the I Ching. Feminists involved with goddess spirituality have been entering theological seminaries in large numbers, and they are writing new history and new thealogy.

As the women's spirituality movement continues to grow, it continues to define itself. One of its greatest struggles and debates is over the question of whether it is to be a fundamentally monotheistic or polytheistic movement. All would agree that it is essential to reclaim from the ruins, to create, dream again, and restore the power of the thousands of ancient goddesses that informed a multitude of ancient cultures. These powerful figures are models in our own becoming. As we understand their strengths, we can more easily claim them as our own. But to invoke, to evoke, to become, to actualize these ancient goddesses is very different than to reduce them to one universal Mother Goddess, or even a Triple Goddess. The claim that a universal Mother Goddess was worshipped widely throughout the ancient world may be a kind of monotheism that only differs in gender from the religions modern Pagans have rejected. It also may be a kind of universalism at odds with Pagan concepts of diversity. Mainstream scholarship—some of it by women—is continuing to deal strong blows to the idea of such a universal religion. There is very little evidence—other than intuitive—to support such a claim anyway. On the other hand there is no denying the power and strength of ancient and modern goddesses from a thousand cultures and no denying the many ancient cultures where women wielded power. There is also no denying that the world will change as women take up their roles as priestesses once again.

III. *Other Neo-Pagans*

Religions from the Past— The Pagan Reconstructionists

Outside of the various Witchcraft traditions, the most prevalent forms of Neo-Paganism are groups that attempt to re-create ancient European pre-Christian religions.

Church of Aphrodite

In the United States the first reconstructionist Neo-Pagan organization was the Long Island Church of Aphrodite, established in West Hempstead, Long Island, on May 6, 1938.

Gleb Botkin, founder and priest of the church, was the son of the court physician to the last Russian Tsar. After Botkin came to the United States he wrote several novels about Russia before and during the Revolution. Some of them, such as *The Real Romanovs*, concern the last days of the royal family; others depict the lives of students, priests, and more ordinary folk. But the theme of goddess worship drifts through many of them. The titles themselves are revealing—*The Woman Who Rose Again* (about Anastasia); *Immortal Woman; The God Who Didn't Laugh;* and *Her Wanton Majesty.*[1]

All the novels, dating from 1929 to 1937, involve women who inspire men to worship them, and men who are tempted and allured by the "divine feminine." In two of the novels the Pagan religious ideal is stated directly: the protagonist becomes a worshipper of

233

Aphrodite. *Immortal Woman* (1933) is the story of Nikolai Dirin, the son of a Russian priest, who flees to America shortly after the Russian Revolution and becomes a world-famous conductor. His musical ability is inspired by a vision of Aphrodite and by the remembrance of a real woman, a playmate from his youth. His dreams and daydreams lead him to reject his Russian Orthodox upbringing and to adopt the Aphrodisian religion:

> The more he studied, the more convinced he became that his Goddess was no myth, that millions upon millions of human beings had worshipped her for thousands of years and that many continued to worship her in the present.[2]

Another novel, *The God Who Didn't Laugh*, is the most autobiographical of Botkin's works. It is the story of a Russian man who studies to be a monk, but is visited early in life by a vision of Aphrodite and, again, by actual women who seem to embody that vision. At one point, the protagonist imagines a world of Greek temples of white marble where naked worshippers sing hymns, burn incense, and fall asleep on the grass after laying wreaths of roses at Aphrodite's feet.

While training for the priesthood, he is repeatedly instructed that women are the "Vessels of the Devil" and that he must reject all his experiences with them as dirty, repulsive, and sinful.[3] Just before his ordination he realizes that his feelings toward women were the purest and most sacred he had ever experienced. He begins to find Christ at fault for thinking of women with disgust. At the end of the book he leaves the monastery with ambivalent feelings.

Gleb Botkin converted his vision into reality when he established the Long Island Church of Aphrodite in 1938. He had only about fifty followers. He created three different liturgies and he held worship services four times a week, before an altar with a replica of the Venus de Medici. Behind the statue was a purple tapestry. There was incense of frankincense and myrrh. Nine candles were placed on the altar, as well as the symbol of the church, the planetary sign for Venus.

In 1939 Botkin told a reporter for the *New York World-Telegram* that the purpose of the Aphrodisian religion was "to seek and develop

Love, Beauty and Harmony and to suppress ugliness and discord." The principle of Christianity, he said, was to suppress desire in order to develop the spirit; but the religion of Aphrodite sought to develop the spirit through antithetical principles. Botkin conceived of nature as good. He considered hate, selfishness, and jealousy "unnatural." While in theory he idealized sex as a "divine function," in practice he was conservative and concerned lest the church "attract neurotics and those emotionally unstable."[4]

Botkin envisioned the Aphrodisian religion as a formal structure, complete with church, clergy, and liturgy. Unlike most Neo-Pagans today, he believed in monotheism and creed and dogma. *Belief* was considered necessary for salvation; one had to come into a "correct relationship" with the Goddess. During the services worshippers chanted their creed before the altar:

> Blessed thou art, O beautiful goddess; and our love for Thee is like the sky which has no bounds; like eternity which has no ending; like thy beauty itself that no words could describe. For we love Thee with every atom of our souls and bodies, O Aphrodite: holiest, sweetest, loveliest, most blessed, most glorious, most beautiful Goddess of Beauty.[5]

Botkin died in 1969, and none of his five children carried on the faith.[6] But one man who did was W. Holman Keith, a former Baptist minister who attended services at Botkin's church in the early 1940s and became a convert. He wrote *Divinity as the Eternal Feminine* (1960), and has continued to write articles for Neo-Pagan publications. Keith is considered to be one of the true elders of the Neo-Pagan movement, but his views, like those of elders in many religions, are not very similar to the views of younger Neo-Pagans.

Keith described Botkin as a man who seemed to dislike both communism and democracy and to be for "some kind of Theocratic rule through the Aphrodisian religion." In an article in *Green Egg* he observed that many of Botkin's views would not coincide with those of most Neo-Pagans today.

> Freedom of conscience took second place for him to a rightly informed conscience from childhood on. . . . He did not believe in natural immortality . . . but in conditional immortality. The soul must come into the

right relationship with the Goddess if it is to escape extinction. . . . Rev. Botkin was a monotheist in his doctrine of Deity. . . . Rev. Botkin was not cooperative with other Pagan sects. He believed that he had the Goddess truth in his teaching in all its purity.[7]

In many of these beliefs, Keith wrote, Botkin was more in line with the ancient mystery traditions than most Neo-Pagans would admit. Keith finally left Botkin's church in a dispute over its dogmatism and today is an elder in the Neo-Pagan group Feraferia.

Feraferia: The Beautiful Jewel That Lies in Its Box

"How do you like New Crete?"
I blushed and said slowly: "Why ask me, Mother?"
"Mothers often ask their children questions to which they already know the answers."
"Oh, well—it isn't really beyond criticism. Though the bread's good and the butter's good, there doesn't seem to be any salt in either."
—ROBERT GRAVES, *Watch the North Wind Rise*[8]

In 1949 Robert Graves created a fictional utopia called New Crete in a book titled *Watch the North Wind Rise*. New Crete, he wrote, came into existence during a period filled with wars and revolutions, culminating in a nuclear war. An Israeli philosopher, concerned with the survival of humanity, recommended the creation of anthropological enclaves, each of which would represent a stage in the development of civilization.[9] Each enclave was to be sealed off from the world for generations, communicating only with an anthropological council that studied the reports from these societies to determine which of them were viable and where civilization ultimately went wrong.

The enclaves devoted to the Bronze Age and early Iron Age became so successful that they were resettled on Crete. A new society evolved and, with it, a new religion devoted to the Mother Goddess, Mari, a religion similar to pre-Christian European Paganism, complete with agricultural festivals and mysteries. The new society on Crete was seen as "the seedbed of a Golden Age."[10]

But the society of New Crete was not perfect. Although much different from the bureaucracy to which we are accustomed, it was no less authoritarian. Nothing outside the dictates of poetry could be manufactured; nothing purely utilitarian. Rigid patterns of custom ruled the country's five classes. The protagonist, an Englishman from the 1940s, is sent for by the Goddess to shake the society up a bit, to put a little salt in the bread and butter, as the above quote suggests, and bring about the winds of change and freedom.

Graves was writing fiction, of course, but the idea of a Goddess religion emerging after a cataclysm is not uniquely his. Many Neo-Pagans told me they envisage a similar outcome, and several spoke to me of the Hopi prophesies of a Great Purification. Many of them seemed to feel that only a great catastrophe could bring about the seeds of change from which a new society could be created. "Look at the freak weather phenomena all around us," was a comment I heard frequently. "Mother Nature is beginning to take things into her own hands." Certainly the utopian vision that is central to a number of Neo-Pagan religions makes sense only in a world far different from the present one. And there is at least one group that could fit Graves's description of a new Goddess religion awaiting the blessed cataclysm. That religion is Feraferia, founded by Frederick Adams.

What Fred Adams has in mind is having this magnificent reconstruction of a very ancient Goddess religion, which is a finished product—polished and sitting encapsulated on an upper shelf.

After the cataclysm, who is going to have faith in Christianity? So we simply pull it down from the shelf and say, "Look, Feraferia! We've gone through Hell; so let us celebrate the return of the Kore, the Maiden Goddess from Hell!"

—ED FITCH, Gardnerian priest

Of the many groups I have encountered, Feraferia is one of the most difficult to describe. Feraferia—the name is derived from Latin words meaning "wilderness festival"[11]—is the most intricately formed of the Neo-Pagan religions in the United States. As the quote by Fitch implies, it is a jewel, an artistic creation, the private vision of one man, which sits like a beautiful crystal on a shelf, highly admired but mostly from afar. It is never contaminated by offshoots, or schisms, or changes, or even by many followers who might spread it too thin. As the sound of its name implies, it is a religion of both wildness and delicateness. Considered by its small following to be the aristocrat of Neo-Paganism, it has all the advantages and disadvantages that the word "aristocrat" implies.

Frederick Adams is a kind and gentle man who has spent most of his creative energies as an artist, astrologer, and researcher into archeology and geocosmic lore (such as ley-lines and henge construction). He lives in Los Angeles with his partner, Svetlana Butyrin, in a small house covered with his artwork. When I visited them, I was welcomed with a short ritual in English and Greek. I was given a drink that tasted of cinnamon and mint, and a dish of fresh raspberries. The house radiated peace and beauty, and there was a frailty about Adams as he sat barefooted in a blue robe; I came away with the feeling that he had been buffeted by a harsh world that would not accept his sensitivity.

They were evicted from their former dwelling place several years ago after neighbors told their landlord about strange religious activities. Robert Ellwood described this home:

> A visitor to Frederick Adams' home is made immediately aware that this is no ordinary suburban house. The front porch is full of signs and symbols from out of the past—wreaths, crossed sticks, painted stones. In the backyard trees have been planted and given names. There is a henge—a circle of forked sticks oriented to the pole star and the rising sun. The group has a larger henge in the mountains to the north. Within the house are shrines to sun and moon, and a shrine room whose floor is a large wheel on which the passing days and seasons and motions of the planets are marked with stones. Here, the important news is not what comes in the paper, but what nature is doing.[12]

Fred Adams described Feraferia in *Earth Religion News:*

> Feraferia is a Paradisal Fellowship for the loving celebration of Wilderness Mysteries with Faerie style, courtly elegance, refinement & grace. The Great Work of Feraferia is the lyrical unification of Ecology, Artistry, Mythology and Liturgy. In such Love-Play-Work many Women & Men achieve reunion with Great Nature, each other, and their own Souls, before and after the Transition we call "Death." . . . Wilderness is the Supreme Value of Religion and Life! Feraferia offers, perhaps for the first

time in known history, a Poetic Liturgy and Altruistic Theurgy of Holy Wilderness.[13]

Much of Feraferian philosophy is connected to a body of utopian thought. It did not spring full blown from the head of Zeus, or even Fred Adams. Adams was the artist, but the vision shows the influence of many sources: the utopian novels of William Morris (*News from Nowhere*), Robert Graves (*Watch the North Wind Rise*), William Hudson (*A Crystal Age*), and several others[14]; writers on nature and wilderness, particularly John Muir and Henry David Thoreau; the archetypal psychologists (C. G. Jung, Erich Neumann, J. J. Bachofen, Karl Kerényi); surrealist artists and philosophers; naturalist and nudist movements; *The White Goddess*; and perhaps most of all, the work of Henry Bailey Stevens, whose *The Recovery of Culture* provided Adams with the philosophical basis for the paradisal vision of Feraferia.

Stated simply, the basic idea in *The Recovery of Culture* is that human beings have forgotten their primate origins and that this primate past, far from being a time of violence, was, in fact, the paradise of which all the myths speak. Stevens, a horticulturist, argues that the ancestors of human beings lived peacefully in trees for millions of years. It was no accident, he says, that the legends speak of Buddha's gaining enlightenment under a tree. Eden, Avalon, the Garden of Hesperides, all these visions of paradise hark back to a time before the last ice age, a peaceful time before the beginnings of animal husbandry, the eating of meat, and blood sacrifice. This paradise was no myth, but a real period of peace and plenty. The myth of the Fall was simply the story of the end of that era. The story of Cain and Abel was the story of the cropper versus the herdsman, of human beings steeling themselves to the necessity of throat cutting.

According to Stevens, grazing animals had caused the infertility of the soil, creating deserts out of gardens. "Only through gardens," he wrote, "can the neolithic civilization be understood." He added:

Green plants form a marvelous partnership with animal life . . . they purify the air for us, giving us the vital oxygen and themselves using the carbon dioxide which we throw off. Thus there is literally a magic circle between the plants and men. This relationship has reached its most intimate form in the food-bearing trees, which fed the primate family throughout its physical evolution and became the principal inspiration of its culture.[15]

For Stevens, history began at the point where matters turned wrong. And all the great reformers in history were, in effect, attempting to turn civilization back on course. Pythagoras, Tolstoy, Wagner, Shelley, and Shaw all attempted to return humankind to a vegetarian, frugivorous existence. The end of that existence was the fundamental factor responsible for the wrong turning of civilization, the fundamental cause of wars, famines, and other catastrophes.

Stevens advocated that we "take up again our membership in the primate family," since a properly developed plant-human ratio could make of the world "a new and more marvelous Garden of Eden."[16] He hinted that one mechanism to bring all this about could be a new world religion. Frederick Adams clearly designed Feraferia to be this religion.

Adams's first direct experience of the Goddess came in 1956, while he was doing graduate work at Los Angeles State College. Before that he had explored the work of Robert Graves and C. G. Jung. He had immersed himself in occultism and ceremonial magic, and had long had a love for ancient Greece and the myths of the gods and goddesses. He also loved wilderness and had begun to draw and paint feminine religious figures.

On a spring day, during a period when he was rereading Robert Graves and studying anthropology and the works of Mircea Eliade, Adams was walking across the college campus, he told me, when "It flashed upon me! The feminine aspect of deity, the femininity of divinity. I realized at that moment that the divine feminine is the most important, most valid, most world-shaking truth that we can possibly realize. It came out of the blue, and I just started walking crazily in circles, thinking, 'That's it, that's it, She is It.'"

After that, Adams began a series of notebooks on a new theology. Their theme was that the Goddess was the only spiritual force and Jungian archetype capable of reuniting humanity's instincts with the biosphere, nature, and the cosmos. It had to be done through the feminine modality. This did not mean the masculine would be excluded, but the balance could be restored only *through* the feminine.

A year later, in 1957, Adams and some friends formed the group Hesperides, which preceded Feraferia. Adams wrote a pamphlet, "Hesperian Life—The Maiden Way," which has been revised several times. The latest edition, 1970, remains the best explanation of Feraferian philosophy.

> There is a way of life for Man which allows him to remain Man and yet also be an integral part of Nature. This way of life was abandoned not yesterday, not even in the space of many hundreds of years. It was disrupted and given up thousands of years ago. . . .
> But the Way once existed in the world. It had hardly survived infancy when the urban-hierarchical-militaristic culminations of the different Neolithic phases of human History abruptly ended its career. However, the Way survives and smolders, imaginally, in the collective depths of the Human Psyche. If one taps these depths, dredges up the lost images of the Way, and takes them seriously, she or he is usually stigmatized as a hopeless romantic, or even worse.

Adams argued that the vision of Hesperian life still existed, to a limited degree, in various reform movements—nudist, naturalist, vegetarian, utopian, and so on. But these movements always failed because they functioned separately, and also because they lacked a "strong religious center."

The elements needed to create the Hesperian life included organic gardening, with emphasis on tree crops; promotion of forestation and reverence for the Tree as the Guardian of Life; a diet of fruit, nuts, berries, and leafy vegetables; reverence for all animal, vegetable, and mineral life; no more use of animals as chattel and pets; the promotion of regionalism with small villages and palaces, as opposed to cities; outdoor living, preferably in warm climates where only a minimum of clothing is necessary; a reverence for health and natural medicine; the end of all divisions between "mind work" and "body work"; the end of rigid scheduling and regimentation, of arbitrary coercion, codified laws, and penalization; the elimination of artificial conditions that generate competitiveness, insensitivity, and indifference; the elimination of hierarchy, authoritarianism, and inequality of work; the implementation of safeguards against overpopulation and overorganization; the maximization of "free creative play and erotic development"; and finally, the elimination of "all purely utilitarian, instrumental, automative devices and activities as loveless and disruptive of the *living* Cosmos."[17]

Adams was clear in his disdain for most modern technology, as well as in his belief that apocalypse could be avoided only by willing an end to industrialism. "The only task remaining," he wrote, "for our overestimated, painfully inflated engineering, is to clear the Earth of its own debris and trappings, systematically and gradually over the next several hundred years. Otherwise the clearing of the Earth must be violent, for a clearing there will be."

Fred Adams and Lady Svetlana described to me their vision of the future. It is far removed from the world of today, and far removed from their own life in Los Angeles. They envision a planet that would support a human population of ten to twenty million, living off horticulture, similar to the paradise pictured by Stevens. It would be "an egalitarian aristocracy, based on arborial culture," since tree crops, they argued, produce more food per acre with less work than corn or wheat or livestock. This new aristocracy would be most feasible in a warm and fruitful climate, like Java or California. Lady Svetlana told me, "We think communities should have no more than a thousand people, all self-sufficient, since trees, when you get them going, are not hard to take care of. You could sing and dance as you picked the fruit and nuts. It's totally nonviolent." Fred Adams said that, in his fantasy of the future, nation-states would erode into temple-palace estates. These would exist amidst garden groves that would graduate into wilderness. Each temple would be connected with every other by ley-lines,* like the ancient sites of Britain. Vast tracts of land would be returned to their wild state. The population would be lowered drastically, either by sensible human measures or by the actions of the Goddess which, he told me, had already begun

---

* The theory that important ancient British sites are aligned, that they are linked by prehistoric trackways (ley-lines), was formulated by Alfred Watkins in his book *The Old Straight Track* (London: Methuen and Co., 1925). More recently, the theory has become well known through the works of John Michell. In *The View over Atlantis* (London: Sago Press, 1969), a book that has enjoyed the same kind of fame among occultists as Louis Pauwels' and Jacques Bergier's *Morning of the Magicians*, Michell argues that the entire planet is marked with traces of prehistoric engineering, and that the straight tracks, or ley-lines, of Britain are one such form. A British magazine, *The Ley Hunter*, has been devoted to the study of leys, megaliths, folklore and cosmology. Janet and Colin Bord's *Mysterious Britain* (London: Garnstone Press, 1963, pp. 175–206) also takes up the question of leys.

in earthquake activity and weather phenomena. "She will strike back," he said. "She is not going to let the whole biosphere be torn apart by nuclear maniacs."

The vision of Feraferia is of a Paganized world, but one that is far from primitive. Adams told me that it was his firm belief that if relatively small numbers of people lived in climates that were suitable and did not engage in destructive practices such as "animal husbandry and warfare," a high culture would be conceived, exemplifying the best of ancient cultures such as Crete.

I asked Adams and Lady Svetlana for their views on the future of cities. They hoped that permanent cities would cease to exist, replaced by large cultural and sacramental centers where people would come together for seasonal festivals and cultural events. "Why then," I asked them, "does Neo-Paganism grow up in cities?" I had noticed that the Neo-Pagan movement, like the ecology movement, is mostly an urban phenomenon.

"I'll tell you why," Adams replied. "Most people who live on the farm are always fighting nature. They don't have the aesthetic distance to see other possibilities of relating to nature. Who, after all, started writing sensual literature during the early decades of this century? Who talked about freeing the sensual nature? D. H. Lawrence, an Englishman, a man from a country where people were more uptight and less sensual than anywhere else. Sometimes reversals have to come from their complete opposite; the yin gives rise to the yang, and the yang gives rise to the yin. I've known many people from the farm who can't sense Thoreau's love of wilderness; they can't sympathize with it because they are struggling with nature due to what we feel is a false agricultural approach."

And Lady Svetlana added, "We call this false approach the corn-cattle-battle syndrome."

Frederick Adams lives in Los Angeles, a city far removed from the Feraferian vision. His life and actions exemplify the contradictions that sometimes afflict a Neo-Pagan. He is a man who functions best as Pagan priest, magician, teacher, and artist in a world that has no use for these vocations. Gentle, peaceful, almost an innocent, Adams made his living for many years as a caseworker for the Los Angeles County Welfare Department. He told me that the problem of living a split life, of trying to do meaningful nonalienating work, had been with him constantly since 1957. "All my life I have sensitized myself to be a visionary artist in a magic circle," he said. "I used to spend all my time thinking about the Goddess and the Gods. Then I had to go into the freeway world." Adams told me that he had often been subjected to harassment on the job because of his unorthodox religious beliefs. It was still his goal to find work that was not psychically damaging, and to leave Los Angeles. Neither goal seemed to be around the corner.

Adams often writes poetically, sometimes in language that few can understand. Much of it presumes a knowledge of esotericism and occultism. Occasionally, it falls into a social-science jargon.[18] A woman once wrote to him, "You need to get some of this stuff down to grade school level . . . or don't you intend for the common people ever to understand it?" The answer to that question is complicated. Fred Adams clearly believes that the philosophy and theology of Feraferia are all of one piece and cannot be separated or watered down. Still, he did publish a piece called "Feraferia for Beginners" in an issue of *Earth Religion News.* He wrote that the religion celebrated "the processes of Nature as a whole" and worshipped them as "a family of Gods issuing from a cluster of Goddesses."

> Feraferia is a mystery religion in the most ancient sense because it teaches that Life in Nature cannot be reduced to logical formulae and that it is really wrong to try to do so.
>
> The Divinities of Feraferia may appear as mighty spirits that people can feel surging through them, uniting them with Earth and Sky; or as radiantly beautiful bodies, as in myths and dreams; or as those mighty intelligences that dwell in the different forces of Nature.
>
> The main sources from which the Queendom of the Gods has reached Feraferia are associated with ancient Britain, Greece, and Minoan Crete, although all wholesome Pagan Ways, such as the American Indians, ancient Egyptian and Eastern ones, have influence . . .
>
> From Temples of the Earth Mother and Soul Daughter, like Eleusis, a wonderfully refined sense of Mystery has flowed secretly through the centuries from ancient Greece to us. And from the excavation of places like the Palace of Minos, on the island of Crete, the beautiful Earth devotions of the peaceful Minoans can now inspire and educate us. In our time of ecological crisis, we really need these original root-systems of Nature Religion.[19]

After it appeared, a number of people wrote to Adams that they were more confused than ever. Adams laughed when he told me this and said, "After that I gave up. I told myself, 'You have a convoluted, schizoid mind and you just have to accept it.' " We should bear this in mind as we approach his writings.

According to Feraferian thealogy, the center of the universe, of all universes perhaps, is the Arretos Koura, an ancient Greek phrase for the ineffable bride, the Nameless Maiden. The Arretos Koura spins a cosmic dance from which all things come into existence, each of them unique and particular. The Nameless Maiden is not the "One" from which all things leave and return; she is, rather, the "transcendent unique," the creatrix of all uniqueness. All the entities she creates interrelate with her, but never lose their individual essence. Thus, she represents polytheistic wholeness as opposed to monotheistic unity. An analogy to this might be a symphony, where each note is differentiated, but the whole is something beyond a "unity."

Under the Arretos Koura are what Adams has called "the Goddess-given Gods." These are the archetypal beings—Mother, Father, Son, Daughter. Feraferia is unlike many other Neo-Pagan revivals in emphasizing the Young Maiden rather than the Mother Goddess. Feraferia deemphasizes the paternal and maternal aspects of life, which imply relationships based on a notion of authority. Lady Svetlana said, "We don't want to think that authoritarianism is the primal thing in the universe."

The Korê—the Maiden Goddess—is at the center of Feraferia's paradisal vision. In Adams's view only a new religion that worships the Maiden Goddess—beauty, creativity, and desire—and that "draws strength from all the mysteries of Immanent Nature and the flesh," can bring the vision into reality. It is she "who is the ultimate image of delicacy and nonviolence, of playfulness and sensitivity and childlikeness. From such an archetype a society might develop in which no matriarchs or patriarchs would exist, and people would not develop hard and fast hierarchies."

Adams stated this idea in an essay called "The Korê."

To inform the dawning Eco-Psychic Age of Aquarius, wherein celebration will determine subsistence, a long repressed image of divinity is re-emerging: The Merry Maiden, Madimi, Rima, Alice in Wonderland,

Princess Ozma, Julia, Lolita, Candy, Zazie of the Métro, Brigitte, Bar-
barella, and Wendy—a grotesque and incongruous assembly at first
sight—are all early harbingers of the Heavenly Nymphet. She alone may
negotiate free interaction between the other three anthropomorphic divinities of the Holy Family. These are the Great Mother, Who dominated
the Old and New Stone Ages; the Great Father, Who initiated the Early
Patriarchal Era; and the Son, who crystalized the megalopolitan mental-
ity of the Late Patriarchal Era. It is the Dainty Daughter of the Silver
Crescent who will transmute the saturate works of Father and Son to
wholeness in the Maternal Ground of Existence, without sacrificing the
valid achievements of masculine articulation. And She accomplishes this
without a crippling imposition of parental or heroic authority images.
How delightful to behold her tease and tickle Father and Son into respectable natural, Life-affirming Pagan Gods again.[20]

Adams argued that the central problem of our time is how to reconcile "the primal parents," the Mother and the Father, the yin and the
yang. The dominance of the Father excludes the Mother, but, said
Adams, the Mother principle includes the Father, and must take
precedence.

The emphasis on the feminine yin meant freedom for both yin
and yang in their fusion. "In Yin," he wrote, "Yin and Yang find full
scope for the expansion of Life between them. This means Yin, in
some transcendent-immanent way, is TAO."

Within the Holy Family of four, it is the Daughter who brings
about their harmony.

The Mother is Source and Center. The Son is creative separation,
opening and outgoing. The Father is full outwardness, withdrawal and
particularization. The Daughter or Holy Maiden is Creative Return, con-
figuration, form. But the Daughter as Nameless Bride of ancient Eleusis is
also the Mysterious Wholeness of the Four which consists in their dynamic separateness. We are initiating the Age of the Daughter, the Korê
Age. (Korê is another name for Persephone, the Goddess of Spring and
the Dead, Daughter of Demeter—the Great Mother, in the Eleusinian
Mysteries.) The Korê Age will bring about the re-synthesis of the Maternal Whole of the Sacred Family.

It is only through the Maiden, Adams argued, that the balance can be
restored in a way that will elevate freedom, playfulness, sensuality,

and the imagination. The flaw of Christianity—and of most of the Eastern religions—is that they sought to create a balance through the Father principle, and were forced to do so through asceticism and the images of a pure, castrated male. Such an image, he wrote, would only continue the "Age of Analysis." In contrast, the Maiden Way would provide the necessary spiritual cohesion to begin a shift in history that would end "the prisons of hierarchy and the garbage heaps of industrialism." And this "Great Shift" or "Great Return" to the feminine could be seen by anyone who carefully examined the news of the day, or took a look at recent films, or novels, or essays, or poetry, but all "with an inner eye sharpened by the depth psychology of C. G. Jung."

In *Hesperian Life and the Maiden Way* Adams wrote that all previous attempts at revolution were trying to return to some contemporary aspect of the Goddess, but failed because they could not rid themselves of "mechanization, hierarchy, exploitation of animals, [and] sex repression." He argued that such an impulse had inspired Marx to talk about the "withering away of the state"; it was present on banners depicting the Virgin of Guadalupe during the Mexican Revolution. But the Maiden Goddess was never acknowledged as the guiding spirit of these reforms. Neither liberal education, nor totalitarian propaganda, nor the education of an elite vanguard, nor the victory of science and technology could ever bring this revolution about. "Only a great Religious Revolution, springing from the very broadest collective base of the Human Soul, can spread rapidly enough and thrust deeply enough without cataclysmic consequences to win the whole Human Race back to its Root Sense of the Organic Feminine Balance, and its natural destiny of Hesperian Life."[21]

> All life on Earth participates in
> the dance of Moon and Sun.
> And we, engendered in the oceans,
> feel in our blood the pull of
> our Moon upon the tides.
> We are sunlight transformed by
> trees into fruit and plasm, and we
> are so intimately of the Earth that
> our collective dream is paradise.
> Thus we are moved to celebrate

the ceaseless play of the seasons
and to ensoul ourselves,
landscape and heaven.[22]

—FREDERICK ADAMS

Frederick Adams has lived in the wilderness, and Feraferia has participated in reforestation work, regarding wilderness as "the supreme value of religion and life."[23] Feraferia has stressed its spiritual link with ecology, stating that the lyrical unification of ecology and religion is its prime task. Adams has written that "The only way to reunite Mankind is to reunite Mankind with Nature. Mankind will become humane toward Man only when he becomes humane toward all nature."[24]

Feraferia's first article of faith has been a belief that from wildness springs love, wonder, and joy, and that, as the famous quotation from Thoreau goes: "In wildness is the preservation of the world." Adams has written that the primary cause of alienation and most psychological disorders is the severing of humanity from wilderness. Poetry, ritual, dance, and song unite the inner and the outer: they link "visionary nature within and ecological nature without," microcosm and macrocosm. Adams emphasizes techniques that lead to a feeling of connectedness to the natural world. These include not only ritual techniques for producing ecstasy but techniques to reconnect one to the living cosmos—knowledge of wilderness, ecology, astronomy, astrology, and henge construction. Since all nature is sacred space, the planet and sky are Feraferia's temple. Adams has devoted many articles to building temples in nature, orienting them to the four directions and the positions of the stars and planets. "Land-Feeling," wrote Adams, "is absolutely essential to the Spiritual Reclamation of Man to Nature in Her hour of crisis," and building a henge or "topocosmic mandala" promotes a feeling of "Land-Sky-Love."[25]

Feraferian rituals are oriented toward the play of the seasons and the transformations of the Maiden Goddess and her lover and son as the year progresses. Adams writes:

Our Earth, a very great Goddess in artistic communion with The Cosmic Korê, displays the magnificent pageant of the seasons. . . .

The year is a continual courtship between Moon and Sun. On May Day . . . Moon and Sun become engaged. At this time flowers are in full bloom. On the first day of Summer, They are married: fruits are forming. In the middle of Summer, Lammas, The Goddess and God are on Their Honeymoon: fruits are ripening.

On the first day of Autumn, Moon Goddess and Sun God come home: the fruits are dropping, crops being ingathered. At the middle of Autumn, Hallowe'en, the Divine Lovers prepare for the long Winter sleep of all Nature: leaves and seeds are settling to soil.

On the first day of Winter, Yule, the Goddess suddenly reawakens. She finds The God has mysteriously departed, but She is pregnant with The God of the coming year, really the same God, the Lord Sun Himself. . . . Yule is when the Sun starts North again, thus promising that Spring will follow the long cold rest period of Winter.

At the middle of the Winter, Candlemas, The Goddess emerges from Her Royal Bedroom, The Great Earth-Sphere, and prepares to give birth to The Sun God again as an infant: enscaled buds stand out on bare branches.

Then, on the first day of Spring, Ostara, She does give birth to the baby Sun: fragile buds emerge from their scales in the dewy Sunrise of the year. The Goddess bathes in Her magic fountain and becomes a girl again. She and The God grow up together, very rapidly. Once more They become engaged on May Day, when buds are opening into flowers.[26]

Feraferia lays great emphasis on sensuality and eroticism, but by these words Adams does not mean genital sex. Rather, Feraferia stresses the idea that human beings should open themselves up to their own sensual nature, to the landscape, the earth, and sky, as well as to all other beings. Feraferia, like a number of Neo-Pagan groups, talks about sensuality as a sacrament, as the "feast of the Goddess and the Goddess-given Gods."

Feraferia distrusts modern technology much more than does any other Neo-Pagan group. Adams and Lady Svetlana feel that most mechanization has disrupted the flow of human life so that humanity is no longer in tune with the pulse of nature's own rhythms: solar, lunar, and the circadian rhythms of our bodies. Adams told me that he hopes for a new science—a small, highly refined technology embodying solar energy, laser technology, and a combination of forms—some of it old, known to the megalithic stone builders, and some of it new. In one flight of imagination Adams told me of his fantasy of priests and priestesses creating orgone energy in great ley-line temple centers through the use of highly developed sex magic.

Some Neo-Pagans have called the Feraferian vision unrealistic, as well as too blatantly antitechnological. Others have criticized its vision of nature as "unnatural" because it accepts only the calm, refined, elegant, peaceful, and romantic aspects of nature. These Pagans believe that nature has a dark side, that the destruction caused by storms, the killing of one species by another, are part of nature's laws and necessary for life. Adams told me, "Evolution is now maintained on this planet by predation and competition. There may be other principles for regulating evolution on other planets that are not as cruel as those on earth."

Feminist Neo-Pagans have criticized Feraferia for emphasizing a glamorous, seductive, playful goddess. And both Fred and Svetlana have said that women should not make themselves less glamorous; rather, men should make themselves more childish, more delicate. Svetlana said, "Wilderness is highly decorative. We should emulate her beauty."

But the main criticism by Neo-Pagans is that Feraferia is primarily an artistic creation rather than a functioning religion. In practice, it has had few followers. Feraferia emerged out of Hesperides during the 1960s; it was incorporated in 1967 and reached its height in the early seventies. Even then, it had an active group of only about fifty people (occasionally more appeared for big festivals), of whom only twenty or thirty were initiates. Feraferia has been very selective in accepting initiates.

In 1971 Robert Ellwood wrote about Feraferia:

Serious members are typically people who have been involved in pacifist, ecological and utopian movements. They seem in Feraferia to find a religious expression adequate to what has long been their real spiritual concern. . . . Adams's exercise of the leadership role has illustrated the problems inherent in this vocation. The vision is preeminently his, and he has himself done most of the writing, created most of the art and devised most of the rites. In some ways he approaches religious genius, and undoubtedly without his labors the movement would not exist. . . . It is essentially a circle around a charismatic leader and has no real structure otherwise. It is not clear whether at this point it has any potential to survive him as a sociological entity. Yet there are those who feel that his personality stifles the creativity of others in the evolution of Feraferia, albeit he is a mild and winsome person whom all love and revere. Some feel his vision is so personal and intricate it does not communicate as easily as it should. Some have been through Feraferia and left to establish their own henges and forms of neopaganism, though no off-shoots have yet attained real structure.[27]

At least one person told me he left Feraferia when Adams began to insist on *belief* in its thealogy. One couple, the Stanwicks, left to form an autonomous Feraferian group called Dancers of the Sacred Circle. Even though the circle around Adams is small, he continues to develop his artistry and vision. He and Lady Svetlana have continually stressed the need to keep the vision pure. They are openly elitist. Lady Svetlana said, "We want to keep it small because it is so precious, like a diamond; you can't just throw gems to the wind. Everything is worked out in so much detail that if any detail is changed ideologically, it would be very upsetting." And of course, Feraferia *is* like a necklace of precious stones, intricately worked out: the religion is very detailed, complete with rituals, calendar, thealogy, and vision. Adams has said that he doesn't think the vision will even begin to be realized until after his lifetime. He says that Feraferia's aim should first be to find a territory, a sanctuary, where the Hesperian vision can be actualized. Then the training of priestesses should begin.

Feraferia's purpose, according to Adams, is to save the earth and return humanity to a state of harmony with nature; to begin a transformation that will end with the dawning of a new culture throughout the galaxy, focused on the Korê. In Ellwood's words, its purpose is clearly "to recover an ecstatic vision of wholeness and unity which utterly respects the reality of the particular. It brings together not only man and nature, but man and each seasonal and geographic particular of nature, and also man and each style of his own consciousness—masculine and feminine, analytic and dream, vision and fantasy."[28] But, says Adams, the vision must be freely accepted; never imposed. "If we impose it, we'll abort the attempt. We will become monsters and lose our historic mission to save the planet from disaster and to convince the Goddess to let us reenter Her Queendom."

By 1986, activities by Feraferia were pretty minimal. Fred Adams and Svetlana Butyrin were no longer partners. For a while Lady Svetlana was holding public services, but these were in abeyance when the revised edition of this book went to press. Adams says he is still involved in research; he occasionally does rituals and leads discussion groups.

The Sabaean Religious Order: Rite as Art

One night, during a Midsummer Solstice festival held in a city park, a friend of mine observed the Neo-Pagan phenomenon for the first time. Afterward my friend remarked, "It was lovely. Sweet. Almost Edwardian."

Those words grated upon me, because I agreed. I have always felt that a Pagan celebration should be powerful, energizing, ecstatic—never merely "sweet." Seasonal festivals should suspend the dictates of convention and dissolve, however temporarily, the bonds of time and space. I remember being mesmerized many years ago by a Zuni corn festival in Colorado which lasted from morning until night. My attention never wandered from the dancers for that period of many hours. I have only rarely achieved such rapt attention during the rites of Neo-Pagans and Witches.

That this should be so is not surprising. It is the dilemma of modern life, a dilemma that arose with the destruction of the Pagan-folk-peasant traditions of Western Europe. The rise of Neo-Paganism in the United States must be understood as, in part, a search by uprooted Westerners for their own roots and origins, for a vibrant, rich culture equal to the cultures of tribal peoples and the great ancient civilizations. The Neo-Pagan movement is tied in ambiance if not in fact to those movements that seek to retain, preserve, and strengthen traditionalist cultures in Europe—the pan-Celtic movement, for example. It is no coincidence that many of the non-Gardnerian Witchcraft groups label themselves "Irish Traditionalist," "Scots Traditionalist," or "Welsh Traditionalist."

Many Neo-Pagans are drawn to Native American traditions, to

Voodoo and Santeria. These Pagan traditions are a much larger phenomenon than Neo-Paganism. People who are drawn to Neo-Paganism usually do not have a vital, indigenous tradition and are seeking to recover their roots, to rediscover folk tales, stories, songs, and dances that have largely vanished in the last hundred years.

Neo-Paganism in the United States is primarily a white phenomenon because it is a revival of Western European Paganism. Many blacks and Latins who are engaged in the same process—searching for roots—are drawn to Voodoo, Santeria, and Candomblé, all of which combine African religious and magical practices with elements of Roman Catholicism. (In Haiti the religion of the French colonialists and slavemasters mixed with the religions of the Dahomeans, Ibos, and Magos to produce Voodoo. Elsewhere in Latin and South America the Yoruba religion mixed with the religion of the Spanish and Portuguese colonialists, creating Santeria and—in Brazil—Candomblé).

These traditions are often more vital than the groups we have been discussing, simply because they took form within whole cultures and communities. But most white North Americans lack a culture that is still tied to the earth and its seasons. The Neo-Pagans are attempting to rebuild a whole new culture from a pile of old and new fragments. When they are honest with themselves, they admit their impoverishment; for even if their small groves and covens succeed, it will take generations to create successful ritual forms.

At present, some of the most powerful rituals in the United States take place in the theater, in modern dance performances, sporting events, or occasionally certain public events such as some rock concerts of the 1960s.

In 1977 the New York Shakespeare Festival performed Aeschylus' *Agamemnon* in a production where the ritual elements and the powerful music of Elizabeth Swados overshadowed the play. Swados and director Andrei Serban had spent several years investigating the emotional impact of Greek tragedy. The rhythmic chanting of the chorus and the use of gongs, drums, flutes, pots of flame, and smoking torches provided a powerful ritual experience.

Other dramatic, political, or cultural happenings have evoked power through ritual techniques. However, only occasionally has this power been present during the rituals of Neo-Pagans. This is not surprising, since the Neo-Pagan priesthood is in its infancy, picking up small pieces and discovering things often by chance.

Devlin, the Witch from California, once remarked to me, "Unfortunately, the raising of power is an accidental occurrence among us most of the time. In ancient Ireland the music of pipes and drums and harps was essential to the success of the rites. And so, I must say, was ritual drunkenness and ritual sex. I do not respect many 'public' Witches because I find among them a lack of ecstatic experience which I think marks these people as having incomplete traditions. And I hope that, in time, these incomplete forms will give way to complete forms."

During my travels around the United States I attended many rituals, ranging from the full-moon ceremonies of small Witch covens and visits to private and personal shrines, to large, public, seasonal festivals attended by hundreds. Some were totally captivating. Often the simplest were the most powerful. But frequently, I felt that something was missing.

One of the most important exceptions to this was a wedding ritual in Chicago at the Temple of the Moon of the Sabaean Religious Order, a religious order inspired by ancient Basque, Yoruba, Sumerian and Babylonian sources. Like Feraferia, the Sabaean Religious Order comes out of the vision of a single man, Frederic M. de Arechaga, who is called Odun, but his vision is far different from Frederick Adams's.

When I went to Chicago in the fall of 1975 I found so many rumors circulating about the Sabaean Religious Order that it was impossible to sort them out. Everything I had read about the order was confusing, almost as if Odun had sought to surround it with mystery. My first encounter was symbolic.

I had just arrived in Chicago and went to visit an old friend, the former editor of an underground newspaper—now defunct—and a veteran of many unusual experiences. This man had no particular interest in "the occult," and I thought he would not easily succumb to fear of the unknown. But as we were walking on the North Side in Chicago, my friend began to cross the street in order to avoid passing a small magic shop. On the sidewalk in front of the shop were various magical symbols drawn into the concrete. I asked him why we were making this detour. He said that the owner of the shop was very strange, and was said to have put broken glass on his roof to prevent children from climbing. He described him as "weird and unpleasant." He waited on the other side of the street while I entered El-Sabarum, the occult supply store of the Sabaean Religious Order and one of the five or six places in Chicago I was determined to visit.

In the next few days several occultists also warned me to be wary of Odun. I was told he practiced negative magic and performed animal sacrifices. I could find nothing to substantiate the first charge; the second was true—all animal food consumed in the temple had to be killed ritually. But since I was not a vegetarian, I felt I could hardly complain of this practice, any more than I might complain of the kosher laws of the Jews.

My own meeting with Odun (pronounced Ordun) was cloaked in mystery. There was a series of phone calls in which it was never clear whether Odun was in or out. I was kept waiting in a back room of the temple building, filled with statues and paintings. While I waited, a young woman in purple stockings practiced operatic arias on a piano. An hour later Odun arrived with six or seven members of the order, all carrying large grocery bags filled with food—a preparation for a wedding. Odun was dressed casually in jeans, a shirt, and sweater, but all were white, as might be required of an initiate into Santeria, which in fact he was.

Finally our interview began. I felt somewhat at a loss, having much less to go on here than with any of the other groups I'd met—a few articles, some confusing pages by Hans Holzer, and a bagful of rumors, some of them perhaps true, others perhaps the product of jealousy. My confusion had been aided and abetted by Odun's evident love of weaving a bit of mystery around him. I came away with a wealth of impressions, a sense of great creativity and variety, but also the feeling that the group was hard to pin down, that I was missing certain signals.

Odun has described Sabaeanism as a philosophy of action that states that human beings should live in the present, identifying with those principles that are unchanging even in the face of death. One such principle would be the pursuit of knowledge, since knowledge, he observed to me, is the one thing we are not born with, but which we take with us when we go. Sabaeanism, he has said, is a system of thought that can be applied to all aspects of life.

According to an article in the order's occasional publication, *Iris*, Sabaeanism is "a unique philosophy" that "extends back in time 6000 years or more, and as a living undogmatic principle is evasive when put into impersonal written words." Sabaeanism was originally part of an effort "to preserve an antediluvian philosophy by means of deliberate hieroglyphics superimposed on the illusion of star groups in the heavens."[29] According to Berosus, a Babylonian historian, the last antediluvian kings were ordered to write down all history and deposit their writings at Sippar, the city of the sun god, Utu. This was to be no earthly city, since man-made and natural disasters would destroy such writings. So the city of the Sun God was really the heavens, and the history was recorded in the stars. Thus, astronomy evolved as the most important feature of Sabaeanism, along with astrology, temple building, and the study of the relation of place, time, and celebration to the planets and stars. "Sabaeanism" means worship of stars or star lore. But the Sabaean Religious Order has been involved in a large number of activities that have nothing to do with astrology and astronomy. Odun told me that Sabaeanism came to Egypt at the time of Menes (1st dynasty), and later emissaries brought it westward. He told me that during the seventeenth century, during the slave trade, it was brought to the New World and that is why the tradition has deep ties with Santeria.

Odun's background in the arts seems to be the key to the order's richness and mystery. He has been a choreographer and a designer. He told me he worked with the Lyric Opera of Chicago and designed jazz pianist Ahmad Jamal's nightclub, the Alhambra. I once watched him work with a dancer during a wedding rehearsal in the temple. He ran and leapt and directed her until she moved gracefully to the music of the small temple orchestra. From the little I saw, Sabaean rituals are the most complex and beautifully organized of any Neo-Pagan group I visited. The use of music and dance was truly inspiring. The order has mounted mystery plays; they have synthesized art, dance, song, and ritual to a height I have not seen elsewhere. In addition, there are classes in herbalism, magic, and astrology. The priesthood seems small, with certainly less than a dozen members, but I noticed that many Chicago Neo-Pagans came to work with Odun for a period of time. Most of the Pagans I met in Chicago had dealt with the order—some favorably, some not favorably—and many had been influenced by Odun.

Frederic de Arechaga came to the United States from Spain. He changed his name to Odun Arechaga after his initiation into the mysteries of the god Obatala. He told me that he inherited the Sabaean tradition from his mother, but, whatever its origins, it bears the stamp of his own artistry. The order consists of the small supply store, El-Sabarum, which opens in the late afternoon and seems to cater to members more than the general public. El-Sabarum also runs a mail-order service and an occasional newsletter. Behind the shop is the temple, some space for classes, and living quarters for the priesthood. The temple was completely designed and built by members of the order and is the focus for religious gatherings small and large.

Sabaean theology describes God or the Gods as *Am'n,* a word that is said to mean the hidden, numberless point. Unlike the word *God,* the word *Am'n* can be singular or plural; it suggests neither maleness nor femaleness. The Am'n are seen as a Source, but hidden like the wind, which can be felt but not seen. An article in *Iris* observed that the Am'n "cleanse the imagery of deity to its original premise of self-metamorphosis; man's ultimate responsibility to himself."[30]

The Am'n are seen as total knowledge; they are "indifferent, amoral and pure source." They are "above being adored." They "do not exist for the morbid preoccupation of a fanatic. But rather as avenues that can develop the individual to an awareness of himself and the universe that hitherto has remained unearthed."

For the sake of convenience, the Am'n can be divided. Odun told me that the order represents the Am'n symbolically as five different goddesses. "Poetically we use the term *goddess.* After all, the female is a formidable symbol for creation. We always know who the mother is, and even the mother does not have to know who the father is. Still, the idea of creation must not be misunderstood. We are not feminists. The entire universe is *not* based on the feminine precept. The incident of sex or gender which comes about in an incarnation is only a necessity or need of evolution. Divinity is sexless. The most ancient descriptions of gods are androgynous. But it is very hard for people to concentrate on the abstract. That is the whole purpose of mythology, to familiarize yourself with certain mysteries in an unmysterious way through storytelling."

The order also divides the Am'n to represent various races, seasons, philosophies, and theologies. The Red Goddess represents Autumn and the peoples native to this continent. The White Goddess represents winter and Caucasians. The Black Goddess represents the spring and blacks. The Yellow Goddess represents the summer and Orientals. And the Blue Goddess represents leap year, the day between the years, and the races and peoples beyond earth.

The Am'n are also used to represent five aspects of philosophy—logic, aesthetics, ethics, politics, and metaphysics—and five aspects of theology—atheism, pantheism, polytheism, monotheism, and henotheism. The Sabaean Religious Order adheres to henotheism as the most inclusive. A henotheist is person who worships one god *without excluding the existence of others.*" A henotheist," Odun said, "is a person who relates to deity in a personal way. For a time, one might be attuned to Venus; at another time, to Saturn." An article in *Iris* explained further;

> As a henotheist, a Sabaean can related to an individual imagery that particularly reflects himself. . . . However he never forgets that there is another imagery he can [use] if it comes to pass that he changes and no longer can identify with the image he so fondly admired.[31]

Odun described henotheism as the "ultimate wheel of the five-pointed star which would begin with atheism, go through pantheism, polytheism, monotheism, and finally end up with henotheism before beginning all over again." These five theisms, he observed, relate to all of human knowledge, to the five aspects of philosophy.

"Atheism seems to relate to logic (the idea that this is this and that is that). At the point when a person realizes that there is a form and a movement to things, this brings about a sense of aesthetics and leads a person to pantheism (the feeling of a tree, of a flower, of the wind). When a person comes to the realization that these feelings, these 'spirits,' have a kind of personality, this leads to polytheism, and the sensing of these diverse points of view and individualities leads a person to a sense of ethics. At this point, people often begin to manipulate reality and to move in one direction or another. Thus they come to politics and monotheism. At the point when a person realizes there is something beyond all this, they develop a sense of metaphysics and become henotheists."

Odun said that one could be an atheist and still be a Sabaean, although, later, an atheist woman told me that she had left the order because she felt that her views were too far removed from the general conceptions of the priesthood.

Odun calls the Sabaean Religious Order a kind of finishing school and says that learning about the ancient philosophies and mystery traditions is equivalent to learning to be civilized. "We do not believe in teachers," he told me. "The purpose of a priesthood is to be a catalyst, to sustain a strength for people who come to it so they can be vitalized." Most people, he said, are unable to read the ancient books properly and to open themselves to the ancient myths. But despite his stress on ancient knowledge, Odun points out that the order is not anachronistic. There is no purpose to living in the past or attempting to mimic ancient times; most religions failed precisely because they did not take into account the metamorphosis of people, nations, mind. "The object of life," he told me, "is to know yourself, to learn, to become, to grow; it's the becoming divine, the principle of the mystery of deification. *Sabaeanism* is simply a term given to our people. But they are people who follow their own heads. They are not hung up on a book or on a prophet. They are not idolators of books. They know there are many different paths within Sabaeanism."

The feeling one gets in visiting the order is of a constant stream of diverse activities. Odun told me that the one thing that was not allowed was wasting time. "We are constantly busy. We build. We teach. We do research. We write mystery plays. We choreograph. We teach dancers. We *are* a source."

My visit to the Sabaean Religious Order culminated in a magnificent wedding ceremony, or "eclipse," as the Sabaeans call it—literally, the movement of one planet in front of another. The length of an eclipse is decided by divination. If a couple decides to join for a period of years, it is called a solar eclipse; if for a period of months, a lunar eclipse.

The ceremony I attended in the late fall of 1975 was the solar eclipse of a priestess in the Sabaean Order. She was marrying a man who had no connection with the religion. It was, ritually speaking, the most beautiful wedding I have ever seen, surpassing a magnificent traditional country wedding I once attended in England.

The eclipse took place in early evening in the Temple of the Moon behind the small occult supply store run by the order. A door in the shop opened into a large high-ceilinged room lined with two rows of tall gray columns, each topped with a statue of a white elephant. The columns were ringed with wreaths of ferns and daisies. A brownish-gold curtain cut the inner portion of the temple in half.

Before entering the temple, we took off our shoes. Inside, on one side of the curtain, the bride sat on a golden chair covered with a soft animal skin. Her head was covered by a light yellow silk veil that fell loosely in folds like an Arab burnoose. A wreath of ferns and gardenias held it in place. Her dress, which she had made herself, was translucent light yellow with long silk tassels. She was barefooted and held in her hand a single white gardenia. All the women sat beside her—friends, mother, and the groom's mother. On the other side of the curtain, seated on a silver chair, sat the groom with all the men around him. According to Sabaean lore, the woman is symbolized by the sun, and the man by the moon. In this it differs from most Neo-Pagan traditions.

After a while, Odun Arechaga appeared, dressed in white satin priest's garb and a large white cap. He held a long white feather in one hand, and in the other a beautiful sistrum, an ancient musical instrument. Odun spoke of the Am'n. He then told a story. It was a pre-Hellenic myth that forms much of the basis for the Orphic mysteries, often called the Pelasgian creation myth. It went something like this:

"In the beginning the goddess Eurynome, mother of all things, arose naked from chaos, not finding a place upon which to stand. Moving through space she grabbed hold of the north wind and, catching that gust that moved behind her as she turned, she rubbed both winds between her hands to create the great cosmic serpent Ophion.

"No sooner had life breathed into his nostrils and he saw those divine limbs than did he lust to couple with her. But the action of time was slower for him than Eurynome. Whilst he still saw the divine naked matrix she in fact had metamorphosed into a dove and had laid a large silver egg that shone with divine eminence.

"Ophion, desiring to satisfy his lust, wrapped himself around this egg seven times. But so tightly did he coil that the egg split in two!

"Out tumbled a heaven of a thousand suns and moons without number. Planets and comets, nebulae and galaxies of stars!

"Ophion, stupefied and proud, boasted to the very plenum of his creation. He gorged himself on the self-adulation of genetrix and claimed the sole authorship in creation. He looked down upon Eurynome as a mere functionary of his great work.

"Instead, Eurynome bruised his head with her heel, and kicked out his teeth for this presumption. She split his sex as male and female and placed him on the many thousand worlds he created so that in time he can justify and merit that position he once had.

"Since then it seems that all male seeks female so as to regain a fragment of his other half, and somewhat nostalgically we are awed with the expanse of the night heaven, looking out there knowing not where we have come."[32]

The meaning of marriage is the reuniting of these two halves. To achieve this unification, both partners must die symbolically, they must abandon their individualities and become one. This death and rebirth, then, was the ritual we would witness. And we would do more than witness it, for Odun said that there could be no "observers" present but only those who were willing to participate fully in the rite. Those who did not wish to participate were asked to leave. No one left.

Odun began to shake the sistrum and to move in and out beneath the columns. He gave one candle to the bride and one to the groom. He told them to stand if they still wished to be united. The mothers of the pair stood with the bride, the fathers stood with the groom. The room was darkened. The temple orchestra played dark Middle Eastern themes intensely and rhythmically. There was a predominance of bells and drums. Suddenly, Odun pulled down the silken dividing curtain. It fell on top of the pair, covering them. Odun wrapped the curtain around them. He led them around the pillars in a slow dance, then down a flight of stairs and into a ceremonial chamber. There, out of sight, the couple did various rituals which we did not see. Meanwhile we danced circle dances.

Then the temple priests strewed barley and rice in patterns across the temple floor. While the music continued, the pair, still bundled together, was led up the stairs and through and around the pillars. They were taken into another chamber for divinations, and finally, into a third room where a bed waited, covered by elaborate spreads. They were left alone to consummate the marriage while, outside, the women danced together to send energy to the bride and the men danced together to send energy to the groom. Then we waited while a temple dancer, the one I had seen work with Odun several days before, danced for us with graceful, sensual movements. After a time, the couple opened the door and emerged. All the women danced with the groom and all the men with the bride.

Then the feast began, and what a feast it was! The bride and groom sat at either end of a long table covered with a cloth. Young priests, dressed in white, brought forth a large cauldron that stood on a tripod. With great ceremony they threw spinach and romaine lettuce into the cauldron from large straw baskets. To the sound of cymbals and drums, lemons were ceremoniously squeezed, eggs were shelled and tossed into the mixture, along with anchovies and salt. The priests poured vinegar and oil from large carafes. Finally, one of the young priests rolled up his long sleeves, thrust his arms deep into the cauldron, and tossed the enormous salad. Odun took a lettuce leaf and gave it to the bride, who approved it. Then all the guests dug in with their hands.

That was merely the beginning. It was followed by a procession of courses—vegetables, fish, beef, and fowl—from shrimp in sauces, deviled eggs, and stuffed clams to plates of stuffed grape leaves, sweet fried plantains, pita bread with various dips, tomatoes and peppers, and platters of pigeons, oysters, chickens, and geese. Each set of dishes had been prepared by the priests; they appeared with the flourish of cymbals and drums, and each course was washed down with a strong, foamy punch. In the midst of the banquet came the ritual meal of the bride and groom, and in contrast to our feast, it was simple. Two fish were broiled and served with parsley. Dessert included carrot cakes, wedding cakes and puddings, honeycombs dripping in honey, rows of papayas, persimmons, pomegranates, figs, and dates.

During the feast I came across a bowl of enormous goose eggs. I picked one up and gazed at it, to remind myself later that this had been a feast out of a fantasy. Finally, I could contain myself no longer. I walked up to Odun and said, "This is the most amazing feast I have ever seen, barring the banquet scene in Fellini's *Satyricon.*"

Odun gave me a wry smile and said with a touch of affected humorous contempt, "Remember *Satyricon* was *merely* a movie."

The Sabaean Religious Order is located at 3221 Sheffield Street, Chicago, Illinois 60657. There are also small chapters located in Ohio, Philadelphia, San Francisco, and Fort Lauderdale. There are regular weekly services at the Chicago Temple. The Temple has been furnished with a blend of Egyptian and Saracenec decor, with Hathorian columns. Odun has continued his own research, traveling to Egypt and Greece, to study the inscriptions on the walls of the temples at Edfu, Denderas, Abydos, and Philae.

The Church of the Eternal Source

Feraferia and the Sabaean Religious Order each sprang from the vision of one person. The power of these two groups reflects the energy, charisma, and talent of their founders.

The Church of the Eternal Source (CES), a federation of Egyptian cults, stands in contrast—devoid of charismatic leadership. Instead, it centers on the power, artistry, and beauty of a culture—ancient Egypt. Involvement in CES depends on a direct personal, intellectual, and emotional encounter with the force of Egypt, with its gods, with the beauty of its art. Most members usually had such an encounter at an early age, perhaps in a library or a museum, or through a book or a film. Since relatively few people in our culture have had such a fortunate experience, the Church of the Eternal Source is very small.

Many of the founders and priesthood of CES have similar stories: early identification with ancient and classical cultures—Greek, Roman, Egyptian—and an early religious bent. Don Harrison, one of the founders of the Church of the Eternal Source, is a commercial artist whose home is decorated with exquisite hand-carved replicas of Egyptian works of art. Harrison began carving statues of gods and models of temples as a child. Later, he was converted to Catholicism and entered a Benedictine monastery. Then he rebelled, declared

Christianity "anti-life," and left the monastery a confirmed Pagan, determined to reestablish the ancient religions. Influenced by Gore Vidal's novel *Julian*, in 1967 he founded the *Julian Review*, one of the earliest Neo-Pagan journals. Believing that the ancient Egyptian religion was too esoteric for most people, he joined Michael Kinghorn in founding the Delphic Fellowship, a group devoted to Greek Paganism. In the meantime, he began a six-year project to create a full-size replica of the throne chair of Tehutimes III, hand-carved in two thousand pieces of ivory and rare woods. Finally, when the Church of the Eternal Source was established in 1970, after much study, Harrison declared himself a priest of the Egyptian god Thoth and began to reestablish the Thoth cult.

Jim Kemble had planned a career as an Episcopalian priest, but later became enamored of the classical religions of Greece and Rome. In high school he performed secret ceremonies to the old gods. He would walk to the beach in California and drop wine and bread into the sea, invoking Zeus, Poseidon, Bacchus, and Pluto. After 1970 he came upon CES, and the gods he had worshipped merged into the figure of Osiris. He began to study Egyptian history and religion and became a priest of Osiris, reviving the Osiris cult.

Elaine Amiro, a priestess of Neith, was fascinated as a child by native American and Egyptian cultures. She was attracted to the desert and at various times kept many strange animals, including iguanas, bobcats, monkeys, ocelots, and alligators. She taught Navajo children in New Mexico and studied the Navajo religion although, she told me, "as an Anglo, I was barred from learning much of the rites."

After returning to her home in Massachusetts, Amiro said, she discovered the Goddess at the end of a period when her life had "just seemed to fall apart." One day she was looking in an encyclopedia at the names of Egyptian gods and goddesses. "One name caught my attention," she wrote me, "and I kept coming back to it. I had never heard of the Goddess Neith before. I wondered why I was so attracted."

Neith, writes Amiro, was the great lady who was mother and daughter to Ra, the sun god, who "brought forth herself in primeval time, never having been created." She was the "first to give birth to anything, when nothing else had been born, not even herself."

Amiro found that her name matched Neith's numerologically, and several strange experiences convinced her that Neith was her spiritual guide. She wrote that after this discovery her creative energies seemed set free. She began to paint, to write poetry, even to carve statues. "Life has never meant more to me than when I rediscovered ancient Egypt and the Goddess. All my talents began to surface. I was amazed at the number of things I could do and do rather well." She began doing healings. Amiro, the mother of three children, teaches elementary school. She told me that she has made Egypt and other ancient cultures come alive for children.

Later she found out about the Church of the Eternal Source and established the cult of Neith at her home in West Wareham, Massachusetts. "I finally discovered who I was and what my job on earth was—to be a servant and priestess of Neith." Only after this, she said, did she really begin to live.

Harold Moss was one of those most instrumental in founding the church. One could say that CES began in fun, as a series of Egyptian costume parties originating with a group of students known as the Chesley Donovan Science Fantasy Foundation (CD). The group was formed in 1953, when Harold Moss, now secretary of CES, was in high school in California. A CES pamphlet described the Chesley Donovan Foundation as "an elitist science fiction club and atheist organization." Its members "quoted Thomas Paine and Willy Ley and Robert Heinlein, read horror comics, wore military helmets with meat cleavers implanted in them to social functions and school, and used 'normal,' 'average,' and 'Christian' as swear words."[33]

Harold Moss is a warm and compassionate man who works as an engineer in the daytime and by night lives in a house whose walls are covered with shelves of classical records. We spent a long evening talking, listening to Bach cantatas, and looking at pictures of the California desert. Harold told me that he had long been fascinated by the sophisticated cultures of the ancient Egyptians, Greeks, and Romans.

"Just precisely how I became aware of Egypt is pretty clear to me. I did a lot of reading as a child and I loved to go to the movies. I was aware of the Arabian Nights stories, and movies such as *The Thief of Baghdad*, and even the old *Cleopatra*—as corny as it was. Roman epics fascinated me.

"I remember I particularly liked the idea that ancient people wore few clothes. I thought clothes were stupid and ridiculous and even as a child I kept trying to take them off. The Hebrews always seemed to wear too many clothes, whereas the Romans and the Egyptians ran around naked, and this made a lot of sense to me as a child.

"But mainly, I was captivated by the sense of beauty of the Egyptians. I find I am using this phrase a lot these days. I was utterly captivated by this magnificently developed sense of beauty. I felt there was no possibility that anything could be wrong with a people who could manifest such beauty."

In 1954, after seeing the film *The Egyptian*, Moss went to the library and read James Breasted's *History of Egypt*. The child of Theosophists, Moss was brought up as a free thinker, and it was natural for him at the time to identify with Akhenaten and the religion of Aten, finding it to be a kind of Pagan rationalism. "I was under the spell of Breasted," Moss said, "with all his highly fictionalized accounts of Akhenaten as the lonely progressive in a world of hidebound people who were worshipping blindly, through habit. Akhenaten was the one who dared to think, to do something different, to be unusual. So, of course, he was the proper hero for an eighteen-year-old."[34]

Members of the Chesley Donovan Foundation adopted Akhenaten as their hero and began to wear ankhs. Moss pursued his interest in Egypt with his friends, who may not have taken it as seriously as he did. As the years progressed, he came to realize that he was captivated by *all* of the Egyptian religion, not just Akhenaten. By 1967 he had rebelled against Akhenaten's monotheism, declared himself a polytheist, and immersed himself in the classic cult of Horus, the god of light.

Moss and a number of friends had started a tradition of Egyptian summer costume parties in 1964. Eventually, they were scheduled to coincide with the ancient Egyptian New Year's celebration in mid-July. By 1970 Moss had come into contact with other Pagans, including Feraferia's Fred Adams and various Wiccan groups. He met Don Harrison and Sara Cunningham, a priestess of Wicca, and together they founded the Church of the Eternal Source officially on August 30, 1970. It was incorporated the next January. Sara Cunningham later left CES and returned to Wicca.

The Church of the Eternal Source considers itself to be the *refounded* religion of ancient Egypt, authentic in spirit, scholarly, and intense. An early CES leaflet proclaims:

> The Church of the Eternal Source is the refounded church of Ancient Egypt. We worship the original gods of mankind in their original names in the original manner as closely as possible. This religion produced in Ancient Egypt a golden age of peace, happiness, tranquility, and accomplishment unmatched since. . . .
>
> Nothing stands still. . . . Our work is to establish a constantly evolving synthesis of ancient and modern knowledge under the direct guidance and in direct contact with the Eternal Gods. . . .
>
> How can we reconcile a polytheistic faith to the "modern" ideas on religion? It is true that the central religious experience is unity with the universe. . . . But the distinctness of the Gods is a fact of our revelation. Like the facets of a precious jewel, each of them should be approached separately. . . . The human spirit is beautiful only when it is free. The diversity of the Gods commands a deep commitment to human diversity.[35]

But what does it mean to be authentically Egyptian today? CES understands that the answer to that question is complicated, and that it can easily be misunderstood by those who think of ancient Egypt simply in terms of pyramids, burial customs, bureaucracies, and powerful pharaohs.

The priesthood of CES sees Egypt as the first truly religious culture and to them "Egyptian" means remaining true to the spirit of the ancient religion, a spirit exemplified by three things: ecumenicism, polytheism, and the mythopoetic view.

CES encourages its students to continue any religious practice they have found meaningful in the past. "We think our general viewpoint is more meaningful, more powerful and more satisfying, but whatever of value you have found we will urge you to keep. . . . Our purpose—the purpose of true religion—is to help you become *more*; not to tell you a lot of things you have to give up, nor to insult you, nor try to terrorize you."[36]

What, then, is this more meaningful, more general viewpoint? First of all, it holds that the Egyptian gods are not "Egyptian" in any national sense of the word. CES has no ties with the present-day

Arab world. It views Egypt today as a place that has been devastated and violated by unbelievers and infidels. The sanctuaries have been desecrated; the shrines are in ruins. The Egyptian gods are seen as eternal forces, and all modern religions are simply aspects of the Egyptian view narrowly focused. For example, modern Judaism may be seen as a cult of Ra, Christianity as a cult of Amen-Ra-Harakhte constructs—personifications. . . . Do the gods exist? Yes. The conceptualization of polytheistic divinities is a useful way of explaining the kind of contact we *do* have with the transpersonal and transinfinite forces of life. These forces are beyond human conception, but to us, to people, *as though there were gods.* "Still," Moss added, "the gods are real."[39]

CES is adamantly polytheist. "Polytheism," a CES pamphlet states, "accepts a concept of Divinity based on the plurality of the Gods in human perception." What a Christian might call God, a priest of CES might call "the gods"; but both stand for the totality of divinity.

> There is surely a single source of Divinity, but this abstraction when translated into human institutions often results in the worship of the Ego, or in an enantidromia, a dualistic split, with "God" in an exalted position placed in opposition to Man and everything human. A polytheistic concept, on the other hand, can embrace the religious experiences of Monotheism and Pantheism also: we view Divinity as a balance of distinct divine vectors.[40]

In this very Jungian view, the parts of a human being are infinite. Likewise the parts of "the gods." When they are brought into harmony, health results; sickness comes when they are in disarray. In this scheme the goal of life would be to bring one's own individuality into balance with these forces, into harmony with *Ma'at*, a word the ancient Egyptians used to describe the preexisting original order of the universe.

Unlike many of the "new" religions, CES does not print its own religious books. There is an occasional pamphlet and the magazine *Khepera*, which for a time was published in the pages of *Green Egg*. But generally CES relies on the basic texts of scholarship on Egypt and the best translations of ancient texts.

If CES has one basic recommended introduction to the study of Egypt, it is Dr. Henri Frankfort's *Ancient Egyptian Religion*. Frankfort stresses that to understand Egypt we have to begin to understand the mythopoetic outlook, a totally different way of perceiving reality, and dispense with our evolutionary bias. Whereas most Westerners are used to the idea of revelations from a single God transmitting with a touch of Isis thrown in, Buddhism as a cult of Amen. "This," wrote Moss to a Protestant clergyman, "makes perfect sense, explains why men disagree, and gives us the ultimate answer to ecumenicism—freedom."[37]

The priests of the Church of the Eternal Source have often said that there is more of the truly Egyptian in Nepal, or in a Hopi pueblo, than in late Egyptian texts, which are tainted by foreign elements. CES encourages dressing in the Egyptian manner, learning hieroglyphics, using Egyptian dates and names, but at the same time it upholds the view that "the Egyptian culture we imitate was ancestral to the present culture of all Western nations," and that therefore understanding of and respect for all religious practices are beneficial.[38]

I asked Harold Moss how he looked at the gods. "I'm a Jungian introspectionist," he said. "The Egyptian gods and goddesses represent one central truth, the ancients "admitted side by side certain *limited* insights, which were held to be *simultaneously* valid, each in its own proper context." There was no single truth, no central dogma, no single coherent theory to explain reality, no one holy book. Frankfort wrote that this habit of thought, which is so unlike our own, "agrees with the basic experience of polytheism." The universe is alive with multiple forces. The question of their "unity" does not arise. There are many gods and they are immanent in nature.[41]

In addition, Frankfort writes that many of our assumptions about Egypt are incorrect. For example, it is wrong to say that Egyptian religion evolved from more primitive forms, or that modern religions evolved from Egyptian forms that were more primitive. Nor was the worship of animals and animal gods a transitional phase toward the worship of human forces. Frankfort argues that the Egyptians viewed the universe "as a rhythmic movement within an unchanging whole" and believed that only the changeless participated in divinity. Since animals, unlike humans, have no history, and since the lives of animals change little in comparison with those of humans, animals shared more in divinity, in the eternal, than did humans.

Like Frankfort, the members of CES have a view of Egypt that is very different from the popular conception, which, they are quick to point out, has been distorted by Egypt's conquerors. For example, we commonly think that in Egypt all religious power was invested in a priesthood, and that priests always functioned as intermediaries between a worshipper and the divine. But Harold Moss contends that this is a mistaken view; Egyptians had personal shrines and worshipped individually. One tenet of CES is that people should contact the gods daily. The priests are used for exceptional circumstances. Moss told me, "It's controversial whether the Egyptians were really that sacerdotal. I think they were less so than Catholics today. The religion was political, but not in the sense of a state arm to oppress. The priesthood functioned to advise in all major undertakings. It oversaw rituals for fertility, for the rising and setting of the sun. The religion had the same ethical base as the Hopi religion—the great national festivals were for the purpose of securing the bounty of nature."

Moss also told me that CES did not follow Egyptian burial customs and practices; his own travels to Egypt convinced him that those customs were conditioned by the environment of the Nile Valley and had continued to be practiced there long after the religion had faded. Most members of CES favor cremation and the return of their ashes to the earth. "The real question," Harold said, "is what of the ancient Egyptian religion is truly for all the world and not simply for the Nile Valley? What parts of this religion fit in with the life of the United States?" He concluded that these questions must be solved by practice, not dogma. "We're trying to avoid the mistake of the Christians. They started out with a whole lot of writings which they then spent the rest of their existence defending and trying to live up to."

In practice, the Church of the Eternal Source is a federation of independent cults, each led by a priest or priestess who maintains services for a particular deity—such as Horus, Osiris, Isis, Thoth, Neith, and Bast—supervises initiatory procedures of that cult, and corresponds or meets personally with those students who express interest.

Each cult is autonomous. Rituals are held separately. Most students reach CES through correspondence with one of its priests or initiates, who advise a course of study. Books and later rituals are suggested. If at a certain point a student makes a commitment to a particular deity, the study program is tailored in that direction.

The church has had no more than five to eight functioning priests and priestesses, several full initiates, about twenty serious students, fifty financial supporters, and an additional hundred on the mailing list. Since dues are twelve dollars a year, the financial resources of the church are virtually nonexistent, and expenses are paid by the priests, who work at regular jobs. The church has had functioning chapters in New York, California, and Massachusetts, and most of their activity has been the correspondence with students in the United States, Britain, Canada, and Africa. The Egyptian New Year's party continues, and has developed into an ecumenical Pan-Pagan gathering for many Neo-Pagans in California.

Religious practice in CES is centered on the personal shrine, which is created by each individual and may or may not be devoted to a particular deity. In addition to study of Egypt and worship at the shrine, members of CES are encouraged to learn psychic and divinatory arts ("Divination reminds us on a day-to-day basis that the macrocosm and the microcosm—the universe and man—are interrelated in function"), to produce works of art with Egyptian symbolism, to explore the wilderness and nature, and to involve themselves in community actions.

A church pamphlet, "Our Modern Practice of the Ancient Egyptian Religion," states:

> Tell us what you want, what you seek, and we will provide the maximum assistance possible. Our purpose is to aid each person to become her or his own Priestess or Priest, to aid each person in the attainment and fulfillment of her or his own vision and Goddess or God experiences.

The pamphlet says that the church provides information and instruction about "things Egyptian" and various occult techniques, but all from the following general standpoint: The church does not manipulate or coerce its members. "Power" is understood to mean a sense of wholeness that comes from living in harmony with the flow of the universe (Ma'at). The church does not believe that power shared is power lost, but rather that knowledge is increased as it is shared. There are no secrets. CES does not claim to teach "Ultimate Truth," which, according to the pamphlet, "is endlessly discovered for and by one's self, throughout one's existence and incarnations."[42] Moss reiterated this point by observing, "When a person assumes that his or her revelation is the only true one, it only says that this person has had very few religious revelations and hasn't realized how many there are." The pamphlet goes further:

> We enjoy different peoples' being different and do not teach sameness, conformity, or a rigidly bound system, but rather encourage diversity and "varieties of religious experience."
> We seek to help to open one to learning more and to heal the damage done by various religious and political systems that seek to degrade and use people. . . .

Harold Moss once observed that the Church of the Eternal Source faced one great hindrance as a religious organization—it lacked charismatic individuals. Its appeal has always been to intellectuals who enjoy scholarly pursuits. "My own approach to religion is intellectual," Moss told me, "and since I am writing most of the introductory letters to people, as secretary of the church, this is a stumbling block. The only people the church has gathered are those who have been captivated by this force which reaches through Egyptian art across the centuries and which seduces people. Then a person has to be driven to want to understand what sort of intellectual force produced such a culture.

"Our smallness is a source of disappointment to some of us. The number of people who are interested in ancient Egyptian religion is rather limited. But we have made a beginning." Moss became reflective and began to talk about why he has not lost his fascination with ancient Egypt. "I have always been wrapped up with the idea of permanence and commitment. And Egypt was a very conservative society, where obligations were often life-long, and where permanence and commitment were stressed. In our society, we often collide with one another like molecules in a gas; we interact briefly to form submolecular species and then go our separate ways. This is all part of the unfolding of the universal life force to understand itself, and I understand this intellectually, but it bothers me. Perhaps Egypt becomes, for me, a kind of utopia, where things never change."[43]

If the Church of the Eternal Source remains small, its importance for Neo-Paganism is disproportionately great, for it emphasizes more clearly than any other Neo-Pagan group a commitment to diversity, multiplicity, and freedom. Writing to *Green Egg* several years ago, Moss summed up the essence of CES:

> Many people I think are disappointed in us because we are not the most mysterious of the mysteries. They think Egypt was like that, from the testimony of her conquerors. But Egypt was actually one of the most uncomplicated places that ever was, and religion was no exception. . . . The power of Egypt was closeness to the Earth. Her religious symbols were all of the Earth. Her religious acts were all celebrations of the cycles of the Earth. That is what I/we mean when we say: "We are all Egyptians." The true living "Egyptians" are the American Indians. . . .
>
> Many today seek the true Gods, the Egyptian wisdom, in dark rooms, arcane studies, ferocious secrecy. If they reach their goal they will find themselves standing in the sun under a clear blue sky, on the banks of a river—5000 years ago—singing and dancing for joy, heart brimming with love, mind afire with certainty of the harmony between the Gods and Man, of the brotherhood and sisterhood of all life.[44]

In 1985, Harold Moss told me, "For us, there is no change in our operations. We are a little more active now than then, and we have some new people. Philosophically we are (being Egyptians) unchanged, except that our mailing address zip+4 is 91510–7091."

Odinism, Asatru, and Norse Paganism

When *Drawing Down the Moon* appeared in 1979, one of its most glaring oversights was the omission of Norse Paganism. While I had received many publications relating to Odinism—*The Runestone, The Raven Banner*, and others—I found myself in a quandary. Some of the information I received was from groups genuinely seeking a Norse Pagan path, but there were other groups clearly using Odinist symbols and mythologies as a front for right-wing and even Nazi activities. I even had a neighbor, around the corner from me, who was a leading member of a Nazi political party and who was communicating his religious ideas in the forum of the

Green Egg. His cramped apartment on Ninety-third Street was crammed with books—one wall was filled with Nazi regalia and literature; the other wall was filled with books on the occult, with particular emphasis on Norse and German (and Vedic) mythology.

In addition, the common notion within much of the Pagan movement was that Norse Paganism was filled with such people. And since the Odinist Pagan community is generally more conservative in its values and ideas *anyway*, stressing concepts like family, courage, and warrior virtues, it was easy to become confused. In the end I just gave up, deciding it was a can of worms I just didn't want to open.

But Pagans interested in Norse mythology just won't go away. There are serious seekers, there are organizations that are flourishing, there is some good scholarship, and there are a host of publications with a Norse and Germanic orientation. While many of the values may not be my own, it is important that this path be represented fairly. It is also important to remember that there are even places where indigenous Norse Paganism continues. For example, public Pagan worship was outlawed in Iceland over nine hundred years ago, but the ancient restrictions were repealed in 1874. In 1972, Nordic Paganism was officially recognized as a legitimate and legal religion.

The problem of being confused with Nazism is one that almost all Odinists have to confront. As Alice Rhoades, an editor of *Boreas*, a journal of Northern European Paganism, said to me, "You will always find fringe people attracted to Paganism. Just as Witches have to contend with the occasional news report of weirdos torturing animals and calling themselves Witches, we in Norse Paganism have our own fringe types. There's been a general assumption that the Norse religion is connected with the Nazis because the Nazis used Norse symbols. And Neo-Nazis sometimes get attracted to Odinism, because the trappings are the same." And Prudence Priest, the editor of *Yggdrasil*, wrote me, "How are we ever to reclaim the swastika—symbol of both Thor's hammer and the wheel of the sun (and dating back thousands of years before Hitler's perversion of it)." Rhoades told me of putting on a Norse ritual at a large Pagan festival and finding that many who came to it were wary that it "would be negative," an impression that was only dispelled by the ritual itself.

As with Neo-Pagans from all cultures, people attracted to Scandinavian and Germanic forms of Paganism often come to it as part of a search for their own ancestral roots. Alice Rhoades told me, "My family is

Scandinavian, and as I was growing up, my mother read me the Norse myths, and they remained my favorite ones." After attending an extremely conservative Christian college in Texas, Rhoades decided she was not a Christian. She studied different religions, became interested in the occult, and, through a poetry teacher, began learning about Paganism. "The minute I realized Paganism was the religion for me, and that it was OK, and not weird, I *immediately* went back to the Norse gods, which had been in the back of my head all this time. There was never a question. I just knew. I thought, 'I can really believe in these guys again!' Perhaps it was the way I was raised, or perhaps I just had these images in my head."

The largest and most successful organization promoting Norse Paganism in the United States is the Asatru Free Assembly (AFA), which was started by Stephen McNallen in 1971. "I had wandered out of high school in rural Texas," McNallen told me, "and had shaken off Catholicism because it conflicted with my basic instincts. I sampled many religions, read about Wicca, looked into Crowley, but none of it clicked. Then I ran across a novel about the Vikings. In retrospect, it wasn't a great novel, but the Vikings, in contrast with the monks, were real; they were alive. They had all the intensity and courage. It was clicking into something I already believed, but it was still awhile until I became aware that you can choose your gods."

McNallen says that many of the main Odinist groups (the Odinist Fellowship, the Odinist Committee in England, Asatruarfolks in Iceland, and the AFA) started within a very few months of each other, with no knowledge of each other's existence. Perhaps it was "a wind blowing through the World Tree," he said. The AFA publishes *The Runestone*, a quarterly journal, as well as assorted books and tapes on the religion, mythology, rituals, and values of Asatru. Every year the AFA holds an annual three-day festival called the Althing. It is held in a rural setting and is filled with rituals, fellowship, music, and feasting. The AFA also has a system of guilds to encourage fellowship and the sharing of skills: the artists' guild; the brewing guild; the warrior guild; the computer/ shamanism guild; the writers' guild; the sewing guild; even the aerospace technology guild.

Some people involved in Scandinavian, Germanic, and Norse Paganism prefer the word Asatru to Odinist (since Odinist refers to only one in a large pantheon of deities). Asatru means "belief in the gods" in Old

Norse, or, more correctly, loyalty to the Aesir—one of the two races or groups of gods in Norse mythology. The other group is the Vanir. The Aesir consists of gods many people will find familiar: Odin, who is often seen as the high god, a kind of All Father principle; his wife, Frigga; his son Thor; Tyr; Balder; and many others. The Aesir, in Scandinavian myths, are a race of sky gods. They are generally the more aggressive and outgoing, the movers and shakers. The Vanir consist of the gods of the earth, of agriculture, fertility, and death. The most well known are Frey and Freya (the terms are somewhat similar to Wiccan notions of the Lord and Lady, and there are some people involved in Norse Paganism who have concentrated on the Vanir). The Vanir also include Nerthus and Njord. The myths tell of a time way in the past when the Aesir and the Vanir warred. Later, the two pantheons merged. Most people involved in Odinism and Norse Paganism are very polytheistic, preferring to honor all the gods, Aesir and Vanir.

On one level the gods are examples and models—inspirations, self-aware personifications of the forces of nature. On another level, McNallen says, "they are a numinous logic-defying reality, something apprehended only by means of symbols, something that speaks to us on deeper levels where words are inadequate. Studying the Gods, we can all add richness and power to our religious lives by tapping this ancient, non-verbal wisdom."

In a pamphlet titled "What is Asatru," McNallen describes the spiritual beliefs of Asatru as:

> We believe in an underlying all-pervading divine energy or essence which is generally hidden from us because it surpasses our direct understanding. We further believe that this spiritual reality is interdependent with us—that we affect it, and it affects us.
>
> We believe that this underlying divinity expresses itself in the forms of the Gods and Goddesses. Stories about these deities are like a sort of code, the mysterious "language" through which the divine reality speaks to us.[45]

The gods are honored in daily rituals, and there are seasonal celebrations on the solstices and equinoxes and other ancient festival days. Some have told me that rituals are often sparser than those in Wicca. There are some groups that do circle rituals, using different symbols for the elements—perhaps a sickle or cakes for North, a spear or rune wand for East, a sword for South, a horn for the West. Many groups do not find the circle form of ritual appropriate. Some groups celebrate six of the eight traditional Pagan sabbats, having a six-spoked wheel of the year, rather than the eight of many Pagan traditions.

Whenever you talk to people who are involved with Odinism, they will carefully distinguish themselves from other forms of Neo-Paganism, and only a few of them interact with the larger Pagan community, go to festivals, or engage in ecumenical activities. Part of this is because they do not see themselves in any way as part of a universal movement; in fact they do not believe in universal religions. Stephen McNallen has written that the various branches of humanity have different ways of looking at the world and that this is natural. McNallen wrote to me:

> We're not eclectic. You won't find tarot or astrology or I Ching incorporated into Asatru—not because they're not valid or powerful, but because they aren't *ours*. This isn't to say of course that an Odinist can't utilize these systems as an individual, but they're not a part of Asatru.
>
> A second difference is that we are so intimately involved with the idea of ancestry as to be almost a "Norse Shinto."

This is where it gets complicated and problematic. Many of the Odinists I spoke with and much of the literature I read put a heavy emphasis not only on ancestry but on a belief in the primacy of genetics, as well as a belief that certain aspects of the soul are transmitted down the family line, that reincarnation comes within race, tribe, and family. In looking at the Jungian idea of archetypes, several articles in *The Runestone* have observed that Jung's original idea was that these archetypes were not culturally transmitted but inherited genetically.

One member of the AFA told me, "We are not racists, but we are racially aware. I look at my children's red hair and freckles and think how many generations it took for them to get that way. I want them to be the same color as me." To which I refrained from replying, "Suppose it was just a random mutation?" A woman in AFA told me that she had never had a black person apply to be in her group, but she would wonder why they weren't interested in "their own religious roots." This is completely at odds with, for example, Isaac Bonewits' Druid group. "Most of the black people in the group have more Celtic blood than I do," he observed. Speaking personally, if religious impulses and archetypes are transmitted genetically, I would never have been influenced by Athena and Artemis, and this book would never have been written. As David James, also a member of the AFA, once observed to me, "It's rather funny, there are a whole bunch of Jews in the Celtic groups and a whole bunch of us Celts in the Norse groups."

Despite observations like these, members of the AFA believe that duty to one's ancestors and kin is a holy duty that comes first. Blood *is* thicker than water. Thus an AFA member would score low on Kohlberg's morality test, where morality is rated by how far you put the good of all people above the good of those you are personally tied to. "This way of looking at things is contrary to the dogma of this day," McNallen observes, but he contends, "We know in our hearts . . . Ancestry is better than schemes which would deny these truths and propose a formless, alienated and unnatural universalism."[46]

In talking about Asatru as a very ancestral religion, with bonds that are genetic, "even paragenetic," McNallen concedes that "it can easily be misinterpreted." "How do you prevent misinterpretations?" I asked. Partly by explaining over and over again, he said. "We used to get people who thought we were out to save the white race. But we are not for putting anyone down. We are simply for the spirituality of our own people. This is a real religion. It is not a front for any political group." McNallen says that while a lot of Odinists in the past were attracted for political and cultural reasons, a real religious development has been taking place with interest in magic, ritual, and runes.

But while the AFA stresses the religious aspects of Norse Paganism and downplays the political, some Odinist organizations have a different view. The Odinist Fellowship, for example, devotes much of its journal, *The Odinist*, to political and philosophical articles on subjects ranging from attacks on liberalism to a defense of the original goals of apartheid. Instead of avoiding these political discussions, the Odinist Fellowship meets them head on. It is frankly racist, although they would probably prefer the term "racialist." One article had these words: "The most distinguishable feature of Odinism is that for the first time a religion has declared itself founded upon the concept of race, with its correlation to culture and civilization. Without race there is nothing; therefore our first duty is a study of race and the significance of Aryan people to world history."[47] Thankfully, you don't find these kinds of sentiments in AFA literature.

If there are differences between Neo-Pagans and Odinists in regard to beliefs about ancestry, politics, and race, there are also some differences in values. A leaflet describing the values of the AFA lists them as follows:

> Strength is better than weakness
> Courage is better than cowardice
> Joy is better than guilt
> Honor is better than dishonor
> Freedom is better than slavery
> Kinship is better than alienation
> Realism is better than dogmatism
> Vigor is better than lethargy
> Ancestry is better than universalism.

In general, Odinism attracts people who are more politically conservative than the majority of Neo-Pagans. They are uncomfortable with feminism, anarchism, and diversity in sexuality and life style. Of course, there are also conservatives in the general Neo-Pagan community. But all in all, there's less vegetarianism and more alcohol as opposed to other mind-altering methods. There's a stress on martial arts and on warrior values. (The Vikings are seen as freedom fighters, not robbers.) The AFA has, in the past, advertised in *Soldier of Fortune*. McNallen disagreed with my label "conservatism," saying that modern society didn't have much to conserve. "We are seeing the decline of the West," he said, "we are living in the ruins." Still, as Ariel Bentley, a woman in the AFA, put it to me, "I'm no longer a bleeding heart liberal," and Alice Rhoades said, "There's stress on independence, courage, on not being pacifistic. The idea that life is a struggle and that's fun, so go out and *do* it. It's definitely not a meditative religion." I asked her if she agreed with those ideas, and she said: "If someone came for me in an alley, I'd rather wipe 'em out, than rehabilitate them. In the 60s it was uncool to have those thoughts and I repressed them. But I realized I was lying to myself."

In describing the most recent Althing, Ariel Bentley described workshops, presentations by the guilds, rituals, feasting, songs around the campfire, and a sumbel—a Germanic ritual in which a drinking horn filled with mead is passed around and each person toasts, recites a poem or song. It is a place where the psychic storehouse of a group can be brought into the present. "There were songs, stories, prayers, bragging and boasting." "Bragging and boasting?" I queried. "Yes," she said. "Bragi is the god of poetry. All my life," she said, "I was trained not to blow my own horn. But in Asatru, it is considered fine, a way of linking oneself to one's ancestors."

Like most Neo-Pagans, Odinists do not believe in sin and regard guilt as a destructive rather than useful concept. In an article called "Joy is better than Guilt," McNallen writes that guilt is a tool for forging a brave new world, filled with docile, interchangeable units. In Asatru, the gods inspire one to a different view.

> Odin, pragmatically breaking the rules to safeguard the worlds of gods and men; Thor, indulging his appetites without shame or fear; Frey and Freya, reveling in healthy sexuality; these are powerful, liberating models casting off the chains of restraint. By invoking them into our lives we can experience the joy of existence in a world where strength, ambition, competence, and pleasures are not fettered with alien, life-denying bonds.[48]

While Odinists tend to be more conservative than most Neo-Pagans, their religion puts them at odds with the mainstream conservative culture. Stephen McNallen has written that the religion of Asatru is under assault by Christian fundamentalists. "After a period of religious tolerance that has lulled us for several decades—a tolerance that has protected both the best and worst in American behavior—it is apparent that we are entering a time when we of Asatru are going to meet greater and greater resistance from the powers that rule this country." McNallen notes that there is some irony in this situation, because "Many of the values championed by those who would oppress us are values with which we can readily identify, such as a strengthened family, less bureaucratic intervention in the life of the individual, and the rest. Unfortunately," he adds, "it was the followers of the pale Galilean who coopted the movement back to traditional values more in keeping with those of our Folk—and we, who follow the gods that hallowed those values, stand to be crushed, if the new inquisitors have their way."[49]

Another distinction between much of Neo-Paganism and Odinism is the relative position of male and female gods. In fact, many Pagans simply dismiss Norse Paganism as "patriarchal." "People ask me, 'How can you be a woman in Asatru?'" Alice Rhoades told me. "It is true that there are more patriarchal aspects, after all, the head god is Odin. But I would call it 'balanced,' with a certain leaning toward male gods. It is true more men have been attracted to it than women, but that seems to be changing. And while some people in Asatru have traditional role models in mind, I have not found men to be hostile to me as a woman. I have only had encouragement, and I am not a traditional woman. I'm independent, I'm unmarried, I'm an actress. Remember that in ancient Norse culture, women had much more freedom than in Greece or Rome. Women could own property, divorce their husbands and take back their dowry. It's true the most visible gods are Odin and Thor, and they have warrior values. They are very macho gods—so they appeal to men and more men join the group and people say it's a male religion. But I'm hoping more women will become visible."

Women in Odinism also reminded me that the Norse goddesses are powerful figures. Freya, for example, may be a goddess of love and procreation, but she is also a warrior, a goddess of passion and change. Writes Stephen McNallen in *The Runestone*:

> Lest we fall into the snare of thinking of the Lady of the Vanir in the somewhat predictable female roles of sex goddess or promoter of the perpetual pregnancy, we must remember her fiercer side. . . . When we recall that she chooses half the battle-slain, when we reflect on her links to the valkyries, when we consider her many parallels with Odin, we are led to conclude that Freya's martial abilities must be formidable. . . . Her message is simple: women too, can be strong, assertive, and full of fight. As Frey tells men that they can be lovers AND fighters, Freya says the same thing to women.[50]

Alice Rhoades and Maddy McNallen, Stephen's wife, both told me there is beginning to be a determined effort to foster the role of the goddesses in Norse Paganism, to "redress the balance."

Another organization devoted to Norse and Teutonic Paganism is the Heathen Way in San Francisco. They have a sacred grove called Wotanwald; they put on seasonal gatherings and publish *Yggdrasil*, a journal of Heathen culture, ethos, and mythology. *Yggdrasil* describes Odinism/neo-Heathenism as a religion with a deeply felt spiritual link to the land, the forests, the seas, our ancestors, our successors, and to the celebration of the life experience. Its principles are honesty, honor, the value of one's word, keeping a healthy environment, placing principle above gain, and leading a worthy life. While many Norse and Odinist groups have kept to themselves, finding their ways too different from most of the Pagan movement, Prudence Priest, editor of *Yggdrasil*, has written extensively in Pagan periodicals.

Recent Notes

Perhaps the main difference in the Pagan movement today, as a whole, compared to the movement that existed in the middle and late 1970s is that, at that time, the organizations described in this chapter, as well as CAW and the Reformed Druids, were the main influences in creating a Neo-Pagan consciousness. These organizations set the terms of the debate and led the discussions that were developed in Pagan journals. The leaders of these organizations (with the exception of the Sabaean Order which never really participated in the broader Neo-Pagan community) developed many of the key concepts and theories that have become generally accepted.

Today, this has all changed. These organizations, those that still exist, do not participate in the continuing Pagan dialogue. Instead, Wiccan organizations have come to the foreground as the primary form of Neo-Paganism in America and these organizations now dominate the discussion. It's important to remember, however, that the reason the Pagan movement in the United States is so rich and varied and presents such a unique perspective to the world is primarily because of the non-Wiccan influences that were so dominant in earlier years.

10

A Religion from the Future— The Church of All Worlds

Someday, people may speak of the last two thousand years as "The Christian Interlude."

—Tom Williams, priest,
Church of All Worlds

My first meeting with the Church of All Worlds took place on a cold day in late October 1975 in a small house in a predominantly black suburb of St. Louis. Eight or nine people sat around a long low table that was covered with large stacks of freshly printed pages. The house was decorated simply—beds and sofas covered with Indian print spreads, cushions on the floor, posters on the wall.

In a large enclosure of hand-carved wood and glass, four reptiles (rock pythons and boa constrictors) reposed quietly. A yellow flag lay draped over the top of the cage. "Don't tread on me," it stated, with its coiled serpent below. On a shelf, toy dinosaurs stood amid a collection of fossils, seashells, rocks, and bones.

The sound of friendly chatter mingled with the rustling of pages, the steady firing of a stapling machine, and the occasional crunching of popcorn, which was being passed around in a large bowl. On the inside of the doors of the house, only a few feet from shelves littered with books and records, a sign read, "Did you remember to dress?"

The sign was quite appropriate. Only one person in the room was wearing any clothes, a fact that didn't seem particularly noticeable after a few minutes. The house was very warm, and undressing seemed to be one way to be comfortable. But everyone—dressed or undressed—was engaged in the business of the day, which was sorting, collating, stapling, and mailing the seventy-fourth issue of *Green Egg*. This peculiar journal had become one of the most important sources of information on Neo-Paganism, and until recently it played a key role in facilitating communication among Neo-Pagan groups.

The *Green Egg* Mailing Party was an eight-times-yearly event of the Church of All Worlds. This particular party lasted for two days, with people wandering in and out for a few hours here and there.

Now, describing a religion founded by a prophet or under the leadership of a central charismatic figure is easy. The words of the founder and the praises of the followers are the story. But since most Neo-Pagan religions—certainly the most interesting ones—are leaderless groups with multiple voices, even contradictory positions, it is difficult to describe them without leading readers down an easy path where they can all too quickly slip on their own assumptions. By starting out with a description of a nude gathering, even a business-like one, I may already have led you in a wrong direction.

Almost every time (and there is one notable exception to this) an outsider has attempted to write up the Church of All Worlds (CAW), he or she has misunderstood and misrepresented it, probably because CAW refuses to fit into any easy set of boxes. Mircea Eliade refers to CAW briefly in his essay "The Occult and the Modern World":

> A rather unusual sect, even judged by the standards of the contemporary understanding of the occult, is the Church of All Worlds, founded in 1961, by two students at Westminster College in Missouri, after reading *Stranger in a Strange Land*, by the noted science fiction writer Robert A. Heinlein. The members greet each other with the phrase "Thou art God."[1]

Hans Holzer, a popular writer on the occult, implied that there was an unfortunate amount of controversy and bickering in *Green Egg*, and he disparaged the group for basing its vision "on the work of a prolific and popular science fiction writer" and "not on any ancient tradition."[2] A Neo-Pagan group that takes its myths from the past seems obvious. One that looks to the future is something else again. But Holzer's criticism is simply not valid. In fact, science fiction and fantasy probably come closer than any other literature to systematically exploring the central concerns of Neo-Pagans and Witches. Such writers of science fiction and fantasy are bound less than any others by the political, sexual, and racial mores of their society. In recent years some science fiction writers (notably women—Ursula K. Le Guin, Joanna Russ, Pamela Sargent, Vonda McIntyre[3]) have even gotten beyond the traditional sexism of the genre to look anew at men and women. Science fiction has been the literature of the visionary; it has been able to challenge preconceived notions about almost everything, while at the same time attending to fundamental questions of the age. No wonder, then, that not only do many Pagans and Witches read science fiction, but some of them write it. In my travels I came across four well-known science fiction and fantasy writers who were members of Neo-Pagan groups. Of the four, only one—Robert Anton Wilson—was public. The remaining three did not wish to have their identities disclosed.

There has always been a relationship between science fiction and the occult, but it has often baffled serious scholars. Mircea Eliade writes: "The literature of *fantasy* and the fantastic, especially in science fiction , is much in demand, but we still do not know its intimate relationship with the different occult traditions."[4] Neo-Pagans often mentioned science fiction. "Science fiction/fantasy readers tend to think of things in terms of the galaxy as a whole," one wrote to me, "rather than think in a local or national sense." Another said, "Readers are usually more acutely aware of the problems of ecology, utopia (and dystopia), and changes brought about by technological advancement."

"Science fiction," Isaac Bonewits told me, "is the one element in my life most responsible for my not being a racist or a cultural bigot," and Aidan Kelly said, "Science fiction is the major literature of the most intelligent people in this country at this point. The only authors who are coping with the complexity of modern reality are those who are changing the way people perceive reality, and these are authors who are tied in with science fiction."

Science fiction might even be called a form of divination. Certainly history offers many examples (H. G. Wells, Jules Verne) where such divination was accurate. Robert Scholes in his essays on science fiction, *Structural Fabulation*, writes: "To live well in the present, to live decently and humanely, *we must see into the future*," and he observes that good science fiction allows us to leap from worlds we know to quite different worlds and thereby illuminate our situation. This is done through the techniques of defamiliarization and estrangement. Using such techniques, we are able to see the universe anew. Scholes, from the halls of academia, utters pure Neo-Pagan sentiments:

> We are now so aware of the way that our lives are part of a patterned universe that we are free to speculate as never before. Where anything may be true—sometime, someplace—there can be no heresy. And where the patterns of the cosmos itself guide our thoughts so powerfully, so beautifully, we have nothing to fear but our own lack of courage. There are fields of force around us that even our finest instruments of thought and perception are only beginning to detect. The job of fiction is to play in these fields. . . .[5]

The Church of All Worlds has called science fiction "the new mythology of our age" and an appropriate religious literature. Tom Williams, a former editor of *Green Egg* and a priest of the church, wrote that science fiction could evoke a new age by generating new metaphors and an infinite array of new possibilities. Reality is "a construct," a product of unspoken beliefs and assumptions that seem unalterable simply because they are never questioned. "It is from the oppression of overwhelming consensual reality constructs that the mythology of science-fiction/fantasy so frees us. It does this in two ways: one, the most obvious, by offering us alternate reality constructs, and two, by revealing to us the *way* in which realities are made." The true function of myth, he said, is not simply to explain the world in some simple form that a "primitive" can understand, but like art, music, and poetry, to *create* the world. Williams argued that both Neo-Paganism and speculative fiction were based on the expansion of human consciousness and both arose at the same time.

Today, he wrote, we have a rare privilege—to choose consciously the myths we wish to live by and to know "that the world which is evoked is dependent on the mythic structure of a people and can literally be anything from the oil and bombers and pollution of the Pentagon and Kremlin to the Magic Wood of Galadriel."[6]

The Church of All Worlds has been called everything from a "subculture science-fiction Grok-flock'"[7] to a "bunch of crazy hippie freaks." But the real origins of CAW lead back to a small group of friends who, along with untold numbers of middle-class high-school and college students in the late 1950s and early 1960s, became infatuated with the romantic, heroic, compelling right-wing ideas of Ayn Rand. It is a sign of the peculiarity of North American consciousness that thousands of young students, at one time or another, have become possessed by her novels—*Atlas Shrugged*, *The Fountainhead*, and *Anthem*.

Jerome Tucille, in his witty, tongue-in-cheek tour of the libertarian right, *It Usually Begins with Ayn Rand*, could not have been more precise in his choice of title. He noted that Rand's works were particularly appealing "to those in the process of escaping a regimented religious background." Despite the author's rigid philosophy of Objectivism, in her fiction she stirred a libertarian impulse and *Atlas Shrugged* became a "New Marxism of the Right."

> If Marxism, with its promise of a proletarian utopia, was tailor-made to the aspirations of the working-class crusader, Objectivism and its ethic of self-sufficiency and achievement was intoxicating to the sons and daughters of the middle class, graduating from college at the end of the Eisenhower era.[8]

It was easy to be swept up by the intense struggles of Rand's artists and creators, who stood larger than life, battling government and bureaucracy. Recently Karl Hess, the former speechwriter for Barry Goldwater who later became an anarchist on the left, observed to me, "At a time when no one made arguments, when intelligence was undervalued, when smart kids were looked down on, Ayn Rand seemed to say to them, 'You're important.' She seemed to have a philosophical system with a rigorous structure at a time when no one wanted to talk sensibly at all. She scratched that peculiarly American strain—ironically, the same strain scratched by Emma Goldman. She was appealing, even if her philosophy was better expressed by others, such as Max Stirner, and her writing style seemed to come straight from Jack London."

The novels of Rand were seeds that sprouted and bore many strange fruits, most of which must have horrified her. CAW is certainly such an example. It is a religion, and Rand has consistently been intensely atheist. It has long considered ecology the supreme religious activity and study, and the harmony of human beings in the biosphere the goal of highest priority. Ayn Rand, on the other hand, has praised pollution as a sign of human progress. Her heroines have wept with joy at billboards and saluted smokestacks, regarding them as a sign of the human struggle against nature. She calls people concerned about ecology "antilife" and "antimind," and condemns Native Americans as "savages." She has even called smoking cigarettes a moral duty that aids the capitalist system.[9]

The ironies of life are many, I thought, after speaking to Karl Hess, a renegade from Rand as well as from Goldwater. He was building, by hand, a solar-heated house in West Virginia. I wondered about the founders of CAW, some of whom voted for Goldwater in 1964, the same year I was arrested on the steps of Berkeley's Sproul Hall. CAW can only be understood within a broad libertarian framework, but one that is hard to define within our traditional political notions of "left" and "right."

CAW began in 1961 when a young group of high-school friends, including Lance Christie, later a priest of CAW, began discussing the novels of Ayn Rand. Six months later, now college students, they began to explore the self-actualization concepts of Abraham Maslow. In the beginning, as Christie described these discussions, they were "dialogue/fantasies over the ills of the world," and, much as in the plot of *Atlas Shrugged*, these friends fantasized "a withdrawal of creative, unenculturated people to a remote place to await Armageddon." Christie wrote, "After Babylon had fallen again, we saw ourselves as coming forth to rebuild the world along rational lines."[10]

After Christie entered Westminster College in Fulton, Missouri, he began ESP experiments with a new acquaintance, Tim Zell, who later played a key role in the formation of CAW.

Maslow's attraction stemmed from his theories about the characteristics of those he called "self-actualizers"—people who perceived reality more clearly than others. They accepted themselves without unnecessary guilt or shame, and tolerated—even gravitated toward—the new, the ambiguous, and the unknown. They were spontaneous and natural, with a sense of humor that was neither hostile nor sick. They tended to be independent and at ease in solitude; they were ethical; they had social feeling; they had a wide perspective, a sense of wonder, and a sense of the mysterious. But Maslow's "self-actualizers" were, he found, alienated from ordinary convention. They felt detached from the values of the culture. Maslow referred to such persons as "aliens in a foreign land,"[11] a phrase that struck a deep chord in Christie, Zell, and their friends.

Combining Maslow with Rand (some might think it a most unlikely combination), Christie envisioned an educational institution that would produce "Ayn Rand heroes, alias Maslonian self-actualizers."[12] In Rand's capitalist utopia of *Atlas Shrugged*, brilliant industrialists, creative artists, and pirates against the poor waited until the dross of civilization killed themselves off, or, more correctly, became so weakened that a takeover was possible. But at Westminster College, with the introduction of Maslow, Rand's right-wing utopia got turned on its head: change the system, educate for intelligence, and Randian heroes and heroines can be the norm.

In the next year the group read Robert Heinlein's *Stranger in a Strange Land*. Christie later wrote that reading the novel, he was "seized with an ecstatic sense of recognition. It is as if I had found in completed form the ideas which I was trying to jell on my own."[13]

The novel tells of Valentine Michael Smith, who was born of Earthparents on Mars and raised there by aliens. When he returns to Earth as an alien, Smith looks at the planet with amazement. For example, he wonders if the grass minds being walked on since, after all, "these live." In general, he expresses the philosophy of someone in tune with the universe.[14]

Only one writer has begun to comprehend the subtleties of the Church of All Worlds. He is Robert Ellwood, Jr. His book, *Religious and Spiritual Groups in Modern America*, devotes a chapter, "The Edenic Bower," to modern revivalist Neo-Pagan groups. He is, incidently, Eliade's one source. Ellwood writes of Heinlein's novel:

> The principal purpose of a Martian's life is to "grok," to intuit the "fullness" of something completely from within.
>
> When Smith was brought to Earth, he seemed at first out of place. He did not understand elementary things, yet the deep things of character and Earth's wisdom he could accurately intuit in a moment. He moves about the Earth at once guileless and wise. . . .
>
> Eventually Smith created a religion, the "Church of All Worlds," for his companions. It took the form of paradisical communities called "Nests," in which the best of both planets was brought together. In the Nests they could learn Martian, and be initiated into the lore and psychic skill of that planet. They also joyfully practiced sexual love within the family of the Nest.

Ellwood wrote that *Stranger in a Strange Land* was one of the bibles of the youth of the sixties, for in a real sense they felt they were Martians on Earth. . . .

> Childlike and mystical, lovers of beauty and harmony and magic, impatient of materialistic values and moral codes, they too seemed not to fit, almost to have dropped from another world. Many, like Smith's friends, were seeking with eager desperation an alternative life style, other modes of relationship between man and nature, and different ways of understanding the relationship of consciousness and cosmos.[15]

In *Stranger in a Strange Land* the most profound ceremony is waterbrotherhood, the sharing of water, during which each person "groks" the other's godhood and an empathic bond is formed between them. In April 1962 Zell and Christie shared water together, and during the next fall the concept of a waterbrotherhood, called Atl, emerged among this group of friends now living in Fulton, Missouri.

In a sense, the waterbrotherhoods seemed to create Maslow's self-actualizers, and the statement "Thou art God," used in Heinlein's novel, expressed what Christie and his friends had sensed in the works of Ayn Rand. They began to criticize Rand's philosophy at the many points where it conflicted with Maslow, and decided that intelligence was more important than doctrine.

The name *Atl* was said to come from an Aztec word for water that also had the esoteric meaning of "home of our ancestors." The closeness of Atl to words like *Atlas, Atlantic,* and *Atlantis* was also noted. Water was seen as an appropriate symbol of life, since the first organisms came into existence in water and water is essential to life. Atl had its own emblem, the *tiki,* based on the Caribbean water god Ruba-tiki. One Atlan called the tiki "a not-for-sale sign" to hang on one's life. Atl soon had a logbook, an inside journal called *The Atlan Annals,* and a student paper called *Atlan Torch.*

But Atl was never a formal, rigid organization. Lance Christie said the relationship of Atlans to one another was like "the ties between siblings" in a large family. They were " a group of friends around the country who shared a desire to explore human potential and social structure and to give each other emotional support"—an extended family in a world of nuclear families. "When the chips are down," wrote Lance, "the family defends and shelters its own," but there are, he added, "no 'parents' in Atl. One's own judgment maintains in their place." Atl was conceived to have no leaders and no followers. Besides being a family, it was also a dream, and Zell wrote: "We do not 'belong' to it. . . . *Atl* belongs to us, the dreamers."[16]

The small group of Atlans, never greater than a hundred, saw themselves as the promoters of alternatives that would lead to the creation of human beings with godlike potentialities. Atlans attempted to infiltrate Mensa. They concerned themselves with educational experiments, studying the Montessori system and the works of A. S. Neill. They had a strange fascination with IQ and personality tests. Just when these tests began to be adversely scrutinized by radical critics, the Atlans were using them experimentally in their search for new Atlans. Still, tests were not primary; Atlans became Atlans by the same process we have seen in regard to Pagans generally, a process of coming home, an intuition.

Atlans were, above all, survivalists. They encouraged their "members" to learn such diverse skills as "speedreading, memory training, karate, yoga, autosuggestion, set theory, logic, survival training and telepathy."[17] Atlans saw themselves as brighter, more active, more creative, more in need of stimulation and interaction, and more able to make their own rules than other people. They often considered themselves outcasts, a "leper colony," dangerous because they were uncompromising and refused to fit into the general "sociological matrix."

Politically, they were hard to define. One Atlan described himself as a "left-wing-type democrat"; another said he favored "dictatorship without oppression"; a third said she hated "the NAACP, ban-the-bombers, farm subsidies, and social 'sciences.'" Zell wrote that his dislikes included the military, missionaries, isms, labels, commercials, atomic annihilation, and "original sin." His greatest wish for the world was for the "full and controlled use of all the powers of ESP and PK for the entire human race."[18]

Atl was not revolutionary in the ordinary sense of the word; it did not proselytize, and one Atlan wrote that "the happiness of this group can be assured without harming the rest of the world." Still, Atl's reading list was filled with visionaries of diverse and contradictory stripes: Neill, Maslow, Fromm, Leary, Huxley, Heinlein, Rand, *The Realist*. Some Atlans, like Zell and Christie, had visionary goals. They had short-term aims like establishing a press, a school, a nudist colony, a coffee house. In the long term their goals were, as Lance wrote, "to work toward a world along the lines seen in those books, a world where the children of Man may walk the hills like Gods."

Others disagreed and felt Atl should have no real purpose "except to maintain communication" between friends. As Lance observed:

> Atl is not a unitary movement with a rigid dogma and a narrow, specific Cause. It is a vast, heterogeneous assemblage of ornery, cantankerous, intelligent, independent, unenculturated human beings who have an indefinable something that sets them apart and binds them together. Expecting all Atlans to agree at any given time on anything is a classic example of wild-eyed optimism.[19]

The Church of All Worlds grew out of Atl in 1967. It was conceived, according to Christie, as a "living laboratory" to work out problems in communal living, philosophy, and communication. As in Heinlein's novel, the Church had a structure of nine circles, each named for a different planet. The Church was "Tim Zell's baby,"[20] Christie wrote at one point, and much of what came to pass was the evolution of Zell's own vision, with which not all Atlans sympathized. Nor was sympathy considered obligatory.

From the beginning, Zell's description of Atl was "a society dedicated to the maximal actualization of human potential and the realization of ultimate individual freedom and personal responsibility." Within a few years the Church of All Worlds would only slightly rephrase that to proclaim that CAW was, in fact, a Neo-Pagan religion "dedicated to the celebration of Life, the maximal actualization of Human potential, and the realization of ultimate individual freedom and personal responsibility in harmonious eco-psychic relationship with the total Biosphere of Holy Mother Earth."[21]

The real story of CAW is how contact with the ecology movement and other groups and research into the history of ancient and "primitive" peoples (the worship of the Mother Goddess, etc.), transformed into a Neo-Pagan religion an organization originally based on the visions of a science fiction writer, a psychologist, and a right-wing philosopher who hated with a passion all forms of reverence for nature and all forms of religion. And the transformation revolved around the word *Pagan*.

In 1967 Tim Zell was using "Pagan" to describe the idea of CAW. In 1968 Paganism, as expressed in *Green Egg* (then a single-page newsletter), was a "life affirming religion without supernatural elements, such as were the Dionysians, the Epicureans, the Stoics, the Druids, the Transcendentalists, the Existentialists."[22]

How, we might ask, did this word *Pagan* come to include newly emerging nature religions? Until the late 1960s the word had been used to designate either an ancient or indigenous tribal religion or an irreligious, immoral approach to life.

The change may have been due largely to Kerry Thornley, a man who appears in the next chapter in a most amusing role. Thornley, under the unlikely name of Omar Ravenhurst, helped found a complex of delightfully bizarre and surrealist Neo-Pagan groups— among them the Erisians, the Discordian Society, the POEE, the Erisian Liberation Front—all devoted to the Greek goddess of chaos and strife, the Lady Eris. In 1966 Thornley, calling himself "Young Omar," wrote an article for a communitarian group called Kerista. He noted that B. Z. Goldberg, in his book *The Sacred Fire*, had observed that one function of primitive religions had been to provide refuge and relief; to lift temporarily the taboos of the society. Goldberg, according to Omar, wrote: "What was forbidden at large in the bush not only was permitted, but in fact, became a duty in the temple of the gods."[23]

Taking off from Goldberg, Omar said that since the Jewish and Christian traditions were not credible in this age of science, they should be abandoned. He wrote:

> Let us forget them. Instead, let us look at the jobs of the far less intellectual, but far more constructively functional religions of old. These were the "pagan" religions—the religions that survive to this day in England and the United States as "witchcraft."

Pagan religions "both stabilized and overthrew the social structure." Modern psychotherapy, sensory awareness workshops, and existential games were attempting to do the same thing and had, most likely, been reintroduced into society for a similar purpose. To Omar, science provided confirmation of Paganism as "an institutionalized cultural countertrend" and paved the way for the return of Paganism as a legitimate social force.

As for Kerista, that group espoused spontaneity, community, eroticism, and liberty. Omar wrote that the aims of Kerista and Paganism, in general, were strongly opposed to dogma and creed:

> Kerista is a religion and the mood of Kerista is one of holiness. Do not, however, look for a profusion of rituals, dogmas, doctrines and scriptures. Kerista is too sacred for that. It is more akin to the religions of the East and, also, the so-called pagan religions of the pre-Christian West. Its fount of being is the religious experience and that action or word or thought which is not infused with ecstasy is not Kerista. And Kerista, like those religions of olden times, is life-affirming.[24]

Kerista disappeared and Young Omar became involved with the vagaries and intricacies of the Lady Eris, but he was perhaps the first person, at least in the United States, to use the word *Pagan* to describe past and present nature religions. Some have actually alleged that the entire Neo-Pagan movement is an Erisian Plot (see next chapter and Robert Wilson and Robert Shea's *Illuminatus*). At this time the word *Pagan* was also being used by Witchcraft covens in the

United Kingdom and the United States. It found its way into the publications of the Witchcraft Research Association in 1964 and 1965. But most revivalist Witches were using the term to describe the ancient religions of the British Isles and Continental Europe and their own religious practice as Witches, not the Neo-Pagan phenomenon outside the Craft revival.[25] It took a catalyst to create a sense of collectivity around the word *Pagan*, and in the United States the Church of All Worlds and its *Green Egg* filled this role. It was Tim Zell who picked up the term from Young Omar's article.

For this reason alone the Church of All Worlds deserves a large place in this story. CAW was not the first Neo-Pagan group in the United States. As we have seen, Gleb Botkin's Long Island Church of Aphrodite may well have been the first, and Feraferia was probably the first group to espouse polytheism openly. But CAW helped a large number of distinct groups to realize they shared a common purpose, and this gave the phenomenon new significance. Until then, each group had existed on its own, coming into contact with others only at rare events like the Renaissance fairs in California or science fiction conventions. CAW and Tim Zell, by using terms like *Pagan* and *Neo-Pagan* in referring to the emerging collectivity of new earth religions, linked these groups, and *Green Egg* created a communications network among them.

The Church of All Worlds was formally chartered in March 1968. It rented a building for meetings and began publishing *Green Egg*. At this time it came into contact with Feraferia and a number of Witchcraft covens, and began to involve itself in the growing environmental movement. In the earliest issues of *Green Egg* Paganism was seen as encompassing transcendental meditation and liberal unitarianism. But contact with these groups changed CAW's conception of Paganism.

At first, CAW was most inspired by Feraferia's vision. In 1969 CAW was using Feraferia's calendar and its greeting "Evoe Korê!" hailing the Divine Maiden. It was Feraferia's Fred Adams who coined the term *eco-psychic* to explain Neo-Paganism's religious ecology. Zell wrote that Feraferia had developed virtually all aspects of a Pagan religion—myths, rites, ceremonies, celebrations, and an eco-psychic vision of truly gigantic proportions—whereas the Church of All Worlds had concentrated more on ethics, psychology, sociology, human development, and morality. An alliance seemed to Zell most natural.

Green Egg became more serious in tone, as befitted the newsletter of a church with a mission. CAW began to look seriously at the questions of rite, ritual, and myth. Fred Adams wrote:

> It is the Neo-Pagans' Destiny to supply the *"Cult-Culture-Cultivation"* foundations for the now rising, yet psychically rootless Conservation Action Movement(s). Not only must we re-implant the *Soil* of *Holy Earth.* We must also re-implant the Human Soul & Body! Thus reforestation as Celebration for one thing—Pagan celebration. . . . The gap between work and play must be closed.
>
> These two Turtle-Back movements must be joined: 1) Panerotic Freedom and 2) Wilderness Conservation.[26]

CAW and Feraferia jointly founded the Council of Themis, a Neo-Pagan ecumenical alliance. They invited all groups working for "the realization of the eco-psychic potential" of human beings and nature to join. The council was short-lived, dissolving after a dispute involving questions of philosophy, organization, and leadership.

Tom Williams, a priest of CAW, described to me the slow transformation of the church. He had joined in 1968, after stumbling across a sign advertising a meeting that read: "You may be a Pagan and not know it." Having considered himself a "Pagan" (as opposed to "Christian") for many years, and having a deep love for Greek mythology, Williams was interested. "I found out that there were other people who called themselves Pagans, but it took a while, because CAW did not accent its connection with earth religions in the beginning. Since the church came out of a conglomeration of Heinlein and Rand, it had to evolve."

Williams remembered that CAW's original attitude toward occultists was uniformly negative; Williams even remembered pulling a few harmless practical jokes on local occultists and ceremonial magicians in the area. "In the beginning," he said, "one might have been *justified* in calling CAW a science-fiction Grok-flock, but things began to change. We began to work with the Coalition for the Environment in the community. We began to meet people who were into Witchcraft, the modern Craft. At first I did not understand what the Craft was all about. I had more or less lumped it together with spiritualism and ceremonial magic. But then, gradually, we began to realize that there was *something here*, involving a connection with the ancient and modern earth religions. I think exposure to these things awakened something within us that apparently had been there for quite some time without us knowing it. I think it was a process of discovery. We had always felt we were the outcasts, the dispossessed. Of course, we had some of this feeling in the beginning, as the title *Stranger in a Strange Land* implies. But when we recognized that our emotional feeling lay with the planet; that there was a real distinction between the path of things and the path of the heart, these feelings went further than they had in the beginning."

In 1970 Williams wrote that the church was placing a greater emphasis on ecology and on the idea of a reverent identification with nature. "We are basically life-affirming and nature oriented as opposed to the anti-life, spirit oriented, anti-nature religions of the Judeo-Christian tradition. . . . Hence the only word for us is Pagans—the lovers of trees, the mad dancers in moonlit groves, the reverers of our beloved Earth for the mere fact of her immediate intoxicating existence."

The idea of linking a number of Neo-Pagan groups was not merely "to flee the smokestacks, stifling gases and filth that man has surrounded himself with in his 'pursuit of happiness,' " but to build in a positive way, "to create the dream of eco-psychic-land-sky-love-body-Wilderrealm," a time when all would "walk the Green Hills of Earth [a reference to another Heinlein novel] as Gods in the paradisal garden of Great Nature!"[27]

Another CAW priest, John McClimans, of the Chicago nest, also talked to me about the church's growth and evolution. He said, "When CAW was started, we used the word *Pagan* to mean non-Christian, even anti-Christian." But as the group spread out and came into contact with other groups, that changed. "The next thing I knew, I was a *real* Pagan instead of an anti-Christian type of Pagan. . . . There was a change of attitude, a change of value. I remember I felt it inside my head. I suddenly felt we were in the midst of the creation of something entirely new, something that offered us a way out of all the shit around us."

These transformations ended CAW's relationship with Atl. Many

Atlans had no wish to involve themselves with the church, objecting to CAW's relationship with the occult—tenuous though it was—as well as CAW's unconventional tendencies. While the church was never officially interested in conversion, some Atlans objected to what they felt was its missionary zeal. Tim Zell's hair and beard got longer. Occasionally, he would carry his lovely pet boa constrictor, Histah, around his shoulders when speaking in public. In 1972 Tim, Histah, and Julie, the woman he lived with, took the part of Cerridwen and Cernnunos and won a prize at the Costume Ball of the World Science Fiction Convention in Los Angeles. Two years later Tim and his present partner, Morning Glory, won another prize at the world science fiction convention in Washington (Discon) for their portrayal of two characters in Philip José Farmer's novel *Flesh*. Both Morning Glory and Tim had their pet serpents with them and they both looked quite dazzling. It was episodes such as these that led a number of Atlans to dissociate themselves from the church on the grounds that they did not want to be involved in a "public spectacle." As McClimans observed, "Most of the people in Atl were confirmed agnostics. They had no use for anyone who could even conceive of a theistic universe." He remembered once trying to explain Neo-Pagan philosophy to a former Atlan who had a Ph.D. degree in philosophy. McClimans said his friend didn't want to hear about it. "If it wasn't Kant, if it hadn't made the big time, it was worthless. My friend only wondered how I could be so stupid."

I asked if Atl still existed. "Yes," he said, "in a small way." McClimans told me that in the last two years he had been accepted by total strangers in another state simply because he possessed an Atl tiki. Some members of the original Atlan group left Missouri and settled elsewhere. According to one story, they purposely chose a state with low population density, one that might prove fertile ground for innovative political and social changes. There are still Atlan nests, but they do not wish to be publicly known. Apparently, the goals remain the same.

As for the Church of All Worlds, during the next few years it began to evolve its own philosophy, which is quite distinct from the philosophies of Feraferia and other Neo-Pagan groups. Tim Zell began writing about the planet Earth as deity, as a single living organism, and this became the Church of All World's central myth. Since

1971, the myth has been revised constantly and has become a unique eco-religious perception.

In the first article, "Theagenesis:* The Birth of the Goddess,"[28] Zell wrote that all religions should be considered subjectively "true," as should all opinions. Personal reality was necessarily subjective, so a belief was "true" by definition. He observed:

> A Voudou death-curse is as real to its victim, and as effective, as being "saved" is to a Christian fundamentalist, or the kosher laws are to an Orthodox Jew. A flat Earth, with the stars and planets revolving around it, was as real to the medieval mind as our present globe and solar system are to us. Hysteric paralysis and blindness are as real to the sufferer as their organic counterparts. The snakes and bugs of alcoholic and narcotic deliria are real to the addict, and so is the fearful world of the paranoiac. From the standpoint of human consciousness, there is no other reality than that which we experience, and whatever we experience is therefore reality—therefore "true."

Only when we compare our subjective experiences with the experiences of others and come to a consensus of reality, Zell wrote, do we arrive at a more objective truth, although even the consensus of a community is often subjective. While all religions are subjectively "true," their objective truth depends on how much they themselves depend on blind faith, dogma, tradition, and authority. A religion that could accommodate itself to new discoveries and changes, hold dogma and creed to a minimum, and encourage curiosity and questioning would stand a good chance of holding up under objective scrutiny. With this idea as background, Zell described the ancient Pagan religions:

> The Paleo-Pagans, diversified though they were, held among them certain common viewpoints. Among these were: veneration of an Earth-Mother Goddess; animism and pantheism; identification with a sacred region; seasonal celebration; love, respect, awe and veneration for Nature and Her mysteries; sensuality and sexuality in worship; magic and myth; and the sense of Man being a microcosm corresponding to the macrocosm of all Nature. These insights, however, were largely intuitive, as

* Originally Theogenesis but changed in later printings for obvious reasons.

science had not yet progressed to the point of being able to provide objective validation for what must have seemed, to outsiders, to be mere superstition.

These attitudes, Zell wrote, take on entirely new implications in the twentieth century. He took the reader on a long tour through biology, cell division, reproduction, and evolutionary theory. The central idea of this tour was that all life had seemingly developed from a single cell that divided and subdivided, passing its cellular material on and on. All life was interconnected, part of a single living organism.

"Literally," wrote Zell, "we are *all* 'One.' The blue whale and the redwood tree are *not* the largest living organisms on Earth; the entire planetary biosphere is." This organism Zell called "Terrebia" (later changed to Gaea). He began to make analogies between her and other living organisms. Like all organisms, Terrebia, or Gaea, was composed of many organs; she had her own forms of specialization. Each animal and plant was "the equivalent of a single cell in the vast body of Terrebia." And "each biome, such as pine forest, coral reef, desert, prairies, marsh, etc., complete with *all* its plants and animals," was the equivalent of an organ. And, just as in a human being each organ contributes to the total coherence of the being, similarly, in Gaea, you cannot "kill all the bison in North America, import rabbits to Australia, cut or burn off whole forests" without disrupting the integrity of the whole. To anyone viewing the earth as a living being, ecological principles became obvious.

Unlike the views of many evolutionists, Zell's was not open-ended but progressive. At first, he saw humans as the nervous system of the planet, among the last to evolve and the most complex. Human beings were the stewards of the planetary ecology of Gaea. But Zell soon changed this view. He concluded that all sentient life functions collectively as the nervous system of the planet, and that the primary "brain" function may well belong to the cetacea, and not to human beings. Zell saw modern humans as a cancer on the planet, cells multiplying out of control. At one point he even postulated nuclear war as a kind of ghastly radiation treatment that he hoped could be avoided.

The ultimate potential of Gaea was the telepathic unity of consciousness between all parts of the nervous system, between all human beings, and, ultimately, between all living creatures. Evolution to such a point would be similar to Pierre Teilhard de Chardin's emerging planetary consciousness, "the Omega Point," although without Teilhard's Christian trappings. The evolutionary goal is a total telepathic union, a destiny like that described by Arthur C. Clarke in *Childhood's End*, but without the loss of individual consciousness and sense of self. When the Omega Point or *Apotheasis* is reached, the planetary organism Gaea will truly awaken.

In this context, Zell redefined divinity and deity as the fulfillment of potential, as "the highest level of aware consciousness accessible to each living being, manifesting itself in the self-actualization of that being." Thus, the cell is God to its components; the tissue is God to the cells, and so on. And a human being manifests a wholly new level of awareness, organization, and "emergent wholeness." Of this level of organization, Zell wrote, "We find it appropriate to express recognition of this Unity in the phrase: Thou art God."[29] And since all beings are connected biologically, all eco-systems express a new level of awareness. Mother Earth herself can be seen as God. Zell wrote:

> Indeed, even though yet unawakened, the embryonic slumbering subconscious mind of Terrebia is experienced intuitively by us all, and has been referred to instinctively by us as Mother Earth, Mother Nature (The Goddess, The Lady.)[30]

God became Goddess, as had so intuitively been understood for centuries. In a later article Zell noted:

> Countless mystics, poets, shamans and children the world over have through all ages had their lives uplifted and transformed by the appearance or vision of She whom they have named Isis, Ceres, Rhea, Dana Gaea, Oestra, and in the Christian lands, Mother Mary. She whom we know as the All-Mother; The White Goddess; The Great Goddess; Mother Nature, Mother Earth. She is a real living Being, and like all living Beings, She too has a Soul-Essence which we can perceive, although "translated" into images familiar to our limited imaginations. . . .
> And just as every cell in our own bodies contains the essence of the Whole in the genetic code imprinted within the intricacies of the double

helix DNA molecule, and as indeed each cell in my own body is Tim Zell, so does every living plant and creature share in the essence of the Whole of Mother Earth. To each we can rightly say, "Thou Art Goddess."[31]

The publication of "Theagenesis" was followed by a number of other articles. In "Biotheology" Zell wrote that, since we are all Goddess, deity should be conceived of as "immanent," not transcendent; deity is within. He wrote:

We see that the Humanists are right; God is Mankind. Also correct are the Pantheists in their recognition that God is all Nature. Even the Christians touch upon the truth when they realize that God is "revealed in the forests, the glens, the meadows. . . ." The "religious experience" of mystics, which seems to show them "the naked face of God," is actually an experience of coming into complete attunement with this highest level of aware consciousness. . . .

Such an experience could be brought about by fasting, religious or sexual ecstasy, or hallucinogens. In all cases, "the experience itself appears to be identical, an experience of total beingness, of ecstatic revelation." To anyone having such an experience, Zell wrote, the phrase "Thou art God" becomes obvious. Heinlein's idea of "groking" was "a kind of total empathic understanding in which identity of subject and object merge into One." Thus, "to grok something," wrote Zell, "would be to relate to it with one's full potential." This, he said, was something that happened naturally with plants and animals. Only human beings seemed not to know who they were and to act accordingly, and this human failing was perhaps at the root of all human suffering. It is why, he wrote, there is so little species awareness, life awareness, and environmental awareness among human beings today.

This awareness *was* known to many ancient celebrants, the Pagans, the "naked dancers of moonlit groves" who were put to death by monotheists. "Monotheism," wrote Zell, "is a synonym for genocide," and yet, the new Pagans emerged in "the midst of the most monolithic, monotheistic state ever erected," rejecting transcendent deities and finding deity where it was all along, within each person.[32] The cosmic purpose of Neo-Paganism is to facilitate that increased awareness—to work for it by supporting all ecologically oriented movements, establishing alternative communities, demonstrating alternate possibilities for survival on the planet, and, ultimately, awakening Gaea, the Goddess, the planetary mind.

Zell's articles had a strong influence on the development of the Church of All Worlds. Lance Christie wrote of them:

> You've begun the creation of a myth, and a most livable one at that. It is a myth which defines a role for man and answers a lot of mystic questions. It seems to fit very well within the total tradition of man's symbols and myths, expressing in clearer and expanded form a theme as old as consciousness can remember.

Christie viewed the myth as a beginning, adding, "I still think we need to explore Jung et al. to get the whole concept within a full psychological/anthropological perspective. . . . Be that as it may, the world view you are creating is compatible with objective consciousness and science in a way no other religious myth is. . . ."[33]

Several years after the articles were written, *Newsweek* magazine, as well as a number of less popular journals, mentioned the work of British scientist James Lovelock, who had posited the "Gaia hypothesis": the living matter on earth, air, oceans, and land was all part of a system that Lovelock called after the Earth-Mother Goddess, Gaia. He said that this entire system seemed to "exhibit the behavior of a single organism—even a living creature," and argued that the biosphere was able to exert control over the temperature of the earth's surface and the composition of the atmosphere. *Newsweek* stated that the "Gaia hypothesis" was, in the main, "an elaboration of general ecological notions of close relationships between living things and their environment," but that Lovelock had carried this idea further, saying, "in man, Gaia has the equivalent of a central nervous system. We disturb and eliminate at our peril. Let us make peace with Gaia on her terms and return to peaceful coexistence with our fellow creatures."[34] Zell entered into a short correspondence with Lovelock, comparing their world views.

The concept of Gaea was never, officially, a dogma of CAW. There were, and still are, no dogmas. But the effect of "Theagenesis; The Gaea Hypothesis" on CAW's history and on the thoughts and goals of church priests, priestesses, and members has been extraordinary. All the CAW members I interviewed felt that the goals of Neo-Paganism were enormous, involving a total transformation of Western society. In contrast, only half the other Neo-Pagans I interviewed thought in such sweeping terms.

Tom Williams once told me that CAW's goal was to change the world. "After all," he said, laughing, "why be petty?" Another time he said that one goal of Neo-Paganism was to learn to see ourselves "as a total entity—rational and irrational at once, within a total environment, and with a total identification with all life."

Carolyn Clark, a priestess in CAW, told me, "If there *is* an ultimate goal or purpose, it has to be the purpose of achieving Chardin's Omega Point, the union of consciousness with all living things." And Zell, as might be expected, said the ultimate goal was "totally and completely to transform human consciousness and planetary consciousness." When I asked if he had anything less ambitious in mind, he smiled and said, "Anything less is not quite enough."

"It is a choice between Apocalypse or Apotheasis," Morning Glory said to me. "The purpose of Neo-Paganism is to put us back on the track; we took a wrong turning somewhere around thirty-five hundred years ago. But our purpose is not to compromise, to rework, to integrate ourselves back into the culture, but rather to be a viable alternative to it. Now that is a challenge that many of us are not going to be up to. I myself have nightmares about it. Still, that is the challenge. That is where it lies, because there is no way to reform the system."

"For me," John McClimans told me, "the idea of theagenesis is *it!* But I don't want CAW to be enclosed by it. As long as we truly stay open for others to come in and show us other ways, the theagenesis idea is sure to be modified, or someone will show us something that seems better entirely."

While many members of CAW see their church as "a total, holistic, cultural alternative to the entire fabric of Western Civilization,"[35] the Gaea hypothesis remains hypothesis. The Church of All Worlds has only one real dogma—its belief that it has no beliefs.

Most people find the idea of a religion without creeds difficult. Many within the Church of All Worlds have thought about a new definition of religion. They confronted the problem from the very beginning, particularly when describing Neo-Paganism to people who they felt were their kind of people, but who were hostile to the idea of all religions. As Zell explained, "Most of the people who think in ways similar to us, have been turned off by conventional religions. This is the greatest problem we have. Ten years ago, if someone had presented me with Neo-Paganism and put it in terms of a 'new religion,' I would have had nothing to do with it. And yet here I am. We had to get a new definition of religion. Because everywhere else religion is defined in Judeo-Christian terms; it means belief in a supreme being, heaven, hell, and so forth. And none of us believe in any of that, yet we consider ourselves deeply religious. We slowly came to understand that religion is a form of relinking, of increasing consciousness and communication. Worship is a form of communication, of communion. And communication can only be between equals. It can't be abasement, a bowing down before something greater. When I make love with a woman, when I sleep under the trees, when I compost my garbage, all these things can be acts of worship."

With this different understanding of religion, the Church of All Worlds began to formulate a concept of its relationship to Neo-Paganism and to the Pagan religions of the past. CAW members saw themselves as a family, a kind of tribe. The ancient Pagan religions were seen as tribal religions, based on custom and tradition rather than on dogma and belief, grounded in what one *did* rather than in what one *believed*. Zell made a distinction between what he called philosophical religions (taught by prophets and formulated into creeds) and natural religions (the evolving, indigenous folk or Pagan religions of particular peoples). The former, he wrote, were artificially constructed; the latter emerged out of the processes of life and nature, and continued to evolve organically.

Philosophical religions are like buildings: an architect (prophet) gets an inspiration (revelation) and lays down his vision in blueprints (prophecy; scriptures). Then contractors, carpenters, masons, etc. (disciples and followers) build the building more or less according to his specifications. It is *made* of non-living materials, and does not *grow* naturally; it is assembled. When it is finished, it cannot grow further, and begins to deteriorate, until it is eventually so outmoded and rundown it is demolished to make way for new buildings. A world of philosophical religions is like unto a city, with all the problems (hunger, war, hatreds, crime, pollution, disease) of a big city, and for much the same reason: unnaturalness.

A Pagan religion, on the other hand, is like a tree: it emerges alive from the Earth, grows, changes (both cyclically in seasons, and continually in upward and outward growth), bears flowers, fruit, shares its life with other living beings. It is not made, or designed according to any blueprint other than genetic. And when, after many thousands of years, perhaps (for many trees are potentially immortal, never dying of old age), it should come to the end of its time, it does not pass from the world entirely, for its own progeny have, in the interval, begun to spring up all around, again from the Earth, and again, similar yet each unique. A world of Pagan religions is like a forest.

Included in natural religions would be animism, totemism, pantheism, much of Witchcraft, all indigenous religions of Africa, Australia, and America and the old religions of the Celts, the Gauls, the Norse, and the fairy faith in Ireland. Zell wrote:

> The old Pagan religions were never "created." . . . What little we can trace indicates a descent from Paleolithic and Neolithic fertility cults, hence the common symbols of the Earth Mother Goddess and the Horned God, representing, respectively, the vegetable and animal life of the Earth. We find them therefore unanimous in their veneration of Nature and their sensual celebration of life, birth and death as expressed seasonally in aspects of sexuality.
>
> All the Great Festivals of Paganism, wherever they may be found, correspond in common with the Solstices, Equinoxes, and other natural annual cycles of life (animal mating seasons, planting, harvest). Most of these remain with us today in more or less disguised form as the so-called "Christian" holidays of Christmas (Yule), Easter (Ostara), May Day (Beltane), Thanksgiving (Harvest Home), Halloween (Samhain) and even Groundhog's Day (Oimelc). In addition to these six, there are two others, Midsummer and Lugnasadh, comprising a total of eight Festivals (or Sabbats as they are known, under different names, in Witchcraft).[36]

Another CAW member who sought to describe the nature of Neo-Paganism was Lewis Shieber, who divided religions into two categories—those that functioned from a base of "Tribal/Tradition" and those that functioned from a base of "Dogma/Belief." The latter, said Shieber, were, more often than not, based on a "universal" idea. Such religions were often large, evangelistic, and based on a powerful but closed system. The religions based on "Tribal/Tradition" were usually small ones, functioning out of a local "cultural matrix." In such religions *participation* in tribal actions was emphasized; it was never that important to *believe* in the myths and legends of the tribe. In Judaism, for example, Shieber noted that one could disbelieve in God, as long as you followed the tradition. "All primitive Pagan religions have this [Tribal/Tradition] base," Shieber wrote, adding, "Thus many sometimes contradictory beliefs may be held by individuals without harm to the religion as long as the *identification with the Tribe and tribal practices is strong.*"

Tribal/Tradition religions stressed social and personal interaction. The governments in these societies were often "basically anarchistic," tribal order being maintained by "conventions and discussion leading to consensus." The Church of All Worlds falls into the Tribal/Tradition category. While "there are some practices and ideas which have been associated with CAW," he wrote, "all these associated things are unofficial and not even accorded the name of tradition."

CAW's antipathy toward dogma is typical of many but by no means all Neo-Pagan groups. Feraferia, for example, has, as we have seen, definite beliefs and creeds, and even with CAW there was a temptation to "require belief in the poetic and useful vision of Tim Zell's 'Theagenesis' theory." Shieber concluded that CAW as "tribal religion" could never claim universality, and therefore would always be small. "We must assume," he said, "that we are a guest people in a possibly unfriendly nation and act accordingly."[37]

Many people in CAW talked about the strange position of being a priest or priestess in a church that stresses lack of dogma. John McClimans told me that those who remain in CAW are usually people who don't want someone in the middle—between themselves and the discovery of their own God/Goddess within. "You're the Goddess. I'm the Goddess. When a person becomes aware of that idea; when they begin to conceive that this might even be a tentative possibility, they're hooked. They don't need someone else to tell them how to touch "god" or "goddess." They may need someone to give them the impetus to put their hand on the pulse; but once they've felt it, they don't want you there anymore. Once their hand is there, they are going to say, 'Get away, so I can feel it without you interfering!' "

Besides a tribal/tradition base and lack of dogma, most members of CAW feel that all the new Pagan religions, from Feraferia and CAW to the Witchcraft covens, hold certain other values in common. To describe this common thread, Zell used Fred Adams's term, "eco-psychic." As we have seen, it was Feraferia that first put forth the idea of a life of religious ecology and Fred Adams worked out elaborate rituals to complement such a life. An early statement from the Council of Themis put the idea this way:

> Everything we encounter in the Biosphere is a part of Nature, and ecology reveals the pattern of this is-ness, the natural relationships among all these things and the organic unity of all of them as a Biospheric Whole. . . .
>
> Of all man's secular studies, ecology comes closest to bringing him to the threshold of religious relationship to his world. Ecology not only confirms the wonders of form and function that other secular studies have revealed, but it brings these into organic union with each other as one dynamic, living Whole; and it points out the conditions for the well-being of both this overall Unity and the parts that comprise it.
>
> An intensive realization of these conditions, and of one's own immediate role in their sustainment and development, brings one to the threshold of religious awe.[38]

The Church of All Worlds, like Feraferia, sees Neo-Paganism as a response to a planet in crisis. And if science fiction provided the myths and vision for CAW, ecology is the supreme religious study. A Pagan religion means a life of harmony with the earth, not a set of rituals. The ritual is nothing less than a truly integrated life.

Carolyn Clark put it this way: "It has to become second nature. So that when you take the garbage out to your compost heap, there's this moment of awareness and attunement between yourself and the collective unconscious of the Earth; so that as you throw it on the heap, you think, 'Say there, Mom, I'm feeding you.' " But unlike Feraferia, CAW's support of ecology is coupled with support for sophisticated technologies, as long as they are based on an understanding and respect for eco-systems. As might be imagined, CAW has also consistently supported space exploration.

In keeping with Arthur C. Clarke's famous remark that any highly developed technology is indistinguishable from magic, I often heard church members quote a remark made by Tom Williams: "You gotta admit, any magic that can erase an entire city from the face of the Earth in a single instant, well—that plenty big Ju-Ju, B'wana!"[39] Similarly, Zell observed to me, "Magic is the science you don't understand, the science you don't take for granted. Science and magic are both approaches to understanding the universe. If you have a theory to explain something, it gets called science. If people don't understand something, or lack a theory to explain it, they label it 'magic.' " In general, members of CAW see Neo-Paganism as a religious philosophy that combines intuitive *and* rational modes of thought.

Lance Christie wrote in *Green Egg* that the problem with modern technology was not the inventions themselves but a "mechanical world picture," a mechanistic view of the universe. He noted that against this picture many people such as Mumford and Dubos had opposed an "organic world picture." CAW, according to Christie, was uniquely able to combine "a scientific skepticism and rationality with an acceptance of that which is non-analytic and non-rational in human experience."[40]

Since most members of CAW are visionaries, anarchists, and religious ecologists, they have naturally gravitated to "alternative" forms of energy—solar, wind, and so forth. But they have always supported scientific inquiry in order to broaden and enrich our ways of thinking, not to obliterate them. Scientific inquiry has never been seen as contradictory to psychic development or magic. The ancient Pagan peoples are seen as sources of skills that can be learned to advantage by modern Neo-Pagans. CAW has always had its eye on ancient dolmens, as well as civilizations light years away. The Church, Ellwood noted, has become "a lively meeting of an old Pagan world view, the provocative images of some modern novels and biophilosophic reflection, and a group of vigorous, socially experimental young adults."[41] CAW has a history of attempted communes, group marriages, Heinleinian sex experimentation, and even vows of poverty, all in an atmosphere where the only sin is hypocrisy (sin is an act against God, and Thou art God) and the only crime is "that which infringes against another."[42]

Most CAW members do not see themselves as "political"; many define themselves as "apolitical" or even "antipolitical." Zell has been known to assert that all "real" revolutions are concerned with changes of consciousness rather than shifts of power. Like interplanetary explorers in science fiction novels, CAW has entered new universes, created new social systems, and new kinds of human and interspecies relationships. But it has yet to establish any real relationship to human beings on this planet.

Until recently, the Church of All Worlds was set up with a nine-circle structure. One advanced through the levels by progressive involvement and participation, as well as study and getting through CAW's long reading list, as interesting and filled with contradictions as any I have ever come across. For example, to move from the fourth to the fifth circle, a person had to read seven books listed in the basic bibliography, including one on perception, one on Native American religion, and one from a section called "Homo Novus." In addition, the person had to begin some form of psychic training (anything from Arica to Akido would suffice) and write a long paper comparing three different religions, one of which should be Neo-Paganism. The process of advancement was conceived of as continuous and never-ending. No one, not even Tim Zell, had ever made it to the ninth circle.

Groups within the church are called "nests"—another practice taken from *Stranger in a Strange Land*. Each nest is autonomous. Most decisions are arrived at by consensus. I visited meetings of two of the St. Louis nests in the fall of 1975. At each one there were twelve to fifteen people. The Dog Star Nest met in the nude. The meeting I attended concentrated on shamanism. I participated in a beautiful Native American ritual, followed by CAW's very simple ritual of watersharing, the clearest reminder of CAW's Heinleinian orgins. A goblet of water is passed from one to another. All share this cup and say appropriate phrases to one another: "May you never thirst," "Drink deeply," "Thou art God," "Thou art Goddess."

The other nest, led by Don Wildgrube, met clothed and was experimenting with sensitivity awareness techniques. Most CAW members are in their late twenties and early thirties. But there are members in their late teens, and at least one member in his sixties. Members include psychologists, engineers, bus drivers, salesmen, and students. Most are white, middle-class, and college educated. And, unlike many Neo-Pagans, the vast majority come from Protestant backgrounds.

One scholar of Neo-Paganism, the Reverend J. Gordon Melton, a Methodist minister from Chicago who has been studying new Pagan religions for several years, said that the majority of Neo-Pagans are ex-Catholics, followed by ex-Jews. The abundance of ritual in Neo-Pagan groups may appeal to Catholics and Jews, whose religions included much ritual. Protestants, however, have little experience with ritual, according to Melton, and do not seek it. He has described CAW as the Neo-Pagan group with the most ex-Protestants, the least ritual, and the greatest tendency to proselytize, even to the point of having religious tracts. His perception of this one group seems accurate, but in my own experience in the Neo-Pagan movement, there are equal numbers of ex-Catholics and Protestants, with a smaller number of Jews. I also found many who had been deprived of any religious ritual as children.

It was clear that one of the most important reasons for CAW's existence was a response to a need, a lack, a longing. The bond that united past and future visions within the church was a yearning for a real culture. "A common thread in Neo-Paganism," said priestess Carolyn Clark, "is nostalgia, a yearning to get back to a time when people seemed more in control of their own lives, and societies, while complex, had a definite cultural pattern, not this weird shifting kaleidoscope that's called American culture."

Morning Glory Zell expressed it this way: "We're orphans, we're bastard mongrel children in a beautiful land that isn't really ours. We're grafted and transplanted, saddled with a tremendous guilt for everything from strip mines and city dumps to the death of the people who lived here before. One of the reasons for CAW's success is that everyone identifies with being a Stranger in a Strange Land. The only people who have a real tradition here are the Native American people. There is much to identify with them. But it is not our tradition. We were never chanted the chants and rocked in the cradle and told the working rhythms and rhymes. Most of us were raised in concrete and steel, totally removed from the seasons around us. Some of us smiled when the air would get a certain taste from burning leaf smoke and we felt that stirring inside of us. But nobody else noticed it; they walked on past. Some of us are attuned to the same rhythms as indigenous people, but we have no traditions. We live in an impoverished culture. We have to create our culture from scratch."

By 1978 much had changed in the Church of All Worlds. There were CAW nests in Chicago, St. Louis, Atlanta, and Milwaukee. There were other nests in Indiana and Illinois. New priests and priestesses had been ordained. But CAW's role as catalyst for the Neo-Pagan movement had ended, at least temporarily, with the death of *Green Egg*.

How important *Green Egg* was to the Neo-Pagan community is a matter of controversy. There are many who welcomed its death with a sigh of relief. But others, including myself, believed that it was a key to the movement's vitality and that its death in 1976 was a blow from which the movement is only now recovering.

There were eighty issues of *Green Egg* spanning nine years. In each issue fully a third of the fifty to sixty pages were devoted to letters from various types of Pagans, Neo-Pagans, Witches, occultists, ecology activists, anarchists, and libertarians—among others. The writers of letters ranged from Neo-Nazi James Madole, head of the National Renaissance Party, to advocates of Timothy Leary's theories of space migration and life extension.

Unlike most mainstream intellectual magazines, where issues become narrowly defined by a more or less reigning ideology, *Green Egg,* both in its Forum and in its articles, had maintained a hands-off, free-for-all policy. Debates raged on the merits of Velikovsky's theories, the place of technology, the teachings of Aleister Crowley, the evidence for ancient matriarchies, and hundreds of other issues, with emphasis on ecology, ethics, tribalism, magic, science fiction, and the relationship of human beings to the planet. *Green Egg* served to create the sense that hundreds of diverse and even contradictory groups were part of an eclectic movement with certain common goals.

It is popular today to talk about "synergy"—a combination that has a greater effect than the simple addition of its components—and that perhaps best describes the effect of *Green Egg*. It connected all the evolving and emerging goddess and nature religions into one phenomenon: the Neo-Pagan movement.

But the goals of many of these groups were diverse, even contradictory. To those with a conservative life style, CAW seemed to be a bunch of crazy anarchists. The *Green Egg*'s hands-off policy created controversy. Increased contact between groups led at times to an increase in internal bickering. When *Green Egg* ceased publication at the end of 1976, a number of Neo-Pagans and Witches told me they were glad because now there would be more tranquillity in the movement. And perhaps there is. Many groups began "sticking with their own" and with those others they felt close to. They simply ignored the rest of the movement.

Tom, Tim, and Morning Glory left for the West Coast. Those who stayed in St. Louis, at least the majority, remained loyal to their CAW nests and friends. Many felt that *Green Egg* had never served the CAW community as well as it had the Neo-Pagan community as a whole. There are other Neo-Pagan journals, and new ones have appeared, but none has as yet attempted to become a vehicle for interaction and communication among the various movement groups. As a result, most covens and groves have relied on an informal communications network of letters, phone calls, conferences, informal meetings, and, occasionally, larger ecumenical gatherings. For two years, the community was more "tranquil" but definitely less vital. It is only in the last year that these new decentralized forms of organization are bearing new fruit. (See Chapter 12.) The CAW organization is in a state of flux. The old requirements for advancement have been scrapped and the present leadership is thinking about proposals for a new structure.

Meanwhile, Tim and Morning Glory Zell converted a school bus into a home for themselves, their two snakes, a possum, a tarantula, and a rat colony—food for their snakes and spider. They spent a year in Oregon writing, lecturing, and teaching. They formed a coven called Ithil Duath. Morning Glory was quoted in a local Oregon newspaper as saying, "We realize that we don't have 'The Way.' After all, that's been done. . . . We want to restore the role of the shaman (or witch) in our culture. . . . We really must return the Goddess to the earth if we are to keep a balance and avoid ecological apocalypse. . . ."[43] Tom Williams moved to Palo Alto.

In 1977 Tim and Morning Glory moved to northern California. In the spring of 1978 they wrote to me: "We are living in a pioneer community comprising twelve square miles of Sacred Wilderness somewhere in the mountains of Ecotopia." They call their place "the magic land." They live in their converted school bus with Tanith, a six-foot-long Boa, Ananta, an eleven-foot-long Burmese python, and two tarantulas—Charlotte and Kallisti. They conduct seminars in the local community and they earn a bit of money making ceramic figures. They described their life as simple, with almost no expenses other than food and fuel. Of their present life they wrote:

> About 150 people are living in homesteads among these hills. A beautiful, anarchic, nature-oriented community has been evolving here over the past five years and we want to be a part of it.
>
> Here, no horns honk, no traffic rumbles. It has been raining a lot and our springs flow with Mama's very own sweet clear waters, direct from Her bosom to our tap. The air is sweet with the aroma of flowers, wild irises, blue-eyed-grass, hyacinths, buttercups and stork-bills.
>
> Since hunting was abolished on the land, the deer have gotten downright casual about naked hippies and will just stand and watch you go by. They often graze right in back of our bus and pay little attention when we open the back door and watch them. It's wonderful living in a place where we (as humans) are *not* the terror of every living thing.
>
> Often, on our walks, we will come upon a log cabin or a teepee hidden deep within the forest. Always, we are invited in for a smoke, some food, news, conversation and company. On the Outside, it is the 1950's down in the valley below, but up here in the mountains, it is a strange time-warp linking 1878 with 1968.

The Zells said that their land has become a place of pilgrimage for many Pagans and that they plan a large number of new projects. These include a monastery ("or perhaps we should call it an Omnistery") and the Ecosophical Research Society for research into philosophy, history, and theology. This society will eventually publish a newsletter, *Amargi*. Finally, Morning Glory's dream is the Bene Gesserit,[44] a shamanic training and initiation center that will offer correspondence courses. Graduates would come to the land for wilderness shamanic training, culminating in a vision quest and initiation. But these projects lie in the future. "We are still stunned," they wrote to me, "as to how to reach our old readership." Meanwhile, they continue to share their dream, a longing to expand possibility and potential, or as Tim once told me, the desire "to eat the fruit of both trees, to recover the sense of the Home."

Recent Notes

The Church of All Worlds no longer exists in St. Louis. "I don't feel bad about CAW dying," Don Wildgrube told me, "I loved it. If it hadn't been for Tim, I wouldn't have been in any of this. But the world evolves, and Paganism evolves. Tim once wrote that Pagan religions are like trees, they grow, they bear flowers and fruit, and when they have served their purpose, they die, but they leave their progeny." Don Wildgrube is now the priest of a Craft coven.

There is a group in Milwaukee that calls itself the New Reformed Church of All Worlds, but it doesn't really resemble the old CAW. The one place the CAW does exist is in California where it functions as an umbrella organization for a number of specific groups. These include the Ecosophical Research Association, Lifeways, a ritual and teaching organization, and Forever Forests, the environmental organization created by Gwydion Pendderwen. After Gwydion's tragic death in a car accident in 1982, his will specified that his land and Forever Forests be left in the care of a group of stewards. Forever Forests continues to have its annual tree planting each New Year's weekend. A connected group of city dwellers— the Urban Ents—involve themselves in local environmental actions. Forever Forests also manages Annwfn, Gwydion's land, which has become a retreat center. Money has been raised by the continued sales of Gwydion's two albums, T-shirts, and various publications. And in 1986 there are rumors that *Green Egg* will rise again.

As for Tim (who changed his name to Otter) and Morning Glory Zell, their saga has taken amazing twists and turns since *Drawing Down the Moon* was first published; their journey has included creating and patenting a process for creating unicorns—the unicorns that have been exhibited at the Ringling Brothers Barnum & Bailey Circus are their creation—and even a search for mermaids which took them to the South Seas.

In the late 1970s, the Zells came across the work of W. Franklin Dove. Beginning in 1935, Dove, a biologist at the University of Maine, wrote several articles in scientific journals describing various attempts to create single horned animals and documenting his own efforts. It is not generally known that during the first week of a horned animal's life, the horn buds are only attached to the skin; they have not yet attached themselves to the skull. Dove observed that all unicorns have been developed by a surgical procedure (a very minor one—since it only involves the layers of the skin) in which the horn buds are moved to a central position.

The Zells began looking at the ancient pictures of unicorns; they noticed that the earliest depictions were more goatlike than horselike. They theorized that unicorns may well have been produced, an ancient process once known and lost, and they speculated that ancient herders might well have found a one-horned creature useful in protecting their flocks. They also believed that creating a unicorn would be a powerful magical symbol that would say to millions: "If a unicorn exists, why then anything is possible. I can even change my own life."

The Zells created a number of unicorns from various breeds of white goats. For several years, Otter and Morning Glory made the rounds of renaissance and medieval fairs with several of their adorable creatures. Children were photographed with the unicorns, and the animals were treated more lovingly than 99 percent of male goats on this planet. In the winter the unicorns roamed on Coeden Brith, the same magical land in Mendocino where Nemeton was founded, adjacent to Annwfn, where Gwydion lived until his death, and where Forever Forests still makes its home. To see the unicorns wandering around seemed miraculous, even if in humorous moments one might find oneself calling them "unigoats." But on a magic morning on the land, they did seem to have wandered in from faerie.

Attitudes among Pagans differed. Most people took the unicorns Lancelot and Bedevere, and the five or six other creatures who appeared, to their hearts. And the Zells continued barely to eke out a living despite unicorn postcards, the Living Unicorn Calendar, and various public appearances.

A few Pagans were disturbed by the unicorns. Does making a unicorn "real" destroy the power and romance of the myth, some asked? Is it appropriate for members of a Pagan religion to alter surgically an animal—even if the operation only involves cutting flaps in the skin and moving the horns toward the center?

In 1984, the Zells signed an agreement with Ringling Brothers Barnum and Bailey Circus. The circus bought four of the unicorns. Under the terms of their contract Otter and Morning Glory were not allowed to talk to the press for three years. The Zells received $150,000, although by the time lawyers, agents, trainers, and debts were paid, less than a third of the money was left.

Once the circus had the animals they proceeded to shroud them in mystery. They never admitted there was more than one but claimed the unicorn had mysteriously "appeared" in Texas. They showed the unicorn with pomp, glitz, and ceremony but refused to tell its true history. At a New York press conference, when a reporter pointed to evidence of the Zell's existence, the question was ignored. Almost none of the many news accounts, fueled by protests by the ASPCA, ever got the story right. One *New York Post* reporter finally found the Zells but sensationalized the story by describing their rural setting as a hideout secured by gun-toting sentries.

In April 1985, Alison Harlow came to New York and we decided we would go to the circus and see an old animal friend. As glittering human butterflies swung from high wires, the unicorn Lancelot appeared on a movable cart, a woman in a pink gown standing by his side. He was followed in the procession by eager children who rode in white carts. His hair had been oiled. It had been kept long—making him seem more goat-like than usual. I don't know the reason, but I would surmise that they wanted to hide his genitalia. As the procession advanced, Alison started giggling and whispered to me, "To think, that's the same little fellow that once pissed on me," and we all broke up. But one row down, a five-year-old boy told his mother, "It really *is* a unicorn—it *is!*" So, perhaps, the Zells' magic was working.

The Zells started a new organization called the Ecosophical Research Association. ERA, they said, would study and explore the territory of the archetype, the basis of legends and the boundaries between the sacred and the secular. One prime area of research would be crypozoology—the identification of unknown animals such as the Loch Ness Monster, Unicorns, Bigfoot, and Mermaids.

Taking some of the money from their first crypozoological adventure, and convincing other backers to put in the rest, they planned an expedition to New Ireland in Papua, New Guinea, to look into stories of possible mermaid sightings. They chartered a boat and assembled a group of fourteen adventurers to look for the mysterious "ri." "You doubt?" wrote Otter in a Pagan journal, "O ye of little faith . . . remember the lesson of the Unicorn."

But when they arrived in New Guinea, they quickly found out that the indigenous word for mermaid, *ri*, was the same word as that used for the aquatic creature called the dugong. The mermaid was a dugong. It was not as happy an ending as the creation of the unicorn and they returned home penniless.

There was something breathtaking about the Zells' trip to the South Seas, staking the only real money they had ever gotten on a grand research adventure. For me, hearing about it as I took my daily subway ride to the office, it seemed bold and grand. There were others who simply thought that the Zells had lived in the magical wilderness so long that they had simply lost touch with reality. When they returned, they were asked to leave Coeden Brith. The owner felt some of the unicorn money might have been better spent in helping to pay the taxes or to make land improvements. The Zells now live in Ukaiah. But who knows where the next adventure will take them.

Religions of Paradox
and Play

"*Large parts of the Neo-Pagan movement started out as jokes, you know,*" Robert Anton Wilson, author, Witch, and a former editor of *Playboy*, told me one day. "Some of the founders of NROOGD will tell you their order started as a joke; others will deny it. There is a group that worships Mithra in Chicago which started out as a joke. The people in many of these groups began to find that they were getting something out of what they were doing and gradually they became more serious."

There have always been spoofs on religion. But religions that combine humor, play, and seriousness are a rare species. A rather special quality of Neo-Pagan groups is that many of them have a humorous history. As we have seen, the Church of the Eternal Source, a serious attempt to revive the ancient Egyptian religion, began as a series of yearly Egyptian costume parties. The Reformed Druids of North America began as a humorous protest movement against a regulation at Carleton College requiring attendance at chapel. The Elf Queen's Daughters, a network of "elves" located mostly in the Far West, sent out each week three pages of quite beautiful poetic prose, most of it composed by automatic writing. "Most of it's nonsense," they told me. "We don't take it too seriously." In Minneapolis a group calling itself the First Arachnid Church began to publish hilarious leaflets calling for the worship of the Great Spider and the

True Web.[1] It was pure satire and a great parody of fundamentalist Christian leaflets. But it was also pure Neo-Paganism. And, most preposterous of all, there is the worship of Eris, goddess of chaos and confusion, recently popularized in the science fiction trilogy *Illuminatus*.[2]

Since we live in a culture that makes a great distinction between "seriousness" and "play," how does one confront the idea of "serious" religious groups that are simultaneously playful, humorous, and even (at times) put-ons? How *seriously* can we take them?

The relationship between ritual and play has long been noticed. Harvey Cox, in *Feast of Fools*, develops a theory of play, asserting, like others before him, that our society has lost or mutilated the gift of true festivity, playful fantasy, and celebration. In 1970, when an interviewer asked Cox about the "rise of the occult," he replied that astrology, Zen, and the use of drugs were "forms of play, of testing new perceptions of reality without being committed to their validity in advance or ever." When the interviewer observed that sociologist Marcello Truzzi had called the occult "trivial" because people were not serious about it, Cox replied, "That's exactly the reason it's *important*. People are playing with new perceptions."[3]

The classic study on play was written in 1944 by Johan Huizinga. "Human civilization," he says, "has added no essential feature to the general idea of play." Both animals and humans play, and play is irrational, defying logical interpretations. Yet the "great archetypal activities of human society are all permeated with play from the start." Further:

> You can deny, if you like, nearly all abstractions: justice, beauty, truth, goodness, mind, God. You can deny seriousness, but not play. . . . Play only becomes possible, thinkable and understandable when an influx of *mind* breaks down the absolute determinism of the cosmos.

Huizinga writes that play and ritual are really the same thing and that all sacred rites, mysteries, sacrifices, and so forth are performed in the spirit of play, that poetry is a play function, and that all these things may well be serious since "the contrast between play and seriousness proves to be neither conclusive nor fixed . . . for some play can be very serious indeed." In addition, "The outlaw, the revolutionary, the cabalist or member of a secret society, indeed heretics of all kinds are of a highly associative if not sociable disposition, and a certain element of play is prominent in all their doings.'"[4]

In the light of these words we can look at two Neo-Pagan groups that have combined seriousness with play: the Reformed Druids of North America and the worshippers of Eris. These two groups, while differing in almost every way conceivable, illustrate the idea that once you embark on a journey of change in perception, even when you start this journey as "play," you can end up in waters far different from those you may have originally intended to enter.

The Reformed Druids of North America (RDNA) began in 1963 at Carleton College as a humorous protest movement directed against the school's requirement that all students attend a certain number of religious services. Since "attending the services of one's own religion"[5] was one way to fulfill this requirement, a group of students formed the RDNA to test it. The group was never intended to be a true alternative religion, for the students were Christians, Jews, agnostics, and so forth and seemed content with those religions.

In 1964 the regulation was abolished but, much to the surprise—and it is said, horror—of the original founders, the RDNA continued to hold services and spread its organization far beyond the college campus. One of the founders, David Fisher, who wrote many of the original rituals, is now an Episcopal priest and teacher of theology at a Christian college in the South, having apparently washed his hands of the RDNA. Many of the original founders considered Reformed Druidism not so much a *religion* as a philosophy compatible with any religious view, a method of inquiry. They certainly never considered it "Neo-Pagan."

The original basic tenets of Reformed Druidism were:

1. The object of the search for religious truth, which is a universal and a never-ending search, may be found through the Earth-Mother; which is Nature; but this is one way, one way among many.

2. And great is the importance, which is of a spiritual importance of Nature, which is the Earth-Mother; for it is one of the objects of Creation, and with it do people live, yea, even as they do struggle through life are they come face-to-face with it.

These tenets were often shortened to read

1. Nature is good!
2. Nature is good!⁶

The original founders seemed to hold the fundamental idea that one should scrutinize religion from "a state of rebellion," neither embracing traditional faiths nor rejecting them. They intended RDNA to avoid all dogma and orthodoxy, while affirming that life was both spiritual (Be'al) and material (the Earth-Mother) and that human beings needed to come to a state of "awareness" through unity with both spirit and nature. The founders also seemed to distrust ritual and magic, sharing the prejudices and assumptions of most of the population.

RDNA has always had a sense of humor. The *Early Chronicles* of the Druids, as well as many later writings, are written in a mock biblical style. Here, for example, is a description of how the regulations at Carleton were abolished:

1. Now it came to pass that in those last days a decree went out from the authorities;
2. and they did declare to be abolished the regulations which had been placed upon the worship of those at Carleton.
3. And behold, a great rejoicing did go up from all the land for the wonders which had come to pass.
4. And all the earth did burst forth into song in the hour of salvation.
5. And in the time of exaltation, the fulfillment of their hopes, the Druids did sing the praises of the Earth-Mother.⁷

Similarly, the original "Order of Worship" has many similarities to a Protestant religious service, complete with invocations and benedictions. Reformed Druids are not required to use these rituals and—as is true of so many Neo-Pagan groups—participants have created new rituals to take their place. I did attend an RDNA ritual in Stanford, California, that sounded not much different from a number of liberal Christian services I have attended, despite its being held in a lovely grove of oaks. But when I described this ritual to another leader of a Reformed Druid grove, he merely laughed and remarked, "It all depends on who's doing the ritual. A service by

Robert Larson [Arch-Druid of an Irish clan in San Francisco and a former Christian Scientist] often sounds like Christian Science. My services are influenced by my own training in Roman Catholicism. Besides, most religious ceremonies follow the same kinds of patterns. It is natural to find similarities." The Reformed Druid movement is extremely eclectic, to say the least.

The festivals of the Reformed Druids are the eight Pagan sabbats we have come across before: Samhain, the Winter Solstice, Oimelc (February 1), the Spring Equinox, Beltane, Midsummer, Lughnasadh (August 1), and the Fall Equinox. The rituals are held (if possible) outdoors, in a grove of oaks or on a beach or hill. The officiating Druids often wear robes—white is traditional, but other colors are acceptable. During the ritual, which can include readings, chants, and festival celebrations, the waters-of-life are passed around and shared to symbolize the link between all things and nature. (During the ritual I attended in Stanford, California, the waters-of-life was good Irish whiskey. Whiskey in Gaelic means 'waters of life.') All worship is directed toward nature and various aspects of nature retain the names of the Celtic and Gaulish gods and goddesses:

> Dalon Ap Landu, Lord of the Groves
> Grannos, God of Healing Springs
> Braciaca, God of Malt and Brewing
> Belenos, God of the Sun
> Sirona, Goddess of Rivers
> Taranis, God of Thunder and Lightning
> Llyr, God of the Sea
> Danu, Goddess of Fertility

The "paganizing" of the Reform Druids came as a great surprise to many, and some of the originators regard it as a regression. But from its inception there has been much in RDNA that is Neo-Pagan in nature. The "Order of Worship" includes hymns to the Earth-Mother, to Be'al, and to Dalon Ap Landu, lord of the groves, as well as ancient Welsh and Irish poems. This is fertile ground for anyone with a love of nature, an interest in Celtic lore and myth, and a love of poetry, music, and beauty.

Once the initial protest was over, the most important aspect of Reformed Druidism had to be that it put people in touch with a storehouse of history, myth, and lore. Isaac Bonewits, Arch-Druid of

the Mother Grove of the NRDNA in Berkeley (see below) and certainly an avowed Neo-Pagan, told me, "Over the years it grew and
mutated, much to the horror of the original founders, into a genuine
Neo-Pagan religion. There were actually people who were worshipping the Earth-Mother and the old gods and goddesses, who were
getting off on it and finding it a complete replacement for their traditional religion." Bonewits, Larson, and one or two others played a
large role in this change in direction.

At present there are branches of Reformed Druidism in at least
seven states. The grove at Carleton has existed on and off to this day
as a philosophic path open to the members of many different reli-
gions. There are also non-Pagan RDNA groves in Chicago, Ann
Arbor, and San Jose. In addition, there are a number of Neo-Pagan
branches. Calling themselves the New Reformed Druids of North
America (NRDNA), these groups include Norse Druids in San
Diego, Zen Druids in Olympia, Wiccan Druids in Minneapolis, Irish
Druids (with services in Gaelic) in San Francisco, Hassidic Druids in
St. Louis, and various Eclectic Druids in Oakland, Berkeley, and Los
Angeles. All these groups are autonomous. Bonewits has publicly
stated that Reformed Druidism can survive only if it recognizes its
own nature, which is that of a Neo-Pagan religion.[8]

The NRDNA, unlike the RDNA, is Neo-Pagan. And Isaac's Eclectic Druid grove in Berkeley requires the members of the priesthood
to declare themselves Neo-Pagans and make a commitment to the
religion. His grove, writes Bonewits, "is avowedly Neo-Pagan" and
defines itself as:

> . . . an Eclectic Reconstructionist Neo-Pagan Priestcraft, based primarily
> upon Gaulish and Celtic sources, but open to ideas, deities and rituals
> from many other Neo-Pagan belief systems. We worship the Earth-
> Mother as the feminine personification of Manifestation, Be'al as the
> masculine personification of Essence, and numerous Gods and God-
> desses as personifications of various aspects of our experience. We offer
> no dogma or final answers but only continual questions. Our goal is in-
> creased harmony within ourselves and all of Nature.[9]

Bonewits publishes a newsletter, *The Druid Chronicler*, available
from Box 9398, Berkeley, California 94709. He has also published a

book, *The Druid Chronicles* (*evolved*), which gives the history of Reformed Druidism, the liturgy, and much more.

The Hassidic Druids were formed in 1976 and the group is made up primarily of former Jews who wish to keep certain aspects of Hebrew and Yiddish culture but want to avoid the oppressive nature of what is in many respects a patriarchal theology. They add Yiddish and Hebrew sources to the Gaulish and Celtic ones. They have a set of additional scriptures called the *Mishmash* and the *Te-Mara*, which, in Reformed Druid tradition, satirize in a good natured way the scriptures—this time the Talmud. Most of it is both humorous and profound.[10]

The Reformed Druids have never been a large movement. Even now, with two different branches and twelve different groves, the active members probably number no more than a hundred. Yet they seem to illustrate an important point: When one combines a process of inquiry with content of beauty and antiquity, when, even as a lark, one opens the flow of archetypal images contained in the history and legends of people long negated by this culture, many who confront these images are going to take to them and begin a journey unimagined by those who started the process.

Recent Notes

By 1985, most of the reformed Druid groups were moribund. A few groups are still flourishing. There's a Druid group in Seattle and a lively group in Berkeley, California—the Live Oak Grove. This group publishes *A Druid Missal-any*, has planted a sacred grove, and is doing research into Gaelic rituals.

Meanwhile, after a long absence from the Pagan scene, Isaac Bonewits has started his most ambitious Druid project yet: *Ar nDraiocht Fein* (Our own Druidism). He has started a new journal, *The Druid's Progress*, and, by the time the second issue was out, scores of people were joining the process of slowly, carefully creating a new form of Neo-Pagan Druidism.

Bonewits told me, "It started out as a simple network for a few dozen people who wanted to coordinate research on the old religions of Europe. Then more and more people wanted rituals and clergy training. Now it's a collective act of creation. With the help of 200 people we're creating a new religion."

Bonewits said that he came to realize that the Reformed Druids was not an appropriate vehicle, at least not for him. "Most people in the RDNA were Zen anarchists," Bonewits said. "They had a philosophical approach, applicable to any religion. Most of the RDNA were not Pagans. They resented me and felt I was infiltrating their group."

In *The Druid's Progress*, Bonewits lays out his vision of *Ar nDraiocht Fein*. It would be an attempt to reconstruct, using the best scholarship available, what the Paleopagan Druids actually did, and then try to apply such knowledge to creating a Neo-Pagan religion appropriate for the modern world. It would use the scholarship of authors like George Dumézil, Stuart Piggot, Anne Ross, and Mircea Eliade. It would create rituals and liturgy and would set up a complex training program to achieve excellence. It would "keep nonsense, silliness and romanticism down to a dull roar," he told me. "After all, the Druids had some unpleasant customs which I have no intention of perpetuating. They were headhunters, for example. But it is important to know where you are coming from if you are going to claim you are connected to certain ancestors or traditions. If you say you are a 'Druid' you ought to know what kind of people they were and what kinds of thoughts they had. Then you can pick and choose what parts make sense in modern America."

Bonewits' vision of Druidism is not entirely Celtic or even Pan-Celtic, but Pan-European. It would include all the branches of the Indo-European culture and language tree—Celtic, Germanic, Slavic, Baltic, even pre-classical, archaic Greek, and Roman. While most people are aware that fragments of Druidism seem to have survived in parts of Wales and Ireland, some of them surviving in disguise through the institutions of the Celtic Church and among bards and poets, research done by Russian and Eastern European folklorists, anthropologists, and musicologists, writes Bonewits, "indicates that Paleopagan traditions may have survived in small villages, hidden in the woods and swamps, even into the current century! Some of these villages still had people dressing up in long white robes and going out to sacred groves to do ceremonies, as recently as World War One!"[11] Much of this research has been published in Soviet academic literature and has never been translated. Bonewits believes that this material, combined with Vedic and Old Irish sources will provide most of the missing links in reconstructing Paleopagan European Druidism. Translating these sources will be one of ADF's tasks.

One of the most important aspects of *Ar nDraiocht Fein* is its training system, which is based on a series of levels or circles, somewhat like the organization of the old Church of All Worlds. You can move forward and (if you lose knowledge or skills) backward! Since the Indo-European clergy were supposed to be the intelligentsia of their culture—the poets, the musicians, the historians, and the astronomers, the training for each level includes drama, music, psychic arts, physical and biological and social sciences, counseling, communications, and health skills. Languages are also emphasized. Bonewits is partial to Irish but is seeking scholars in all European languages. Along with many others, he has come to believe that when you invoke a deity in the language their original worshippers used, you get a more powerful magical response.

Bonewits has always been extremely opinionated and often difficult, even egotistical, but he remains one of the most interesting Pagans around. In talking about Druidism, he says flatly that there is no indication that the Druids used stone altars. They did not build Stonehenge, the megalithic circles and lines of northwestern Europe, the Pyramids, or have anything to do with the mythical continents of Atlantis or Mu. What's more, he will not accept what he considers to be the questionable scholarship of Louis Spence, Margaret Murray, Robert Graves, H. P. Blavatsky, and others.

While the local druid groves will have lots of autonomy, Bonewits makes no apologies for the fact that this group will have a structured hierarchy and that Bonewits will be the Arch-Druid. He told me, "I'm being extremely out front about running it as a benevolent dictatorship. I get a lot of feedback, but I make the final decision. These are the rules of this game. You can criticize them, but the rules of the game are the rules of the game. If you don't want to play by them, you should probably start your own Druid group, and I hope you succeed. Some people will think that makes me autocratic," he laughed, "and they're probably right."

Reaction to this approach in Pagan periodicals has ranged from attacks: "Bonewits has come out with *his* plea in the wilderness. 'Support me and I'll be your Guru.' Give me a break Isaac" (*Pegasus Express*) to great praise: "This is actually a good approach for a young organization whose founder wishes it to proliferate and generally be successful" (*Panegyria*). Appearing at major Pagan festivals, Isaac has had a rousing response. Clustering around him on an evening, you might find an intense discussion, or three Celtic harpists playing for each other and exchanging information. His training program has gotten many people talking. Several priests and priestesses in other traditions, feeling that their own training was haphazard, have talked about incorporating elements of his system into their own groups. Several local Druid groves have already formed. There is clearly a thirst for structured study and scholarship within the Pagan movement and *Ar nDraiocht Fein* is one group that is going to try and fill that need. The pendulum always swings.

If a number of Neo-Pagan groups began in a spirit of play and, while remaining true to that spirit, grew more serious, there is one Neo-Pagan phenomenon that will never become too serious: the Erisian movement and groups connected with it that have been engaging in absurdist and surrealist activities for the past seven or eight years.

In a way, it's ridiculous even to talk seriously about the Erisians, a group, or collection of groups, that has called itself a "Non-prophet Irreligious Disorganization" that is "dedicated to an advanced understanding of the paraphysical manifestations of Everyday Chaos,"[12] and at other times has stated, "The Erisian revelation is not a complicated put-on disguised as a new religion, but a new religion disguised as a complicated put-on."[13]

The Discordian Society was founded (if one can call it that) in 1957 (or 1958—even this primary confusion has never been cleared up) by Greg Hill (Malaclypse the Younger) and Kerry Thornley (Omar Ravenhurst). After the initial "Erisian Revelation" (see below), Malaclypse the Younger went on to start an Erisian Neo-Pagan Paradox Cult called the Paratheoanametamystikhood of Eris Esoteric (POEE), and in 1970 POEE published the *Principia Discordia, or How I Found Goddess and What I Did To Her When I Found Her.* The first edition—there have been five—was five photocopies; the second was quickly offset in New Orleans, and the third was printed in Tampa. By now, at least several thousand have been distributed. Omar Ravenhurst went on to form his own Erisian organization, the Erisian Liberation Front (ELF). The *Principia* puts the story of the beginning of the Erisian movement this way:

THE BIRTH OF THE ERISIAN MOVEMENT

The Earth quakes and the Heavens rattle; the beasts of nature flock together and the nations of men flock apart; volcanoes usher up heat while elsewhere water becomes ice and melts; and then on other days it just rains.

Indeed do many things come to pass.

HBT; The Book of
Predictions, Chap. 19

THE REVELATION

Just prior to the decade of the 1960s, when Sputnik was alone and new, and about the time that Ken Kesey took his first acid trip as a medical volunteer; before underground newspapers, Viet Nam, and talk of a second American Revolution; in the comparative quiet of the late 1950s, just before the idea of RENAISSANCE became relevant . . .

Two young Californians, known later as Omar Ravenhurst and Malaclypse the Younger, were indulging in their habit of sipping coffee at an all-night bowling alley and generally solving the world's problems. This particular evening they were complaining to each other of the personal confusion they felt in their respective lives. "Solve the problem of discord," said one, "and all other problems will vanish."

"Indeed," said the other, "chaos and strife are the roots of all confusion."

FIRST I MUST SPRINKLE YOU
WITH FAIRY DUST

Suddenly the place became devoid of light. Then an utter silence enveloped them, and a great stillness was felt. Then came a blinding flash of intense light, as though their very psyches had gone nova. Then vision returned.

The two were dazed and neither moved nor spoke for several minutes. They looked around and saw that the bowlers were frozen like statues in a variety of comic positions, and that a bowling ball was steadfastly anchored to the floor only inches from the pins that it had been sent to scatter. The two looked at each other, totally unable to account for the phenomenon. The condition was one of suspension, and one noticed that the clock had stopped.

There walked into the room a chimpanzee, shaggy and grey about the muzzle, yet upright to his full five feet, and poised with natural majesty. He carried a scroll and walked to the young men.

"Gentlemen," he said, "why does Pickering's Moon go about in reverse orbit? Gentlemen, there are nipples on your chest; do you give milk? And what, pray tell, Gentlemen, is to be done about Heisenberg's Law?" He paused. "SOMEBODY HAD TO PUT ALL OF THIS CONFUSION HERE!"

And with that he revealed his scroll. It was a diagram, like a yin-yang with a pentagon on one side and an apple on the other. And then he exploded and the two lost consciousness.

Eris—Goddess of Chaos,
Discord & Confusion

They awoke to the sound of pins clattering, and found the bowlers engaged in their game and the waitress busy making coffee. It was apparent that their experience had been private.

They discussed their strange encounter and reconstructed from memory the chimpanzee's diagram. Over the next five days they searched libraries to find the significance of it, but were disappointed to uncover only references to Taoism, the Korean flag, and Technocracy. It was not until they traced the Greek writing on the apple that they discovered the ancient Goddess known to the Greeks as ERIS and to the Romans as DISCORDIA. This was on the fifth night, and when they slept that night each had a vivid dream of a splendid woman whose eyes were as soft as feather and as deep as eternity itself, and whose body was the spectacular dance of atoms and universes. Pyrotechnics of pure energy formed her flowing hair, and rainbows manifested and dissolved as she spoke in a warm and gentle voice:

"I have come to tell you that you are free. Many years ago, My consciousness left Man, that he might develop himself. I return to find this development approaching completion, but hindered by fear and by misunderstanding.

"You have built for yourselves psychic suits of armor, and clad in them, your vision is restricted, your movements are clumsy and painful, your skin is bruised, and your spirit is broiled in the sun.

"I am chaos. I am the substance from which your artists and scientists build rhythms. I am the spirit with which your children and clowns laugh in happy anarchy. I am chaos. I am alive, and I tell you that you are free."

During the next months they studied philosophies and theologies, and learned that ERIS or DISCORDIA was primarily feared by the ancients as being disruptive. Indeed, the very concept of chaos was still considered equivalent to strife and treated as a negative. "No wonder things are all screwed up," they concluded. "They have got it all backwards." They found that the principle of disorder was every much as significant as the principle of order.

With this in mind, they studied the strange yin-yang. During a meditation one afternoon, a voice came to them:

"It is called THE SACRED CHAO. I appoint you Keepers of It. Therein you will find anything you like. Speak of me as DISCORD, to show contrast to the pentagon. Tell constricted Mankind that there are no rules, unless they choose to invent rules. Keep close the words of Syadasti: 'TIS AN ILL WIND THAT BLOWS NO MINDS. And remember that there is no tyranny in the State of Confusion. For further information, consult your pineal gland."

"What is this?" mumbled one to the other, "A religion based on the Goddess of Confusion? It is utter madness!" ... And amid squeals of mirth and with tears on their cheeks, each appointed the other to be high priest of his own madness, and together they declared themselves to be a society of Discordia for whatever that may turn out to be.[14]

The *Principia* was composed from articles and ideas that Greg Hill (Mal) collected during communications with co-conspirators. In 1969 Mal started the Joshua Norton Cabal. (Emperor Joshua Norton lived in the late 1800s in San Francisco. He declared himself emperor of the world and issued his own money, and, proving that one *can* often create one's own reality, much of San Francisco humored him—accepted his money in bars and so forth. It is said that thousands came to his funeral.) Other Erisian cabals formed. At one point there were rumored to be more than twenty, although some may have had a membership of only one. Since radical decentralization is a Discordian principle, it is impossible to know how many Discordians there were and are, or what they are doing. Most of these cabals engaged in various nonviolent, absurdist, revolutionary, magical, and surrealist endeavors. A number of these "actions" were done under the name of the supposed "Bavarian Illuminati," a rather mysterious organization founded by Adam Weishaupt in 1776. The Erisian "Illuminati" have mostly been the inspiration of someone known as Thomas Gnostic. Similar actions were initiated by ELF. Omar Ravenhurst, for example, invented a Do-It-Yourself Conspiracy Kit, complete with assortments of stationery bearing dubious letterheads. Robert Anton Wilson, a leading Discordian (sometimes known as Mordecai the Foul), described one such action.

Omar would send a letter to the Christian Anti-Communist Crusade on Bavarian Illuminati stationery, saying, "We're amused you've discovered that we've taken over the Rock Music business. But you're still so naive. We took over the business in the 1800s. Beethoven was our first convert."

A number of these Discordian actions found their way into the underground press in the late sixties and early seventies. They were not, Wilson told me, "hoaxes," for "a hoax suggests something that's done out of adolescent perversity. I regard them rather as educational projects. We are teaching people that there are alternate realities."

Discordianism is an anarchist's paradise. One of its mottoes is "We Discordians Shall Stick Apart." And all you have to do to become a member of the Discordian Society is (1) decide it exists and (2) include yourself in it. Greg Hill has described himself as a "Transcendental Atheist" who has always been interested in absurdist religion and, discovering that the ancient Greeks had a goddess of confusion, decided it was the funniest thing he had ever heard. But POEE is a priesthood of sorts, and you can become a priest by (as you might expect) declaring yourself one. POEE has thousands of wallet-sized "Pope Cards."

Wilson (Mordecai) has described himself as a "Transcendental Agnostic," although, he added whimsically, "There are many me's." He recently told an interviewer from a science fiction magazine:

I'm an initiated witch, an ordained minister in four churches (or cults) and have various other "credentials" to impress the gullible. My philoso-

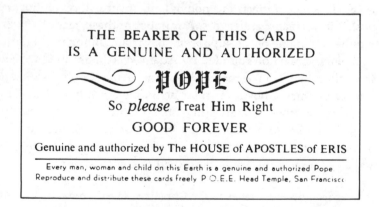

THE BEARER OF THIS CARD
IS A GENUINE AND AUTHORIZED

∾ 𝔓𝔬𝔭𝔢 ∾

So *please* Treat Him Right

GOOD FOREVER

Genuine and authorized by The HOUSE of APOSTLES of ERIS

Every man, woman and child on this Earth is a genuine and authorized Pope
Reproduce and distribute these cards freely P.O.E.E. Head Temple, San Francisco

phy remains Transcendental Agnosticism. There are realities and intelligences greater than conditioned normal consciousness recognizes, but it is premature to dogmatize about them at this primitive stage of our evolution. We've hardly begun to crawl off the surface of the cradle-planet.[15]

Wilson, along with another Erisian named Robert Shea, co-authored *Illuminatus*, a three-volume science fiction/occult/conspiracy novel that takes place in an Erisian framework. Its success in both science fiction and occult circles may prove to be the springboard for more Erisian activity, although the opposite could just as easily occur. In fact, one Erisian magazine in New Jersey published a notice dissolving the local Erisian cabal. The reason: "Since the beans were spilled in the proverbial manner (see *Illuminatus*) it is necessary to retreat to a more esoteric position."[16] Meanwhile, Malaclypse has given notice that the Eris in the *Principia* and the Eris in *Illuminatus* are *not* the same Eris.

Whichever Eris you choose, she always seems to take the form of paradox, and an Erisian notice printed in *Green Egg* said that the Erisian path generally appealed to those who have "an affinity toward taoism, anarchy and clowning; who can feel comfortable in a Neo-Pagan context; and who probably have a tendency toward iconoclasm."[17]

And Discordianism plans to stay humorous. Wilson says, "Much of the Pagan movement started out as jokes, and gradually, as people found out they were getting something out of it, they became serious. Discordianism has a built-in check against getting too serious. The sacred scriptures are so absurd—as soon as you consult the scriptures again, you start laughing. Discordian theology is similar to Crowleyanity. You take any of these ideas far enough and they reveal the absurdity of all ideas. They show that ideas are only tools and that no idea should be sacrosanct. Thus, Discordianism is a necessary balance. It's a fail-safe system. It remains a joke and provides perspective. It's a satire on human intelligence and is based on the idea that whatever your map of reality, it's ninety percent your own creation. People should accept this and be proud of their own artistry. Discordianism can't get dogmatic. The whole language would have to change for people to lose track that it was all a joke to begin with. It would take a thousand years."

The Erisian position on humor has always been clear, and to prove it, here is another section from the sacred scriptures, the *Principia*.[18]

THE DISCORDIAN SOCIETY
Joshua Norton Cabal
San Francisco

THERE IS NO ENEMY

ANYWHERE.

GREYFACE

In the year 1166 B.C., a malcontented hunchbrain by the name of Grey-face, got it into his head that the universe was as humorless as he, and he began to teach that play was sinful because it contradicted the ways of Serious Order. "Look at all the order about you," he said. And from that, he deluded honest men to believe that reality was a straightjacket affair and not the happy romance as men had known it.

It is not presently understood why men were so gullible at that partic-ular time, for absolutely no one thought to observe all the *disorder* around them and conclude just the opposite. But anyway, Greyface and his fol-lowers took the game of playing at life more seriously than they took life itself and were known even to destroy other living beings whose ways of life differed from their own.

The unfortunate result of this is that mankind has since been suffering from a psychological and spiritual imbalance. Imbalance causes frustra-tion, and frustration causes fear. And fear makes a bad trip. Man has been on a bad trip for a long time now.

It is called THE CURSE OF GREYFACE.

The Curse of Greyface and The Introduction of Negativism

To choose order over disorder, or disorder over order, is to accept a trip composed of both the creative and the destructive. But to choose the creative over the destructive is an all-creative trip composed of both order and disorder. To accomplish this, one need only accept creative disorder along with, and equal to, creative order, and also be willing to reject destructive order as an undesirable equal to destructive disorder.

The Curse of Greyface included the division of life into order/disorder as the essential positive/negative polarity, instead of building a game foundation with creative/destructive as the essential positive/negative.

He has thereby caused man to endure the destructive aspects of order and has prevented man from effectively participating in the creative uses of disorder. Civilization reflects this unfortunate division.

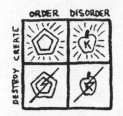

POEE proclaims that the other division is preferable, and we work toward the proposition that creative disorder, like creative order, is possible and desirable; and that destructive order, like destructive disorder, is unnecessary and undesirable.

Seek the Sacred Chao—therein you will find the foolishness of all ORDER/DISORDER. They are the same!

Principia Discordia or How I found Goddess and what I did to Her when I found Her

And yet Erisianism should not be treated frivolously. Greg Hill told me his experiences with Eris had been quite profound. Although it started as an atheistic joke, his perceptions began to change.

"Eris is an authentic goddess. Furthermore, she is an old one. In the beginning I saw myself as a cosmic clown. I characterized myself as Malaclypse the Younger. But if you do this type of thing well enough, it starts to work. In due time the polarities between atheism and theism became absurd. The engagement was transcendent. And when you transcend one, you have to transcend the other. I started out with the idea that all gods are an illusion. By the end I had learned that it's *up to you* to decide whether gods exist, and if you take a goddess of confusion seriously, it will send you through as profound and valid a metaphysical trip as taking a god like Yahweh seriously. The trips will be different, but they will both be transcendental. Eris is a valid goddess in so far as gods are valid; and gods are valid when we choose them to be. The Christian tradition has become so totally alienated from reality in the Western world that people have had to start inventing their own damn gods. Some people are doing it seriously and it is validly working. The Neo-Pagan phenomenon is an example. Another path would be transcendental atheism: using atheism as a spiritual path. The phenomenon of Eris is a hybrid between the two. She is an absurdist deity who shows that nonsense is as valid as sense, since Eris is as preposterous a deity as ever invented. Yet, if you pursue her, it can be a valid spiritual experience that can carry you to the point where you no longer relate to things in terms of deities and nondeities."

For Wilson also, Discordianism is a perceptual game, a means of expanding one's perception of reality. The Discordian position, he has written, "demands, then, continuous motion. To stop at any one metaphor and establish it as dogma is to put the mind in chains." He adds, "Although Discordians move about the country and the world constantly, in many guises, there is always one major Discordian ashram in the San Francisco Bay Area 'on the site of the beautiful future San Andreas Canyon.' The only way to remain sane is to *know* that the ground below you is pure Void."[19]

I asked Malaclypse, "What's Omar Ravenhurst doing these days?" He said, "Ravenhurst has recently been in a state of extreme discord. We were talking about Eris and confusion and he said, 'You know, if I had realized that all of this was going to come *true*, I would have chosen Venus.'"

Recent Notes

Discordians and Erisians are very much present in the Pagan community today. They make their presence known at Pagan festivals, and there are several journals with a Discordian point of view.

The Pagan community is one of the only spiritual communities that is exploring humor, joy, abandonment, even silliness and outrageousness as valid parts of spiritual experience. Oz, a Craft priestess from New Mexico, wrote these words to me only days before the final revisions for this edition of my book were due:

> The Pagan movement is exploring social change in a way that I don't see it done anywhere else. We are living with nudity, sexual freedom, license for experimentation, freedom of thought and a loose, fun joy that is unique.
> I don't see other "magickal" people developing a culture of boisterous joy. To

find in expression, silliness, outrageousness, pushing the limits—to find that in this there is spirit. If you think about the dual meaning of the word "spirit" for a moment, I think you have it. I now get much of my intellectual and even spiritual stimulation from people who are not Witches or Pagans, but when I want to be around people with whom I am comfortable living my life the way I like to live it, who are being exceedingly open about everything from soup to nuts, who won't think you're crazy if you express a silly desire and act on it, I hang out with Pagans.

There are now many places where you can find alternatives to patriarchal Christian culture, places that are open to the mystical and the feminine. What exists in Paganism is the exposure to others that aren't afraid to dream a different dream and try to live it.

We're not following anybody. We're like explorers on a new planet in some ways. And we say as Discordians say, "Don't make plans."

12

Radical Faeries and the Growth of Men's Spirituality

In the last eight or nine years, alongside the enormous and continuing growth of women's spirituality, there has sprung up, in almost parallel fashion, a small spiritual movement among men. This movement is connected with the feminist critique of patriarchal notions of religion and authority, and with the attempt of both gay and straight men to create a new definition of maleness.

Many men within Neo-Paganism have asked the question, "What is our role to be?" This question is not being asked very much within the British-based traditions of Wicca. In fact, many men within the dualistic traditions of the Craft, where the Goddess and the God are given equal, if polarized, roles, simply feel that the pendulum has swung too far and that the male aspects, the "God" aspects of the Craft, have been neglected. But among the less insular parts of the Pagan movement, and among men who have considered themselves feminists, or aligned with the feminist critique of our society, there has been a strong pull toward re-examining the role of men, with a view to reclaiming a non-sexist, but whole and strong, male nature.

For example, there is a Pagan newsletter called *Brothersong*, formerly called the *Brothers of the Earth Newsletter*. In the Yule 1983 issue, the editor

338

describes himself as a bisexual man whose primary relationship is with a woman. He also has a four-year-old daughter. "This is without exaggeration a very difficult and troubling time for men and boys with regards to the relationship between the sexes," he writes. He says that he has publicly identified himself as a feminist, spoken out against rape and pornography, and participated in demonstrations. But increasingly, he says, he feels disappointment and pain. While describing positive connections between men and women, he feels a need to express "anger at the rejection that I and an increasing number of changing men feel about being purposefully isolated and excluded from the opportunity of working with our Sisters on issues which concern us all." He adds that "the continual lumping together of all men as the enemy" which he had previously only identified as a "separatist position" is very prevalent throughout the feminist movement. He says that he is not challenging the need for "women's space"; he understands the reasons for rage, pain, and distrust toward men, but he writes that he also hears the pain and anguish of changing and loving men whose reborn and beautiful spirits have begun to languish and die in isolation. "And I hear," he writes, "the pain of Brothers who are aimlessly searching for alternatives and whose confused and oppressed natures need yet to be challenged and healed."[1]

The editor of *Brothersong*, Gary Lingen, believes that men must accept responsibility for their own transformation, and they must connect with each other to achieve that goal. Brothers of the Earth was created to be a network—a separate place for men and boys to celebrate and empower themselves, a place to examine and celebrate the cycles of life and the passages of men's lives.

In the past, ideas about men's roles have been examined deeply by intellectuals like Jean Paul Sartre and Simone de Beauvoir, but these ideas seldom filter down to the culture at large. Today, the man who has been speaking most publicly about these questions is the poet Robert Bly. For the last few years, Bly has lectured across the country on the subject of men. Articles sharing his views with readers have found their way into magazines like *New Age*. Bly says that over the last twenty years, many men have begun to acknowledge their feminine side; often they have become more nurturing and gentle. But often these men seem incomplete; they lack energy.

In his lectures, Bly often uses a fairy tale sometimes called "Iron John." In this story, there is a kingdom far away where men are constantly disappearing in a forest, and no one knows why. Finally a stranger comes to the kingdom and sets out to find the answer. He finds a strange hairy Wildman, and he pulls him up from a deep pool. The man is put in a cage. For Bly, this hairy man represents the deep and dark part of man's psyche, a part of their natures with which they must reconnect if they are to be whole. Getting in touch with the feminine gives men one key to their nature, but, says Bly, the Wildman holds the other key.

In a second part of the story, a child loses a golden ball and it rolls into the cage of the Wildman. To get the ball, the child takes the key to the cage from under his mother's pillow and lets the Wildman out of the cage. For Bly, the golden ball is the unity of our natures, a unity that we usually only experience as children. Bly suggests that, for men, the golden ball lies within the deep, dark, primal field of the Wildman; that men, to become whole, must go deep into this place of the true masculine. To do this, men must confront the ancient mythologies, must in some way move against the forces of Western civilization, must leave the force field of the mother and the force field of collective male society and, as the initiate, confront the Wildman alone. In this way, says Bly, men will gain their true fierce energy, but it will not be a strength based on chauvinistic concepts of domination and control.[2]

There are many different perspectives in the search for new male roles, but in an article in the April/May 1986 *Utne Reader*, writer Shepard Bliss says that two viewpoints emerge as dominant: the feminist and the mythopoetic. The feminist approach (led by organizations like the National Organization of Changing Men) emphasizes the problems of sexism and patriarchy. The mythopoetic tradition, led by Robert Bly, argues against certain aspects of the feminist critique. Our society may be sexist and even male dominated, says Bly, but patriarchy means "the rule of the fathers," and our society is characterized by an absence of fathers.[3]

Within the Pagan community, many men are awakening to their need to explore these realms. This is a movement that is not bound by sexual preference. It involves heterosexuals and homosexuals. But just as the women's spirituality movement received some of its strength, its push, its most dynamic energy from lesbian women, gay men have often been at the forefront of developing this new view of male spirituality. Just as women from the mixed branches of Paganism were forced to confront an energetic movement of women's religion and were changed by it, many men within Paganism and the Craft are now having a similar experience.

And the several thousand who go to the large festivals every year and bring what they have learned back home to countless others have been greatly affected by those who are known as the "radical faeries" (or fairies). From lingerie "tea dances" to explosive encounter sessions between gay and heterosexual men, the radical faeries have brought changes to the Pagan community.

The Radical Faeries

The movement of radical faeries began around 1978. Its official beginning can be traced to a 1979 gathering, a Spiritual Conference for Radical Fairies that was held at a desert sanctuary near Tucson, Arizona. A couple of months earlier, Arthur Evans—whose book *Witchcraft and the Gay Counterculture* argued that gay men needed to look at the connections between gay spirituality and the old Pagan nature religions—held a faerie circle in a redwood forest. This led to a conference, "A Call to Gay Brothers," in Arizona. As one writer wrote in *RFD*—the journal that has most consistently detailed the growth of faery spirituality—"the conference was issued as a 'call' in the Sufi sense." Those who were ready to hear the call would come.[4]

The gathering, and the subsequent growth of radical faery spirituality, came out of a deep spiritual need. As one man told me recently, "We all wanted something that we didn't have and we desperately wanted it, but we didn't know what it was." Jody, a man who has been involved with shamanic forms of Witchcraft for a number of years, told me that before meeting with the radical faeries, his experiences in gay culture had left him frustrated, angry, and disillusioned. "When I first 'came out,' I experienced this rush—'I can finally love, I can finally have sex, I can finally express myself.' But in many ways the gay culture did not serve my needs. I felt that, in many ways, it was an oppressive parody of straight culture. It takes place primarily in bars, where music is loud and people are not encouraged to talk, or form bonds or care for each other. It imitates the worst of heterosexual culture. I found I had to become a different person to get laid, and I didn't like that at all. I became ashamed and I wondered, 'Is this the best we have to offer?' "

Jody went to the second faerie gathering, held in the mountains of Colorado. "When I arrived," he told me, "I knew I was home. This is my culture. These are people who don't become someone else in order to make love. They live their sexuality in a way that is very connected to the earth."

At the first faerie gathering in Arizona, the rituals were often completely spontaneous and unplanned. At one point, a man said that one of his urges was to go out into the desert with buckets of water and cover himself with wet sand. In the end, forty men went with him on a Sunday morning. "What started out to be a lighthearted romp," writes one, "turned into a serious tribal affair. Something about the nudity and the primitiveness of the chanting and the ambiance of the gathering triggered a primal urge in them all and the chanting became more real." A bystander, taken by the spirit of the gathering, took off his clothes and started down the bank.

> Immediately there was a sense of initiation. They held him on their shoulders—a completely white body amid the mud people. They lowered him into the ooze and covered him over. They held him up high again and began to chant. After they put him down another spontaneous dance broke out. It was truly watching a tribal ritual. Even the photographs I've seen since are uncanny—like right out of National Geographic. The men in the photos aren't accountants or teachers or movie cameramen or lawyers or students or radical leftists or physicians or clerks or postal workers. They're members of the same tribe. It did not escape anyone how leveling the mud was. They were all the same and they got an electric sense of unity and power from it.[5]

Another man, describing the curious onlookers, wrote, "I saw tourists with Nikons standing on a bluff above us, stealing our visions to sell and felt maybe how aborigines feel when they find their faces in National Geographic."[6] A third participant observed, "Joyously caked with mud and with several dozen of my brothers—singing, dancing, shouting—I evoked a sensation of timelessness that I sometimes feel during especially satisfying love making, that I am in touch with something thousands and thousands of years old. This skeptical Marxist-Buddhist-Unitarian has become a true believer in the Fairy Spirit."[7]

There was one large, structured ritual—the Great Faery Circle. It began with a torchlight procession, parading through the Arizona desert, to the sound of flutes. "The moon grows full; we dance in its light,"[8] wrote one. Another said, "In the twilight the gathering . . . was extraordinary. There was no self-consciousness, everyone seemed to anticipate doing a great work and they began clapping and chanting as the musicians began to play. . . . As soon as they got away from the compound and into the desert under the moon, they became quiet, and as soon as they entered the wash with its scraggy trees and low mesquite bushes, power seemed to enter them."

A small wire cage was brought out. "There were things we had come with—thoughts, ideas, anxieties, fears, anything which chained or shackled us—we would not be taking back to our other world with us. These were whispered, spoken, screamed into the cage and never let out again. As the cage began to make its way around the circle, spontaneous chants began. . . . A low hum began but quickly moved into more agitated, coarser, emotion-filled cries. Hisses and isolated screams—and then came the most frightening of all—the animal noises. From seemingly nowhere, howls, barks, growling, roars, began softly and grew to a terrifying proportion. . . . It died as quickly as it had started and was replaced by a soft keening. I have never experienced so many people in harmony, nor had so much gooseflesh.

"When the cage had been around the circle, the leader took it to the center, and held it up, over his head. Slowly he walked around the fire so everyone could see what they were throwing away and then, with a great shout, he flung the cage and everything it contained far into the desert darkness."[9]

"In the beginning," Peter Soderberg, a radical faerie from Iowa told me, "we had no answers, we cried a lot, and laughed a lot, and sometimes we were cruel to each other. Living in a culture that has this idea that the physical and the spiritual are split, we didn't even have a vocabulary for speaking about what we needed. When we say 'spiritual' in our society, it usually doesn't encompass my flesh, the food I eat, the art I make, and the pleasure I get from my friends. But what I came to understand quickly was that being around faeries was the first safe place for me." And Don, another faerie man added, "We wanted a family, not a club, not an organization." Peter chimed in, "a place that we could be really honest with each other in this really direct way that scares people."

One important impulse behind the notion of radical faeries was the idea that there had to be something beyond assimilation. Just as radical feminists wanted to go beyond women attaining equal rights in a man's world, toward a notion that feminism implied a totally different reality, a different language, a different attitude toward power and authority, this group of gay men saw their own movement as implying a totally different view of the world, with different goals and different spiritual values than the "straight" world. Harry Hays is said to have once put it something like this: "People who are trying to be accepted by the 'straight' world pander to the straights, saying, 'We're really just the same as you, the only thing we do different is what we do in bed.' No," says Hays, "the only thing we do the *same* is in bed."

In an article in *RFD* called "A Sprinkling of Radical Faerie Dust," Don Kilhefner writes that the dilemma facing gay men is "our assimilation into the mainstream versus our enspiritment as a people. . . . There is a reality to being Gay that is radically *different* from being Straight. . . . It is real. We can feel it in our hearts and in our guts."[10] But where does one find role models for such a person? One article in *RFD* suggests:

> We gays cast our nets out into the mythic sea, searching for our own lost archetypes, our spiritual role models . . . those symbols of the human psyche which we may claim as emblematic of our particular way of being.[11]

Gay men began looking at the role of the shaman, the berdache, and the bardajo. Writing in *RFD*, J. Michael Clark described the magical and spiritual role of the "berdache" in certain tribal cultures. Berdache was a term, first popularized among French explorers, which came to mean a person of one sex who assumes the role and status of the opposite sex. This person was socially accepted in these cultures and often was considered to have an enhanced spirituality. Similarly, other writers in *RFD* and elsewhere noted the role of homosexuality, cross-dressing, role changing, and androgyny in shamanic cultures and the fact that it is often easier for someone who is not tied down to specific gender roles to walk between the worlds.[12]

"We are the equivalent of Shamans in modern culture," said Peter Soderberg, during an interview at the 1985 Pagan Spirit Gathering. "Many gay men want to be middle-class Americans. They want to be respected as human beings and they want their sexuality to be ignored. But radical faeries are willing to live on the edge. We feel there is a power in our sexuality. You know there is a power there because our culture is so afraid of us. And there is a lot of queer energy in the men and women most cultures consider magical. It's practically a requirement for certain kinds of medicine and magic. The Pagan movement doesn't give credit to this, or even know about it, but then, there's a lot of heterosexism in modern Neo-Pagan culture."

Similar ideas were expressed to me by Jody, as we sat in a forest in the Berkshires at the 1985 COG Grand Council. "Look," he told me, "if most of the traditions of Wicca have been destroyed, gay spirituality has been totally eradicated. After all, think of the origin of the word 'faggot,' we were burned along with the Witches. Our magic was destroyed. It was not preserved like indoor ceremonial magic was preserved."

Jody quoted from *Visionary Love* by Mitch Walker;[13] he said that a door can be opened when you have psychic knowledge of male and female united within yourself. You then form a oneness that is a gate which connects you with the sexuality of nature creation. Jody believes that the elements of play and shape-changing so necessary for magic come more easily when you are one body instead of two, when the idea of gender doesn't come between you and the various parts you might play. "It is simply easier," he told me, "to blend with a nature spirit, or the spirit of a plant or animal, if you are not concerned with a gender-specific role."

Radical faeries seem preoccupied with questions of process and form. Just as feminist women have been struggling with questions about auuthority, forms of leadership, decision making, language, and control, these gay men seem to spend much of their time struggling with the same kinds of questions. "Process *is* content," Peter told me. As a person who has always felt content was more important than form, I was dismayed. But in Peter's view, society's violence begins at the place where creativity and self-expression is controlled. "In our system of male dominance," he told me, "there is an unexpressed contract that says: 'It is safer to control energy than it is to experience energy.' In our society men are the 'control' referents, and women the 'experience' referents." On the most superficial level this would mean: "Women are feeling people. Women must be controlled." But on a subtler level Peter believes that this system exists within every human being. We tend to control our experiences, instead of participating in them and acting from them.

In contrast, faerie reality says, "It is more enjoyable to experience energy than to control energy," that the need for violence will disappear as creativity and real self-expression increase. Faerie gatherings, at their best, would be places where experimentation with new social forms could take place. They would not be a place for set rituals or workshops given by "leaders." Writes one man: "Spirituality has to be discovered . . . by each individual. Even the Native American cultures with a highly spiritual worldview did not 'teach' it. Instead, the young of the tribe, as part of their initiation, went on a vision quest to seek their own personal experience with the spirit realm."[14]

When they come to conferences about men, or participate in Pagan festivals, radical faeries often promote what might be called Discordian or Erisian energy (see Chapter 11). They have been the public anarchists. As the main, formal ritual was about to begin at a recent Pagan gathering, a group of faery men stood at the entrance to the circle, calling out, "Attention! No spontaneity! We're the spontaneity police!" In general, they have been uncomfortable with formal workshops, with discussions by "leaders," with models that are top-down or front-to-back. They do not want "elders," or parental authority figures. Above all, they want to elevate the transformative power of play.

At the Pagan Spirit Gathering, Peter told me, "If you want to come to the faery camp, bring lots of clothes, bring lots of toys. If you bring things that are fun, you will find out what the process is about. It's the flip side of our culture. It seems nonsensical but it makes perfect sense." "Patriarchy, in a nutshell," said Don, "is about taking control. It permeates everything in our culture, including Paganism." If the problem is control, they see spontaneity and play as the antidotes. "There's lots of laughter and gossip among the faeries," said Don. "We love to share and we hate secrets."

The first Pagan gathering where there was a significant presence of gay men was the Pan-Pagan Festival in 1980. The presence of feminist women like Z Budapest combined with the men created explosive divisions and change. One afternoon at the gathering, Z Budapest led a circle of some sixty women. For many women at the campsite in Indiana, it was their first experience in an all-woman ritual. Z had enlisted the aid of a group of men, many of them gay, to protect the perimeter of the circle, since the camp was adjacent to a public camping area, and many at the ritual went skyclad (or nude).

The ritual began with a procession past a lake. Women holding branches of flowers walked through the camp singing. Many Pagans heard for the first time the words that would soon become one of the best-known festival chants:

> We all come from the Goddess, and to her we shall return, like a drop of rain, flowing to the ocean.

The women gathered in a circle, chanted, danced, and wove webs of brightly colored yarn to symbolize their connection with each other. Unbeknownst to the women in the circle, one of the organizers of the festival was so angered and upset by the all-woman skyclad ritual that he tried to break through the circle of men guarding the rite, in order to pull his wife and child out. The controversy was one of several—all of them confrontations over politics or life style—that led to the breakup of the ecumenical council that had put on this gathering for four years. Three separate factions put on festivals the next summer.

Since 1981, at the Pagan Spirit Gathering, and at many other festivals—from Georgia to Ontario, from Massachusetts to New Mexico—there have been workshops and rituals for men. There have been faerie circles, but there have also been rituals and workshops where men of different sexual persuasions have come together, sometimes explosively, often joyously, and frequently with some unease.

One of the most unusual new developments at festivals has been the "tea dance." When it first appeared at a festival put on by the Athanor Fellowship, it seemed strangely out of place—disco music, alcoholic beverages, and dressing up in lingerie and crazy clothes. It seemed more suited to the gay community on Fire Island, not a wooded setting filled with Witches, vegetarians, and ecology buffs who rarely drank anything stronger than wine. The Athanor Fellowship—a group with few gays in it—found the dance so successful that it began to take it around from gathering to gathering until an enormous number of Pagans had let down their hair, dressed in costume, put on wigs and makeup, and had simply let loose. And no one will ever forget the moment when the quiet, poetic, retiring, and definitely heterosexual Jim Alan of Circle Farm appeared dressed as a stunning woman with silver gloves and a blue bodice.

"I remember someone saying the other night," Jody reflected, "that when he first entered the Pagan community, you could not even touch another man. And there were regular polarity checks in circles—you know, boy, girl, boy, girl. There's been a wonderful loosening and blossoming in the last few years, but there is also much resistance.

"I remember one meeting of men, at a gathering, where I decided I would come in a dress. I was asked to give 'the gay perspective.' I talked about the evils of competitive aggression, how it alienates men from each other. When I was finished, one man rose to speak. 'I love women and I get along with other men,' he said, 'but I'm a *man*, understand?' And I said, 'Look buddy, *I* am a man. A *strong* man. A man who knows how to get what he wants, and I don't have to stomp on others to get it. And nobody backs me down.' "

But thinking over the last few years of Pagan gatherings, Jody observed, "I do think we have a place here, a voice here and I think it's the voice of the faery spirit coming through these men." And writing after a week-long festival in 1982, another man observed, "This is difficult and delicate work we are doing. There are many changes that we need to make, much violence we need to transform and lots of old hurts we need to face. It is a sturdy, easily-found playfulness we are headed toward. . . . But this journey being taken by men of all persuasions (plus a few that we haven't managed to persuade yet) is just beginning."[15]

Some of the men I spoke to—both gay and straight—argued that their journey to freedom was even more difficult than the journey of women. "If you think it's hard to free yourself from being the oppressed, think how much harder it is to free yourself from being the oppressor," Jody insisted. "Why so?" I asked. "Because the role is entirely played out inside yourself. You have no one to say, 'get off my back.' With men, the oppression is all inside, and to root it out, you have to open up men's ability to feel." "Women have also internalized their oppression," I observed. "Yes," said Jody, "but men have been cut off from their hearts; there is no communication between their heads and their hearts and oppression is only possible when one no longer feels the result of one's actions on people and other creatures."

Jody and many of the faeries believe the time is ripe for men's liberation and they believe that gay men will have a special role to play, just as gay women have had a unique role to play in the liberation of women. They are convinced that they have liberated themselves from many of the things most men don't even realize oppress them. They believe they know how to be simultaneously strong and vulnerable. "Finally," said Jody, "we have the ability to play. Men who are stuck in the role model of the stern, mature adult never truly engage in creative play.

"So think about the tea dance," he said at the end. "All those men and women in crazy lingerie, dancing weirdly and loving it! Five years ago, it would never have happened. It's wonderful! Think of all the new ideas they may now have, now that they have found a way to get beyond their locked perceptions of role and place."

IV. *The Material Plane*

13

Scholars, Writers, Journalists, and the Occult

All statements are true in some sense, false in some sense, meaningless in some sense, true and false in some sense, true and meaningless in some sense, false and meaningless in some sense, and true and false and meaningless in some sense.
—Principia Discordia[1]

To account for the current resurgence of occultism in the popular culture of America by means of any monistic psychological or sociological theory is to oversimplify the reality of the many movements.
—MARCELLO TRUZZI[2]

There is an old psychiatric saying: People who are in Freudian analysis have Freudian dreams, people in Jungian analysis have Jungian dreams, and people in Adlerian therapy have Adlerian dreams. Our experience of the world often reflects the influences under which we find ourselves. The categories we use to define an experience often determine it.

When we look at what the media might call "the occult explosion"—of which the revival of Witchcraft and Paganism is certainly a part—this perception rings particularly true. This "explosion" or "resurgence" is a confusing and ambiguous subject, and almost everyone has a superficial explanation that usually conforms to his or her previous experience and beliefs. Stereotypical notions are rampant about most subjects that become fads for a time, and occultism, magic, Paganism, and Witchcraft are no exception.

A psychologist might attribute this resurgence to the need of certain neurotics to regress to a beatific infant stage. A professional humanist might bemoan the "rise of the irrational" and "the trend toward anti-intellectualism." A Christian fundamentalist might be troubled by the "reawakening of the demonic," and a Marxist writer might be distressed by the attempt of a wealthy leisured class to dissipate the forces of dissent by promoting ideas that mystify the "real" issues and lead to decadence and narcissism. There is an "occult explosion" nightmare to fit every ideology. And on the other side, occultists share an equal number of paradisal dreams and fantasies about the importance and ultimate benefits of their efforts.

Distortions that circulate about occult groups are generally of two types. The first and more easily dismissible is what might be called the "Exorcist–Rosemary's Baby" view put forth by much of the press and by fundamentalist Christian groups. Although books, articles, and scholarly studies have shown this view to be pure fiction (with the exception of an occasional sick individual), the feeling persists that those who practice Witchcraft or occultism are engaged in something fearful, pernicious, illegal, and immoral. This image has a long history. It is nourished by the media because it sells. But more important, this image encourages a fear of the unknown that blunts most people's curiosity and adventurousness.

These negative feelings are widely shared, even by well-educated people. I have told many hundreds, perhaps thousands, of people about my travels around the United States to various Witchcraft covens and Neo-Pagan groups, and the response was usually "Weren't you afraid? Wasn't it dangerous?" This assumption was so common, and stood at such odds with the facts of my travels, that it seemed to be a clue to a general misperception. The facts were simple. I met with representatives of over a hundred groups. The majority were previously strangers. My only negative experience came when a coven of Witches walked out on me after a political disagreement. Such an event could have happened anywhere, and was certainly no more likely to occur among Witches than anyone else.

Another type of image circulates primarily among intellectuals and must be looked at seriously. This is the view that occult groups are trivial, escapist, anti-intellectual, antipolitical, narcissistic, amoral, and decadent. These charges do not come from the sensationalist press. They appear in the works of highly regarded writers and scholars, in *The New York Review of Books, Commentary, Partisan Review.* Many of the ideas in these articles filter down into ordinary "educated" conversation, becoming the basis for the rigid, defensive, and hostile reactions that many people exhibit when they talk about the occult.

Of course, there is a group of writers who have consistently praised the occult revival, viewing it as a seedbed of innovation. There are also critiques by anthropologists, sociologists, historians, and psychologists that contain few stereotypes. These writings reveal the occult world to be complex, with many themes and many layers, a world richer and far different from that portrayed in the press, in most books, in the dinner-table conversation of certain intellectuals and, for that matter, in the simple-minded postures of certain occult writers.

This chapter serves two main functions: it summarizes some of the standard arguments surrounding the revival of occult and magical groups, and it makes accessible a number of lesser known articles and less rigid ideas and perceptions.

One thing should be made clear at the start. There is no consensus on why there is a resurgence of Witchcraft and occultism, and some people even doubt whether such a resurgence exists. There are any number of fascinating theories and speculations, many of which contradict each other. For example, in 1971 there appeared a rather unexceptional popular study of new religious sects by Egon Larsen. The book, *Strange Sects and Cults,* takes a pseudo-psychological approach and describes the rise of these sects as "a subconscious protest against the faculty of thinking. . . ." Larsen argues that these new sects are peopled by a "simple kind of soul." Such people's "personalities never mature"; they remain frightened and bewildered by rigorous mental activity.[3] Several years earlier Richard Cavendish had observed the exact opposite in *The Black Arts,*[4] a study of occult and mystical practices. Cavendish wrote that people who enter mystical groups are generally seeking to take the Apple from the Serpent; they want to eat of the tree of knowledge and become "as gods." He claimed that the typical magician or mystic, far from being a simple person, is attempting to become "the complete man." Such persons, he wrote, throw themselves into all kinds of experiences, both good and evil. They tend to regard all experience as potentially rewarding.

Here are some more examples. The Reverend J. Gordon Melton, whose Institute for the Study of American Religion has amassed perhaps the largest existing collection of modern Craft and Neo-Pagan publications, has written that control and manipulation are absolutely essential to the magical world view.[5] An opposing view has been expressed many times by Mircea Eliade, Theodore Roszak, and others who believe the occult revival regards the universe as *personal*, alive, numinous, mysterious, and beyond manipulation.

The anthropologist Marvin Harris has argued that occult ideas have been used as a weapon of survival by the wealthy classes to stifle the rational growth of protest and dissent. In contrast to this view, Eliade and Edward Tiryakian have argued that many artists and writers have used the occult as a weapon to fight against the bourgeoisie.

In 1977 the scientist Carl Sagan told a symposium at the Massachusetts Institute of Technology that part of the blame for the rise of occultism and irrationality rested on an educational system that had failed to show students the mysteries and wonders of science. Meanwhile, sociologist Marcello Truzzi was writing in a series of articles that the rise of the occult was, paradoxically, a *vindication* of the scientific world view and that most occultists had not rejected science at all, but were furthering the process of secularization by making once-feared aspects of life (the occult, the paranormal) easily comprehensible and benign.

In looking at a wide variety of theoretical viewpoints in the next few pages, we might do well to heed the words of one editor of a Neo-Pagan journal who wrote to me bluntly: "I don't think Pagans share *any* beliefs! And no Witches think alike!" We should also remember Susan Roberts, the journalist who was forced to throw up her hands and exclaim, "Witches defy categorizing," but then went on to say that Witches did not like to wear hats and shoes, that Witches were nonconformists, that Witches were conventional on the surface, that Witches were clean, that Witches were not "hippies," and that Witches didn't go to psychiatrists. There are, of course, Witches who like hats and shoes, who go to therapists, who are "hippies" (whatever *that* means), and there are probably even some who lead superficially unconventional lives but are conformist way down deep.[6]

Theories that attempt to explain the growth of new magical and religious groups fall into several categories:

1. Theories that see this growth as evidence of regression, escape, or retreat.

2. Theories that see this growth as a positive reaction to, or rebellion against, the limitations of Western thought or the excesses of modern technology, that generally view occult* ideas as energizing and innovative.

3. Theories that do not easily fit either of these categories.

---

* The word *occult* and the phrase *occult resurgence* are being used broadly. Technically, the word *occult* first appeared in 1545 (Oxford English Dictionary) and it meant that which is hidden or is beyond the range of ordinary apprehension and understanding. Later, the word began to be used as an umbrella description to cover such studies as astrology, alchemy, and magic. A recent (and much quoted) sociological definition of the occult was formulated by Edward A. Tiryakian, in his essay "Toward the Sociology of Esoteric Culture." He wrote:

> By "occult," I understand intentional practices, techniques, or procedures which (a) draw upon hidden or concealed forces in nature or the cosmos that cannot be measured or recognized by the instruments of modern science, and (b) which have as their desired or intended consequences empirical results, such as either obtaining knowledge of the empirical course of events or altering them from what they would have been without this intervention. . . .[7]

Many of the articles discussed in this chapter are directed specifically at various recent phenomena, including the growth of the occult, Witchcraft, "the consciousness movement," new therapies, and new religious sects. Very few are directed specifically at Witches, and Neo-Pagans have generally been ignored by scholars. It could be argued, for example, that Cavendish's comments on those who enter magical groups apply to magicians generally, but do not apply to members of those religious sects discussed by Larsen, and that the members of those sects *are* bewildered and immature, unlike most magicians. I tend to doubt it, but a plausible case could be made. It could also be argued that revivalist Witches and Neo-Pagans differ in so many ways from the subjects of these articles that these critiques, both positive and negative, just don't apply.

This may be a good argument for a scholarly journal, but most people, and this includes most intelligent nonspecialists, lump all these phenomena together. And many of the writers do the same thing. The article that speaks of the "growth of the irrational" is often talking about many kinds of groups. For these reasons the term *occult resurgence* is used here broadly.

Regressions and Retreats:
Psychological and Political Approaches

Some writers who attempt to analyze the growth of the occult talk in terms of a *retreat* or a *regression* and portray the sect member or occultist as a neurotic individual whose actions can best be explained in psychoanalytical terms. At the most simple level, the psychological approach can be seen in writers like Larsen, who view the various groups as simple souls, devoid of the possibility of growth and maturity. I am also reminded of a well-known New York psychiatrist who has been known to mutter "Schizophrenics!" whenever the subject of religious sects turns up in conversation. Andrew Greeley and William McCready have described a similar reaction:

> The conditioned reflex of many social scientists when someone raises the subject of mystical ecstasy or confronts them with a person who has had such an experience is to fall back on psychoanalytic interpretations. The ecstatic is some sort of disturbed person who is working out a personality problem acquired in childhood. That settles the issue in most instances. They "know" that the ecstatic episode is in fact some sort of psychotic interlude.[8]

Despite the prevalence of these kinds of analyses, a number of psychological interpretations deserve serious consideration. In 1966 Raymond Prince and Charles Savage wrote that mystical states represented a regression to an earlier stage of adaptation, that the feeling of unity is a reexperience of unity felt by the infant nursing at the mother's breast. This analysis formed the basis for many criticisms of the youth movement of the 1960s.[9] But Prince's view of mystical experience is not so negative as the idea of "regression" implies. In "Cocoon Work: An Interpretation of the Concern of Contemporary Youth with the Mystical" (1974), Prince wrote that the increase in people seeking mystical experience could best be explained as a self-imposed rite of passage, a "cocoon work," in which contemporary young Americans were creating a place and time for their own metamorphosis in a society that lacked a clear and acceptable image of the adult.

Prince observed that psychologists had offered two main interpretations of mystical states. The first (outlined in the earlier Prince and Savage paper) said that mystical states were a regression in which the ego descended to the earliest level of experience where the universe is simple and trustworthy. The second hypothesis was that mystical states are a form of deautomatization: the mystic restores to a state of new awareness and sensitivity those actions that have been ignored and have become automatic.

In turning to the growth of new religious groups, Prince gave the movement a name—"Neotranscendentalism." Many of the characteristics he attributed to it would apply well to some Neo-Pagans: lack of dogma, exaltation of the body as a temple, interest in new types of social and economic relationships, and cooperative forms of living. Prince saw this movement as a *rite de passage* in a society that had no rituals for the passage from childhood to adulthood. People became engaged in this cocoon work and then, after a time, took up their normal responsibilities in society.[10] (A less charitable description would be that most young rebels eventually sell out.)

One trouble in applying these arguments to Neo-Pagans is that, unlike the sixties youth culture that Prince describes, most adherents of Neo-Paganism are adults whose lives—with the exception of their religious practices—are fully integrated into the mainstream of society.

But why should the occult be seen as a regression at all? Part of this tendency comes from a fairly long standing anthropological thesis, originally put forth by A. L. Kroeber and George Devereux, that spiritualists and shamans were village psychotics who were given a unique role in primitive societies.[11] In recent years this idea has come under attack by scholars in a variety of fields—Claude Lévi-Strauss, Mircea Eliade, and Jerome Frank, among many others—but it continues in a watered-down form on the popular level. Hence the widespread notion that occultists and mystics are simply "mentally ill."

Dr. E. Fuller Torrey writes that this "sickness" myth had its origins in the colonialism of the eighteenth and nineteenth centuries, and in the reductionist ideas applied to primitive societies. He argues that many well-known anthropologists were themselves in psychoanalysis at the time they formulated their theories, or at least were profoundly affected by psychoanalytic theory. They were, observed Torrey, ill disposed to see their own analysts as "analogous to those strange people in other cultures who are chanting and shaking a rattle." But in point of fact, writes Torrey, spiritualists and shamans "do the same thing as psychiatrists and psychologists do, using the same techniques, and getting about the same results."[12]

Why not, instead, view the shaman as Eliade does when he writes that the shaman's imitiation of animal cries "betokens the desire to recover friendship with the animals and thus enter into the primordial Paradise?"[13] Is the desire for such a paradise a regression? Greeley and McCready think not:

> We humans are inextricably caught up in the physical, chemical, and biological processes of the universe. We swim in an ocean of air, held by gravity to the planet earth and sustained in life by oxygen, carbon, and nitrogen cycles. We are indeed distinct from everything else, but only up to a point; and those psychiatrists who seem to think that an experience of profound awareness of how much one is involved in the natural processes is a regression to childhood have apparently come to think of themselves as archangels who live quite independently of the life processes of the universe.[14]

The assertion that the growth of mysticism and occultism is a *retreat* is primarily a political argument, made most forcefully by Marxist theorists and other progressives. Briefly stated, the critique goes something like this: Occultism, new religions, interest in magic, and so forth are tendencies that promote superstition and downgrade scientific and intellectual ideas. Worse, these ideas devalue the material struggles in the real world and aid reactionary forces by promoting confusion and a false picture of reality. The occult is a powerful weapon of mystification.

Many writers have presented such arguments. One is Marvin Harris, professor of anthropology at Columbia University and author of a fascinating book, *Cows, Pigs, Wars and Witches: The Riddles of Culture*, published in 1974. Harris uses the last chapter, "The Return of the Witch," to launch a strong attack on all the most publicized proponents of the counterculture, in particular Theodore Roszak, Charles Reich, and Carlos Castaneda.

Harris writes that the "modern witch fad blunts and befuddles the forces of dissent."

> Like the rest of the counter-culture it postpones the development of a rational set of political commitments. And that is why it is so popular among the more affluent segments of our population. That is why the witch has returned.

Harris waxes eloquent in his fury against those members of the counterculture who, ten years ago, attempted to levitate the Pentagon by magic during the antiwar demonstrations in Washington. He seems to have taken them literally; he certainly does not understand their sense of humor and understanding of metaphor. He argues that their disdain for rationality and objectivity is dangerously "stripping an entire generation" of intellectual tools. In this he sounds much like Larsen. He accuses supporters of the counterculture of ethnocentric thinking and amoral relativism.

> I contend that it is quite impossible to subvert objective knowledge without subverting the basis of moral judgements. If we cannot know with reasonable certainty who did what, when, and where, we can scarcely hope to render a moral account of ourselves. Not being able to distinguish between criminal and victim, rich and poor, exploiter and exploited, we must either advocate the total suspension of moral judgements, or adopt the inquisitorial position and hold people responsible for what they do in each other's dreams.

But Harris's main argument is that occultism and mystical thinking promote the idea that one can change the course of history by changing consciousness rather than by changing the material conditions that, he believes, create consciousness. To Harris these movements are dangerous because "they prevent people from understanding the causes of their social existence."[15] Such doctrines are very useful to inequitable social systems.

Another writer making a similar argument is Edwin Schur, in his book *The Awareness Trap: Self-Absorption Instead of Social Change.* Schur charges that the "awareness movement" (another catch-all phrase that includes most of the groups we are talking about) addresses the problems of the affluent, the white middle class, and diverts the poor from advancing their real collective interests.[16]

But the most serious critique of this type, joining a psychological and a political perspective, comes from Christopher Lasch, who has written several articles on the "new narcissism" in America for *The New York Review of Books* and *Partisan Review*. Lasch argues that a "retreat to purely personal satisfactions," one of the main themes of the seventies, is reflected in everything from occultism to jogging, from the new therapies to the revival of fundamentalist Christianity. According to Lasch, these new movements, unlike the millennarian movements of the waning Middle Ages which were concerned with social justice, all include a wish to forget the past, to live only for the moment. They go no further than a search for instant gratification and a kind of survivalism.

The picture Lasch paints of the present culture is one in which people "veer between unthinking political commitments and a cult of the self, between a wholesale rejection of politics and a rejection of personal life as a bourgeois self-indulgence." While Schur characterizes the members of these movements as complacent, Lasch shows them as self-preoccupied and desperate.

Lasch argues that every age has its own forms of mental illness, which simply mirror, in exaggerated form, the basic characteristics of that age. In Freud's time the dominant mental illness was hysteria and obsessional neurosis. These, writes Lasch, "carried to extremes the personality traits associated with the capitalist order at an earlier stage in its development—acquisitiveness, fanatical devotion to work, and a fierce repression of sexuality." In our age, by contrast, the dominant illnesses have been schizophrenia and "borderline" personality disorders. These, he writes, seem to signify a societal change from inner-direction to narcissism. According to Lasch, narcissism and its traits—pansexuality, hypochondria, corruptibility, shallowness, the inability to mourn—are simply the best way of coping with a warlike social environment where friendships and family life are hard to sustain, where relationships are shallow, where there is no sense of historical continuity, and where consumption and glamour are emphasized.[17]

Occultists as Rebels and Innovators

The counterthrusts to these types of argument come from a number of sources. Some writers, such as Roszak, see the current occult resurgence as, in part, a protest against a sterile technocratic ethic. Industrial society has produced its opposite: a yearning for the sacred, the communal, the spontaneous. Others, such as Edward Tiryakian and Mircea Eliade, see the occult as providing, both historically and in the present, fresh images for many artistic and political movements. Esoteric culture, writes Tiryakian, "with its fantastic wealth of imagery and symbolism, is multivalent in terms of the political expressions that can be derived from it."[18] He observes that all kinds of groups from the Sinn Fein to the Nazis made extensive use of occult images. These ideas do not belong to reactionaries any more than they belong to progressives.

Both Tiryakian and Eliade mention symbolist poets and surrealist writers like André Breton, Louis Aragon, and Paul Eluard, all of whom were committed to radical politics as well as to occultism.[19] The entire surrealist movement seems to speak directly against the arguments that occultism and magic are antipolitical per se. Breton and the surrealists spoke out strongly against what they considered to be the three prime evils: realism, industrial rationalism, and the bourgeois social order.*

Another writer who has compared the growth of mysticism, particularly among young people, with the surrealist and Dadaist movements is Nathan Adler. He writes that in both cases dreams, hallucinations, and chance were used as "an antidote to the increasing sterility of industrial and mercantile life."[20] He makes a careful distinction between the surrealist movement and the group he is writing about—the youth culture of the early seventies—believing the latter to be anti-intellectual. In my own experiences with Witches and Pagans I have come across very little anti-intellectualism.

---

* While visiting Neo-Pagans in Chicago, I was led to the studio of Robert Green, a surrealist painter who uses magical rituals to renew his creative energies. Green made a distinction between *religion*, "which relies on belief," and *magic*, "which is a process to renew the subconscious." He told me that both magic and surrealist art seek to "liquefy the mind," to liberate the mind from imprisoning dogmas. He said that the problem with the rational mode was that it imposed unacceptable limits. The purpose of surrealism was "liberation period. Liberation of the mind, but also, of all human existence." Green told me that surrealists have always maintained a critical analysis of society. They have always been "political." Magic and occultism in no way contradict this, he said, so long as they are kept free of dogma and fixed beliefs.

Tiryakian has written that the occult, now, as in the past, seems to function as a "seedbed," a source of change and innovation, that ultimately affects the arts, the sciences, and politics. He notes that while it is customary to regard the occult as marginal, atavistic, an odd deviation from the modernization process, another way of viewing esoteric traditions is to see them as the source for new paradigms, catalysts for modernization that appear in both the "build-ups" and the "break-downs" of history—in the Renaissance, for example, or during the waning of the Roman Empire.[21]

As for Harris's charge that the growth of the occult leads to befuddlement, retreat, and reaction, Roszak counters with these words: "It is not transcendent experience that should be rejected but its invidious employment and attendant obfuscation of consciousness." The real evil, he writes, lies in "setting transcendence *against* the earth, the body, the city of man, *for the sake of protecting* criminal privilege."[22] Good magic, he maintains, is rather like good art. Bad magic and bad art simply mystify; good magic and good art lay open the mysteries for all.

Still another positive view sees the occult resurgence as a healthy refusal to be content with the finite. Harriet Whitehead, as we have seen, has written that this refusal is the result of a conviction that there are gaps and deficiencies in the Western mode of comprehending reality. The search and exploration of the occult is an attempt to get at the order that lies at the bottom of things, to discover the "really real."[23]

Is occultism a retreat from the world? It must be said that few occultists, Pagans, and Witches spend much time debating this question (or, for that matter, reading these articles). But the debate is taking place in the women's movement. As we have seen, a number of women have disposed of the entire notion of a split between spiritual and material reality by simply saying that it is a mistaken notion born of patriarchal thinking. They see ritual and magic as a connecting force, like art and poetry. If there is a necessity for art, why not for ritual? Artists are merely a bit more respectable these days than magicians and creators of rituals.

Other Theories of More Than Passing Interest

Some of the most interesting thoughts on contemporary occult movements have come from historian Mircea Eliade, whose more than twenty published works range from mythography to investigations of shamanism and Witchcraft. In 1976 the University of Chicago Press published a collection of Eliade's essays under the title *Occultism, Witchcraft, and Cultural Fashions,* one of the sanest books on these topics to appear in years. Three essays bear directly on the themes of this book. Two are considered here; a third was discussed in Chapter 4.

In "Cultural Fashion and History of Religion" Eliade investigates the extraordinary popularity in France of the magazine *Planète,* and of the philosophy of Pierre Teilhard de Chardin. The arguments in this essay can easily be applied to most recent occult groups. *Planète* was started by Louis Pauwels and Jacques Bergier, two authors who became famous in 1961 with the publication of *Morning of the Magicians,*[24] a book that combined politics, occultism, science fact, and science fiction. It raised quite a furor in France and became the basis for much excited discussion in the United States, particularly within the counterculture. *Planète* was founded with money earned by the book. The magazine also contained a mixture of magic, science, politics, and speculation.

Eliade argues that in France, after the Algerian War, there was a "profound malaise among the intellectuals." They had become tired of living in the "gloomy, tedious," historical moment, but Sartre and other existentialist writers had taught French intellectuals that this was the only responsible thing to do. *Planète* presented a total contrast, offering a new, "optimistic and holistic outlook" in which the universe was mysterious and exciting, and in which occultism and science combined to create infinite possibilities. The world was no longer doomed to be absurd; human beings were no longer condemned to be estranged and useless. One was no longer committed to constant analysis of one's own existential situation; instead, one was committed to the infinite process of evolution.

Eliade argues that the philosophy of Teilhard de Chardin became popular in France for similar reasons. Teilhard looks at the world from a cosmic viewpoint in which human history is a small part of an infinite progressive evolution.* Eliade writes that Teilhard's universe is "real, alive, meaningful, creative, sacred." Teilhard, despite his Christian symbolism, is really a pantheist who ignores sin and evil and who views human and planetary evolution as progressive, optimistic, and infinite. Eliade writes:

> One cannot even go back to a romantic or bucolic approach to nature. But the nostalgia for a lost mystical solidarity with nature still haunts Western man. And Teilhard has laid open for him an unhoped-for perspective, where nature is charged with religious values even while retaining its completely "objective" reality.[25]

How does Eliade sum up the ideas of those people who read *Planète* with eagerness and find themselves interested in the ideas of Teilhard? These people reject existentialism, are indifferent to history, exalt physical nature, and hold ultimately *positive* feelings toward science and technology. What is more, their antihistoricism is not really a rejection of history but "a protest against the pessimism and nihilism of some recent historicists," coupled with a "nostalgia for what might be called a macro-history—a planetary and, later, a cosmic history."

Eliade echoes Lasch, but from the other side. The indifference to history produces an ultimate optimism as opposed to the survivalism born of desperation depicted by Lasch.

Eliade's essay "The Occult and the Modern World" focuses more specifically on the history of occultism and its current popularity. After discussing the nineteenth-century occultist Eliphas Levi, who was largely responsible for the vogue of occultism in France, Eliade writes that the generation of French occultists that followed Levi wanted to regain humanity's spiritual perfection as it was "before the fall." This occult movement "did not attract the attention of competent historians of ideas of the times but did fascinate a great number of important writers, from Baudelaire, Verlaine, and Rim-

---

* For a look at how one Neo-Pagan group, the Church of All Worlds, has adapted, modified, and expanded on the ideas of Teilhard, see Chapter 10.

baud to André Breton and some of the postsurrealist authors, such as René Daumal."

The use of occult themes by these writers took one of two paths. Those who wrote before the second half of the nineteenth century, writers such as Balzac, Schiller, and Goethe, all "reflected a hope in a personal or collective *renovatio*—a mystical restoration of man's original dignity and powers." The second and later path, taken by such writers as Rimbaud, Baudelaire, and Breton, was the use of occult themes as "a powerful weapon in their rebellion against the bourgeois establishment and its ideology." Implicit in this rebellion was a rejection of Judeo-Christian values and the social and aesthetic sensibilities of the day.

> In the occult traditions these artists were looking for pre-Judeo-Christian and pre-Classical (pre-Greek) elements, i.e., Egyptian, Persian, Indian, or Chinese creative methods and spiritual values. They sought their aesthetic ideals in the most archaic arts, in the "primordial" revelation of beauty. . . .
>
> To conclude, from Baudelaire to André Breton, involvement with the occult represented for the French literary and artistic avant-garde one of the most efficient criticisms and rejections of the religious and cultural values of the West—efficient because it was considered to be based on historical facts.

Eliade feels that the current occult scene is distinguished from the past occult resurgence in certain important ways. The present occult explosion was "anticipated" by a new wave of scholarship and understandings made principally *not* by writers and artists, as in the previous era, but by historians of ideas. These contributions include the decoding of esoteric manuscripts found in the Dead Sea caves, new monographs on Jewish Gnosticism, new studies of Chinese, Indian, and Western alchemy, new investigations of the Hermetic traditions, and new research into shamanism and Witchcraft. This contemporary scholarship has, according to Eliade, "disclosed the consistent religious meaning and cultural function of a great number of occult practices, beliefs, and theories, recorded in many civilizations, European and non-European alike, and *at all levels of culture.*" He argues that these new studies have led to great changes in think-

ing among scholars. He gives a number of examples, the most perti-
nent of which, for our purposes, is the change in thinking on the
question of the origins of Western European Witchcraft.

We have seen Eliade's argument previously. In brief, eighty years
ago most historians considered that Western witchcraft was the invention of the Inquisition. The covens, the reports of orgies, all the
various accusations, were regarded as either "imaginary inventions
of neurotic persons or declarations obtained from the accused during
the trials, especially by means of torture." In contrast, Margaret
Murray argued that Witchcraft was an ancient pre-Christian fertility
religion. Although her method and information were wrong, he
writes, her assumption "that there existed a pre-Christian fertility
cult and that specific survivals of this pagan cult were stigmatized
during the Middle Ages as witchcraft" was, in fact, correct and has
been borne out by more recent investigations of Indo-Tibetan and
Romanian materials.

Returning to the recent occult resurgence, which, he notes, is centered on the urban middle class, Eliade writes that both of the older
themes, the rebellion against Western religious values and the search
for renewal, reappear. But, he contends, the most important aspect
for all groups from astrologists to Satanists is the hope for an individual and collective *renovatio*, or renewal. "It is primarily the attraction of a *personal* initiation that explains the craze for the occult," he
writes. And all these groups imply, "consciously or unconsciously,
what I would call an optimistic evaluation of the human mode of
being."[26]

One of the most important books to chart the rise of new religious
movements in the United States is the 1974 Princeton University
study *Religious Movements in Contemporary America*. Among the most
unusual articles in this large volume is anthropologist Edward
Moody's study of Satanism, "Magical Therapy: An Anthropological
Investigation of Contemporary Satanism."* Moody spent two years
as a participant-observer at the Church of the Trapezoid, a branch of

---

* *Drawing Down the Moon* does not include a study of Satanism because it is not
primarily a Neo-Pagan phenomenon. Satanists (Bonewits's "Neogothic Witches")
take their myths from Judeo-Christianity. Most worship Satan as a symbolic figure of
rebellion against Christianity. Moody's article is relevant here because it answers a
broader question: Why are occult and magical groups so appealing?

Anton LaVey's Church of Satan. Moody set out to answer the question, "Why do people become Satanists?" After two years he concluded that Satanists find that something they call "magic" works for them, that they accomplish many of the goals they set out to achieve. But *how* this magic works proved to be very complex.

From the start, Moody found himself beset by difficulties. He could not find any "traditional sociological pigeonhole" into which the Satanist could be placed. He found members who were "successful" in life and those who were "failures." He found rich members and poor ones, representatives of all classes and political persuasions. The only characteristic common to all the members he observed was a behavioral trait that placed them outside the cultural "norm." Many of them displayed a lack of knowledge of the "rules of the social game" and often felt unable to "make the system respond."

Moody observed that magic training for the new Satanist recruit was a combination of many practical skills designed to build up the ego and lessen feelings of guilt and anxiety. The techniques and rituals were a combination of psychodrama, tips on social manners, advice on how to make oneself more attractive, and techniques to strengthen confidence.

Moody observed a sample subject, "Billy G.," over a period of many months. He watched this young man change from a person whose level of anxiety was so great that he could not even speak to a member of the opposite sex into a more "normal" young man who could interact with men and women, both inside and outside the church. Billy G. slowly worked through various rituals, many of which were composed of behaviorist techniques to lessen anxiety.

In one example Moody gives a new twist to that fact of contemporary Satanism most played up by the press: the nude woman who acts as the altar. In the beginning Billy G. finds this setting so disturbing that he stands at the back of the room. In succeeding weeks he moves closer. Finally, Billy G., the son of fundamentalist missionaries, is able to stand next to this woman, to talk to her, to hand her a goblet or in some other way participate in the ritual without feeling ill at ease. He is given encouragement; he is told that his sexual feelings are natural and not to be denied, as his previous education had taught him. Eventually, he is able to meet women and to go out with them. He becomes socially successful. The magic works.

Ironically, Moody shows that the Church of Satan, certainly one of the less "acceptable" occult groups, actually functions as a normalizing force, a socializing force within the larger society. It functions much like therapy and it apparently succeeds. Moody comments on Billy G.:

> If he attributes this new-found power and success to magic rather than to the insights of sociology, anthropology, or psychology, it is because such an interpretation is more in accordance with his world view and the categories of understanding which he uses to give structure and meaning to his world.
>
> In fact, it is sometimes difficult to argue against his interpretation. If psychology explains personal interactions in terms of hypothesized "forces" at work, forces which are known and measured only through the perception of their effects, then how is that different, the Satanist asks, from magic? Satanists say, with some justification, "When magic becomes scientific fact we refer to it as medicine or astronomy." (LaVey, 1969).

Moody ends his paper by encouraging the growth of the Church of the Trapezoid and arguing that such institutions socialize individuals for whom traditional therapy has failed and, paradoxically, serve to bring people closer to cultural norms. Why is there a growth of magical groups today, Moody asks. He says that it is "an attempt by various people to regain a sense of control over their environment and their lives." It is important to note what Moody is *not* saying. He is not employing the standard cliché that people become occultists to gain power over others, although, of course, some may join for that reason. He is not saying that such people want to retreat from the world. Instead, he is saying that they join these groups in order to gain a sense of self-mastery, to be in control of their own lives *in the world*. Moody concludes:

> This seems to be a time when many of the gods of the Western world, like the old traditional gods of the urbanizing African, are being challenged. God is dead, but that means not just the Judeo-Christian god but also the gods of progress, science and technology. We put our faith in

"him," but now the god of progress is discovered to be a two-faced Janus about to extract a terrible price for our progress and comfort; the god of science has failed us and has not created the paradise we were led to expect, free from disease and ignorance and death. Instead he threatens us with destruction with either the apocalypse of atomic conflagration or a slow death by chemical pollution. The god of technology reveals his "true" face and our streams die, our lakes atrophy, and the very air is turned into a subtle poison. . . . In such time the people look to new gods or try to refurbish the old ones. . . .

Now that external sources of truth, the experts and scientists, have failed us, many people have begun to look within themselves for their source of wisdom and security. Some have begun to reassert the necessity of finding personal solutions. In a certain sense witchcraft* is a product of these needs. If the world of the Satanist is a criterion, the Satanist is training himself to be assertive and powerful *as a individual.* Although he draws a sense of security from his association with powerful forces, he is finding inner sources of strength. He is casting off the need for powerful gods to protect and care for him, insisting that he is strong enough to care for himself. He commands the gods and does not beseech them. He is turning from an ethereal and other-worldly orientation to a somewhat more realistic assessment and concern with the mundane and real world.[27]

Moody's point that the occult functions as a rationalizing force is made in another article, "Urban Witches," in which he argues that much that is called magic is actually a learning process of social behavior and interpersonal games. Magic, he writes, allows its practitioners to cope better "with the everyday problems of life, with the here and now."[28]

But the writer best known for a somewhat similar position is the sociologist Marcello Truzzi. In 1972, in an article "The Occult Revival as Popular Culture," Truzzi wrote that the revival of occultism involved a broad spectrum of individuals, many of whom were "not the simple identity-seeking variety that some have portrayed them to be." Truzzi argued that occultists tend to be playful with ideas that were once greatly feared and that therefore the rise of occultism is

---

* Moody does not distinguish between Witchcraft and Satanism, a flaw in this otherwise excellent essay.

evidence of a victory over the supernatural. He wrote: "What we are seeing is largely a demystification-process of what were once fearful and threatening cultural elements."[29]

In another paper, "Toward a Sociology of the Occult: Notes on Modern Witchcraft," Truzzi wrote that Witchcraft groups have, in general, very little supernaturalism. He found most occultism to be naturalistic and pragmatic, "a kind of deviant science." He noted that most occultists seek scientific validation of their claims and regard themselves as scientific in a philosophical sense, working within an "ultimate purview of scientific understanding." Truzzi observed:

> In this sense, it would appear that there has been a kind of secularization of magic in adaptation to the modern scientific and naturalistic world view. Thus, what were once described in the occult literature as supernatural psychic forces are now examples of extra-sensory perception of a kind basically examinable and potentially understandable in the psychologist's laboratory.[30]

Taken collectively, these articles present a wealth of diverse viewpoints. These writers give the lie to the simple stereotypes about "the occult" that most of us unconsciously imbibe—that it is irrational, escapist, retreatist, and so forth. These articles show that whatever is going on here is much more complicated than most people generally allow.

Recent Notes

Journalists have written a few sensitive articles on Paganism and Wicca in the last few years but, in the main, the newspapers and wire services are only interested in a few kinds of stories—sensational descriptions of Witches' gatherings, stories involving criminal charges or activities, clashes between Witches and Christians, and something cute (or occasionally even good) for their Halloween feature.

If you look at a news database, like *Nexus*, and you pull out the approximately fifty newspaper, magazine, and wire service stories on Witchcraft that have been collected over the past five years, you will find that there were really only five stories.

1. The Helms and Walker bills. Senator Jesse Helms put forward an amendment (#705) to an appropriations bill. The amendment would have denied tax-exempt status to religious groups that practiced or had a primary interest in Witchcraft or Satanism. Pennsylvania Congressman Robert Walker also put forward a bill that would have amended the Internal Revenue Code in a similar way. This bill only mentioned Witchcraft. The Helms bill was killed in a conference committee of the House and Senate. In 1986, the Walker bill is still pending.

2. Many stories about the Ravenwood Church of Wicca, in Atlanta, where a twenty-three-year-old shot a teenager. There were also several later stories about how Ravenwood had won a court battle over property taxes.

3. Coverage of the trial of the late Loy Stone, a Witch who was accused of murder after a group of teenagers rode by his house to cause mischief and to "see the devil worshippers" on Halloween. Shots rang out. A teenager was murdered. Loy Stone was acquitted.

4. Stories about a gathering of Witches in Amarillo, Texas, in 1980. More than three hundred fundamentalists picketed the gathering, singing hymns, and there was even a bomb threat.

5. A few stories about perverted individuals in New Jersey who killed animals and called themselves Witches.

I could find only two other stories about Witches listed in the *Nexus* files going back over the last five years.

14

Living on the Earth

The circle is a nice defensive mechanism to get away from the twentieth century and you need an escape point in this day and age. But we must also respond to the rest of our life on the outside. If we are not an alternative, we are not living our religion. It is as pure and simple as that. We are not a transcendental religion. We are not trying to transcend nature. Our religion is reality.

—MARK ROBERTS, Dianic priest

Most Neo-Pagans and Crafters have never done any serious thinking about the implications of their belief system. Most of them—like most Americans—are extremely shallow about religion. Take some of the basic issues that are tearing apart American Christianity—abortion, euthanasia, the morality of war—most Pagans have not thought through on a logical basis what their belief systems really mean in making practical decisions in day-to-day life.

—ISAAC BONEWITS, occultist and writer

Many Neo-Pagans will tell you that their religion is a "way of life." There is no separation between the spiritual and the earthly; there is no retreat from the world of matter. A British Witch once observed to me brightly, "Your head in the clouds, your feet on the ground, *that's* the proper place for an occultist."

Neo-Pagans do not live in ashrams. Most live in city apartments and suburban homes. A smaller but growing portion live on farms and in rural areas. While there has been an important move to buy land and create Pagan nature sanctuaries, this is still, by and large, a movement of people who live very much within the modern world. The temple of a Wiccan priestess is most likely either her home, a secluded back yard, or a neighboring park. Unlike those who enter highly organized and highly financed religious groups, Neo-Pagans do not, as a rule, live in a sympathetic religious community. They do not live apart. They do not live in a Neo-Pagan world. They often have quite "ordinary" jobs, raise ordinary families, and live very normal lives.

What then does it mean to call oneself a Pagan, or Neo-Pagan, or Witch in our society? What does this "way of life" look like? How different is it? Does it make a difference? To us? To others? To the world? If the primary bond between Pagans is one of imagination, does this bond make any difference in the "real" world? Does it affect the daily living of Pagan folk?

Furthermore, how do Pagans face the struggles of working and living in the United States? What do their lives look and feel like? Are they wealthy? Are they poor? Do they find contradictions between their spiritual values and their material realities, between their professional lives and their religious lives? Are they forced to split their personalities and lead double lives? If so, does it bother them?

For example, what do these participants in newly created or newly revived religions of nature think of modern civilization, modern technology? Are they antiscience, as so many scholars assume? Have they forsaken the cities and run off to the land? What are their views on ecology? How do they answer the standard accusation that occultism is an escape from reality, a cop-out from the vital issues of the day? Are they concerned with politics? Or do they believe that politics is a waste of time? Are they concerned with the transformation of society as well as the transformation of the self?

All these seemed to be proper questions to ask a modern Pagan living on the Mother's Earth. And strange it was in 1976 to find that most of these questions had never been asked or answered, despite the many books on modern Witches and the sprinkling of books and essays on Neo-Paganism. Most books had focused on the "beliefs" of Pagans, on stories and anecdotes of psychic experiences, on descriptions of initiation rites and seasonal festivals, and on the history of the worship of ancient deities. But none had asked how comfortable these Pagans were with the world around them.

In seeking answers to some of these questions, I typed up a question-naire with more than seventy questions. The questionnaire was published in *Green Egg*[1] and became the basis for the interviews I conducted around the country. Several Pagan groups used the questionnaire as a basis for discussion topics. All told, I received about one hundred replies.

In 1985 I passed out another much shorter questionnaire. It was published in *Panegyria* and passed out at three Pagan festivals. One hundred ninety-five were returned.

Coming to Terms with One's Own Biases

I came to Neo-Paganism out of a search for a celebratory, ecological nature religion that would appease my hunger for the beauty of an-cient myths and visions without strangling my mind with dogmas or cutting off the continuing flow of many doubts. In a family of agnos-tics, atheists, and Marxist humanists I was a secret childhood wor-shipper of the Greek gods and goddesses. But later I was heavily influenced by the politics of the sixties and early seventies. I was jailed and convicted in Berkeley, teargassed in Chicago, and nearly killed in Mississippi. Still later, as a journalist, I witnessed political trials and covered political demonstrations, and I twice visited Cuba and the German Democratic Republic. I have come to understand that all things are interconnected. I reject *nothing* in this past, neither the jails nor the goddesses, neither the moonlit rituals nor the politi-cal activism and analysis.

My views have changed during the last fifteen years. It would be fair to say that I now tend toward a "longer," more "cosmic" view of the world, and that my politics are more decentralist, if no less radi-cal. Still, I did not come to Neo-Paganism out of a *rejection* of or es-cape from the political. Instead, Paganism seemed to me a philosophy that could heal the breach between the spiritual and the material. If ecology studied the interrelatedness of all living things and their environment, Neo-Paganism seemed to be a religion that would celebrate those interrelationships, that would heal into syn-thesis all oppositions: primitive and civilized, science and magic, male and female, spirit and matter.

Given this position, I was drawn to those writers who perceived a split in humanity's consciousness and sought to heal it. In particular,

I was drawn to the works of anthropologist Stanley Diamond, especially his book *In Search of the Primitive* (1974).

Diamond argues not only that the spread of modern civilization has conquered and imperialized primitive peoples, but that it is "ultimately man's self, his species being, which is imperialized." Civilized humanity, by losing touch with the primitive, the primary, lost and subordinated what was essentially human within itself. The central question, Diamond writes, is, "What part of our humanity have we lost and how and why we have lost it and how and in what form we may regain it." It is clear that primitive societies had their disadvantages, but it is also clear that many of them allowed for more participation in community life and that many primitive religions were more in tune with human existence. "The sickness of civilization," Diamond observes, consists in "its failure to incorporate (and only then to move beyond the limits of) the primitive." The split in modern consciousness is so destructive that it can be healed only by "a revolutionary transformation," equal "in scope and depth to that which initiated civilization about 5,000 years ago." The first task of anthropologists—and, by extension, all people—is to become critics of their own culture.[2]

Hundreds of other writers have discussed the split between mind and body, that split which historian E. R. Dodds called the most far-reaching and perhaps the most questionable of all the gifts we received from classical culture.[3] Lynn White placed the blame on Christianity. Theodore Roszak wrote eloquently on the perils of objectifying nature to the exclusion of ecstasy, and B. Z. Goldberg described that ecstasy in *The Sacred Fire*. Neo-Paganism, it seemed, was a philosophy that could join ancient and modern values. As Pagan writer Allen Greenfield observed to me, "The future must be built from the best material of past and present, and on the grave of those elements in both which were/are adverse to human life and living." Neo-Paganism seemed also to be a religion and way of life that allowed one to regain kinship with nature without sacrificing one's individuality or independence.

These influences, among many, led me to certain assumptions. Neo-Pagans, it seemed to me, had turned to new and old nature religions for nourishment and inspiration at a time when the degradation of nature and the artificiality of the environment were among the supreme facts of life, particularly in urban and suburban areas, where most Neo-Pagans—and most people in the United States —lived.

Since Pagans often looked to the past for *sources* of inspiration, I assumed that they, like myself, would have an ambivalent and troubled attitude toward modern civilization. I assumed that they would be critical of much modern technology and would distrust linear concepts of progress. I assumed that the majority would be fervent ecologists, that most (given the prominence of female deities) would be sympathetic to feminism and would favor decentralized and regional forms of governance. I also assumed that Neo-Pagans, critical of the society around them, would find their lives filled with contradictions that they would be trying to resolve. They would see Neo-Paganism as an alternative to much of the status quo, and even a vehicle for ultimate transformation. And finally, I assumed that the excesses of Neo-Pagans would be my own: a tendency to ludditism and to romanticizing the past.

Many of these assumptions turned out to be false, but they were natural ones to make—not only because of the philosophical influences that informed my own journey but because such views have always been central to the political movements of indigenous peoples. Journals like *Akwesasne Notes*, for example, the newspaper of the Mohawk Nation at Akwesasne in upstate New York, have always taken such a critical perspective.

Akwesasne Notes:
A Voice for Natural People

It can be argued that *Akwesasne Notes,* a newspaper with over seventy thousand subscribers, is the most far-reaching journal promoting a Neo-Pagan perspective. Sixty thousand copies of *Gnostica* were sent out, with three thousand paid subscribers. *Green Egg* never had more than two thousand. *Circle Network News* has about six thousand. But is *Notes* Neo-Pagan? Doesn't the official newspaper of the Mohawk Nation at Akwesasne represent a voice of Native Americans? Isn't it, if anything, the voice of one indigenous or, to use Bonewits's term, Paleo-Pagan group? The answer is, not entirely.

Originally *Notes* was a newspaper that reported on the ferment in

Native American communities, and it continues to do this with great effectiveness. Over the years, starting in 1969, with the occupation of Alcatraz by a group of Native Americans, it chronicled the development of the American Indian movement. It reported on the situation at reservations throughout North America. It described with unparalleled excellence and accuracy the occupations, arrests, trials, shootings—all facets of Native American political struggles in North America. In addition, it combined religious traditionalism and political radicalism in a unique way.

Eventually, as one editor told an interviewer, "we began to realize that it was not going to be sufficient to remove an oppressor off our backs. We had to discover something positive. We had to recreate a destroyed way of life."[4] Soon *Notes* came to embrace a viewpoint more universal than Native American traditionalism. The newspaper advertised itself as a voice for all "Natural" as well as Native people, the voice of people who were trying to live lives in tune with the natural world and the "Laws of the Creation." Many of its articles pointed out that people in North America—natives and non-natives alike—were caught up in complicated social processes that they did not understand, processes that were destroying them physically and spiritually. The newspaper took the position that Western culture was impoverished, artificial, and diseased—"a cancer." Western culture offered visible ease and convenience, but at a price that was indirect and invisible, except to those who had purified themselves by returning to a less artificial way of life. The flushing of a toilet was visible and direct; the lowering of water tables and pollution of waters was often invisible and indirect.

Many articles in *Notes* stressed a central theme: the pervasive penetration of artificiality into daily life, coupled with the loss of diversity and freedom. As one *Notes* editor remarked, after traveling around the country with the Native American group White Roots of Peace,

> We find the same things in New York and California. We find the same things in Northern Canada and Southern Florida. Everything has become standardized. Why should people on the Pacific Ocean be listening to the same music and the same commentators as people on the Atlantic? . . .

Now, if people want to put all their eggs in one basket, that is their business. But when you recall that there were hundreds of native nations . . . , native languages, native systems of government, you will realize what a rich diversity there was of human culture. And of course, in nature, where there is diversity, there is the greatest richness of life and where there is conformity, such as the planting of one crop that can be wiped out by one weevil or one fire or one fungus, that is not a way for life, but something that ultimately brings death.[5]

The task at hand was to define and begin to free oneself from consumer culture. The newspaper saw itself "at war with the most destructive forces ever assembled in the history of mankind," but in "a unique position to raise the most critical questions," to voice concerns about survival that were generally unspoken.[6]

Notes did not romanticize the situation of Native Americans, as many whites tend to do. It often pictured the ancient traditions as fragmented, much like those of modern Witches. Most "Indians" were as much the victims of Western culture as most whites. But Native American traditions were seen to contain many answers to the problem of how to live a human life on the North American continent. Most important, the conditions and problems were universal problems of survival, of "being human-human beings," that other political movements had failed to address.

What did it mean to be a "Natural" person? Quite a few Neo-Pagans would identify with the description in a *Notes* editorial:

If we look about us at the Natural World, we can see that many people call themselves the Natural or Real People. The people who call themselves by these names know that they are a part of the Creation—they know that they are real in the way that the Oak Tree is real . . .

The Oak Tree gives of its Oxygen so that the Rabbit may breathe, and the Rabbit gives of its flesh that the Fox may live. . . . All things, in their real ways, support life. It is only when beings leave their real ways that they cease to support Life. . . .

The People of the Natural World are the spiritual proprietors of the Universe, not because they possess the things of Creation, but because they celebrate them. . . . The way of being of the Natural People is the active participation in the daily celebration of Life supportive processes. That is why they do not call theirs a religion, but rather a Way of Life. . . .

And we, who would be Real People, are those who must now struggle to regain those real ways, not in words or ceremonies, but in reality.[7]

How did one "regain those real ways"? Many articles conceded that it was almost impossible, the job of a lifetime, since most people's lives were enmeshed in a web of contradictions that clouded true perception. To take one example, an article describes the plight of a Native American farmer whose cattle are dying of chemical poisoning from the nearby Reynolds aluminum plant. Once his cattle begin to sicken, the farmer is forced to find outside work. Where can he find it? Why, at the Reynolds plant, of course, the company that is destroying his way of life. His understanding becomes clouded when he becomes thankful to get the job. "How can you fight something that you work for?" The article adds, "The monster gives you no choice. It pokes you in the eye at the same time that it fills your wallet and it destroys your garden and cattle at the same time that it offers you jobs."[8]

Another writer describes the progress of his family and neighbors during a rent strike in a large Eastern city. After a long struggle that takes up most of their energies, they win a difficult court case and possibly will soon own the building themselves. Is this a victory? The writer begins to notice the knotweed that threatens the foundations of their building. Eventually these houses will decay. His family has stopped planting lettuce in the front-yard garden because the lead from passing automobile exhausts will coat the lettuce and build up in the body of their child. What does it really mean, he asks, to fight for an artificial reality? He continues:

> The folks I live with have already abandoned the more gross forms of greed and consumerism. But we have been schooled from birth to think that ownership and control are the only alternatives to weakness and failure, and those lessons remain deeply etched in our minds. What frightens us about winning this house from the landlord is that our inner desire to possess could keep us from recognizing when the time has finally come to desert it.

The writer notes that he has begun to change his perceptions. While he remains a political activist, he no longer feels that the overall struggle is simply between warring classes. He now believes that the issue is survival (everyone drinks the water), he admits his fear and ignorance of "the natural world to which we must head for survival," and he asks himself, Will I become so caught up in the survival struggles of the artificial world that I forget what the real issues are?[9] The idea that one must constantly strive to attain clarity on these issues is a constant theme in *Akwesasne Notes*. Rarihokwats, editor of the paper until 1977, told an interviewer:

> A person in this culture may be very sympathetic and outwardly moral. They would never consciously hurt a human being. They may feel very bad about native people. Yet, just by the flick of a switch that turns on their air conditioner, they may cause native people in James Bay or Black Mesa to be moved off their land in order to produce the power that is turned on. . . .[10]

Other articles in *Notes* have spoken eloquently about religions of the earth. While it should be clear to readers of this book that modern Witches are creating their traditions from fragments, using past sources for inspiration but mixing them with modern creativity, many whites tend to assume that most Native Americans, in contrast, possess *complete* traditions. *Notes* shows Native Americans in a similar struggle to revive natural religions that have been suppressed over centuries. The position of many Native Americans does not seem so far removed from that of modern-day European descendants of the ancient Celts, although it can be argued that more of the ancient traditions have survived on the American continent, since the arrival of Christianity here is a more recent event.

Several articles in *Notes* have underscored the idea that there is a nonexploitative European heritage, embodied, one article noted, in "the old tribal/peasant heritage of Europe (still not absolutely corrupted, even today),"[11] as well as in the philosophies of Rousseau, Voltaire, and others. Many Neo-Pagans are searching in that "old tribal/peasant heritage" for their cultural roots. In this they are much like Native Americans who newly adopt traditionalist values. After all, as Leo Martello has remarked on many occasions, "If you go far enough back, all of our pre-Judeo-Christian or Moslem ancestors were Pagans."

It is striking how many of the *religious* values expressed in *Akwe-sasne Notes* come close to the ideas of many Neo-Pagans. For example, in an article called "The Non-Progressive Great Spirit" a writer observes:

> Our entire existence is of reverence. Our rituals renew the sacred harmony within us. Our every act—eating, sleeping, breathing, making love—is a ceremony reaffirming our dependence on Mother Earth and our kinship with her every child. Unlike Christians, who dichotomize the spiritual and the physical, put religion in its compartment, and call the physical world evil and a mere preparation for a world to come, we recognize the "spiritual" and the "physical" as one—without Westerners' dichotomies between God and humankind, God and nature, nature and humankind, we are close and intimate and warm with Mother Earth and the Great Spirit. Unlike Christian belief, which claims that our species is both inherently evil and the divinely ordained ruler of Earth, we know that, being of our sacred Mother Earth, we are sacred.[12]

This statement is close to words I heard over and over again from Neo-Pagans.

But on matters that are *not* connected with religious values, most Neo-Pagans have fundamental differences with most of the positions taken in *Akwesasne Notes*. Many articles in *Notes* reject much of Western technology, viewing it as "extractive" and therefore exploitative and disharmonious.[13] Neo-Pagans, in contrast, often express positive feelings toward modern technology, and almost everyone I talked to had astonishingly positive attitudes toward science, the scientific method, and Western modes of thinking.

Many articles in *Notes* have described cities as "unnatural" since they must transport many necessaries for survival from outside their boundaries. While some Neo-Pagans took a similar view, I found among them many staunch defenders of city living.

Several articles in *Notes* have talked extensively about the traditionalist view that nothing advances or progresses, that time is spherical, and that the Western linear notion of time has been partly responsible for producing a society based on exploitation. A few Neo-Pagans accepted this view. Many rejected it. Most had never thought about it.

Finally, *Notes* has taken the position that we are in a time of great crisis; that the next forty years will use up those resources produced by the extractive technologies; that new and alternate technologies will not meet growing needs, or easily and quickly replace the present ones; and that these hardships will be increased by weather changes and food shortages. Noting the ancient Hopi prophecies of a Great Purification, articles in *Notes* have taken the position that the natural world is going to "purify itself" no matter what we do. They have simply asked the question, "Will we know how to survive in the natural world when it is the only one left?" While many Neo-Pagans struggle over the issues of ecological destruction and nuclear war, many of them do not accept the Akwesasne model. The majority accept much of modern technology and urban life. Most would not agree with the idea that we all, as it were, are working for Reynolds.

Working and Living in the World

Susan Roberts, in her book *Witches, U.S.A.*, states that Witches "are mostly middle-class Americans who, on the surface, live quietly and unobtrusively in the mainstream of American life." But, she says, privately they are nonconformists. They defy categorizing and "can never be measured with any degree of accuracy." Publicly, "most witches . . . appear to the world to be conventional men and women. They fit themselves into society as comfortably as they can." Roberts says that all Witches do share one trait—they have never lost the simple wonder and curiosity of small children. She also concludes that most Witches are not religious rebels; that is, they have not come to the Craft out of a rejection of a previous religious upbringing.[14]

In my interviews with all types of Neo-Pagans, including Witches, two statements of Roberts rang completely true: they defy categorizing, and they maintain a childlike wonder at the world. I found many religious rebels, and many who had made peace with their religious past. I found former Catholics who still took communion and others who had harsh words for all organized religion. I found every conceivable life style, occupation, and financial position, and I found remarkably diverse political viewpoints.

But when asked, Neo-Pagans were adamant in insisting that they were "different" although often the differences were subtle and hard to express. "What *are* the common traits of Pagans?" I asked. The answers I received included, again, that sense of childlike wonder, acceptance of life and death, attunement to the rhythms of nature, sense of humor, lack of guilt-ridden feelings about oneself and about the body and sexuality, genuine honesty, and unwillingness or inability to play social games.

"We tend to include people who seem to be in touch with the essence of life," Alta Kelly told me as she lounged on a sofa in her house in Oakland. "Witches may be frivolous in some ways. They certainly have their problems in day-to-day living, but they have a quality of eternalness about them. They feel comfortable with living and dying, and that's something I find lacking in folks who are non-Craft."

Others told me that being a Pagan was simply a more comfortable, freer, friendlier way to be. "I can cope with loneliness and solitude, whereas most of my neighbors must surround themselves with noise," said one woman who lived in a small town. "And psychic phenomena no longer seem supernatural," she added. Feminist Witch Z Budapest told me, "Trees talk to me. My plants are telling me right now that they could use some more water. I am surrounded by my ancestors and by spirit friends. The sky kisses me. I can talk to stones, and sometimes clouds part if I ask them to."

This feeling that Pagans have a friendly relationship to the universe, that they feel a vital contact with natural forces, came home to me most forcefully when I received a letter from a friend who had visited Z's little shop in Los Angeles, The Feminist Wicca. This friend was not a Pagan. In the summer of 1977 she had walked into the shop several times out of curiosity. She wrote:

> It's my reaction to that place, those people, that's got me confused. On the one hand, the teachings seem a trifle silly and the rituals seem like just words, meaningless in themselves. My rational mind argues this way for hours. But then I feel a current when I am there, a force that surrounds us. It's alive, it pulsates, it ebbs and flows like the waxing and waning of the moon. . . . I don't know what it is, and I don't know how to use it. It's like being near an electric current, very near, so near you can hear it humming and crackling, but not being able to tap into it.

I know it must be a wonderful thing to be able to use it, or open one-self to it completely, for just being aware of it makes me feel wild and excited and very much alive, more alive than at any other time in my life.

And then I remembered, at various times in my life, having this same sensation—of being on the verge of something tremendous, but never quite knowing what it was, where it was coming from, or what to do with it. Stuck without a vocabulary to describe it, as it were, it slipped away from me again and again until I thought it a thing of childhood, which I'd put behind me forever. Quite a pleasant surprise to find that not only is it still alive in me, but that others feel it too! To know that there are people who, though they speak of it in terms my rational mind rebels at, have felt the flow like me.

Others expressed it more simply. Alison Harlow, a computer consultant, said, "I think we're a lot more fun. We use ourselves better. We're clear in how we want to live. We play fewer games determined by other people. We are free to choose our roles and find ways to live in accordance with our feelings." She thought a minute, laughed, and added, "Paganism says I am alive and therefore I am good and the Goddess rejoices in my joy. The more I celebrate life, the happier She is, the happier I am." Still others said that becoming Pagan had allowed their imaginations to flower. A successful scientist told me, "A few weeks after I had entered the Craft, I was driving home, looking at the mountains. I said to a friend, 'Those mountains are alive. You can almost see the Indians marching through them.' My friend said, 'Wow, two months ago you would never have said a thing like that to me.'"

Most Neo-Pagans are white and from middle-class backgrounds, but that does not necessarily mean that most live middle-class lives. I found an enormous range in financial position and style of living, often within the same city or within the same group. In 1976, these were the occupations people listed.

Housewife (9)	Chemist
Farmer (4)	Medic in military
Salesperson (4)	Social psychologist
Nurse (3)	Landowner
Writer (3)	Library assistant
Student (3)	Graphologist
Psychologist or Counselor (3)	Computer systems analyst

Unemployed (3)
Publisher (2)
Electrical engineer (2)
Engineer (2)
Metalurgist (2)
Secretary (2)
Welfare department worker (2)
Teacher (2)
Editor of technical magazine (2)
Run occult shop (2)
Retired (2)
Armed Forces (2)
Guided missile research
TV producer
Bartender

Girl Friday
Underwater archeological
  fieldworker
PhD candidate
Professional psychic
Radio announcer
Silversmith
Travel agent
Real-estate agent
Run Witchcraft shcool
Living on alimony
Work for government (HEW)
Machinist
Bill collector[15]

Two years later the government worker left for the land and two of the farmers left for town. The woman living on alimony died. The Ph.D. candidate received his degree. There are probably other changes. Many (20 percent) did not describe their work.

There was a great division between those who said they worked merely to survive and those who found meaning and satisfaction in their work. There was also a great division between those who had an integrated identity and were fairly public about their beliefs while on the job and those who led separate lives, with two different sets of associates. While some found unpleasant discrepancies between their working life and their Pagan/Craft identity, others felt no sense of contradiction, and in a few cases accepted and even enjoyed the double life.

A striking number of Neo-Pagans worked in scientific and technical fields, and all felt there was absolutely no conflict between their scientific work and their belief in, or use of, magic. A doctor of physical chemistry, working at a major corporation in a high position, told me, "Science is the study of natural phenomena. Witchcraft is learning to live in this world on a natural basis. There is a lot in common. It's all one world. The energies we study in science are the same energies we work with in Witchcraft."

This chemist is the priestess of one of the most active Gardnerian covens in the United States. She is a fine example of someone whose work life and religious life are totally distinct. As she described it, her life was equally divided between the two occupations. She enjoyed her professional life; she enjoyed her Craft life. "I have found no way to integrate the two, at this stage of the game," she said at one point. "I absolutely refuse to mix them," she said at another. But another priestess, referring to this woman, put it more bluntly: "Despite her Ph.D. and successful position, she lives in mortal terror that her employers will discover that she's a Witch."

I asked this scientist how her two sets of associates differed. She replied, "The Craft is a way of life. It's a way of being yourself, of feeling comfortable. You don't have to fight natural tendencies. People in the Craft appreciate you for what you are. They don't put guidelines and restrictions on you. I am constantly struck by how open and honest people in the Craft are about who they are and what they feel about things. Whereas in my mundane life as a scientist, showing your individuality is not really accepted."

Alison Harlow is, in contrast, open and public about her beliefs. I asked her if she found any contradictions between her work and her religious life.

"No," she said. "I am a systems analyst which, on one level, seems contradictory. But I feel that the work that I do is basically intellectual work. It does not put a drain on my resources of empathy, sensitivity, and magical perception. I have all of that available to me when I go about, in a sense, my "real" life of relating to people as a Witch and a priestess." She added that science and magic were simply "subjective" and "objective" sciences, and that different sets of tools were needed for each.

Ed Fitch, who has written some of the most beautiful Pagan rituals ever published—the Pagan Way rituals—composed most of them on a bus that took him to work at a military base. "Didn't you find *that* a contradiction?" I asked him.

"Not at all," he replied. He told me that in his experience some of the best Neo-Pagans were, by profession, either technocrats or in the military.

On the other hand, the late Craft bard and priest Gwydion Pendderwen spent many years working for the Internal Revenue Service and the Department of Health, Education and Welfare. Finding such work troublesome and filled with contradictions, he finally left those jobs to live a rural life in Mendocino County. He once said to me, "You get up in the morning, go to work for eight hours a day, turning off your psyche. The hardest part for most Witches and Pagans is that they have to lead two separate lives. They are doubly victims because they have the desire to be free, but most of them do not have enough trust in themselves, or in the gods, if you will, to get out."

Aidan Kelly, of NROOGD, observed to me that the question of contradictions was often skirted by Pagans, and understandably so. "A lot of jobs in this society are life-denying. And anyone who has a strong sense of ethics is going to be faced with difficult personal problems about working in a great many jobs in this society. It's unfair to be too idealistic about this. What people generally do is compartmentalize. They set up a mental wall and refuse to look at the problem because it hurts and seems unsoluble."

Others in the movement have been less charitable. New York Witch Leo Martello has publicly stated that any Pagan who works for the government or the military is hypocritical. "There were no Witches in Watergate," he once wrote to me.

Only six of those who answered this question had jobs related to occult practices. Most felt that it was important to have a livelihood totally separate from magical pursuits, and that becoming involved in the "magic racket" was ultimately corrupting. One of the most thoughtful answers to this question of work came from a machinist in St. Paul, Minnesota:

> Like a lot of old-fashioned Anarchists and Communists, I'm a skilled worker who relates almost entirely to the work I do rather than to the employer I work for, and always refuse promotions that would force me to relate to the power structure.* If a significant number of my co-workers are political leftists, I'll work with them openly on various political projects, like radicalizing an existing union local, or founding one from scratch. If not, I keep my mouth shut on the job. (Not really a difficult thing to do, since my job requires me to bend over a machine at least three-quarters of the time anyway.)
>
> I was originally trained in the biological sciences and worked in the field for a few years, but couldn't take the frustration of being forced into

---

* In several interviews I was told that the person had refused a promotion for similar reasons.

being an active participant in the "Rape of Nature," knowing the whole time that improvements, when they came, wouldn't come from within the field but would be entirely political. (Also, that no significant improvements will come until ecological and economic necessity forces them, probably not in my lifetime.)

So I work at reasonably well-paid working-class jobs, the sort of thing where no one questions my background much when I apply for work (either you have the skill or you don't, and if they suspect you're faking your background, they just assume you're coming off a messy divorce or a stretch in the penitentiary for some barroom brawl, like practically everyone else).

I received a lot of criticism for this from my friends, but I still think my method of making a living is what's best for me. Sure, I could make my living through "the magic racket" if I wanted to, but I saw what that did to my aunt and uncle, and I don't think it's a good idea. The same goes for trying to make a living as a professional writer—most of the writers I know don't make much money at it, work much harder than I do, and worse yet, end up compromising themselves. If you make your living by either magic or the arts, you have to go out of your way to relate to and please "straight people." The longer you do this, the harder it is to keep these conscious compromises from influencing your thinking and the development of your personality. I prefer to keep my life compartmentalized, doing work that can't very easily contaminate my personality because it's essentially neutral and without meaning, either positive or negative.

As for going back to the land, most of the counterculture back-to-the-land ventures I've encountered so far were so obviously doomed to failure there was little one person could do to save them, so I was afraid to get involved.

Yes, there are obvious complications and contradictions involved for any Aquarian when it comes to "making a living" in this society, and I know of no easy solutions. Whatever approach you use, it takes a lot of work and a lot of self-discipline to survive both physically *and* develop an Aquarian personality. There don't seem to be any shortcuts: most of the obvious "solutions" are illusions.

Urban or Rural?

Most Neo-Pagans live in urban areas and most, but not all, plan to stay there. "Why does Paganism grow up in cities?" I asked. "Because most *people* live in cities," was the most common reply. "Because strange ideas grow up in cities," was another. "Because books are printed there," was a third. Publisher Carl Weschcke put it this way: "Most covens are urban covens. As long as we're talking about a *live* religious phenomenon, it's going to occur primarily in urban areas, just because that's where people are and that's where the need is. We will not all leave the city and go back to the land. The cities will either have a healthy future or we will have to condemn ninety percent of the population to extinction."

It is clear that Weschcke differed greatly with the Feraferian vision of ten to twenty million people living in a horticultural paradise; he also differed with a number of Neo-Pagans who felt that urban populations were condemned. Not all Pagans agreed with Weschcke, but his was the majority view.

Many of the people I questioned believe that new ideas enter through cities. A man from the Midwest wrote, "The breakdown of Piscean culture and the developing of Aquarian culture is occurring in the big cities. Aquarians gravitate there because they are freer to develop there."

Another common thread was the idea that the disadvantages of city living produced a reverence toward nature (the same idea was expressed by Fred Adams in an earlier chapter). Alison Harlow told me, "Urban Pagans feel most uprooted, most alienated from nature. Those in the country are living quietly. They don't need to talk about it. They don't know we're around. Maybe they don't need us." A Gardnerian priestess from New York told me that cities had access to new ideas and intellectual stimulation and that "sensitive urban people, surrounded by concrete, would feel more urgently the lack of living greenery, and lack of contact with Earth and her seasons, and might therefore try to reestablish contact on a ritual or intellectual basis through a Pagan religion." She also wrote that "in the anonymity and aloneness of a city the tribal format of a Pagan religion might prove an acceptable substitute for the extended family and fulfill the need for traditions and belonging." Another priestess, Bobby Kennedy, from Ohio, expressed a similar idea. "City dwellers," she told me, "are so isolated from nature that they need to venerate it more because it's so far away from them. Most religions, as far as I'm concerned, answer a need for something that's missing."

"Is it contradictory to celebrate a harvest festival in the city?" I asked her.

"No," she said. "We are still eating the harvest. November is the only time pomegranates come around. That's something to celebrate!"

A few felt that cities inculcate false and romantic ideas about nature. Penny Novack said, "Neo-Paganism grows up in cities because that's where colleges, libraries, and bohemian centers are, places which foster weird ideas." But she added, "I dislike cities. I dislike the nature blindness that city environments encourage. I dislike the romantic fear and the silly adulation which city life seems to link with Nature when it does consider Her."

A surprisingly large portion of urban Neo-Pagans defended present-day city life and felt there were possibilities for a truly human urban life in the future. "I'm a computer programmer," Harlow told me. "There aren't many computers sitting around under oak trees. I like computers and many other aspects of urban life. I do think the city, as it has come to be in this civilization, is as much of an abomination as many other aspects of our civilization. But that does not mean I think cities are, per se, terrible. I think that we, as a species, are theoretically capable of building cities that are wholesome and healthy and authentically spiritually satisfying places to live."

Chicago Gardnerian priestess Donna Shultz told me that she likes city living; she enjoys indoor rituals, and believes strongly that "it is possible to live in the middle of the city and be in harmony with the land as long as you commit yourself to certain principles." Lady Cybele, the "Fam-Trad" Witch from Wisconsin, put it simply: "The Goddess lives under concrete as well as in the mountains."

The strongest statement for city living came from Leo Martello, who lives in a small Manhattan apartment with his two dogs. He has no car. He rarely uses a telephone. His house is filled with numerous occult artifacts and curios, but he lives simply. He said; "I'm a New York City chauvinist. I love this city. I live two blocks from Central Park which I frequent often, walking my dogs. I know where to pick wild crabapples, as well as blackberries, grapes, nuts, mulberries, dandelions, and many wild fruits, vegetables, and herbs. I am an extremist. I prefer to live in the most exciting city in the world, or to have a place of my own in the country as far away from other people as possible. Anything in between bores me."

Some urban Pagans saw great advantages to leaving the cities, but even they felt that country living did not necessarily make for a rev-, erent attitude toward nature. Carolyn Clark of the Church of All Worlds said, "It's not enough to say, 'When you live on the land you will have a reverent attitude toward nature.' I just came back from a weekend on the farm with my inlaws. Despite the fact that they make their living from the land, they are totally divorced from it. They are not personally involved with their crops. They will say, 'Well, the almanac says such and such, so let's do this.' Most people don't consider the earth to be their mother. They don't see it as a living organism—it's just a lot of dirt and animals are just 'critters,' not beings with whom you interact."

Mark Roberts of Dallas expressed a similar idea. "Often a person in the country lacks an awareness of the country. Many farmers today are far more technocratic than people with front yards and gardens. A farmer in today's society is often the very worst technician with his superplows and super poisons. It's not whether or not you have a farm. It's how you relate to the earth. You don't need acres. The minute you plant an outside window box, all of a sudden, rain is no longer something that fouls up the traffic when you go to work; it's something the earth needs. You become responsive to the cycles and needs of the earth."

A few did express the desire, often a fantasy, to leave the cities, or at least have the option to do so. And six of those I interviewed had either just left the city or did so not long after I talked to them (Gwydion Pendderwen; Otter and Morning Glory Zell; Tom Williams; Bran and Moria). Others said they were fearful that the cities had no future; they were impressed by theories that predicted a coming ice age, long cold winters. Still, the majority planned to stick it out. As one person wrote to me, "Neopaganism *is* the back-to-the-land movement. But for all of us to depart immediately for what's left of the forest *would* be a cop-out. Good or bad (and it *is* bad) the contemporary action is, largely, in the cities. And that's just the hard truth of it." (The only group that said fifty percent of its people were rural was the School of Wicca.)

Attitudes toward Technology and Science

In contrast to the views expressed in *Akwesasne Notes*, and contrary to my own expectations and the assumptions of various scholars, the majority of Neo-Pagans are optimistic about the uses of science and modern technology. Furthermore, while they may take inspiration from the past, they do not want to return to it. Many, in fact, do not view the past positively at all. They were quite adamant on this point. Perhaps they reacted strongly because I expressed forcefully my own ambivalences and my surprise at their seeming complacency. My own Pagan journey had been highly colored by the writings of Theodore Roszak and Stanley Diamond and by the vast ecological literature of the early seventies. To me every "advance" seemed to have its heavy price.

Among those who felt differently was Leo Martello, who wrote from New York: "A Pagan life as currently and loosely defined is *not* a return to the mud hovel." And Lady Cybele of Madison told me, "I'm all for technology, as long as it doesn't destroy the earth in the process. I'm very happy with technological advances. I'm very happy to climb in my car and drive two hundred miles to see Pagan friends." She began to laugh and added, "It's a bummer flying my broom in the winter. Besides, modern conveniences have eliminated a lot of drudgery. Modern technology has freed up time so people can develop philosophical pursuits."

Gwydion Pendderwen, the Craft bard, said, "There is a tendency among some Pagans to want to be back in, let us say, sixth-century Wales instead of wanting a *transformed* world. Going back to sixth-century Wales is a fantasy that is dear to me. It's part of the archetypal dream. But that is all it is. Nobody really wants to go back into the past, except a bunch of space cookies. It is not modern technology that is desensitizing. It is the misuse of it that is. I would not throw out my tape recorder for a bunch of lutes. I can use both to make music."

Some of those I questioned told me that the misuse of technology could be prevented if the right consciousness were present and the profit motive absent.

Several northern Californian Pagans saw the potential for a useful ecological technology. Sharon Devlin, as we have seen, was one.

Caradoc, of Berkeley, was another: "Technology is not good or evil; it depends on whether it's used for profit or not"—a traditionally radical view. Others, when asked these questions, offered common clichés. "Don't throw the baby out with the bath water," one person told me. "We can use technology up to the hilt; up until now we have let it use us." "After all," said another, "the occult is itself a technology, a psychotherapy for healthy people, a technology for self-evolution." One woman mused over a past life she felt she had known in a highly technical world. "I like technology," she said. "I am used to more of it." And one man wrote to me that, despite poisoning and pollution, "Intuition leads me to identify high technology and large populations with the new age. Technology is our creation and we can control it." The bluntest statement of all came from Herman Slater, Craft priest and owner of the Magickal Childe, a New York occult shop. He wrote to me:

> The good old days were not so good. We have lost nothing. We have just taken the names of old religions and applied modern forms and ideals that would not stand up to the original barbaric worship we claim to emulate.
>
> I look to the past for some of the simplicities of life, but to the future for the realization of my ideals. I don't feel we have lost anything except the primitive trappings of the old ways.

Very few people were concerned about the idea that modern technology costs a heavy price in desensitization. "We are dulled by technological overload," wrote Pagan writer Allen Greenfield, who observed that technology had "many gifts" but that our "high-energy culture was dehumanizing and alienating." Theos, the Gardnerian priestess from Long Island, said, "I haven't found that technology has posed a threat to my daily activities, but I see the hostile uses of the art catching up with the beneficial uses. Technology by and of itself is not evil. What we should be concerned with is the misuse and prostitution of technology for dehumanizing or other purposes, which hits us in many areas of our lives—nuclear weapons, automatic manufacturing processes which eliminate jobs, computers which store information that invades the privacy of one's life, chemical and bacteriological 'weapons,' and so on. It is impossible to ignore it."

Most reflective of all was priestess Morgan McFarland of Dallas. "Our civilization has tricked us into accepting as normal or natural things that are not. We only have flashes of insight and we are no longer producing real individuals, but cookie-cutter stereotypes."

McFarland spoke also of her fear that television was destroying the "secret kingdom" of children's street games and play rituals, "the only place where *real* ritual still exists," and she told me she often felt that it was almost impossible to attain a clear perspective. "I know that I am so involved in a life style filled with modern technological conveniences that I do not really know what I need and what I could do without, what Pagans really need, and what we could do without." Then, as we talked into the early hours of the morning, this priestess of three flourishing Dallas covens, a woman who struck me as one of the most perceptive coven leaders I had encountered during my travels, told me how deeply aware she was of contradictions in her own life. "The Craft is a way of life," she said softly, "but that does not mean that we live it, that I live it. It is something I strive toward."

The late Bonnie Sherlock expressed similar feelings. She was a bright, lovely, lonely woman in her forties who lived in the small town of Lander, Wyoming. Along with a small group of friends, Sherlock had published *The Medicine Wheel*, a small, sensitive Neo-Pagan journal that had never gone out to more than a hundred people. She had also presided as priestess in a coven that combined Celtic and Native American traditions. They called themselves the Delphians. A diabetic, dependent on extensive medication, she died in the fall of 1976. Her witty letters to *Green Egg* ceased, along with *The Medicine Wheel*.

Less than a year before she died we sat in her tiny, cozy house and talked. She talked about the initiation she had received, years before, into a Native American tradition. Despite her diabetes, she had gone on a three-day fast and vision quest that landed her in the hospital and nearly in the grave. Recalling the experience, she said it had been worth it. She would do it again in a minute. "I'm not in tune, always, with the life I would like to lead," she told me, pointing to her medications. She said that there was no history of diabetes in her family and called her illness "a disease of civilization," aided in its course by commercial foods, sugars, and additives. "The Craft is a way of life. It is a religion that celebrates life and love of nature. But there are times when I am not living it, when I step in and out of it."

She told me of her fantasies. They were simple. She said that she would like to be a caretaker of gardens, of temples with gardens where flowers bloomed and waters constantly flowed. It was February. Wyoming seemed a desert that lay under snow.

Bonnie Sherlock and Morgan McFarland were among the few who shared the feeling of identity with that cattle farmer who now worked at the Reynolds plant. But these feelings were not widely shared.

Despite the deep division in opinion about modern technology, almost everyone talked of the need for a return to the "primal," the unconscious, the "primitive"—but a "primitive" *within*, not a "primitive" that one *went back to*. Tony Andruzzi, a Witch of Sicilian origin and former stage magician, told me, "A Pagan is a believer in the primitive," but for him this meant a return not to the world of the primitive but to the roots of things. This did not necessarily conflict with a technologically advanced society, he said, although he added that, if it did conflict, the society should be destroyed. Sitting in a room decorated with red and black velvet, Andruzzi said, "A Pagan is a believer in the values of self-survival, in literally sitting down in the swamp, knee deep in mud, and becoming a part of it, letting it become a part of one; of becoming earth, of becoming stars, of becoming a piece of something that encompasses beyond understanding a part of the spectrum of all we know.

"We have subjugated that. We have to shear away, we have to tear out the rock wall, the crypt of our social, psychological being. We need to get back to a more elemental way of being, of living with our environment. We must protect that flame from all wind or threat. We must allow the growth of that diamond chip of god within us.

"We have to get back to a more elemental way of of *being*, not feeling, of *being*. I mean a living with our elements, a living with our environment instead of being superior to it."

Morgan McFarland's partner, Mark Roberts, expressed a similar point of view: "It's not a matter of going back into the past. It's getting off the sidewalk onto the earth. Walking out on the earth is not walking into the past; it's simply relating to what's there." The most important training for a Pagan, he thought, was that which opened the senses and allowed one to get back to the "untracked and un-trained level of our senses." But again, Pagans were split on the question of whether or not our ancestors had had an easier time coming to their senses in a world vastly simpler.

Turning to the question of "scientific" versus "magical" thinking, almost everyone I questioned felt that there was no conflict between the two; and most would have agreed with Robert Anton Wilson's humorous saying; "Advertising, Magic and Behaviorism all say the same thing—invoke often!" But two of the most important Pagan theorists made a careful distinction between scientific research done by scientists and what they called "the religion of science" or "Scientism" or "Scientolatry."

"There is no fight between 'science' and 'magic,' " Aidan Kelly said. "But there is a fight between two different kinds of religions, one of which often falsely claims to be science." He went on:

"I remember that I first thought about this over a year ago, when the American Humanist Association came out with their manifesto against astrology. The real clue was this—the newspapers reported the manifesto as if it were a pronouncement by the American Acad-emy of Science on the discovery of a new planet, as if this were the scientific opinion of scientists speaking as scientists. But in fact, the manifesto was the dogmatic *opinion* of members of the American Humanist Association, speaking as members of a secular religion, the major religion among intellectuals in America today.

"This religion of scientolatry is usually referred to as science. But it is not. The first two dogmas of this religion are, first, that it is not a religion at all, but a purely rational philosophy. The second dogma is that all other religions are purely superstition. And intellectuals who do not subscribe to this religion are discriminated against.

"Unfortunately, the rebellion against the spiritual poverty of scientolatry, often ends up becoming a mistrust of science itself and a mistrust of any kind of technological development. This is a con-fusion. There is a great deal of wistful archaicism going on in this society, going back to the way it used to be. That is a fantasy. Science is a method, a technique. And technology is very useful. The prob-lem is not with the tools, but with this idolatrous attitude toward science, this secular religion that denies all other aspects of being human."[16]

Another who expressed this view was Isaac Bonewits, who described himself as a "materialist" as well as an occultist, adding, "I just have a somewhat looser definition of matter than most people." Bonewits told me that he preferred to take a "practical approach" in analyzing psychic phenomena. In his opinion, most such phenomena were caused by physical organisms interacting. "Now the interaction may be an energetic reaction rather than a material reaction, but it's still being caused by a physical phenomenon." He added, "I'm a naturalist rather than a supernaturalist. I believe the gods have a mechanistic as well as a spiritual existence, that they follow certain laws and patterns of behavior. But reality is consensual. People define what reality is. In my personal definition of it, I include the fact that you can come up with a moderately logical explanation for everything that happens, provided that you are not hung up on using only Western logic."

What about Aidan's distinction between "science" and "scientolatry," I asked. Bonewits concurred: "Scientism is the worship of nineteenth-century science. It is also the unthinking acceptance of any statement made by any man wearing a white lab coat. That's scientism, and it's a very strong religion in America, mostly among mediocre scientists. You'll find very few topnotch ones who are scientistic in thinking. It's the second-level ones who are terrified of the occult."

This distinction was stressed over and over by Neo-Pagans. They expressed anger *not* at "science" but at the "religion of science." Allen Greenfield said that science contains many truths, but the "scientific establishment is an organized faith that contributes heavily to our present sorry state as a civilization." And CAW priest Don Wildgrube answered my question by saying, "Science is a tool—but when it becomes a god, a religion, that is something else."

Despite most Pagans' positive attitudes toward science and technology, real differences have surfaced from time to time, occasionally leading to open conflict between Neo-Pagan groups. Since most Neo-Pagans, like most people, don't often think about the ethical and political implications of what they are doing, the differences often lie unexpressed. Occasional conflicts between groups seem, on the surface, to be mere personality conflicts (and some, of course, *are*), but many reflect real and complex philosophical differences.

One example was a dispute that came to be known as the Council of Themis War of 1972, perhaps the worst conflict to take place within the Neo-Pagan community. It was made worse by inaccurate reporting in several Witchcraft books.[17]

Ostensibly, the issues in the dispute were twofold. The Council of Themis was an ecumenical meeting of some twenty Neo-Pagan groups that wanted to issue statements of common purpose. The dispute revolved, on the one hand, around the drug and sexual practices in Berkeley's Psychedelic Venus Church and the attitudes toward animal sacrifice in another group, the Hellenic Order; and, on the other hand, around unilateral actions taken by two members of the Council to expel these two groups without discussion and without the consent of all member groups. But underlying these issues were philosophical differences on the questions of sexuality, drugs, authoritarianism, and technology.

During this dispute there was an interesting exchange of letters between Feraferia's leading lady, Svetlana Butyrin, and CAW priestess Carolyn Clark. Svetlana observed:

> I have my doubts about incorporating technology into any Pagan system; of course, Feraferia totally rejects modern technology and the scientific experimental method. The only allowable science is strictly observational—not manipulative.

To this Carolyn Clark replied:

> . . . . even when Australopithecus picked up a stick and used it to kill food, he was using technology. I believe our argument is over *degree*. To what extent can we go with our technology and still retain eco-psychic equilibrium? . . . I doubt it is possible/probable to survive on Mother Earth without manipulating Her. Manipulation She doesn't seem to mind. She is, in fact, responding favorably to my manipulation of our back yard into an organic garden. Hurting Her is something else again.[18]

Ecology

In retrospect I see that I should not have been so surprised that many Pagans favored technology, since most of those I talked to were highly imaginative, were avid readers of science fiction, and tended to put their ideals and fantasies in as many future settings as past ones. My own views began to change and adapt. I had a more receptive attitude toward technology, science, and cities after conducting these interviews. This did not happen, however, when I touched upon another subject—ecology.

Again, it must be said, I came with a strong bias. As a person who had entered the Craft in part because it was "an ecological religion," I assumed that an ecological concern would be one of the two or three unifying bonds among all Neo-Pagans, one of the unarguable points. My reasoning was a bit simple: The worshippers in a religion that venerated nature would surely consider the protection of the earth a religious duty. I also tended to the position that anyone who did not feel this way either was not a "real Pagan" or was a person who had not begun to make connections between belief and daily life. It would be dishonest to say that I have changed my position.

Verbally, most of those I interviewed agreed that "a reverence for the earth and nature" was a common bond between Pagans. A Neo-Pagan from Florida told me, "Pagans are close to the earth, have a love for her, and are certainly concerned when she is polluted." Leo Martello wrote, "Neo-Paganism is a pre-Judeo-Christian religion of nature worshippers: spiritual ecologists." Morgan McFarland said, "A Pagan world view is one that says the Earth is the Great Mother and has been raped, pillaged, and plundered and must once again be celebrated if we are to survive. Paganism means a return to those values which see an ecologically balanced situation so that life continues and the Great Mother is venerated again. If nature disappears, all my spiritual efforts go up in smoke. Both ecology and Paganism seek a restoration of the balance of nature. If you're not into ecology, you really can't be into Paganism." Morgan's partner, Mark Roberts, was even more emphatic. "We should live our religion," he said. "If our land is being poisoned and we don't relate to the poisoning, there is a very large error factor there. Ecology should not be an arguable point within the Craft. If our goal is seeking kinship with nature and the nature we are seeking kinship with is being poisoned, then we must become religious militants. We should be the chaplains of the ecology movement, at the least, if not in the front ranks of the fight."

Almost everyone spoke somewhat in this vain. Moria, a priestess from California, told me, "We are here to preserve what little is left of nature and of freedom. We are learning to live with nature, learning to live in tune with the seasons, tuning into the life forces of plants, animals, and people." The Ph.D. chemist told me that if there was a goal of the movement it was "the salvage of the earth." Carl Weschcke, the publisher, stated it clearly: "A Witch can't think of nature as something to be conquered. . . . Paganism is a response to the planet as a whole. The clearest thing about Pagan philosophy is its awareness of need: that the planet is in crisis and that we must get back in tune with the natural world. We must live within nature." And still another respondent told me the goals of Neo-Paganism would be "to fight the destruction of the natural world, as well as promote the individual spiritual advancement of each person." Finally, I asked Bonewits if there were certain positions that most Neo-Pagans and Crafters would "have to come to." "Yes," he said. "I think one would wind up being very concerned about environmental and ecological matters," although, he added wryly, "Most Neo-Pagans are too loose and liberal to be fanatic about *anything*, including their own survival!"

This comment may have been the truest of all, for despite this widespread verbal agreement there was a deep split between Pagans whose commitment to ecological principles was strong and practical, and those whose commitment was limited to a religious vision. The former often felt the latter were not living up to their commitments. The latter generally felt that no extreme measures were needed. The real difference was political—between those who believed that a complete change in life style or economy or consciousness was needed, and those who felt such a change was unnecessary or undesirable or something that would evolve by itself, given time.

Quite a few spoke against any kind of militant action to save the environment. "The principles of the Craft," said one priest from the

Midwest, "are more universal than environmental. The same planting, growing, ripening, harvesting, storage, and quiet period that nature goes through we go through in our own lives, even in the city. They may not be as apparent, but these same cycles are here in almost everything we do."

This coven priest then expressed to me opinions I have heard from many people in the United States since the "energy crisis" and accompanying ecological backlash—although those people were not Pagans. "I am pulling a little ways away from ecology. The environment is constantly changing. The minute you plant a seed in the ground, you have altered the environment. It's really not a matter of man trying to rape the earth. We simply do not yet know the results of our actions and reactions. Yes, the Craft is involved in ecology, but I do not think it is a major Craft problem."

Roberta Ann Kennedy, the Craft priestess from Ohio, told me, "I see people in the Craft talking about ecology, but not living it. I believe there's a problem, but until it gets a lot worse nobody's going to do anything about it." She added, "I'm judging from my own behavior," and told me that she enjoyed her comforts and would find it hard to change her way of living. Theos, the Gardnerian priestess from Long Island, told me that she could not "recall any persons seeking membership in my coven via the ecology route." She observed, "If there is any connection at all, I would think it is based upon a growing awareness that the earth is a living and breathing entity as opposed to a pile of lifeless dirt. As such, it should be recognized as having dignity, treated with respect; it must be given rest and replenishment. I don't necessarily agree that the public relates this to Paganism, however such beliefs are alien to many of us within Paganism, and presumably, once 'infected' with the concept of a living Earth-Mother, the natural 'next step' for some people might be to seek out a concept of life which incorporates such ideas." But, she concluded, since no one had entered her covens via this route, she was "stabbing in the dark" on this question.

Most of the strong statements supporting ecological militancy came from Neo-Pagans involved in groups other than Witchcraft—groups like the Church of All Worlds and Feraferia. The most militant statements came from Penny Novack, for many years a leader of Philadelphia's Pagan Way. Penny told me she found a great difference between those she labeled "Pagans" or "celebrants" and those she labeled "occultists." "Many occultists can't really plug in to the earth," she maintained. She felt the movement should involve itself heavily in ecological activities and had failed to do so because most people "did not make connections" and remained on a "pretty fantasy trip."

In a long letter to *Earth Religion News* Penny described how the Pagan Way had been created, and expressed her feelings of frustration at the philosophical divisions that had split the group apart. When the Pagan Way began, in 1970, she said, it was designed to be a "poetic, mystic pagan group based on the seasonal celebrations." It was loose, eclectic, with a series of post office boxes in several states and a set of rituals for seasonal celebrations. It was "adamantly celebrant."

> The entire idea was the celebration of the yearly round with festival behavior and simple, joyous ceremonies. It was not required that those attending be strongly cognizant of the religion and certainly not that they have an interest in the "occult" or even "Witchcraft." . . . We assumed those who were aware would, as the seasons passed and they were exposed to Her gracious beauty, grow from within, in reverence for Nature and for the glory of life. I will not say this was a failure. In a few cases it worked beyond my wildest dreams. But then the occultists began to make themselves felt . . . and . . . the number of plain, ordinary folk dwindled.

The world, she observed, needed less Witchcraft training circles and more celebrant nature worshippers. She concluded:

> Our Mother is in trouble, folks. Although the Earth and Moon will doubtless survive, the living flesh of our world biosis is endangered by mankind, by that devouring cancer which is humanity. It is up to those of us who are aware of this to turn from petty ego-trips. . . . . We must join the ecologists and philosophers of the holistic universe and our native American Indian brothers and sisters in their desperate attempts to change the consciousness of all people no matter what "religion" they profess.[19]

Penny described the ecologists and celebrants as "essentially anarchists." She described the others as concerned with hierarchy. As she saw it, the free spirits melted away and the opportunity for an ecologically aware Pagan group vanished.

When I last spoke to Penny she and her husband were calling themselves Judeo-Pagan Taoists. She said she was disillusioned; she felt there was little chance for a Neo-Paganism that would unite with the ecology movement. She had converted to Judaism, the religion of her husband, because, she said, she believed in tribal religions. She felt a hunger for a tribe. She had hoped the Neo-Pagan movement would provide it, but so far it had not. Before I left, the Novacks told me, "The Pagan movement will grow, we think. But will it awaken people's earth consciousness? Because, if people's earth consciousness does not awaken, we are dying!"

So I asked Penny, "How, then, *do* you get people to relate to nature?"

And she replied, "I would trick them into going into the wilderness with me. And maybe we'd get lost. And maybe we would get cold. And perhaps we would have to trap and find herbs and learn basic things, like how you bury your shit. And by the time they got back, they would be so pissed at me they would never go anywhere with me again. But they would know the earth!"

As we sat around at the Novacks' house, relaxing, Penny pulled out a stack of *Akwesasne Notes* and pointed out articles to me. I opened one of them. It read:

> Ecology is not continuing the exploitation of the earth in a "clean way," it is the development of non-exploitative relationships with the creation. . . . Ecology will never take place without a massive reordering of the social and economic structure of the United States.[20]

Clearly, a position that assumed the necessity of political and economic *and* religious transformation was not typical of the Pagans I had encountered. The Novacks, perhaps. Few others.

As we have seen, the Church of All Worlds and Feraferia have consistently taken a militant position on ecology, although they have differed on the question of technology and on ultimate vision. The Church of All Worlds has published many articles on the *religious* nature of all ecological activities, and articles in *Green Egg* have often talked about "the murder of the planet" or "Terracide." According to one article, CAW was seeking to end the destructive course of events by engaging in various organizing activities, by seeking to live close to nature, and by emphasizing the values of decentralism and small-village life.[21]

A number of Pagans held up to me other models for ecological sanity. Among these were the works of Murray Bookchin, the anarchist writer whose book *Our Synthetic Environment*, had appeared in 1962, well before the ecology craze. Bookchin advocated a decentralized society composed of moderate-sized cities and involving a highly developed system of what we call alternate technologies—solar, wind, etc. This future would neither be a return to the past nor a "suburban accommodation to the present." Ecology, wrote Bookchin, "refers to a broad, philosophical, almost spiritual, outlook toward humanity's relationship to the natural world. . . ." Such an outlook could "heal the wound that was opened by humanity's split with nature thousands of years ago;" if it were aligned with a view that advocated diversity and decentralization.[22]

Another book that Pagans thrust into my hands was Ernest Callenbach's *Ecotopia*, a utopian novel that takes place in the Pacific Northwest in 1999, after northern California, Oregon, and Washington have seceded from the United States and have established an ecological stable-state system. The new society is democratic, decentralist, filled with separatist and communitarian values. New technologies (like biodegradable plastics) exist alongside certain delightful primitivisms, and a Pagan religion of tree worship is subtly alluded to but never detailed.[23]

These two works reflected some of the ideas that I came across many times in my interviews. But few of those I spoke to considered any of these models seriously. Most continued to subscribe, consciously or unconsciously, to the majority American view in these matters. The nature paradise was vision—no less, no more.

Politics

Differences between Pagans in regard to ecology really come down to differences in regard to "politics," although that word may seem to many Neo-Pagans a bad choice, since so many of them described themselves as "apolitical," while espousing very political views. Ed

Fitch observed to me, "You find in Paganism the strangest mixture of people. You find revolutionaries and radicals. You find former army intelligence types, maybe even active CIA types. This is because they are all action-oriented. They crave something new. They crave dignity and adventure. They want to know what's just over the next physical or intellectual or emotional hill. All these people work together, thoroughly enjoy each other's company, and ignore each other's politics."

This statement holds true not only for Neo-Paganism but for other movements and groups that are bonded primarily by imagination. It holds true for science-fiction fans and for members of the Society for Creative Anachronism—the medievalist society. Among such groups *nothing* is taken for granted, politically or philosophically. Nothing is "given," and nothing is assumed as common ground. You are as likely to meet up with a monarchist as with a Marxist. The views expressed in various Pagan journals, most particularly *Green Egg*, were especially free-ranging and diverse. At the same time, they were seldom analytical or theoretical (since there was no common theory). An issue of *Green Egg* might have a long essay on the theories of Velikovsky, an article on tribal communes, a long essay on DNA, a reprint from an organization dedicated to saving the whales, an article from *Akwesasne Notes*. There was less common ground assumed in *Green Egg* than in any other publication I had ever seen. The same holds true for Neo-Pagans generally.

When I asked one hundred Pagans to list their political positions, the assortment was astonishing. There were old-style conservatives and liberals, a scattering of Democrats and Republicans, twenty different styles of anarchists (ranging from Ayn Randists to leftist revolutionaries), many libertarians, a couple of Marxists, and one Fascist. Despite this range, the majority were not very self-critical and many defined "politics" in a very narrow way.

"Politics" means something very different in the mainstream of American society from what it means on the fringes. The questions I asked—Are you political? do you think there is a political aspect to Paganism?—were, I saw later, badly framed. Many of those who said they were apolitical were, by another definition, highly political.

For most of America, despite the events of the last twenty years, "politics" means such things as voting, political campaigns, the actions of Congress, lobbying. Those Pagans who defined politics in this fashion—and many did—generally told me that Neo-Paganism was totally removed from politics and should remain so. The comments of Theos were typical: "I think that most of the people in my coven are not very active participants in any political movement. I suppose that they vote, but I don't find that the topic ever comes up in conversations we have. I myself owe no allegiance to any one political philosophy or party, at times abstaining from the whole scene when it turns me off."

On the other hand, most feminists, most militant ecologists, and most people who had gone through the sixties understood "politics" to be something akin to "the decisions that affect our daily lives." These people often said that Neo-Paganism was intensely political.

Most Neo-Pagans felt that their religion presented an alternative world view, but some of them said that this had nothing to do with "politics," while others felt that "politics" and "world view" were synonymous and that a change in world view implied a change in politics. Others felt there was a great distinction between "political" and "spiritual" transformation. Still others felt the two were inseparable. Again, these differences had little to do with the tradition one belonged to. Even in the Church of All Worlds, all of whose members described themselves as some sort of anarchist and believed that Neo-Paganism had a transformative mission, there were great differences in how that mission was described. And most felt it was "not political."

To give another example, many felt strongly about ecological problems. Those who felt that such problems were the result of ignorance or apathy would often tell me that ecology was of great concern to Pagans, and then say, "Paganism is apolitical." But those who felt that ecological problems were due to "the patriarchal rape-head" or "the profit motive" would often describe Paganism as very political.

If there was any clear division, it was between two groups: those who saw Neo-Paganism as a vehicle for the transformation of society through a heightened ecological or feminist consciousness, for example, as well as an avenue for personal growth; and those who merely saw the latter. Those who saw Paganism as a transformative vehicle generally tended toward the extremes, both left and right;

they might be "rational anarchists" or "spiritual socialists" or, in Paul Goodman's words, "neolithic conservatives." Those who saw Neo-Paganism as simply a vehicle for individual development tended to be "moderates."

In general, one could not escape the conclusion that Neo-Paganism and the Craft are adaptable to almost any stance on politics. The differences were often extreme, but the Pagans got along well together.

Here are some examples of the range in replies of the many Pagans who disavowed all political connections:

"The least discussed subject in our coven is politics."—The Cyprian, a Craft priestess

"I don't consider myself political. I look at politics like I look at children playing with a revolver. I just hope they don't hurt themselves."—Tony Andruzzi, Chicago magician and Witch

"We are political only in a very oblique way; in that we do present a challenge to certain conventional ways of thinking."—Alison Harlow

"A proper Witch response would be: The government doesn't recognize us, well that's fine, since we don't recognize the government."—Aidan Kelly, in a letter to *Green Egg*

"Paganism is not a threat. It can only offer, persuade, beckon, entice, enchant."—Tony Kelly, a Pagan living in Wales

"The Craft is adaptable to every society it has been in."—Lady Cybele

"I think it's wrong to be politically active. The Craft is part of the same phenomenon of change that's occurring. But it's not a revolutionary movement."—Carl Weschcke, Llewellyn Press

"Politics has absolutely *nothing* to do with what's going on. It's a red herring. Any true revolution is a religious and cultural revolution, a revolution of values. The political situation is really irrelevant."—Tim Zell, CAW

"The political side of the movement is staying alive legally."—Carolyn Clark, CAW

"I'm a conservative. We *are* the establishment. Most Craft people are middle class, reasonably financially secure."—Two members of a coven in Minnesota

Not surprisingly, both the strongest antipolitical and propolitical statements came from Pagans living in the San Francisco Bay Area.

Aidan Kelly spoke for the idea that politics and religion deal with two completely different realities:

"The Craft implies almost an antipolitics. We tend to pick up people who have gotten disillusioned with politics and have discovered that they are throwing energy down a rathole. They realize, 'I could devote my life to this kind of trip and it would not make one iota of difference for the human race.' And they come back from that and start trying to take a broader look at life.

"At this point in my life, I feel that when you try to deal only in terms of political and economic structures, you end up producing, usually, nothing better than a palace revolution.

"The idea of the Craft is not to overthrow the political structure or the economic structure, but the entire culture, the entire civilization. Now, I am not convinced the Craft can do that. I think, at this point in history, a new religion is needed."

Isaac Bonewits also took an antipolitical stance. He told me that his own beliefs were close to Fabian socialism, but that occultists and Pagans should not get involved in politics, with the exception of fighting for legislation that protects religious dissidents and trying to educate the public to understand and tolerate different religious viewpoints.

A few Neo-Pagans felt that no matter what they labeled themselves, most Pagans were on the same political wavelength. As one person wrote to me, "I am an old fashioned left-wing anarchist of the sort that feels that capitalism, Marxism, and liberalism are all facets of one repressive political-economic system. From what I can tell, most Neo-Pagans, whether they call themselves 'Conservatives,' 'Liberals,' 'Anarchists,' or 'Apolitical,' tend to agree more closely with each other and with me on any particular *real* issue than do "Piscean" people on the same issue."

Mark Roberts of Dallas made a similar point: "I was an organizer for the Young Republicans. I also worked for Gene McCarthy. I've carried different labels at different times. I've noticed that many Witches 'feel' their politics. Some are to the right, some are to the left. They generally avoid the middle. Both those on the left and those on the right are aware that change is needed."

And most Pagans, no matter what *their* politics, assumed that most *other* Pagans were liberals. I was often confronted by people who told me they were "conservative, unlike most Pagans," whom they invariably described as "liberals," a word that almost no one used to describe his or her own politics. Many simply refused to be labeled at all.

Of those who felt that Paganism was political, all were residents of the San Francisco Bay Area, or ardent feminists, or ecology activists, or activists on behalf of gay or civil rights. Taken together, they were perhaps one-fourth of the people I interviewed.

Caradoc, a Pagan who lives in a small house in Berkeley, had this to say:

"If one is working within the Craft as anything that is recognizable to me, one is working with a set of values which are totally at odds with the values of this society. This society has replaced the old state religions with a state-supported reality construct. If the Craft is so little different that it doesn't come up with different attitudes, viewpoints, and answers than this culture, then what good is it?

"Craft values say you are basically good. The world is holy. Your body is holy. It isn't a piece of dirt. Evil arises not from some 'force' of evil, but from a misconstrual of that which is good. The only way the Craft can be apolitical is if Craft people do not in their own lives challenge the basic assumptions of the American value system, and, in my own view, if they don't do that, they're not Witches no matter who initiated them.

"I come from a place that sees the Craft as an extremely political thing, as totally bound up with feminism and with the rejection of Christian patristic religious, social, and economic values. The rejection of these values was an inextricable part of the Old Religion. As it should be still. Without them, the Craft loses its soul. You can't take that stance, without being political."

Others who saw Paganism as intensely "political" came from an intellectual universe where it was assumed that all things are interconnected, that *everything* is "political." The strongest statement came from Devlin, the hereditary Witch of Irish descent, a mother, musician, and weaver. It appears in an earlier chapter.

Another person who, while not using the word "political," expressed ideas similar to Devlin's was Gwydion Pendderwen, who told me, "The Craft is a spiritual movement, a psychic development movement, and a movement based on the absolute worth of the individual as opposed to corporate principles. The principles of the Craft don't seem to allow for accommodation with the establishment. In a way, we're trying to have the same rights blacks have asked for: asking that 'Witch' like 'nigger' stop being a pejorative term."

And I must not forget the one reply to my questionnaire that stated it most simply: "Life celebration is always a threat to those bent on destruction."

These replies show that the politics of Pagans were not dependent on their "tradition," but on the community and universe to which they belonged, on their life styles, and the history of their interactions with the world. A Gardnerian priestess in the Bay Area might have far less in common with her counterpart in New Jersey than she would with a feminist Witch in Los Angeles. The differences within their traditions are, it seems, far less important than the differences created by their lives in the world.

Secrets That Can't Be Kept

Some Neo-Pagans, like Carl Weschcke, were entirely open about their religious views and found no problems in being Pagans in the society. Others, like Bran and Moria, found their house stoned or, like Judy Myer, their children taken away, or like Z, their psychic consultations considered illegal, or like Fred Adams, their means of employment put in jeopardy.

The Frosts, of the School of Wicca, were militantly public. Gavin bought and sold pigs in the name of the School of Wicca. Their controversial *The Witch's Bible* was public knowledge, and they were identified with it. One day, during my visit to their farm, we went into a small local lunchroom. I began talking of Witches and covens and, instinctively, given this small farming town of Salem, Missouri, I lowered my voice. Immediately, Yvonne demanded that I speak up loudly. Gavin explained later:

"The people who really get in trouble are the people who are semisecret, that's how rumors start. Be public! The government will defend your right to the bitter end, because that's the way we're set up in the U.S. But if you're private and secret, then people will come around and burn down your barn in the middle of the night. And then who will defend you?"

Gavin and Yvonne felt perfectly comfortable with the system. Said Gavin, "The system is set up to help us, so why not use the system? It's a great system—freedom of speech, freedom of religion, separation of church and state. If you've got a law against fortune-telling or something, why not go down to the local police station and say, 'Hey, I'm into this trip, and I'd like to explain it to you guys.' You get to know them and work with them, and they're not going to give you a rough time no matter what fortune-telling you do."

"Secrecy," Susan Roberts had written, "is their [the Witches'] security blanket."[24] But in fact, while some Witches and Pagans delighted in secrecy, others felt it was a hard necessity. In contrast to the Frosts openness, the Gardnerian priestess–Ph.D. chemist was totally private. To her, secrecy was important, desirable, necessary. This was reflected in her large and comfortable suburban house, where the windows were covered with thick drapes. The sun remained outside. "My religious needs are behind the scenes," this priestess told me. She enjoyed the secrecy. She said, "The secrecy is a major part of my attraction to the religion. It's my nature."

But others felt that the only necessary secrets were private ritual mantras that might give a group identity and cohesion, or certain magical teachings that should be handed out warily, "because you don't give a blowtorch to someone who doesn't know how to use it." Still others told me that there were *no* secrets, since, as one priestess said, "How can you give away the secret of a wheat stalk? Much of what's going on is that simple. It's all lying right there for everyone to see."

Politics and Ecology

In the late 1980s, many of the attitudes described in the previous pages of this chapter have changed. Some of these changes are reflected in answers to a 1985 questionnaire (see Appendix I), and some of these changes are profound.

In particular, there is a lot more political activism among Pagans and a lot more concern with ecology issues than there was when *Drawing Down the Moon* was first published.

Before delving into an area as sensitive as this, it is essential to say, once again, that Pagans are a diverse, individualistic lot. There are Pagans who go camping in RV's with bags of Fritos and there are Pagans who seem to eat nothing but nuts and sprouts. Likewise, there are Pagans who voted for Ronald Reagan as well as Pagans who have put their bodies in front of military trucks. While most of the political activities of Pagans have been about peace and ecology issues, it's absolutely essential to say over and over again that the groups and individuals described below do not reflect the Pagan movement as a whole. Some people—myself included—may wish they did, but they only represent a segment. In a 1984 editorial in *Red Garters*, the official newsletter of the New Wiccan Church, an organization of English Traditional Witches, Allyn Wolfe wrote:

> A quick survey of current Pagan periodicals gives the impression that Witches are: politically liberal, or libertarian; "feminist"; anti-hierarchical; "save-the-whales"; and tolerant of homosexuality. The truth is that right-wing, nuke-the-whales, bomb-the-ruskies-back-to-the-stone-age Witches don't subscribe to such commie-faggot, nouveau-witch, anarchist bird-cage-liner. The following are just a few of the things that Witches DON'T agree on:
> Abortion and Birth Control; Animal Rights; Astrology; Environmentalism; Foreign Policy; Nuclear Armament; Nuclear Energy; Premarital Sex; Politics; President Reagan; Recreational Drug Use; and Vegetarianism. Believe it or not, some of the oldest branches of Wicca do not worship a Goddess! Of course you are free to argue that your fellow Witch SHOULD hold certain views, but it is ridiculous to assert that they DO hold such views. Witches are as diverse in their views as are Christians.[25]

Some Pagans were very upset with this editoral, which was published in at least four different magazines in 1985. Ann Forfreedom called it "bigoted" and "hate-filled." In her view, being anti-feminist, anti-gay, anti-ecology, and politically right-wing is simply not compatible with a Pagan or Wiccan perspective. One group of political Pagans, the Thomas Morton Alliance, even circulated a petition that said they took great exception to Wolfe's views, saying, "It is the very root of Paganism to respect *all* Her living beings," and that there could be no room for racists, sexists, nationalists, or nuclear proponents among those who were "truly Pagan." But I think Wolfe was not, himself, espousing the values above—at least not all of them—but was giving an essentially accurate picture of the true political diversity within Neo-Paganism.

With that caveat in mind, it is still fair to say there has been an amazing growth of political activity, *most* of it in support of alternative, feminist, ecological, "green," or peace objectives. In 1974, at a Gnosticon festival in Minneapolis, Carl Weschcke, the head of Llewellyn Press, led an audience in a meditation for peace and healing of the Earth. It was perhaps the most political Pagan event I had seen that year. More than ten years later, this has changed. There are at present at least five, and probably more, Pagan periodicals with a primary political emphasis—*Pagans for Peace Newsletter*, *The Pipes of P.A.N.* (*Pagans Against Nukes*), *Faerie Fire*, *Heretics Journal Forum*, and *Reclaiming*.

Goddess rituals have taken place in the midst of demonstrations at military bases and nuclear plants. Goddess symbols have been placed, rituals danced, and webs woven at Greenham Common, at the Seneca Encampment for a Future of Peace and Justice, and at similar encampments around the world. Goddess affinity groups have been arrested blocking the Lawrence Livermore Laboratories again and again. Starhawk, whose books *The Spiral Dance* and *Dreaming the Dark* have perhaps reached more women and men than any other books written by a Pagan, has personally been arrested more than fourteen times. *Dreaming the Dark* is a brilliant attempt to merge the insights of coven work with those learned from anarchist anti-nuclear affinity groups. In addition, Reclaiming (the feminist collective where Starhawk remains one of the founders) has taught these ritual and leadership techniques all over the United States and Europe. Moreover, Starhawk is not the only well-known Pagan to involve herself in political action, and face arrest. Several months before his death, Gwydion Pendderwen wrote me these words in a letter, after his own arrest at Livermore:

> I spent three days in jail as a result of the blockade of Lawrence Livermore Lab. It was a very empowering experience, in which I learned that my personal power and greatest potential in healing and reaching people is in music. The brothers, on the way to arraignment, began singing "We won't wait any longer," which I had sung in jail. They prevailed upon me to lead a chorus and sing it as my statement in court. It's in the record, with a men's chorus of 25.

Political rituals have taken place at several Pagan festivals. In 1982, at Pagan Spirit Gathering, I was one of about seventy people who rose early in the morning to do a ritual that coincided precisely with a political action at Livermore. In addition, politically motivated Pagans have created their own gatherings. The Canadian group which publishes the *Pagans for Peace Newsletter* put on a festival camp-out for like-minded people in Ontario last year. In September 1985, the Thomas Morton Alliance, a group of politically radical Pagans in Massachusetts, held a one-day conference. To this meeting, came some of the most religiously traditional but politically radical Pagans—for example, members of Pagansword, a group that calls for the revival of the ancient warrior tradition and has harsh words for most of the Pagans described in this book. Perhaps twenty people came to this meeting. It was very "linear," with position papers being formally presented as opposed to the loose give and take of most Pagan gatherings. Here are some of the views that were expressed: the belief that Paganism is rooted in reality of this world; that Pagans have a moral obligation to defend the planet and the rights of traditional peoples; that Pagans must bow to the leadership of traditional elders; that the eclecticism and anarchism of the Pagan revival is not positive; and that using the ritual and magical techniques of indigenous peoples constitutes "stealing" their traditions. Speaking personally, as a very eclectic, anarchistic Pagan, the meeting was not an easy experience.

It's important to say that these political groups are very small. There is only one Pagan political group of significant size: the thousands of women from Greenham Common to New York to California who are combining political action with women's spirituality and earth reverence. This movement really began with the Women's Pentagon Action group of several years ago that sponsored large rituals encircling the Pentagon to protest nuclear war; it then spread to Europe, to Greenham Common and elsewhere, and then came back to the United States. As an intellectual movement it's also sometimes called "eco-feminism." Some of the people involved in organizing a Green movement in the United States are also looking at the interrelationship of ecology, feminism, and politics. And some of the most militant environmental organizations, like Earth First!, are beginning to explore Pagan ideas.

The broader Pagan movement is only indirectly involved with any of these explorations, but there has definitely been a change in perception over the last ten years. In responding to the question "What are the most important issues facing Pagans today," these were the categories Neo-Pagans mentioned most often in 1985. Items mentioned only once or twice were excluded.

Ecology, healing the Earth, etc.	24
Nuclear war, peace issues	22
The fundamentalist right	21
Surviving as a religion, legitimacy, defending religious freedom	12
Achieving community and unity of purpose	9
Raising Pagan children in a non-Pagan world	7
Training our clergy	7
Public relations, questions of image	7
Feminism, problems of sexism	7
Avoiding becoming a fad	6
Issues of social justice	6
Living in the world without violating our beliefs	5
Accepting diversity	4
Political activism	4
Ethics	3
Spiritual growth and development	3
Avoiding commercialization of the movement	3
Avoiding bureaucracy	3

This is a very different list than you might have had ten years ago. While I haven't done a true statistical analysis, there wasn't, in 1976, that much concern with peace and ecology issues. One thing hasn't changed: Pagans coming out of the women's spirituality movement are still more politically radical; Witches coming out of English traditions are still the most conservative.

In the last ten years many Pagans have become more political for one reason only: their concern with the advance of the Christian right. In the 1985 questionnaires many people expressed concern with attempts to declare the United States a Christian country and with President Reagan's connection with the "Moral Majority." At the time *Drawing Down the Moon* was first published, most Pagans were not thinking about fundamentalism. The general turn to the right has, I think, forced many Wiccans and Pagans into an awareness they might not have once had.

In the fall of 1985, Pagans mobilized to defeat several congressional attempts to deny them religious validity. These attempts came about after ABC aired a television special about Satanism and cult killings. The "20/20" program did not mention the word "witchcraft" even once, but several congressional leaders used this program as a springboard to take actions against Wicca as well as Satanism. Senator Jesse Helms attempted to attach a rider (Amendment 705) to the Treasury, Postal Service, and General Government Appropriations Bill for 1986. A version of this bill, with the amendment, passed the Senate. After an extensive letter-writing campaign, probably the most concerted political effort ever attempted by Pagans, a House-Senate conference committee killed the amendment.

In the House, Pennsylvania Congressman Robert Walker introduced a similar measure, but this time only Witchcraft was mentioned. HR 3389 would amend the Internal Revenue Code so that religious organizations "substantially interested in the promotion of witchcraft," would be denied the tax-exempt status given to other religious groups. As this edition went to press, this bill was still pending.

This is the first time fundamentalists have launched an attack on the legitimacy of Wiccan organizations, and it is partly due to the fact that there are more Pagan and Wiccan legal religious organizations today than ever before. But it's still important to emphasize that these organizations are tiny! The Covenant of the Goddess, the largest cross-traditional federation of Wiccan congregations—about 70—had a budget in 1985 of $10,000. Treasury Department officials are well aware of this. Secretary of the Treasury James Baker III wrote in a letter to Helms, "Several organizations have been recognized as tax-exempt that espouse a system of beliefs, rituals, and practices, derived in part from pre-Christian Celtic and Welsh traditions, which they label as 'witchcraft.' We have no evidence that any of the organizations have either engaged in or promoted any illegal activity."[26] There are plenty of laws on the books to deal with crimes—and cult murderers should be prosecuted. But we should remember that some of the worst cult abuses—Children of God, Jim Jones, Sun Myung Moon—have been the excesses of people who considered themselves Christians, not Witches.

The frightening aspect of this push by the fundamentalist right is that it threatens the protections guaranteed by the separation of church and state. When the government starts defining what constitutes a legitimate religion, all people should beware.

The Helms amendment actually tried to set out definitions of "Witch-craft" and "Satanism," and one of the definitions of "Witchcraft" was simply "the practice of sorcery." Since sorcery is defined by many as "the practice of magic," a law that would deny legitimate religious status to groups that practice sorcery could include most traditional, tribal religions as well as Voudoun and Santeria. Are healing groups practicing sorcery? Even Christian ones? It's a real black hole and it quickly makes you realize the wisdom of this country's founders when they took these kinds of issues out of the hands of the state.

Pagans are also worried for more practical reasons. The tax-exempt status given to religious groups allows lower postage rates so Pagan periodicals can flourish (most of them, however, are already operating at a loss). Legal recognition allows a Wiccan or Pagan priest or priestess to perform legal marriages and be accepted as pastoral counselors in many states. These laws also make it easier to establish nature sanctuaries.

Paganism Approaching the 1990s

In September 1978, at the Association of Cymmry Wicca's Gathering of Tribes festival in Helen, Georgia, Selena Fox read a position paper from *Circle*. In summary, the paper said that the "Earth Religions Movement" was undergoing its rite of passage, its coming of age, after passing through a rocky adolescence. The future would include:
—An increase in the number of Pagans willing to appear in the media and willing to take an active, public position.
—An increase in the number of Pagan newsletters and published books.
—An increase in communication between different traditions and groups.
—An increase in festivals and conferences.
—An increase in contact between Pagan and Craft groups and other "new age" groups.
—The emergence of self-supporting Craft communities, businesses, enterprises.
—The sharing of music and art.

In 1986, this wish list is simply an accurate tally of things that have in fact happened. Here is what the present looks like.

GROWTH

Almost everyone believes the Pagan movement is growing by leaps and bounds, but no one knows what the figures are. Many people have made a guess, but few have tried to make a systematic count. J. Gordon Melton, who heads the Institute for the Study of American Religion, headquartered in Santa Barbara, California, posed the following question in a survey of Pagans five years ago: Do you own a copy of *The Golden Dawn*? Since only 15,000 copies of this book had ever been published, Melton used the percentage who said "yes" as a base to then extrapolate the number of Neo-Pagans in the United States. He came up with 40,000. Most people would double that number now. Other estimates have gone as high as 100,000.

Starhawk, whose book *The Spiral Dance* may have created hundreds of ritual groups (perhaps more than all the Gardnerians and Alexandrians combined), says that she feels there has been enormous expansion. "Everywhere I go, people are crowding lectures and workshops—albeit on a small scale. People are always coming up to me and telling me that they read my book and started a coven. Many people are doing rituals from other traditions as well—Native American and Shamanic. In Canada, I found many people doing Pagan rituals on the islands off Vancouver, British Columbia; Paganism seems to be growing in a grounded way."

There are now at least one hundred Pagan periodicals. Many of them are better produced and better written than before and many exist for a longer period of time. There has also been a burst of creativity in the arts and in music. There are at least twenty records and tapes by Pagan recording artists and folk musicians. The presence of large gatherings has created a demand for Pagan artisans, and there has been a true flowering of crafts—clothing, jewelry, herbs, oils.

There has been an outpouring of books with Pagan or goddess-oriented themes. Some of them, usually novels, have entered the mainstream. The most extraordinary example of a book that became a best-seller even though it had thoroughly Wiccan themes and was written by a Wiccan priestess is *Mists of Avalon* by Marion Zimmer Bradley. Here are some other popular books with Pagan themes: *Lammas Night* by Kathrine Kurtz; *The Book of Kells* by R. A. MacAvoy; *Witches* and *Fanny* by Erica Jong. It should be noted that Starhawk's *The Spiral Dance* had sold about 50,000 copies by the end of 1985 and *Dreaming the Dark* had sold about 30,000 copies. *Drawing Down the Moon* had sold about 30,000 copies.

SANCTUARIES, LEGAL RECOGNITION, AND INSTITUTIONALIZATION

One very significant trend in the last ten years is the growth of legally recognized Pagan religious groups—groups that have all the tax-exempt privileges and other rights of religious organizations. One has only to look at the resource section of this book under "groups" to see how true this is. Whether we are talking about COG or Circle or the Church of Wicca, we are often talking about groups that have made a decision to be incorporated as tax-exempt religious bodies. While the vast majority of Pagan organizations are tiny, with extremely low budgets, tax-exempt status eases the fight to obtain legal Pagan marriages, allows reduced postal rates, and makes it easier to establish nature sanctuaries.

The movement to establish Pagan/Craft sanctuaries comes out of several needs: the desire to have land where rituals can take place in privacy, the desire to have access to wilderness settings, and the desire to protect wild areas. Circle Sanctuary, Coeden Brith, Annwfn, Eclectia, and Camelot of the Wood are but a few of the names of Pagan nature sanctuaries.

Most Pagan and Wiccan groups still meet in living rooms or in public parks, and in most covens you still bring food or wine, rather than give a donation. But the number of correspondence courses, Wiccan businesses, attempts to buy land, and attempts to set up a temple or seminary have increased exponentially. While much of this seems positive—the victory of Pagans to attain the rights given to all bona fide religious groups in this country—a few things seem worrisome.

One of the things that has distinguished Neo-Paganism from the many religious cults has been the strict separation of the religion from profit. In fact, one of the things that attracts many people to Neo-Paganism is that it is not primarily a religion of temples or paid clergy. "Money seldom passes from hand to hand," I wrote in one of the first paragraphs of this book. But in 1986, there is a raging debate within Paganism on the "money issue" and there are many Pagan groups that are businesses as well as religious organizations.

In many traditions of Wicca, teaching the Craft for money has always been strictly forbidden—a violation of Craft Law. There have always been exceptions to this, from Maxine Sander's ritual groups in England to the many correspondence courses on Witchcraft that are advertised. But these were never considered the norm, and many people looked at them askance. But now, the number of people teaching and charging for workshops on ritual and magic has increased tenfold. There is a funny saying in the Pagan movement: "The difference between Pagan and 'new age' is one decimal point." In other words, a two-day workshop in meditation by a "new age" practitioner might cost $300, while the same course given by a Pagan might cost $30. While Pagan workshops still cost only a fraction of similar "new age" seminars, there's no telling what could happen if, Goddess forbid, Paganism became really popular.

While the "Craft Laws"—writings which some argue are probably only forty years old—forbid the taking of money, other more indigenous Pagan religions charge large fees for initiations: Santeria and Voudoun, for example. There are beginning to be priests and priestesses within Neo-Paganism who firmly believe that a clergy should be supported, that if Paganism ever wants to develop a truly skilled clergy, there will have to be people who work at their religion all day and who do not spend most of their hours programming computers, waiting on tables, or selling books. Z Budapest asks for a tithe from women to support her work. Isaac Bonewits also believes that a clergy can function only if there is community support and funding. Often the division on this issue comes between those who work in the Craft full time and therefore need some means of livelihood and those, like myself, who work at other paying jobs in the "real world."

The greatest challenge in the next years will be defining how to walk the very fine and problematic line between the beneficial and negative aspects of institutionalization. The question comes down to: Can you support yourself through the Craft without being corrupted? The history of religions in this society doesn't offer too many good examples. The growing institutionalization of Paganism is, at this point, a fact, and there are some blessings that come with it. But it is important to remember many people come to Paganism precisely because it is fundamentally anarchistic and uninstitutionalized and because, even now in the era of yuppies, most celebrations are free of charge—just as they would be if they were happening within your own family, or tribe.

Meanwhile, most Neo-Pagans are not thinking deeply about these issues. They are fighting the more practical battles to achieve legitimacy, without exploring what that might mean farther down the road. In New York State, for example, the ACLU helped a group of Pagans turn over a rule that insisted that "certain" religions could register only two ministers. And in 1985, Pagans mobilized against various attempts by the fundamentalist right to prevent Witches from using the tax-exempt status allowed to all bona fide religious groups.[26]

PAGAN FESTIVALS: THE SEARCH FOR A CULTURE OR A TRIBE

When *Drawing Down the Moon* was published on Samhain 1979, the principal mode of communication was through newsletters. Finding Pagans was not easy. It took determination and luck. There was a feeling, often communicated by covens and groves, that this hard and long search was part of the growth process. When you were ready, your teacher or group would materialize. The upside of this was that when you did find a group, even if it wasn't quite the right group, you still were committed. The downside was that people were often alone and completely isolated in their search for years. And if the group they entered was inappropriate, unacceptably hierarchical, or the leaders were simply on a power trip, there was often no recourse.

I think my own search was not untypical. I came across an English Pagan journal, *The Waxing Moon*, and eventually corresponded with an English coven. But, turning to my own community, I was reduced to looking through ads in the *Village Voice*. I entered an occult shop, only to find out that it was a front for La Vey's Church of Satan. I finally saw an ad for a lecture series on Witchcraft at a Brooklyn church and visited yet another occult store, finally happening upon a Pagan study group that was linked to a Celtic-oriented coven. At the time I began I did not know there were a dozen excellent Pagan newsletters. In fact, a member of this Celtic coven, hinting great mystery, told me that the newsletter, *Green Egg*, was an "insiders' journal" available only to advanced students. I had no idea that the United States was filled with active and creative Pagan groups.

It is still a difficult process to find an appropriate group, but it is now much easier to enter the Pagan community, to attend rituals and workshops, and to encounter an extraordinary number of different Pagan traditions. Some people do this without ever belonging to a coven or grove. Their route to the Pagan community is through festivals. As one person told me, "There are people who have searched for years. I went to a festival and met ten people who are my friends five years later. It took me four years to get invited to a ritual. At my first festival I saw four rituals in five days."

Festivals have completely changed the face of the Pagan movement. It is the one most enormous and striking change that has occurred since *Drawing Down the Moon* was first published. Festivals have created a national Pagan community, a body of nationally shared chants, dances, stories, and ritual techniques. They have even led to the creation of a different type of ritual process—one that permits a large group to experience ecstatic states and a powerful sense of religious communion. And while perhaps less than 10 percent of the Pagan community goes to festivals, the importance of the information brought back to the many hundreds of small groups all over the United States, Canada, and beyond far outweighs the number of people who may actually attend one or more major festivals in a given year.

There had been large gatherings before the late 1970s, but except in California almost all were indoors and at hotels. Often they were sponsored by a large organization like Llewellyn, the publishing company, which for many years put on Gnosticon and several smaller conferences. These events, which took place in Minnesota, were geared to a diverse mix of people—occultists, astrologers, magicians, Pagans, and Wiccans. Carl Weschcke, the head of Llewellyn, has always had a personal interest in the Craft, but his publishing company makes its bread and butter on occultism and "new age" subjects. Most of those who attended these gatherings were more Christian than Pagan, but many Pagans—Otter and Morning Glory Zell, Isaac Bonewits, Alison Harlow, for example—met with each other at Llewellyn events.

One of the most beautiful rituals I ever attended, the handfasting of Otter (then Tim) and Morning Glory Zell, took place at such a festival in Minneapolis in the spring of 1974. I also remember an amazing experience at a Fall gathering, when twenty Pagans simply decided to go skinny dipping in the hotel pool some time well after midnight; I remember it as an ecstatic event. The pool was empty. There were no hotel employees around. A sudden decision, pulling off our clothes, jumping in. The water so cool and fresh. It seemed right out of the Garden of Eden when Otter and Morning Glory let their two pet snakes—a python and a boa constrictor—out of their cage to enjoy the pool with us. Very few people saw us, except for a tourist from India, who immediately joined us in the pool, accepting it as a natural part of American culture. (Although I think he was greatly disappointed when an orgy did not follow.) I do not think the Hyatt House Lodge was amused, however, for Llewellyn's next festival took place elsewhere. Carl Weschcke was probably not pleased either; it seemed too much of a hippy vision for his sensibilities.

Another organization with a history of indoor gatherings is the Church and School of Wicca. Since the late 1970s, they have held an annual Samhain Seminar, with workshops, rituals, and guest speakers. In the past, the gatherings have been primarily for the students of their correspondence school. Approximately 40,000 students have taken some part of their course of study.

In California, the mid-seventies were filled with gatherings. The Pagan organization Nemeton was founded in 1972, and a year later an overnight Summer Solstice gathering was held on the land at Coeden Brith. About 150 people attended, including many in the NROOGD tradition. In the desert near Los Angeles, overnight ritual gatherings have been held since 1970, starting with a small group and growing to hundreds. In the Bay area, NROOGD pioneered large public and semi-public seasonal celebrations and each fall, starting in 1968 and continuing to the present, NROOGD presents its recreation of the Elusinian Mysteries. For the fortunate hundred or so who attend, one can relive the Goddess Persephone's abduction and descent into the underworld as personal initiation: one can stumble into the dark cave, groping and struggling to find the way, one can eat of the promegranate seed.

But all of these gatherings did not in themselves lead to the Pagan festival phenomenon. The indoor festivals were too much like ordinary conventions to create a real community feeling, and many of the outdoor festivals were geared to one group, or tradition, or school and so did little to create a broad ecumenism.

Outside of California, one of the first organizations to think about an outdoor camping festival was the Midwest Pagan Council. The Midwest Pagan Council was originally organized in 1976 among groups in the Chicago area. Most of these groups came from the same English-based Wiccan tradition, but many of them had gone their own way and there was some friction between the groups. "Our goal was uncertain," Ginny

Brubaker, an organizer of many Midwest festivals, told me. "But we felt there were tensions between us and we should at least be talking to each other."

Originally, the idea may have been to celebrate one of the two summer sabbats together—Lammas or the Summer Solstice. Christa Heiden, a Pagan priestess currently studying theology at a Unitarian seminary, remembers suggesting that there be instead a special festival that would not interfere with individual coven celebrations—a Pan-Pagan festival that would celebrate unity in diversity. Ginny Brubaker remembers Dick Clark, another council member saying, "Why don't we all go camping?" So, she said, "we put some notices in a few publications and used a few of our mailing lists and lo and behold, 80 people showed up.

"In retrospect, we weren't very organized. Our campsite wasn't reserved, and we ended up with chicken for 300 people. We decided that if we ever did it again, we would do it right, and in 1978 we had 150 people."

Even at the very first Pan-Pagan festival in 1977, many things were in place. The program included lectures, workshops, a main ecumenical ritual, a mystery play, and lots of music. For a while the numbers seemed to double each year. The largest Neo-Pagan and Wiccan outdoor camping festival ever held in the United States took place in 1980, sponsored by the Midwest Pagan Council and the Covenant of the Goddess. Almost six hundred attended the four-day festival.

Other groups began organizing around the same time. The Georgian tradition started annual gatherings in Bakersfield, California. In 1978, southern Pagans in the Church of Y Tylwyth Teg organized a festival at a private retreat in the mountains of Georgia. It was called the Gathering of the Tribes. By 1979, there were beginning to be ecumenical festivals in many parts of the country, but no one really thought these gatherings would change the face of the Pagan community.

Reaction to the festivals has been explosive. In 1985, there were at least fifty annual regional or national gatherings with a Pagan or Wiccan focus. Groups like the Covenant of the Goddess even have a huge booklet giving details on how to organize a successful festival. Why did festivals catch on? Probably most critical was the fact that outdoor festivals established a sacred time and space—a place apart from the mundane world, where Pagans could be themselves and meet other people who, although from a variety of traditions, shared many of the same values. Many festival organizers have told me that the most frequent feedback they receive is the comment "I never knew there were other people who believed what I believe, let alone several hundred at one place. I never knew that I could come totally out of the closet and be what I am openly." This feeling of being at home among one's true family for the first time is the fundamental reason that festivals have spread throughout the country. As one organizer told me, "It's a trip to the land of faery, where for a couple of days you can exist without worrying about the 'real' world. It seems absolutely logical that people would come to a festival and see all this and say, 'Let's go home and make one ourselves.' "

Some things are more possible in a small group, other things in a larger one. The small coven has an intimacy that no large tribal village will ever share. But large gatherings have their own special energy. Certain things can happen at festivals. I remember at Pan-Pagan 1980, witnessing for the first time, although people told me it had occurred the year before, the beginning of spontaneous group ritual processes: the leaping over bonfires, the rising and falling of ecstatic chanting and dancing, lasting until the early morning hours. For those of us whose previous ritual experience had been running around a small circle while Carmina Burana played on the living room stereo, this was heady stuff.

"I remember," Ginny Brubaker told me, "I was working in a Wiccan group where you weren't even supposed to talk to people in other groups. Going to festivals changed everything. The kind of gurudom that tries to censor sources of information is totally destroyed by this kind of event. You ain't going to keep 'em down on whatever your farm is after they've seen all the possibilities. Even if you snicker at 80 percent of the workshops and rituals, there's going to be that other 20 percent that makes you say, 'I wonder why we don't do that.' "

Within a few years, a body of chants, songs, and techniques for working large group rituals was known to thousands of people from coast to coast. This knowledge has affected the conduct of small groups. "Our coven changed," Ginny Brubaker told me. "We started using more songs and chants in ritual. We had only done a few before and they were very boring. Suddenly we had all this music." Since the Erisians and Discordians were making their presence known at festivals (see Chapter 11), there was a lot more humor. "Meetings became more fun, there was more playfulness. And our group got exposed to new psychic techniques like the Bach Flower remedies. Our ritual style loosened up. Our ritual garb changed."

Festival organizers had to learn new methods. When ten people are chanting in your living room and you want a moment of silence, it's very easy to make that suggestion known; when there's a group of two hundred dancing in the open air, you suddenly understand the usefulness of drums. Organizers became skilled at facilitating large rituals and at running large community meetings, adapting techniques from tribal gatherings. As years have gone by, the festivals have developed a feeling of their own. At first people would bring a simple sign or draw a pentagram on their tent. Now the campsites often have the flavor of a country fair, with poles and banners and hand-designed flags. There has also been an explosion of crafts and music, now that there is a large audience with which to share these things. At the first festivals, only the local occult bookstore sold its wares. Within a few years there were scores of jewelers, robe makers, sellers of incense, T-shirts, herbs, Pagan buttons and bumper stickers, and beautiful arts and crafts. Tapes of original music, and occasionally albums, proliferated. Festival concerts and variety shows got better and better.

Many people were really not prepared for the results of Pagan ecumenism and community building. At Pan-Pagan '80, groups confronted each other that had never conceived the possibility of working or being together. Sometimes there were political fireworks. For example, at the time of Pan-Pagan '80, the movement of Radical Faeries was just beginning. Several gay men came to the gathering to share their perspective. There were several gay workshops at a festival that only two years before had been unwilling to even mention a gay workshop in its brochure.

Many of the people in the Midwest Pagan Council were uncomfortable with the large and growing feminist segment of the Craft and many firmly believed that there should never be separate male and female events at a public festival. Yet at Pan-Pagan '80, Z Budapest led more than sixty women in a skyclad ritual. Many of these women came from more conservative traditions that stressed the duality of deity and the polarity of male and female energy. Many of these women were forever changed by their experience. Z Budapest changed as well. She not only used men to guard the perimeter of the circle (the first time men had ever had a role in her rituals), but, as she observed later, she had spoken to more men in that weekend than she had in her entire life. In the years since, there have been many more feminist and Dianic Witches at large ecumenical Pagan gatherings and women from the British traditions have made appearances at all-women events. Throughout the Craft, there has been a flowering of women's and men's separate mysteries.

Some people could not accept these kinds of changes in the Pagan community. Deep differences in philosophy, politics, attitudes toward sexuality and life style, even differences in class, surfaced as the festival ended and a number of groups left the Midwest Pagan Council. The next year, three different Midwest festivals occurred, one put on by the Circle, another by those remaining in the Midwest Pagan Council, and a third by a group called Epiphanes. While there has never been a festival quite as large as Pan-Pagan '80, the Pan-Pagan Festival continues as a wonderful event. The largest festival these days is the Pagan Spirit Gathering, organized by Circle and held in Wisconsin during the week of the Summer Solstice.

After the Pagan Spirit Gathering of 1981 and 1982, Circle published a booklet of reflections, essays, and poems written by some of the hundreds who had participated. Many of the things that were written could well be said about most current festivals; the booklets provide a window into the special festival realm.

The organizers spoke of creating a magical village, a special place where songs, dreams, meditations, rituals, food, ideas, work, fun, and future visions would be shared. And many who came did indeed speak of living those few days in a dream. "Each one passed through a portal, and was transformed," wrote a woman from Milwaukee. "Each one gave their quest a name, and in the fires, nightly searched. Like the grasses we were nourished there. Like the trees, learning the wind's dance, we sought our earth-bound fruition, rooted and reaching, drinking in the sweet rain."[27]

Another woman wrote: "To go out walking and not have the fear of ravenous glances, cat-calls, come-ons, and other unasked for responses. To feel the sun, wind, fire, and water on my naked body without feeling vulnerable to physical or psychological attack. To be able to chant and sing loudly with the power of my lungs. To dance and move with the strength of all the muscles in my body. To feel that I can be whoever I am with total acceptance and unselfconsciousness—and to have that feel as natural as breathing."[28]

A man from Chicago wrote these words: "It was twilight and there was a gentleness in the air. As I heard the distant sounds of flutes and drums, I felt a thrill of recognition, as if something I had felt fleetingly in rare moments of my life, something beautiful beyond words to describe, something I had sought for, was beckoning to me. . . . I felt the music flow throughout my body and felt grounded in the earth. . . . But it was not the music, but some feeling or energy behind it, a communion of consciousness that infused it. It was the same feeling I've had whenever I've felt closest to a vision of spiritual and social wholeness."[29]

These festivals, like many others, have certain guidelines. All participants are expected to put in work shifts at childcare, firewood gathering, gatekeeping, health care, and security. Many of the rituals are cooperatively planned. "Who could have imagined," wrote Dierdre Pulgram, of the Athanor Fellowship, "that a group of 250 strangers camping together for a long weekend in the wilderness of Wisconsin could have formed a community with such a strong sense of group identity. It seemed like such an ideal. You think, 'People can't come together for such a short period and really become a unit.' What happened over that weekend was magick. From the moment we arrived, we were drawn into the feeling of it."[30]

Many people wrote about how difficult it was to return to their ordinary life. "It felt hard to adjust . . . upon my return home. I still felt so open and free. The festival has the effect of opening the doors inside me that I keep closed most of the time."[31] "I carry that Magick Village home with me in my heart," wrote another. "With the Cree Indians I sing, 'There is only beauty behind me. Only beauty is before me.' Carrying this vision of beauty in my heart changes my life. There is a new depth of my being; a new primal dimension of spirit which allows me to shake off the sophistication of the twentieth century American and to hark back."[32]

In the 1985 questionnaire, I asked Neo-Pagans about their thoughts on the impact of festivals on the community. It's only fair to say that the 195 people who answered the questionnaire are a biased sample. Most of the questionnaires were handed out at large festivals. Perhaps only 10 percent of the community goes to festivals, but over 85 percent of those who responded to the questions had been to at least one large gathering. Still, there were a number of criticisms. Some people said the festivals were elitist and that many people with nine-to-five jobs found it impossible to go. Although festival fees are not huge ($30–$50 for a three-day weekend), if you have a family or must travel great distances, the expenses can be exorbitant. Time is another precious commodity. Most people with regular jobs can't take five days off to commune in the woods.

One person argued that festivals give people a false sense of security and acceptance. Another said that festivals foster a certain commercialism, a concern with pretty robes and jewelry. "They focus on the socially extroverted," one complained. "There's too much lust in the dust," said another. "It's hard for the elderly and the disabled to go camping," said a third.

But the most serious critique of the festival phenomenon was that it was changing the basic structure of Pagan and Craft groups. "The coven is losing its magic," a priestess wrote to me. Covens and groves are no longer as central as the festivals and large networking organizations. Since people can enter the Pagan community through festivals and never feel the need to commit themselves to a group, festivals tend to break down the authority of coven leaders. Much of this may be very good, but there is a price. "At one time covens were given time and the required space to develop their own identity. They had time to seed. But now, with organized groups waiting for members, a temporarily dissatisfied student never takes the time to sort things out. They just split. The easy availability of networking prevents a student from staying and working things out." In addition, this priestess wrote, "There is a tendency to replace one hierarchy with another. The new celebrities are the authors, the musicians and the leaders of large networking organizations."

"You know," Ginny Brubaker said to me thoughtfully, "in the long run, the festival movement will be held responsible for destroying the uniqueness of traditions. Nobody is as isolated or as 'pure' as they were ten years ago. Everybody is stealing from everybody else. That's real good for the survival of our religion as *a whole*, but in another ten years no one's going to know what a Gardnerian was." Others disagree with that prediction. The English traditions are flourishing, they say, and staying very much intact.

Most of those who have attended festivals not only love them but feel that they are the most important and inspiring part of the Pagan phenomenon. Most of the people who answered the questionnaire said that festivals were important because they exposed participants to new ideas, challenged assumptions, ended isolation and loneliness, reduced divisiveness among traditions and groups, renewed people's energy, provided stunning proof that unity can be achieved amid diversity, and, beyond all, proved that an alternative culture is possible—even if it lasts for only a weekend or a week. As one respondent wrote: "It is absolutely crucial for our identity that we can be a part of something larger than a coven. Festivals disempower the idea, just lurking below the surface of our consciousness, that we and our goals and our visions are somehow deviant."

Haragano, an English traditional priestess, put it this way:

> Pagan festivals are the meeting of the tribes. You come from different parts of the country, from different trainings, and traditions. You may have read some of the same books. You meet people from all spiritual backgrounds and all levels of spiritual growth. You see the whole spectrum of our belief and practice in a few days. Gardnerians and Dianics, Druids and Faeries, all acting like neighbors.
>
> Everyone's finding out how much of their own beliefs they are really comfortable with. You start to discard things because they encumber your own reaching out to someone who is spiritually valuable. Perhaps you are homophobic, and suddenly the person who is making the most sense at a meeting, whose ideas pierce your heart, turns out to be gay. Or perhaps you arrive with a fear, and there are a whole bunch of workshops that strip away that fear and after dancing and worshipping you go away from the festival, having your personal demon exorcised.
>
> And you find that you are not alone and you understand this three dimensionally. You have danced it, sung it, cried it, let it loose through every possible human sense.
>
> These large groups come together for such a short period of time, but that's when the gods dance. We meet the Goddess and the God in everyone and in ourselves.

SHAMANISM

One of the most significant changes within the Pagan community in the last five years has been the attempt by modern Wiccans and Neo-Pagans to merge their practices and traditions with the methods of shamanism. There are now a number of traditions calling themselves Shamanic Wicca, Shamanic Craft, and Wiccan Shamanism. A few groups, like the Church of Seven Arrows, have considered themselves shamanic for many years, but more recently there has been an explosion of Pagan groups interested in shamanic exploration. The Athanor Fellowship, Circle, and the Earth Song Community all use the word shamanic to describe some of what they are doing. In Scotland, Kalledon Naddair, the editor of *Inner Keltia*, has been giving workshops on "Pictish Shamanism" and drumming. Most of this is wonderful and reflects the fact that the Pagan community is actually trying to explore ecstatic states. There is a misguided tendency, however, for anyone who has had an experience with altered states to consider him or herself a shaman.

Of course, Pagans are not the only people exploring this path. Carlos Castaneda's "Don Juan" novels popularized shamanism for millions of people. Books by Black Elk and various traditional medicine people have also become popular. In the 1960s, Leary and Alpert's *Psychedelic Review* looked at the pharmacopoeia of shamans. The Rainbow Family Gatherings and the gatherings of the largely white Bear Tribe have offered certain experiences to thousands. In the 1970s, the anthropologist Michael Harner did extensive research into those techniques of shamanism that use drumming. His teaching of these techniques has led to the formation of dozens of groups that consider themselves engaged in shamanic exploration.

The word *shaman* is one of those words, like *Witch*, that means something different to everybody. The term itself comes from a word used by a Siberian tribe. But as Michael Harner once put it, the word can best be defined as a method to open a door and enter a different reality. A shaman is someone who enters an altered state of consciousness and goes on a journey in order to gather knowledge from a different reality. The knowledge depends on a deep connection with the forces of nature—with the spirits of plants and animals. The methods used to enter this altered state depend on the culture. Some cultures use drugs; more cultures use drumming and ecstatic dancing. What many Wicca traditions call the eightfold paths of power—chanting, dancing, trance, wine, and sexuality among others—is another way of talking about methods to enter altered states.

In the last five years, Pagans have begun exploring some of these pathways. The most common, and a feature of many recent Pagan festivals, is ecstatic dancing, drumming, and chanting, often lasting for hours. There has been an increased interest in fasting, vision quests, and sweat lodges, and there is also more interest in working with nature spirits and earth energies.

In most cases, Pagans are blending European Pagan symbolism—the holidays, the elements, the directions, the deities—with animism, ecstatic techniques, and some ideas from tribal cultures worldwide. In an article in *Circle Network News*, Selena Fox wrote about her own path which she calls "Wiccan Shamanism."

> I am a traveler between the world of Daily Life and the Otherworld which is the land of Dreams, Visions, and Spirits. I journey into the Otherworld for a reason—to bring back healing and knowledge to apply to Daily Life, helping others, myself and the Planet.
>
> I see the Divine in all things. My friends and allies include not only humans but also plants, animals, rocks, winds, waters, fire, stars, and other life forms. I commune with the Source some call "God" as both Mother Goddess and Father God, for both aspects are necessary for the Unity.
>
> The main focus of my Shamanic work is healing. I was called to this path as a young child in Dreams and Out-of-Body experiences, but I didn't begin my work until my adult years when I started Healing myself. To do this, I journeyed alone into the Pit of my Shadow Self and came face-to-face with my problems and hang-ups; with my doubts, fears, disillusionments, rejections, angers, and hurts; with all my false self images. Words cannot begin to express the misery, the utter despair, the powerlessness I felt during this time. Yet coming apart was essential; it enabled me to break through the barriers which I had formed and let others form in my psyche that had kept me from being one with my true Self. In the deepest Darkness, I felt the Light on my own Inner Self beginning to shine through. I focused on that Light and slowly emerged from the Pit, stronger and more integrated than ever before, and with the power to heal others as well as myself.[33]

There are some people who question the use of certain shamanic techniques within the Pagan community. Some people argue that Pagans don't have the traditions with which to use these methods wisely. In an article in a 1985 issue of the *Georgian Newsletter*, Brandy Williams writes that too many Pagans go off to the mountains camping for a weekend and then make portentous statements about their visions:

> We are not Native. We do not resemble Natives. We are not any of us prepared to be shamans. How could we be? Modern Americans, Neo-Pagans among them, lack the supporting context in which shamanism functions. We have not lived in a single place for many generations. We are removed from the web of interaction with the natural world; the rhythms of our daily movements

do not relate us to earth and sky, weather, seasonal changes, sources of our food. Our language does not structure the natural world into sacred space, either in vocabulary or in categories of thought. Our grandparents did not know one another, and did not transmit to us a body of oral tradition in that language which reinforced those concepts of the sacred and prepared us for shamanic experience. Our art forms do not express those concepts or depict those experiences. We do not have shamanic role models.[34]

Williams says that Pagans cannot comprehend the shamanic journey; they have no symbol systems with which to understand the changes the Shaman undergoes. "We are fakes and we are thieves," she says. "Thieves because we claim a spiritual legacy which belongs to a more or less intact set of disparate peoples. . . . That is to my way of thought, the most contemptuous way we could possibly relate to the indigenous peoples of this continent."

A few Pagans have even gone further and suggested that Pagans stop giving "shamanic workshops" or using sweat lodges and vision quests. They argue that anyone not from a genuine tribal culture does not have the training or background. But one of the problems with this argument is that many of the indigenous cultures are not intact. Recently, Michael Harner gave a workshop to a group of people from tribal cultures who felt that many of their own traditions and teachings had been lost and that they would gain knowledge from recent scholarship.

What's more, shamanism is not the sole property of any particular indigenous culture. I think Michael Harner's view is correct—that these methods are remarkably similar worldwide, whether they are used by indigenous peoples in Australia, Lapland, the Amazon Jungle, or Eastern Europe. Harner argues that the reason that cultures thousands of miles apart with different kinship structures, religious ideas, and ecological requirements developed strikingly similar shamanic techniques is that over thousands of years, through empirical trial and error, these techniques worked from culture to culture, as a means of healing, of finding lost children, of finding animals and sources of food.

While Wiccans and Pagans who are exploring the shamanic path must respect and learn from the traditions of others, and avoid the pitfalls of Western arrogance, this worldwide search is really a quest for our own lost traditions, traditions which were, from all we can tell, not so very different from the practices of traditional cultures today.

Most people who have gone on any shamanic journey return with a deeper respect for all nature, a more profound understanding of the unity of all things and a more urgent sense of the need to heal the planet. Any exploration that leads in this direction must be seen as important and positive. Instead of looking in musty Books of Shadows, Pagans are turning to the best teacher of all—Nature Herself.

CHILDREN

Children are beginning to have a prominent place in Paganism. Pagan festivals have begun to include activities for children. There are special Pagan periodicals catering to children's interests and there are organizations and newsletters for parents concerned with the issues of raising Pagan children in a non-Pagan world.

PROFESSIONALISM

One of the most frequent and just criticisms that emerged from the questionnaire about the Pagan community was that it didn't have a service structure. Several people interested in community and parish service ended up leaving the Craft and returning to their former religions. Several people who needed help with alcoholism or other social problems found no place in their own religious community to get help and were forced to go elsewhere. In recent years, there has been a growing effort by Pagans to get professional training. Psychologists and counselors already rank fourth highest among job titles for Pagans, but there are many more who are beginning to get serious training in the helping professions. In addition, many Pagan groups are becoming interested in community service issues.

SCHOLARSHIP

Some Pagans and Witches are beginning to do serious scholarship. A surprising number are studying religion seriously and entering divinity programs across the nation. There are at least three Wiccan priestesses at Harvard Divinity School in 1986 and at least a dozen women involved with goddess religion at the Graduate Theological Union in Berkeley.

This increased interest in religious study and scholarship is beginning to be reflected in the articles appearing in Pagan journals. One Pagan journal, *Iron Mountain*, is totally devoted to scholarly articles.

THE UNITARIAN CONNECTION

There have been goddess-oriented rituals within the Unitarian Church for a number of years. In 1982, I attended moon rituals led by Unitarian women in a suburb of Boston. I have heard emotional and moving stories of celebrations of women's spirituality involving hundreds of Unitarian women. The Unitarian Universalist Association (UUA) has held various convocations on women and religion. I know at least three UUA ministers who are openly Pagan and there is also a group called CUUPS (Coven of Unitarian Universalist Pagans) operating in the Boston area. Some Unitarians are a bit uncomfortable about all this. Some Unitarians consider themselves Christians and others, who are not very religious, find that "this witchcraft stuff," smacks of superstition.

But the Unitarian Church remains one of the only places that Pagans and women involved with goddess religion can enter the organized ministry. A Wiccan priestess currently enrolled in a Unitarian seminary in Chicago estimates that there are more than a dozen priestesses enrolled at Unitarian seminaries across the United States. And we must not forget that Beacon Press—a Unitarian publishing company—is the publisher of this book and books by Starhawk, Mary Daly, and a host of other authors involved with women's spirituality.

In an essay written in February 1985, four months before he was to be elected president of the Unitarian Universalist Church, William F. Schulz wrote that there has been "a religious revolution" in the Unitarian Church, that, "to put it in symbolic terms, Ashtar, the Goddess, had been issued invitation where formerly only Lord Jehovah dared to tread." Schulz said that the Women and Religion resolutions passed by the UUA General Assemblies in 1977, 1979, and 1980, "must first be appreciated THEALOGICALLY." He said the resolutions laid the basis for a new kind of Unitarian Universalism and there were at least five implications: that religion is to be experienced, as opposed to being understood in terms of right and wrong beliefs; that the religious experience is personal and found in ordinary experience; that personal religious experience can be shared in community; that creation is a whole; that human beings are not rulers or even "stewards" of nature, but co-creators with all living things; and that from this kind of spirituality flows a commitment to peace and justice. Among the most interesting suggestions made by William Schulz was the creation of a new hymnal that would reflect feminist spirituality through words, songs, and liturgies.[35]

INCREASED CONTACT BETWEEN PAGANS AND OTHER SPIRITUAL GROUPS

Pagans are not only making contacts with Unitarians, but there is a continuing, active dialogue between Pagans and members of many other religions and often a sharing of ritual activities. I personally joined with a Rabbi to perform a "mixed" marriage rite. There are Pagans who have been the featured speakers at Sunday services in Christian churches. One Pagan group even presented a lecture at a Morman church. Interfaith councils have begun to include representatives from the Pagan community and Pagan speakers have joined "new age" conferences and seminars. Pagan ritual techniques and methods of ecstatic dance and trance are being used by many mainstream religious groups, which usually call them "celebratory" rather than "Pagan."

A CREATIVE TENSION: ECLECTICS VS. TRADITIONALISTS

Some people will tell you, "the difference between now and five years ago, is that now everyone is an 'eclectic.' " Others will insist that many former eclectics are now searching for more formal traditions, and that the more hierarchical British traditions of Wicca are flourishing in the United States. Both are true. On the one hand, there is much more spontaneity everywhere. There are many new traditions and many amalgams of traditions. On the other hand, many people are yearning for a sense of formal structure. Gardnerian covens are proliferating and organizations like the New Wiccan Church are growing. There are good arguments on both sides.

Haragano, one of the leaders of the New Wiccan Church, gave me the best argument I have ever heard for traditionalism. "We do the same service over and over. And throughout the world, wherever the English-speaking Craft celebrate, one can know that over the three days of a full moon, or solar festival, somewhere, a Craft circle is in the midst of its ritual. So we join together in a circle that encircles the globe.

"On a personal level, it lets our conscious mind not be distracted, it lets the spiritual work take place. That doesn't happen for some people if you change the circle every time. So we are sticks-in-the-mud traditionalists. We do the same thing over and over and over and over again. But for the most part, it brings us contentment and the joy of linking with hundreds and hundreds of other circles who are doing the same thing, or so closely to it, we could walk right into their circle and pick up the next word."

The yearning for structure, for formal rituals and a system of learning remains a common theme, particularly among those who have had no structure for years, as well as those who have recently entered the community and do not have memories of authoritarian groups, obsessions over lineage, untruths about origins, and other abuses that were common ten years ago. But for every person who desires a more formal system of training, there is one who tires of the present teacher and wants a more personal, unmediated, and direct source to the divine.

Epilogue

Guard the Mysteries; constantly reveal them.
            —From a poem by the late Lew Welsh,
                now a popular Craft saying

It is primarily the attraction of a personal initiation that explains the craze for the occult.

            —MIRCEA ELIADE[1]

The eminent archeologist George Mylonas, director of the excavations of My- cenae, involved himself deeply in the final excavations of Eleusis, which was the site of the Eleusinian Mysteries for two thousand years. During that time multitudes of woman and men from all over the world of the ancient Greeks participated in the rites of Eleusis and, if we can believe the poets, playwrights, and philosophers, drew great strength from them. Pindar wrote: "Blessed is he who hath seen these things before he goeth beneath the hollow earth; for he understandeth the end of mortal life, and the beginning (of a new life) given of God."[2] Cicero, Sophocles, and Aristotle likewise extolled the Mysteries. Greek and Roman political figures such as Pericles, Hadrian, Marcus Aurelius, and Julian considered their experiences there moving and joyful. And some of the most profound passages in the plays of Aeschylus were considered so close to the essence of the Mysteries that the playwright came under the scrutiny of Athe-

439

nian law until it was proved that he had never been initiated, and therefore could not have revealed the Mysteries in his works.

Mylonas, being a scholar of the twentieth century, was forced to study merely their remains. He concludes *Eleusis and the Eleusinean Mysteries* with sorrow and longing. He laments:

> For years, since my early youth, I have tried to find out what the facts were. Hope against hope was spent against the lack of monumental evidence; the belief that inscriptions would be found on which the Hierophants had recorded their ritual and its meaning has faded completely; the discovery of a subterranean room filled with the archives of the cult, which dominated my being in my days of youth, is proved an unattainable dream since neither subterranean rooms nor archives for the cult exist at Eleusis; the last Hierophant carried with him to the grave the secrets which had been transmitted orally for untold generations, from the one high priest to the next. A thick, unpenetrable veil indeed still covers securely the rites of Demeter and protects them from the curious eyes of modern students. How many nights and days have been spent over books, inscriptions, and works of art by eminent scholars in their effort to lift the veil! How many wild and ingenious theories have been advanced in superhuman effort to explain the Mysteries! How many nights I have spent standing on the steps of the Telesterion, flooded with the magic silver light of a Mediterranean moon, hoping to catch the mood of the initiates, hoping that the human soul might get a glimpse of what the rational mind could not investigate! All in vain—the ancient world has kept its secret well and the Mysteries of Eleusis remain unrevealed.[3]

Eleusis has puzzled scholars for centuries. Much has been discovered about the preparatory and public celebrations, the preliminary processions and purifications, the Demeter-Korê myth cycle, and the nature of certain processions and lesser rites. Karl Kerényi, C. G. Jung, M. F. Nilsson, W. K. C. Guthrie, Mylonas, and other scholars have created a large storehouse of intuitions and speculations. Many scholars would now agree with Kerényi that a profound religious experience must have occurred, repeated year after year, a psychic reality that succeeded again and again.[4]

The vision of Mylonas standing, empty in spirit, in the moonlit ruins of Eleusis stayed with me through all my explorations of Neo-Paganism and the Craft. This is not surprising, since the Craft (and a number of other Neo-Pagan religions as well) has always claimed to be a mystery religion, although exactly what that means is not always clear even to the participants.

At one level, I think, all mystery traditions involve processes of growth and regeneration, confrontations with birth, death, the source of life, and the relationship of human beings to the cosmos. In connection with these ideas a number of Neo-Pagans and Witches have foresworn the words "Pagan" and "Witch," saying that they regard their religion as "the revival of the mystery tradition." A New York coven writes that rituals are really the reenactment of "cosmic drama," allowing the participant to enter "into the drama of life itself, of joining with the gods in an achievement of universal advantage, so that growth (which is the true magic) is achieved."[5]

If, with Aidan Kelly, we define the Craft as "the European heritage of Goddess worship,"[6] the connections with the mysteries of Demeter and Korê become clearer. Above and beyond the murky area of historical and geographical connections, the philosophical connections are real. What little we know of the Mysteries seems to indicate that these rites emphasized (as the Craft, at its best, does today) *experience* as opposed to *dogma*, and *metaphor* and *myth* as opposed to *doctrine*. Both the Mysteries and the Craft emphasize initiatory *processes* that lead to a widening of perceptions. Neither emphasizes theology, belief, or the written word. In both, participants expect to lead normal lives *in* the world, as well as attain spiritual enrichment.

How can one explain the plight of George Mylonas? Aidan notes that the Athenians distinguished between lesser and greater Mysteries.

The Great Mysteries of Eleusis were, in large part, archetypical of the Mystery religions. According to Karl Kerényi, when Athens annexed Eleusis about 600 B.C.E. and made its Mysteries the state religion of Attica, the Athenians passed a law to protect the secrecy of the Mysteries. This law, however, distinguished two types of secrets, the "Lower" and the "Higher." The "Lower secrets" were those that could be told to another person by word, gesture, or whatever; these were called *ta aporrheta*, "the forbidden," and the law applied only to them—hence their name. Why didn't the law apply to the "Higher secrets"? The latter were called *ta arrheta*, "the ineffable," and it was recognized in the law itself that these secrets could not be communicated except by the Mysteries themselves; hence they needed no protection by a mere law.[7]

It is the *process* and the *experience*, not the secrets, that are the mystery of the Mysteries. Even were a secret chamber found in the depths of Eleusis, or had the basic rituals been inscribed, the Mysteries would defy discovery. This explains why, for over two thousand years, even during times of Christian domination, there were no revelations by converts, no statements from ex-initiates.

Mysteries, observe two Neo-Pagan writers, are "stages of growth in consciousness of the sacred universe, not secrets":

> A mystery can't be told or even easily shown someone, while a secret can be told to just about anyone and they can tell it to somebody else. And it will be the same secret. And yet there seem to be an amazing number of people who seem to believe the two terms to be synonymous. . . .
>
> The truly frustrating thing about the mysteries is that they cannot be taught, they must be experienced. In fact, telling most people the surface-seeming substance or "secrets" can blind them to the depth of the real mysteries, the great sea of the untellable, the unsayable. . . . As with a zen monk, the teacher must "trick" the neophyte into awakening. . . .
>
> If it were as easy as telling to introduce someone to the mysteries, then those who have perceived them would simply *tell*, and all people would become wise and awake. . . . But when people try to *tell*, the things that are said are either understandable but not true or true but not understandable. They are image-illusion, they are empty baskets.[8]

Mylonas is, then, a potent symbol. We are all searching among the ruins. He is all of us who have admitted our spiritual impoverishment, hoping that objects, words, and inscriptions will give us clues to things that can be learned only through experience. What Mylonas (and most of us) have been denied is the experience of being "tricked" into this initiatory process. We are forced to rely merely on our intellectual tools, which will not allow us to enter certain hidden chambers. The secret that Neo-Paganism seems to have begun to learn over the past ten years is this: If the methods for creating such experiences have been lost, the way to find them again is to create them again.

Appendix I

The 1985 Questionnaire

In the summer of 1985, I distributed 450 questionnaires at three different Pagan festivals. Fifty questionnaires were distributed at the Rites of Spring celebration in Massachusetts. Three hundred copies of a longer questionnaire were handed out at the Pagan Spirit Gathering in Wisconsin, and one hundred copies were distributed at the Festival of Women's Spirituality in Oregon. One hundred ninety-five questionnaires were returned to me. However some of these were copies of the originals, and at least fifteen responses arrived after the questionnaire was published in the journal *Panegyria*. Replies came in from thirty states and, to my amazement, I even received two responses from Australia.

This was not the kind of extensive and complex questionnaire I used at the beginning of my research in 1975. It was really designed to get feedback from Pagans and Wiccans on a series of questions: (1) What changes have there been in the last seven years? (2) What are the most important issues facing the Pagan and Wiccan communities? (3) What is the most important thing you want to tell the public about Paganism and the Craft? (4) What are your feelings about the word "Witch"? Can it ever be truly reclaimed? (5) What has been the impact of Pagan festivals on the community? There were also questions on occupation, former religion, attitudes toward drugs, and a question on what had led them to choose this path. Here are the results.

Religious Upbringing

It used to be a common assumption—made by me and many others—that the Pagan and Craft movement was filled with a majority of ex-Catholics and ex-Episcopalians. The reasoning went something like this: People who enter the Craft have a love of ritual and a hatred of dogma. Often they had early experiences with the beauty of rituals in Catholic or Anglican ceremonies but rebelled against many of the teachings and the notion of sin.

The Rev. J. Gordon Melton originally made this assumption (see p. 311) but later conducted his own survey and found out otherwise. In a paper presented in 1980 to the Society for the Scientific Study of Religion, meeting in Cincinnati, Ohio, Melton said that he and others had hypothesized that in religious background, the Neo-Pagan Movement was 50 percent Catholic, 25 percent Jewish, and 25 percent Protestant and others. But in his own survey, using 178 returned questionnaires, Melton found that the religious background of the Pagan community mirrored the national religious profile of America very closely, the only departure was that Jews were doubly represented. Melton found:

Catholics	25.8%
Protestant and Sectarian	42.7%
Jewish	6.2%
Non-religious	10.1%
Other	15.2%

In my own survey, of 166 people who answered the question, I found:

Catholic	39	23.5%
Anglican or Episcopalian	15	9.0%
Other Protestant	65	39.2%
Mixed (Catholic and Protestant or Catholic and Episcopalian)	13	7.8%
Jewish	9	5.4%
Unitarian	5	3.0%
Non-religious	14	8.4%
Other (Greek Orthodox, the Craft, etc.)	3	1.8%
Religious Science, Science of Mind, etc.	3	1.8%

Path to Paganism

I asked people how they entered this religion. I suggested several routes that people had mentioned in interviews, including ecology, occultism, and interest in magic, feminism, mythology, science fiction, the SCA (Society for Creative Anachronism), folklore, music, and psychology. Many people put more than one answer down. Out of more than 195 responses, the following is a tally of the results:

Feminism	36
Interest in occultism or magic	31
Reading books (books mentioned included *The Spiral Dance* (7), *Drawing Down the Moon* (6), *When God Was a Woman* (2), *Positive Magic*, *The White Goddess*, *Womanspirit Rising*, *The Complete Art of Witchcraft*, *Holy Book of Woman's Mysteries*, *Witchcraft the Old Religion*)	27
An interest in science fiction or fantasy	18
An interest in ecology, a feeling for nature	16
Society for Creative Anachronism (SCA)	11
The result of a religious or philosophical search	10
An interest in psychology	9
An interest in folklore	8
An interest in mythology	5
Had psychic experiences	5
Being in the woods or living on the land	5
Stumbled into a class or occult shop	5
A rejection of Christianity	4
Childhood experiences, memories, having an imaginary playmate	4
Family tradition or influence of a family member	3
An inner feeling—drawn to it since being a child	3
The Frosts' correspondence course	2
Interest in anthropology	2
Interest in politics	2
Interest in art, reading art history	2
Always loved ritual, did spontaneous rituals as a child	2
Born that way	2
Studying comparative religion or theology	2

Went to a festival, or saw an ad	2
Had a past life experience	2
Influence of a friend	2
Day dreams	1
Did my dissertation on the subject and got hooked	1
Interest in music	1

Occupation in the Mundane World

As Gordon Melton noted in his 1980 survey of Neo-Paganism, "while Pagans seem to the casual observer to be 'counter-cultural' types, they are, in fact, basically white-collar, middle-class professionals." Their job profiles are pretty unusual, with an amazingly high percentage in computer, scientific, and technical fields. Here's how respondents to the 1985 questionnaire make a living.

Computer programmer, system's analyst, or software developer	21	Own small business	4
		Social worker	4
		Bookkeeper, accountant	4
Student (either college or graduate)	16	Unemployed	4
Secretary/clerical	12	Massage, dance or body work	4
Psychotherapist or counselor	10	Occult/book supplier, book seller	4
Teacher, professor, instructor	9	Scientist	4
Writer	8	Technical writer	3
Housewife	7	Forestry, landscaping, gardening	3
Typesetter, typographer, printer	7	Welder, machinist	3
Priestess, teaches Wicca or Occultism	6	Waitress	3
Salesperson	6	Manager, business executive	3
Craftsperson	5	Doctor, chiropractor	2
Nurse	5	Law clerk	2
Artist	5	Nanny	2
Auditor, financial or market analyst	5	Courier	2
		Cook	2

Other 18
  technician, real
  estate, anthropologist,
  bus driver, factory
  worker, postal worker,
  filmmaker, astrologer,
  librarian, carpenter,
architect, lawyer, word
processor, security
officer, actress,
professional dominatrix,
labor union consultant,
tattooist

The most unusual finding in this job survey was that so many people involved with Paganism were in technical fields. Out of 195 answers, 28 people or roughly 16 percent were either programmers, technical writers, or scientists—and I'm not even counting the lab technicians or the students who said they were studying computer programming. The finding was not totally surprising since people in the Pagan community have noticed the large numbers that seem to work in computer fields. So the questionnaire also asked the question: what percentage of people in the Pagan community work with computers, and what, if any, relationship exists between a Pagan or Craft philosophy and an interest in computers.

The answers ran the gamut from people who felt the question was ridiculous—that computers were inimical to Paganism—to those who were convinced that 80 percent of the Pagan community actively used computers and that there was an important and striking relationship between the two. The answers were fascinating, ranging from the practical to the esoteric.

1. Computers are like magic.

"Symbolic thinking and patterning are essential to magical thinking. Like magic, computers work in unseen ways to accomplish tasks." "Like magic, computers require a procedural and logical mind, yet sometimes defy logic." "A computer is like a sigil." "Computers often seem to be living entities." "Computers are elementals in disguise." "They are the new magic of our culture." "Pagans are beginning to view the products of the human mind as sacred, what else could possibly be sacred to a largely urban people?" "Coupled with modems, computers are the oracles of the future." "If you learn the obscure and arcane magic words, you can force a powerful entity, whom many people fear, to do your bidding." "Magic is metaphorical, like programming."

2. Paganism is a pragmatic and practical religion.

"Scientific, sensible, reasonable people are drawn to computers; it makes sense that they would be drawn to a scientific, reasonable, sensible religion." "Witches believe if it works use it. They are pragmatic, not dinosaurs. Save the old, use the new. Computers are practical." "Logical people will not tolerate an illogical religion like Christianity, but will accept a prelogical or alogical faith."

3. Computers are simply where the jobs are these days.

"Computers were developed so people like us could earn a living," says Bonewits. "It's just a job." "Computers are the easiest way for an educated person to make a living."

4. Computers are simply the best way to communicate, they are practical tools.

"They are the networks for the new age." "They give us more time to grow, study, be creative." "They help us put out newsletters which are Paganism's main way of communicating." "A tool for decentralization and dissemination of information."

5. Paganism provides a balance to people who are heavily involved in linear forms of reality, and vice versa.

"It's a balance of left and right brain." "Computers are getting away from the earth, and Paganism is getting down to it." "Computer folk want a religion that allows them to get 'hands on' with their souls and 'debug' themselves by their own efforts. No packaged software for these 'self-programmers.' Paganism offers a spirituality that uses instrumentalities (ritual) under the control of the self." "People who work with computers and are often removed from nature in their work, turn to Paganism as a reaction to the sterility of their world." "After working with the mind and the intellect, one needs a religion of the senses, the emotions, the world."

6. Oddball people are attracted to both.

"Both attract slightly unenculturated, solitary, creative thinkers." "Both types like mental games." "It takes us less time to adapt to new ideas." "Both types distrust authority." "Both types are on the leading edge." "Pagans are playful by nature, and the computer is the most endlessly fascinating toy ever invented." "Computer people and Pagans often lack social skills and have had painful experiences with family relationships, leading them to seek alternatives to 'normal' society."

There were a few people who disagreed with any attempt to find a relationship. They wrote things like: "A truly Pagan world would not have computers, but if we are oppressed by them, we have the right to fight back with them." Others said, "Neo-Pagans tend to be faddish, so are computers." "Don't be ridiculous, most Pagans are therapists or gardeners." "Educated, intelligent people have computers—they also have cars." "The only correlation is intelligence."

Public or Secret

The questionnaire asked how public or secretive Pagans were about their spiritual practices. While it's hard to characterize many of the answers strictly, 57 people said they were fairly public ("I wear a pentagram," or "I have a 'pagan and proud' bumper sticker on my car"), 58 people took a middle-of-the-road position ("I'm public except at work," or "All my friends know, but I don't tell my family"), 39 people said they were "very secretive." I considered someone who said, "Only close friends know," to be secretive. I considered someone who said, "My co-workers and family know," to be public. If someone said, "I use Goddess in public and Witch in private," I tabulated them "middle-of-the-road."

I think it is fair to say that, in general, people are much more willing to be public than they were five years ago and that despite the efforts of fundamentalists Paganism is much more accepted as a bona fide religion by the media and by ordinary Americans.

So how necessary is secrecy in the late 1980s? It depends on who you are and where you live and what you do for a living and the basic way you approach people. There are Pagans who have problems in the most open communities and Pagans who have no trouble at all in small communities in the Bible Belt. However, in recent years there have been more attempts by fundamentalists to attack Pagan and Wiccan groups directly. Stone circles have been desecrated, and fundamentalists have tried to break up several large public rituals given by Starhawk and Luisa Teish. In Atlanta, vandals destroyed a stone circle and altar on private land and, later, local rednecks disrupted a circle by the Grove of the Unicorn. Near Minneapolis, another stone circle was destroyed by fire and crosses were erected on the site. At least one Pagan networking organization was infiltrated by fundamentalists and the mailing list used to attempt to persuade members to abandon the Craft. There are still people losing child custody battles or losing their jobs because of the charge of "witchcraft." Despite this, the public at large is more aware of Neo-Paganism today than at any time previously, and there are many Pagans who are willing to be completely public about their beliefs.

Drugs

At the time *Drawing Down the Moon* was first written, there was a very strong anti-drug stance in most of Wicca, although among those interested in shamanism, there was a belief in the occasional use of mind-altering substances to achieve altered states. While grass was occasionally used recreationally by Pagans, just as it was by many other people, there were strong strictures in all the covens I attended about no drugs in ritual. The basic ideology was that drugs were unnecessary and that one could get the same altered effects through trance, chanting, dancing, and other legal and honorable methods. The position taken by Sharon Devlin (that Pagans should get more experience and training in ecstatic states, using all the traditional methods—sex, drugs, etc.) was a very, very minority position.

But at the same time that there were heavy warnings against the use of mind-altering substances, and strict rules in every coven I visited, there was some very occasional, private use of psychedelics. One long-time Pagan priest, now deceased, developed a complex and deeply spiritual event called the "Faery Shaman Ritual." This was a long ceremony, with prior fasting and much preparation. It involved sufi dancing, face painting, and a visionary journey into the realms of faery in order to contact your own totem animal. Psychedelics were sometimes used in this ritual.

I, myself, participated in a Faery Shaman Ritual in 1980. It was an extremely choreographed, very controlled, and incredibly beautiful experience. The ritual had been planned well in advance, and there were several people present whose sole function was to make sure that the people undergoing the ritual would be all right.

Several people have attempted to create similar ritual experiences for Neo-Pagans, but not always with as great success. There is now a consensus within the Pagan community that these experiences can happen only with an incredibly knowledgeable and experienced teacher, and the Pagan community has not yet evolved a group of teachers with that kind of wisdom. There is also a consensus that these kinds of rituals must never be done at public gatherings or festivals. The possibilities for abuse are too great.

So why mention it at all? The reason for including a question about mind-altering substances in the questionnaire was that in recent years there has been an increased interest in shamanism and all techniques of consciousness alteration. Many Craft traditions are calling themselves Shamanic Wicca and although these traditions almost always use chanting, drumming, and ecstatic dancing rather than drugs, it seemed important to see what attitudes toward mind-altering substances now exist in the community at large.

Fifty-six respondents said "never, never, ever, ever use drugs." In particular, a large number of women involved in Goddess-worshipping groups advocated a completely chemical-free existence—no alcohol, no caffeine, no drugs. A majority of the people in the British traditions of Wicca also said, "Don't use!" These people stressed that the Craft can achieve the same altered states without psychedelics. These people stressed that drugs were "more trouble than they were worth" and that a cloudy mind was the worst thing possible in magic.

All these responses stressed the negative. For example: "I don't think there are any Euro-American Pagans with the necessary discipline or training to use these substances. They have no place in Pagan ritual, with the possible exception of rituals led by an authentic Native American medicine person. In our modern, detribalized, commoditized world, without tribal laws, drugs became a tool of depoliticization." Another wrote, "Despite their historical validity, and value, we cannot afford to be associated with them." A third responded: "I do not condone using any consciousness-altering substances. The Craft is enough of a high and using such crutches cripples the person." Several people said they would not voluntarily work in a circle with someone who was on drugs. As one woman said, "I have never needed to chemically alter myself to communicate with the Great Ones."

Seventy-six respondents, the largest group, stressed that it was a matter of individual choice and said that these substances were "occasionally, very valuable," were traditional in many cultures, but they warned that these substances were dangerous and must be used discretely and never publicly. All these respondents opposed recreational drug use and distinguished it from occasional sacred use in ritual or initiatory experience. A few made a big distinction between natural psychedelics (mushrooms, peyote) and synthetic psychedelics (LSD), accepting the use of the former but not the latter. Again, almost all warned against drug abuse and cautioned that no one should ever be asked to experiment with these substances against his or her will.

Even those who agreed with the occasional use of psychedelics wrote things like, "They must be used under scrupulous supervision, not circulated like joints at a party." "They are powerful tools which should never be used for recreation." One person observed, "They are useful to demonstrate the existence of other modes of consciousness, but the same effects can be achieved through ritual and psychic training."

Thirteen people supported the use of "sacred substances" as a "powerful tool," as long as they were used in sacred contexts. As one person put it, "They represent an incontestable contact with 'magical/ visionary' experience and will be used no matter what anyone says. They demand the development of new ethics and rules for safe conduct—ethics and rules that have been too slow in coming." Another said, "They are very potent sacraments. When used properly (set and setting), they offer the most easily accessible contact with sacred space. Unfortunately many abuse or use them in a party atmosphere." "LSD woke me up," one woman wrote. "It shook me out of the pabulum consciousness with which I had been raised and showed me a world of possibility." "They are gates to the other world, holy agents of self-knowledge," wrote another.

But even the most ardent advocates of psychedelics urged extreme caution. "I learned a lot from my use of LSD and peyote, but I am very conservative in my ideas about others using them," one wrote. Others stressed that it was important that drugs not be used to substitute for genuine ritual experience. Nor were they a substitute for hard discipline and spiritual work. "They were important in my past," one wrote, "but now I prefer ceremony, fasting, and the sweat lodge to achieve the same ends." Another noted, "Let's face it, these things are dangerous. In supervised settings, they can bring enlightenment, but this can also be achieved through study and meditation. I prefer the longer and safer path to enlightenment." "They may be invaluable," someone else wrote, "but like chain saws, powerful tools hurt fools." Yet another observed, "If the object is to expand the mind, it is violence to blow the mind."

And despite whatever value these substances may have, many Pagans emphasized the legal problems connected with them. As one person noted: "It is too complex, there are too many variables, and Pagans should remember that drug busts are often used to smash unpopular groups."

The Most Important Thing You Want to Tell People

Perhaps the most surprising finding was the almost total unanimity expressed by people when they answered the question, "What is the most important thing you want to tell the public about Paganism and the Craft?"

More than half the responses (76) could be summarized by the following paragraph:

"We are not evil. We do not worship the Devil. We don't harm or seduce people. We are not dangerous. We are ordinary people like you. We have families, jobs, hopes, and dreams. We are not a cult. We are not weird. This religion is not a joke. We are not what you think we are from looking at T.V. We are real. We laugh, we cry. We are serious. We have a sense of humor. You don't have to be afraid of us. We don't want to convert you. And please don't try to convert us. Just give us the same right we give you—to live in peace. We are much more similar to you than you think."

Fifty-four respondents talked about the beauties of a Pagan religion. Wrote one woman, "I would show them a flower, a stalk of wheat, a lake and a mountain unspoiled, a rising sun, a crescent moon and I would say, 'This is where we get our religious inspiration. It's loving, caring, and

healthy. One can become in tune with natures' cycles and with the self."
Another wrote, "The only thing they have to fear from us is the breaking
down of the walls that keep them trapped and the knowledge that the
Kingdom of Heaven really is within you just like Brother Jesus said."

Others stressed that Pagans were gentle, loving people, who love the
earth and its creatures, and that the religion is a pathway to greater
understanding. "It allows one to account for everything and deny
nothing," was one reply. "It presents the best possible pattern for the
understanding of personal power and responsibility. It can open all the
doors that lead anywhere." "Paganism is a gift of life to life herself,"
wrote a woman. Still others wrote, "It's a loving, healing, nurturing, soul-
searching experience." "To some of us the world looks different when the
universe is female." "It's planting gardens, loving the planet, being
concerned with truth and honesty, and reclaiming parts of ourselves that
have been cut off." "It's just another path to the center." "It says that
magic is alive and that dreams can come true. Just listen, and you will
hear your heart dance to the piper's song as does ours." "Mirth and
reverence is the key. We have a tremendous amount of fun. We have
religious services and everyone howls with laughter. We dance, we yell,
we sing, we weep, we talk about serious matters. We leave less tired than
when we came. We are filled with the spirit of life." And still another
said, "When bewildered or in doubt, dance in circles, scream and
shout. . . . The most useful route to the higher self is through the lower
self."

Eight people said they wanted to tell the public that the planet was in
danger, that Mother Nature needed to be defended, and that Paganism
provided some important answers. "We are responsible and ethical
people," wrote one person, "following a spiritual path with valuable,
even crucial perspectives on our relationship to the earth and its other
creatures. We understand the magical capacity to transform ourselves and
our community." Another simply wrote, "Help! The Earth is in danger!"
A third responded, "We are among the religions most concerned with the
fate of nature." And one person observed wryly, "There ain't no Devil
and there ain't no Angels, just corporate criminals playing with tanks."

Six people stressed the issue of diversity above all else, noting that the
United States was founded on the principles of religious freedom. Several
observed that diversity was central to Paganism. "Fundamental to our
understanding," wrote one, "is the notion that we can live with

differences." Another offered a quote: "One source, many paths. One truth, many explanations." A third offered, "We are an affiliation of individual shamans each following their own dreaming. The many dreams are one." Yet another observed, "We are a very diversified, undogmatic community, more into perceiving than believing. Artistic, psychic, Pagans seek refuge from the arrogant belief in One Way."

Changes

For me, the most important question on the questionnaire was "What changes have you seen in the Pagan community in the last seven years, in other words, since the publication of *Drawing Down the Moon*?" This is the question that seems most relevant to a second edition. There is no way to quantify these answers. They go all over the map. But there were definitely certain themes and certain disagreements. And there were at least thirty different subjects that people mentioned.

—There has been a population explosion within Paganism. There are at least 50,000 to 100,000 active self-identified Pagans or members of Wicca in the United States. (Remember, there are about 180,000 Unitarians and about 40,000 Quakers.)

—There are many more good books and materials available. There is more serious scholarship both by Pagans and by the academic community—and occasionally they're the same people.

—There are more skilled people within the movement. There are more older people.

—There is more attention to the needs of children within the community. There are more children within the community.

—There is more acceptance of Paganism in the larger culture. In a few communities there is almost total acceptance. A few books on the Goddess have even entered the mainstream. Anthropology and folklore have brought Paganism to the universities, and magical imagery has caught the attention of millions in films like *Star Wars* and *The Dark Crystal*.

—Less persecution.

—At the same time there is more of a Christian fundamentalist backlash.

—More Pagans are "out of the closet." There's been better press coverage, better public presentations of Paganism. Some people noticed less publicity in general, which they said was good.

—There has been less secrecy, less paranoia, less suspicion, more open circles and classes.

—More communication between groups. More networking. More newsletters (about one hundred). More legal Pagan organizations. More sanctuaries. More access. More gatherings.

—Festivals. The impact of festivals, in particular national festivals, was noted by many (see festival section in Chapter 14). In brief, people noticed increased sharing between traditions, the creation of a body of nationally shared Pagan chants, songs, and rituals, the growth of ecstatic dancing, and the phenomenon that festivals and networks have become more important than established groups as an entry point into the Pagan community.

—*The Spiral Dance*. Many noted the impact of Starhawk's work and the thousands that have been brought into the community through her books. Several noted that those who came into the community through reading her books often have a different set of values and politics than those who have entered the community through more "traditional" ways.

—The growth of the feminist Craft and feminist covens. More acceptance of feminism in the larger Pagan community. More older women's covens. More rural women's covens. While at least two people attacked the feminist Craft as sexist and talked of an increasing female militancy, many more people noticed the passing or lessening of separatism in the women's spiritual community. As one woman put it, "Women are now out in the community with confidence, energy, and visions to share with a dearth of enlightened men." Others noticed links between lesbian and straight women. "There's more balance," observed another.

—The dominance of Wicca in the Pagan community as opposed to other types of Paganism that were dominant ten years ago (CAW, Feraferia, Church of the Eternal Source).

—More acceptance of gays within the Pagan community and the rise of the Radical Faery movement.

—Increasing interest in shamanic and tribal paths. The growth of at least three different strains of Shamanic Wicca as traditions. A growing interest in non-European traditions; a melding of Western magical traditions with new trance techniques. More reliance on experiential and intuitive forms of working. There were at least two people who expressed dismay at this phenomenon and at what they saw as the tendency to "steal Native American traditions and ceremonies."

—The beginning of attempts of Pagans to work with other religious and "new age" groups; ecumenism and explorations of activities of service in the community. The increasing use of Pagan ceremonies and celebrations of the Earth as sacred by Unitarian and other religious groups. The increased use of ecstatic dancing by Christian, Jewish, and, of course, Sufi groups. The use of ritual circles by many non-Pagan groups. More dialogue between Pagans and other spiritual groups.

—Less dogma; less, or at least more intelligent, bickering; fewer holy wars; less ego-tripping. Less guru following. Less narrow-mindedness. Less crazies, less flashy robes and flamboyance. Less thrill seekers. Less paraphernalia. More serious grappling with real-world issues. Less fantasy. More maturity.

A minority disagreed and said they found

—More ego-tripping, more paraphernalia, more flakes. More commercialism, more materialism. And one person said, "The good are better and the bad are worse."

—More political activism by Pagans—in particular, more ecological and anti-nuclear activity.

—Eclecticism. Here was the greatest amount of controversy and disagreement. A majority said eclecticism was the best thing that had happened to the Pagan community—resulting in more openness, more sharing, more creativity, and less narrow-mindedness. It had also encouraged techniques of community building and had fostered the creation of a national Pagan community. Many said that eclectics were at the forefront and that the "traditionalists were on the defensive." Several noticed the growing acceptance of self-initiation and self-dedication. But there were also many long and emotional essays expressing concern about losing the good parts of the traditional Craft, and several people expressed the view that eclecticism often reflects an unwillingness to do the hard work needed to make progress on a spiritual path.

Others said that traditional Wiccan groups were on an upswing, particularly with the development of cross-traditional English Tradition organizations like the New Wiccan Church. Several eclectics said they were becoming more traditional and feeling a need for more structure. One person said there were more eclectics, but they were now becoming more traditional and one priestess observed, "People are more interested in traditions than they were five years ago, but the traditions are less rigid than they were." Another wrote, "The above ground are more eclectic and the below ground have pulled back out of sight and are practicing more traditionally." One coven leader said this: "We are becoming very scattered. When I entered the Craft, we were all searching for an established system or an individual who could give us direction. Now people seem interested only in creating their own religion. We all do this, but first you need understanding of self, discipline, and direction from a structured system. There is more knowledge available now, but instead of it being an advantage, people are lost in a sea of knowledge. We need a resurgence of some form of traditional beliefs, in the sense of moorings to guide those entering the Craft." Another wrote, "People are less willing to make compromises and yield to the need of the group. They are aware of the breadth of opportunities. Is it so valuable to be some kind of eclectic?"

On the other hand, many people said that eclecticism had resulted in less blind belief in the old myths, less hierarchy, less "grand-motherism" and a growing understanding that there were very few—if any—direct descendents from thousands of years ago. Many noted the value of creative innovation and the melding of traditions. Many said they were glad that the importance of succession had lessened. Several said there was more emphasis on creativity and real religious consciousness, instead of relying on the writings of Gerald Gardner and Margaret Murray. And one person noted that priests and priestesses were beginning to be valued not on the basis of "degrees" but on the effectiveness of their healing, channeling, and ritual abilities.

—A significant attempt to create a national movement with legal recognition, sanctuaries, and communities. "We have created a culture," wrote one, "or at least, a subculture."

Oh That Vexing "W" Word

Almost all the people who answered the questionnaire considered themselves "Pagans." Seven did not, including Gavin and Yvonne Frost, who have never agreed with the use of the word "Pagan." Several city-based Witches also wrote that the word "Pagan" with its root meaning "country dweller" did not really fit their reality. But almost everyone else said the word was absolutely appropriate to describe their religious path.

People defined the word "Pagan" in many different ways, but most agreed that Pagans were members of pantheistic, tribal, shamanistic nature religions, and that modern Neo-Paganism embodied a respect for the earth and nature's laws and a conception of deity as immanent.

Several people simply defined Paganism as any religion outside Judaism, Christianity, and Islam. Several others defined a Pagan as anyone who worships the old gods of any culture. Some simply talked about belief in a goddess or a goddess and a god, but most expressed the notion that Paganism involves multiple deities and a concept that the earth is sacred. Several said that Pagans base their religion on the laws of nature rather than the teachings of a "divinely" inspired individual or group. Many expressed the idea that a Pagan has a duty to defend Mother Earth. Many expressed a belief in the material world as sacred and said a Pagan does not seek to transcend that world. Others emphasized the sentience and aliveness in all nature, the importance of attunement to the earth and to the lunar, solar, and seasonal cycles, as well as the need for human communities to once again have the experience of ecstatic celebration, rites of passage, and mystery traditions. Many talked of their love of the earth, their respect for all life, and their awareness of the living spirit in all things. Several mentioned the idea of working with nature, not against her, of understanding power as something that comes from within as opposed to the structures of domination that constitute "power over." Still others mentioned the idea of the earth as a living organism, as Gaia. Other qualities mentioned were life affirming, fun-loving, non-dogmatic, flexible, pragmatic, and ecstatic.

About two-thirds of those who answered the questionnaire considered themselves Witches. I asked them whether the word *witch* would ever be reclaimed? What did they think about this word *witch*? As we saw in an earlier part of this book, the word *witch* is a very difficult word, with bad connotations not only among Christians but even among anthropologists and many tribal peoples. Are modern Witches called Witches because Margaret Murray said so? Because the inquisitors called Pagans Witches? Or are there deep, important, archetypal reasons for modern Wiccans to use this word, with its notions of power, wisdom, healing, independence, and female strength?

The Pagan community is divided over this word, although many more would reclaim it than abandon it, and those who would keep the word are more emotionally committed than those who would forsake it. Among the themes expressed over and over again by those who think the word *witch* is absolutely essential are the following:

1. Abandoning the word is equivalent to abandoning the millions that were hanged and burned during the Inquisition. Several people mentioned the Jews during Hitler. "In Nazi Germany," one wrote, "no Jewish person would have dreamed of changing the name of their religion. We shouldn't accommodate other people's prejudices, but challenge those biases." Another entry picked up the same theme. "Forty years ago, they nearly wiped out those named Jews. They were more successful a few hundred years ago in wiping out those named Witches. We must reclaim our ancestors and restore their good name." Remembering the Inquisition was a recurrent theme. "The word carries a part of our past. It would be dangerous to forget it and leave it behind."

2. It is the very things that make the word "uncomfortable" that give the word its importance. "The words of comfort are usually not the words of power," wrote one. "For years, I fought against the term 'Witch,'" wrote a graduate student in religious studies. "I wanted the juice without the term. Now I think Starhawk is right—the 'juice' goes with the term." A woman wrote, "For me, the association with women, tradition, and power are important. I also think a reaction of discomfort to the concept of Witch is an appropriate one. The path of Witchcraft is a path into the unknown, which usually makes people uncomfortable. A Witch deals with forces that are potentially dangerous and should be credited as dangerous, not hidden under sweet blandishments. Witch is a radical

concept, pertaining to the root, essential, inherent, basic. To deradicalize the concept of Witch by using a different name would fully be cutting off our roots." Another woman wrote, "I like the word. . . . It's on the edge."

3. Many women said the word had simply claimed them and that there was no other word that brought together the concepts of women and solitary wisdom, isolation, healing, and power. As one woman wrote, "I use the word because it speaks of women with power. Few other words put women together with power." "It feels right to say 'Witch,' right from the souls of my feet!" wrote someone else. "It has a feeling that rings true," wrote another. "It emphasizes my woman self, wild, free and strong." "It is essential to what I am," said yet another, "a woman acting to empower herself and others. Until I say 'Witch' as easily as 'The Old Religion' or 'I follow Wicca,' I am not yet accepted for all that I am." Still another woman wrote, "We should educate people that 'Witch' is not evil but ancient and positive. The first time I called myself a 'Witch' was the most magical moment of my life." One woman noted that in our patriarchal system any strong, assertive woman is already called a Witch, "so we should keep the word and remember why we use it." Another respondent observed, "They will call us Witches anyway, we might as well claim the word with pride."

4. Some people liked the word because of its association with mavericks, outcasts, and the unconventional. One person wrote, "Witches were seen as acting against the best interest of society because their actions were against the best interests of the reigning theocracy. Theocracies demand conformity, control learning and language. At present, our situation is more flexible than it was in the past, as we have two theocracies—the scientific and the Christian—at war with each other."

5. Many people liked the word because of its association with the idea of ancient healers in touch with hidden forces in nature.

Many Pagans and Wiccans expressed reservations about the word *witch*. The most frequent was the notion that there are so many stereotypes surrounding the word that it's impossible to explain one's religion unless one has several hours to spare. Many people told me, "When I have a limited amount of time to tell someone my viewpoint, it's just a lot easier to omit the word 'Witch.'" "I call myself 'Witch' in private," wrote one person, "but to do so in public invites confusion."

Said another, "The use of the word brings up more trouble than it resolves." "It takes too much energy to counter old images," said a third. Quite a number of questionnaires used phrases like the following: "It works against us in public contexts." "It does more harm than good." "Definitions are created by a majority consensus. The tiny Pagan community cannot hope to alter the majority definition of the word 'Witch.' " "It's a stumbling block. It's become a trigger word like 'Kike' or 'Nigger.' It can set you apart."

The most important argument against the word *witch* is that it just doesn't communicate the reality of the Pagan experience to most of the public, whereas a less loaded word often does. Haragano, an elder in the New Wiccan Church, told me, "I prefer not spending a third of my first contact with somebody explaining away the bad connotations. I don't see myself as an apologist, spending my life reclaiming the word. I live my religion. Within the New Wiccan Church, we identify ourselves to each other as Witches, but to the general public we are elders in our church. The word 'Witch' is a big red flag. When people get to know us, we'll tell them; we'll tell them what makes us what we are and that gives a more three-dimensional explanation than any apology for a word. Everyone is reacting to a little badge that we put on ourselves. This is taking up so much energy we could be using to connect with each other." This is in stark contrast to the views of someone like Laurie Cabot, the "official" Witch of Salem. She and other Salem Witches have often said, "You can walk the streets of Salem in a black robe and pentagram and feel totally safe. That's because for thirteen years we've been on the front lines every day as public Witches."

Some people noted that even anthropologists use the term *witch* negatively and that the word has bad connotations among many tribal peoples. Others told me, "Look, the word 'Witch' is not a word from us, it was given to us by 'you know who.' The word doesn't cut it. Leave the past to the past." This is very similar to something Isaac Bonewits once said: "Maybe Gerald Gardner and Doreen Valiente made a mistake when they used the word to describe what they were doing, because the creative seed they planted that blossomed into the Neo-Pagan movement had nothing to do with anything that had been called 'Witch' in the English language before."

There's another problem. For most people, the word *witch* means someone with magical powers—and not the kind of "power from within" that people such as Starhawk are talking about. There is also the dilemma that not even everybody in the Craft means the same thing by the term *witch*. For some, it's a specific initiatory religion, for others it is something that happened to them the magical moment someone looked them in the eye and said, "Thou Art Goddess, baby . . . This is it!"

Many of those who felt uncomfortable with the word *witch* said they felt more comfortable with "Pagan" or "Wiccan" or "Shaman." Many said they believed in using it "privately with people I trust," but "judiciously with outsiders." While a great number of feminist Witches say the term is essential and necessary, a great number of Witches from English traditions say "abandon the name." One man wrote, "I don't think 'Wicca' is such a good term either. Too many nuts using the name. And I resent non-British traditionalists using 'Wicca.'" Another man from a British tradition said flat out, "Witch refers to a rather specific class of English or British traditional religion. There was a north central tribe called the Hwicea around the eighth century. Feminist Witchcraft with a Goddess and no God is not Witchcraft." The problem with this position, even were it reasonable, is that there are only a few thousand British traditional Witches in the United States—ten thousand at the most. The number of people who understand the word *witch* in a Jungian, archetypal sense and who feel the word's connection with the hidden, primal forces of nature probably number in the millions. That is why, in the end, the arguments against the word *witch* are usually tactical, and the arguments for the word *witch* are usually spiritual. The arguments against the word are never quite able to counter the deep feelings expressed by those who consider the word a part of their essence.

After I facilitated a workshop discussing this topic at a Pagan festival, an essay by a woman named Oreithyia arrived in the mail.

> I am not a Pagan; I am a Witch. And for many, many of us, Uncle Gerald and Aunt Doreen have nothing at all to do with how or why we are Witches.
>
> Over the last ten years there have been women who have cast the circle, howled at the moon, danced the Spiral, invoked the Goddess in her myriad forms; women who have gathered together in groups of three or three hundred to celebrate the turn of the seasons; to pour handfuls of rich, brown earth over a map of nuclear waste dumps, missile silos, and power plants.
>
> Women who have sat together, pained and fierce, calling the wind, asking Her aid, sweeping up, in great gentle swirls the dirt and degradation and fear clinging to the woman in that circles' center, the woman who, three days

before, had been attacked on the mid-afternoon country roadside as she jogged along. Again and again the wind came up, the house fairly sang with the force of it moving through the gaps in the clapboard siding; the women sang the wind's song to add to their strength. It was a howl of pain, a howl of mourning. It moved and grew. It became a song of fury, an Amazon battle call, the sound of the sacred axe swung round and round to turn the tide. The sound, and the constant evocation, invocation, incantation of the one who, for this night, in this place, for this purpose, wrapped herself in indigo, taking on the mask of the Dark Mother. Together, the Wind and the Women and the Dark One, together they lifted off layer upon layer of filth. Together they called to the woman who was its center, together they forged the fury and the love that coursed through the pain, transforming what had been rendered numb back into wholeness and self-respect.

What had been broken they began to heal. The power for the healing rested where it belonged, in the person of she who must be healed. The work was half done. Now was the Contract recalled. "Whatever you do shall return to you, threefold." They called the wind anew; called and envisioned the pain that had been inflicted, the fear that had been created, the self-loathing that the attempted rape had birthed. They watched all these twine, furious, in the air. They sent it whipping around, faster and faster, repeating the Contract, chanting the Law with each spin. Spinning her hand in time to the chants, gathering that other darkness to her, the Dark One rose.

"We know not who he is," she called, "or where he makes his home." Her whole body swaying, now with the energy she sought to contain, to focus, she turned slowly, looked deeply into the eyes of every woman in the room. Seeking the group will. Had even one faltered, she was to re-direct the storm, send it howling out to the open sea, bringing harm to none. They had agreed to this.

But there was not one who turned away, not one who did not meet her gaze. The storm had begun in another's hands, in another's mind, another's action. The storm belonged to him.

And, beginning now to echo the voice of the storm, holding the heart of the storm in the palm of one hand, she held the fury high, high above her own head, ". . . aaiiieeee . . . Aiieee . . . AAAIIIEEEEEEEE . . ." and spinning, cast the storm back to the winds, sending it down the mountain to find its home.

"Home!" she charged, "home to the one who called you! We recall the Contract. Let the results of his acts rest not with this woman, but in his own life. Let the self-hate, and the fear, and the pain find their true home. We ask for nothing beyond what is just. Only let him understand, at some time, in some way, that his actions cannot be disconnected from their results."

The ritual went on a while longer. There was tea for the woman in the center, and soft, strong arms to hold her. More than one breast to rest against. More than one set of hands to rub her back, massage her shoulders, catch her tears, see her safely to sleep.

None of these women have ever considered what they did as arising from anything beyond the wisdom they find in their own Woman's soul. They, we, have found our roots in the great Mother Tree, looking back through our own, our Women's heritage. We look to the Amazons of Scythia and Dahamey, we look to the names we find buried in forest and desert and ocean; names found in the ashes. Sometimes they are the names of Goddesses, sometimes they become names of Goddesses. Sometimes, the names are our own. We look, most important of all, into each others lives. We ask ". . . what does the world look like when I sing the Goddess in my heart . . . ?" and then act, whenever we can, from that place. And it is from that place we define ourselves as Witches. Pagan is a word that some of our kin, for a variety of excellent reasons, have chosen to use. It is not the word we choose.

Within this context, Uncle Gerald and Aunt Doreen may be perceived as distant family. Some of us go and visit. Some of us never do. Sometimes the ones who visit return home with stories of what our cousins are up to; how it is sometimes so familiar and sometimes so foreign. Often we return having learned something. Often we have taught something.

I continue to enjoy the improved trust and communication between groups of us, Pagans, Witches, Shamans, Wicce. I continue to relish what makes us different. I enjoy the visits and honor the lessons. But there is no question that we come to some of the same places along different routes. And for many of us, the word "Witch" speaks less about how we do what we do, and more about the fire inside.

Appendix II

Rituals

Space limitations prevent me from reprinting many of the beautiful and varied rituals and poems that modern Pagans have written in the last ten years. I include five here. They may give you some idea of this literature.

*Woman-Charms: A Litany**
by Morgan McFarland

I AM THE WHITE DOE WHO SEVEN TIMES FLEES.

I am pure and fleet, for I know that capture is Death to my Soul.

I AM A GREY FLOOD UPON WHICH THE BOAT IS TOSSED.

I ebb, and I flood, and my water is uneasy.

I AM A VIOLENT WIND THAT STIRS THE DEPTHS.

I rise up in anger from my uneasy slumber.

I AM A SUN-SPIKE RIPPING THROUGH THE CLOUDS.

I shall give forth the pure ray of reality.

I AM A BIRD OF PREY WHO PROTECTS HER BROOD.

I am cunning and canny and give shelter to my children.

I BRING FORTH TERROR AS THE NIGHT-CROW.

I guard the boundaries and seek the enemy from his corners.

I AM DENSE SMOKE AND HEAVY FIRE.

I cloud the reason of Man and elevate she who would brave my flame.

I AM THE FIRE-FORGED SWORD WHOSE BLADE IS BLOOD-TEMPERED.

I am the Amazon who never wounds, but destroys the usurper, row upon row.

* Part of an unpublished manuscript of rites for women.

I AM WISER THAN THE CIRCLING SALMON WITHIN THE HOLY POOL.

I am the hazel nut that feeds the Wicce and spells the lore in her ear.

I AM THE VARIECOLOURED SNAKE WHO CROWNS THE HILL OF INSPIRATION.

I inflict the deadly sting upon the heavy-footed and uninspired.

I AM THE THICKET THAT WILL HIDE NEITHER THE BOAR NOR THE ROEBUCK.

I am the Daughter who wields the spear of the Sacred Name.

I AM A TIDE MORE VIOLENT THAN ITS WAVES SPEAK.

I am the terror in the shingle's rattle against the crumbling cliffs.

I AM THE SEA WAVES WHOSE CREST IS BRILLIANT FOAM.

I shall not be stopped, and I shall ceaselessly eat away the enemy shore.

WHO KNOWS THE SECRETS OF THE UNHEWN DOLMEN?

I, who am Woman: for its stones are my living, and its portal, my heart.

I, who am Woman: for I am the structure that opens to give Life passage.

I, who am Woman: for I am also the door that takes Life into Death.

I AM PRIESTESS AND WOMAN.

I am my Mother's Daughter.

Litany of the Earth-Mother*

O Earth-Mother, Thou of uncounted names and faces, Thou of the many-faceted Nature in and above All, Nature Incarnate, Love and Life fulfilled; look favorably upon this place, grace us with Your Presence, inspire and infuse us with Your powers; by all the names by which You have been known, O Earth-Mother:

COME UNTO US.

Thou Whom the Druids call Danu—

COME UNTO US.

Thou Who art Erde of the Germans—

* From the Hasidic Druids of North America (HDNA); published in *The Druid Chronicles (Evolved)*, ed. Isaac Bonewits (Berkeley: Drunemeton Press, 1976).

COME UNTO US.
 Thou Whom the Slavs call Ziva—
 Thou Who art Nerthus of the Vanir—
 Thou Whom the Poles call Marzyana—
 Thou Who art Frigga of the Aesir—
 Thou Whom the Romans call Terra—
 Thou Who art Diana to the Etruscans—
 Thou Whom the Persians call Kybele—
 Thou Who art Iphimedeia, Mighty Queen of the Greeks—
 Thou Whom the Egyptians call Nuit, Star Mother—
 Thou Who art Ninmah of Sumeria—
 Thou Whom the Hittites call Kubala—
 Thou Who art Mami-Aruru of Babalon—
 Thou Whom the Caanites call Arsai—
 Thou Who art Our Lady of Biblos in far Phonicia—
 Thou Whom the children of Crete call Mountain Mother—
 Thou Who art Yemanja of the Umbanda—
 Thou Whom the Dahomeans call Erzulie—
 Thou Who art Shakti and Parvati of India—
 Thou Whom the Tibeteans call Green Tara—
 Thou Who art Kwanyin of China—
 Thou Whom the Nipponese call Izanami—
 Thou Who art Sedna and Nerivik of the Eskimos—
 Thou Whom the Pawnee call Uti-Hiata—
 Thou Who art Cornmother of the Plains—
 Thou Whom the Navaho call Estanatlehi—
 Thou Who art Ometeotl and Guadalupe in Mexico—
 Thou Whom the Islanders call Hina-alu-oka-moana—
 Thou Who art the Great Mother, the Star Goddess, the All
  Creating One—
 Mother of All, we call upon You—
 Terra Mater, Mater Sotier, Earth-Mother—
COME UNTO US!

Self Blessing*

This ritual should be performed during the new moon, but it is not
limited to that phase. Need, not season, determines the performance.

There is real power in the Self Blessing; it should not be used other than in time of need and should not be done promiscuously.

The purpose of the ritual is to bring the individual into closer contact with the Godhead. It can also be used as a minor dedication, when a person who desires dedication has no one who can dedicate him. This self blessing ritual may also be used as a minor exorcism, to banish any evil influences which may have formed around the person. It may be performed by any person upon himself, and at his desire.

Perform the ritual in a quiet place, free from distractions, and nude. You will need the following:

1. Salt, about one quarter teaspoon.
2. Wine, about an ounce.
3. Water, about one-half ounce.
4. Candle, votive or other.

The result of the ritual is a feeling of peace and calm. It is desirable that the participant bask in the afterglow so that he may meditate and understand that he has called the attention of the Godhead to himself, asking to grow closer to the Godhead in both goals and in wisdom.

When you are ready to begin, sprinkle the salt on the floor and stand on it, lighting the candle. Let the warmth of the candle be absorbed into the body. Mix the water into the wine, meditating upon your reasons for performing the self blessing.

Read the following aloud:

BLESS ME, MOTHER, FOR I AM YOUR CHILD.

Dip the fingers of the right hand into the mixed water and wine and anoint the eyes,

BLESSED BE MY EYES THAT I MAY SEE YOUR PATH.

Anoint the nose,

BLESSED BE MY NOSE, THAT I MAY BREATHE YOUR ESSENCE.

Anoint the mouth,

* This was written by Ed Fitch in the late 1960s, and designed to be an introductory ritual for those who are searching and investigating the Pagan path.

BLESSED BE MY MOUTH THAT I MAY SPEAK OF YOU.

Anoint the breast,

BLESSED BE MY BREAST, THAT I MAY BE FAITHFUL IN MY WORK.

Anoint the loins,

BLESSED BE MY LOINS, WHICH BRING FORTH THE LIFE OF MEN AND
WOMEN AS YOU HAVE BROUGHT FORTH ALL CREATION.

Anoint the feet,

BLESSED BE MY FEET, THAT I MAY WALK IN YOUR WAYS.

Remain . . . and meditate for a while.

Pagan Ritual for General Use*

A circle should be marked on the floor, surrounding those who will
participate in the ceremony. An altar is to be set up at the center of
the circle. At the center of the altar shall be placed an image of the
Goddess, and an incense burner placed in front of it. Behind the
image should be a wand fashioned from a willow branch. Candles
should be set upon the altar . . . a total of five, since one is to be set at
each quarter and one will remain on the altar during the rite.

When all the people are prepared they shall assemble within the
circle. The woman acting as priestess shall direct the man who acts
as priest to light the candles and incense. She shall then say:

The presence of the noble Goddess extends everywhere.
Throughout the many strange, magical,
And beautiful worlds.
To all places of wilderness, enchantment, and freedom.

She then places a candle at the north and pauses to look outwards,
saying:

The Lady is awesome.
The Powers of death bow before Her.

The person closest to the east takes a candle from the altar and
places it at that quarter, saying:

* Another introductory ritual by Ed Fitch.

Our Goddess is a Lady of Joy.
The winds are Her servants.

The person closest to the south takes a candle from the altar and places it at that quarter, saying:

Our Goddess is a Goddess of Love.
At Her blessings and desire
The sun brings forth life anew.

The person closest to the west takes a candle from the altar and places it at that quarter, saying:

The seas are the domains of our Serene Lady.
The mysteries of the depths are Hers alone.

The priest now takes the wand, and starting at the north, draws it along the entire circle clockwise back to the north point, saying:

The circle is sealed, and all herein
Are totally and completely apart
From the outside world,
That we may glorify the Lady whom we adore.
Blessed Be!

All repeat: Blessed Be!

The priest now holds the wand out in salute towards the north for a moment and then hands it to the priestess, who also holds it out in salute. She motions to the group to repeat the following lines after her:

As above, so below . . .
As the universe, so the soul.
As without, so within.
Blessed and gracious one,
On this day do we consecrate to you
Our bodies,
Our minds,
And our spirits.
Blessed Be!

Now is the time for discussion and teaching. Wine and light refreshments may be served. When the meeting has ended, all will stand and silently meditate for a moment. The priestess will then take the wand and tap each candle to put it out, starting at the north and going clockwise about the circle, while saying:

> Our rite draws to its end.
> O lovely and gracious Goddess,
> Be with each of us as we depart.

> The circle is broken!

Beltane Ritual (May 1)*

I

Spiral-circle dance.

II

First priestess: (*Casts circle.*) The heaviness of winter has ended. Let us rejoice in the budding Earth and the beauty of the Maiden now ascendant. (*Lights altar candles and incense.*) We light the Beltane fires and celebrate the fertile warmth and light of our Lord and the renewed and renewing powers of light, energy, and love that are our Lady of May.

III

Second priestess: We celebrate the fragrant spring air, the soft May breezes that refresh the Earth and Her children.

First priestess: We celebrate the gentle fire of the sun in spring, whose caressing warmth awakens the Earth and Her children.

Third priestess: We celebrate the cool, damp spring rains, those sparkling showers that give sustenance to the Earth and Her children.

Fourth priestess: We celebrate the Earth. In the full bloom of Her maidenhood, She gives life to all of Her children.

---

* This ritual took place on Beltane, 1978, in Central Park in New York City. The four priestesses were members of a group called Manhattan Pagan Way. They wrote the ritual. About thirty-five people attended. This exemplifies the kind of spring ritual a group of city Pagans might attempt.

IV

Third priestess: O source of joy and love, O Goddess of all beginnings, come and join us, for this is the season of new growth. O
Lady of May, refresh our senses, make us whole, replenish the
earth.

Second priestess: At the equinox, I awakened. Then I had the power
to melt the winter. But now I am in the fullness of my maidenhood, and I am wild with joy!

See how the buds burst into bloom. See how all of my animal
creatures are drawn together in love and pleasure. Feel how my
beauty tempts you all to forget your daily chores and celebrate
with me.

Drink in this season fully, for my maidenhood is fleeting, and it
will seem to you as if it were only an instant, and then it will be
gone. The heavy heat of the summer will be on you, and I will be
the Great Mother once again.

V

First priestess: (*Displays wine.*) We celebrate the dizzying sweetness
of the spring that now blossoms around us. Bless this, our offering
of May Wine, and as we taste its fullness, teach us to sow your
seeds in love and joy.

Fourth priestess: (*Displays bread and sprouts.*) We celebrate the cycle
of life renewed. From seed to bud to flower to fruit to seed. A perfect circle. These are the beads of Her necklace! (*People in center
share, then take wine, bread and sprouts around circle.*)

VI

Third priestess: Now, as the warm spring renews the Earth and our
lives, let's remember how our predecessors celebrated Beltane.
The hearth fire of each home would be extinguished. Then the
whole community would gather for a festival. As the celebration
ended, each householder would take home some coals from the
communal bonfire, to rekindle the hearth at home.

First priestess: Hearth fire is not forest fire. The dangerous is made
domestic by skill and experience.

Hearth fire cooked their food and warmed their homes. It stood
for safety and comfort. It still represents the warmth of the

heart—the friendship and caring that come from the center of the person.

Hearth fire is simple, familiar, unspectacular. It is the polar opposite of fireworks. Safety, comfort, friendship. Love "to the level of every day's most quiet need, by sun and candle light."

Fourth priestess: The winter strained us. The city was bleak and gray. The cold was painful. We wrapped our bodies and pulled in our senses. We got through.

Now, in the softness and beauty of spring, we shed the layers of clothing from our bodies and open our senses again. Together, today, we pool the warmth of our joy in the spring. We will take a portion of our shared warmth home with us, to renew our everyday lives.

VII

Cauldron dance, to "The Lady's Branle" or "She will bring the buds of spring," music traditional, words by Hope, published in Songs for the Old Religion.

VIII

Second priestess: We thank you for the flourishing of new life and for the feast of spring that is the freshness of your presence. Blessed be!

The circle is ended. Merry meet, merry part.

Appendix III

Resources

CURRENT NEWSLETTERS AND JOURNALS

The Pagan Movement is fast-changing and always in flux. Some of the journals listed below may be defunct; some may be located at new addresses. Please send a self-addressed, stamped envelope (SASE) with your inquiry.

What do you do when confronted with more than one hundred journals? Well there are many strategies you can follow. Here are a few suggestions. Send for sample copies of a few that sound interesting. Subscribe to a few of the journals that have a lot of dialogue and controversy. While the quality of these magazines changes, at the time I am writing this, *Panegyria, The Georgian Newsletters,* and *Harvest* have been filled with debate. You might want to subscribe to *Circle Network News,* the prime Pagan networking journal; you might first want to look for journals in your region of the country; or you might want to look for journals that focus on your area of greatest interest: feminism, Druidism, and so on.

If you come across this book after 1989, these listings will be more than three years old. One thing you might consider doing to obtain more current information is writing for the *Circle Guide to Pagan Resources.* Circle is an international resource center of nature spirituality, located near Madison, Wisconsin. Every year or two, Circle publishes a fine guide to Pagan groups, periodicals, musicians, artists, and suppliers. Its guide is more comprehensive than the one here, although some of the listings are different in each. Send an SASE for current price to Circle, P.O. Box 219, Mt. Horeb, Wisconsin 53572. You can also write to me (Margot Adler, P.O. Box 20182, Cathedral Station, New York, New York 10025-9992), since I plan to keep abreast of new developments.

Akwesasne Notes. "A Journal for Native and Natural Peoples." Published five times a year. No fixed subscription price, but donations requested. This is an extremely important journal detailing the struggles of indigenous and traditional peoples both in this country and around the world. Articles on the values of religious traditionalism, political and ecological battles, and the fight to retain native lands. Address: Mohawk Nation, via Rooseveltown, New York 13683.

All My Relations. A Pagan newsletter for the Turtle Island Community. Articles, seasonal observance, celebrating the rainbow bridge which connects European and Native American traditions. Published eight times a year. Subscription: $5/year. Address: *All My Relations*, General Delivery, Milner, British Columbia VOX ITO Canada.

All Ways Free. A free networking magazine published by people connected to the Rainbow Family of Living Light. It acts as a forum for the sharing of heartsongs, dreams, visions, and the realization of peace; gives updates on the events of the world; it seeks to bring about increased awareness about difficulties and problems facing the planet, as well as potential solutions, progress, accomplishments. "We have chosen not to sell *All Ways Free*, or any space within it. Instead it flies on love, energy, money, and materials freely given. With this process we hope to bring about a shared vision of love, peace, justice, and freedom, through a strong, broad, common unity." Articles, letters, poems. Many articles about native struggles and prisoner's rights. Address: *All Ways Free*, P.O. Box 3433, Ann Arbor, Michigan 48106-3433.

Ancient Ways. "Ireland's Pagan Alternative Magazine." Articles, editorials, letters, poetry, magic, herb lore, seasonal celebrations, sacred sites. 75p/issue. Write for current subscription price. Address: *Ancient Ways*, c/o The Alchemist's Head Bookshop, 10 East Essex St., Dublin 2, Ireland.

Annals of Earth. A publication of Ocean Arks International and the Lindisfarne Association. A continuation and extension of the *Annals of Earth Stewardship* and of the *Lindisfarne Letters.* Ocean Arks was incorporated in 1982 to disseminate the ideas and practice of ecological sustainability throughout the world. Lindisfarne, founded in 1972, is dedicated to fostering "the emergence of a new global culture." The journal is essentially a coming together of the work of William Irwin Thompson (Lindisfarne) and John and Nancy Todd (New Alchemy Institute). The journal has a biological perspective and stresses appropriate technology. Articles on philosophy, ecological problems and solutions. Subscription: $10/year, tax deductible contribution to either Ocean Arks International or the Lindisfarne Association, Inc. Address: *Annals of Earth*, 10 Shanks Pond Road, Falmouth, Massachusetts 02540.

Arachne. A magazine published by the Matriarchy Research and Reclaim Network (MRRN), a network of women exploring spirituality and doing research. Address: *Arachne*, c/o A Woman's Place, Hungerford House, Victoria Embankment, London WC2 England.

Awen. "A new magazine of Keltic-Pagan poetry." Named after the primal Kymraeg Goddess for poetic inspiration, the magazine is devoted to publishing the rich stream of modern-day Celtic and Pagan poetry. Published by Kaledon Naddair, who publishes *Inner Keltia.* $5 for each issue. Address: Kaer Eidyn, 8 Annandale Street, Edinburgh, EH7 4AN, Alban (Scotland).

The Bard. A hereditary-Welsh journal of Celtic religion. Published to coincide with the four Celtic festivals by the Annwn Temple of Gwynfyd. The journal and the Temple are concerned with the presentation of a family-based Celtic religion. "We do not pretend to practice ancient Celtic religion—only Celtic religion as it survived as folk religion. Our main focus, then, is the presentation of our family religion's teachings, beliefs, practices, while showing how they evolved and their basis in ancient Celtic belief. . . . We conceive our journal as a traditional Celtic publication. . . . We are not neo-Pagans and our journal is not a neo-Pagan creation. It is a traditional Pagan publication; we consider ourselves traditional Celtists (Our family religion is called, by us, *Celtism*)." Celtic history, lore, poetry, rituals, festivals. Subscriptions: $9/year in U.S. and Canada; $12/year foreign airmail (U.S. funds or U.S. money order only); $3.50 for sample copy. Checks payable to: R. A. DeVowe. Address: Annwn Temple of Gwynfyd, 5102 N. 16th Dr., Lot #3, Phoenix, Arizona 85015.

The Beltane Papers (TBP). "A Journal of Women's Spirituality and Thealogy," and *TBP*'s *Octava*. *The Beltane Papers* is published four times a year and *Octava*, the seasonal newsletter supplement, comes out eight times yearly. Articles, letters, scholarship, art, poetry, dreams, magical journeys. This is an amazingly wonderful, beautifully produced and well-written journal oriented toward women's spirituality. Each cover could be framed, and there is much wisdom within the pages. "We focus on women's religion and try to uncover, to grasp, what that really is, or could be. That search necessitates inquiries into the history of women's religions (but for 'history' read also archaeology, anthropology-gynopology-myth, arts, literature, etc.). We feel that our material must range from the scholarly (footnotes and bibs, so information can be traced back to sources—very important) to the experiential to the creative/artistic. Our deepest concern is the psychic empowerment of women, which we believe will inevitably result in a rebalancing of the feminine/masculine principles in the world." The journal is dedicated to "Aphrodite of the Warm Eyes and to Diana of the Compassionate Arms." Subscriptions: $10/year; $18/two years; $20/ foreign or first class; samples—*TBP* $2.50 and *Octava* $1.25. Editors: Helen G. Farias and Judith G. Maxwell. Produced by the New Moon Collective. Address: P.O. Box 8, Clear Lake, Washington 98235.

Boreas. A newsletter of Northern European Heathenism. Articles, reviews, graphics, news; often scholarly, seldom solemn. Published approximately twice a year by Oak and Ash and Thorn. Subscription: $6 for four issues; $2 for sample issue. Address: *Boreas*, P.O. Box 1182, New Haven, Connecticut 06505.

The Broomstick. A bimonthly national feminist political journal by, for, and about women over forty. Articles, news, poetry, art, networking, letters. "A magazine of older women's personal experiences and positive images of ourselves and our struggles; a network of over-forty women taking a stand against ageism and sexism and developing our understanding of our lives. We repossess the BROOMSTICK as a symbol of our strength and unity. It stands for many aspects of our lives and interests: SKILLS—homemaking and paid jobs; CHANGE—the new broom sweeps clean; POWER—the witch flies on the broom; HEALING—witches were the ancient healers; CONFRONTATION—exposing what society calls ugliness." Subscriptions: $15/year; $20/year in Canada (U.S. funds); $25/year overseas; $3.50 for sample copy. Address: *Broomstick*, 3543 18th St., San Francisco, California 94110.

Brothersong. A Journal for the Brothers of the Earth. A bi-yearly journal which explores and celebrates men's mysteries and positive male energy. Brothers of the Earth and its journal is "for gentle, yet strong, caring, and changing men who acknowledge and celebrate their connection to the Earth/Nature—to each other, to women/ mothers, sisters, friends, lovers, daughters, and to children, and all other living things." Brothers of the Earth is open to males of all ages, cultures, and sexual orientations who are interested in exploring, creating, and celebrating a positive male, earth-centered, and life-affirming spirituality. The *Brothersong* is published at the Winter and Summer solstices. *Brothersong* appears as a bulletin on the remaining six Sabbats. Subscriptions: $20/year for journal and bulletins in U.S. and Canada; $25/year overseas; $5.00 for a single issue (bulletin $1.50). Checks payable to Brothers of the Earth. Address: Brothers of the Earth, P.O. Box 13158, Minneapolis, Minnesota 55414.

Caer Rhiannon Newsletter. A Pagan and Craft newsletter for networking, training, and support, serving the greater Riverside–San Bernardino–Pomona Valley area of southern California. Many subscribers are solitary Pagans and Witches. Articles, poetry, original rituals, magic, Pagan parenting, reviews, seasonal notes. One of the persons involved with Caer Rhiannon is Ed Fitch, who was very instrumental in the early Craft revival in this country. Caer Rhiannon also sponsors two university-based Pagan groves, one at Riverside City College and one at U.C. Riverside. Published four times a year. Subscription: $6/year. Checks payable to Jo Ann Adams. Address: Caer Rhiannon, P.O. Box 5261, Riverside, California 92517.

Cainteanna na Luise. A quarterly journal of modern Druidic arts. "The concern of *CnL* is the multiplicity and mutability of reality, linked with ancient Celtic mythopoetica. *CnL* believes that most 'druidism' today has nothing to do with ancient form, but that much can be learned by going to scholars and Irish sources. *CnL* emphasizes the study of Irish (Gaelige), as a thaumaturgic—liturgical language, believing a person's language determines his/her reality." Articles, linguistic discussion, book reviews. 16–24 pages. Subscriptions: $9/ year in U.S. and Canada; $11/year overseas; sample issue: $3 in the U.S.; $4 elsewhere. Checks must be made out to John Kellnhauser. Address: *Cainteanna na Luise*, 805-85 Wellesley East, Toronto, Ontario, M4Y 1H8, Canada.

The Cauldron. "An independent pagan journal of the Old Religion founded in 1976." Articles on Wicca, Paganism, earth mysteries, sacred sites, book reviews, history, festivals. This is one of the most respected British Craft publications. The journal is dedicated to presenting a broad spectrum of Pagan belief. It has a wide readership throughout the Pagan movement. Published four times a year. Subscriptions: £2/year; $6/year in U.S. (bills only). Address: M. A. Howard, 4 Llysonnen Cottages, Llysonnen Road, Carmarthen, Dyfed, SA 33 5ED Wales, United Kingdom.

Changes Journal. "The magazine of Future Magick. Devoted to the experimental study and application of the ancient and modern Spiritual Arts." Its thesis is that "Esoteric Psychology, in all its forms, is the keystone that will enable new age ideas, alternative life styles and technology, and all other facets of the Aquarian Conspiracy to fuse together into the viable, honorable new culture that is our shared dream." A combination of new age, Pagan, and magical ideas. Leary, Wilson, Crowley, mythology, festivals, artwork, announcements. While not specifically Neo-Pagan, it tells philosophers to spend "less time in sterile thinking and more time howling chants around a fire in moonlight," and it tells Pagans to stop pretending to be wizards and spend some time thinking about what that would really mean, "so you would stop being regarded as stupid kooks and instead be regarded as Wise Kooks." Published somewhat erratically, but generally twice yearly. Subscription: $5/ year; $3 for sample copy. Address: *Changes Journal*, P.O. Box 734, State College, Pennsylvania 16801.

Changing Men. A journal devoted to issues in gender, sex, and politics. This magazine was formerly called *M. gentle men for gender justice*. It is a publication committed to a new vision of masculinity and to "an anti-sexist politics which envisions a world free of sexism, racism, militarism and economic exploitation." Articles, poetry, reviews, letters, fiction, a directory of men's groups. Well produced and well written. A recent issue had serious articles on men and war, rape, jocks within the men's movement, "the third gender," androgyny, as well as a beautiful retelling of the Theseus myth. Published three times a year. Subscription: $16 for four issues. Address: *Changing Men*, 306 N. Brooks St., Madison, Wisconsin 53715.

The Changling Times. A sporadic neophilic journal in the Discordian tradition. Not exclusively Pagan, but earth religions, space exploration, Leary, Crowley, new age, and magical subjects. Articles, fiction, poetry, events. Published occasionally. Address: *Changling Times*, A.C.E., 1643 Lee Road, #9, Cleveland Heights, Ohio 44118.

Children of the Earth. A newsletter by/for/about Pagan families. Subscription: $5 for four issues. Published on irregular schedule. Participation encouraged. Address: P.O. Box 116, Berkeley Springs, West Virginia 25441-0116.

Circle Network News. One of the largest, best, and best-known Pagan newspapers—filled with articles, rituals, illustrations, invocations, contacts, news, photos, herbal formulas, reviews, magical development exercises, chants, and other material contributed by network members. Emphasis on Wicca, shamanism, Goddess-worship, positive magic, and related Pantheistic ways. Published quarterly. At this point Circle can lay claim to being the largest, most visible, and most important Pagan networking organization around. Circle has taken on the responsibility for being a contact center for Pagan folk throughout the United States and around the world. Subscriptions: $9/year bulk mail in U.S.; $13/year first class in U.S. and Canada; $17 airmail elsewhere (U.S. funds); $3 for sample copy. Address: *Circle*, Box 219, Mt. Horeb, Wisconsin 53572.

Clothed With The Sun. The quarterly journal of clothes-optional living. This is not a Pagan magazine, although it has included sympathetic articles on Wicca and feminist spirituality. Naturist philosophy, with its attitude that the natural, naked body is beautiful and healthy, seems to connect with Pagan ideas. A glossy magazine, 80–100 pages with photographs, articles, an updated guide to nude beaches and recreation, legal battles, and many surprises. Did you know there is a whole community in France, even a bank and a grocery store, where you can go nude? Did you know there's a nude Christian church? Subscription: $18/year; $5 for single copy. Address: The Naturists, Inc., P.O. Box 132, Oshkosh, Wisconsin 54902.

Converging Paths. A newsletter focusing on the traditional ways of Wicca, its roots and current directions. Published four times a year. Articles, rituals, poetry, columns. Membership: $13/year. The newsletter also facilitates *The Rowan Exchange*, a Pagan letter exchange, confidential contacts forwarding service. Membership: $9/year. Address: *Converging Paths*, P.O. Box 63, Mt. Horeb, Wisconsin 53572.

Council of the Magickal Arts. A quarterly Craft journal containing articles, poetry, herbalism, humor, magic, news, reviews, and announcements related to the Council. Subscriptions: $7/year; $2 per issue; $13/year for membership in the Council which includes the newsletters. Send SASE for membership information and a copy of the bylaws. Address: *Council of the Magickal Arts*, 5920 Bissonnet #113, Houston, Texas 77081.

Covenant of the Goddess Newsletter. Published eight times a year on the Sabbats. Articles, poetry, announcements, humor, rituals. Subscriptions: free to members; $15/year donation for non-members. Address: *COG*, P.O. Box 1226, Berkeley, California 94704.

Cultural Survival Quarterly. A magazine that since 1976 has addressed issues of both immediate and long-term concern to indigenous peoples throughout the world. Seeks to inform and stimulate action on behalf of tribal people and ethnic minorities. This is the best source for any modern Pagan to find out about the destruction of indigenous Pagan societies on this planet. Well produced, complex, and detailed articles, 70–100 pages. Subscriptions: $3 for a single issue; $20 for membership (which includes magazine). Address: Cultural Survival, 11 Divinity Ave., Cambridge, Massachusetts 02138.

Dawntreader. A Pagan journal published very occasionally by the Children of the Dawn. Address: P.O. Box 6245, Albuquerque, New Mexico 87197-6254.

Dragonsmoke. The annual offering of the Church of the Dragon, published by Two Wolves Press, a publishing house which "exists to further the evolution of the new age and light, love and laughter." One of its ads proclaims: "It's *Green Egg*, *The Equinox*, and the *Village Voice* all in one." A complex, large journal, wonderfully produced, with beautiful graphics. Each issue is bound, signed, and numbered. Articles on Witchcraft, Thelema, fantasy, nature, Cthudhu, magic, philosophy. Also poetry and art. Organizations connected to *Dragonsmoke* include Coven of the Dragon, a hereditary Craft tradition made up of only blood-related members: Dragonhenge Sanctuary, a non-profit organization working toward the creation of a metaphysical center and wildlife sanctuary. Subscription: $10 an issue. Editor: Tiffany Yvonne St. Moonstar. Please enclose SASE with all inquiries. Address: *Dragonsmoke*, P.O. Box 65, Mt. View, California 94042.

A Druid Missal-Any. The publication of the Reformed Druids of North America (RDNA). News, articles on the festivals and on various aspects of Druidism, ancient and current. Published eight times a year on the Druid High Days. Subscription: $3.50/year. Address: Bodfish, P.O. Box 142, Orinda, California 94563.

The Druids' Progress. The journal of Ar nDraiocht Fein ("Our own Druidism") edited by P. E. I. Bonewits. Scholarly emphasis. Bonewits is creating a Pan-European reconstructionist tradition of Neo-Pagan Druidism. The journal is opinionated, intellectual, fascinating. The organization is hierarchical—or at least not democratic to the point of overthrowing the Archdruid (Bonewits) himself—but really good for people searching for a structured form of study on the Druidic path. Discusses beliefs, linguistics, training, history, research, art, music, ritual. Subscription: $20 for four issues minimum donation (Canada $30; overseas $40). All subscriptions start with the first issue. Checks payable to P. E. I. Bonewits. Address: P.O. Box 9398, Berkeley, California 94709.

Earth First! The Radical Environmental Journal. Not specifically Pagan, but militant earth consciousness. Earth First! is a direct-action environmental group working to develop a biocentric worldview and to preserve natural diversity. Earth First! believes not only that it is not enough to preserve what wilderness remains but that roads must be closed, clearcuts rehabilitated, dams torn down, and extirpated species like the grizzly and wolf reintroduced, in order to recover the natural diversity and empowering spirit of Earth. The journal is an independent entity within the broader Earth First! movement. The structure of Earth First! is anarchistic. It uses confrontation and direct action and civil disobedience to fight for wild places. It believes that most of the environmental movement was co-opted in the 1970s and continues to accept an anthropocentric worldview. In contrast, Earth First! works to develop a "new bio-centric paradigm: Deep Ecology." Published eight times a year (on the Sabbats). Subscriptions: $15/year; $25/year first class; $25/year overseas surface; $40/year overseas airmail. (If you're totally broke, they'll probably send it to you anyway.) Address: *Earth First!*, P.O. Box 5871, Tucson, Arizona 85703.

EarthSong. "A Journal of Earth Awareness and Magickal Spirituality." A quarterly journal in newspaper format with emphasis on the arts, scholarship, anthropology, tribal cultures, magical practice, ecology, Pagan parenting, rites, and customs. Also poetry, reviews, and resources. Subscriptions: $10/year U.S. bulk mail; $14/year U.S. first class; $18/year overseas airmail; $4 per sample issue. Checks payable to *EarthSong*. I've seen one terrific issue of this journal. Address: EarthSong Publications, P.O. Box 5628, Baltimore, Maryland 21210.

Environmental Ethics. A scholarly journal with lively debates on the philosophical aspects of environmental problems, often focusing on issues such as ecology, religion, public policy, animal rights, wilderness and species preservation. Subscription: $18/year for four issues. Address: *Environmental Ethics*, Department of Philosophy, University of Georgia, Athens, Georgia 30602.

Faerie Fire. "A Journal for the Ancient Pagan Warrior Tradition as Revolutionary Activism." A radical political/spiritual synthesis. The editors write that the spirit of the ancient warrior tradition "has been too long ignored by those in the new pagan underculture, and this has led to an unbalanced approach to our role as pagans in this age. We are realists and revolutionaries, not romantic adventurers, and thus do we found an activist nucleus around which a true warrior society can coalesce. Our name (Faerie Fire—a shifting, elusive light seen over fens and desolate places at night) implies recognition of the world-historical defeats sustained by those who led Europeans in the ancient ways of humanity at the hands of emerging patriarchal imperialism: we have been reduced to but a shadow of our former power and influence. But the tide has turned, and though we are still a shadow, we are now a shadow of the future rather than of the past. . . . And that which we are a shadow of remains the same—the Spirit of Life, which is resistance to oppression." Leaflets also available on topics ranging from "Who Was Robin Hood?" to "Paganism and Technology." Subscription: free to all who want it. Please send a few postage stamps for each issue, to cover cost of mailing. Address: *Faerie Fire*, c/o Pagansword, St. 432 (Dept. R), 263A West 19th St., New York, New York 10011.

The Faerie Folk Newsletter. A quarterly Wiccan publication published by Lady Eilonwy and the Children of the Moon Grove. The grove is part of Y Tylwyth Teg (The Faerie Folk), an ancient Welsh tradition. Articles, poetry, rituals, herbs. Subscription: $5/year; $1 for sample copy. Checks payable to Mary Santangelo. Address: *The Faerie Folk Newsletter*, c/o Lady Eilonwy, P.O. Box 100585, Ft. Lauderdale, Florida 33310.

Fifth Estate. A quarterly journal out of Detroit that Sam Wagar (*Pagans for Peace Newsletter*) calls "the very best critique of technology and the technologic worldview" that he's ever seen. It analyses language, technophilia, modern society, and much more. Subscriptions: $5/year in U.S.; $7/year elsewhere. Sample copies available. Address: *Fifth Estate*, Box 02548, Detroit, Michigan 48202.

Forsooth. The newsletter of the East Kingdom Soothsayer's Guild. This publication aims to be quarterly and is published for the members of the Guild and others interested in Forecasting. It is not an official publication of the Society for Creative Anachronism (SCA), but the Guild is an SCA Guild. Subscription: 25 cents per issue. Address: Diccon Frankborn, P.O. Box 589, Bladensburg, Maryland 20710.

Ganymede. The newsletter of the Tayu Center for Gay Spirituality. Published quarterly and mailed free to all who request it. The Tayu Center was founded in 1976 by Daniel Ennis. It is based on the belief that "Gayness represents a necessary role in the universal balance: that of mediation or harmonization between the active and passive forces. Thus Gays play an important part in every human society; and in the spiritual life of humanity as well." A small newsletter with news, announcements, and an opening article or meditation. Address: Tayu Center, P.O. Box 11554, Santa Rosa, California 95406.

Georgian Newsletter. Published monthly by the Georgian Church (Church of Wicca of Bakersfield). Originally founded by the late George Patterson. A very chatty, newsy publication, filled with letters, jokes, communications from members, serious articles mixed with humor, contests, announcements. Many years ago, I thought this was a cute but fairly shallow newsletter, but it has gotten better and better, offering meaty articles and lots of serious news and debate. Subscriptions: $8/year; $16/year overseas surface mail; $32/year foreign air mail. Address: Georgian Church, 1908 Verde, Bakersfield, California 93304.

Gnosis. A journal of the Western Inner Traditions. It was founded to provide a regular forum and resource for people who are exploring the esoteric spiritual and occult traditions of the West. Articles, interviews, and book reviews cover a range from the mystical traditions of the Judaeo-Christian-Islamic matrix to the Hermetic traditions of neoplatonism, magic, freemasonry, alchemy, etc. *Gnosis* is interested in the emerging balance between masculine and feminine in western spirituality as well as in the insights of depth psychology. Published twice a year. Subscriptions: $20 (U.S.) for surface mail; $30 (U.S.) airmail. $5 for sample copy. Foreign orders must be paid by check in U.S. funds drawn on a U.S. bank or by international money order. Address: *Gnosis*, P.O. Box 14217, San Francisco, California 94114.

Goddess Rising. "A journal of Womyn's Spirituality." Published quarterly, at each Solstice and Equinox by Goddess Rising Wicce Shop, for womyn only. The shop describes itself as a "center of matriarchal womyn—identified spirituality" with a focus on Dianic Wicce, ritual, healing, and "rediscovering and reclaiming the Goddess within each of us—our power and strength as womyn." Subscriptions: $5/year; $7/year outside U.S.; $1.25 for sample copy. Free to any womyn in jail or unable to pay. Address: 4006 1st Ave. NE, Seattle, Washington 98105.

The Great Write. quarterly journal of ideas. Emphasis on reflective commentary, Pagan theology, religious poetry, original research, translations of ancient Pagan prayers and theology, media reviews, and humor. Subscription: $6 for four issues; $2 for sample issue. Some back issues available. The journal is mailed in a plain brown wrapper. Address: *The Great Write*, P.O. Box 409024, Chicago, Illinois 60640.

Green Alliance Newsletter. Articles on ecology, land usage, antinuclear activities, women's issues, appropriate technology, Green politics, and an exploration of the spiritual dimension of those subjects. Subscription: $10/year; $2 for sample issue. Address: *Green Alliance Newsletter,* P.O. Box 55, Cooma, Australia.

Green Letter. An educational forum devoted to reporting on the activities of the Green Movement. Lots of news items from various regions. Editor: Jerry Gwathney. Address: *Green Letter,* P.O. Box 9242, Berkeley, California 94709.

Green Line. A wide-ranging discussion magazine from the United Kingdom that focuses on Green issues and philosophy, as they relate to Britain. Subscriptions: 5 pounds for 10 issues; $5.50 overseas. Address: *Green Line,* 34 Cowley Road, Oxford, OX4 1HZ United Kingdom.

Harvest. A Neo-Pagan journal devoted to bringing together the fruits of many traditions and belief systems as well as covering news of interest to the Pagan and Wiccan communities. "Our main theme is Modern Wicca/Neo-Paganism, how it relates to our daily lives; its past, present, and future, and the myriad belief systems, lifestyles, knowledge systems, myths, magicks and discoveries that are a part of this." Articles and letters, herbs, ecology, megalithic sites, tarot, Goddess-worship, poetry, rituals, reviews, recipes, puzzles, networking, art, songs, announcements. It has a particular interest in networking with Pagans west of the Boston area. One of the better Pagan journals, the "one" to get in the Northeast. Published eight times a year since 1980. Subscription: $10/year in U.S. and Canada; $16/year overseas; $2 for a sample copy. Address: P.O. Box 228, S. Framingham, Massachusetts 01701.

Heresies. "A Feminist Publication on Art and Politics." Each issue of this journal has a different theme—for example, music, racism, architecture, performance. People are still talking about the issue on goddesses and spirituality. Anarchists, socialists, lesbian feminists, all get a chance to argue the issues surrounding feminist culture. A well-produced journal. Subscription: $15 for four issues. Address: *Heresies,* 1306 Canal Street Station, New York, New York 10013-0867.

Heretic's Journal Forum. This publication is founded on the concept of the need for a synthesis of liberationist spirituality with revolutionary politics. A low-budget, one-person effort by Ron Heresy, who says he was raised in a radical, working-class family, became involved in politics and Marxism in the 1960s yet was psychic as a small child and interested in psychic phenomena. As an adult, he decided there couldn't/shouldn't be a contradiction between these two spheres. Heresy calls himself a "Green libertarian Communist and a Sethian Pagan." *HJF* is a reader-participation magazine for the purpose of exploring these issues in a dialogue—or multilogue—format. The *Forum* is $10 a year; $8 if you contribute to the magazine by writing a letter or article. Address: Heretic's Journal, P.O. Box 12347, Seattle, Washington 98111.

The Hidden Path. "A Voice of Gardnerian Covens." This journal is limited to Gardnerians. You must be an initiate of the Gardnerian Tradition or a Gardnerian High Priestess must vouch for you. Articles, poetry, rituals, letters, debate. Published four times a year. Subscription: $10/year. Address: *The Hidden Path*, c/o Windwalker, P.O. Box 793 F, Wheeling, Illinois 60090.

Inner Keltia. "The Leading Journal of the Keltic Renaissance." A well-produced, illustrated journal devoted to "re-animating virtually every aspect of Keltic-Pagan culture and spirituality." Each issue is more than 100 pages, with articles, poetry, reviews, news, designs, music, history, festivals, symbolism, rituals. Each issue is $6 in the U.S.; $7 in Canada; £2 in Great Britain. The editor is Kaledon Naddair, who believes that the "Ancient Shamanistic Wisdom of the Druids is being re-born, and it is taking many Native Pagans very much deeper into Initiation than Wicca or Crowley-mania ever could!" Naddair also publishes two other journals. The first is *The Pictish Shaman*, a magazine which "focuses on the Initiatory Wisdom of the Primal Kelts—the Kruithni/Ffichti/Picts." Approximately 80 pages, illustrated. Same prices as *Inner Keltia*. The second is *Awen*, a poetry magazine featuring religious, mythological, erotic, and romantic poetry from the leading Celtic-Pagan poets. Approximately 80 pages, illustrated; $5 an issue. Address: Kaer Eidyn, 8 Annandale Street, Edinburgh, EH7 4AN, Alban (Scotland).

Iron Mountain. A journal of magical religion. A semiannual journal devoted to the exploration and study of religious traditions, both ancient and contemporary, which emphasizes magical, metaphysical, and shamanic elements. Scholarly papers, essays, journalism, book reviews, letters, critiques, and poetry. A serious, thoughtful journal. Doreen Valiente, Aidan Kelly, Isaac Bonewits, and many others have published here. Subscriptions: $9/year; $16/two years; $3 for sample issue. Address: Artemisia Press, P.O. Box 227, Florence, Colorado 81226.

Isian News. A quarterly networking magazine from the Fellowship of Isis (FOI). For members only. Articles, news, rituals, reviews, letters, announcements of interest to members, news of members and FOI. Sister Centers. Subscriptions: $7.50/year; $8.50/year airmail. The Fellowship of Isis invites inquiries for membership. Send three International Reply Coupons or $2 to cover postage. Address: Cesara Publications, Clonegal Castle, Enniscorthy, Eire.

Jots. "The Journal of the Senses." Published quarterly by the Elysium Institute, a naturist organization with its own seminars, gatherings, and publications. The magazine's purpose is "to broaden public recognition of the naturalness and rightness of the human body and its functions; to eliminate the attitude of guilt and shame toward natural processes of life." Articles on health, sex, spirituality, nudism, men, women, natural living. Subscriptions: $4/year; $8/year overseas; sample copy: $1; $2 (foreign). Address: Elysium Institute, 814 Robinson Road, Topanga, California 90290.

Journal of Women & Religion. Published biannually by the Center for Women & Religion of the Graduate Theological Union. Membership: $30/year or $18/year for students. Address: *Journal of Women & Religion*, 2465 LeConte Avenue, Berkeley, California 94709.

Kindred Spirits Quarterly. "An optimistic journal for Pagans and all good friends of Mother Earth, presenting writings on: present day Paganism and environmental consciousness, the old nature religion, earth magic, herbs and herbalism, permaculture, ecology, shamanism and healing." This is a wonderful, truly amazing journal put out by rural Pagans in Australia. The artwork is spectacular and original. There's lots of stuff on indigenous cultures and Green activities. The magazine seems warm and authentic, and what's more, they make the word "networking" seem more than a buzz word—they often feature other Pagan journals, they reprint various articles, and they really emphasize supporting other Pagan ventures. Subscriptions: $6/year in U.S.; $4/year in Australia; $2 for sample issue. Address: *Kindred Spirits Quarterly*, P.O. Box 101, Bega, New South Wales, 2550, Australia.

Lady-Unique-Inclination-of-the-Night. This wonderful Goddess-oriented publication is no longer publishing, but many back issues are still available. The journal was started in 1976, after Kay Turner spent a year in Mexico and Guatemala, trying to track down the great Mayan Moon Goddess—the name of the journal is one of her many names, indicating the movement into the dark phase of the moon. The journal started as a sanctuary in book form, "where the Goddess would be revealed to all women and men. Our feminist orientation led us to an ideology of feminine sacred imagery which attempted to get at the positive power of feminine representation— through research, poetry, essays and art." Wonderful essays, poetry, and pictures. Cycles 1 and 2 are out of print; cycles 3, 4, and 5 (approximately 88 pages each) are $4 each; one of the most beautiful issues (cycle 6—approximately 148 pages) is entirely devoted to women's home altars. This issue is available for $6. Checks payable to Kay Turner, c/o *Lady Unique.* Address: *Lady-Unique,* SSB 3.106, Folklore Center, University of Texas, Austin, Texas 78712.

L'Étoile. Bulletin Officiel de la Wicca. A French Wiccan journal. Address: Wicca Française, 6 rue Danton, 94270 Le Kremlin Bicêtre, Paris, France.

Llewellyn's New Times. Llewellyn has been in the occult publishing business for many years. Their magazines have sometimes been merely catalogues to sell their occult books, occasionally flowering into good journals with a lot of Pagan influence. A previous journal, *Gnostica News,* was, under Isaac Bonewits' brief editorship, one of the leading Pagan journals. *Llewellyn's New Times* has a new Pagan editor—Stephanie Fox, so good things are in store. Articles on magic, astrology, Wicca, new age sciences, Paganism, reviews. Published every eight weeks. Subscription: $2 for two years or free to active mail-order buyers of Llewellyn products. Address: Llewellyn Publications, P.O. Box 64383, St. Paul, Minnesota 55164-0383.

The Littlest Unicorn. "A Pagan journal devoted to Children, their Parents, and the Child within each of us." This newsletter exists to fill a gap in Pagan-oriented material dealing with the issues that children born of Pagan parents must deal with and provides help for parents trying to raise Pagan children in the modern world. A delightful newsletter from the Rowan Tree, the same people who publish *The Unicorn.* Published eight times a year. Subscriptions: $7/year in

U.S.; $8/year elsewhere. Address: The Rowan Tree, P.O. Box 8814, Minneapolis, Minnesota 55408.

The Lunar Calendar. This beautiful Goddess-oriented calendar has become a tradition. It has been published for more than ten years by Nancy Passmore and Luna Press. Besides the phases of the moon and beautiful illustrations depicting many different goddesses, it includes lunar, tree, and herbal lore as well as poetry and astronomical information. Cost: $11, plus $2 for postage and handling. Address: Luna Press, Box 511, Kenmore Station, Boston, Massachusetts 02215.

Lunarway. A quarterly networking newsletter for the Earth Song Community. It features seminars, classes, news, reports from area groups, retreats, and festivals given by various members of the community. Also poetry and reviews. The Earth Song Community was born in 1982, in Baltimore. Its membership extends throughout the mid-Atlantic region. Membership is $13/year. The newsletter is free to members; $4/year for non-members; $1.50 for sample issue. Make checks out to Earth Song Community. Address: Lunarway, P.O. Box 16251, Baltimore, Maryland 21210.

Magical Blend. This is a glossy "new age" quarterly magazine that is not specifically Pagan but explores many spiritual possibilities. It accepts the premise that society is presently undergoing a fundamental transformation. "A new world is being born and whether this birth is to be an easy or difficult one will depend largely upon the individual. It is our aim to chart the course this transformation is taking and to assist the individual to cope with and contribute to the birthing process." Articles on mysticism, human potentials, holistic health, healing, art and poetry, fantasy, music, ritual. Subscriptions: $12/year; $16/year overseas. Address: *Magical Blend*, Magazine Dept., P.O. Box 11303, San Francisco, California 94101.

Magickal Unicorn Messenger. A quarterly newsletter published since 1980 by the Temple of Wicca, for the purpose of reaching the Pagan community, with education, entertainment, and news. Published four times a year on the major sabbats. Articles, reviews, poetry, news, festivals. Very good on current events. Subscriptions: $7/year in U.S. and Canada; $8/year (U.S. funds) overseas surface mail; $13/year (U.S. funds) overseas airmail; $2 for sample issue. Editor: Samantha Pugh. Address: Temple of Wicca, P.O. Box 1302, Findlay, Ohio 45839.

Moccasin Line. The magazine of the Northwest Indian Womens Circle, a nonprofit organization of Indian women involved in projects and activities which address the special needs and problems of Indian women and their families. Subscriptions: $15/year in U.S.; $25/year overseas. Address: Northwest Indian Womens Circle/*Moccasin Line*, P.O. Box 8279, Tacoma, Washington 98408.

Mond-Blume (formerly the *Wicca-News*). A German Wiccan journal. Herbal lore, moon magic, poetry, and articles. Subscription: 3,50DM. Editors: Arivey and Levannah. Address: Mellerstr. 59a, 4800 Bielefeld 1, West Germany.

Moonkind. "A new graphic magazine of timely, informative, and entertaining features, especially for Wiccaens, Pagans and others who respect nature's laws. . . . Promoting the balance and harmony of nature in ourselves and our environs. . . . A magazine for the children who kneel before the magick moon." Send SASE for information to: The Oaken Door, P.O. Box 31250, Omaha, Nebraska 68132.

Moonstone. A nonprofit poetry and prose magazine published at Candlemas, Beltane, Lammas, and Hallowe'en. "We try to keep the spirit of Pagan poetry alive in Albion." Contributions welcomed. Subscriptions: 2 pounds for five issues; $2 for sample copy (U.S.). Address: BM Moonstone, London WCIN 3XX England, United Kingdom.

Newaeon Newsletter. A Thelemic newsletter dedicated to the work of the present aeon of Horus, the Crowned and Conquering Child, and the 93 current. Its deepest concerns are the establishment of Thelema in the world and setting the record straight about the character of Aleister Crowley. Unfortunately, the two issues I've seen were mostly devoted to attacks on other Thelemic groups and the various O.T.O.'s, whose journals, in turn, are often just as vituperative. It's terribly sad, particularly since there are lines in *The Book of the Law* that do seem divinely inspired. Subscriptions: $6.66/year (six issues); $9.99/year overseas. Address: *Newaeon Newsletter*, P.O. Box 19210, Pittsburgh, Pennsylvania 15213.

The New Celtic Review. "The Quarterly Journal of the Golden Section Order Society for the Preservation of Celtic Lore." This Druid revivalist group puts out a beautifully produced journal, many pages are hand-lettered. Celtic news, festivals, philosophy, poetry, bardic lore, artwork. Subscriptions: $6/issue in U.S.; £3/issue in United Kingdom. Address: The G.S.O. Society, BM Oak Grove, London WCIN 3XX England, United Kingdom.

New Options. A newsletter that investigates new political ideas and approaches that go beyond those of the traditional left and right. While not Pagan, it focuses on libertarian, Green, and what it calls "post-liberal" ideas. A widely reprinted article advocated a "star-trek" as opposed to "Star Wars." Perhaps the most controversial article advocated that local communities decide the issue of school prayer—a solution that most Pagans wouldn't find palatable. Always opinionated, always interesting. Published every four weeks. 8 pages. Articles, letters, book reviews, debate. Subscriptions: $25/year in U.S.; $32/year first class and Canada; $39/year elsewhere. $2 for sample issue. Editor: Mark Satin. Address: P.O. Box 19324, Washington, D.C. 20036.

No Governor. "The zine of Illuminated Anarchism." Published by Robert Shea (co-author with Robert Anton Wilson of *Illuminatus!*). Not exactly Pagan, but a discussion of libertarian and anarchist ideas, with definite Erisian overtones. 18–20 pages. Subscriptions: $2 for each issue; $10 for six issues. Checks should be made out to Robert Shea. Address: Green and Pleasant Publications, P.O. Box 319, Glencoe, Illinois 60022.

The Odinist. The journal of The Odinist Fellowship. Published eight times a year. Articles, poetry, political essays, history, reviews, Odinist dates of distinction. This journal is much more "political" than the other Norse and Odinist publications listed here. Very frankly anti-liberal and racist: "What is in the heart of every Odinist is primarily the preservation and advancement of the Aryan racial type, with this people continuing to derive maximum benefit from the genius of their culture without this passing away as in former eras." Past issues have had articles on the Vikings, apartheid, racial politics, liberalism, women, the problem of Christianity. Responding to the charge that *The Odinist* espouses "Nazi politics," the journal calls such a charge "a cheap shot." It does consider National Socialism a legitimate topic for analysis, discussion, and criticism, "regarding it neither as a divinely-inspired panacea nor as the embodiment of all evil." I have often felt that racial and political issues lie embedded, unexpressed, in much (though not all) Odinist material. In this journal they're right out front. Subscriptions: $5/year; $6/year in Canada; $8/year overseas. Address: The Odinist Fellowship, P.O. Box 1647, Crystal River, Florida 32629.

Of a Like Mind. "A quarterly newspaper for spiritual ♀." Articles on dreams, tarot, astrology, wellness, herbs, goddesses, herstory, psychic development, the Craft, and extensive networking section. *OALM* is also a spiritual network dedicated to bringing together ♀ who follow a positive path to spiritual growth. Its focus is on Goddess religions, ♀'s mysteries, Paganism, and earth connections from a feminist perspective. This is the newspaper that will put you in touch with an enormous number of goddess-centered organizations, newsletters, shops, and celebratory groups. It has the best feminist spirituality listings found anywhere. Published quarterly. Subscriptions: sliding scale; $13/Nymph; $21/Maiden; $33/Crone. Add $5 for first class or outside U.S. Network membership: add $15 to subscription. Sample copy is $3. Address: *Of a Like Mind*, P.O. Box 6021, Madison, Wisconsin 53716.

On Wings. A newsletter published by Women in Constant Creative Action (W.I.C.C.A.). Women in Constant Creative Action provides the means in which women can meet together locally in small groups for supportive growth and learning. Each of these local groups are called Wings. Subscription: $16/year for non-members. Address: Women in Constant Creative Action, P.O. Box 201, Monmouth, Oregon 97361.

OPEC News. A quarterly networking newsletter published by the Ozark Pagan Ecumenical Council (OPEC). 15–20 pages. Articles, poetry, cartoons, film and book reviews. Subscriptions: $8/year; $10/year in Canada and overseas; $1 for sample copy. Address: OPEC, P.O. Box 605, Springdale, Arkansas 72764.

Outer Court Communications. Published bi-monthly by Our Lady of Enchantment. Articles on the meaning of the sabbats, rituals, spells, contacts. Subscriptions: $12/year in U.S.; $16/year elsewhere. Address: Our Lady of Enchantment, P.O. Box 1366, Nashua, New Hampshire 03061.

Pagana. (See *Pagan/Occult/Witchcraft Special Interest Group of Mensa* listed under Groups.)

Pagan Parenting Network. Published by the same people who put out *Pipes of Pan.* A newsletter devoted to the issue of bringing up Pagan children in a non-Pagan world. Subscription: £2/year. Address: Nicola Miles, 'Blaenberem', Mynyddcerrig Nr. Llanelli, Dyfed, Cymru SA15 5BL (Wales, UK).

Pagan Parents League Newsletter. Another newsletter for Pagan parents. Articles, letters, editorials. The newsletter is free but donations are welcomed to help defray costs (stamps preferred). Address: Pagan Parents League, c/o Belinda, P.O. Box 423P, Bay Shore, New York 11706.

Pagan Spirit Alliance Newsletter. A quarterly networking newsletter available to members of this Pagan friendship network within Circle Network. Members share opinions and personal experiences on various topics in each issue. Members include Pagans from around the U.S.A. and some other countries. Send SASE for membership information to: Circle, P.O. Box 219, Mt. Horeb, Wisconsin 53572.

Pagans for Peace Newsletter. The newsletter of a small, loose network of politically involved Pagans. It was founded to provide a free space for those who feel isolated as spiritual people in the radical community and as political people in the Pagan community. Peace, ecology, animal rights, feminist and gay liberation, native struggles. A Pagan spiritual-political synthesis. Published roughly each full moon. Available by donation or free upon request. Send SASE to Sam Wagar, Pagans for Peace, P.O. Box 6531, Station A, Toronto, Canada M5W 1X4.

Paganspoof. This is a one-time-only spoof on Pagan periodicals. If you're getting bored with most of the journals listed here, this will give you a chuckle. Cost: $3. Write to Moonstone Publications, Our Lady of the Woods, P.O. Box 176, Blue Mounds, Wisconsin 53517.

Pagan Unity News. "A publication devoted to Paganism as the Old Religion and recognition of the Duality in One." Its purpose is to unify Pagan individuals and groups of all traditions by establishing a "common ground" for all interested members and friends of the Pagan community to share information, ideas, techniques, and traditional lore. Published quarterly. Articles, news, herb lore, networking, festivals. Subscriptions: $8/year; $10/year outside U.S. and Canada; $2 for a sample copy. Address: The Northern Way, Inc., 45 South LaVergne, Northlake, Illinois 60164.

Pagan Web. A diverse network of Alabama covens, ritual and study groups, and solitaries. "We are a discrete mechanism for Pagans to meet each other." Pagan strength web, phone tree. Occasional parties and rituals. Address: *Pagan Web*, c/o Lodestar Books, 2020 B 11th Avenue South, Birmingham, Alabama 35205.

Panegyria. A Pagan-oriented journal and newsletter published by the Aquarian Tabernacle Church, Inc. Articles, news, letters, legal reports, contacts, reviews, announcements, debate, and local happenings. Some of the best controversy and debate anywhere in Pagan journals. While the emphasis is on Wicca, one enthusiastic subscriber wrote: "Your publication has the same joyous feel that *Green Egg* did when it was still in publication in the 60's and 70's." I'm not sure I'd go quite that far, but it's definitely on the way. Published eight times a year. Subscriptions: $8/year in U.S.; $16/ year foreign airmail. Sample copy sent free on request, but 3 oz. postage appreciated. Address: *Panegyria Journal*, P.O. Box 85507, Seattle, Washington 98145.

The Pegasus Express. A Pagan/Craft newsletter. Articles, poems, herb lore, mythology, stories, astrology, reviews. Published eight times a year. Subscriptions: $6/year; $1 for sample copy. Make checks out to Ellen Hansen. Address: *The Pegasus Express*, Rt. 3, Box 962-H, LaBelle, Florida 33935.

The Pictish Shaman. "A periodical Journal entirely devoted to the Druidical Shamanistic Initiation techniques of the Picts." Includes poetry, tree lore, symbolism, Celtic meditation methods, news, reviews. Subscription: $6 an issue ($7 in Canada). Published by Kaledon Naddair, who also puts out *Inner Keltia*. Address: Kaer Eidyn, 8 Annandale Street, Edinburgh, EH7 4AN, Alban (Scotland).

Pipes of P.A.N. "Published by Pagans Against Nukes, an activist organization dedicated to the banishment of nuclear technology from our earth and the re-establishment of a culture that lives in harmony with her. We seek to coordinate pagans, of whatever land and tradition, in political and magical work, to achieve this end, that the Earth be Greened Anew." Well produced—a political and spiritual synthesis. Articles on sacred sites, fiction, events, poetry, art. Published quarterly at the fire festivals. Subscriptions: 4 pounds/ year surface mail; £7/year airmail; £2 & .50p per copy. If you are sending U.S. or Canadian money, send an extra $2, because they have to go through currency exchange. Address: *Pipes of P.A.N.*,

'Blaenberem,' Mynyddcerrig, Llanelli, Dyfed, Cymru SAI5 5BL (Wales, UK).

Potlatch. An occasional small bulletin of one or two pages focusing on folk customs, natural ways, and community events. Also involved with community service issues. Send SASE to: Lee Allen, P.O. Box 4674, Chicago, Illinois 60680.

Priest/ess. A journal published by Our Lady of the Woods, a Wiccan ministry and resource center. Aims to be quarterly and focuses on the project of creating a Wiccan residential seminary to train members of the Craft in coven leadership and magical skills, using resources and expertise from a wide variety of traditions. Subscription: $13 donation a year. Address: Our Lady of the Woods, P.O. Box 176, Blue Mounds, Wisconsin 53517.

Quest. A journal concerned with all practical aspects of the Western Mystery traditions. Published quarterly since 1970. Articles on magic, Witchcraft, divination, ritual, reviews, events, personal experience, and all aspects of modern practical Western occult matters. Subscriptions: £3.50/year; $10/year in U.S.; sample issue: £1; $2 in U.S. (bills only). Editor: Marian Green. Address: *Quest*, BCM–SCL QUEST, London WCIN 3XX, England.

The Quill and the Unicorn. An irregularly published small newsletter for anyone interested in Paganism and the Old Religion. Poetry, letters, networking, reviews. Subscription: $6 for six issues. Address: *The Quill and the Unicorn*, Route 3, Box 113, Magee, Mississippi 39111.

Rags to Witches. This is a journal published eight times a year by Charles Arnold. The magazine is dedicated to community building and information sharing. Articles, letters, reviews, poetry and Craft news. Subscription: $13/year; $2 for an issue. Send SASE to: Charles P. Arnold, 26 Pendeen Avenue, Toronto, Ontario, Canada.

Reclaiming Newsletter. A political and feminist Pagan newsletter. Reclaiming is a collective of San Francisco Bay Area women and men working to unify spirit and politics. Reclaiming describes their vision as "rooted in the religion and magic of the Goddess—the Immanent Life Force" and their work as "teaching and making magic—the art of empowering ourselves and each other." The newsletter is published four times a year and contains articles, poems, letters, reviews, announcements. Subscriptions: sliding scale—$4–$15 for one year; $8–$30 for two years. If you are on a very low income and cannot donate you can still request the newsletter. Address: Reclaiming, P.O. Box 14404, San Francisco, California 94114.

Red Garters of California. "The Official Newsletter of the New Wiccan Church of California." The NWC is a non-profit, religious organization dedicated to promulgating English Traditional Wicca in its various traditions. Articles, announcements, poetry, news. The Office of the Summoner publishes a minimum of eight issues per year (on no official schedule), as a function of the membership and mailing lists of the NWC of CA. Subscriptions: free to NWC of California members. Please inquire as to current non-member subscription rate. Address: New Wiccan Church, P.O. Box 162046, Sacramento, California 95816.

RFD. "A Country Journal for Gay Men Everywhere." A reader-written journal for gay men which focuses on country living and encourages alternative life styles. Articles often explore the building of a sense of community, radical faerie consciousness, the caring for the environment, as well as sharing gay men's experiences. Members of the *RFD* collective have written, "We are the iconoclasts of our time. We work to break the worshipped stereotypes in the general society as well as the gay subculture." Neo-Paganism and faerie spirituality are important parts of this journal. Well produced, 60–80 pages. Poetry, articles, letters, fiction, art, photographs. Published quarterly. Subscriptions: $12/year; $18/year first class; $4.25 for a sample issue. Address: *RFD*, Running Water, Rt. 1, Box 127-E, Bakersville, North Carolina 28705.

Rocky Mountain Pagan Journal. A newsletter particularly geared to the Rocky Mountain area, with the purpose of collecting and disseminating information relating to Neo-Paganism, ceremonial magic, shamanism, astrology, metaphysics, and related sciences. Articles, poetry, music, Pagan parenting, book and movie reviews, upcoming events, notices, humor. This is a good journal; the one issue I've seen had everything from tips for astronomers to a long article on Pythagorean magic. Subscription: $15/year (six issues); $3 for sample copy. Editors: Gary Dumbauld and Kyri Comyn. Address:

Rocky Mountain Pagan Journal, P.O. Box 620604, Littleton, Colorado 80162.

The Runestone. "A journal of the ancient, yet ever new, religion known as Asatru. It is dedicated to that religion and to the values of courage, freedom and individuality which are associated with it." Articles on history, ancestry, rune lore, values, the gods, seasonal festivals, reviews, letters, poetry, announcements. Published quarterly by the Asatru Free Assembly. Subscriptions: $9/year in U.S. and Canada; $12/year overseas airmail. Address: AFA, P.O. Box 1754, Breckenridge, Texas 76024.

SageWoman Magazine. A feminist, grass-roots quarterly centered on women's spirituality. "We hope to continue and expand on the traditions of *WomanSpirit* and *Country Woman* to provide a space for women of all ethnic and cultural backgrounds to share women's wisdom and women's mysteries. *SageWoman* is dedicated to strengthening our inner visions and using these visions to transform our world. Articles, poetry, short fiction, book reviews, rituals, music, and letters. Subscription: $13/year. Address: *SageWoman Magazine*, P.O. Box 1478, Hillsboro, Oregon 97123.

Sanctuary Circles Newsletter. A regional networking newsletter published eight times yearly for Pagans in Wisconsin and neighboring areas. News and announcements of events sponsored by Circle and other area groups. Subscription: $5/year (issues mailed first class). Address: Circle, P.O. Box 219, Mt. Horeb, Wisconsin 53572.

Seasonal Silver. A newsletter whose purpose is to "express a love of Nature and a basically Humanitarian point of view. That whatever our beliefs, our gender, our color, our sexual preference, or whatever makes us unique individual human beings; we CAN get along and love each other. And we can love and respect Her; our Mother, the Earth." Not exclusively Pagan, but a decidedly Pagan/ Wiccan slant. Poetry, mythology, herbs, editorials. A small, lovely newsletter. Subscriptions: $8/year; $2 per issue. Make checks payable to Dorothy C. Pfaff. Editor: Donna Lyon Rhose. Address: *Seasonal Silver*, P.O. Box 189, Alpharetta, Georgia 30201-0189.

Shadowplay. A journal of Neo-Paganism, Wicca, magic, divination, celebration, art, poetry, and good times. Also reviews, letters, rituals, graphics. 52 pages. A good networking journal that offers more evidence that a wide range of Pagan and Craft activity is happening in Australia. Published quarterly. Subscriptions: $10/year in Australia; $12/year overseas seamail; $16/year overseas airmail; sample issue: $3; $3 seamail; $4 overseas airmail. Address: *Shadowplay*, P.O. Box 343, Petersham, New South Wales, 2049, Australia.

Shaman's Drum. "A Journal of Experiential Shamanism." Published by the Cross-Cultural Shamanism Network, an educational organization dedicated to fostering a shamanistic consciousness and to promoting understanding between various healing traditions, disciplines, and people. Articles, book reviews, opinion, interviews, rituals, resource listings. A well-produced and very much needed journal. Subscriptions: $15/year in U.S.; $20/year in Canada; $24/year overseas. Address: *Shaman's Drum*, P.O. Box 2636, Berkeley, California 94702.

SheTotem. "A Women's Magic Newsletter." The editor of *SheTotem* calls it a feminist-oriented magazine for everyone. "The name 'SheTotem' came from an allusion to the idea that each person has an animal or plant or spirit protector who comes to them in times of need and gives them the attributes of that totem. This is a time of stress and people are forgetting that they can reach out to these strengths and wisdoms. *SheTotem* hopes to help them remember, to let them know that they are strong." Published quarterly by Panic Press and the Council of the Blue Moon. 16–20 pages. Articles, art, reviews, poetry, humor. Subscriptions: $8/year; $2 per issue (but they love to trade and barter). Address: *SheTotem*, P.O. Box 27465, San Antonio, Texas 78227-0465.

Silver Elves. Not exactly a publication, but a monthly mailing of Elven Magical Love Letters. Once called the Elves of the Southern Woodlands, or the Sylvan Elves, this whimsical bunch now lives in California. The letters are free for the asking, but they request first-class postage stamps to cover costs, and an occasional letter telling them how you like the mailings. They write, "We do not seek to convert anyone, since in our view, only the elven have any interest in being elves. Yet in many, their elfin natures slumber and for these we sing the songs of awakening. . . . Whether there ever were elves is not as important to us as the fact that by manifestation, will and burning desire, we are Here Now. We feel ourselves to be the genetic and spiritual descendants of all the gentle folks through the ages whose cultures have been oppressed, obliterated and absorbed. . . . All the oracles tell us that the Age of Faerie returns and for this we both work and await in playful anticipation." Address: (put "please forward" on the envelope—they move a lot) *Silver Elves*, P.O. Box 2035, Guerneville, California 95446.

Sphaera Imaginatio. A journal dedicated to the Goddess, focusing on magic, mythology, Wicca, starseed, and divine wisdom. Emphasis on imagination, poetry, articles, drawings, reviews. 40–50 pages. Published two times a year. Subscription: suggested donation is $6 for three issues. Editors: Cammonette, Orion. Address: *Sphaera*, P.O. Box 7293, Lincoln Acres, California 92047.

Spirit Within News. A newsletter published by the Coven of Dawn, a prison ministry. Articles, rituals, poetry, astrology, herbs. Subscription: $8/year or whatever you can give. Published six times a year. Address: Anubis-Amen-Ra, c/o David E. Chamberlain, P.O. Box A, Thomaston, Maine 04861. This very simple and lovely journal is published by a coven in a prison. They would appreciate any donations of old books and candles. Candles must be sent to the prison chaplain, Rev. Wayne Gustafson (same address).

Starlight (and *Sirius*). These two newsletters (the first in English, the second in Finnish) are published by Sirius, a fellowship and Isis-based grove which follows "what one could call a Fenno-Egyptian tradition, as it uses a common mythology for some of its rituals." As far as is known, Sirius is the only grove in Finland at the moment. It is not very large, but it is very active, having attended the annual Festival for Spirit and Knowledge for four years, and arranging a Fantasy Egypt exhibition in 1985. Subscription: $4/four issues surface mail; $5/four issues air mail. Address: Center of the Star Goddess, c/o Sirius, P. O. Box 452, Helsinki, Finland 00101.

Survival. A bimonthly publication of the Church and School of Wicca. While the magazine is directed primarily at students of the School of Wicca, *Survival* has become better and better over the years. It now claims to be the oldest surviving regularly published occult newspaper—and you don't see a lot of Craft journals vying for that title. Articles, poetry, letters. Subscription: $12/year or $3 an issue. Address: *Survival*, c/o School of Wicca, P.O. Box 1502, New Bern, North Carolina 28560.

Synthesis. A newsletter and journal for social ecology. A source of news about green/bioregional/social and deep ecology issues. Subscription: $7.50 for 10 issues; $3.75 for 5 issues; $10 outside U.S. Address: *Synthesis*, League for Ecological Democracy, P.O. Box 1858, San Pedro, California 90733.

Tara. The official newsletter of the Tara Vagran tradition. A Wiccan journal that attempts to synthesize Eastern and Western ancient traditions. Five issues per year. Subscriptions: $12/year in U.S.; $15/year elsewhere. Address: *Tara*, 427-3 Amherst St., Suite 234, Nashua, New Hampshire 03061.

Telewoman. "A Woman's newsletter." *Telewoman* is a national lesbian networking newsletter with an emphasis on resources and contacts for women who write poetry and fiction, women in the arts and photography, and women whose spiritual perspectives are central in their everyday lives. A very intimate magazine that aims to stay small enough to maintain a personalized relationship with any woman who writes. If a poem or piece of fiction is rejected, feedback and suggestions will be given. Poetry, beautiful graphics, book reviews, art, letters, links between country and city lesbians. Subscription: $20/year; $2 for sample issue. Address: *Telewoman*, P.O. Box 2306, Pleasant Hill, California 94523.

Thesmophoria. "Voice of the New Women's Religion." The newsletter of the Susan B. Anthony Coven No. 1, of which Z Budapest is Priestess. Published 8 times a year, at the sabbats. Letters, announcements, poems, articles. Subscriptions: sliding scale of $7–$10/year; $13.25/year outside the U.S. Address: Susan B. Anthony Coven No. 1, P.O. Box 11363, Oakland, California 94611.

Thunderbow. "A synthesist Neo-Pagan Shamanic orientation monthly national newsletter published by the Church of Seven Arrows." It has been published since 1977 as a national forum for Craft-Practitioner idea-exchange and interface between Craft and non-Craft persons having common interests or concerns. It includes articles, news items, magic, science, opinions, events, researches, and forecasts from a number of sources and traditions. A very unique, opinionated newsletter which (although it has occasionally attacked me and close friends of mine) is always, always, filled with fascinating tidbits of science and magic. Subscription: $6/year. Address: Church of Seven Arrows, 4385 Hoyt St. #201, Wheatridge, Colorado 80033.

The Unicorn. A delightful little newsletter which has been around since 1977. "A publication for those who live the cycles of the Earth, who take this planet as the altar for our religions, and who are not afraid of labels the Christian majority and the Establishment might place upon those of us who strive to emulate Nature." Lots of poetry, lovely artwork, articles, herbs, tarot, reviews, letters, news. Published eight times a year. Subscriptions: $10/year in U.S.; $14/year elsewhere. Address: The Rowan Tree, P.O. Box 8814, Minneapolis, Minnesota 55408.

Unicorn. "Magie, Schamanismus, Wege zur Erde." A glossy magazine of magic, shamanism, and Earth mysteries. Subscription: 12DM/issue. Editor: Jorg Wichmann. Address: Horus-Buchlandlung, Bismarckstr. 19, D-53 Bonn 1, West Germany.

Utne Reader. While in no way a Pagan journal, this is the "Readers Digest" of the alternative press. Each issue contains at least 128 pages of the best and most unusual articles from everywhere. Recent issues have been chock full of controversial pieces on the environment, women's issues, and many topics of deep concern to Pagans. They take articles from everywhere, including community newsletters and places you have never heard of. Sections are often organized by theme, grouping a bunch of articles with conflicting and/or complementary points of view. If I was stranded on a desert island with only one magazine in the world, this is the one I would choose. Published six times a year (and it takes at least a month to get through each issue!). Subscriptions: $18/year; $23/year in Canada and Mexico; $28/year elsewhere; $4 for a single issue. Address: *Utne Reader*, P.O. Box 1974, Marion, Ohio 43305.

The Vigil. A Pagan/Craft journal from the people who once published *New Pagan Revival* and *Craft News Brews*. *The Vigil* is published on an irregular basis. It is published by an English Traditionalist Coven, the Coven of the Sacred Oaks, "for the purpose of preserving the balance of nature in ourselves and our environs, to encourage and strengthen the common bond between all Earth Religions." Articles, news, graphics. Promises to be lively and filled with controversy. The editors took a five-year hiatus from the Pagan community, and the community has changed enormously in that time. They say they want to stir things up a bit. By the time you read this, *The Vigil* may have evolved into a larger magazine called

Moonkind. That's the plan. Subscriptions: $8.50/year; $10/year first-class mailing. Address: The Oaken Door, P.O. Box 31250, Omaha, Nebraska 68132.

Vor Tru. A magazine dedicated to the restoration of Asatru, with a focus on Icelandic and Scandinavian approaches. Articles, news, ancestral lore. Subscription: $8/year (cash only). Address: *Vor Tru*, 2922 S. Marvin, Tucson, Arizona 85730.

Vultur. "A paper for the unorthodox and unshackled individual!" Articles on libertarian philosophy, esoterism, free science. Published irregularly. Free to prisoners. $1 suggested donation for all others. Will exchange publications. There are also several other publications for prisoners: *Nemesis*, a resource paper; *Anathema*, a series of leaflets to help prisoners; *Z.*, a listing of open-minded/libertarian prisoners. All free to prisoners. Write: C.P. 95, Stn. Place D'Armes, Montreal, Quebec H2Y 3E9 Canada.

The Web. The newsletter and literary journal of the Women's Spirituality Network of Portland, Oregon. The Web is dedicated to providing a forum for networking among women of all spiritual traditions and inclinations. Women are encouraged to submit written and graphic material for publication. Articles, news, artwork, letters. Donations appreciated. Address: *The Web*, P.O. Box 2885, Portland, Oregon 97208-2885.

The White Light. The official journal of the ceremonial order, the Temple of Truth. Articles by currently practicing Adepti, historical items, humor, satire, ads, and notices of interest to the student and practitioner of Ceremonial Magick. Subscriptions: $5/year inside U.S.; $8/year overseas airmail; $1.25 for sample copy. Address: *The White Light*, P.O. Box 93124, Pasadena, California 91109.

Whole Earth Review. A quarterly journal published by the people who put out *The Whole Earth Catalog*. Excellent articles on ecology, appropriate technology, community organizing, spirituality, and politics. Wonderful book reviews and catalog of sources. Subscription: $18/year. Address: *Whole Earth Review*, 27 Gate Five Road, Sausalito, California 94965.

The Wiccan. The newsletter of the Pagan Federation, a national and international free association of Pagans and Crafters. The newsletter was founded in 1968 and is "produced by the Craft for the Craft and sympathizers, seeking to build fellowship and to consolidate the self-image of the Old Religion of Western Europe as a valid path of personal development and for the evolution of mankind." Published at least four times a year. Subscriptions: £2/year; $6/year in U.S. for four issues airmail. Address: *The Wiccan*, BM Box 7097, London WC1N 3XX England.

The Wiccan Way. A quarterly newsletter with articles, news, poetry, puzzles, cartoons, notices. Subscription: $5.50/year; $1.75 for sample copy. Address: Diana, P.O. Box 347, Seldon, New York 11784.

Wiccan Rede. A quarterly, Pagan/occult magazine in a bilingual format: half the articles are in Dutch, the other half in English, and summaries in the second language accompany the articles. *Wiccan Rede* is mostly concerned with in-depth articles about Pagan philosophy, heritage, Craft practice, and personal ideas, insights, symbology, etc. Published quarterly. Articles, comments, book, music, and film reviews. Subscriptions: $8/year in U.S.; £4.50/year in U.K.; sample copy: $2; £1.50. Address: *Wiccan Rede*, P.O. Box 473, 3700 Al Zeist, Holland.

Wiggansnatch. "A Neo-Pagan literary magazine." Essays, fiction, comics, satire. Emphasizing personal experience over theory. Magic, myth, dreams, spirit. Sample: $2. Subscriptions: $6 for four issues; $7 in Canada; $8 overseas. Address: *Wiggansnatch*, P.O. Box 20061, Seattle, Washington 98102.

Wildfire. A quarterly networking magazine published by the Bear Tribe Medicine Society. This magazine evolved out of *Many Smokes*, a journal of Native American culture and vision, which the Bear Tribe published for more than twenty years. Articles on ritual, healing, native rights, communities, sacred sites, reviews. The new journal will provide networking sections for jobs, projects, travel, cottage industries, partners, and land. Subscriptions: $5/year in U.S.; $10/year in Canada and overseas. Address: *Wildfire*, The Bear Tribe, P.O. Box 9167, Spokane, Washington 99209.

Wild Magick Bulletin. A quarterly newsletter published by the Elf Lore Family, a multi-traditional networking organization working to provide "a common ground land base for the study and practice of Heathen/Pagan/Natural ways in Southern InDiana." Information, contacts, festivals, events. Subscription: $5/year. Address: Elf Lore Family, ELF, P.O. Box 1082, Bloomington, Indiana 47402.

The Wise Woman. A national quarterly journal of feminist issues, feminist spirituality, Witchcraft, other Goddess lore, and feminist Witchcraft. Published around the solstices and equinoxes. "The Wise

Woman includes women and men on the cutting edge of change, trying to create a world free from sexism, racism, agism, imperialism and patriarchal religious views." Articles, news, events, reviews, Pagan art and poetry, songs, inspirational women in the past and interviews with inspirational women of our own time, holy days, psychic development, editorials, and more. Subscription: $6/year (U.S. funds only); $2 for a sample copy. An excellent and empowering journal that combines feminist activism and feminist spirituality. Editor: Ann Forfreedom. Address: *The Wise Woman*, 2441 Cordova St., Oakland, California 94602.

Wodenwood. A generic Pagan newsletter with Druidic leanings. Articles, poetry, book reviews, rituals, music, recipes, and editorials. Published approximately four times a year. Subscription: $1.50 for single issue; $6/year. Address: *Wodenwood*, P.O. Box 33284, Minneapolis, Minnesota 55433.

Woman of Power: A Magazine of Feminism, Spirituality, and Politics. An international, multi-racial, multi-cultural quarterly publication. Themes for the first few years include: Issue One, "Womanpower," Spring 1984; Issue Two, "Envisioning a Feminist World," Summer 1985; Issue Three, "Woman as Warrior," Winter 1986; Issue Four, "Woman of Color: A Celebration of Power," Fall 1986; Issue Five, "Healing," Winter 1987; Issue Six, "Art as Activism," Spring 1987; Issue Seven, "International Feminism," Summer 1987; Issue Eight, "ReVisioning the Dark," Fall 1987. This is an incredible, inspiring magazine, with some of the most beautiful artwork I have ever seen in a journal. Unbelievably well produced! The articles, the poetry, and graphics are simply amazing. *Woman of Power* believes that the ancient spiritual voice of woman is now speaking its long-hidden wisdom and becoming an active force for the conscious evolution of the world. Its statement of philosophy says in part, "We believe that if we are to survive as a species it is necessary for women to come into power, and for feminist principles to rebuild the foundations of world cultures. . . . *Woman of Power* honors the work of woman as visionary as we transform our inner world, thus recreating our symbolism, imagery, values, and beliefs. We also honor the work of woman as activist as we transform our outer world, by recreating our personal lives and relationships, our communities, and our world." Subscriptions: $22 for four issues;

$24 for four issues surface mail in Canada and all other countries; single issues: $6 plus $1 postage in U.S., or plus $2 postage internationally. Write for airmail rates. Address: *Woman of Power*, P.O. Box 827, Cambridge, Massachusetts 02238-0827.

WomanSpirit. While no longer publishing, this pathbreaking journal of women's spirituality has ten years of back issues available. All forty issues produced regularly from Fall Equinox 1974 through Summer Solstice 1984 can be ordered. Back issues are $3 an issue, except for those that are out of print which can be obtained in photocopy for $5 each. For current information on which issues are what price send an SASE to: *WomanSpirit*, Wolf Creek, Oregon 97497-9799.

Womanswork/Spirituality. A Summer Solstice project of Womanswork Connection. This is not a newsletter but a classified directory with listings and ads, combined with lovely intimate stories from women. A previous directory, *Women of Interest/Women's Spirituality*, came out in 1984. There may be further directories by the time you read this. Write: Womanswork Connection, P.O. Box 2282, Darien, Connecticut 06820.

Wood & Water. "A Goddess Inclined Eco-Pagan Magazine." Mythology, legends, folklore, the preservation of sacred groves and wells, poetry, art, reviews, news. Published quarterly. Subscriptions: £3.50/year (UK), £6/year airmail. For overseas, send equivalent in cash only. Sample issue 85p posted. Address: *Wood & Water*, 4 High Tor Close, Babbacombe Road, Bromley BR1 3LQ, Kent, England, United Kingdom.

Yggdrasil. A quarterly journal focusing on Heathen culture, religion, ethos, and mythology. Yggdrasil is the world ash tree in Norse mythology whose roots and branches hold up the universe. Norse and Teutonic orientation. Articles, sagas, lore, runes, poetry, reviews, fiction. Published by the Heathen Way. Subscriptions: $6/year in U.S. and Canada; $8/year elsewhere; $2 for sample copy. Checks payable to Prudence Priest. Address: 537 Jones, #165, San Francisco, California 94102-2007.

GROUPS

There is no way to catalog the thousands of groups in America today—let alone elsewhere—that have a Pagan or Craft focus. For example, the *Guide to Pagan Resources* published by Circle includes approximately two hundred groves and covens—and these are just the ones that have chosen to list themselves with Circle. What you will find below is a very eclectic guide to an assortment of groups, centers, regional and national networks. In most cases I am not listing individual covens but am sticking to larger groups. The current Circle guide will have a larger and more complete, although somewhat different (and less annotated), list. Please remember that most of the people you will contact have regular jobs and a limited amount of time. Enclose a self-addressed, stamped envelope with any request for information.

In the event that you are new to all of this, and have justifiable worries about contacting strange groups, here are a few words of advice. I know something about most of these groups—but not all of them. I have never, personally, had an ugly experience in contacting a group, but there is always a first time. While Pagan groups are not cults (they do not try to "convert" you, or brainwash you, or take over your life), any person open enough to be on a spiritual quest is in a somewhat vulnerable position. There are also many people who talk a good line but have not worked out some deep emotional problems. The leader of one Wiccan group that I praised to the skies (fortunately the group has dissolved) ended up on a total guru trip and even expected sexual favors from some of the members of his group. We all make mistakes. I should also say that there are some groups here (only a few, thankfully) that I find objectionable—a couple of them are racist or sexist. They are included because this is supposed to be a fairly comprehensive resource guide. I have also tried to describe them objectively.

In *Real Magic*, Isaac Bonewits published what he called his "Cult Danger Evaluation Frame." He lists fifteen things to look at when you are thinking about a specific group. You can give each item a score from 1 to 10. As a general rule, he says, the higher the numerical score of a given group, the more likely it is to be dangerous. He notes that while many of the scales in the frame are subjective, the evaluation frame is founded on modern ideas of humanistic psychology concerning the nature of mental health and personal growth, as well as being based on Bonewits' own experience. Whether you are evaluating the Unification Church or the local Pagan grove, it's worth considering the fifteen issues mentioned below before you make your plunge.

CULT DANGER EVALUATION FRAME

by P. E. I. Bonewits

1 2 3 4 5 6 7 8 9 10
low   high

1. INTERNAL CONTROL, amount of internal political power exercised by leader(s) over members. 1_____

2. WISDOM CLAIMED by leader(s); amount of infallibility declared about decisions. 2_____

3. WISDOM CREDITED to leader(s) by members; amount of trust in decisions made by leader(s). 3_____

4. DOGMA, rigidity of reality concepts taught; amount of doctrinal inflexibility. 4_____

5. RECRUITING, emphasis put on attracting new members; amount of proselytizing. 5_____

6. FRONT GROUPS, number of subsidiary groups using different names from that of main group. 6_____

7. WEALTH, amount of money and/or property desired or obtained; emphasis on member's donations. 7_____

8. POLITICAL POWER, amount of external political influence desired or obtained. 8_____

9. SEXUAL MANIPULATION of members by leader(s); amount of control over sex lives of members. 9_____

10. CENSORSHIP, amount of control over members' access to outside opinions on group, its doctrines or leader(s). 10_____

11. DROPOUT CONTROL, intensity of efforts directed 11_____
    at preventing or returning dropouts.

12. ENDORSEMENT OF VIOLENCE when used by or 12_____
    for the group or its leader(s).

13. PARANOIA, amount of fear concerning real or 13_____
    imagined enemies, perceived power of opponents.

14. GRIMNESS, amount of disapproval concerning 14_____
    jokes about the group, its doctrines, or leader(s).

Quite frankly, if you find that any group listed here has anything but a low score according to this evaluation frame, it shouldn't be in this book. Some groups will have a lot of structure, formal training, and a fair amount of hierarchy. A few groups may even have fairly charismatic leaders. Others will be leaderless, anarchistic, and make their decisions by consensus. But none of these organizations should ever censor your sources of information, control your life, decide on your friends, insist on sexual favors, demand exorbitant amounts of money, or try to prevent you from leaving. Thankfully, most Pagan groups believe that you are the mistress of your fate and that the only real initiation (and power and knowledge) comes from within. Thou Art God/dess. While some charge fees for workshops and courses, many more do not. A Pagan belief structure makes abuses more difficult—but not impossible. So with those words in mind, here are the listings.

Amber Web. Amber Web is a men's network in Laurel, Maryland. "Our focus is on weaving a web of communication based on like hearts and the love that connects us as brothers. We strive to help our brothers find that spiritual essence within that transforms our images of masculinity. We facilitate men's circles and sweatlodges." Sponsors meetings and celebrations in the Baltimore and Washington, D.C. area. Contact: Raven and Mateo, P.O. Box 5128, Laurel, Maryland 20707-0984.

American Civil Liberties Union. Certainly not a Pagan organization, but every minority religion's best friend. The ACLU fights to protect freedom of religion as well as freedom of the press, the right to privacy and personal autonomy. This national civil liberties organization has branches in most states and in many major cities. Worth joining—you might need them some day. Address: ACLU, 132 West 43rd Street, New York, New York 10036.

The Aquarian Tabernacle Church. The Aquarian Tabernacle Church was founded in 1979 by Rev. Pete Pathfinder. It is a new tradition, although based on English traditional Wicca. It is a tradition of stewardship of the land and of service to the Pagan community as a whole, to Pagans in the Pacific Northwest and beyond. In setting out to provide some of the things often lacking in the Pagan community, the Church operates the Center for Non-traditional Religion, the Aquarian Tabernacle Chapel, the Hecate Shrine, and the Retreat House in the Cascade Mountains of Washington. There is also an outdoor circle of Menhirs standing in a grove of stately old Cedar trees. These facilities are regularly made available to all religious groups, including the non-affiliated who have need of such a meeting place. Any organization which concerns itself with spiritual well-being, life-enhancement, and tolerance of the beliefs of others may be permitted the use of these facilities. The Aquarian Tabernacle Church has a publishing arm, Pathfinder Press, and puts out an interesting newsletter, *Panegyria*. Address: Aquarian Tabernacle Church, P.O. Box 85507, Seattle, Washington 98145.

Arachne. A women's circle and network dedicated to creating a safe and sacred space for women in the Pagan community. The core group is centered primarily in the Maryland/D.C. area with other members located along the East Coast. Circles focus on empowering women. "Our rituals are eclectic and transformative." Arachne sponsors classes and occasional open gatherings. Contact: Arachne, P.O. Box 5128, Laurel, Maryland 20707-0984.

Ar nDraiocht Fein ("Our own Druidism"). A Druid Fellowship that practices a form of Indo-European reconstructionist Druidism, started by P. E. I. Bonewits. ADF, says Bonewits, will be a Neo-Pagan religion based on solid (but imaginative) scholarship in the fields of linguistics; Indo-European studies; comparative religion; archeology; anthropology; Celtic, Norse, Baltic, and Slavic studies; history; musicology; and polytheology. ADF will be developing a slow, careful, and steady stream of training for Druidic clergy. It will have a carefully structured hierarchy, based on actual skills and knowledge obtained and demonstrated. The organization publishes *The Druids' Progress*, available for $20 or more donation for four issues (U.S. bulk rate; Canada $30; overseas $40). Checks payable to P. E. I. Bonewits. Address: ADF, P.O. Box 9398, Berkeley, California 94709.

The Asatru Free Assembly. A non-profit, tax-exempt religious corporation dedicated to Scandinavian/German Paganism. "Long before Christianity came to Northern Europe, the people there had their own religions. One of these was Asatru. It was practiced in the lands that are today Scandinavia, England, Germany, France and the Netherlands." The AFA is dedicated to promoting that religion "and to the values of courage, freedom, and individuality which are associated with it." The AFA is a membership organization; it publishes *The Runestone* and other materials and sponsors an annual festival—the Althing. Membership is by application and is granted to those who adhere to the organization's stated goals and beliefs and who pay yearly dues. Address: AFA, P.O. Box 1754, Breckenridge, Texas 76024.

The Association for Consciousness Exploration. An organization in Ohio providing services in the fields of magic, alternative life styles, new age studies, mind-sciences, and other related subjects. Founded in 1983 by members of the Chameleon Club, ACE has provided programs of an educational, spiritual, and recreational nature to the Greater Cleveland Area and the public at large. This organization puts on the Starwood Festival and the Winterstar Symposium. Their guest lecturers include many Pagans as well as such people as Robert Anton Wilson and Timothy Leary. ACE runs a center for inner exploration and stress management featuring classes in memory and concentration, meditation, parapsychology, and consciousness exploration and provides members and guests with biofeedback equipment, a sensory isolation tank, controlled sensory stimulation devices, and an extensive reference library. Address: ACE, 1643 Lee Road, #9, Cleveland Heights, Ohio 44118.

Association of Cymmry Wicca. A non-profit religious association that includes groups from a variety of traditions. A democratic confederation that works for world peace, healing of Mother Earth and evolving of self. Members accept twelve basic precepts. There is a yearly meeting and ritual work. Send SASE to: P.O. Box 1866, Athens, Georgia 30603.

The Athanor Fellowship. A network of groups ("a coven of covens") that work together in the Glainn Seidhr Order of Shamanic Witchcraft. It derives its fundamental symbols and patterns from the traditions of the ancient Celtic and Germanic peoples, but its practices are largely original and focused on the realities of the modern world. "We approach Witchcraft not so much as a religion, but as a form of Shamanism which, we believe, is more likely in keeping with its ancient practice." The Glainn Seidhr Order is based on a system of nine levels of initiation—each involves completion of specific mental, physical, and psychic work. The Athanor Fellowship is composed of seven covens (five in the greater Boston area), as well as some solitary practitioners. A council of elders oversees the magical direction of the group. There are also several guilds: bards, artisans, wordsmiths, dancers, diviners, providers. There is also a much larger outer circle of the Fellowship, the EarthSpirit Community, which is best known for putting on the Rites of Spring Pagan festival. Address: Athanor Fellowship, P.O. Box 365, Medford, Massachusetts 02155.

Avalon. Avalon is a center of learning and instruction established to serve the Milwaukee Pagan community. Avalon offers public rituals, workshops, lectures, and a place to network. "We are diviners and healers, celebrators of life and seekers of truth, dedicated to the highest magickal ideal: the realization of human potential. We believe the Mystery Traditions of the West shall lead us to a new wisdom for the era now beginning." Address: Avalon, P.O. Box 18423, Milwaukee, Wisconsin 53218.

CASHEW (Children's Astral Sanctuary of Healing Earth Wisdom). An organization dedicated to networking Pagan and Wiccan resources in the Southwest, primarily New Mexico. It provides a research library, workshop space, and legal Pagan marriages. Send SASE to: Cashew, P.O. Box 26414, Albuquerque, New Mexico 87125.

Center for Shamanic Studies. This is an organization founded by the anthropologist Michael Harner, who has spent many years studying and teaching shamanism. The center sponsors workshops in shamanic training throughout North America and Europe. "The workshops in shamanic training focus on the principles of 'core shamanism,' the universal basics of shamanic practice that can be utilized in one's personal life in contemporary Western society, especially for the restoration of personal spiritual power and self-confidence, for personal health and well-being, and for a new sense of spiritual integration with our planet and all species. Methods are also learned for helping others, for in shamanism helping others is the path to helping oneself." Harner teaches that Shamanism is a method of using altered states to enter another reality and, during this journey, gather knowledge. Harner uses drumming—a sonic driving technique—to achieve an altered state. As a result of Harner's work there are dozens of groups in the United States and Europe that come together to continue shamanic exploration. Membership is offered in the Center for Shamanic Studies, and members receive a quarterly newsletter. Address: Center for Shamanic Studies, P.O. Box 673, Beldon Station, Norwalk, Connecticut 06852.

Center of the Divine Ishtar. A Goddess fellowship founded in 1982 for Pagan individuals who honor Goddess/es in their worship. It is primarily focused on Witchcraft, but there are non-Craft members, and different traditions and styles are represented. The organization sponsors Pagan celebrations, classes, and networking. Address: Center of the Divine Ishtar, P.O. Box 9494, San Jose, California 95157.

Chameleon Club. A group of individuals involved in new age and magical networking. "Founded May 5, 1978, their motto is *Change!*, their spirit is undaunted, their energy is phenomenal, and their number is far from legion." They are magicians of many paths, teachers of many reality perspectives, and joyous entertainers. Their efforts include the periodical *Changling Times* ("dedicated to the expansion of the frontiers of your consideration"), the production of musical tapes, video tapes, the Dark Horse Tarot, Chameleon Cubes, and an acoustic musical group called Chameleon. They are the originators of the Association for Consciousness Exploration and creators and staff for most of its events, including the Starwood Festival and the Winterstar Symposium. The Chameleon Club also considers itself an extended family in the style of the Pranksters; its members can be found from Cleveland to Alabama, from California to New York. The club's founder, C. C. Rosencomet, says there are many other groups like the Chameleon Club, but they all reside in parallel universes. Address: Chameleon Club, 1643 Lee Road, #9, Cleveland Hts., Ohio 44118.

Church of All Worlds. (See Chapter 10.) The *CAW* today is radically different from the organization that existed ten years ago as documented in *Drawing Down the Moon.* "In our early years we were concerned with outreach. Through regular meetings and events and through the publication of *Green Egg,* we were primarily concerned with attracting and involving new people to our concepts of religion and personal growth. In recent years, we have been concentrating on actually doing the things we talked about doing." *Forever Forests* was chartered as a subsidiary organization, whose purpose was to plant trees and increase people's awareness of ecological issues. The *Ecosophical Research Association* was chartered to investigate myth and legend and how they relate to today's world. The recreation of unicorns is the best known example of ERA's efforts. *Nemeton* is the publishing arm of CAW, presenting albums, songbooks, and newsletters. There are plans for the return of *Green Egg* as a national magazine. *Lifeways* has become the teaching arm of the Church, dedicated to the study of consciousness, healing techniques and magical ritual. The spiritual home of CAW is Annwfn, located in the mountains of Mendocino County, California. The land is maintained as a sacred space, where people can "experience magic and enter the realm of faerie." The CAW today dedicates itself to bridging the seemingly ever-widening gap between women and men, science and religion, heaven and earth. Address: The Church of All Worlds, P.O. Box 212, Redwood Valley, California 95470.

The Church of Seven Arrows. The Church of Seven Arrows was established in 1975 as a Universal Life Church congregation. Its goals include providing information, introductory experience, and training in the practices and concepts of old religions and ancient sciences (magic, divination, etc.). It seeks to provide information, aid, and guidance to any who seek greater knowledge of themselves, the universe, and the higher powers. Its tradition is shamanic, and here are a few of its principles: There is no one path of spiritual and religious practice that is proper for everyone; "The Universe, and Each Being Therein, all be Mirrors Reflecting Each Other and the Creator; As Above so Below; Each Being is, as a Spirit, a Living Medicine Wheel of Infinite Beauty, Capability, and Power." The Church of Seven Arrows offers several basic study series. There is no tuition. It publishes books, conducts seminars, does ceremonies, and publishes a national newsletter, *Thunderbow*. Address: Church of Seven Arrows, 4385 Hoyt St., #201, Wheatridge, Colorado 80033.

Church of the Eternal Source. "The Church of the Eternal Source is the refounded church of Ancient Egypt. We worship the original gods of mankind in their original names in the original manner as closely as possible. Our work is to establish a constantly evolving synthesis of ancient and modern knowledge under the direct guidance and in direct contact with the Eternal Gods." A polytheistic federation of Egyptian cults founded in 1970. See pages 263-273 for details. Address: Church of the Eternal Source, P.O. Box 7091, Burbank, California 91510-7091.

Circle. Circle is a non-profit resource center serving people interested in magic, metaphysics, and nature spirituality. Circle was begun in 1974 by Selena Fox and Jim Alan, who continue to direct its many services along with Dennis Carpenter who coordinates publication projects. Circle's headquarters are at Circle Sanctuary, a two hundred-acre nature preserve in southwestern Wisconsin, about thirty miles from Madison. Circle coordinates Circle Network, an international information exchange and contact service for Wiccans, Neo-Pagans, Pantheists, Goddess researchers, Shamans, Druids, Eco-Feminists, Native American Medicine People, Seers, Odinists, Ceremonial Magicians, and others on related paths. Circle publishes a sourcebook—periodically updated—the *Circle Guide to Pagan Resources*, which lists periodicals, groups, artists, musicians, and suppliers. Circle also publishes a quarterly newspaper, *Circle Network News*, and coordinates a Pagan friendship network, the Pagan Spirit Alliance which has its own newsletter. Circle also runs seminars, workshops, training in magic and herbcraft, and at least once a year runs a special weekend retreat for Pagan ministers. Circle sponsors a number of gatherings, the most famous is the International Pagan Spirit Gathering which takes place on private land near Madison, at the time of the Summer Solstice. Circle's ministers perform Pagan marriages and rites of passage, hold monthly spiritual healing circles, and do private counseling. Address: Circle, Box 219, Mt. Horeb, Wisconsin 53572.

Clan of Y Tylwyth Teg. An initiatory/adoptive training system with outer court, inner court, training, and working groups. Y Tylwyth Teg is duality-oriented, with both robed and skyclad groups. There is also a developing farm community, Camelot of the Woods. There are nine levels of membership in YTT, there are training groves and a correspondence course in Welsh Witchcraft. "We are relinking ourselves with Nature, the Great Spirit, the Welsh God/desses and other humans. Our world is a circle of beauty, of freedom, of learning awareness and harmony." Send SASE to: Church of Y Tylwyth Teg, P.O. Box 1866, Athens, Georgia 30603.

The Council of Isis Community—The Witches of Salem. Over 40,000 people have come in contact, through workshops and classes, with Laurie Cabot, the Official Witch of Salem. About 2,000 of these live in Salem. The Council of Isis Community holds open gatherings on some of the major sabbats. For thirteen years, the Witches of Salem gave a public Halloween ball, and two years ago more than forty Salem Witches marched in Salem's Heritage Day Parade. They have also raised money for the Chamber of Commerce by putting on ritual dramas; they have donated toys to local hospitals and have worked with other community groups. While some of the Wiccan community have been uncomfortable with Laurie Cabot's flamboyance—black robes, Egyptian eye makeup, and lots of jewelry— Laurie and the Witches of Salem put it this way: "For 14 years we've been out on the front lines every day as public Witches. You can walk the streets of Salem in your robe and pentagram and feel absolutely safe." Address: Council of Isis Community—Witches of Salem, c/o Crow Haven Corner, 125 Essex St., Salem, Massachusetts 01970.

The Council of the Magickal Arts. The organization was started in 1980, to provide a means of communication between various traditions. It publishes a newsletter four times a year and holds two general meetings a year. It has done charitable service in the community, providing food and clothing and aiding battered women. It also puts on Moontalks, monthly Sunday meetings which include a lecture or workshop and a covered dish dinner. Moontalks were originally started by Nexus International (a networking group in Dallas) several years ago. One group within CMA, Flamekeepers, an Isian tradition coven, sponsors new moon celebrations that are open to the public. There is also a newly formed church, Our Lady of the Sacred Flame. Membership in the Council is open to any person or group that practices magic in the light and love of the Goddess and/or God. Membership dues are $13/year and include a subscription to the newsletter. Send SASE for membership information and a copy of the bylaws. Address: Council of the Magickal Arts, 5920 Bissonnet, #113, Houston, Texas 77081.

The Covenant of the Goddess. The Covenant of the Goddess is a cross-traditional federation of some seventy Wiccan covens in fifteen states that have joined together to win recognition for the Craft as a legitimate and legally recognized religion. COG was born at Coeden Brith on the Summer Solstice in 1975. The Covenant is incorporated as a non-profit religious organization in California, though it has grown to be a nationwide organization of covens and solitaries of various traditions sharing in the worship of the Goddess and the Old Gods and subscribing to a common code of ethics. Decisions are usually arrived at by consensus. When consensus cannot be reached a vote is taken. Each member coven has one vote. Each coven also has the power to veto. COG publishes a newsletter of Craft and Pagan news, announcements, articles, poetry, and humor. Each year, COG holds its Grand Council as part of a national festival, which is open to the whole membership as well as Pagans and Witches who are not part of COG. A coven can apply for membership if it is a cohesive, self-perpetuating group that has been meeting monthly or more often for at least six months; the group believes and follows a code of ethics compatible with that of the Covenant; the coven has three or more members who have been formally accepted into the clergy; and the focus of the group's ritual and thealogy is the worship of the Goddess and the Old Gods (or the Goddess alone). Address: COG, Box 1226, Berkeley, California 94704.

Cultural Survival. An organization which, since 1972, has supported projects on four continents, specifically designed to help indigenous peoples survive, both physically and culturally, the rapid changes which contact with expanding industrial society brings. Cultural Survival has provided legal and medical assistance, bilingual education, cultural centers, as well as involvement in educational campaigns and research projects. It publishes a magazine, *Cultural Survival Quarterly*, and many papers and special reports. It is a membership organization, and it actively seeks contributions and support. Address: Cultural Survival, Inc., 11 Divinity Avenue, Cambridge, Massachusetts 02138.

Daughters of the New Moon. Not a coven, or even Wiccan, but a growing group of women in the Denver, Colorado, area who are celebrating women's mysteries. Currently the mailing list contains about two-thirds Pagan and one-third sympathetic onlookers. "We come together to share our secrets and to form a bonding group of women of like minds, and hope through this activity to identify ourselves as female, especially as this relates to our religious impulses." Meetings, discussions, sharings, rituals. Address: Daughters of the New Moon, P.O. Box 65, 1525 Sherman St., Denver, Colorado 80203.

The Earth Song Community (ESC). A networking organization in the Mid-Atlantic area that was formed in 1982 in association with Silver Web. ESC is now an independent association of groups and individuals in the Maryland/D.C./Virginia area. It keeps members aware of resources, both magical and mundane, offers moral support and community gatherings and festivals. ESC puts out a networking newsletter, *Lunar Way*. Membership is $13/year. Some organizations within ESC include: Silver Web, Rainbow Web Grove, Moon Web, Circle Aeyrie, and Keepers of the Holly Chalice. Contact through Earth Song Community, P.O. Box 16251, Baltimore, Maryland 21210.

The EarthSpirit Community. A non-profit religious organization that serves as the outer circle of the Athanor Fellowship. Its original purpose was to help foster a Pagan community in the Boston area. EarthSpirit offers several semi-public celebrations throughout the year and sponsors workshops, concerts, talks, and classes. There are approximately 150 members and several hundred more receive mailings. There is a frequent free networking newsletter, *EarthSpirit Community Newsletter* (donations are appreciated), and an occasional journal, *Crossroads*. There is also a monthly study group—Mooncircle. The most important event organized by EarthSpirit is the Rites of Spring Pagan gathering, held on Memorial Day weekend in May, near Boston. Address: The EarthSpirit Community, P.O. Box 365, Medford, Massachusetts 02155.

The Eleusis Foundation. A non-profit organization formed to support and sponsor the retrieval and recreation of ancient ritual art, and the exploration and adaptation of living shamanic traditions. "Ritual art . . . is a means of breathing new life into ancient wisdom. Ancient forms and modern techniques are woven together by artists, musicians, dancers, performers, martial artists, and individuals walking the path of the Old Religion of Europe or Native America. Performance is integrated with participation to inspire a transformative experience by bringing the viewer/participant into contact with those spiritual qualities and values which have been for too long lost and which are deeply essential to the survival of the Earth and the rebirth of the human spirit and its cultural expressions." The Foundation sponsors large public seasonal events—Beltane, Yule, and Summer Solstice celebrations. These events explore the creation of sacred space; the influence of the cycles of the seasons; myths of death and rebirth; the role of violence; the power, wisdom, and beauty to be found within concepts of divinity as feminine; the mysteries of balance between male and female and masculine and feminine aspects of divinity; the depth of love as the context of universal relationship between humanity and the natural world. "The challenge is to enrich and to embolden, to reawaken the human heart to its place in the web of life." Address: The Eleusis Foundation, c/o Phillis W. Curott and Rodger Parsons, 85 Eastern Parkway, #2E, Brooklyn, New York 11238.

The Elf Lore Family. "A multi-traditional networking organization designed to bring together any and all evolutionary wee-folk into a working web of positive planetary citizens (the Meek—not the "weak"—shall inherit the earth). Our main thrust is toward Whole-Earth healing thru the re-planting of the gardens, sacred groves, and magickal meeting grounds around our sphere. We are a practical craft organization, with emphasis placed on personal and individual doing and grounding of the Divine Dream within us all." The Elf Lore Family (ELF) is a not-for-profit educational experiment. One of its main efforts is toward the creation of Lothlorian, a nature sanctuary and survival education center, but it encourages all sanctuary efforts. As of 1986, ELF said it had about three hundred members. ELF describes itself as a cooperative collective where decisions are made by an Elder Council, by means of consensus. The Elf Lore Family publishes a newsletter, *Wild Magick Bulletin*. They also put on four annual networking festivals in Indiana. Address: Elf Lore Family, P.O. Box 1082, Bloomington, Indiana 47402.

The Elmwood Institute. The Elmwood Institute was founded by Fritjof Capra and developed with a circle of colleagues—among them Ernst Callenbach, Hazel Henderson, Charlene Spretnak, and many others. Its primary purpose is as a forum for "ecothinking"—to provide analyses of the merits and limitations of previous thinking patterns. For example, the thinking that tolerates the risks of nuclear war. Through small gatherings, conferences, and publications, the Elmwood Institute generates and communicates alternatives and seeks to obtain broadbased responses to them. While it is in no way a "Pagan" organization, it is presenting itself as an intellectual resource base for the Green movement, and it has as one of its main goals "furthering the convergence of politics, ecology and spirituality." It has sponsored symposiums on the Greens, on science and ethics, and on the "new paradigm." Address: The Elmwood Institute, P.O. Box 5805, Berkeley, California 94705.

The Fellowship of Isis (FOI). An organization "dedicated to spreading the religion of the Goddesses throughout the world, and in the ideals of Love, Truth, Beauty and Abundance; and in the reverence for all forms of life, animal, plant and mineral. It rejects the principle of sacrifice in any form, whether actual or symbolic." Membership is open to all people (including children) and there are no fees or vows of secrecy. As of May 1986, there were 6,342 members in 57 countries. Many members have founded FOI Sister Centers; there are more than 192 in 27 countries. The Fellowship of Isis was founded on the Vernal Equinox in 1976 by Laurence Durdin-Robertson and his wife, Pamela, and his sister Olivia Robertson at their family home, Clonegal Castle. There is a temple to Isis and shrines to other deities. The Fellowship is organized on a democratic basis. It is not exclusivist. It is open to all. Members are free to maintain other religious allegiances. Membership includes Christians, both Catholic and Protestant, Hindus, Buddhists, Shintoists, numbers of Wiccan groups, those still holding to the indigenous religions of Africa and America, and those now restoring the ancient religions of Babylon, Egypt, Greece, Rome, and the Celtic and Norse lands. Members keep in contact through the *Isian News*. The Fellowship of Isis also publishes a directory, a liturgy, many rituals, and books on the goddesses of various parts of the world. Information on membership can be obtained by sending three International Reply Coupons or $2 to cover postage to: Fellowship of Isis, Clonegal Castle, Enniscorthy, Eire.

Feminist Spiritual Community. A community of women in Portland, Maine, that meets weekly "to affirm women's heritage and our own experiences; to celebrate our dreams and our rooted-ness in the empowering sources of creativity and goodness; to support one another and learn to value differences; to explore our visions and give voice to them in art, theology, study, and action." Each Monday there is a simple ceremony of naming, healing, and empowering. Meditation, singing, telling stories, exploring ideas, planning activities. Contact: Feminist Spiritual Community, P.O. Box 3771, Portland, Maine 04104.

Feraferia. (see Chapter 9) Although Feraferia no longer exists as an organization, Fred Adams is still involved in pursuing his research. Address: P.O. Box 4163 Eagle Rock Station, Los Angeles, California 90041.

Forever Forests. A non-profit, tax-exempt organization dedicated to the restoration of ecological awareness and Earth stewardship through reforestation. "We are an organization dedicated to education about ecological issues with a spiritual perspective. Our focus is often on forests and trees because forests are the single most important endangered area on the planet. We feel that trees are crucial to the survival of the planet. Planting trees is a spiritual empowering act as well as an investment for the future. Our purpose is to teach through example and hands-on activities: tree-planting, sanctuary maintenance, networking, workshops and festivals. When we plant trees we are planting dreams for the future." Forever Forests was started by the late Pagan bard Gwydion Pendderwen and is located on the sacred land of Annwfn in Mendocino County, California. Sponsors an annual tree-planting gathering on a weekend close to

New Years. Send SASE to: Forever Forests, Box 212, Redwood Valley, California 95470.

Free Spirit Alliance. An alliance of covens, collectives, and solitaries of varying traditions in the Mid-Atlantic area. "We are bound together by a spirit of community and awareness, to share knowledge and celebrate our different paths." The Free Spirit Alliance holds quarterly community meetings and seasonal open rituals. They publish a newsletter, *Free Spirit Rising*, and sponsor an annual festival near Lammas (July/August). Projects include: Pagan Prisoners Network, S.O.U.R.C.E. (Sisters of Unity ReClaiming the Earth), and the Capital Hill Political Watch. Contact: Free Spirit Alliance, P.O. Box 25242, Baltimore, Maryland 21229.

Goddess Rising. A non-profit educational and spiritual organization which seeks to empower women, encourage female leadership, and educate both women and men about psychic development and feminist Witchcraft. Goddess Rising sponsors special classes and workshops and sells cassette tapes of speeches and workshops at the *Goddess Rising Conference*, held in Sacramento, California, in March 1982—a major, well-publicized conference of feminists, Witches, Goddess-worshippers, Pagans, and curious Christians. Donations are tax-deductible. Send SASE to: Goddess Rising, 2441 Cordova St., Oakland, California 94602.

Greenpeace. An international environment organization involved with the protection of wildlife and anti-nuclear activities. Address: 1611 Connecticut Avenue, NW, Washington, D.C. 20009.

The Greens. Green political movements are forming in many parts of the world. While the original movement and its most powerful expression remains in West Germany, Green movements are sprouting up in the United States, England, over much of Europe, and elsewhere. It may seem strange to list the Greens in a book on Pagan spirituality, but there is a spiritual dimension to Green politics, although it is often not articulated. Core Green beliefs include creating a sustainable culture and looking at the interrelatedness of all nature. They place ecology in a primary position, and key values include ecological wisdom, decentralization, grass-roots democracy, community-based economics, global responsibility, inclusiveness, feminist values, personal and social responsibility, and non-violence. Green groups are exploring the deep questions—how we live our lives, our values in work and love, and our connections with all living processes. Some resources include:

—*Committees of Correspondence.* An annual contribution of $15.00 will make you a participating member of the National Committees of Correspondence network and entitle you to receive quarterly newsletters, notices of Green gatherings, and support for your local organizing efforts. Address: National Clearinghouse, Committees of Correspondence, P.O. Box 30208, Kansas City, Missouri 64112.

—*East Bay Green Alliance,* P.O. Box 9242, Berkeley, California 94709.

—*"Green Politics: The Spiritual Dimension."* A lecture presented by Charlene Spretnak, October 1984, E. F. Schumacher Society, Box 76, RD3 Great Barrington, Massachusetts 01230. Also take a look at *Deep Ecology,* an anthology edited by Michael Tobias, Avant Books, 1984; and *Deep Ecology* by Bill Devall and George Sessions, George M. Smith, Inc., 1984.

—*New England Committees of Correspondence,* P.O. Box 703, White River Junction, Vermont 05001.

—*New York Greens,* c/o Joan Shapiro, 83 Wooster St., New York, New York 10012.

Grove of the Unicorn. An American Eclectic tradition grove, founded in 1979 by Galadriel in Atlanta, Georgia. The grove has new moon and sabbat celebrations which are open to all positive celebrants of any tradition. Full moon circles are open to initiates only. Seekers are given a thirteen-week introductory course on the principles of Wicca. At the end of this time the seeker and the group decide if staying with the group is appropriate. If they do stay, there is at least a year of training before initiation. There is a rigorous written and oral examination, and the decision on initiation is made by all members of the Inner Circle. The grove also seeks positive interaction with the public through written materials, radio and television interviews, and "opening the door" to all who seek to learn more of the religion. Address: Grove of the Unicorn, P.O. Box 13384, Atlanta, Georgia 30324.

Heartland Pagan Association. A non-profit organization that was created in 1984 to purchase and operate a Pagan land preserve near Chicago, to create a library and research facility, to present Pagan and "new age" speakers, and to promote seasonal festivals. The association is a membership organization: membership is $15/year or $150/lifetime. Heartland sponsors a Beltane feast, a summer festival, a harvest gathering, a Samhain/Witches Ball, weekend camp-outs, and co-sponsors the Gaia Festival with the Elf Lore Family. Members have voting rights in connection with decisions, activities, and land purchases. They have use of all research facilities and discounts on all Heartland, Gaia, and many other events. There are also special interest groups (SIGS), including mead making, folk dance, folk magic, biofeedback training, women's and men's groups. Most Heartland events are public and non-Pagans are welcomed. The organization also publishes a newsletter. Address: Heartland Pagan Association, 2237 West Morse Avenue, Chicago, Illinois 60645-4850.

Hernesgaard Pagan Circle. A Pagan circle in Englewood, Colorado, based on the Gardnerian tradition, with a lot of "borrowing" from other Neo-Pagan traditions. Particular attention is given to the need for a reliable and safe outlet for young adults who are interested in non-Christian spiritual paths rather than the more readily available sensational avenues. Most Pagans are reluctant to invite teens into their groups. Kyri Comyn and Gary Dumbauld, who lead Hernesgaard, believe that teenagers between fourteen and eighteen are becoming very aware of themselves as spiritual as well as physical beings, that they have a boundless energy which is not completely under their control as yet, and that they are quite capable of making rational and intelligent choices regarding their own spiritual welfare. Strict guidelines: permission from guardian, personal interview, no drugs or alcohol. Address: Hernesgaard, P.O. Box 620604, Littleton, Colorado 80162.

The Institute for the Study of American Religion. This institute was founded by Dr. J. Gordon Melton, and it probably contains the best library of Pagan and Craft publications and materials anywhere in the world. This is the place to go for anyone doing serious research on the Pagan revival. There is a comprehensive collection of British and American Wicca, Pagan and magical periodicals going back to the 1960s, over 1,500 books, booklets, and pamphlets generated by the movement, as well as newspaper and magazine articles. The Institute moved in June 1985 to Santa Barbara, California. Its research collection of 28,000 volumes along with its periodicals and files are now a part of the special collection of the University of California at Santa Barbara. Dr. J. Gordon Melton remains as director and is also a visiting scholar in the Department of Religious Studies of the university. Inquiries concerning the collection from interested researchers should be addressed directly to the Institute at P.O. Box 90709, Santa Barbara, California 93190-0709.

Maidenspirit. A Pagan, non-profit, non-prophet information, education, and referral service serving the Pacific Northwest in particular. Maidenspirit holds workshops and semi-public rituals. Address: c/o Eridani Productions, P.O. Box 47111, Seattle, Washington 98146.

The Matriarchy Research and Reclaim Network (MRRN). A women-only network involved with spirituality and research. Also publishes *Arachne* magazine. Address: MRRN, c/o A Woman's Place, Hungerford House, Victoria Embankment, London WC 2, England.

Midwest Pagan Council. An incorporated association of Pagan groups in the greater Midwest area, founded in November 1976. The Midwest Pagan Council sponsors the Pan Pagan Festival, the longest running annual Pagan camp-out gathering in the U.S. Address: Midwest Pagan Council, P.O. Box 313, Matteson, Illinois 60443-0313.

Moonweb. A network of Witches and Pagans who join energies together in peace and healing efforts. Send SASE to: Bone Blossom, 983 Haven Avenue, Redwood City, California 94063.

The New Wiccan Church. The New Wiccan Church (NWC) was originally established in California as the Neo Celtic Church. Its name was changed in 1973 when its members restricted their practice to traditional British Witchcraft. The New Wiccan Church now has branches in four states, with numerous local branches. The NWC of America and its various state, area, and city branches are secret, non-profit, religious organizations dedicated to promulgating English traditional Wicca in its various traditions, rites, forms, and orders. Membership is open to initiated Wiccan of the following traditions: Alexandrian, Algard, Gardnerian, Georgian, Kingstone, Majestic Covens, Majestic Order, Silver Crescent, Taran, and other similar British traditions. All Wiccans, Pagans, and Neo-Pagans are welcome to contact them. The New Wiccan Church does not initiate but will forward inquiries for admission. Addresses: New Wiccan Church, National Office, P.O. Box 162046, Sacramento, California 95816; NWC of Oregon, c/o NWC, Washington; NWC of Washington, P.O. Box 30511, Seattle, Washington 98103; NWC of California, P.O. Box 421044, Sacramento, California 95842; NWC of Wisconsin, P.O. Box 64, Mt. Horeb, Wisconsin 53572.

NEXUS. NEXUS International is a Wiccan/Pagan networking organization which was born in 1980 as a source of energy, love, and support of two Wiccans who were facing an unjust, threatening situation. It has grown into a healing network, a place to share and send energies connecting Wiccans and Pagans with supportive love and energies when and wherever they are needed. In addition to energy alerts, NEXUS serves as a connecting link for outreach, helping seekers to find those of like mind in their area. NEXUS also works to clean up and rectify the image of Wiccans and Pagans—an educational service for the world-at-large. NEXUS sponsors Moontalks, open meetings. NEXUS has functioning groups in Texas, Colorado, and California. Membership: $13/year single membership; $20/year for families. Address: NEXUS, P.O. Box 532256, Grand Prairie, Texas 75053.

Northern Way, Inc. A Norse Pagan incorporated organization (NFP) for education, research, and the religion of Asatru as a way of life. Affiliated with the Asatru Free Assembly and the Midwest Pagan Council. The organization publishes *Pagan Unity News*. Address: Northern Way, Inc., c/o 45 S. LaVergne, Northlake, Illinois 60164.

The Oaken Door. An organization started by a group of English Traditionalist Witches which serves as a vehicle for many publications and services. Headed by Bob and Marsha Clark, the Oaken Door once published the *New Pagan Revival Magazine, Craft News Brews*, and the *Mailing List*. It now publishes *The Vigil* and *Moonkind*, as well as having several networking services, a directory, and a correspondence course. There is also a working group, Coven of the Sacred Oaks. Address: The Oaken Door, P.O. Box 31250, Omaha, Nebraska 68132.

Odin's Folk. The official newsletter of the *Arizona Kindred*. The Arizona Kindred is one of the largest Asatru groups in the U.S. It seeks "the full restoration of the Old Norse Religion known as Asatru (sometimes as Odinism). . . . Our group is strictly religious and non-political." Write for information: Arizona Kindred, P.O. Box 961, Payson, Arizona 85547.

The Order of Osiris. A religious order "founded on the Wisdom and Ethics revealed in ancient Egypt by the Son of God, Osiris, the Universal Christ, who incarnates in all generations as Krishna, Buddah, Dionysus, Jesus." The Order utilizes ancient Egyptian rites and other universal rites. The Order establishes Osirian Christian Temple Assemblies and meditation circles which meet weekly. Retreats and community service are maintained by religious members and clergy. New members undergo a one year training for confirmation. Confirmed members may apply for clergy training which is open to women and men over 21. All members pledge at least $10 per month. The Order was founded in 1980 as a religious order and church. There are 171 members in the United States, Africa, and Europe. Weekly meetings; healing and renewal services twice a month. *The New Horizons News* is published for members. For application write: Order of Osiris, P.O. Box 4084, Roselle Park, New Jersey 07204.

Oregon Pagan Association. An organization for Pagans at the University of Oregon or living in and around Eugene. It was started in 1981 by Stephanie Fox. Networking, public education, workshops, rituals. Address: Oregon Pagan Association, c/o ERB Memorial Union, University of Oregon, Eugene, Oregon 97402.

Our Lady of Enchantment. A seminary of Wicca located in Nashua, New Hampshire. Holds Friday-night church meetings twice monthly and public sabbats. Also classes, services, library, counseling, priesthood and group leadership training. Address: Our Lady of Enchantment, P.O. Box 1366, Nashua, New Hampshire 03061.

Our Lady of the Woods. A National Wiccan Ministry and Resource Center. For many years, Our Lady of the Woods has combined counseling, educational programs, publications, and crafts. Under the leadership of two priestesses—Amber K and Catelaine—Our Lady of the Woods is undertaking to create a Wiccan residential seminary, where members of the Craft can come to study the arts of magic and the skills of coven leadership for a week, a month, a summer, a year, or longer. The seminary will draw on material and faculty from every Wiccan tradition possible. Our Lady of the Woods also hopes to create a center for self-healing and the education of healers—in herbalism, nutrition, energy channeling, and many traditional and alternative healing arts. You can write for information: Our Lady of the Woods, Box 176, Blue Mounds, Wisconsin 53517.

The Pagan Anti-Defamation League. A British organization dedicated to correcting the misconceptions, distortions, and untruths about Paganism that have emerged unchallenged from the media. It seeks to show that "Paganism—the natural faith of Britain and Northern Europe, whose three main forms are Wicca, Odinism and Druidism—has reverence for the sanctity of the Earth, its peoples and the natural cycles of life and the seasons. . . . Whenever Paganism is defamed, we shall bring the true facts to the attention of those responsible, in order that the correct version may be published. No more misrepresentation. Defend our ancient heritage." Address: Prudence Jones and Nigel Pennick, BM Box 7097, London WC1N 3XX England.

Pagan Counseling Network. A loose correspondence network for practicing Pagans who are also involved in the "helping professions." A chance to share a psychological understanding of why magic works, and a magical understanding of why the various helping professions work. Members send materials to the editor who collects them and sends them out to participants. A kind of postal encounter group, or postal peer supervision group. Write: Ginny Brubaker, 1532 West Victoria, Chicago, Illinois 60660.

Pagan Federation (PF). An organization, centered in England, that seeks to provide contact between the Craft of the Wise and genuine seekers of the Old Ways. It was founded, as the Pagan Front, in 1971, by senior members of four branches of the Old Religion of Wisecraft, and it continues as a Craft organization today. There are a number of PF discussion groups throughout Britain and the PF also publishes *The Wiccan.* Although founded by Witches, you do not have to be a Witch to join. Anyone who finds sympathy with the three principles below is welcome to apply: (1) love and kinship with Nature, participation in the cosmic Dance of Goddess and God, woman and man, yin and yang, rather than the customary attitude of aggression and domination over Nature; (2) the Pagan ethic, "Do what you will, but harm no-one." This is a positive morality, not a list of thou-shalt-nots. Each person is responsible for discovering his or her own true nature and is committed to developing it fully in harmony with the world; (3) reincarnation in some form, as taught by many faiths throughout time, including the Druids and Witches. What we are is the substance of *this* Nature, *this* world, not of some far-off beyond. To join, send SASE with details of yourself and your interest in Paganism. Overseas: 3IRCS please. Address: The Pagan Federation, BM Box 7097, London WC1N 3XX, England.

Pagan/Occult/Witchcraft Special Interest Group of Mensa. An international network of persons interested in Nature religions, Witchcraft, magic, and related topics. Non-Mensans may join as associate members, with all privileges, including the newsletter *Pagana*. *Pagana* features articles, news, art, reviews, letters, announcements, contacts, calendar of events. Published about six times a year since 1980. A large forum section with lots of letters and debate. A good networking journal. Subscriptions: $12 for six issues; $20 for ten issues; $18 for six issues overseas airmail. Send $1 and a double-stamped business-size self-addressed envelope for sample information packet. Make checks payable to Pagans SIG. Address: *Pagana*, c/o Valerie Voigt, P.O. Box 9494, San Jose, California 95257.

Pagan Parents League. An organization of networking, information exchange, and mutual support among Pagans who have children. Address: Pagan Parents League, c/o Belinda, P.O. Box 423-P, Bay Shore, New York 11706.

Pagans for Peace. A small, loose network of politically involved Pagans scattered around Turtle Island. It was founded to provide a free space for those who felt isolated as spiritual people in the radical community and as political people in the Pagan community to come together for discussion of similarities and differences, to network projects, and generally to end feelings of isolation. The group has no "party line," although many are anarchist-inclined, and areas of political involvement include animal rights, prisoner support, the peace movement, support for native struggles and for feminist and gay liberation. Address: Sam Wagar, Pagans for Peace, P.O. Box 6531, Station A, Toronto, Canada M5W 1X4.

Pagan Spirit Alliance. A networking association within Circle Network of Pagans interested in ecumenical concepts of spirituality. Members connect with each other through a quarterly *PSA Newsletter* and through correspondence. See the listing under Circle for more details.

Reclaiming—A Center for Feminist Spirituality. Reclaiming is a collective of San Francisco Bay Area women and men working to unify spirit and politics. "Our vision is rooted in the religion and magic of the Goddess—the Immanent Life Force. We see our work as teaching and making magic—the art of empowering ourselves and each other. In our work, we train our voices, bodies, energy, intuition, and minds. We use the skills we learn to deepen our strength, both as individuals and as community, to voice our concerns about the world in which we live and bring to birth a vision of a new culture." Reclaiming gives workshops, runs a summer apprenticeship program, conducts public rituals, and publishes a newsletter. All decisions are made by consensus, and classes are usually run by pairs. There have also been study groups on substance abuse, and there is a strong commitment to alcohol-free and drug-free ritual space. Reclaiming also has an events line: (415) 849-0877. Address: Reclaiming, P.O. Box 14404, San Francisco, California 94114.

Re-formed Congregation of the Goddess (RCG). The vision of RCG is to be a viable international ♀'s religion which provides the benefits and recognition of an organized religion to its members, "while finding ♀ centered ways to express our dreams." It is organized in the state of Wisconsin as a not-for-profit corporation. The name the Re-formed Congregation of the Goddess was chosen to "reflect the matriarchal origins of ♀'s religion. . . . The name . . . acknowledges that this is not the first time ♀ have recognized the need to express their intuitive and spiritual selves in a supportive structure with other ♀. We are not beginning to find each other and our spiritual beliefs for the first time, but are re-membering and re-forming the ancient congregation of the Goddess." *Of a Like Mind*, a newspaper and international network for spiritual ♀, is a project of RCG. RCG plans workshops, conferences, and training sessions. It also provides legal recognition and credentials so that ♀ can perform rituals celebrating lives, deaths, bondings, and experience. Address: RCG, P.O. Box 6021, Madison, Wisconsin 53716.

Reformed Druids of North America—Orinda Grove (RDNA). There are at least four RDNA groves functioning at the time this edition went to press: Post Oak Proto Grove in Texas; Birch Grove in New Hampshire; Greenwood Grove in Washington; and this grove in Orinda, California. They have planted a sacred grove, and they publish *A Druid Missal-Any*. While they still use much of the standard RDNA service, they are incorporating elements from Celtic and Indo-European material; members are learning Gaelic, Scots, Welsh, Cornish and looking into ancient sources and recent archeological discoveries. Address: Bodfish, Box 142, Orinda, California 94563.

The Rowan Tree. A Mystery School, "in some senses following the Traditions of the Essenes and of Pythagorus, yet also in communion with those of Tibet. Our focus is on a synthesis of modern approaches to the ancient mysteries. We are a literary tradition of Wicca, and are a non-profit organization devoted to the survival of the Mysteries, and to providing a Priest/esshood to the world that is trained in healing, in counseling, in knowing how to preserve the Earth." For a sample packet which contains the most recent issues of the group's two publications, *The Unicorn* and *The Littlest Unicorn*, an informational letter about the Rowan Tree Church, the Rowan Grove, and other information, send $2.50 to: The Rowan Tree, P.O. Box 8814, Minneapolis, Minnesota 55408.

Sabaean Religious Order. A complex religious tradition combining Egyptian, Sumerian, and West African elements developed as Latin Santeria (see Chapter 9 for details). The Order was founded by Odun Arechaga and bears his artistic stamp. Services every week; elaborate seasonal rituals in a beautiful temple in Chicago. Several chapters elsewhere. Address: Sabaean Religious Order, 3221 North Sheffield Street, Chicago, Illinois 60657.

Sacred Erinnyes Grove and Nature Center. An eclectic Wiccan grove open to Pagans and other magical seekers in Michigan. Address: 1805 Pierce Road, Chelsea, Michigan 48118.

Silver Web. A Pagan resource center and Shamanic Witchcraft clan. The center focuses on networking among groups and individuals in the Maryland/D.C./Virginia area. Educational programming and community festivals. Silver Web publishes *EarthSong*, a quarterly journal of Pagan culture and spirituality, and holds several community festivals including the annual Harvest Survival and Healing Gathering in August. The clan, legally incorporated as Temple of the Silver Web, currently consists of two groves: Rainbow Web Grove, a service-oriented group, and Moonweb, a women's bardic grove focusing on lunar mysteries. There are also independent members. Address: Silver Web, P.O. Box 5628, Baltimore, Maryland 21210.

Sisterspirit. Sisterspirit was formed in December 1985 to create a place where women could share and celebrate their spirituality. Weekly meetings alternating celebration with discussion. Address: Sister-Spirit, 2804 N.E. 42nd, Portland, Oregon 97213.

Southwest Earth Festival Association (SWEFA). An organization that puts on Pagan festivals in the Southwest, usually in New Mexico. Festivals include the Enchanted Mountain Gathering, as well as Beltane and Yule gatherings. Send SASE to: SWEFA, P.O. Box 26414, Albuquerque, New Mexico 87125.

Temple of the Elder Gods (TOTEG). A non-profit religious corporation founded by Joseph B. and Joanna B. Wilson. TOTEG is an American tradition of the Old Religion which embodies Shamanic philosophy and technique. "We believe that the Earth, our Mother, is the living body of the Goddess and that all manifestations of animate and inanimate life on this planet are our siblings. We recognize the different aspects of the Goddess and God in the seasons of the year and in our natural environment. We devote the energy of our circles and our everyday actions to healing the Earth Mother." TOTEG is a membership organization and also publishes a newsletter, *The Waxing Moon*. Send SASE to Temple of the Elder Gods, P.O. Box 4172, Sunland, California 91040.

Temple of the Silver Crescent. The Temple of the Silver Crescent (formerly of Silver Web Raith) is a legally incorporated religious organization of Shamanistic/Ritualistic covens in the Baltimore/Washington, D.C. area. "We focus on healing, Web energy, and sound and movement as magical tools." Silver Crescent members are active as networkers in *Free Spirit Alliance*. The organization offers pre-initiatory classes to serious-minded students and occasionally sponsors open rituals and celebrations. Contact: Silver Crescent, P.O. Box 5128, Laurel, Maryland 20707-0984.

The Temple of Truth. This is not a Pagan group, but a ceremonial magick order, one which, "unlike most other Orders and Magickal Lodges, is essentially unstructured. It has no 'grades,' issues no pretentious certificates, and has no fixed curriculum. . . . The Temple of Truth takes no part in political quarrels which sweep through the contemporary American Occult scene. Likewise, we abjure most of the 'traditional' secrecy which all too frequently hides ineptitude and selfishness on the part of those purporting to know it all." Students can select their course of study and rate of progress. Emphasis on individual practice. Membership in the Temple is non-exclusive. "Motivation should be desire for spiritual development rather than 'powers'—usually over others—in lieu of Self-Control." The Temple of Truth is sponsored by the Light of Truth Church, a duly licensed and incorporated religious institution. "We do proselytize the basic dignity of Man, and we recognize the subjectivity of what most people call 'truth.'" Send SASE for information. Address: The Temple of Truth, P.O. Box 93124, Pasadena, California 91109.

The Thomas Morton Alliance (TMA). A small group of Pagans who believe in political activism as Pagans and who believe they have a responsibility for protecting Mother Earth. Thomas Morton was a historical figure in early colonial America. He is supposed to have settled in Massachusetts in the 1620s. He was an opponent of puritanism, an ally of the American Indians, and is supposed to have raised an eighty-foot May Pole at his home called Merry Mount. The TMA describes itself as a group that comes "from diverse traditions and backgrounds, but we are bound together by the conviction that we must translate into action our commitment to Mother Earth and all her living beings—action that will ultimately transform a society which constantly takes from the Earth into one which balances taking with giving back." The TMA's slogan is "Earth Religion, Earthly Concerns!" TMA supports the rights of indigenous peoples to self-determination everywhere in the world. It also opposes racism, ageism, sexism, classism, and colonialism. Address: The Thomas Morton Alliance, 7 Marlboro Street, Newburyport, Massachusetts 01950.

Women In Constant Creative Action (W.I.C.C.A.). Located in Oregon, W.I.C.C.A. is an organization devoted to women's spirituality. It was formed out of the need of women for a support group, to aid in spiritual and creative growth. It describes itself as a paradox—a loosely knit/tightly structured organization that is more of an organism, one that is waiting for each woman's energy to become, but is already. It is made up of small, local groups (called Wings) that meet weekly, offering supportive interaction, study materials, and experiential exercises. Woman In Constant Creative Action has a spiritual base, expressed through metaphysical exercises. Every meeting has an energy circle. There are also monthly retreats, celebrations, and gatherings. A newsletter, *On Wings*, is published monthly. Send SASE for membership information. Address: Women In Constant Creative Action, P.O. Box 201, Monmouth, Oregon 97361.

FESTIVALS AND GATHERINGS

Some festivals are like old friends—they've been around since the 1970s. Some of them are new and just getting started. While some of the friendliest are smaller regional gatherings, the larger national festivals, like Pagan Spirit Gathering, have become a place for people from all over the country to meet, exchange stories, share ideas, and renew friendships. Festivals are where Pagans come to exult in the knowledge that they are not alone, to find others with similar interests, to join with others in ecstatic celebration, and to learn different ways of doing ritual and work. To find out the most current information about festivals, there is a calendar of events that is published six to eight times a year by Larry Cornett. It is available by subscription for $3/year. Write to: Larry Cornett, 9527 Blake Lane, Apt. 102, Fairfax, Virginia 22031.

Here are some of the more permanent festivals.

Althing. An annual summer celebration sponsored by the Asatru Free Assembly. For AFA members and "all those true to the Gods of the North." Emphasis on Norse and Teutonic Paganism. Workshops, rituals, bardic revelry, bragging and boasting, feasting, fun, and fellowship. Usually held in a wilderness area in Texas. Send SASE to: AFA, P.O. Box 1754, Breckenridge, Texas 76024.

Ancient Ways Festival. A festival held Summer Solstice week in northern California. Rituals, workshops, music, camping. Pagan/Wiccan focus. Send SASE to: Covenant of the Goddess, P.O. Box 1226, Berkeley, California 94704.

Australian Wiccan Conference. An annual gathering usually held near the Spring Equinox (that's fall in the U.S.) in Southern Australia. Camping, rituals, Equinox celebrations. Write: Wiccan Conference, P.O. Box 62, O'Halloran Hill 5158 South Australia.

Celebration of Manhood. An annual weekend gathering for men that takes place during the fall. Send SASE for information to: NEXUS, P.O. Box 532256, Grand Prairie, Texas 75053.

Celebration of Summer. A festival celebration and gathering in Texas, sponsored by NEXUS, P.O. Box 532256, Grand Prairie, Texas 75053.

Celebration of Womanhood. An annual gathering in Smithville, Texas, for women in the Craft. Takes place the weekend prior to Valentine's Day. Send SASE for information: Judy Haskell-Carusone, 5920 Bissonnet, #113, Houston, Texas 77081 or NEXUS, P.O. Box 532256, Grand Prairie, Texas 75053.

Church of All Worlds Beltane Festival. Takes place on the weekend closest to Beltane. The festival includes an all-night Walpurgisnaught bale fire, pagents, nature walks, and May Pole dance. Send SASE to: Church of All Worlds, Box 212, Redwood Valley, California 94570.

Council of the Magickal Arts Beltane Festival. An annual festival held the weekend closest to and preceding Beltane in Crosby, Texas. Contact: Judy Haskell-Carusone, 5920 Bissonnet, #113, Houston, Texas 77081.

Council of the Magickal Arts Samhain Weekend. An annual festival held the weekend closest to and preceding Samhain in Crosby, Texas. Contact: Judy Haskell-Carusone, 5920 Bissonnet, #113, Houston, Texas 77081.

Covenant of the Goddess Grand Council. The Covenant of the Goddess is a cross-traditional federation of some seventy Wiccan covens in fifteen states that have joined together to win recognition for the Craft as a legitimate and legally recognized religion. Every year COG holds a grand festival at the time of their yearly Grand Council. The festival is usually held at a secluded campground or resort and moves to a different area of the country each summer. In addition to the council meeting, the program includes workshops, rituals, music, arts, and crafts. Send SASE to: Covenant of the Goddess, P.O. Box 1226, Berkeley, California 94704.

Eleusis Foundation Festivals. The Foundation sponsors large public seasonal celebrations in New York City at Beltane, Yule, the Summer Solstice, and on other occasions. The celebrations combine ancient and modern forms of ritual art and include dancers, musicians, artists, and performers. The events explore the creation of sacred space, the cycles of death and rebirth, feminine and masculine aspects of divinity, and the relationship between humanity and the natural world. Send SASE to: The Eleusis Foundation, c/o Phyllis Curott and Rodger Parsons, 85 Eastern Parkway, #2E, Brooklyn, New York 11238.

Elf-Fest. A five-day magical convention in late May, sponsored by the Elf Lore Family. "Calling together all Elfin folk, Faeries, Dwarves, Giants, Hobbits, Wise-Women, Mages, Sages, Hermits, Heathens, Bards, Druids, Shamans, Warriors of the Rainbow . . . and to all honest folk who believe that the forgotten ways of old may hold the secret to the future." Magick and mirth, elf-lore, workshops, market, tribal drumming, bardic music and tales, poetry circles, sacred rites and rituals, woodland explorations, shamanic journeys, sweat lodge, healing circles. Send SASE to: ELF, P.O. Box 1082, Bloomington, Indiana 47402.

Elusinian Mysteries. Every year since the late 1960s, NROOGD—the New Reformed Orthodox Order of the Golden Dawn, has presented a re-enactment of the Demeter/Persephone myth. Usually held at the seashore, and usually involving one's own symbolic descent and rebirth, this can be a truly magical experience. The one-day gathering takes place in September, close to the time these ancient mysteries were celebrated. Send SASE to: NROOGD, c/o C.O.G., P.O. Box 1226, Berkeley, California 94704.

Enchanted Mountain Gathering. A four- to five-day festival usually held in early August, in a mountain wilderness area of New Mexico. Camping, workshops, music, sweat lodge, rituals, celebrations. For magical folk with a focus on tribal peoples. Send SASE to: SWEFA, P.O. Box 26414, Albuquerque, New Mexico 87125.

Esotericon. An occult, magic, science fiction, and fantasy convention. It is held each January, near Martin Luther King's birthday, at a hotel in New Jersey (near New York City). Selena Fox, Marion Zimmer Bradley, Kathrine Kurtz have been guests. Address: Esotericon, P.O. Box 22775, Newark, New Jersey 07101.

Festival of Women's Spirituality. A three-day August festival sponsored by Women In Constant Creative Action (W.I.C.C.A.). Women only. Workshops, rituals, music, dance, bazaar, networking. Takes place in a beautiful wilderness setting in Oregon. Send SASE to: W.I.C.C.A., P.O. Box 201, Monmouth, Oregon 97361.

Forever Forests Tree Planting. Forever Forests was started by the late Pagan bard, Gwydion Pendderwen. The gathering takes place on a weekend close to New Year's Day on the sacred land of Annwfn in Mendocino County, California. "Through planting trees we renew our connection with the Earth and reaffirm our belief in the future. We share magic, music and merriment: hard work, hot tubs and hope." Send SASE to: Forever Forests, Box 212, Redwood Valley, California 95470.

Free Spirit Festival. A weekend camp-out festival in late July or early August. Workshops, music, rituals, child care, sweat lodges. Contact: Free Spirit Alliance, P.O. Box 25242, Baltimore, Maryland 21229.

Front Range Pagan Festival. An annual regional summer festival, usually held in the mountains of Colorado. Workshops, rituals, music, magic, campfire, activities for children, bazaar. Rural camping setting. Festival organizers wish it to continue as a small, intimate gathering, and so it is by invitation only. Send SASE to: L. R. Martin, 1950 Trenton Street, #540, Denver, Colorado 80220.

Gaia Festival, A Celebration of Planetary Consciousness. Co-sponsored by the Elf Lore Family and the Heartland Pagan Association. Camping, rituals, workshops, barter, songs, feasting. Takes place in the Midwest. Contact: Gaia Registration, c/o Heartland, 2237 West Morse Avenue, Chicago, Illinois 60645-4850.

Gathering for Life on Earth. A gathering in Ontario that focuses on political-spiritual synthesis and networking of Pagans involved in peace, feminist, Green, gay, native, and anti-nuke issues. Takes place in rural, camping setting in July. Donations accepted to cover cost. Write: Pagans for Peace, c/o Sam Wagar, P.O. Box 6531, Station A, Toronto, Canada MSW IX4.

Goddess Gathering. An annual festival usually held on the weekend of the Summer Solstice in Ohio. Workshops, performances, rituals, trade fair, music, bonfires, camping. Send SASE to: Temple of Wicca, P.O. Box 1302, Findlay, Ohio 45839.

Harvest Festival—A Faerie Gathering. A nine-day autumn festival in mid-October for gay men, for women, children, and friends. Rituals, bonfires, camping. Held in Tennessee. Send SASE to: Short Mountain Sanctuary, Rt. 1, Box 98A, Liberty, Tennessee 37095.

Harvest Moon Celebration. A fall festival in California. Rituals, workshops, and celebrations. Sponsored by the Pallas Society, P.O. Box 4983, Chatsworth, California 91313-4983.

Harvest Survival and Healing Gathering. A festival that is usually held during the second week of August. Sponsored by Silver Web, a resource/networking center, and Pagan Clan whose Craft is known as Shamanic Craft, which operates a legally recognized Temple. Four days in a Pagan forest village environment, with rituals, celebrations, theatre, village councils, music, artists and merchants, sweat lodge, activities for children. Send SASE to: Silver Web, P.O. Box 5628, Baltimore, Maryland 21210.

The Long Dance. I am using these three words to stand for many different ceremonies, rituals, and dances led by Elizabeth Cogburn. While she is not really connected to the Neo-Pagan community, her work touches many of its themes. Elizabeth Cogburn believes that rituals and ceremonies are "intended to restore, deepen and enlighten our human awareness—our sense of living presence—in and of the One Universal Intelligence (God) as it manifests through and among us. . . . The Sacred Theater of the Long Dance is an enactment in microcosm of the grand FACT of manifest life—that uniqueness and diversity may live and thrive together in one interrelated wholeness with great strength and beauty. . . . Living ritual is the great transformation technology of the human race. . . . The changing of the form of our own human consciousness from its raw, ignorant, undisciplined, uninitiated state, to the refined enlightened, creative, benevolent instrument it is meant to be."

Elizabeth Cogburn does many different dances in various parts of the country each year. Another central concept of her work is using ceremonial to find "a better game than war," finding ways to create a dynamic, vital exciting world beyond war. Conflict, says Cogburn, is built into nature as a propelling force of evolution. Peace is not the absence of conflict. Human beings need courageous exploits, trials, stories of struggles and victories. Cogburn is creating ceremonies where creative conflict can take place, where "we consciously choose our stories and our hero models. . . . The proving ground is self-knowledge and creative relationship with equals. The adversary is within ourselves." Write for information: Elizabeth Cogburn, 6741 Edgewood Drive, N.W., Albuquerque, New Mexcio 87107.

Medicine Wheel Gathering. The Bear Tribe has many gatherings throughout the year. Rituals, Native American dance, story-telling, and other activities. Write for information: Bear Tribe, P.O. Box 9167, Spokane, Washington 99209.

Michigan Women's Music Festival. The largest gathering of women and music anywhere. Takes place in August. While not a Pagan festival, this gathering brings together thousands of women. Send SASE to: P.O. Box 22, Walhalla, Michigan 49458.

Mt. Franklin October Gathering. An Australian gathering that takes place on the last weekend in October (near Australia's Beltane). Takes place in the crater of a dormant volcano. Camping, workshops, rituals. Focus on Paganism, Wicca, Ceremonial Magic. Write: October Gathering, P.O. Box 54, Castle Maine, Victoria, Australia 3450.

National Women's Music Festival. An annual feminist music festival that is more than twelve years old. This three-day gathering takes place early in June in a campus setting in Bloomington, Indiana. Besides the abundance of women musicians, this festival includes a writer's conference and a series of workshops on women's spirituality. Music, workshops, open mike. Address: National Women's Music Festival, P.O. Box 5217, Bloomington, Indiana 47402.

Northwest Fall Equinox Celebration. A festival for all who love Mother Earth. Rituals, workshops, music, dancing, crafts, networking, outdoor camping in the midst of the Columbia Gorge region. Stonehenge replica nearby. Sponsored by A Voice of the Goddess. Write for information: A Voice of the Goddess, P.O. Box 13072, Portland, Oregon 97213.

Pacific Circle Gathering. A Pagan and Wiccan festival in Southern California held in the middle of June. Workshops, rituals, camping. Send SASE to: Pacific Circle Gathering, P.O. Box 9513, N. Hollywood, California 91609.

Pagan Spirit Gathering. A week-long festival in Wisconsin around the time of the Summer Solstice, sponsored by Circle. Large camp-out village atmosphere. At present, the largest (approximately four hundred) and most ecumenical Pagan festival in the United States. The focus is on building a week-long community, experiencing nature, sharing work and celebration. Rituals, workshops, village meetings, sweat lodge, wonderful music sharing, ecstatic dancing, men's and women's circles, activities for kids. This gathering attracts people from all over the United States, as well as Canada and beyond. It's becoming more and more international, a place to meet and interact with different Pagan folk and different Pagan traditions from all over. A wonderful way to see the multiplicity of Pagan paths. Send SASE to: Circle, P.O. Box 219, Mt. Horeb, Wisconsin 53572.

Pan-Pagan Festival. One of the oldest outdoor Pagan gatherings. It's been around since 1977. Sponsored by the Midwest Pagan Council, an association of Pagan groups in the Midwest. The focus is on sharing knowledge, celebrating life, and attuning oneself to the Lord and Lady through communion with nature and each other. Send SASE to: Midwest Pagan Council, P.O. Box 313, Matteson, Illinois 60443-0313.

Panthea. A three-day fall retreat in New York State. "We tend to be more participatory and intimate but less rowdy than Pagan 'festivals.'" Rituals, camping, exposure to different Pagan traditions. Write: National Alliance of Pantheists, P.O. Box 622, Farmington, Maine 04938.

Pantheistic Festival. An annual festival in the Ohio-Pennsylvania area. Lectures, workshops, seminars, rituals, psychic fair, bazaar. Send SASE to: The Church of Universal Forces, P.O. Box 03195, Columbus, Ohio 43203.

Radical Faeries Equinox Gathering. A festival to celebrate the Fall Equinox for gay men and friends. Held in North Carolina. Bonfires, rituals, camping. Send SASE to: RFD, Rt. 1, Box 127E, Bakersfield, North Carolina 28705.

Radical Faeries Solstice Gathering. A gathering for gay men and friends held on the weekend of the Summer Solstice in North Carolina. Rituals, bonfires, camping. Send SASE to: RFD, Rt. 1, Box 127E, Bakersfield, North Carolina 28705.

Rainbow Gathering. This is not a strictly Pagan festival, but it is a huge, yearly "new age" camping festival with workshops, music, meditations, rituals, bonfires. Takes place in early July. If you go to this festival, you will believe the 1960s never ended. There are as many as six thousand people at these yearly gatherings which take place in different parts of the country each year. An alternative Utopian Village. Some say this is the most amazing festival on the planet in this current era. Absolutely free. Send SASE to: the Rainbow Family Tribal Council, P.O. Box 5577, Eugene, Oregon 97405. There are also many regional rainbow gatherings on the Summer Solstice. Write: Colorado Rainbow, P.O. Box 9847, Denver, Colorado 80209; Great Lakes Rainbow, P.O. Box 4133, Ann Arbor, Michigan 48106; Rainbow Outreach, P.O. Box 75263, Washington, D.C. 20013; Southern Rainbow, c/o Katuah, Rt. 2, Box 132, Leicester, North Carolina 28748.

Rites of Spring. This festival, sponsored by the EarthSpirit Community, takes place on Memorial Day weekend. One of the best annual Pagan gatherings anywhere, and definitely the best festival in the Northeast. Most recently the gathering has taken place in a beautiful woodland setting, with cabins nestled in the forest. Rituals, workshops, bonfires, sweat lodge, swimming, activities for kids, village meetings. The people who have come year after year have become an extended family. Issues of building community are primary. Send SASE to: The EarthSpirit Community, P.O. Box 365, Medford, Massachusetts 02155.

Rites of Spring & Beltane (May 1) Bash. A nine-day faerie gathering for gay men, women, children, and friends. Rituals, bonfires, camping. In Middle Tennessee. Send SASE to: Short Mt. Sanctuary, Rt. 1, Box 98-A, Liberty, Tennessee 37095.

Samhain Festival. A Pagan, Wiccan, magical street festival, held on the weekend near Samhain. Rituals, music, singing, entertainment. Sponsored by the Magickal Childe, 35 West 19th Street, New York, New York 10011.

Samhain Seminar. A weekend gathering, sponsored by the School of Wicca, that may well lay claim to the title of oldest annual Wiccan festival. It was started in 1974, by Louise and Loy Stone. Rituals, workshops. It takes place in a different part of the country each year and involves not only students from the School of Wicca but people from many different Craft traditions. Send SASE to: School of Wicca, P.O. Box 1502, New Bern, North Carolina 28560.

Samhain Witches Ball. A real Witches Ball with costumes and dancing. Held near All Hallows' Eve. Sponsored by Enchantments, 341 E. 9th St., New York, New York 10003.

The Solitary Convention. A gathering for those who work singly and alone, to talk, listen, and share experiences. A small gathering usually held in August. The convention is sponsored by the Aquarian Tabernacle Church and is usually held at their Retreat House in the woods near Seattle, Washington. Workshops, rituals, music. Send SASE to: Aquarian Tabernacle Church, Inc., P.O. Box 85507, Seattle, Washington 98145.

Sommarsthing. A festival of Norse and Teutonic Paganism that takes place over the July 4th weekend in California. Camping, workshops, rituals, bardic sharing. Send SASE to: Sommarsthing, P.O. Box 185, Camptonville, California 95922.

The Spiral Dance. A large, beautifully choreographed, and artistic ritual and dance, created for Pagan celebration by Reclaiming. It takes place near Samhain but doesn't happen every year. Send SASE to: Reclaiming, P.O. Box 14404, San Francisco, California 94414.

Spiral Gathering. A Southern Pagan Renaissance Lunarfest. A beautiful festival held in September, at a wilderness setting in Georgia. A very special festival with rituals, bonfires, sweat lodge, workshops, networking, community spirit, music, and even good home-cooked food. Lodging in rustic cabins. Sponsored by the First Humanist Church of Atlanta, P.O. Box 8264, Atlanta, Georgia 30306.

Spring Equinox Mysteries Festival. A recreation of the Elusinian Mysteries in underground chambers, held annually over Easter Weekend and sponsored by the Aquarian Tabernacle Church. Heated buildings at seaside retreat. Rituals, music, discussions, arts, crafts, and networking for the Pagan Community. Send SASE to: Aquarian Tabernacle Church, Inc., P.O. Box 85507, Seattle, Washington 98145.

Starwood Festival. A summer festival in central Ohio that combines Pagan, "new age," magical, and often Erisian elements. Among the frequent guests: Robert Anton Wilson and Robert Shea, authors of *Illuminatus!* In the past, the site of this annual magical camping gathering has been a clothes-optional natural recreation park with lakes, hiking trails, and many other facilities. Workshops, rituals, films, classes, concerts, bonfires, ecstatic dancing. Send SASE to:

Association for Consciousness Exploration (ACE), 1643 Lee Road, #9, Cleveland Heights, Ohio 44118.

SWEFA—Beltane. A one-day festival held on a weekend day near May 1st, in the mountains near Albuquerque, New Mexico. Sponsored by the Southwest Earth Festival Association. Maypole, music, feasting, rituals, and celebrations of May. Send SASE to: SWEFA, P.O. Box 26414, Albuquerque, New Mexico 87125.

SWEFA—Yule. A Yule celebration and craft fair held on a weekend day just before the Winter Solstice, in Albuquerque, New Mexico. Continuous live entertainment, evening ritual, and pot-luck feast. Send SASE to: SWEFA, P.O. Box 26414, Albuquerque, New Mexico 87125.

Wic-Can Fest. A festival in a beautiful rural setting near Toronto usually held on the last weekend in May. This has become "the" festival in Canada. Workshops, rituals, music, revelry. Camping, some cabins. Send SASE to: Wic-Can Fest, 3090 Danforth Ave., P.O. Box 105, Scarborough, Ontario M1L 1B1 Canada.

Wild Magick Gathering. A three-day harvest festival usually held at the Fall Equinox by the Elf Lore Family and friends. "A meeting place for all manner of fair folk." Rituals, workshops, camping, celebrations. Send SASE to: ELF, P.O. Box 1082, Bloomington, Indiana 47402.

Winterstar. A February winter festival held in a ski resort in central Ohio. Workshops, rituals, music. The festival has both a Pagan and new age focus, with topics ranging from the occult to consciousness exploration. Sponsored by the Association for Consciousness Exploration (ACE), 1643 Lee Road, #9, Cleveland Heights, Ohio 44118.

BIBLIOGRAPHY

This is a very eclectic and personal bibliography, which makes no attempt to be complete. It attempts to be a rough guide to some of the better books on modern Neo-Paganism, Wicca, and Goddess spirituality. Many of the books footnoted in *Drawing Down the Moon* are not listed here. In fact, I've tried to emphasize many of the books that came out around the time or after this book was first published. A more complete bibliography on Goddess spirituality can be found in *The Politics of Women's Spirituality*, edited by Charlene Spretnak. This booklist gives some of the standard works and a number of my more recent favorites. It's given with the notion that someone new to Paganism, Wicca, and Goddess spirituality might like to have a small guide giving some of the choices available for further exploration.

Adair, Margo. *Working Inside Out, Tools for Change* (Berkeley, Calif.: Wingbow Press, 1984). This is one of the best books focusing on applied meditations, affirmations, and pathworking. The author has been involved in political struggles for many years and is a teacher of meditation as well. There are exercises for building community, healing yourself, dealing with past traumas, working through relationships, and envisioning a different world, to mention just a few.

Apuleius, Lucius. *The Golden Ass.* Many different translations exist, including ones by Jack Lindsay (Bloomington: Indiana University Press, 1960), Robert Graves (New York: Farrar, Straus & Young, 1951), or W. Adlington trans. of 1566 (Cambridge, Mass.: Harvard University Press, 1955). As a friend of mine put it, this is either the first Goddess novel or the oldest one still in print. Apuleius was an initiate of Isis, and the book was written in the second century A.C.E. The vision of Isis near the end of the book is poetic and inspired.

Bolen, Jean. *Goddesses in Everywoman, a New Psychology of Women* (San Francisco: Harper & Row, 1984). A popular book by a practicing psychiatrist who uses the archetypal images of the Greek goddesses—including Athena, Hera, Hestia, Artemis, Demeter, and Persephone—as a method of personal exploration and growth.

Bonewits, P. E. I. *Real Magic* (Berkeley, Calif.: Creative Arts Book Company, 1971, 1979). A no-nonsense guide to magic and psychic reality by a feisty, opinionated, knowledgeable practitioner. The only man to receive a major in magic from the University of California—and his degree is signed by Ronald Reagan! Witty, entertaining, with a sprinkle of arrogance.

Bracelin, J. L. *Gerald Gardner: Witch* (London: Octagon Press, 1960). The only biography of Gerald Gardner. Rumored to have really been written by Idris Shah. Filled with wonderful anecdotes about Gardner's life. Somewhat of an apology. Not great literature.

Bradley, Marion Zimmer. *The Mists of Avalon* (New York: Knopf, 1983; Del Rey, 1984–85). One of the only books on Goddess spirituality to make the *New York Times* best-seller list. A powerful retelling of the Arthurian legend from a feminist and Pagan point of view. A stirring and satisfying novel that has reached a broad audience.

Cameron, Anne. *Daughters of Copper Woman* (Vancouver, British Columbia: Press Gang Publishers, 1981). Matriarchal legends from the indigenous peoples of Vancouver Island. Simply and beautifully told.

Christ, Carol P. *Diving Deep and Surfacing: Women Writers on Spiritual Quest* (Boston: Beacon Press, 1980). Another excellent book on women's spirituality.

Christ, Carol P., and Judith Plaskow. *Womanspirit Rising, a Feminist Reader in Religion* (San Francisco: Harper & Row, 1979). An excellent sourcebook in feminist theology, including selections from Starhawk, Mary Daly, Merlin Stone, Naomi Goldenberg, Zsuzsanna Budapest, Rosemary Radford Ruether, and many others.

Downing, Christine. *The Goddess, Mythological Images of the Feminine* (New York: Crossroad Publishing Co., 1981). A scholarly and personal journey. The author has a background as a Jungian analyst as well as a professor of religious studies. The book explores the relationship of the classical Greek goddesses to who we are and who we might become.

Ehrenreich, Barbara, and Dierdre English. *Witches, Midwives and Nurses* (New York: Feminist Press, 1963). A groundbreaking small booklet, linking the persecution of women, the persecution of Witches, and the rise of the medical profession.

Eliade, Mircea. *Occultism, Witchcraft and Cultural Fashions* (Chicago: University of Chicago Press, 1976). Some of the most sensible, intelligent, and perceptive essays on occultism and Witchcraft ever written. Once you've read this, take the big leap and try his massive tome on shamanism!

Evans, Arthur. *Witchcraft and the Gay Counterculture* (Boston: Fag Rag Books, 1978). This book, one of the harbingers of the Radical Faery movement, is an attempt to find, understand, and reclaim Gay history and to uncover its links to pre-Christian spiritual traditions. A controversial book that links the persecution of Gays with the persecution of Witches and the routing out of Paganism by Christianity.

Farrar, Janet and Stewart. *The Witches Way* (London: Robert Hale, Ltd., 1981, 1984). Published in the United States as *A Witches Bible*, Vol. I, II (New York: Magickal Childe, 1985). The most complete versions of the Gardnerian and Alexandrian rituals ever published. Stewart Farrar is a former journalist who became an initiate of Alex and Maxine Sanders and then wrote a book, *What Witches Do*, which was one of the better early books on Wicca. Since then, Stewart Farrar has written many occult novels, as well as begun his own coven with his wife, Janet. Some Witches are angry that, yet again (this is at least the fourth time), someone has published a large portion of the Gardnerian rituals in violation of oath. But this book is the most accurate version and even has Doreen Valiente's blessings and contributions. The book also has many chapters on the history and practice of Wicca. Lots of good, practical knowledge from two experienced coven leaders.

Forfreedom, Ann and Julie Ann. *The Book of the Goddess* (1980). Available from Ann Forfreedom, Goddess Rising, 2441 Cordova St., Oakland, California 94602. Personal experiences of the Goddess, poetry, illustrations.

Fortune, Dion. *The Sea Priestess* (New York: Weiser, 1978). Dion Fortune has written many novels, as well as many books on practical occultism. Within the novels, Pagan initiatory themes are dominant; in her nonfiction they are not. All the Pagan novels are interesting, especially *Moon Magic* and *The Goat Foot God*, but *The Sea Priestess* is very special, portraying the power of ritual and initiatory experience in a way that words are seldom able to express. None of these novels really work as *novels*, but *The Sea Priestess* works despite its structural flaws. Students at the beginning of a spiritual search find this novel particularly powerful.

Gardner, Gerald B. *Witchcraft Today* (New York: Citadel Press, 1955). One of the books that started the Wicca revival. First published in 1954, after the repeal of the last Witchcraft Acts in Britain, the book lays out the view that Witchcraft was the survival of the ancient Pagan religion of Western Europe and that Gardner was himself initiated in 1939 into one of the surviving covens in the New Forest. There's a whole lot of questionable scholarship, but if it wasn't for Gardner, *Drawing Down the Moon* would never have been written, and most of us Wiccans would not be around.

Gardner, Gerald B. *The Meaning of Witchcraft* (New York: Samual Weiser, 1959). Published in 1959, this is a much more comprehensive book than *Witchcraft Today* and is a further expansion of Gardner's views.

Glass, Justine. *Witchcraft, the Sixth Sense* (North Hollywood, Calif.: Wilshire Book Company, 1970). When I was entering the Craft in the early 1970s, this was the book that everyone recommended as the best introduction to Wicca. Sensible, well-written, sensitive.

Goldenberg, Naomi. *Changing of the Gods: Feminism and the End of Traditional Religions* (Boston: Beacon Press, 1979). Another excellent book on the rise of women's spirituality and the problems patriarchal religions have failed to address.

Graves, Robert. *The White Goddess* (New York: Farrar, Straus & Giroux, 1948, 1966). A great work of poetic prose, often confused for scholarship. A massive, mythic framework for the Great Goddess in hopes of her re-emergence. An important book in the history of the Wiccan revival.

Griffin, Susan. *Woman and Nature: The Roaring Inside Her* (New York: Harper & Row, 1978). A deep and dark and powerful work. The book starts with the observation that men often consider themselves separate from nature and superior to matter, whereas women are considered closer to nature. The form is a kind of intuitive poetic prose. One of the most extraordinary aspects of the book is a simple listing of dates in history, showing the proximity (and implied connection) between the scientific revolution, the "age of enlightenment," and the most dreadful persecution of Witches. This is a deeply angry, passionate book. Its controversial thesis demands a lot of thought. The writing is exquisite.

Jong, Erica. *Fanny* (New York: New American Library, 1980). There have been only three recent best-sellers to feature a priestess of the Goddess or a Witch from a Wiccan perspective. This is one of them. Fanny is a feisty, bawdy character. Some feminists have attacked the rape scene in the book, as playing into the notion of women as passive, but I personally loved the book.

Mariechild, Diane. *Mother Wit: A Feminist Guide to Psychic Development* (Trumansburg, N.Y.: The Crossing Press, 1981). A wonderful and poetic guide to psychic work. Exercises and affirmations done with great sensitivity.

Merchant, Carolyn. *The Death of Nature: Woman, Ecology and the Scientific Revolution* (San Francisco: Harper & Row, 1980). A more scholarly and less poetic exploration of some of the same issues explored by Susan Griffin in *Woman and Nature*.

Miller, David. *The New Polytheism, Rebirth of the Gods and Goddesses* (New York: Harper & Row, 1974). Miller uses the Greek gods and goddesses as archetypal images to discover a new world of multiple values. While his reliance on classical Greek imagery is limiting, his political and philosophical insights on the relationship of polytheism to politics and society is illuminating and liberating.

Murray, Margaret A. *The Witch-cult in Western Europe* (London: Oxford University Press, 1921, reprint 1962). Much of the scholarship is now considered questionable and certainly controversial. Other parts are incontrovertible—including much of the history of folk traditions and the continuation of Pagan customs. This is where the Wicca revival really began.

Patai, Raphael. *The Hebrew Goddess* (Philadelphia: Ktav Publications, 1967). A wonderful book that shows the rich heritage of Goddess images in Jewish culture. Patai shows that the Hebrews continued to worship the Canaanite goddesses of old. Patai looks at the place of the Shekinah, of Lilith, and explores the battles between patriarchal and matriarchal forces within Jewish history and tradition.

Robinson, James, editor. *The Nag Hammadi Library* (San Francisco: Harper & Row, 1977). The Gnostic writings unearthed at Nag Hammadi. An incredibly important series of documents, especially for women interested in sources for Goddess religion. For example, "The Thunder, Perfect Mind," is one of the most amazing invocations of the feminine and dates back at least to the second century.

Spretnak, Charlene. *The Politics of Women's Spirituality* (Garden City, N.Y.: Anchor Press, 1982). Charlene Spretnak has edited almost 600 pages of essays charting the rise of the Feminist Spirituality Movement. A wonderful source book filled with scholarship and controversy. Poetry, prose, excellent bibliography.

Starhawk. *Dreaming the Dark, Magic, Sex and Politics* (Boston: Beacon Press, 1982). This is an amazing book that joins the insights of the direct action non-violent peace movements with the insights of the Wicca coven. Drawing on her own experiences with groups, doing ritual, doing protest actions, spending time in jail, the book is a rich body of source material for working with groups, particularly groups that combine a spiritual and political perspective. The appendix on the history of the "Burning Times" is extraordinary, combining the insights of English labor historians such as Christopher Hill with the scholarship of feminist writers.

Starhawk. *The Spiral Dance, A Rebirth of the Ancient Religion of the Great Goddess* (San Francisco: Harper & Row, 1979). This book came out the same day as *Drawing Down the Moon*. If you haven't read it, it should be the next book on your list. Simply, one of the best books on modern Wicca, filled with theory, practice, rituals, exercises, and beautiful descriptions. As with all of Starhawk's work, a beautiful interweaving of spiritual and social concerns.

Stone, Merlin. *Ancient Mirrors of Womanhood*, Vol. I, II (New York: New Sibylline Books, 1979). A collection of goddess legends from all over the world, arranged culture by culture. The book has a feminist point of view and includes much source material.

Teish, Luisah. *Jambalaya, The Natural Woman's Book of Personal Charms and Practical Ritual* (San Francisco: Harper & Row, 1985). The only book by a publicly avowed American Voodoo priestess. Teish is a powerful lady, who lays a lot of stereotypes to rest. Lots of information on Yoruba goddesses, magic, and ritual working.

Valiente, Doreen. *An ABC of Witchcraft Past & Present* (New York: St. Martin's Press, 1973). A wonderful source book. All writings by Doreen Valiente can be counted on to be lucid and well written. She is the best to come out of the "Gardnerian" tradition of Wicca, and some of the rituals of that tradition bear her stamp. See also *Witchcraft for Tomorrow* (New York: St. Martin's Press, 1978).

Walker, Mitch, and Friends. *Visionary Love: A Spirit Book of Gay Mythology and Trans-Mutational Faerie* (San Francisco: Treeroots Press, 1980). Many of my friends in the Radical Faery movement say this book is the book to begin with. Also take a look at *The Faggots and Their Friends Between Revolutions* by Larry Mitchell (New York: Calamus Books, 1977).

Weinstein, Marion. *Positive Magic; Occult Self-Help* (Custer, Wash.: Phoenix Publishing Company, 1981). A very good introductory book on magical working from a totally non-manipulative point of view. Includes everything from Astrology to I Ching to Wicca. Chapter 8, "Words of Power, the Work of Self-Transformation," is so valuable it alone is worth the price of the book. Techniques of affirmation are clear and beautifully described. Some people will find Weinstein's approach too saccharine, with almost no acknowledgment of the darker side of life, but the book is a great ethical antidote to the thousands of worthless pages published every day promising readers power, money, love, and glory through the control of others.

Notes

CHAPTER 1:   PAGANISM AND PREJUDICE

1. Craft/Pagan publications (either currently being published or appearing within the last twenty years) include: *The Crystal Well, The Waxing Moon, Nemeton, Green Egg, Korythalia, The New Broom, The Hidden Path, Medicine Wheel, Earth Religion News, The Witches Broomstick, Wica Newsletter, The Witches Trine, Star-Child, Insight, Quest, Revival, The Wiccan, Florida Aquarian, Northwind News, The Black Lite, Survival, Iris, Julian Review, The Harp, Witchcraft Digest, Psychic Eye, Seax Wica Voys, Word to the Wise, Gnostica, The Enchanted Cauldron, Khepera, Esbat, Moon Rise, Wicca Times, Georgian Newsletter, Runestone, Women's Coven Newsletter, Druid Chronicler, Castle Rising, Caveat Emptor, Pagan Renaissance, The Coming Age, The Cauldron, The Covenstead, The Unicorn Speaks, The Summoner, The Sword of Dyrnwyn, Old Gods and New Devils, The Heathen, Raven Banner, Shrew, The Pagan Way.*

2. "Neosacral" was used, for example, by Andrew M. Greeley in "Implications for the Sociology of Religion of Occult Behavior in the Youth Culture," in *On the Margin of the Visible: Sociology, the Esoteric and the Occult,* ed. Edward A Tiryakian (New York: John Wiley & Sons, 1974), p. 295. First presented as a paper at the 1970 annual meeting of the American Sociological Association; "Neotranscendentalist" was used, for example, by psychiatrist Raymond Prince in "Cocoon Work: An Interpretation of the Concern of Contemporary Youth with the Mystical," in *Religious Movements in Contemporary America,* ed. Irving Zaretsky and Mark Leone (Princeton: Princeton University Press, 1974), p. 263.

3. Most Neo-Pagan groups meet in *groves, circles,* or *covens.* The word *nests* is used to describe groups within the Church of All Worlds. The word *vortices* has been used by the Elf Queen's Daughters.

4. "In various suburban basements around the country young marrieds peel off their clothes (thus becoming 'sky clad') and jump within a nine-foot circle to celebrate a witches' sabbat" (Andrew M. Greeley, "The Devil, You Say," *New York Times Magazine,* [Feb. 4, 1973], p. 15).

5. Originally called Craftcast Farm, it became The Holy Order of St. Brigit in 1977.

6. Aleister Crowley, *Magick in Theory and Practice,* privately published in Paris in 1929. Recently published in *Magick,* ed. John Symonds and Kenneth Grant (London: Routledge Kegan Paul, Ltd., 1973), p. 131. Crowley spells magic with a *k* to distinguish it from stage magic. Many magical practitioners do likewise. I do not.

7. Bonewits's definition of magic is not simply "folk parapsychology," a phrase he has used effectively in TV interviews, etc. Bonewits considers magic "an art as well as a science that has to do with the methods people have developed over the centuries for getting their psychic talents to do what they want them to do" (taped letter, winter 1978). My own tendency is to smudge the line between the psychological and the psychic. Bonewits disagrees: "It's true that it is often hard to make a fine line between where the psychic starts and the psychological ends, but it is a distinction that still has to be made from time to time. Most people who have a sloppy definition of magic (or a definition that makes it impossible to distinguish it from art or psychology) are usually not very good occultists who don't have much in the way of psychic talent."

8. Edward Gibbon, *The Decline and Fall of the Roman Empire* (New York: Modern Library, 1932), I, 725–26. In a footnote (Chapter XXI, note 174), Gibbon writes that *pagan* derives from the Greek παγή, signifying fountain and the rural neighborhood surrounding it. It became synonymous with "rural" in Rome and came to mean *rustic* or *peasant.* With the rise of the Roman military, *pagan* became a contemptuous epithet meaning *nonsoldier.* The Christians considered themselves soldiers of Christ and those who refused the sacrament of baptism were reproached with the term *pagan* as early as the reign of Emperor Valentinian (365 C.E.) and the word was introduced into Imperial law in the Theodosian Code. After Christianity became the official religion of the Roman Empire, the ancient religion lived on in obscure places and, writes Gibbon, "the word pagans, with its new signification, reverted to its primitive origin." It was then applied to all polytheists in the old and new world. It was used by Christians against the Mohammedans, the Unitarians, etc.

9. Gore Vidal, *Julian* (Boston: Little, Brown and Company, 1964), p. 497.

10. *The Julian Review* was published by the Delphic Fellowship, a Neo-Pagan group, now defunct. *The Julian Review* was founded in 1967 by

Don Harrison. Shortly thereafter, Harrison met Michael Kinghorn and together they founded the Delphic Fellowship, which considered itself to be the voice of resurgent Greek Paganism. Today, Harrison is a priest in the Church of the Eternal Source (see Chapter 9).

11. Prince, "Cocoon Work," p. 264.

12. "The First Epistle of Isaac," *The Druid Chronicles* (*evolved*) (Berkeley: Berkeley Drunemeton Press, 1976), 2:4.

13. The first quote is from an undated Church of All Worlds tract, "An Old Religion for a New Age: Neo-Paganism." The second quote appears in Bonewits's "The First Epistle of Isaac," 2:2.

14. The *Oxford English Dictionary* observes that the etymology of *religion* is doubtful but that one view connects it with *religáre*—to bind. The *American Heritage Dictionary* observes that *religion*, from the Latin *religió*, is "perhaps from religáre, to bind back: re-, back and ligáre, to bind, fasten."

15. Harriet Whitehead, "Reasonably Fantastic: Some Perspectives on Scientology, Science Fiction and Occultism," *Religious Movements in Contemporary America*, pp. 547–87. The original quote from William James ("His contentment with the finite incases him like a lobstershell") appears in William James, *The Varieties of Religious Experience: A Study in Human Nature*, being the Gifford Lectures on natural religion delivered at Edinburgh in 1901–1902 (New York: Longmans, Green, and Co., Ltd., 1903), p. 93.

CHAPTER 2: A RELIGION WITHOUT CONVERTS

1. Among those books influencing my childhood were: Caroline Dale Snedeker, *The Spartan* (or *The Coward of Thermopylae*) (New York: Doubleday, 1911) and *The Perilous Seat* (New York: Doubleday, 1923); Mary Renault, *The King Must Die* (New York: Pantheon, 1958).

2. For an understanding of Star Trek literature, see J. Lichtenberg, S. Marshak, and J. Winston, *Star Trek Lives* (New York: Bantam, 1975); see also spin-off Star Trek myths written by fans in Jacquelin Lichtenberg, *Kraith Collected*, Vol. I, and issues of *Babel*, a "Trekie" fan magazine.

3. The famous "opium of the people" quote is almost never given in full. My favorite translation is in Christopher Caudwell, *Further Studies in a Dying Culture* (London: The Bodley Head, 1949), pp. 75–76: "Religious misery is at once the expression of real misery and a protest against that misery. Religion is the sigh of the hard pressed creature, the heart of a heartless world, the spirit of unspiritual conditions. It is the opium of the people." For a more accessible version, see Karl Marx, *Selected Writ-*

ings in Sociology and Social Philosophy, trans. T. B. Bottomore (New York: McGraw-Hill, 1964), p. 27.

4. John McPhee, *Encounters with the Archdruid* (New York: Farrar, Straus and Giroux, 1971), pp. 84, 95.

5. Arnold Toynbee, "The Religious Background of the Present Environmental Crisis," *International Journal of Environmental Studies*, Vol, III, 1972. Also published, under the title "The Genesis of Pollution," in *Horizon*, Vol. XV, No. 3 (Summer 1973), pp. 4–9.

6. Lynn White, Jr., "The Historical Roots of Our Ecologic Crisis," *Science*, Vol. 155 (March 10, 1967), 1203–07. Also in *The Environmental Handbook*, ed. Garrett de Bell (New York: Ballantine, 1970), pp. 12–26. Quotations on pp. 19 and 20.

7. See "An Interview with Doris and Sylvester [Vic] Stuart," *Earth Religion News*, Vol. 1, No. 4 (1974), 23–25.

8. Published versions of this ritual—often called "The Charge of the Goddess"—can be found in *The Grimoire of Lady Sheba* (St. Paul: Llewellyn, 1972), pp. 145–47, and in Stewart Farrar, *What Witches Do* (New York: Coward, McCann & Geoghegan, 1971), pp. 193–94. The version on the Stuarts's tape that I heard was written by Neo-Pagan writer Ed Fitch.

9. This attitude toward *belief* is actually not uncommon among writers who treat "occult" subjects. For example, D. Arthur Kelly writes in "Theories of Knowledge and the I Ching," "I cannot say that I 'believe' in the I Ching; rather, I would say that I have learnt a great deal about life and the universe from a contemplation of its 'teachings' " (*Gnostica*, Vol. IV, No. 5 [January 1975], 33).

10. Robert S. Ellwood, Jr., *Religious and Spiritual Groups in Modern America* (Englewood Cliffs, N.J.: Prentice-Hall, 1973), p. 189.

11. In "An Interview with Doris and Sylvester Stuart," p. 24, Sylvester Stuart observes, "I see Wicca as the only hope of the survivors of mankind after there has been a complete breakdown in our present type of society, a breakdown which I see coming in the forseeable future." Stuart said he saw the Craft as a repository for survival skills.

CHAPTER 3: THE PAGAN WORLD VIEW

1. R. H. Barrow, trans., *Prefect and Emperor, the Relationes of Symmachus A.D. 384* (London: Oxford University Press, 1973), pp. 40–41. From an address to Valentinian, Theodosius, and Arcadius. In Latin: "Eadem spectamus astra, commune caelum est, idem nos mundus involvit: Quid interest, qua quisque prudentia verum requirat? Uno itinere non potest perveniri ad tam grande secretum."

2. James Henry Breasted, *Development of Religion and Thought in Ancient Egypt* (New York: Charles Scribner's Sons, 1912), p. 315.

3. Dagobert D. Runes, *Dictionary of Philosophy* (New York: Philosophical Library, 1942), p. 242.

4. *Whole Earth Catalog* (Menlo Park, Cal.: Portola Institute, 1969).

5. Isaac Bonewits, "The Second Epistle of Isaac," *The Druid Chronicles (evolved)* (Berkeley: Berkeley Drunemeton Press, 1976), 2:13.

6. David Hume, "The Natural History of Religion," *Essays and Treatises on Several Subjects* (Edinburgh: Bell & Bradfute, 1825), II, 384–422. Quotations are on pp. 386 and 395.

7. Paul Radin, *Monotheism Among Primitive Peoples* (Basel: Bollingen Foundation, Special Publication No. 4, 1954). Quotations are on pp. 24, 29, 30, and 25.

8. Harold Moss, *Green Egg*, Vol. V, No. 51 (December 21, 1972), Forum section, p. 5.

9. Theodore Roszak, *Where the Wasteland Ends: Politics and Transcendence in Postindustrial Society* (New York: Anchor Books, 1973), pp. 108–09.

10. David Miller, *The New Polytheism* (New York: Harper & Row, 1974), p. 4. Other quotations from Miller are on pp. 5–6, 59–60, vii–viii, ix, and 24.

11. For example, in noting the controversial monotheistic Witchcraft system of Gavin and Yvonne Frost's School of Wicca, Harold Moss of the Church of the Eternal Source observed, "In the discussions with the Frosts, we should remember that polytheism can contain monotheism, but not the other way around. When we say that Witches are polytheists, we are admitting that some of them were and are monotheists. [The Frosts are] monotheist(s) in a polytheistic religion . . . which is perfectly OK!" (*Earth Religion News*, Vol. I, No. 4 [1974], 3–4).

12. James Hillman, "Psychology: Monotheistic or Polytheistic," *Spring 1971* (New York: Spring Publications, 1971), pp. 197, 199–200.

13. Miller, *The New Polytheism*, p. 55.

14. Hillman, "Psychology: Monotheistic or Polytheistic," p. 206. Hillman considers a revival of Paganism a "danger" because it would bring "along its accoutrements of popular soothsaying, quick priesthoods, astrological divination, extravagant practices and the erosion of psychic differentiations through delusional enthusiasms" (p. 206).

15. Miller, *The New Polytheism*, p. 81.

16. Harold Moss, *Green Egg*, Vol. VII, No. 63 (June 21, 1974), p. 28.

17. Robert Ellwood, Jr., "Polytheism: Establishment or Liberation Religion?", *Journal of the American Academy of Religion*, Vol. XLII, No. 2 (1974), 344–49.

18. The next few quotations were culled from answers to a questionnaire

sent out in the mail to various Neo-Pagans during the winter and spring of 1976. The questionnaire appeared in *Green Egg,* Vol. VIII, No. 76 (February 2, 1976), 32–36.

19. Isaac Bonewits, first quote from interview; second from "The Second Epistle of Isaac," *The Druid Chronicles (evolved)* (Berkeley: Berkeley Drunemeton Press, 1976) 1:12. In an editorial in *Gnostica,* Vol. IV, No. 6 (February 1975), 2, Bonewits, with typical humor, added that "monotheistic religions inevitably promote bigotry and chauvinism of all sorts, but let us not forget that polytheistic cultures have also produced chauvinistic behavior.... However, while monotheists are *required* to be bigots, for polytheists, bigotry is merely an exciting option."

20. Harold Moss, *Green Egg,* Vol. VIII, No. 70 (May 1, 1975), 38.

21. Apropos Neo-Pagans as an elite, Bonewits, in an editorial in *Gnostica,* Vol. IV, No. 9 (July 1975), 2, writes that Neo-Pagans are part of the *andermenschen*—the *other people*—as opposed to *übermenschen* or *untermenschen:* "We have always had the *andermenschen*—the odd ones, the different people. We have always had the *andermenschen,* in every society on our planet; they are our painters and poets, our composers and musicians, our dancers and story-tellers, our witches and mediums, our mystics and shamans, our magicians and psychics. These are the strange ones, the people who have dipped their toes into the otherworld and come back raving and enchanting, healing and prophesying, always trying desperately to point toward the new and the inexplicable as the only source of salvation for our poor, confused species."

CHAPTER 4: THE WICCAN REVIVAL

1. Ann Belford Ulanov, "The Witch Archetype," a lecture given to the Analytical Psychology Club of New York on November 17, 1976. Printed in *Quadrant,* Vol. X, No. 1 (1977), 5–22.

2. Elliot Rose, *A Razor for a Goat* (Toronto: University of Toronto Press, 1962), p. 3.

3. Isaac Bonewits, "Witchcraft: Classical, Gothic and Neopagan (Part I)," *Green Egg,* Vol. IX, No. 77 (March 20, 1976), 15. Bonewits's etymological excursion through the word *witch* appears on pp. 15–17.

4. "Witchcraft in Wichita," *The Waxing Moon* (British edition), New Series No. 1 (Samhain 1970), p. 5. *The Waxing Moon* was the journal of the Pagan Movement in Britain and Ireland.

5. Robert Graves, *The White Goddess,* amended and enlarged ed. (New York: Farrar, Straus and Giroux, 1966), p. 14.

6. For a summary of this myth see Raymond Buckland, *Witchcraft from the Inside* (St. Paul: Llewellyn, 1971).

7. Elliot Rose, *A Razor for a Goat*, pp. 8–10. Actually Rose, in humor, puts forth four schools: Bluff, Knowing, Anti-Sadducee, and Murrayite.

8. Margaret A. Murray, *The Witch-Cult in Western Europe* (Oxford: Oxford University Press, 1921), pp. 12, 233, and 236.

9. Margaret A. Murray, *The God of the Witches* (London: Sampson Low, Marston & Co., Ltd., 1933); *The Divine King in England* (London: Faber & Faber Ltd., 1954); *My First Hundred Years* (London: William Kimber and Co., Ltd., 1963).

10. Norman Cohn, *Europe's Inner Demons* (New York: Basic Books, 1975), p. 125. Other quotations are on pp. 104–09, 124, and 258–61. The reference to the Witches International Craft Association refers to New York Witch Leo Martello whose civil-rights activities on behalf of Witches can be read about in his book, *Witchcraft: The Old Religion* (Secaucus, N.J.: University Books, 1973).

11. H. R. Trevor-Roper, "The European Witch-Craze and Social Change," in *Witchcraft and Sorcery*, ed. Max Marwick (Harmondsworth, Eng.: Penguin Books, 1970), pp. 121–23, 127–28, 131–32, 136, 140, and 146.

12. Mircea Eliade, "Some Observations on European Witchcraft," in *Occultism, Witchcraft and Cultural Fashions* (Chicago: University of Chicago Press, 1976), p. 71.

13. Ibid., p. 85. Other quotations are on pp. 75–78 and 81.

14. Lucius Apuleius, *The Golden Ass*, trans. Robert Graves (New York: Farrar, Straus & Young, 1951); also W. Adlington trans. of 1566 (Cambridge: Harvard University Press, 1965).

15. Charles Godfrey Leland, *Aradia, or the Gospel of the Witches* (London: David Nutt, 1899); reprinted (New York: Samuel Weiser, 1974).

16. Jeffrey Burton Russell, *Witchcraft in the Middle Ages* (Ithaca: Cornell University Press, 1972), p. 298.

17. Leo Martello, *Witchcraft: The Old Religion* (Secaucus, N.J.: University Books, 1973), pp. 45–68.

18. Charles Godfrey Leland, *Etruscan Roman Remains* (London: T. Fisher Unwin, 1892).

19. Rose, *A Razor for a Goat*, p. 218.

20. Leland, *Aradia*, pp. 5–7.

21. Jessie Wicker Bell, *The Grimoire of Lady Sheba* (St. Paul: Llewellyn, 1972), p. 145.

22. T. C. Lethbridge, *Witches* (New York: Citadel Press, 1968), p. 9.

23. Buckland, *Witchcraft from the Inside*, p. 50.

24. Doreen Valiente, *An ABC of Witchcraft Past & Present* (New York: St. Martin's Press, 1973), p. 12.

25. Leland, *Aradia*, pp. 104–06 and 111.

26. Aidan Kelly, "The Rebirth of Witchcraft: Tradition and Creativity in the Gardnerian Reform" (unpublished Ms., 1977), p. 274.

27. Graves, *The White Goddess*, p. 488. This is one area where Isaac Bonewits and Aidan Kelly are in disagreement. Aidan wrote to me in the spring of 1978: "Graves says many times in *The White Goddess* that it is a poetic work, and specifically disclaims it as scholarship in the usual sense. Certainly many in the Craft who wouldn't know scholarship from a raven have blithely overlooked this point—but Graves can't be blamed for that."

28. Robert Graves, "Witches in 1964," *The Virginia Quarterly Review*, Vol. XL, No. 4 (1964), 550–59.

29. Patricia Crowther, *Witch Blood!* (New York: House of Collectibles, 1974); Stewart Farrar, *What Witches Do* (New York: Coward, McCann & Geoghegan, 1971); Buckland, *Witchcraft from the Inside*.

30. Valiente, *An ABC of Witchcraft*, p. 153.

31. J. L. Bracelin, *Gerald Gardner: Witch* (London: Octagon Press, 1960), pp. 164–65.

32. Valiente, *An ABC of Witchcraft*, p. 153.

33. Janet and Stewart Farrar, *The Witches Way*. First published in the United States as *A Witches Bible*, Vol. I, II (New York: Magickal Childe Publications, 1984), Vol. II, pp. 283–93.

34. Bracelin, *Gerald Gardner: Witch*, p. 165.

35. Gerald B. Gardner, *High Magic's Aid* (London: Michael Houghton, 1949). The main god mentioned is Janicot. There are indirect references to Isis (p. 172) and "kerwiddeon" (p. 205), and the idea of the priestess representing the "divine spirit of Creation" (p. 120).

36. Valiente, *An ABC of Witchcraft*, pp. 154–55.

37. Gerald B. Gardner, *Witchcraft Today* (New York: The Citadel Press, 1955). First published in 1954 in England by Rider & Company.

38. Valiente, *An ABC of Witchcraft*, pp. 155–57. Many have observed that those portions of the Gardnerian rituals that have been published contain phrases from Ovid, Kipling, Leland, Crowley, and the *Key of Solomon*.

39. Francis King, *The Rites of Modern Occult Magic* (New York: Macmillan, 1970), pp. 176 and 179–80.

40. Rose, *A Razor for a Goat*, p. 230. Other quotations are on pp. 200–01, 204, 206, 210, 217, and 220.

41. *Pentagram*, No. 2 (November 1964), pp. 5, 7.

42. Valiente, letter in *Pentagram*, No. 1 (August 1964), p. 1.

43. Isaac Bonewits, "Witchcult: Fact or Fancy?" *Gnostica*, Vol. III, No. 4 (November 21, 1973), 5.
44. Isaac Bonewits, *Real Magic* (New York: Berkley Publishing Corp., 1972), pp. 129–30.
45. Isaac Bonewits, "Witchcraft," Pt. I, pp. 17–18.
46. Ibid., Pt. II, *Green Egg*, Vol. IX, No. 78 (May 1, 1976), 13–17.
47. Ibid., Pt. III, *Green Egg*, Vol. IX, No. 79 (June 21, 1976), 10.
48. Ibid., p. 7.
49. Ibid., Pt. II, pp. 15–16.
50. Ibid., Pt. III, pp. 5–6.
51. Patricia Crowther and Arnold Crowther, *The Witches Speak* (Isle of Man: Athol Publications, 1965).
52. Victor Anderson, *Thorns of the Blood Rose* (privately published by Cora Anderson, San Leandro, Cal., 1970).
53. Aidan Kelly, op. cit., p. 4.
54. Ibid., p. 18. Other quotations are on pp. 1, 5, and 274.
55. Gertrude Rachel Levy, *The Gate of Horn* (London: Faber and Faber, 1963). Originally published in 1948.
56. Kelly, "The Rebirth of Witchcraft," p. 274. Aidan's summary of the history of Goddess worship is on pp. 281–94.
57. *Iron Mountain* (Summer 1984), 19–29.
58. *Iron Mountain* (Fall 1985), 3–6.
59. Letters from Doreen Valiente, September 12, 18, and November 14, 1985.
60. Bonewits, "Witchcraft," Pt. III, p. 10. Bonewits's arguments may have played a large role in changing the attitudes of many Wiccans on this issue.
61. Hans Holzer, *The Witchcraft Report* (New York: Ace Books, 1973), pp. 135–45.
62. Marcello Truzzi, "Toward a Sociology of the Occult: Notes on Modern Witchcraft," in *Religious Movements in Contemporary America*, ed. Irving Zaretsky and Mark Leone (Princeton: Princeton University Press, 1974), p. 636.
63. Buckland, *Witchcraft from the Inside*, pp. 79–80.
64. Buckland, *Earth Religion News*, Vol. 1, No. 1 (Yule 1973), p. 1.
65. Buckland, *The Tree: The Complete Book of Saxon Witchcraft* (New York: Samuel Weiser, 1974), p. 4.
66. Buckland, *Earth Religion News*.

CHAPTER 5: THE CRAFT TODAY

1. Joseph Wilson, *Gnostica*, Vol. III, No. 11 (June 21, 1974), 17.
2. June Johns, *King of the Witches: The World of Alex Sanders* (London: Peter

Davies, 1969), pp. 10–21; Stewart Farrar, *What Witches Do* (New York: Coward, McCann & Geoghegan, 1971), pp. 1–2.

3. Leo Martello, *Wica Newsletter*, No. 15 (1972), p. 1.

4. *Gnostica*, Vol. II, No. 8 (June 21, 1973), 19.

5. Phoenix, "Gardnerian Aspects," *Green Egg*, Vol. VII, No. 63 (June 21, 1974), 18.

6. Carl Weschcke, "Spirit of the Witchmeet," *Touchstone—Witches Love Letter* (April 11, 1974), 1. This newsletter, edited by Weschcke, was published for the Council of American Witches by the First Wiccan Church of Minnesota, 476 Summit Ave., St. Paul, Minn. 55102.

7. Ibid., February 1974, 5–6, 9.

8. Ibid., Spring Equinox 1974, 3.

9. Ibid., February 1974, 5–6.

10. "Principles of Wiccan Belief," *Green Egg*, Vol. VII, No. 64 (August 1, 1974), 32. Adopted by the Council of American Witches during its spring Witchmeet, April 11–14, 1974, in Minneapolis.

11. *The Witches Trine*, Vol. IV, No. 2 (Lughnasadh, 1974), 7.

12. Sybil Leek, *The Complete Art of Witchcraft* (New York: New American Library, 1973), p. 15.

13. Marcello Truzzi, "Toward a Sociology of the Occult: Notes on Modern Witchcraft," in *Religious Movements in Contemporary America*, ed. Irving Zaretsky and Mark Leone (Princeton: Princeton University Press, 1974), p. 637.

14. Susan Roberts, *Witches, U.S.A.* (New York: Dell, 1971), p. 17.

15. In some traditions, the sword represents air and the wand fire.

16. Helica, letter (New York, November 1977).

17. Farrar, *What Witches Do*, p. 190. Other quotations are on pp. 4 and 22.

18. Doreen Valiente, *An ABC of Witchcraft Past & Present* (St. Martin's Press, 1973), p. xiii.

19. In England the covens that descend from Gardner do not call themselves "Gardnerian."

20. C. A. Burland, *The Magical Arts* (London: Arthur Barker Ltd., 1966), p. 175.

21. "Family of covens" was a term used by a Gardnerian journal that was published from 1974 to 1976 in Louisville, Kentucky.

22. Gerald B. Gardner, *High Magic's Aid* (London: Michael Houghton, 1949); also published in New York by Samuel Weiser (1975); *Witchcraft Today* (New York: The Citadel Press, 1955); *The Meaning of Witchcraft* (London: Aquarian Press, 1959); and Janet and Stewart Farrar, *The Witches Way* (London: Robert Hale, Ltd., 1981), published in the United States as *A Witches Bible*, Vol. I, II (New York: Magickal Childe Publications, 1985).

Today (New York: The Citadel Press, 1955); *The Meaning of Witchcraft* (London: Aquarian Press, 1959).

23. *Georgian Newsletter*, 1908 Verde, Bakersfield, Cal. 93304.

24. Mark Roberts, "An Introduction to Dianic Witchcraft," unpublished Ms., Chap. VI, pp. 1–2.

25. Mark Roberts, "The Dianic Aspect," *The New Broom*, Vol. I, No. 2 (Candlemas, 1973), 17.

26. The correspondence course of Leo Martello would be another.

27. Gavin and Yvonne Frost, *The Witch's Bible* (New York: Berkley, 1975).

28. *Touchstone—Witch's Love Letter* (February 1974), p. 9.

29. Roberta Ann Kennedy, *Green Egg*, Vol. V, No. 51 (December 17, 1972), Forum section, 14.

30. Diana Demdike, "Don't Let Witchcraft Die!" in *Quest*, No. 15 (September 1973), 6. This is the British Witchcraft journal and should not be confused with the U.S. feminist journal of the same name.

31. On the death of Robert Williams see *Green Egg*, Vol. VIII, No. 74 (November 1975), 11; also Vol. VII, No. 65 (September 1974), 3,37; also No. 66 (November 1974), 39–42.

32. Leo Martello, *Witchcraft: The Old Religion* (Secaucus, N.J.: University Books, 1973), pp. 23–27.

33. Isaac Bonewits, "Witchburning . . . Now & Then," *Gnostica*, Vol. III, No. 6 (January 21, 1974), 5–6, 8, 10, 16.

34. Ibid., p. 6.

35. C. A. Burland, *Echoes of Magic* (Totowa, N.J.: Rowman and Littlefield, 1972), pp. 117–18, 132.

36. Letter (name withheld by request), Long Beach, Cal., summer 1977.

CHAPTER 7: MAGIC AND RITUAL

1. Dr. Timothy Leary, quoted in "Neurologic, Immortality & All That," by Robert A. Wilson in *Green Egg*, Vol. VIII, No. 72 (August 1, 1975), 9.

2. "Magick" by the Abbey of Thelema, *Green Egg*, Vol. VIII, No. 75 (December 21, 1975), 19.

3. Isaac Bonewits, "The Second Epistle of Isaac," in *The Druid Chronicles (evolved)*, ed. Isaac Bonewits (Berkeley: Berkeley Drunemeton Press, 1976), 1:7.

4. "An Interview with Robert Anton Wilson," by Neal Wilgus, *Science Fiction Review*, Vol. 5, No. 2 (May 1976), 32.

5. Leo Martello, *Witchcraft: The Old Religion* (Secaucus, N.J.: University Books, 1973), p. 12.

6. See "The First Epistle of Isaac," *The Druid Chronicles (evolved)*, 3:1.

7. Isaac Bonewits, *Real Magic* (New York: Berkley Publishing Corp., 1972), pp. 209, 53.

8. Doreen Valiente, *Natural Magic* (New York: St. Martin's Press, 1975), p. 13.

9. Jacob Needleman, *A Sense of the Cosmos: The Encounter of Modern Science and Ancient Truth* (New York: Doubleday & Co., 1975).

10. Colin Wilson, *The Occult* (London: Hodder and Stoughton, 1971), p. 59.

11. Valiente, *Natural Magic*, p. 33.

12. Dianic Grove training material of the Covenstead of Morrigana in Dallas, Texas, Lesson No. 1.

13. See Bonewits, *Real Magic*, pp. 91–112 and 163–76; "Second Epistle of Isaac," Chap. 6, "The Tools of Ritual."

14. Robert Anton Wilson, "All Hail the Goddess Eris!" *Gnostica*, Vol. 4, No. 11 (September–October 1975), 11.

15. Jane Ellen Harrison, *Epilegomena to the Study of Greek Religion* (New Hyde Park, N.Y.: University Books, 1962), pp. xliv–xlvi.

16. Robert Anton Wilson, "The Origins of Magick," *Green Egg*, Vol. VII, No. 63 (June 21, 1974), 7.

17. Sam'l Bassett ("The Inquisitor"), "An Essay in Divination," *The Witches-Trine*, Vol. 5, No. 2 (Litha, 1976), 7–8.

18. Aidan Kelly, "Aporrheton No. 1, To the New Witch," March, 1973, p. 5. This was part of materials given to new members of NROOGD. A copy of these materials, as well as NROOGD's journal, *The Witches Trine*, is on file with the library of the Graduate Theological Union in Berkeley, California.

19. Isaac Bonewits, taped letter from Berkeley, winter 1978.

20. Bonewits, "Second Epistle of Isaac," 5:5–6.

21. Bonewits, *Real Magic*, p. 175.

22. *The Witches Trine*, Vol. 1, No. 6 (Winter Solstice 1972), 2.

23. Ibid., Vol. 3, No. 4 (Lughnasadh 1974), 11.

24. Ibid., "How We Happened to Get the NROOGD Together (Part I)," 9, 10, 12; Vol. 3, No. 5 (Samhain 1974), "How We Happened to Get the NROOGD Together (Part II)," 18, 19, 21–22.

25. Aidan Kelly, "Why a Craft Ritual Works," *Gnostica*, Vol. 4, No. 7 (March-April-May 1975), 33.

26. I. M. Lewis, *Ecstatic Religion* (Harmondsworth, Eng.: Penguin Books, 1971), p. 205.

27. Kelly, "Why a Craft Ritual Works."

28. Ibid.

29. Ibid.

30. Aidan Kelly, Diary entry, July 6, 1972.

31. Kelly, "Why a Craft Ritual Works," p. 5.
32. Aidan Kelly, "O, That Vexed Question: Is the Craft a Survival, a Revival, or What?" *Nemeton*, Vol. 1, No. 1 (Samhain 1972), 19.
33. Kelly, "Aporrheton No. 1," p. 2.
34. Most of these arguments appear in Aidan Kelly, "Palengenesia," *Gnostica*, Vol. 4, No. 9 (July 1975), 7, 40, 41. Any additions come from interviews.
35. Kelly, "Aporrheton No. 1," p. 1.
36. Kelly, "Aporrheton No. 5, The Craft Laws," April 1973, p. 1.
37. Kelly, "O, That Vexed Question," p. 20.
38. Aidan Kelly, "Inventing Witchcraft" (unpublished Ms., 1985), chapter 7, p. 299.
39. Ibid., chapter 7, p. 293.

CHAPTER 8: WOMEN, FEMINISM, AND THE CRAFT

1. The poem appeared in *WomanSpirit*, Vol. 1, No. 3 (Spring Equinox 1975), back cover.
2. Where did feminist Witches get Laverna from, you may ask? From Charles Godfrey Leland's *Aradia, or the Gospel of the Witches* (London: David Nutt, 1899), reprinted (New York: Samuel Weiser, 1974), pp. 89–98: Leland writes that Laverna is mentioned in Horace, *Epistles*, I, xvi, 59–62.
3. Two examples of conferences on feminist spirituality: Through the Looking Glass, a Gynergenetic Experience, in Boston, April 23–25, 1976; A Celebration of the Beguines, in New York City, October 30–31, 1976.
4. I originally saw this manifesto in mimeographed form, but it has been published, thanks to Robin Morgan, in *Sisterhood Is Powerful*, ed. Robin Morgan (New York: Random House, 1970), pp. 539–43. Quotation on p. 539.
5. Kirsten Grimstad and Susan Rennie, eds., *The New Woman's Survival Sourcebook* (New York: Alfred A. Knopf, 1975).
6. Kirsten Grimstad and Susan Rennie, "Spiritual Explorations Cross-country," *Quest*, Vol. 1, No. 4 (Spring 1975), 49–51.
7. *Country Women* (April 1974), 1. Available: Box 51, Albion, Cal. 95410.
8. Judy Davis and Juanita Weaver, "Dimensions of Spirituality," *Quest*, Vol. 1, No. 4 (Spring 1975), 6.
9. Z Budapest, *The Feminist Book of Lights and Shadows* (Venice, Cal.: Luna Publications, 1976), p. 1. Available from The Feminist Wicca, 442 Lincoln Blvd., Venice, Cal. 90291. Z's spelling of woman as *womon* and women as *wimmin* is intended to take the *man* out of woman.

10. Sally Gearhart, "Womanpower: Energy Re-sourcement," *WomanSpirit*, Vol. 2, No. 7 (Spring Equinox 1976), 19–23.

11. Z Budapest, *Feminist Book of Lights and Shadows*, pp. 1–2.

12. Ibid, pp. 3–4.

13. Friedrich Engels, *The Origin of the Family, Private Property, and the State* (New York: International Publishers, 1967); Evelyn Reed, *Woman's Evolution* (New York: Pathfinder Press, 1975); J. J. Bachofen, *Myth, Religion and Mother Right* (Princeton: Princeton University Press—Bollingen Series LXXXIV, 1973); Helen Diner, *Mothers and Amazons* (New York: Anchor Books, 1973); Erich Neumann, *The Great Mother: An Analysis of the Archetype* (Princeton: Princeton University Press—Bollingen Series XLVII, 1963).

14. Sarah B. Pomeroy, *Goddesses, Whores, Wives, and Slaves* (New York: Schocken Books, 1975).

15. Elizabeth Gould Davis, *The First Sex* (New York: G. P. Putnam's Sons, 1971).

16. Monique Wittig, *Les Guérillères* (Boston: Beacon Press, 1985), p. 89.

17. Paula Webster and Esther Newton, "Matriarchy: Puzzle and Paradigm," presented at the 71st Annual Meeting of the American Anthropological Association, Toronto, 1972. This paper was later published in *APHRA—A Feminist Literary Magazine* (Spring/Summer 1973) as "Matriarchy: As Women See It." A revised version, *Matriarchy: A Vision of Power* by Paula Webster appears in *Toward an Anthropology of Women*, ed. Rayna Reiter (New York: Monthly Review Press, 1975), pp. 141–56.

18. Joanna Russ, *The Female Man* (Boston: Beacon Press, 1986); *We Who Are About To . . .* (New York: Dell, 1975); *The Two of Them* (New York: Berkley Publishing Corp., 1978), among others.

19. Gordon Rattray Taylor, *Sex in History* (New York: The Vanguard Press, 1954).

20. Jean Markale, *Women of the Celts* (London: Gordon Cremonesi, 1975). First published as *La Femme Celte*, Editions Payot, Paris, 1972.

21. Adrienne Rich, "The Kingdom of the Fathers," *Partisan Review*, Vol. XLIII, No. 1 (1976), 29–30, 26.

22. Philip Zabriskie, "Goddesses in Our Midst," *Quadrant*, No. 17 (Fall 1974), 34–45.

23. Robert Graves, *The White Goddess*, amended and enlarged ed. (New York: Farrar, Straus and Giroux, 1966), pp. 484–86.

24. Ruth Mountaingrove, "Clues to Our Women's Culture," *WomanSpirit*, Vol. 2, No. 6 (Fall Equinox 1975), 45.

25. Jude Michaels, "Eve & Us," *WomanSpirit*, Vol. 1, No. 1 (Autumn Equinox 1974), 5–6. In connection with this, I am reminded of the words of the fourth-century Emperor Julian, who observed that the doctrine of

Adam and Eve was unfit for any enlightened mind: "What could be more foolish than a being unable to distinguish good from bad? . . . In short, God refused to let man taste of wisdom, than which there could be nothing of more value . . . so that the serpent was a benefactor rather than a destroyer of the human race." *The Works of the Emperor Julian,* trans. Wilmer Cave Wright, 3 vols. (Cambridge: Harvard University Press, 1961), III, 327.

26. "Voices," *WomanSpirit,* Vol. 1, No. 1 (Autumn Equinox 1974), 38.
27. Carol, Patti, and Billie, "Moon Over the Mountain: Creating Our Own Rituals," *WomanSpirit,* Vol. 1, No. 1 (Autumn Equinox 1974), 30. Robin Morgan's poem appears in *Monster* (New York: Vintage Books, 1972), pp. 81–86.
28. W. Holman Keith, *Divinity as the Eternal Feminine* (New York: Pageant Press, 1960), p. 14.
29. Mary Daly, *Beyond God the Father* (Boston: Beacon Press, 1973), pp. 16–19.
30. Records: Alix Dobkin, Kay Gardner, et al., "Her Precious Love," on *Lavender Jane Loves Women* (1975), Alix Dobkin Project 1, 210 W. 10 St., New York, N.Y. 10014; Cassie Culver, "Good Old Dora," on *3 Gypsies* (1976), Urana Records—ST-WWE-81; Kay Gardner, *Mooncircles* (1975), Urana Records, a division of Wise Women Enterprises, Inc., P.O. Box 297, Village Station, New York, N.Y. 10014—ST-WWE-80.
31. Fran Winnant, "Our Religious Heritage," *WomanSpirit,* Vol. 1, No. 3 (Spring Equinox 1975), 51.
32. Monica, letter to *WomanSpirit,* Vol. 2, No. 7 (Spring Equinox 1976), 62.
33. *WomanSpirit,* Vol. 2, No. 6 (Fall Equinox 1975), 64.
34. Fran Rominsky, "goddess with a small g," *WomanSpirit,* Vol. 1, No. 1 (Autumn Equinox 1974), 48.
35. WITCH documents, in Morgan, *Sisterhood Is Powerful,* p. 546. Other quotations are on pp. 541–43 and 540.
36. Graves, *The White Goddess,* p. 458.
37. Robert Graves, "Real Women," in *Masculine/Feminine,* eds. Betty Roszak and Theodore Roszak (New York: Harper Colophon Books, 1969), pp. 35–36.
38. Keith, *Divinity as Eternal Feminine,* p. 4.
39. W. Holman Keith, "The Garden of Venus," *Green Egg,* Vol. IV, No. 38 (May 7, 1971); *Divinity as Eternal Feminine,* p. 192. See also "The Priestess," *Green Egg,* Vol. VI, No. 60 (February 1, 1974), 28, and "Venus Proserpina," *Green Egg,* Vol. VI, No. 55 (June 21, 1978), 8.
40. Morning Glory Zell, in *Green Egg,* Vol. VII, No. 68 (February 1, 1975), 43.
41. Gearhart, "Womanpower," p. 20.

42. "Woman, Priestess, Witch," *The Waxing Moon*, Vol. 7, No. 2 (Summer Solstice 1971), 3. This Neo-Pagan journal soon changed its name to *The Crystal Well* and was published for many years out of Philadelphia. Today *The Crystal Well* is published (in a different format) out of California.

43. Ravenwolf, "In Defense of Men and Gods," *Earth Religion News*, Vol. 3, Issues 1, 2, 3 combined (1976), 140.

44. Letter from Julie Jay, ibid., p. 11.

45. Morning Glory Zell, *Green Egg*, Vol. VIII, No. 72 (August 1, 1975), 43.

46. Isaac Bonewits, *Gnostica*, Vol. 4, No. 5 (January 1975), pp. 2, 34, 38.

47. Leo Martello, "Witchcraft: A Way of Life," *Witchcraft Digest*, No. 1 (1971), 3. Publication of the Witches International Craft Associates (WICA), Suite 1B, 153 W. 80 St., New York, N.Y. 10024.

48. Margo and Lee, "The Liberated Witch," *The New Broom*, Vol. 1, No. 2 (Candlemas 1973), 10.

49. I. M. Lewis, *Ecstatic Religion* (Harmondsworth, Eng.: Penguin Books, 1971), pp. 31, 117.

50. *The New Broom*, Vol. 1, No. 3 (Lammas 1973), 21, 28.

51. *The New Broom*, Vol. 1, No. 1 (Samhain 1972), 10–11.

52. *Nemeton*, Vol. 1, No. 1 (Samhain 1972), 12.

53. *The New Broom*, Vol. 1, No. 4 (undated), 9.

54. Deborah Bender, "Raising Power in a Single-Sex Coven," *The Witches Trine*, Vol. 5, No. 2 (Litha 1976), 5–6.

55. Barbara Starrett, "I Dream in Female: The Metaphors of Evolution," *Amazon Quarterly*, Vol. 3, No. 1 (November 1974), 24–25. Other quotation on p. 20.

56. Bender, "Raising Power," 5–6.

57. Deborah Bender, letter, summer 1976, Oakland, California.

58. *Women's Coven Newsletter*. Available to feminist Witches from 5756 Vicente St., Oakland, Cal. 94609.

59. Leland, *Aradia*, pp. 4, 6–7.

CHAPTER 9: RELIGIONS FROM THE PAST— THE PAGAN RECONSTRUCTIONISTS

1. Gleb Botkin, *The Woman Who Rose Again* (New York: Fleming H. Revell, 1937); *Immortal Woman* (New York: The Macaulay Co., 1933); *The God Who Didn't Laugh* (New York: Payson & Clarke, 1929); *Her Wanton Majesty* (New York: The Macaulay Co., 1933).

2. Botkin, *Immortal Woman*, p. 184.

3. Botkin, *The God Who Didn't Laugh*, p. 250. Botkin himself at one time

studied for the priesthood in the Greek Catholic Church in Russia: see William Seabrook, *Witchcraft: Its Power in the World Today* (New York: Harcourt, Brace and Company, 1940), p. 343, and the November 15, 1939, edition of the *New York World-Telegram*. When *The God Who Didn't Laugh* and *Immortal Woman* appeared, reviewers did not emphasize the Aphrodisian aspects of the books: see the 25th and 29th annual cumulation of *The Book Review Digest* (New York: H. W. Wilson Co., 1930 and 1934), pp. 105 and 102, respectively.

4. Quoted by Seabrook, in *Witchcraft*, pp. 343–44. See also *Newsweek*, November 27, 1939, p. 32; *Life*, December 4, 1939, p. 101.

5. Seabrook, *Witchcraft*, p. 342. The beginning of the creed goes as follows: "I believe in Aphrodite, the flower-faced sweetly-smelling, laughter-loving goddess of Love and Beauty; the self-existing, eternal and only Supreme Deity; creator and mother of the Cosmos; the Universal Cause; the Universal Mind; the source of all life and all positive creative forces of nature; the Fountain Head of all happiness and joy. . . ."

6. W. Holman Keith, "Obituary for a Neo-Pagan Pioneer," *Green Egg*, Vol. IV, No. 45 (February 3, 1972), 9. Also see Botkin's obituary in *The New York Times*, December 30, 1969, p. 33.

7. Keith, "Obituary."

8. Robert Graves, *Watch the North Wind Rise* (New York: Creative Age Press, 1949), p. 155.

9. Alvin Toffler uses this same idea in *Future Shock* (New York: Bantam, 1971), pp. 390–92. He suggests that the purpose of enclaves such as the Amish communities and preserved sites like Williamsburg, Virginia, is twofold: to provide a place where the rate of change is slower and "future shock" can be escaped, and to provide safety if a technological catastrophe occurs in the larger society.

10. Graves, *Watch the North Wind Rise*, p. 43.

11. Feraferian literature has also said that the name means "wilderness sacrament," "wild festival," and the union of Wilderness and Dream to yield a Life of Eternal Celebration. *Feraferia* (newspaper), Vol. 1, No. 1 (Autumn 1967), 1.

12. Robert S. Ellwood, Jr., *Religious and Spiritual Groups in Modern America* (Englewood Cliffs, N.J.: Prentice-Hall, 1973), pp. 196–97.

13. *Earth Religion News*, Vol. 1, No. 5, 49.

14. William Morris, *News from Nowhere, or An Epoch of Rest* (New York: Monthly Review Press, 1966), first published in Great Britain in 1890; Robert Graves, see note 8; William Hudson, *A Crystal Age* (New York: Dutton, 1906).

15. Henry Bailey Stevens, *The Recovery of Culture* (New York: Harper &

Brothers, 1953), p. 168. Originally published in 1949. Other quotations are on p. 86; the story of Cain and Abel is on pp. 66–67 and 176; the story of Adam and Eve on pp. 82–87.

16. Ibid., pp. 206–08.

17. Frederick C. Adams, "Hesperian Life and the Maiden Way." This paper was originally issued in 1957 and revised in 1970. It is privately published and available through Feraferia. Quotations taken from pp. 1–7.

18. On jargon, see, for example, Earth Religion News, Vol. 3, issues 1, 2, 3 combined, 186: "The Individual Personal: Psycho-Analytic encounter; the individuation process and all inner fantasy production," etc.

19. Frederick Adams, "Feraferia for Beginners," Earth Religion News, Vol. 1, No. 5 (August Eve 1974), 51.

20. Frederick Adams, "The Korê," privately published by Feraferia in 1969. Also appears in Robert Ellwood, "Notes on a Neopagan Religious Group," in History of Religions, Vol. XI, No. 1 (Chicago: University of Chicago Press, August 1971), 134.

21. Adams, "Hersperian Life," pp. 11, 13–16.

22. Frederick Adams, poem published in The Pagan, No. 1 (November 1, 1970), 7. The Pagan had two issues and was published out of St. Louis, Missouri. Adams's poem originally appeared in a privately published article of Feraferia: "Topocosmic Mandala of the Sacred Land Sky Love Year" (1969).

23. From Feraferia's statement, which appears on the inside cover of its journal, Korythalia.

24. Feraferia (newspaper), Vol. 1, No. 1 (Autumn 1967), 1.

25. Frederick Adams, "The Henge: Land Sky Love Temple," Earth Religion News, Vol. 3, Issues 1, 2, 3, combined (1976), 182.

26. Adams, "Feraferia for Beginners," p. 51.

27. Ellwood, "Notes on a Neopagan Religious Group in America," 137.

28. Ellwood, Religious and Spiritual Groups in Modern America, p. 198.

29. Iris, Vol. 3, No. 1 (August 18, 1974), 1, 3.

30. "The Am'n," Iris, Vol. 3, No. 3 (February 1975), 1–2.

31. Ibid., p. 2.

32. For another description of this myth, see Robert Graves, The Greek Myths (Baltimore: Penguin, 1955), I, p. 27.

33. The stories of Jim Kemble, Don Harrison, and Harold Moss appeared in the Church of the Eternal Source's members' newsletter, No. 2 (September 5, 1973), 7–12. CES address: P.O. Box 7091, Burbank, Cal.

34. Harold Moss, taped letter, spring 1977.

35. Green Egg, Vol. VI, No. 55 (June 21, 1973), 17.

36. Introductory leaflet from the Church of the Eternal Source.

37. Letter from Harold Moss to Reverend Gordon Melton, September 18, 1972.

38. "Our Modern Practice of the Ancient Egyptian Religion," a CES pamphlet published in 1974, p. 4.

39. Harold Moss, taped letter, spring 1977.

40. "Modern Practice of Ancient Egyptian Religion," p. 3.

41. Henri Frankfort, *Ancient Egyptian Religion* (New York: Columbia University Press, 1948), p. 4. The other quotation is on p. 13. A good summary of Frankfort appears in the CES pamphlet, "Modern Practice of Ancient Egyptian Religion," p. 8.

42. "Modern Practice of Ancient Egyptian Religion," pp. 2–5.

43. Moss, taped letter, spring 1977.

44. The first paragraph of this quotation comes from a letter by Harold Moss published in *Green Egg*, Vol. V, No. 52 (February 1973), Forum section, 4–7. The second paragraph comes from *Khepera*, No. 1, in *Green Egg*, Vol. VI, No. 56 (August 1, 1973), 24.

45. From a pamphlet, "What Is Asatru," published by the Asatru Free Assembly, p. 3.

46. "Ancestry Is Better Than Universalism," *The Runestone*, No. 50 (Winter 1984), 11.

47. *The Odinist*, No. 92, p. 2. There are other more extreme Odinist Pagan groups. Here are some quotes from a publication called *Quarterstaff*, edited by a Canadian, Jack Leavy. "If we didn't have to worry about Judeo-Christianity and watch our Race being mongrelized, our Celtic culture dissipated, we would still have to contend with the Masons and those who seek One World Government"; "When North American 'Indians' start making incredible land claims, demands for compensation and the right to self-government—including their own courts—we say, 'Wait just a minute!' It's not bad enough that a 'Jew' is credited with (re)discovering America, our People have been on this Continent for at least as long as any of the indigenous Aboriginals. And, an integral body of Celts should be able to make the same demands for recognition etc., from the U.S. and Canadian governments." These quotes came from an analysis of *Quarterstaff* in *The Magickal Unicorn Messenger*, Vol. 5, Issue 2.

48. "Joy Is Better Than Guilt," *The Runestone*, No. 51 (Spring 1985), 11.

49. "The Jesus Flag," *The Runestone*, No. 50 (Winter 1984), 9.

50. "How to Live," *The Runestone*, No. 50 (Winter 1984), 1.

CHAPTER 10: A RELIGION FROM THE FUTURE—
THE CHURCH OF ALL WORLDS

1. Mircea Eliade, "The Occult and the Modern World," a paper delivered at the 21st Annual Freud Memorial Lecture, held in Philadelphia on May 24, 1974. Published in *Occultism, Witchcraft and Cultural Fashions* (Chicago: University of Chicago Press, 1976), p. 62.

2. Hans Holzer, *The Witchcraft Report* (New York: Ace Books, 1973), p. 179. See also Holzer, *The New Pagans* (New York: Doubleday & Co., 1972), p. 120, and *The Directory of the Occult* (Chicago: Henry Regnery Co., 1974), p. 176. Many of the people quoted in this book do not consider Hans Holzer to be friendly to Neo-Paganism. Holzer might have been able to understand CAW a bit better if he had realized that almost all Neo-Pagan groups are based on the creative and artistic efforts of their members rather than on "ancient tradition." The traditions are fragments; creativity is the glue; and CAW has been as inventive as anyone else.

3. See Ursula K. Le Guin, *The Left Hand of Darkness* (New York: Walker and Co., 1969); *The Dispossessed* (New York: Harper & Row, 1974); *A Wizard of Earthsea* (Berkeley: Parnassus Press, 1968); *Planet of Exile* (New York: Ace Books, 1966); Joanna Russ, *The Female Man* (New York: Bantam, 1975); *We Who Are About To . . .* (New York: Dell, 1975); *The Two of Them* (New York: Berkley Publishing Corp., 1978); Vonda McIntyre, *Dreamsnake* (Boston: Houghton Mifflin Co., 1978). Of Le Guin, Robert Scholes, in *Structural Fabulation* (Notre Dame, Indiana: University of Notre Dame Press, 1975), p. 82, writes that her perspective

is broader than the Christian perspective—because finally it takes the world more seriously than the Judeo-Christian tradition has ever allowed it to be taken.

What *Earthsea* represents, through its world of islands and waterways, is the universe as a dynamic, balanced system, not subject to the capricious miracles of any deity, but only to the natural laws of its own working, which include a role for magic and powers other than human, but only as aspects of the great Balance or Equilibrium, which is the order of the cosmos. . . . Ursula Le Guin works not with a theology but with an ecology, a cosmology, a reverence for the universe as a self-regulating structure . . . it is a deeper view, closer to the great pre-Christian mythologies of this world and also closer to what three centuries of science have been able to discover about the nature of the universe.

4. Eliade, "The Occult and the Modern World," pp. 67–68.

5. Scholes, *Structural Fabulation*, p. 75, 38.

6. Tom Williams, "Science-Fiction/Fantasy: A Contemporary Mythology," *Green Egg*, Vol. VIII, No. 69 (March 21, 1975), 5–6.

7. This statement was attributed to Hans Holzer by Carroll Runyon, Jr., head of the OTA, in a letter to Tim and Julie Zell on April 26, 1972. This letter appeared in Zell's "Open Communiqué" to all members of the Council of Themis, May 27, 1972.

8. Jerome Tuccille, *It Usually Begins with Ayn Rand* (New York: Stein and Day, 1972), pp. 14–17.

9. See ibid., pp. 32, 175; also, National Public Radio broadcast of April 18, 1976, as reported in *Akwesasne Notes* (Early Summer 1976), p. 44. Rand's attitudes toward technology and environment are also pretty clearly stated in *Atlas Shrugged* (New York: New American Library, 1959).

10. Lance Christie, "The Origin of Atl," *Atlan Logbook*, p. 23.

11. Abraham H. Maslow, *Motivation and Personality*, 2nd ed. (New York: Harper & Row, 1970), pp. 149–80. Quotation appears on p. 166. It also appears as a selection in the *Atlan Logbook*, p. 64.

12. Christie, "Origin of Atl."

13. Ibid., pp. 23–24.

14. Robert A. Heinlein, *Stranger in a Strange Land* (New York: G. P. Putnam's Sons, 1961; Avon Books, 1962).

15. Robert S. Ellwood, Jr., *Religious and Spiritual Groups in Modern America* (Englewood Cliffs, N.J.: Prentice-Hall, 1973), pp. 200–04.

16. All quotes from *Atlan Logbook*, pp. 1, 14, 17–18 and 23–24.

17. *Atlan Annals*, Vol. 1, No. 1, 5.

18. Political statements of Dagny, Prometheus, Thor, and Adonai in *Atlan Logbook*, individual statements section.

19. Lance Christie, *Atlan Annals*, Vol. IV, No. 2, 6.

20. Ibid., Vol. IV, No. 1, 4, 7. Also, Vol. III, No. 10, 23.

21. First statement, Tim Zell, "Ideals and Principles of Atl, *Atlan Logbook*, p. 11; also appears in *Green Egg*, Vol. 1, No. 2 (March 1968). Second statement is CAW's statement of purpose, which appeared in every issue of the *Green Egg*.

22. *Green Egg*, Vol. 1, No. 1 (March 20, 1968). Zell also described himself as a Pagan in the *Atlan Logbook*, saying, "I am a pagan, considering Atl to be in the vanguard of the new pagan resurgence" (individual statements section).

23. Young Omar, "Kerista's Erotic Ethic and Etcs. (September 4, 1966), reprinted in *Atlan Logbook*, pp. 40–42. Originally published by Kerista Press, Box 34708, Los Angeles, Cal. 90034. Actually, Young Omar paraphrases Goldberg. Goldberg's quote goes as follows: "What was forbidden in ordinary life was allowed in the life of religion. Bonds were broken and taboos raised, once people entered into the temple of the gods." B. Z. Goldberg, *The Sacred Fire* (New York: Horace Liveright, 1930), pp. 36–37.

24. Young Omar, "Kerista's Erotic Ethic."

25. See address by Doreen Valiente, *Pentagram*, No. 2 (November 1964), 5.

26. *Green Egg*, Vol. III, No. 20 (December 29, 1969), 1.

27. *Green Egg*, Vol. III, No. 23 (March 18, 1970), 1. The phrase "the Green Hills of Earth" comes from a story by C. L. Moore (Mrs. Henry Kuttner), and Heinlein used it with her permission in *The Green Hills of Earth* (Chicago: Shasta, 1951).

28. Tim Zell, "Theagenesis: The Birth of the Goddess," *Green Egg*, Vol. IV, No. 40 (July 1, 1971), 7–10. Also published in *The Witch's Broomstick*, Vol. 1, No. 1 (Candlemas 1972), 19–25. Excerpts appeared in Leo Martello, *Witchcraft: The Old Religion* (Secaucus, N.J: University Books, 1973), pp. 102–07. Martello also refers to it in *Black Magic, Satanism and Voodoo* (New York: HC Publishers, 1973), pp. 135–35.

29. Tim Zell, "The Gods of Nature, the Nature of Gods (Part I)," *Green Egg*, Vol. VII, No. 66 (November 1, 1974), 12.

30. Zell, "Theagenesis," p. 10.

31. Zell, "The Gods of Nature," p. 14.

32. Tim Zell, "Biotheology: The Neo-Pagan Mission," *Green Egg*, Vol. IV, No. 41 (August 4, 1971), pp. 7–8.

33. Lance Christie, *Green Egg*, Vol. IV, No. 42 (September 27, 1971), Forum section, 9.

34. *Newsweek*, March 10, 1975, p. 49.

35. From a CAW tract, "Neo-Paganism and the Church of All Worlds," undated.

36. From a CAW tract, "An Old Religion for a New Age, Neo-Paganism," undated.

37. Lewis Shieber, "The CAW and Tribalism," *Green Egg*, Vol. VIII, No. 75 (December 21, 1975), 5–6.

38. Council of Themis statement on the "Common Themes of Neo-Pagan Religious Orientation," *Green Egg*, Vol. IV, No. 43 (December 3, 1971), 11.

39. Tom Williams, "Science: A Mutable Metaphor," *Green Egg*, Vol. VIII, No. 73 (September 21, 1975), 9.

40. Lance Christie, *Green Egg*, Vol. VI, No. 58 (November 1, 1973), 50.

41. Ellwood, *Religious Groups in Modern America*, p. 203.

42. Tim Zell, "Neo-Paganism and the Church of All Worlds: Some Questions and Answers," a CAW tract, undated.

43. *Springfield* (Oregon) *News* (October 27, 1976), p. 3A. See also *Eugene Register-Guard* (October 30, 1976), p. 3B.

44. The term comes from the magical society of priestesses in Frank Herbert's novel *Dune* (Radnor, Pa.: Chilton, 1965).

CHAPTER 11: RELIGIONS OF PARADOX AND PLAY

1. "Trapped!" (a tract from the First Arachnid Church), *Green Egg*, Vol. VII, No. 66 (November 1, 1974), 21–22.
2. Robert Shea and Robert Anton Wilson, *Illuminatus:* Part I (*The Eye in the Pyramid*); Part II (*The Golden Apple*); Part III (*Leviathan*) (New York: Dell, 1975).
3. Harvey Cox, *The Feast of Fools* (Cambridge: Harvard University Press, 1969); "Religion in the Age of Aquarius: A Conversation with Harvey Cox and T. George Harris," *Psychology Today*, Vol. 3, No. 11 (April 1970), 63.
4. Johan Huizinga, *Homo Ludens* (Boston: Beacon Press, 1968), 12. Other quotations on pp 1, 3, 4, and 5.
5. *The Druid Chronicles* (*evolved*), ed. Isaac Bonewits (Berkeley: Berkeley Drunemeton Press, 1976), Introduction, p. 1.
6. Ibid., "The Book of the Law," p. 4.
7. Ibid., "Later Chronicles—Chapter the Tenth," p. 12.
8. Ibid., "The First Epistle of Isaac," 2:12.
9. Isaac Bonewits, "What & Why Is Reformed Druidism in the 1970's," *Green Egg*, Vol. VII, No. 75 (December 21, 1975), 15–17.
10. "Part V: The Great Druish Books," *Druid Chronicles*. All inquiries about various Druid groups and publications can be sent to Box 9398, Berkeley, Cal.
11. *The Druids' Progress*, No. 1, p. 10.
12. These two quotations come from the inside cover of the third and fourth editions of *Principia Discordia, or How I Found Goddess and What I Did to Her When I Found Her*, privately published.
13. Robert Anton Wilson, "All Hail the Goddess Eris," *Gnostica*, Vol. 3, No. 12 (July 21, 1974), 19.
14. *Principia Discordia*, 4th ed., pp. 7–10.
15. "An Interview with Robert Anton Wilson," by Neal Wilgus, *Science Fiction Review*, Vol. 5, No. 2 (May 1976), 32.
16. Thomas J. Walsh, *Beyond the Barrier*, Issue 1, p. 1. Published irregularly out of Irvington, New Jersey. A previous publication was *Patterns of Form*, published by the Morgan Delt cabal.
17. "Erisianism: A Neo-Pagan Path," *Green Egg*, Vol. IX, No. 78 (May 1, 1976), 10.
18. *Principia Discordia*, 4th ed., pp. 42, 63.
19. Robert Anton Wilson, "All Hail the Goddess Eris!" *Gnostica*, Vol. 4, No. 9 (July 1975), 27.

CHAPTER 12: RADICAL FAERIES
AND THE GROWTH OF MEN'S SPIRITUALITY

1. "A Light in the Darkness," *Brothers of the Earth Newsletter*, No. 3 (Yule 1983), 7–9.
2. See "What Men Really Want," an interview with Robert Bly by Keith Thompson, *New Age* (May 1982). See also *Brothers of the Earth Newsletter*, Cycle 2, Issue 5 (Summer Solstice 1984), 9–19.
3. Shepard Bliss, "Bound for Glory," *UTNE Reader*, No. 15 (April–May 1986).
4. *RFD*, No. 22 (Winter Solstice 1979), 59.
5. *RFD*, No. 22, p. 61.
6. *RFD*, No. 22, p. 50.
7. *RFD*, No. 22, p. 29.
8. *RFD*, No. 22, p. 38.
9. *RFD*, No. 22, pp. 62–63.
10. Don Kilhefner, "A Sprinkling of Radical Faerie Dust," *RFD*, No. 24 (Summer 1980), 25–27.
11. Stanley Johnson, "On the Banks of the River Time Looking Inland," *RFD*, No. 43 (Summer 1985), 63.
12. J. Michael Clark, "The Native American Berdache," *RFD*, No. 40 (Fall 1984), 22–30.
13. Mitch Walker and Friends, *Visionary Love: A Spirit Book of Gay Mythology and Trans-Mutational Faerie* (San Francisco: Treeroots Press, 1980).
14. Will Roscoe, "A Call for Dialogue," *RFD*, No. 34 (Spring 1983), 14.
15. *Pagan Spirit Journal*, No. 2 (1983), 41.

CHAPTER 13: SCHOLARS, WRITERS,
JOURNALISTS, AND THE OCCULT

1. *Principia Discordia, or How I Found Goddess and What I Did To Her When I Found Her* 4th ed., p. 40.
2. Marcello Truzzi, "Definition and Dimensions of the Occult: Toward a Sociological Perspective," in *On The Margin of the Visible: Sociology, the Esoteric, and the Occult*, ed. Edward A Tiryakian (New York: John Wiley & Sons, 1974), p. 252. Originally published in *Journal of Popular Culture*, Vol. V, No. 3 (Winter 1971), 635/7–646/18.
3. Egon Larsen, *Strange Sects and Cults* (London: Arthur Barker, 1971), p. 2.
4. Richard Cavendish, *The Black Arts* (New York: Capricorn Books, 1967), p. 3.
5. J. Gordon Melton, *A Dictionary of Religious Bodies in the United States* (New York: Garland, 1967), p. 267. "Manipulation and a manipulative world view is of the essence of magical existence."

6. Susan Roberts, *Witches, U.S.A.* (New York: Dell, 1971), pp. 17–24.

7. Edward A Tiryakian, "Toward the Sociology of Esoteric Culture," *American Journal of Sociology*, No. 78 (November 1972), 491–512. Also in *On the Margin of the Visible*, pp. 257–80. "Occult" is defined on p. 265.

8. Andrew M. Greeley and William C. McCready, "Some Notes on the Sociological Study of Mysticism," in *On the Margin of the Visible*, p. 304.

9. Raymond Prince and Charles Savage, "Mystical States and the Concept of Regression," *Psychedelic Review*, No. 8 (1966), 59–75.

10. Raymond Prince, "Cocoon Work: An Interpretation of the Concern of Contemporary Youth with the Mystical," in *Religious Movements in Contemporary America*, ed. Irving Zaretsky and Mark Leone (Princeton: Princeton University Press, 1974), pp. 255–71.

11. A. L. Kroeber, "Psychosis or Social Sanction" (1940), in *The Nature of Culture* (Chicago: University of Chicago Press, 1952), pp. 309–10.

12. E. Fuller Torrey, "Spiritualists and Shamans as Psychotherapists: An Account of Original Anthropological Sin," in *Religious Movements in Contemporary America*, pp. 330–37. Quotations on p. 331.

13. Mircea Eliade, *Myths, Dreams, and Mysteries* (New York: Harper & Row, 1967), p. 71.

14. Greeley and McCready, "Notes on Study of Mysticism," p. 310.

15. Marvin Harris, *Cows, Pigs, Wars and Witches* (New York: Vintage, 1975), pp. 251, 255, 257–58, 263.

16. Edwin Schur, *The Awareness Trap: Self-Absorption Instead of Social Change.* (New York: Quadrangle, 1976).

17. Christopher Lasch, "The Narcissist Society," *The New York Review of Books* Vol. XXIII, No. 15 (September 30, 1976), 5, 8, 12; also, "The Narcissistic Personality of Our Time," *Partisan Review*, Vol. XLIV, No. 1 (1977), 9–19.

18. Tiryakian, "Sociology of Esoteric Culture," p. 271.

19. Mircea Eliade, "The Occult and the Modern World," in *Occultism, Witchcraft, and Cultural Fashions* (Chicago: University of Chicago Press, 1976), pp. 52–53.

20. Nathan Adler, "Ritual, Release, and Orientation: Maintenance of the Self in the Antinomian Personality," in *Religious Movements in Contemporary America*, p. 285.

21. Edward A. Tiryakian, "Preliminary Considerations," in *On the Margin of the Visible*, p. 3.

22. Theodore Roszak, ed., *Sources* (New York: Harper & Row, 1972), p. 419.

23. Harriet Whitehead, "Reasonably Fantastic: Some Perspectives on Scientology, Science Fiction, and Occultism," in *Religious Movements in Contemporary America*, pp. 547–87.

24. Louis Pauwels and Jacques Bergier, *The Morning of the Magicians*, trans. Rollo Myers (New York: Avon, 1968). Originally published in France in 1960 as *Le Matins des Magiciens* by Éditions Gallimard.

25. Mircea Eliade, "Cultural Fashions and History of Religions," in *Occultism, Witchcraft, and Cultural Fashions*, pp. 10, 13, 16.

26. Mircea Eliade, "The Occult and the Modern World," in *Occultism, Witchcraft, and Cultural Fashions*, pp. 52–53, 57–58, 64–65.

27. Edward J. Moody, "Magical Therapy: An Anthropological Investigation of Contemporary Satanism," in *Religious Movements in Contemporary America*, pp. 380–82.

28. Edward J. Moody, "Urban Witches," in *On the Margin of the Visible*, p. 233.

29. Marcello Truzzi, "The Occult Revival as Popular Culture: Some Random Observations on the Old and Nouveau Witch," *Sociological Quarterly*, No. 13 (Winter 1972), 29.

30. Marcello Truzzi, "Toward a Sociology of the Occult: Notes on Modern Witchcraft," in *Religious Movements in Contemporary America*, pp. 629, 635–36.

CHAPTER 14: LIVING ON THE EARTH

1. *Green Egg*, Vol. VIII, No. 76 (February 2, 1976), 32–36.

2. Stanley Diamond, *In Search of the Primitive* (New Brunswick, N.J.: Transaction, 1974), pp. xv, 10, 122, 129.

3. E. R. Dodds, *Pagan and Christian in an Age of Anxiety* (New York: W. W. Norton, 1970), p. 29.

4. Interview with Rarihokwats, conducted by Natasha A. Friar, July 30, 1975.

5. Ibid.

6. *Akwesasne Notes*, Vol. IX, No. 3 (Summer 1977), 3. (c/o Mohawk Nation, via Rooseveltown, New York 13683.)

7. Fiftieth Anniversary Editorial, *Akwesasne Notes*, Vol. VIII, No. 2 (Early Summer 1976), 4.

8. José Barreiro, "The Damage Close to Us," *Akwesasne Notes*, Vol. IX, No. 3 (Summer 1977), 8.

9. Jonny Lerner, "A Patch of Poison Cabbage," *Akwesasne Notes*, Vol. IX, No. 3 (Summer 1977), 11.

10. Interview with Rarihokwats conducted by Friar. In 1977, Rarihokwats left *Akwesasne Notes* after a complicated political dispute. He is working at present with Four Arrows: A Communications Group of Native People of the Americas, PO Box 496, Tesque New Mexico 87574.

11. Dr. Jack D. Forbes, "Americanism Is the Answer," *Akwesasne Notes*, Vol. VI, No. 1 (Early Spring 1974), 37.

12. Gayle High Pine, "The Non-progressive Great Spirit," *Akwesasne Notes*, Vol. V, No. 6 (Early Winter 1973), 38.

13. See Sotsisowah, "The Sovereignty Which Is Sought Can be Real," *Akwesasne Notes*, Vol. VII, No. 4 (Early Autumn 1975), pp. 34–35.

14. Susan Roberts, *Witches, U.S.A.* (New York: Dell, 1971), pp. 5, 7, 17, 18.

15. This list comes from answers to questionnaires and interviews in 1975 and 1976.

16. See *The New York Times*, September 3, 1975, p. 1; September 11, 1975, p. 40; September 7, 1975, IV, p. 7.

17. In particular, Hans Holzer, *The Witchcraft Report* (New York: Ace Books, 1973), pp. 182–88.

18. Excerpts from these letters appeared in an open communiqué to all members of the Council of Themis from CAW, May 27, 1972.

19. Penny Novack, "Pagan Way—Where Now?" *Earth Religion News*, Vol. I, No. 4 (1974), 35–36.

20. "Why the Indians Weren't Ecologists," *Akwesasne Notes*, Vol. III, No. 9 (December 1971); also reprinted in *Green Egg*, Vol. V, No. 49 (August 11, 1972), 19.

21. Carol Maddox, "The Neo-Pagan Alternative," *Green Egg*, Vol. VIII, No. 70 (May 1, 1975), 17. Also in *Green Egg*, Vol. IV, No. 39.

22. Murray Bookchin, *Our Synthetic Environment*, (rev. ed.) (New York: Harper & Row, 1974), pp. xv, lxxii, 242. Originally published in 1962.

23. Ernest Callenbach, *Ecotopia* (Berkeley: Banyan Tree Books, 1975).

24. Roberts, *Witches, U.S.A.*, p. 19.

25. *Red Garters*, April 1985, p. 4.

26. *Congressional Record—Senate*, September 26, 1985, p. S12174.

27. *Pagan Spirit Journal #1* (Madison, Wis.: Circle Publications, 1982), p. 4.

28. Ibid., p. 8.

29. Ibid., p. 33.

30. Ibid., p. 32. *Circle Network News*, Vol. 6, No. 4 (Winter 1984), 1983.

31. *Pagan Spirit Journal #2* (Madison, Wis.: Circle Publications, 1983), p. 54.

32. Ibid., p. 55.

33. *Circle Network News*, Winter 1984.

34. *Georgian Newsletter*, August 1985, p. 28.

35. William F. Schultz, "What the Women and Religion Resolutions Mean to Me," a paper issued February 1985.

EPILOGUE

1. Mircea Eliade, "The Occult and the Modern World," in *Occultism, Witchcraft and Cultural Fashions* (Chicago: University of Chicago Press, 1976), p. 64.
2. *The Odes of Pindar*, trans. Sir John Sandys (Cambridge: Harvard University Press, 1968), Fragment 137, pp. 592–95.
3. George Mylonas, *Eleusis and the Elusinean Mysteries* (Princeton: Princeton University Press, 1961), p. 281.
4. Karl Kerényi, *Eleusis*, trans. Ralph Manheim (New York: Bollingen Foundation, 1967), pp. 105–74.
5. Statement for beginning a coven by Lyr ab Govannon, spring 1976.
6. Aidan Kelly, "Palingenesia," *Gnostica*, Vol. 4, No. 9 (July 1975), 40. In *Nemeton*, Vol. 1, No. 1 (Samhain 1972), 19, Aidan wrote that one can define the "essence of the Craft as worship of the Goddess."
7. Aidan Kelly, "Why a Craft Ritual Works," *Gnostica*, Vol. 4, No. 7 (May 1975), 32. Aidan has said that he was really paraphrasing Kerényi, *Eleusis*, pp. 24–25.
8. Penny Novack and Michael Novack, *The New Broom*, Vol. 1, No. 4, 25.

Index

Acknowledgments

The author is grateful to the following publishers for permission to reprint excerpts: From *Religious and Spiritual Groups in Modern America*, by Robert S. Ellwood, Jr., © 1973 by Prentice-Hall, Inc. By permission of Prentice-Hall, Inc., Englewood Cliffs, N.J. From *Occultism, Witchcraft and Cultural Fashions*, by Mircea Eliade, © 1976 University of Chicago. By permission of the University of Chicago Press. "The Occult and the Modern World" originally appeared in *Journal of the Philadelphia Association for Psychoanalysis*, Vol. I, No. 3, September 1974. From Edward J. Moody, "Magical Therapy: An Anthropological Investigation of Contemporary Satanism"; Marcello Truzzi, "Towards a Sociology of the Occult: Notes on Modern Witchcraft"; and Harriet Whitehead, "Reasonably Fantastic: Some Perspectives on Scientology, Science Fiction, and Occultism," in *Religious Movements in Contemporary America*, eds. Irving J. Zaretsky and Mark P. Leone, © 1974 by Princeton University Press. By permission of Princeton University Press. From *Europe's Inner Demons: An Enquiry Inspired by the Great Witch-Hunt*, by Norman Cohn, © 1975 by Norman Cohn. By permission of Basic Books, Inc., Publishers, New York. From *An ABC of Witchcraft Past and Present* and *Natural Magic* by Doreen Valiente, © respectively 1973 and 1975 by Doreen Valiente. By permission of St. Martin's Press, Inc., New York. From *Eleusis and the Eleusinian Mysteries*, by George E. Mylonas, © 1961 by Princeton University Press. By permission of Princeton University Press. From "The Religious Background of the Present Environmental Crisis," by Arnold Toynbee, originally published in *The International Journal of Environmental Studies*, 1972, Vol. III, Gordon and Breach Science Publishers Ltd., 41/42 William IV Street, London WC2, England. By permission of the publishers and the Estate of Professor Toynbee. From "The Witch Archetype," by Ann Bedford Ulanov, originally published in *Quadrant*, Vol. X, No. 1, 1977. By permission of the C. J. Jung Foundation for Analytical Psychology, Inc., New York, N.Y. From "Witchcraft: Classical, Gothic and Neopagan," by Isaac Bonewits, © 1976 by *Green Egg*, St. Louis, Missouri. From *The Druid Chronicles (Evolved)*, ed. Isaac Bonewits, Berkeley Drunemeton Press, Berkeley, California, 1976. From *Real Magic*, by P. E. I. Bonewits, Creative Arts Book Company, © 1979 by P. E. I. Bonewits. From *Green Egg*, © 1968–1976 by *Green Egg*, St. Louis, Missouri. From *Gnostica*, © 1973–1975 by Llewellyn Publications, St. Paul, Minnesota. From "The Rebirth of Witchcraft," unpublished manuscript by Aidan Kelly, © 1977 by Aidan Kelly. From "Inventing Witchcraft," by Aidan Kelly, by permission of Aidan Kelly. From "Why a Craft Ritual Works," "Palengenesia," and "She Touched Me . . ." in *Essays Toward a Metatheology of the Goddess*, by C. Taliesin Edwards (Aidan Kelly), © 1975 by C. Taliesin Edwards. From "I.D.," poem by Barbara Starrett, © 1974 by Barbara Starrett. Frontispiece illustration by permission of the Art and Architectural Division of the New York Public Library (Astor, Lenox and Tilden Foundation).